THE
CONSTITUTIONAL LAW
OF
GHANA

Butterworth's African Law Series

No. 1. Essays in African Law, by A. N. Allott, M.A., Ph.D.

No. 2. Law and Justice in Buganda, by E. S. Haydon, B.A.

No. 3. The Native Law of Succession in South Africa, by A. J. Kerr, B.A., LL.M.

No. 4. Judicial and Legal Systems in Africa, edited by A. N. Allott, M.A., Ph.D.

No. 5. The Constitutional Law of Ghana, by F. A. R. Bennion, M.A.

THE

CONSTITUTIONAL LAW

OF

GHANA

By

F. A. R. BENNION, M.A. (Oxon.)

of the Middle Temple, Barrister-at-Law;
Technical Adviser to the Government of Ghana
on the preparation of legislation (1959–1961);
sometime Lecturer and Tutor in Law at
St. Edmund Hall, Oxford

LONDON
BUTTERWORTHS
1962

ENGLAND: BUTTERWORTH & CO. (PUBLISHERS) LTD.
                LONDON: 88 KINGSWAY, W.C.2.
AFRICA: BUTTERWORTH & CO. (AFRICA) LTD.
                DURBAN: 33/35 BEACH GROVE
AUSTRALIA: BUTTERWORTH & CO. (AUSTRALIA) LTD.
                SYDNEY: 6/8 O'CONNELL STREET
                MELBOURNE: 473 BOURKE STREET
                BRISBANE: 240 QUEEN STREET
CANADA: BUTTERWORTH & CO. (CANADA) LTD.
                TORONTO: 1367 DANFORTH AVENUE, 6
NEW ZEALAND: BUTTERWORTH & CO. (NEW ZEALAND) LTD.
                WELLINGTON: 49/51 BALLANCE STREET
                AUCKLAND: 35 HIGH STREET
U.S.A.:   BUTTERWORTH INC.
                WASHINGTON, D.C.: 7235 WISCONSIN AVENUE, 14

PRINTED IN GREAT BRITAIN
BY
PAGE BROS. (NORWICH) LTD.

TO THE
PARLIAMENTARY COUNSEL
OF GHANA

with fellow-feeling

PREFACE

I wrote this book during my spare time while acting as technical adviser to the Government of Ghana on the preparation of legislation during the period 1959–1961. The introduction of the Republic in 1960 made necessary a complete recasting of the law of Ghana, with consequent difficulty for those who had to teach, learn and administer it. To help in this situation I set out out to explain some of the new laws I had helped to prepare. I am not qualified to comment on the political background, nor would it be right for me to do so. My aim has been to expound the provisions of the law as they exist, and to supply some technical help for practitioners, teachers and students who may feel themselves overwhelmed by the recent spate of legislation.

I am conscious that there is some unevenness of treatment in this book. It seemed best to write fully on the matters with which I had been closely associated, leaving it to others to fill in gaps elsewhere. Some of these gaps exist because the law is still in flux. At the time of writing, for instance, the law relating to the armed forces is in the course of a long process of overhaul. Again, new laws on the important subject of co-operatives have been announced but are not yet available. It remains to be seen also whether the 1960 Constitution itself will prove lasting, or whether it will give way to some new device. The time is clearly not ripe for a considered view of the constitutional law of Ghana, but this should not hold up exposition of the law as it now stands.

My thanks are due to colleagues and others who have joined in discussion on the matters here dealt with. For help on particular aspects I must express my gratitude to the following, while absolving them from any responsibility: Mr. K. B. Ayensu, Clerk of the National Assembly; Mr. R. S. N. Bax, of the Auditor-General's Department; Mr. Allan Greenwood, O.B.E., Special Commissioner, Ministry of Local Government; Mr. John Jackson, C.B.E., Senior Local Courts Adviser; Dr. Clive Parry, Fellow of Downing College, Cambridge. I should perhaps add that, while the writing of this book was undertaken with the approval of the Ghana authorities, the views expressed in it are my own and are in no sense official.

F.A.R.B.

FARLEIGH OLD RECTORY, SURREY.
13*th October*, 1961.

Note.—The book was completed in 1961 and stated the law as it existed at the date of the Preface. While passing the proofs for press I have managed to incorporate such corrections as were necessary to bring it up to date to 31st March, 1962, but the reader will, I trust, appreciate that the treatment of these later amendments has necessarily been limited by the space available.

F.A.R.B.

CONTENTS

Preface vii

Table of Cases xiii

Table of Statutes xvii

PART I.—THE REPUBLICAN CONSTITUTION

CHAPTER 1. CONSTITUTIONAL EVOLUTION . . . 3

   1. The Early Period of British Rule, 1821–1874 . . 4

   2. British Assumption of Territories, 1874–1914 . . 17

   3. Colonial Government, 1914–1945 25

   4. Attaining Nationhood, 1946–1960 37

CHAPTER 2. THE CREATION OF THE REPUBLIC . . 74

   1. Legal Difficulties 74

   2. The Constituent Assembly and Plebiscite Act . 80

   3. The Draft Constitution 85

   4. The Constitutional Plebiscite 88

   5. The Enactment of the Constitution . . . 91

   6. Other Acts of the Constituent Assembly . . 97

   7. Inauguration of the Republic 103

CHAPTER 3. THE CONSTITUTION 111

   1. Powers of the People 112

   2. African Unity 120

   3. The Unitary Republic 125

   4. The President 130

   5. Ministers and Cabinet 144

   6. Parliament 146

CHAPTER 3. THE CONSTITUTION—*contd.*

7. The National Assembly 152

8. Public Finance 155

9. Law and Justice 168

10. Chieftaincy 177

11. Public Services and Armed Forces . . . 180

PART II.—THE STATE AND THE INDIVIDUAL

CHAPTER 4. CITIZENS AND ALIENS 187

1. Types of Citizenship 187

2. Loss of Citizenship 199

3. Allegiance 200

4. Entry into Ghana 202

5. Deportation 202

6. Extradition 204

7. Foreign Enlistment 209

8. Diplomatic Immunity 211

CHAPTER 5. LIBERTY AND STATE SECURITY . . . 213

1. Freedom of the Person 214

2. Freedom of Speech 226

3. Freedom of Religion 234

4. Freedom of Movement and Assembly . . . 236

5. Freedom of Association 240

6. Freedom of Property 244

7. Remedies against the State 249

8. Emergency Powers 253

PART III.—LAW-MAKING UNDER THE REPUBLIC

CHAPTER 6. MODES OF LEGISLATION 259

1. Acts of Parliament 259

CHAPTER 6. MODES OF LEGISLATION—*contd.*

  2. Statutory Instruments 262

  3. Other Modes of Legislation 269

  4. Interpretation 272

  5. Publication of Laws 284

CHAPTER 7. LEGISLATIVE FUNCTIONARIES . . . 298

  1. Parliament. 298

  2. The Cabinet 332

  3. Departmental Ministers 336

  4. Administrative Officials 337

  5. Parliamentary Counsel 339

  6. Commissions of Enquiry 346

CHAPTER 8. LEGISLATIVE METHODS: ACTS OF PARLIAMENT 350

  1. The Structure of a Bill 350

  2. Preparation of Bills 363

  3. The Passage of a Bill 370

  4. The President's Assent. 375

CHAPTER 9. LEGISLATIVE METHODS: STATUTORY INSTRU-
    MENTS 381

  1. The Structure of a Statutory Instrument . . 381

  2. Preparation of Statutory Instruments . . . 384

  3. Making of Statutory Instruments 386

PART IV.—COMMON LAW AND CUSTOMARY LAW

CHAPTER 10. THE RECEPTION AND CONTINUANCE OF ENGLISH
    LAW 391

  1. The Position before Republic Day . . . 391

  2. The Present Position 402

CHAPTER 11. CUSTOMARY LAW 408

   1. Section 87(1) of the Courts Ordinance . . . 408

   2. The Present Meaning of " Customary Law " . . 414

   3. Ascertainment of Customary Law. . . . 416

   4. Part VII of the Chieftaincy Act 428

   5. Local Courts 429

CHAPTER 12. INTERNAL CONFLICT OF LAWS . . . 436

   1. The Position before Republic Day. . . . 436

   2. The Application of Law Rules 449

APPENDICES

APPENDIX A. CONSTITUTIONAL ENACTMENTS . . . 467

   The Ghana Independence Act, 1957 467

   The Constituent Assembly and Plebiscite Act, 1960 . 472

   The Constitution of the Republic of Ghana . . . 473

APPENDIX B. GLOSSARY OF TERMS USED IN LEGISLATION . 491

APPENDIX C. ENACTMENTS RELATING TO THE APPLICATION
             OF COMMON LAW AND CUSTOMARY LAW . 498

   The Courts Ordinance (Cap. 4), Part F. . . . 498

   The Courts Act, 1960 (C.A.9), Part III. . . . 500

   The Chieftaincy Act, 1961 (Act 81), Part VIII . . 502

INDEX

TABLE OF CASES

A

Ababio II v. Nsemfoo (1947) 12 W.A.C.A. 127 419
Abbey v. Ollenu (1954) 14 W.A.C.A. 567 .. .. .. 446, 464
Abude v. Onano (1946), 12 W.A.C.A. 102 423
Acquah III v. Ababio (1948), 12 W.A.C.A. 343 .. .. 420, 423
Adedibu v. Adewoyin (1951), 13 W.A.C.A. 191 421
Ado v. Wusu (1940), 5 W.A.C.A. 24 446
Adu v. Kuma (1937), 3 W.A.C.A. 240 422
Akoto, Re (Civil Appeal No. 42/61) 142, 147, 218, 219, 224
Akumanyi v. Pepra (1956), 2 W.A.L. 112 419
Amarfio v. Ayoakor (1954), 14 W.A.C.A. 554 423
Amazone The, [1940] P. 40; 109 L.J.P. 49; 163 L.T. 375; 56 T.L.R.
    266; 84 Sol. Jo. 76; 19 Asp. M.L.C. 351; sub nom Hemeleers-
    Shenley v. The Amazone, Re The Amazone, [1940] 1 All E.R.
    269, C.A.; 11 Digest (Repl.) 630, 532 211
Amissah v. Krabah (1931), 2 W.A.C.A. 30 .. .. .. 416, 423
Amoabimaa v. Badu (1956), 2 W.A.L. 112 419
Amokwandoh v. U.A.C. (1932), 1 W.A.C.A. 179 460
Amuaukwa v. Anyan (1936), 3 W.A.C.A. 22 440
Andoh v. Franklin (1952), (cited in Allott, at p. 263) 439
Angu v. Attah (1956), 1 W.A.L.R. 128 .. 416, 419, 422, 423, 425
Annan v. Bin (1947), 12 W.A.C.A. 177 447
Aryeh v. Dawuoa (1944), 10 W.A.C.A. 188 425
Asenso v. Nkyidwuo (1956), 1 W.A.L.R. 243 431
A.-G. v. Holt (1910), 2 N.L.R. 1 397

B

Balogun v. Balogun (1935), 2 W.A.C.A. 287 417
Bassey v. Eteta (1938), 4 W.A.C.A. 153 423
Bassil v. Honger (1954), 14 W.A.C.A. 569 459
Bickersteth v. Shanu, [1936] A.C. 290; [1936] 1 All E.R. 227; 105
    L.J.P.C. 53; 154 L.T. 360; 52 T.L.R. 290; 80 Sol. Jo. 164;
    Digest Supp. 454
Bonsi v. Adjena (1940), 5 W.A.C.A. 241 438
Brown v. Miller (1921) Full Court Judgements 1920–1921, 50 .. 413

C

Cobbina Ackon v. Solomon (Civil Appeal No. 6/1959), Unreported 442
Cofie v. Ashong (1956), 1 W.A.L. 82 422
Cornish Mutual Assurance Co., Ltd. v. Inland Revenue Commission-
    ers, [1926] A.C. 281; 12 T.C. 864; 95 L.J.K.B. 446; 134 L.T.
    545; 42 T.L.R. 255; 70 Sol. Jo. 343, H.L. 281

D

Dadzie v. Kojo (1940), 6 W.A.C.A. 139 422
Des Bordes v. Des Bordes, Sarbah, F.C.L. 267 397
Diamond Alkali Corporation v. F. I. Bourgeois, [1921] 3 K.B. 443;
    91 L.J.K.B. 147; 126 L.T. 379; 15 Asp. M.L.C. 455; 26 Com. Cas.
    310; 30 Digest (Repl.) 224, 684 425

xiii

Duff Development Co. *v.* Kelantan Government, [1924] A.C. 797;
    [1923] All E.R. Rep. 349; 93 L.J. Ch. 343; 131 L.T. 676; 40
    T.L.R. 566; 68 Sol. Jo. 559, H.L.; 1 Digest (Repl.) 55, *410* ..   211
Dumoga, *Re* (1961) (Misc. 19/60)   218

E

Edet *v.* Nyon Essien (1932), 11 N.L.R. 47   410
Edie *v.* East India Co. (1761), 2 Burr. 1216; 1 Wm. Bl. 295; 17
    Digest (Repl.) 25, *285*   424
Ekem *v.* Nerba (1947), 12 W.A.C.A. 258   ..   ..   423, 448, 461
Enimil *v.* Tuakyi (1950), 13 W.A.C.A. 8   439
Eze *v.* Igiligbe (1952) ,14 W.A.C.A. 61   423

F

Ferguson *v.* Duncan (1953), 14 W.A.C.A. 316   439
Fiscian *v.* Nelson (1946), 12 W.A.C.A. 21   422
Fisher *v.* Swanikier (1889), Redwar 137   397
Fynn *v.* Gardiner (1953), 14 W.A.C.A. 260   460

G

Ghamson *v.* Wobill (1947), 12 W.A.C.A. 181   430, 447, 448, 455, 461
Glasbrook Brothers, Ltd. *v.* Glamorgan County Council, [1925] A.C.
    270; 94 L.J.K.B. 272; 132 L.T. 611; 89 J.P. 29; 41 T.L.R. 213;
    69 Sol. Jo. 212; 23 L.G.R. 61, H.L.; 37 Digest 186, *82*   ..   201
Golightly *v.* Ashrifi (1955), 14 W.A.C.A. 676   ..   412, 417, 425
Goodwin *v.* Robarts (1875), L.R. 10 Exch. 337; 44 L.J. Ex. 157;
    33 L.T. 272; 23 W.R. 915; *affirmed* (1876), 1 App. Cas. 476;
    45 L.J.Q.B. 748; 35 L.T. 179; 24 W.R. 987, H.L.; 17 Digest
    (Repl.) 7, *32* 424, 425

H

Hemeleers-Shenly *v.* The Amazone, *Re* The Amazone. *See* Amazone,
    The
Hilder *v.* Dexter, [1902] A.C. 474; 71 L.J. Ch. 781; 87 L.T. 311; 51
    W.R. 225; 18 T.L.R. 800; 7 Com. Cas. 258; 9 Mans. 378, H.L.;
    9 Digest (Repl.) 185, *1194*   348
Hughes *v.* Davies (1909), Renner 550   421
Humphrey's Executor *v.* United States (1935), 295 U.S. 602   ..   117
Huth *v.* Clarke (1890), 25 Q.B.D. 391; 59 L.J.Q.B. 559; 63 L.T. 348;
    55 J.P. 86; 38 W.R. 655; 6 T.L.R. 373; 2 Digest (Repl.) 412, *768*   135

I

Inspector General of Police *v.* Morlai Kamara (1934), 2 W.A.C.A.
    185   395

J

Jex *v.* McKinney (1889), 14 App. Cas. 77; 58 L.J.P.C. 67; 60 L.T.
    287; 37 W.R. 577; 5 T. L.R.258; 8 Digest (Repl.) 382, *756*   394, 396
Joyce *v.* Director of Public Prosecutions, [1946] 1 All E.R. 186;
    [1946] A.C. 347; 115 L.J.K.B. 146; 174 L.T. 206; 62 T.L.R.
    208; 31 Cr. App. Rep. 57, H.L.; 2 Digest (Repl.) 200, *192*   ..   201

K

Kojo *v.* Anane (1956), 1 W.A.L. 131   423
Kolczynski, *Re*, [1955] 1 All E.R. 31; *sub nom.* R. *v.* Brixton Prison
    (Governor), *ex parte* Kolczynski, [1955] 1 Q.B. 540; 119 J.P.
    68; 99 Sol. Jo. 61, D.C.; 24 Digest (Repl.) 993, *37*   207

Koney *v.* Union Trading Co. Ltd. (1934), 2 W.A.C.A. 188 .. 436, 439, 443
Kwaino *v.* Ampong (1953), 14 W.A.C.A. 250   421
Kwaku *v.* Addo (1957), 2 W.A.L. 306 ..   ..   .. 422, 424, 437, 463
Kwamina Aradzie *v.* Kobina Yandor F.C. 1922, P.91   444
Kwan *v.* Nyiene (1959), G.L.R. 67   453
Kweku Kodieh *v.* Kwani Affram (1930), 1 W.A.C.A. 12   417
Kwesi-Johnson *v.* Effie (1953), 14 W.A.C.A. 254   440
Kudwo Toku *v.* Kofi Ama, Sarbah's Fanti Law Reports, 58   .. 418
Kuma *v.* Kofi, 1 W.A.L.R. 130   426

L
Larinde *v.* Afiko (1940), 6 W.A.C.A. 108   423
Liversidge *v.* Anderson, [1941] 3 All E.R. 338; [1942] A.C. 206; 110
   L.J.K.B. 724; 116 L.T.I.; 58 T.L.R. 35; 85 Sol. Jo. 439, H.L.;
   2nd Digest Supp. 225

M
Mensah Larkai *v.* Amorkor (1933), 1 W.A.C.A. 323 423
Mensah *v.* Takyiampong (1940), 6 W.A.C.A. 188   462
Mensah *v.* Toku (1887), Sarbah's Fanti Law Reports p. 42   .. 417
Morris *v.* Monrovia (1930), 1 W.A.C.A. 70   ..   .. 409, 414, 463

N
Nelson *v.* Nelson (1932), 1 W.A.C.A. 215   ..   ..   .. 422, 423
Nelson *v.* Nelson (1951), 13 W.A.C.A. 248   .. 409, 420, 421, 423, 437,
                                                            438, 439, 441

O
Obeng *v.* Ampofo (1958) (Civil Appeal No. 53/57) Unreported,   .. 394
Okai *v.* Quist (1895), Renner's Report 123   ..   ..   .. 417, 445
Okaikor *v.* Opare (1956), 1 W.A.L. 275   448
Olowu *v.* Desalu (1955), 14 W.A.C.A. 662   459
Oshodi *v.* Brimah Balogun (1936), 4 W.A.C.A. 1   412
Osuagwu *v.* Soldier (1959), N.R.N.L.R. 39   448
Owiredu *v.* Moshie (1952), 14 W.A.C.A. 11   423
Owoo *v.* Owoo (1945), 11 W.A.C.A. 81   ..   ..   .. 417, 422
Owusu *v.* Mantse of Labadi (1933), 1 W.A.C.A. 278   .. 455, 462

P
Parlement Belge, The (1880), 5 P.D. 197; 42 L.T. 273; 28 W.R. 642;
   4 Asp. M.L.C. 234, C.A.; 1 Digest (Repl.) 122, *70*   211
Phillips *v.* Parnaby [1934] 2 K.B. 299; [1934] All E.R. Rep. 267;
   103 L.J.K.B. 575; 151 L.T. 400; 98 J.P. 383; 50 T.L.R. 446; 32
   L.G.R. 270; 30 Cox C.C. 146; Digest Supp.   284

Q
Quansah *v.* Yankum II (1949), 12 W.A.C.A. 435   423
Quayson *v.* Abba (1934), Div. Court 1931–37, 50   423

R
R. *v.* Brixton Prison (Governor), *ex parte* Kolczynski. *See* Kolczynski,
   Re
R. *v.* Hicklin (1868), L.R. 3 Q.B. 360; 37 L.J.M.C. 89; 16 W.R. 801;
   18 L.T. 395; 11 Cox, C.C. 19; *sub nom.* Scott *v.* Wolverhampton
   JJ., 32 J.P. 533; 14 Digest (Repl.) 501, *4838*   233
R. *v.* Godfrey, [1923] 1 K.B. 24; 92 L.J.K.B. 205; 128 L.T. 115; 86
   J.P. 219; 39 T.L.R. 5; 67 Sol. Jo. 147; 27 Cox, C.C. 338, D.C.;
   24 Digest (Repl.) 989, *8* 207

R. *v.* Wilson (1877), 3 Q. B.D.42; 48 L.J.M.C. 37; *sub nom. re*
    Wilson, 37 L.T. 354; 41 J.P. 708; 26 W.R. 44; 13 Cox, C.C. 630,
    D.C.; 24 Digest (Repl.) 989, *9*   207
Ruttmern *v.* Ruttmern (1937), 3 W.A.C.A. 178   422

S
Sackeyfio *v.* Ayichoe Tagoe (1945), 11 W.A.C.A. 73   420
Santeng *v.* Darkwa (1940), 6 W.A.C.A. 52   459
Savage *v.* Macfoy (1909), Renners Reports 504   413
Scales *v.* Pickering (1828), 4 Bing, 448; 1 Moo. & P. 195; 6 L.J.O.S.
    C.P. 53; 11 Digest (Repl.) 115, *90*   282
Scott *v.* Wolverhampton JJ. *See* R. V. Hicklin
Shirley *v.* Fagg (1675), 6 State Tr. 1121; 36 Digest (Repl.) 364, *13*   321
Snia Viscosa Societa, Etc. *v.* S. S. Yuri Maru. *See* Yuri Maru, The
Solomon *v.* Allotey (1938), 4 W.A.C.A. 91   441
Springer *v.* Phillipines Government (1928), 277 U.S. 189   118
Standard Manufacturing Co., *Re* [1891] 1 Ch. 627; 60 L.J. Ch. 292;
    64 L.T. 487; 39 W.R. 369; 7 T.L.R. 282; 2 Meg. 418, C.A.; 7
    Digest (Repl.) 32, *163*   283
Surtees *v.* Ellison (1829), 9 B. & C. 750; 4 Man. & Ry. K.B. 586;
    7 L.J.O.S.K. 335; 42 Digest 773, *2017*   275

T
Tawiah *v.* Kwa Mensah (1934), Div. Court 1931–37, 65   423
Teye Norh *v.* Gbedemah F.C. 1926–29, P. 395   444
The Adama Case (1958), Nat. Ass. Deb. Official Report Vol. II   ..   319,
    327, 328
The Marriage Ordinance, *Re* (1934), Div. Court, 1931–37, 69   ..   417
Tsibol *v.* Kumasi Municipal Council, [1959] G.L.R. 253   ..   252, 280

V
Vanderpuye *v.* Botchway (1951), 13 W.A.C.A. 164   419
Villars *v.* Baffoe (1909), Renner's Reports 549   ..   ..   439, 441

W
Welbeck *v.* Brown (1884), Sarbah F.C.L. 185   ..   ..   412, 425
Wellington *v.* Papafio (1952), 14 W.A.C.A. 49   ..   ..   423, 461
Weytingh *v.* Bessaboro (1906), Renner's Report 428   448
Whicker *v.* Hume (1858), 7 H.L. Cas. 124; 28 L.J. Ch. 396; 31 L.T.
    O.S. 319; 22 J.P. 591; 4 Jur. N.S. 933; 6 W.R. 813; 8 Digest
    (Repl.) 382, *754*   396
Willmott *v.* Barber (1880), 15 Ch. D. 105   464
Wilson, *Re. See* R. *v.* Wilson
Wood *v.* Riley (1867), L.R. 3 C.P. 26; 42 Digest 658, *666*   283

Y
Yamuah IV *v.* Sekyi (1936), 3 W.A.C.A. 57   417
Yerenchi *v.* Akuffo (cited in Kwaku *v.* Addo (1957), 2 W.A.L. 306)   422
Yuri Maru, The [1927] A.C. 906; 43 T.L.R. 698; *sub nom.* Snia
    Viscosa Societa, Etc. *v.* S. S. Yuri Maru, 96 L.J.P.C. 137; 137
    L.T. 747; 71 Sol. Jo. 649; 17 Asp. M.L.C. 322; Digest Supp. ..   409

TABLE OF STATUTES AND
STATUTORY INSTRUMENTS

Note.—Figures in heavy type indicate where the enactment is set out in full.

A. GHANA

Acts and Instruments of the United Kingdom Government relating particularly to Ghana or its predecessors are included under this heading.

Acts of Parliament Act, 1960 (C.A. 7) .. 93, 98, 151, 261, **274**
  s. 1 350
  s. 2 .. .. 151, 350, 352, 356
  s. 3 .. .. 151, 355, 363
  s. 4 .. .. 152, 356
  s. 5 151
    (1)–(3) 376
  s. 6 152
    (2) 378
    (3) 152, 377
  s. 7 .. .. 152, 294
    (1) 378
    (2) 377
  s. 8 (1), (2) 378
  ss. 9, 10 379
  s. 11 (1) 379
    (2) 380
  s. 12 .. .. 350, 356
  Sch. 148, 376, 377
Administration (Foreign Employment) Ordinance (Cap. 23) .. 296
Administration of Estates Act, 1961 (Act 63) 407
  s. 105 (2) 456
Administration of Estates by Consular Officers Ordinance (Cap. 22) 296
Akpeteshi Act, 1961 (Act 77)—
  s. 3 248
  s. 9 380
Aliens Ordinance (Cap. 49) 203
Appropriations of Lapsed Personalty Ordinance (Cap. 24) 296
Armed Forces Act, 1962 (Act 105) 184
Arms and Ammunition Ordinance (Cap. 253) 256
Ashanti Administration Ordinance, 1902 24
Ashanti Confederacy Council Order, 1935 (No. 1) 35
Ashanti Confederacy Council (Amendment) Order, 1950 (No. 147) 43
Ashanti Native Jurisdiction Ordinance, 1924 426
Ashanti Order in Council, 1901 .. .. 24, 34
Ashanti Order in Council, 1906 .. .. 24, 34
Ashanti Order in Council, 1934 34
Ashanti Stool Lands Act, 1958 (No. 28) 72
Authentication Ordinance (Cap. 2) 93
Avoidance of Discrimination Act, 1957, (No. 38) 235, 240
  ss. 3, 4 232
  ss. 5–7 236
  s. 9 .. .. 232, 236

Bank of Ghana Ordinance, 1957 (No. 34) 72
Bills of Exchange Act, 1961 (Act 55) 407
Bills of Lading Act, 1961 (Act 42) 407
Book and Newspaper Registration Act, 1961 (Act 73) 230
British Sphere of Togoland Order in Council, 1923 .. 28, 288
Brong-Ahafo Region Act, 1959 (No. 18) 71
Cabinet and Ministers Act, 1960 (C.A. 3.) 98, 145, 333
   ss. 1, 2 333
   s. 3 334
      (3), (4) 334
   s. 4 335
   s. 5 .. .. 145, 183
   ss. 6, 7 145
Casino Licensing (Amendment) Act, 1960 (Act 24) 153, 377
Chiefs Ordinance, 1904 (No. 4) 20
Chiefs (Recognition) Act, 1959 (No. 11) 72
Chieftaincy Act, 1961 (Act 81) 178, 249, 428, 457, **502**
   s. 4 237
   s. 50 435
   s. 51 235
   s. 58 .. .. **502**
   s. 59 .. .. 424, 454, **502**
   ss. 60–62 .. .. **503**
   s. 63 .. .. **504**
      (2) 457
   s. 64 .. .. **504**
   s. 65 235
   s. 69 (1) 457
Cinematograph Act, 1961 (Act 76) 231
Civil Service Act, 1960 (C.A.5) 42, 98, 145, 180, 181, 183, 331
   s. 6 145
   s. 7 145
   s. 8 145
   s. 23 260
   s. 24 242
   s. 28 .. .. 135, 359, 496
   s. 41 250
Civil Service (Interim) Regulations, 1960 (L.I. 47)—
   reg. 43 242
Civil Service (Structure) Regulations, 1961 (L.I. 139) 181
Cocoa Duty and Development Funds (Amendment) Ordinance, 1954
   (No. 25) 51
Commissioners of Assize and Civil Pleas Act, 1958 (No. 12) 67, 402
Commissions of Enquiry Ordinance (Cap. 249) 346
   s. 5 347
   ss. 10–12 348
   s. 16 347
Compulsory Savings Act, 1961 (Act 70) 245
Concessions Ordinance, 1900 (No. 14) 21, 247
Conspiracy and Protection of Property (Trade Disputes) Ordinance
   (Cap. 90)—
   ss. 3–11 243
Constituent Assembly and Plebiscite Act, 1960 (No. 1) **472**
   s. 1 .. .. **472**
   s. 2 .. .. **472**
      (3) 93
   ss. 3, 4 .. .. **473**

Constitution (Amendment) Act, 1959 (No. 7)—
ss. 3, 4 71
ss. 5–7 70
s. 9 71
ss. 10, 11 66
Constitution (Consequential Provisions) Act, 1960 (C.A.8) .. 99, 100,
112, 150, 180
s. 1 .. .. 99, 153
(2) 99, 102, 154
s. 4 156
s. 5 .. .. 159, 160
s. 9 177
ss. 10, 11 180
s. 16 100
s. 19 101
s. 21 .. .. 99, 108
s. 22 .. .. 61, 153
Sch. 2 .. .. 160, 184, 212
Constitution of The Republic of Ghana **473–490**
preamble 112, 120
art. 1 .. .. 91, 99, 112, 119, 120, 146, 148, 152
art. 2 .. .. 120, 123, 124, 125, 126, 127, 149, 171
art. 4 126
(1) 125
(2) 126
art. 5 .. .. 124, 127
art. 6 .. .. 95, 128, 151, 177
art. 7 129
art. 8 (1) 130
(2) 131, 134
(3) 132, 184
(4) 93, 94, 133
art. 9 .. .. 137, 140, 175
art. 10 .. .. 108, 139
art. 11 .. .. 137, 175
(1) 137
(3) 139
art. 12 .. .. 108, 140, 175
art. 13 .. 109, 112, 120, 125, 140, 141, 142, 143, 148, 168, 177, 234
236
(1) 92, 142, 213
art. 15 144
art. 16 145
(2) 146
art. 17 145
art. 18 143
(2) 134, 135
(3) 144
(4) 175
(5) 143
art. 19 .. .. 144, 160
art. 20 .. .. .. 91, 96, 102, 118, 142, 146, 147, 151, 269
(1) 135, 146
(2) 102, 103, 147, 149, 150, 151, 171, 376
(3) 149, 171
(4) 148, 171
(5) 96, 132, 135, 137, 143, 147
(6) 102, 136, 141, 146

*b**

Constitution of The Republic of Ghana (*continued*)

art. 21	..	152
(1)	..	300
(2)	..	99
(3)	..	91, 153, 259, 322
(4)	..	154, 300
art. 22	..	155
(1)	..	155, 305
art. 23	..	147, 154
(1)	..	305
(2)	..	102, 147, 305
(3)	..	154
(4)	..	148
art. 24	..	152
(2)	..	152, 261
art. 25	..	110, 153, 300
(5)	..	91
art. 26	..	155, 171
art. 27	..	156, 166
art. 28	..	156
(1)	..	156, 157, 158
(2)	..	157
art. 29	..	96, 118
(1)	..	159
(2)	..	160
art. 30	..	118, 165
art. 31	..	118, 161, 162
art. 32	..	161, 164
(1), (2)	..	161
art. 33	..	118, 124, 164
art. 34	..	123, 124, 165, 166
(3), (4)	..	166
art. 35	..	166, 167
(2)	..	92, 167
art. 36	..	167, 171
art. 37	..	160
(2)	..	92
art. 38	..	167
(1)	..	183
(4)	..	160, 167, 184
art. 39	..	103, 167, 404
art. 40	..	92, 103, 132, 136, 151, 169, 272, 405
(c)	..	136
(d)	..	170
art. 41	..	93, 170
(2)	..	168, 170
art. 42 (1)	..	171
(2)	..	93, 170, 171, 172
(3)	..	172
(4)	..	173, 270, 405
art. 43	..	172
art. 44	..	175
(2)	..	183
(3)	..	92, 175
art. 45	..	173, 175
(2)	..	174
(3)	..	183
art. 46	..	149, 150, 175, 176, 184

Constitution of The Republic of Ghana (*continued*)

art. 46 (3)	.. ..	160
art. 47 ..	.. ..	169, 176, 250, 313
(1)	.. ..	176
(2)	.. ..	92, 176
art. 48 ..	.. ..	120, 169, 176
(2)	.. ..	177
art. 49 ..	.. ..	177
art. 50 ..	.. ..	178
art. 51 ..	.. ..	96, 180
(1)	.. ..	94
(2)	.. ..	134, 183
art. 52 ..	.. ..	160, 184
art. 53 ..	.. ..	171, 184
art. 54 ..	.. ..	132, 184
(2)	.. ..	184
art. 55 ..	.. .. 94, 95, 96, 97, 132, 135, 136, 137, 141, 147,	
	170, 171, 172, 270, 271, 272	
(4)	.. ..	171

Constitution (Repeal of Restrictions) Act, 1958 (No. 38) ..	..	69, 78
Constitutional Plebiscite Order, 1960 (E.I. 73)	..	89
Constitutional Plebiscite (Questions) Order, 1960 (E.I. 75)	..	89
Constitutional Plebiscite Regulations, 1960 (E.I 74) ..		89
Constitutional Plebiscite (Symbol) Regulations, 1960 (E.I. 76)	..	90
Consular Conventions Ordinance, 1952, (No. 32)	..	212
Contingencies Fund Act, 1958 (No. 18)	..	166
s. 4	..	69
Contracts Act, 1960 (Act 25)	..	260, 407
Control of Prices Act, 1962 (Act 113)	..	248
Co-operative Societies Ordinance (Cap. 190)—	..	244
Copyright Act, 1961 (Act 85)	..	123, 249
Councils (Northern Territories and Trans-Volta/Togoland) Dis-		
solution Act, 1958 (No. 31)	..	71
Court of Appeal Ordinance, 1957 (No. 35)	..	67
Courts Act, 1960 (C.A. 9) .. 98, 168, 170, 404, 406, 431, 498, **500**		
s. 7	..	172
s. 24	..	177
s. 29	..	172
s. 66 .. .. 449, **501,** 504		
(1) 449, 451, 452, 459, 462		
rule 1 .. 449, 450, 452, 453, 454, 455, 456, 459, 460, 501		
rule 2 .. 450, 452, 453, 454, 455, 456, 459, 460, 461, 501		
rule 3 .. .. 450, 452, 454, 456, 462, 501		
rule 4 .. 450, 452, 454, 455, 456, 460, 461, 462, 464		
(a) 460, 461		
(c) 461, 462		
rule 5 .. .. 450, 452, 456, 461, 462		
rule 6 .. .. 450, 452, 456, 457, 463		
(2)	..	457
(3)	..	457
(a) 455, 463		
(b)	..	464
s. 67 .. .. 426, 427, 428, 431, 432, **502**		
(1) 415, 426, 427, 457		
(2)	..	427
(3) 427, 428		
(b)	..	428
s. 73	..	428

Courts Act, 1960 (*continued*)
s. 98 431
  (1) (f) 20
  (2) 432
s. 99 434
s. 102 432
s. 103 430
s. 104 432
s. 106 (1) 433
  (2) 435
  (4) 434
s. 107 435
ss. 113–117 428
ss. 134–137 432
s. 138 (2) 432
s. 143 (4) 433
s. 144 432
s. 146 (h) 434
s. 147 .. .. 235, 434
s. 154 406
  (3) 214
  (4) 406
Courts (Amendment) Act, 1957 (No. 8) 67
Courts (Amendment) Ordinance, 1957 (No. 17)
ss. 2, 3 67
Courts Ordinance, 1876 (No. 4) 33
s. 19 436
Courts Ordinance, 1935 (No. 7) 33
Courts Ordinance (Cap. 4) 98, 391, **498**
s. 2 413
s. 15 394
s. 16 .. .. 214, 394
s. 17 .. .. 393, 394
s. 25 419
  (5) 418
s. 74 (2) 418
s. 76 420
s. 83 .. .. 391, 392, 393, 394, 395, 397,
        401, 405, 406, 408, 409, 438, **498**
s. 84 .. .. **498**
s. 85 .. .. 391, 394, 396, 406, 436, **498**
s. 86 .. .. 391, 401, **499**
s. 87 .. .. 392, 394, 395, 408, 415, 437, 449, **499**
  (1) 392, 394, 408, 409, 411, 412, 413, 414, 416,
    426, 430, 436, 437, 438, 439, 445, 446, 448, 453, 454
  (2) 417, 420, 421
s. 88 .. .. **499**
s. 89 .. .. 420, **500**
s. 90 418
Sch. 2, Order 38 500
Criminal Code (Cap. 9)—
s. 11 393
s. 345 231
s. 459 229
s. 464 220
Criminal Code, 1960 (Act 29) 216, 249, 350, 492
s. 1 241
s. 4 (c) 234

Criminal Code, 1960 (*continued*)
s. 20 241
s. 23 (1) 240
s. 24 241
s. 39 248
ss. 84–87 220
ss. 88–90 219
ss. 91–95 220
ss. 112–119 233
s. 128 260
s. 180 .. .. 201, 227
(2) 227
ss. 181, 182 .. .. 201, 227
s. 183 228
(1), (2) 230
(4) 138
(11), (12) 228
s. 183A 231
s. 184 .. .. 130, 232
s. 185 228
ss. 189, 191 241
s. 192 229
ss. 196–202 238
s. 204 239
s. 206 256
s. 207 239
s. 208 229
s. 225 234
ss. 280–284 234
s. 296 239
(11)–(13) 236
(16), (21) 239
s. 298 239
s. 314 220
s. 318 (2) 220
Criminal Code (Amendment) Ordinance, 1934 (No. 21) 34
Criminal Procedure Code, 1961 (Act 30) 214, 358, 360, 492
s. 15 (2) 217
ss. 22–31 226
ss. 88, 91 249
s. 94 248
s. 96 217
(2) 216
ss. 97–107 217
s. 296 (4) 130
s. 297 232
(1) 130
ss. 355, 395, 399 237
Customs Ordinance (Cap. 167) 155
ss. 11, 12 388
ss. 41–43 247
Declaration of Customary Law (Akwapim State) Order, 1960 (L.I. 32) 429
Declaration of Customary Law (Dagomba State) Order, 1960 (L.I. 59) 429
Deportation Act, 1957 (No. 14) 72, 203
ss. 3, 4 203
s. 5 (3) 203
s. 9 203

Deportation (Amendment) Act, 1958 (No. 49)—
s. 2 203
Deportation (Amendment) Act, 1959 (No. 65) .. ..
s. 2 .. .. 204, 237
Deportation (Indemnity) Act, 1958 (No. 47) 260
Deportation (Othman Larden and Amadu Baba) Act, 1957 (No. 19) 203, 260

Diplomatic Immunities (Commonwelath Countries) Ordinance, 1957
(No. 22)—
s. 3 211
Diplomatic Privileges Ordinance (Cap. 268) 212
Education Act, 1961 (Act 87)—
s. 19 246
s. 22 234
Elections (Legislative Assembly) Ordinance, 1950 43
Electoral Provisions Ordinance, 1953 (No. 33) .. 49, 153, 302
Emergency Powers Act, 1957 (No. 28) 72
Emergency Powers Act, 1961 (Act 56) 253, 268
s. 2 254
s. 3 (1), (2) 254
(3) 235, 254
s. 5 254
s. 11 253
Emergency Regulations, 1961 (L.I. 144) 255
Exchange Control Act, 1961 (Act 71) 247, 379
Exchange Control Regulations, 1961 (L.N. 133) 384
Excise (Amendment) Act, 1958 (No. 5) 380
Excise (Amendment) Ordinance, 1957 (No. 38) 380
Excise Ordinance, 1953 (No. 31) 380
Excise (Spirits) Regulations, 1958 (L.N. 13) 380
Explosives Ordinance (Cap. 254) 256
Extradition Act, 1959 (No. 56) 205
Extradition Act, 1960 (Act 22) 206
s. 1 207
s. 2 (a), (b) 207
(c) 208
s. 3 (1), (2) 206
ss. 5, 6 207
s. 7 208
s. 8 208
(1) (b) 208
ss. 9–12 208
s. 15 209
ss. 29, 30 207
Sch. 1 .. .. 207, 209
Extradition (Ashanti) Ordinance (Cap. 13) 205
Extradition (Colony) Ordinance (Cap. 12) 205
Farm Lands (Protection) Act, 1962 (Act 107) 248
Flag and Arms Protection Act, 1959, (No. 61) 130
ss. 3, 4 130
Foreign Enlistment Act, 1961 (Act 75) 209
s. 1 210
(2) 201
ss. 2–4, 8 210
Forest Ordinance (Cap. 157) 246
Fugitive Criminals (Northern Territories) Ordinance (Cap. 14) .. 205
Fugitive Criminals (Togoland) Ordinance (Cap. 15) 205
Ghana (Appeal to Privy Council) Order in Council, 1957 (No. 1361) 100

Ghana (Consequential Provision) Act, 1960 (8 & 9 Eliz. 2 c. 41) .. 105
  s. 1 (1), (3) 105
  s. 2 .. .. 100, 105
Ghana (Consequential Provision) (Colonial Stock Acts) Order in
  Council, 1960 (No. 969) 101, 470
  s. 1 101
Ghana (Constitution) Order in Council, 1957 (No. 277) .. 62, 80, 156
  s. 4 (2) 62, 79, 80
  s. 6 62
  s. 7 (1)–(3) 62
    (4) 63
  s. 16 63
  s. 20 .. .. 63, 76
    (1) 76
  ss. 25, 26 .. .. 70, 359
  s. 31 .. .. 74, 75, 76
    (2), (3) 63, 75
  s. 32 .. .. 63, 66, 69, 75, 76
  s. 33 .. .. 64, 69, 75
  s. 34 .. .. 63, 75
  s. 35 .. .. 66, 69
  s. 42 .. .. 79, 82, 83, 472
    (2) 63
    (3) 64
  s. 47 (3) 64
  s. 54 67
    (2) 67
  s. 55 70
  s. 58 157
  s. 59 (1) 161
    (4) 160
  s. 60 (3) 162
  s. 63 71
    (1) 64
    (2) 71
  s. 64 64
  s. 65 50
  s. 66 .. .. 50, 66
  s. 67 .. .. 51, 66, 71
  s. 68 .. .. 66, 71
    (4) 71
  ss. 69, 70 63
  s. 72 (2) 63
  s. 73 63
  ss. 85–87 64
  s. 88 67
  Sch. 3 76
Ghana Holding Corporation Act, 1958 (No. 45) 260
Ghana Independence Act, 1957 (5 & 6 Eliz. 2 c. 6) .. 60, 126, **467**, 469
  s. 1 .. .. 61, 76, 105, **467**
    (1) 67
      (a) 78
    (6) 62
  s. 2 .. .. 67, 68, 190, 191, 192, **467**
  s. 3 .. .. **468**
  s. 4 .. .. **468**
    (2) 469
  s. 5 .. .. **469**

Ghana Independence Act, 1957 (*continued*)
Sch. 1 .. .. 61, 62, 63, 69, 74, 75, 76, 78, 467, **469**
Sch. 2 .. .. 101, 469, **470**
Ghana Nationality Act, 1961 (Act 62) 187, 188
   s. 1 189
   s. 2 192
   s. 3 197
      (4) 198
   s. 4 197
   s. 5 198
   s. 6 .. .. 198, 199
   s. 7 198
   s. 8 198
   s. 9 .. .. 197, 198, 199
   s. 10 199
   s. 11 200
   s. 12 187
   ss. 13, 15 188
   s. 20 195
   s. 21 188
      (1) 197, 198
      (2) 189
      (3) 188
      (4) 197, 198
Ghana Nationality and Citizenship Act, 1957 (No. 1) .. 68, 187,
                        188, 189, 192, 196
   s. 2 (1) 192, 195
   s. 4 189
   s. 5 192
   s. 6 .. .. 195, 196
   s. 7 189
Ghana (Pending Appeals to Privy Council) Order in Council, 1960,
   S. I. 1960 100
Gold Coast Boundaries Order in Council, 1906 24
Gold Coast Colony and Ashanti (Legislative Council) (Amendment
   No. 2) Order in Council, 1949 39
Gold Coast Colony and Ashanti (Legislative Council) Order in
   Council, 1946—
   ss. 4, 5 37
   ss. 34, 38, 40, 49 38
Gold Coast Colony (Legislative Council) Amendment Order in
   Council, 1934 35
Gold Coast Colony (Legislative Council) Order in Council, 1925 .. 30
   s. 15 31
Gold Coast Colony (Legislative Council) Order in Council, 1927 .. 31
Gold Coast (Constitution) (Amendment) Order in Council, 1952
   (No. 455)—
   ss. 3, 5, 8 46
Gold Coast (Constitution) (Amendment) (No. 2) Order in Council,
   1952 (No. 1039) ..
   s. 8 47
Gold Coast (Constitution) (Amendment) Order in Council, 1953
   (No. 1565) 49
Gold Coast Constitution (Amendment) Order in Council, 1955 (No.
   1218) 49
Gold Coast (Constitution((Electoral Provisions) Order in Council,
   1950 43

Gold Coast (Constitution) Order in Council, 1950 .. .. .. 41, 48
  ss. 5–9 42
  ss. 15, 22, 23, 27 42
  ss. 29, 40 43
  s. 50 44
  s. 56 43
  ss. 57, 58, 60 44
Gold Coast (Constitution) Order in Council, 1954 (No. 551) 48, 50, 467, 470
  ss. 5, 7 48
  ss. 13, 16 49
  s. 17 48
  ss. 18, 24, 28 49
  s. 50 (2) 50
Gold Coast (Constitution) Order in Council, 1956 470
Gold Coast Emancipation Ordinance, 1874 (No. 2) 18
Gold Coast Order in Council, 1901 23
Gold Coast Ordinance, 1866 (No. 7) 15
Gold Coast Ordinances Order in Council, 1934 33
Gold Coast Slave-dealing Abolition Ordinance, 1874 (No. 1) .. 18
Houses of Chiefs Act, 1958 (No. 20) .. 66, 67, 71, 410, 411, 420, 426
  s. 16 424
  s. 35 66
  s. 47 71
Houses of Chiefs (Amendment) Act, 1959, (No. 8)—
  ss. 11, 17 71
Immigrant British Subjects (Deportation) Ordinance (Cap. 50) .. 203
Immigration Act, 1957 (No. 15) 72, 202
  s. 4 202
  s. 10 (3) 202
  ss. 13, 15, 16, 19 202
  s. 20 .. .. 202, 203
Income Tax (Amendment) Act, 1962 (Act 110) 245
Income Tax (Amendment) Ordinance, 1952 (No. 18)—
  s. 50 290
Income Tax Ordinance, 1943 (No. 27) 37, 155, 290
Industrial Relations Act, 1958 (No. 56) 242
  s. 16 242
  ss. 28–30 243
  ss. 31, 40 242
Industrial Relations (Amendment) Act, 1959 (No. 43)—
  s. 5 243
Interpretation Act, 1957 (No. 29) 273, 275
  s. 3 393
  s. 35 281
Interpretation Act, 1960 (C.A.4) 99, 101, 273, 281, 294
  s. 1 .. .. 274, 282
  s. 2 .. .. 282, 352, 354
  s. 3 .. .. 282, 363, 383
  s. 4 361
  s. 5 .. .. 275, 277, 355
  s. 6 275
    (1) 277, 278
    (2), (3) 276
  s. 7 .. .. 275, 276
  s. 8 .. .. 84, 275
    (1) 276
      (a) 275

Interpretation Act, 1960 (*continued*)
  (2)   275
  s. 9   ..   ..   275, 276
  s. 10   ..   ..   269, 278
   (1)   174
   (2) 102, 103, 149
  ss. 12–15   278
  s. 17   ..   ..   102, 170, 404, 406, 407, 504
   (1) 405, 406, 458
   (2)   407
   (4) 173, 405
   (5) 132, 406, 416
  s. 18   ..   ..   102, 170, 415, 461, 504
   (1) 427, 457, 463, 501
   (2)   416
  s. 19   278
  s. 20   279
  s. 21   ..   ..   279, 284, 385
  s. 22   279
  s. 23   279
   (4)   155
  ss. 24, 25   279
  s. 26   ..   ..   189, 279
  s. 27   ..   ..   160, 279
  s. 30   279
  s. 32   ..   ..   137, 155, 161, 279, 455
   (1) 252, 274, 406, 407
   (2)   275
Interpretation Ordinance, 1876 (No. 3)   273
Joint Provincial Council (Dissolution) Act, 1958 (No. 51)   71
Judicial Service Act, 1960 (C.A.10) 98, 175, 179, 180, 183
  s. 1   183
  s. 8   ..   ..   174, 359
   (3)   174
Kumasi Municipal Council (Validation of Powers) Act, 1959 (No. 86) 260, 280
Labour Ordinance (Cap. 89)   248
Labour Registration Act, 1960 (Act 9)—
  s. 6   242
Land and Native Rights Ordinance (Cap. 147)   247
Land Development (Protection of Purchasers) Act, 1960 (Act 2)   455, 464
Legal Profession Act, 1960 (Act 32)   174
Legislative Assembly (Powers and Privileges) Ordinance, 1956 (No. 20) 50, 327
Local Courts Act, 1958 (No. 23)   ..   410, 411, 426, 429, 430, 431, 433
  s. 8 (1)   430
  s. 10   431
  s. 11   434
  s. 15   ..   ..   392, 431, 432
   (b)   430
  s. 24   430
  s. 25   431
  s. 28 (1)   433
   (4)   434
  Sch. 1   434
Local Courts Procedure Regulations, 1959   433
  reg. 2   434
  regs. 34, 36   43

Local Courts Procedure Regulations, 1959 (*continued*)
  reg. 37 (b) 435
  reg. 38 435
Local Government Act, 1961 (Act 54) 45
  s. 47 239
  ss. 58, 73 246
  s. 133 252
  Sch. 1 .. .. 45, 239
Local Government (Amendment) Act, 1959 (No. 14)—
  s. 2 72
Local Government Ordinance, 1951 (No. 29) 45
  s. 58 45
Lotteries Act, 1958 158
Lotteries and Betting Act, 1960 (Act 31) 407
Lunatic Asylums Ordinance (Cap. 79)
  s. 14 214
Marriage Ordinance (Cap. 127)—
  s. 48 410
Meetings and Processions Regulations, 1954 (L.N. 415) 237
Merchandise Marks Ordinance (Cap. 178) 249
Ministerial Offices (Resignation) Act, 1959 (No. 42) 70
Ministers' Functions (Justice) Instrument, 1961 (L.I. 154) .. 145
Ministers of Ghana Act, 1959 (No. 77) 69
Municipal Corporations Ordinance, 1924 29
Municipal Councils (Abolition of Traditional Members) Act, 1959
  (No. 15) 72
Municipal Councils Ordinance, 1953 (No. 9) 45
National Assembly Act, 1959 (No. 78) 69, 261, 472
National Assembly Act, 1961 (Act 86) .. 50, 151, 214, 261, 322
  s. 1 .. .. 70, 177, 496
    (1) 262, 302
    (2) 303, 359
  s. 2 .. .. 70, 303, 345
    (2) (a) 359
  s. 3 (1) 305
    (2) 345
  s. 4 303
  s. 5 303
    (2) 145
  s. 6 303
    (4) 331
  ss. 7, 8 303
  s. 11 302
  s. 13 303
  s. 14 .. .. 311, 370
    (2) 321
  s. 16 312
    (2) 317
  s. 17 317
  s. 18 .. .. 38, 164
  s. 19 318
  s. 20 .. .. 233, 259
  s. 21 .. .. 233, 323
  s. 22 325
    (a) 324
    (b), (c) 325
  ss. 23, 24 325
  ss. 25, 26 .. .. 233, 325

National Assembly Act, 1961 (*continued*)
s. 27 .. .. 233, 326
s. 28 .. .. 260, 327
s. 29 (1), (2) 329
ss. 30–35 329
s. 36 .. .. 316, 329
s. 37 329
ss. 38–40 331
s. 41 332
s. 42 .. .. 214, 332
s. 43 332
s. 45 .. .. 260, 332
s. 46 .. .. 300, 304, 305
National Assembly (Disqualification) Act, 1959 (No. 16) 70
Native Administration (Colony) Ordinance 420
Native Administration Ordinance, 1927 32
Native Administration Ordinance, 1932 (No. 1) 35
Native Administration Treasures Ordinance, 1939 (No. 16) .. 32
Native Authority (Colony) Ordinance, 1944 (No. 21) 36
ss. 15–19 46
s. 29 31
Native Authority Ordinance, 1932 (No. 2) 35
Native Authority (Southern Section of Togoland Under United
Kingdom Trusteeship) Ordinance, 1949 39
Native Courts (Colony) Ordinance (Cap. 98)—
s. 10 392
(vi) 392
s. 15 .. .. 392, 447
Native Courts Ordinance, 1935 (No. 31) 35
Native Customs (Colony) Ordinance (Cap. 97)—
ss. 4, 5, 16 235
Native Jurisdiction Ordinance, 1883 .. .. 19, 32
Northern Territories Order in Council, 1901 .. .. 24, 34
Northern Territories Order in Council, 1906 .. .. 24, 34
Northern Territories Order in Council, 1934 34
Oaths Act, 1960 (C.A.12) 98, 144, 174
s. 7 234
s. 8 .. .. 175, 234, 303
Sch. 1 303
Sch. 2 201
Official Publications Act, 1960 (No. 85)—
s. 2 295
Patents Registration Ordinance (Cap. 179) 249
Petitions of Right Ordinance, 1877 (No. 12) 19
Petitions of Right Ordinance (Cap. 18) 99
ss. 4, 6 250
Pharmacy and Drugs Act, 1961 (Act 64)—
s. 41 359
ss. 43–46 247
ss. 50–53 248
Police Force Ordinance (Cap. 37)—
s. 54 (1), (2) 239
Police Ordinance, 1894 20
Police Ordinance, 1922 (No. 10) 20
Police Service Ordinance (No. 37) 20
Poll Tax Ordinance, 1852 12
Post Office Ordinance (Cap. 21 4)—
s. 8 251

Presidential Affairs Act, 1960 (C.A.2) 98, 134
  s. 1 .. .. 102, 134
    (2) 134
  s. 2 .. .. 134, 135
    (1) 69
    (2) 135
  s. 4 145
  s. 5 .. .. 135, 136
  s. 9 251
Presidential Affairs (Amendment) Act, 1960 (Act 8) .. 102, 134
Presidential Elections Act, 1960 (Act 1) 137, 362, 378
  s. 4 138
    (2) 138
  s. 7 138
Preventive Detention Act, 1958 (No. 17) .. 72, 214, 221, 222, 224, 225
  s. 2 .. .. 221, 225
  s. 3 221
    (4) 237
  ss. 4, 5 221
Probate Exemption Ordinance (Cap. 25) 296
Probates (British and Colonial) Ordinance (Cap. 21) 296
Public Accounts (Audit) Rules, 1959 (L.N. 103) 168
Public Holdings Act, 1960 (Act 23) 130
Public Officers Act, 1962 (Act 114) 251
Public Officers' (Liabilities) Ordinance (Cap. 26) 251
Public Officers' Protection Ordinance (Cap. 27) 251
Public Order Act, 1961 (Act 58) 236, 237, 239, 255
  s. 10 (2) 237
Railways Ordinance (Cap. 233) 251
  s. 90 252
Reaffirmation of the Abolition of Slavery Ordinance, (Cap. 107) .. 220
Referendum Act, 1959 (No. 10) 83, 148
Regional Assemblies Act, 1958 (No. 25) 65, 66
Regions of Ghana Act, 1960 (C.A.11) 98, 128
Rent Control Ordinance, 1952 (No. 2) 248
Representation of the People (Women Members) Act, 1959
  (No. 72) 153
Representation of the People (Women Members) Act, 1960 (No. 8) 99, 152, 153
  s. 6 153
Reprint of Statutes Ordinance, 1896 (No. 14) 285
Revised Edition of the Laws (Amendment) Ordinance, 1954 (No.
  35) 289
  s. 2 290
Revised Edition of the Laws (Annual Supplements) Ordinance,
  1938 (No. 37) 289
Revised Edition of the Laws (Gold Coast) Ordinance, 1936 (No. 24)—
  s. 5, Sch. 289
Revised Edition of the Laws (Miscellaneous Provisions) Ordinance,
  1952 (No. 52) 290
Revised Edition of the Laws Ordinance, 1951 (No. 36) 289
  s. 6 290
Revised Edition of the Ordinances (1952–54 Supplement) Ordinance,
  1954 (No. 36) 290
Riot Damages Ordinance (Cap. 46) 249
Road Transport Licensing Ordinance (Cap. 230) 380
Royal Gold Coast Regiment Ordinance, 1929 (No. 25) 25
Royal Style and Titles Act, 1957 (No. 13) 61
Sedition Act, 1959 (No. 64) 72, 228

Separate Representation of Voters Bill, 1951—   79
Slave-Dealing Abolition Ordinance (Cap. 109)   220
Slaves' Emancipation Ordinance, (Cap. 108)   220
Spirits (Distillation and Licensing) Act, 1959 (No. 80)   380
State Councils (Colony and Southern Togoland) (Amendment)
    Ordinance, 1955 (No. 37)   54
State Councils (Colony and Southern Togoland) Ordinance, 1952
    (No. 8)   45
State Proceedings Act, 1961 (Act 51) 99, 249
    s. 1 (1)   250
    s. 2   250
    s. 3 (2)   250
    s. 8   250
    s. 10 (2)   251
    s. 13 (1)   251
    ss. 15, 19   251
    s. 25 (1)   251
State Property and Contracts Act, 1960 (C.A.6)   ..   98, 245, 260
    s. 4 (1), (4)   245
    ss. 5, 6   246
    s. 8 (1)   245
    ss. 9, 10   245
    s. 14   ..   ..   245, 462
    s. 19   247
State Secrets Act, 1962 (Act 101)   229
Statute Law Revision Ordinance (Cap. 3) 1951 (Revised Edition)..   398
Statutory Instruments Act, 1959 (No. 52) 269, 271, 274
    s. 2   ..   ..   266, 275, 407
    s. 3   ..   ..   266, 407
    s. 4   267
        (1) 266, 343
        (2)   267
        (3)   268
    s. 5   268
    s. 6   386
    s. 7   ..   ..   284, 385
    ss. 8, 9   386
    ss. 10–12   388
    s. 13   388
        (1)   387
    s. 14 (1)   269
    s. 15 (1), (2)   381
    s. 16   ..   ..   387, 388
    s. 17   ..   ..   269, 382
Statutory Instruments Order, 1960 (L.I. 9) 267, 341
    para. 2   343
Statutory Instruments Rules, 1960 (L.I. 39)—
    r. 2   381
    r. 3   ..   ..   382, 384
        (2)   382
    r. 4   382
    r. 5   383
    r. 8 (1)   383
        (2)   388
    r. 9 (1)–(4)   384
    r. 10   383
    Sch. 2   493

Stool Lands Boundaries Settlement Ordinance (Cap. 139)—
s. 9 268
Stool Lands Control Act, 1959 (No. 79) 72, 179
Stool Property (Recovery and Validation) Act, 1959 (No. 31) .. 72
Supreme Court (Civil Procedure) Rules (1954 Revised)—
Order 19, r. 31 437
Order 37A 418
r. 11 418
Order 59 .. .. 218, 219, 253
Supreme Court Ordinance, 1876 19
Telecommunications Act, 1962 (Act 112) 231
s. 10 251
Town and Country Planning Ordinance (Cap. 84)—
ss. 9, 10 246
Town Council (Accra) Ordinance, 1943 (No. 26) 35
Town Council (Cape Coast) Ordinance, 1944 (No. 18) 35
Town Council (Kumasi) Ordinance, 1943 (No. 18) 35
Town Council (Sekondi-Takoradi) 1945 (No. 29) 35
Town Councils Ordinance, 1894 (No. 17) 20, 29
Trade Marks Ordinance (Cap. 180) 249
Trade Marks Ordinance (Cap. 181) 249
Trade Unions Ordinance (Cap. 91) 242
ss. 3, 4, 9–11, 14 243
Treason Act, 1959 (No. 73) 72, 201
Trustee Investment in Ghana Government Securities Ordinance,
1957 (No. 13) 101
United Kingdom Designs (Protection) Ordinance (Cap. 182) .. 249
United Kingdom Trusteeship Order in Council, 1949 39
s. 4 128
University of Ghana Act, 1961 (Act 79)—
s. 12 (2) 246
Volta Region Act, 1959 (No. 47) 71
Waterworks Ordinance, 1934 (No. 20) 34
West African (Appeal to Privy Council) Order in Council, 1930 .. 33
West African Court of Appeal (Amendment) Order in Council 1957,
(No. 279) 100
West African Court of Appeal Order in Council, 1928–35 .. 33
West African Court of Appeal Ordinance, 1935 (No. 11) 33
West African (Fugitive Offenders) Order in Council, 1923 206
Widows and Orphans (Overseas Officers) Pensions Ordinance, 1955
(No. 24) 160
Wild Animals Preservation Ordinance (Cap. 246)—
s. 3 295
Wireless Telecommunication Ordinance (Cap. 216) 231

B. UNITED KINGDOM
Abolition of Slave Trade, 1806 (47 Geo. 3 Sess. 1 c. 36) 5
African Company, 1751 (25 Geo. 2 c. 40) 4
African Company, 1782 (23 Geo. 3 c. 65) 4
Air Force Act, 1955 (3 & 4 Eliz. 2 c. 19) 468
s. 225 (1) 468
Army Act, 1955 (3 & 4 Eliz. 2 c. 18) 468
s. 223 (1) 468
Artizans Dwelling Act (1868) Amendment Act, (1879) Amendment
Act, 1880 (43 Vict. c. 8) 352
Bill of Rights (1688) (1 Will & Mar. Session 2 c. 2) .. 119, 216, 322, 399

British Nationality Act, 1948 (11 & 12 Geo. 6 c. 56)   67, 188, 192, 467
  s. 1   187
      (3)   467
  s. 4   ..   ..   190, 191, 194
  s. 5   ..   ..   191, 194
  s. 6   195
      (2)   196
  ss. 7, 8   195
  s. 10   194
  s. 12 (1) 190, 193, 196
      (b)   194
      (2) 193, 196
      (3) 190, 193, 196
      (4) 194, 196
      (5)   196
      (6)   195
  s. 14   196
  s. 30 ..   ..   192, 195
  s. 32 (1) 192, 194, 195
      (5)   188
      (7)   194
  Schs. 1, 3   467
Status of Aliens Act, 1914 (4 & 5 Geo. 5 c. 17)   188
  s. 1   ..   ..   190, 193, 194
British Nationality and Status of Aliens Act, 1943 (6 & 7 Geo. 6 c. 14)   188
  s. 2   190
British Protectorates, Protected States and Protected Persons Order in Council, 1949 (No. 140)   467
  ss. 5, 9 ..   ..   192, 195
  s. 11   196
British Settlements Act, 1843 (6 & 7 Vict. c. 13)   7
British Settlements Act, 1887 (50 & 51 Vict. c. 54)   7
Burma Independence Act, 1947 (11 & 12 Geo. 6 c. 3)   74
Ceylon Independence Act, 1947 (11 & 12 Geo. 6 c. 7)   60
  Sch. 1   77
Colonial Courts of Admiralty Act, 1890 (53 & 54 Vict. c. 27)   ..   75
  s. 4   469
Colonial Development and Welfare Act, 1940 (3 & 4 Geo. 6 c. 40)   468
Colonial Development and Welfare Act, 1955 (3 & 4 Eliz. 2.6)   ..   468
Colonial Laws Validity Act, 1865 (28 & 29 Vict. c. 63)   ..   18, 75, 469
  s. 1   37
Colonial Stock Act, 1900 (63 & 64 Vict. c. 62)   100
Colonial Stock Act, 1934 (24 & 25 Geo. 5 c. 47) 100, 470
Copyright Act, 1911 (1 & 2 Geo. 5 c. 46)   471
  s. 25 (2)   471
  s. 26 (3)   471
  s. 28   471
Copyright Act, 1956 (4 & 5 Eliz. 2 c. 74)   471
  s. 31   471
  Sch. 7 ..   ..   471, 472
Crown Proceedings Act, 1947 (10 & 11 Geo. 6 c. 44)   250
Customs Consolidation Act, 1876 (39 & 40 Vict. c. 36)   351
Diplomatic Immunities (Commonwealth Countries and Republic of Ireland) Act, 1952 (15 & 16 Geo. 6 & 1 Eliz. 2 c. 18)—
  s. 1 (1)   470
      (6)   470
Diplomatic Priviliges Act, 1708 (7 Anne c. 12)   211
Emergency Laws Repeal Act, 1959 (7 & 8 Eliz. 2 c. 19)   471

Extradition Act, 1870 (33 & 34 Vict. c. 52) 205, 206
   s. 2 207
   ss. 6, 17 205
Extradition Act, 1932 (22 & 23 Geo. 5 c. 39) 205, 206
Foreign Enlistment Act, 1870 (38 & 34 Vict. c. 90) 209, 210
Foreign Jurisdiction Act, 1843 (6 & 7 Vict. c. 94) 8, 11, 391
   s. 5 8
Foreign Jurisdiction Act, 1890 (53 & 54 Vict. c. 37) 8
Fraudulent Conveyances, 1571 (13 Eliz. 1 c. 5) 399
Fugitive Offenders Act, 1881 (44 & 45 Vict. c. 69) 205, 206
Habeas Corpus Act, 1679 (31 Car. 2 c. 2) 218, 399
Habeas Corpus Act, 1816 (56 Geo. 3 c. 100) 225, 399
Habeas Corpus Act, 1862 (25 & 26 Vict. c. 20) 218
Import Duties Act, 1958 (6 & 7 Eliz. 2 c. 6) 470
Income Tax Act, 1952 (15 & 16 Geo. 6 & 1 Eliz. 2 c. 10)—
   s. 461 470
Indian Independence Act, 1947 (10 & 11 Geo. 6 c. 30) 74
   s. 6 (2) 77
Interpretation Act, 1889 (52 & 53 Vict. c. 63) 468
Interpretation of Acts, 1850 (13 & 14 Vict. c. 21)—
   s. 1 275
   s. 4 273
Isle of Man (Customs) Act, 1932 (22 & 23 Geo. 5 c. 16)—
   s. 2 470
Land Tax Redemption Act, 1802 (42 Geo. 3 c. 116)
   s. 191 273
Limitation Act, 1623 (21 Jac. 1 c. 16) 437
Merchant Shipping Act, 1894 (57 & 58 Vict. c. 60) 75
   s. 427 (2) 471
   ss. 735, 736 469
Merchant Shipping Act, 1948 (11 & 12 Geo. 6 c. 44)—
   s. 6 (2) 471
Merchant Shipping (Safety Conventions) Act, 1949 (12, 13 & 14
   Geo. 6. c. 43)—
   s. 2 471
Naval Discipline Act, 1957 (5 & 6 Eliz. 2 c. 53) 469
Nigeria Independence Act, 1960 (8 & 9 Eliz. 2 c. 55) 78
   Sch. 1 78
Obscene Publications Act, 1959 (7 & 8 Eliz. 2 c. 66) 233
   s. 1 (1) 233
Overseas Resources Development Act, 1958 (7 & 8 Eliz. 2 c. 23) .. 468
Pakistan (Consequential Provisions) Act, 1956 (4 & 5 Eliz. 2 c. 31) 104
Road Traffic Act, 1930 (20 & 21 Geo. 5 c. 43)—
   s. 15 271
Road Traffic Act, 1960 (8 & 9 Eliz 2 c. 16) 271
Rules Publication Act, 1893 (56 & 57 Vict. c. 66) 264
Ships and Aircraft (Transfer Restriction) Act, 1939 (2 & 3 Geo. 6
   c. 70) 471
Supreme Court of Judicature, 1873 (36 & 37 Vict. c. 66)—
   s. 24 401
      (7) 401
   s. 25 401
      (11) 401
Statute of Distributions, 1670 (22 & 23 Car. 2 c. 10) 456
Statute of Frauds (1677) (29 Car. 2 c. 3) 397
Statute of Westminster, 1931 (22 & 23 Geo. 5 c. 4) 470
   s. 2 75
      (2) 77

Statute of Westminster, 1931 (*continued*)
s. 3 75
s. 4 61
Statutory Instruments Act, 1946 (9 & 10 Geo. 6 c. 36) 264
s. 1 265
Statutory Instruments Regulations, 1947 (S.I. No. 1)—
reg. 2 265
Summary Jurisdiction Act, 1848 (11 & 12 Vict. c. 43) —
s. 11 395
Territorial Waters Jurisdiction Act, 1878—
s. 7 126
Trade to Africa, 1750 (23 Geo. 2 c. 31) 4
Trustee Investments Act, 1961 (9 & 10 Eliz. 2 c. 62) 101
Visiting Forces Act, 1952 (15 & 16 Geo. 6 & I Eliz. 2 c. 67)—
s. 1 (1) 470
s. 8 471
s. 10 (1) (a) 470
Visiting Forces (British Commonwealth) Act, 1933 (23 & 24 Geo. 5
c. 6)—
ss. 4, 8 470
West Africa Act, 1821 (1 & 2 Geo. 4 c. 28) 5
Whaling Industry (Regulation) Act, 1934 (24 & 25 Geo. 5 c. 49) .. 471
Wills Act, 1837 (7 Will 4 & 1 Vict. c. 26) 397
Workmen's Compensation Act, 1906 (6 Edw. 7 c. 58) 271

PART 1

THE REPUBLICAN CONSTITUTION

SUMMARY

		PAGE
CHAPTER 1.	Constitutional Evolution . . .	3
CHAPTER 2.	The Creation of the Republic . . .	74
CHAPTER 3.	The Constitution	111

CHAPTER 1

CONSTITUTIONAL EVOLUTION

The Republic of Ghana lies midway along the Guinea coast of West Africa, being bounded on three sides by former French territories and on the south by the Atlantic Ocean. To the west lies the Ivory Coast Republic, to the north the Voltaic Republic (formerly Upper Volta) and to the east the Republic of Togo. The territories of Ghana consist of those formerly comprised in the Gold Coast Colony, Ashanti, the Northern Territories of the Gold Coast, and Togoland under United Kingdom Trusteeship. The name Ghana was adopted when, on 6th March, 1957, the country became independent of British rule. The name was taken from the ancient negro empire of Ghana in the South-Western Soudan, from which a proportion of the inhabitants of present-day Ghana are believed to derive their ancestry. Ghana became a republic within the Commonwealth on 1st July, 1960.

Although the republican constitution contains a number of original features and represents a clean break with the past, it inevitably perpetuates by way of organic development much of the former constitutional system. It cannot therefore be understood without reference to the growth of the institutions of government which took place during the years preceding the emergence of Ghana as an independent republic. The purpose of the present chapter is to trace briefly the course of this development, beginning with the assumption of jurisdiction by the British Crown in 1821.[1] The history of the four centuries preceding this event is one of great confusion and shifting of populations, in which the tribal systems were being modified by wars and invasions among the Africans themselves and also by the activities of traders from almost every European country. The indigenous constitutional systems are a study in themselves and are beyond

---

[1] For the earlier history, and the general background to the constitutional developments here discussed, see Claridge, *A History of the Gold Coast and Ashanti*, London, 1915; Ward, *A History of the Gold Coast*, London, 1948; *The Cambridge History of the British Empire*. For the later background see F. M. Bourret, *Ghana—the Road to Independence*, 1919–1957, London, 1960.

the scope of the present work. Our concern now is with a type of constitutional law which, while it recognises indigenous customs and has certain similarities with them, is in written form and derives from institutions and modes of legislation unknown to customary law. From this point of view the story begins with the first attempts of the British to provide a system of government in the Gold Coast. Before these were made the British, like the Dutch, Danish and other Europeans, were present merely as traders and missionaries. The British administration, as it developed and as its boundaries were gradually extended to the whole of the territory now known as Ghana, had the effect of welding into one political unit diverse ethnical groups who without its influence might well have remained separate and would certainly not have been subject to what is now the constitutional law of Ghana. The account of constitutional development given here will be a factual one, describing the changes that actually occurred without going very deeply into the reasons for them, the background conditions, or the controversies which have surrounded them.

1. THE EARLY PERIOD OF BRITISH RULE, 1821–1874

From 1821 to 1874 the British possessions on the Gold Coast were, apart from the period 1850 to 1866 (when they were treated as a separate entity), under the control of the Governor of Sierra Leone. His powers were, however, in suspense from 1828 to 1843, when the administration was carried on by a Committee of Merchants in London.

Before 1821 the government of the British trading forts and settlements on the Gold Coast had been vested in the Company of Merchants trading to Africa, as successors to the Royal African Company of England.[1] The most important forts were those at Cape Coast, Dixcove, Accra (Fort James) and Anomabu, and these were kept up by the Crown after 1821. Other forts and settlements, such as those at Winneba, Wida and Apollonia were then abandoned.[2] Interspersed with the British forts there were at this time other fortified depots belonging to the Dutch and the Danish, and used for the protection of their trading activities on the Gold Coast. The administration of the Company of Merchants

---

[1] 23 Geo. 2, c. 31; 25 Geo. 2, c. 40; 23 Geo. 3, c. 65.
[2] Report from the Select Committee on Africa (Western Coast), 1865 (No. 412), p. 39.

had been carried on under a Governor-in-Chief who, with the seven Governors of the more important forts and the Accountant, formed an administrative council. In all, about forty-five Europeans and four hundred and fifty Africans were employed by the Company.[1] Since the slave trade had become illegal for British subjects in 1807,[2] the Company of Merchants had had neither the funds required for maintaining the British forts nor any incentive to maintain them; and a government subsidy had become necessary for that purpose. Allegations were made that this subsidy was misused and that the Company was failing to prevent illicit slave trading. Accordingly an Act was passed[3] by which on 3rd July, 1821, the Company was dissolved and its forts and other possessions vested in the Crown. The Crown was also given power to declare these possessions, and any others on the West Coast of Africa between the latitudes of 20° North and 20° South " which now do or at any time hereafter shall or may belong to His Majesty " to be annexed to or made dependencies on the Colony of Sierra Leone and made subject to its laws.

The Committee of Merchants

The power conferred by the new Act was exercised within a few months when, by letters patent issued under the Great Seal on 17th October, 1821, George IV ordered the existing and future possessions of the Crown on the West Coast of Africa within the latitudes mentioned in the Act to be annexed to and made dependencies on the Colony of Sierra Leone. The Governor of Sierra Leone, Sir Charles McCarthy, arrived in Cape Coast on 28th March, 1822 to assume the government.[4] There followed a period of war and confusion, in which McCarthy was killed in battle with the Ashantis and which was not brought to a close until a peace treaty was signed with the Ashantis in 1831 following their defeat at the battle of Dodowa in 1826. In the meantime the British Government had handed over the administration of the territories in 1828 to a Committee of Merchants selected by the British Government.[5] Local administration was carried on

---

[1] Claridge, *op. cit.*, I, pp. 332–333.   [2] 47 Geo. 3, Sess. I, c. 36.
[3] West Africa Act, 1821.   [4] Claridge, *op. cit.*, I, p. 334.
[5] The reason for this transfer was " the difficulty of maintaining troops in health in that quarter and the enormous expense which would have been incurred in placing the forts in a fit state for defence ": evidence given to House of Commons Select Committee in 1834, cited in J. J. Crooks, *Records relating to the Gold Coast Settlements from 1750 to 1874*, Dublin, 1923, p. 249.

by a President appointed by the Committee, assisted by a council of merchants resident at Cape Coast Castle. An annual subsidy of £4,000 was paid by the British Government. Although theoretically restricted to the forts themselves, the powers thus vested in the Committee of Merchants came to be used on a *de facto* basis in the neighbouring areas. This development was largely due to the administrative and judicial abilities of Captain George Maclean who was appointed President in 1830. By the treaty with the Ashantis in 1831, under which they gave up any claim to suzerainty over the coastal tribes, Maclean had secured the protection and extension of trading activities and peace between Ashanti and the coastal areas.[1] In the more settled conditions which then prevailed, British justice came to be administered among the inhabitants of these areas in a manner which, in the words of Maclean himself, " has had the happiest effect in maintaining peace, encouraging agriculture and commerce, and promoting the civilization of the natives ".[2] He went on to add in perhaps exaggerated terms: " Let but the local government deny or cease to administer even-handed justice to the population for a single day, and the whole country would again become a scene of warfare, rapine and oppression." The British Government declined, however, to regularise this *de facto* jurisdiction until pressed to do so by a Parliamentary Select Committee which reported in 1842. This Committee recommended that the Government of the British forts upon the Gold Coast be resumed by the Crown, and that all dependance on the Government of Sierra Leone should cease, that the forts abandoned in 1828 when the government was handed over to the Committee of Merchants should be reoccupied as helpful in suppressing the slave trade, and that the irregular judicial jurisdiction *de facto* exercised by Maclean and the magistrates at the forts " should be better defined and understood ". This latter aim was to be achieved by means of agreements with the local chiefs and by the appointment of a judicial officer who, in administering justice to the African population, should follow the principles, while not being restricted to the technicalities, of English law and should be allowed a large discretion. The Select Committee expressed the view that the relationship of the chiefs and their peoples to the British Crown should be:

---

[1] For the text of the treaty see Sarbah, *Fanti National Constitution*, London, 1906, p. 153.

[2] Cited Sarbah, *op. cit.*, p. 95.

" not the allegiance of subjects, to which we have no right to pretend, and which it would entail an inconvenient responsibility to possess, but the deference of weaker powers to a stronger and more enlightened neighbour, whose protection and counsel they seek, and to whom they are bound by certain definite obligations."[1]

Resumption of Crown Government

The recommendations of the Select Committee were acted upon, and in 1843 the Crown resumed the government. It did not immediately follow the advice to sever the dependency on Sierra Leone and for a further seven years the Gold Coast settlements were under the control of the Governor of Sierra Leone. A Lieutenant-Governor was appointed for the Gold Coast and Maclean was made Judicial Assessor and Stipendiary Magistrate to carry out, in exercise of his powers as a justice of the peace, the functions suggested for a " judicial officer " by the Select Committee.[2]

The civil establishment was completed by a chaplain, a surgeon, a secretary to the Lieutenant-Governor, a clerk to the Judicial Assessor, and the Commandant at Accra.[3] A Colonial Secretary was added in 1845.[4]

British Settlements and Foreign Jurisdiction Acts

In 1843 two Acts were passed by the British Parliament which enabled the administration of such territories as those on the Gold Coast to be placed on a regular footing. The first of these Acts, the British Settlements Act, 1843,[5] enabled Orders in Council to be made providing for the establishment of laws, institutions and ordinances for the peace, order and good government of " Her Majesty's subjects and others " within the settlements on the African coast. The power thus given could be

---

[1] *Report from the Select Committee on the West Coast of Africa*, August, 1842, pp. iv–vi.

[2] The functions of the Judicial Assessor were exercised *outside* the forts and settlements. " It is to be carefully noted that this external jurisdiction was given distinct from the jurisdiction *inside* the forts, where Captain Maclean and the other magistrates had the ordinary powers of magistrates ": Brandford Griffith, *A Note on the History of the British Courts in the Gold Coast Colony, with a brief account of the Changes in the Constitution of the Colony*, Accra, 1936, p. 13.

[3] Dispatch from Lord Stanley to Lieut.-Governor Hill, 16th December, 1843, given in Crooks, *op. cit.*, p. 285.

[4] Crooks, *op. cit.*, p. 304.

[5] 6 & 7 Vict. c. 13; repealed and re-enacted by the British Settlements Act, 1887.

delegated by royal commissions or instructions to three or more persons within a particular settlement. The second Act, the Foreign Jurisdiction Act, 1843,[1] authorised the exercise of political powers acquired by agreement or usage in territories which had not become part of Her Majesty's dominions by cession or conquest. On 3rd September, 1844, an Order in Council was made under these Acts requiring judicial authorities in the Gold Coast, when exercising jurisdiction among the indigenous inhabitants, to observe such of the local customs as were compatible with the principles of the law of England, and in default of such customs to proceed in all things as nearly as may be according to the law of England. It was also provided that native offenders might be brought for trial and punished at Cape Coast Castle, or else taken to Sierra Leone, in order to satisfy the requirements of s. 5 of the Foreign Jurisdiction Act, 1843.[2]

The Bond of 1844

Commander H. W. Hill, the Lieutenant-Governor, lost no time in reaching the sort of agreement with the local chiefs that the Select Committee had envisaged and thus, on 6th March, 1844, the famous Fanti Bond was signed. By this brief document the chiefs acknowledged the power and jurisdiction which had been *de facto* exercised in their territories adjacent to the British forts and settlements, and declared that " the first objects of law are the protection of individuals and of property " and that human sacrifices, panyarring or the kidnapping of hostages for debt, and other barbarous customs " are abominations and contrary to law ". They agreed that serious crimes should be tried by the Queen's judicial officers sitting with the chiefs, " moulding the customs of the country to the general principles of British law ".[3]

Constitution of 1850

The numbers of the local population which by 1846 acknowledged British jurisdiction amounted to not less than 275,000, scattered over a territory of about 6,000 square miles.[4] This was added to in 1850, when the Danish King ceded the forts of

---

[1] 6 & 7 Vict. c. 94; repealed and re-enacted by the Foreign Jurisdiction Act, 1890.

[2] See Brandford Griffith, *op. cit.*, pp. 12–13.

[3] For the text of the Bond see Claridge, *op. cit.*, I., p. 452.

[4] Report of Lieut.-Gov. Winniett, 20th February, 1847, cited Crooks, *op. cit.*, p. 305.

Christiansborg, Augustaborg Fredensborg, Kongensteen and Prindsensteen, together with various houses and plantations, to the British Crown for a payment of £10,000.[1] In the same year the forts and settlements on the Gold Coast once again ceased to be dependencies of the Colony of Sierra Leone, the British Government belatedly following the advice of the Select Committee of 1842. This marked a considerable constitutional advance, with the Gold Coast being given its own Governor and both a Legislative Council and an Executive Council. Thus institutions were set up which, over a period of a hundred and ten years, were to evolve into the President, National Assembly and Cabinet of today. The change was effected by a Royal Charter dated 24th January, 1850, and made under the British Settlements Act, and which revoked the letters patent of 17th October, 1821.

The Legislative Council

The Legislative Council consisted of the Governor and at least two other persons designated by Royal Instructions or warrants. By an exercise of the powers of delegation conferred by the Act, the Legislative Council was required to make:

> " all such laws, institutions and ordinances as may from time to time be necessary for the peace, order and good government of our subjects and others within the said present or future forts and settlements in the Gold Coast "

subject to rules and regulations made by Order in Council and to the right of the Crown to disallow any such ordinances in whole or in part, and with a saving for the future exercise of legislative power by Act of Parliament or Order in Council.

Royal Instructions issued at the time of the appointment of Governor Hill on 1st April, 1851, designated as members of the Legislative Council in addition to the Governor, the Judicial Assessor, the Collector of Customs and two merchants. In 1853 the Collector of Customs was replaced by the officer holding the post of Colonial Secretary.[2] The Instructions continued by laying down rules for the conduct of the Legislative Council. The Governor was to preside, and the quorum was to be three. Standing Orders were to be established. No law was

---

[1] Convention signed 17th August, 1850, and presented to Parliament in 1851.

[2] Royal Instructions, 12th February, 1853.

to be passed or question debated unless proposed by the Governor, though other matters might be recorded in the minutes with a statement of reasons by the member concerned. Ordinances were to be styled " Ordinances enacted by the Governor of our Forts and Settlements on the Gold Coast, with the Advice and Consent of the Legislative Council thereof " and were to be drawn up " in a simple and compendious form, avoiding, as far as may be, all prolixity and tautology ". The Governor was required to withhold assent to any Ordinance which was repugnant to any Act of Parliament or to the Royal Charter or Royal Instructions, or which interfered with Christian worship, diminished the public revenue, authorised money to be raised by lotteries, permitted divorce, provided for a gift to the Governor, prejudiced private property, taxed the trade or shipping of the United Kingdom in a manner from which other traders would be exempt, or subjected persons not of European birth or descent to disabilities which were not imposed on Europeans. Apart from Ordinances for raising the annual financial supplies or otherwise providing for matters where delay would cause serious injury or inconvenience, no Ordinance was to come into effect until the Royal pleasure had been made known.

The Executive Council

The Royal Charter of 1850 authorised the Governor to summon an Executive Council to assist him in the administration of the government. The Royal Instructions of 1851 provided that, in addition to the Governor, the Executive Council was to consist only of the Judicial Assessor and the Collector of Customs, the latter being replaced in 1853 by the Colonial Secretary. Where additional advice was needed on a particular matter extraordinary members could be co-opted by the Governor. Again, rules were laid down for the conduct of the Executive Council. The Governor was to preside and the quorum was to be three. Except in trivial matters the executive powers of the Governor were only to be exercised by the advice and consent of the Executive Council, unless the case was one of emergency, or unless consultation might cause material prejudice to the Crown. This rule was, however, qualified by a provision which enabled the Governor to act in disregard of the opposition of the Executive Council provided the matter was reported to the Secretary of State in London. As with the Legislative Council, no matter could be discussed unless it had been proposed by the Governor, although other members could require points they wished to make to be entered in the minutes.

The Royal Charter also empowered the Governor to make grants of Crown land for public or private purposes, and to constitute and appoint judges, commissioners of oyer and terminer, justices of the peace and other judicial officers, and remit punishments and grant pardons. By the Royal Instructions he was required, to the utmost of his power, to:

> " promote religion and education among the native inhabitants . . . and that you do especially take care to protect them in their persons, and in the free enjoyment of their possessions, and that you do by all lawful means prevent and restrain all violence and injustice, which may in any manner be practised or attempted against them, and that you take such measures as may appear to you to be necessary for their conversion to the Christian faith, and for their advancement in civilisation."

Poll Tax Ordinance

Although the Gold Coast territories were thus provided with a system of civil government it was still not clear how far it could be taken to extend to the local population. The Act of 1843 under which the Royal Charter was made was limited to the " forts and settlements " and this limitation of course extended to the Charter, although its effect was uncertain. The Bond of 1844 contained no such agreement to yield legislative power as would have formed the basis for an Order in Council under the Foreign Jurisdiction Act. Since it soon became clear that the duties imposed on the Governor in relation to the local inhabitants would require the expenditure of greater sums than could be obtained from the abortive customs duties and the British Government subsidies, the question of whether there was power to tax the local inhabitants arose in an acute form. Whatever the legal powers of the Governor and Legislative Council might be, it was clear that the yield from any tax was likely to be small unless the co-operation of the chiefs was obtained. Accordingly, on 19th April, 1852, the Governor, Major S. J. Hill, summoned a meeting at Cape Coast Castle of " the chiefs and headmen of the countries upon the Gold Coast under British protection ". It was resolved:

1. That the meeting " constitutes itself into a Legislative Assembly, with full powers to enact such laws as it shall seem fit for the better government of those countries ".

2. That the meeting be recognized by Her Majesty's Government as legally constituted, that it be called the Legislative Assembly of native chiefs upon the Gold Coast, that it be presided over, assembled, prorogued and adjourned by the Governor, and that its enactments, when sanctioned and approved of by the Governor, shall immediately become the law of the country, subject to Her Majesty's approval, and " be held binding upon the whole of the population being under the protection of the British Government ".

Having assumed its law-making functions, the meeting went on to impose upon the local inhabitants an annual poll tax of one shilling sterling for the support of the Government. In consideration of annual stipends to be paid by the Government, the chiefs agreed to give " their cordial assistance and the full weight of their authority " in supporting the measure. Taxes could be sued for and obstruction was made an offence punishable by imprisonment or fine, one half of any fine to be paid to the local chief. The revenue was to be devoted to the public good, the education of the people, the general improvement and extension of the judicial system, and the improvement of communications and medical services. The resolutions were confirmed by the Governor.[1]

The poll tax was not a success. Until 1861, when it ceased to be collected, the total gross yield was only £30,000, an average of just over £3,000 a year, from which many expenses had to be deducted. Nor did the Legislative Assembly of native chiefs flourish; in fact it never met again.[2]

Establishment of Supreme Court

By the Supreme Court Ordinance, a regular Ordinance made in 1853 by the Governor with the advice and consent of the Legislative Council, the Supreme Court of Her Majesty's Forts and Settlements on the Gold Coast was established. It was to be presided over by a Chief Justice, being an English, Irish or Scottish barrister, and was given a civil and criminal jurisdiction within the forts and settlements equivalent to that of the Courts of Queen's Bench, Common Pleas and Exchequer at Westminster. It was also given Admiralty jurisdiction, but no jurisdiction in

---

[1] Poll Tax Ordinance, 1852.

[2] Claridge, *op. cit.*, I, pp. 481, 495. A similar assembly met at Accra shortly afterwards, which also imposed a poll tax; see the recital to the Poll Tax Ordinance of 10th May, 1858.

equity.[1] J. C. Fitzpatrick, the Judicial Assessor, was appointed by the Ordinance as the first Chief Justice, holding both posts until his resignation the following year.[2] Provision was made for an appeal to the Governor and Legislative Council from decisions of the Judicial Assessor.

In 1856 the areas in the Gold Coast under British protection were given formal recognition, under the name of the " protected territories ", by an Order in Council made under the British Settlements and Foreign Jurisdiction Acts. This provided somewhat obscurely that, in respect of civil or criminal matters (including in particular bankruptcy and insolvency) arising within the protected territories and in regard to which there was a *de facto* British jurisdiction exercisable " without the co-operation of any native chief or authority ", the Supreme Court and magistrates were to have the same jurisdiction as if the matter had arisen within one of the forts. Where the jurisdiction could only be exercised with the co-operation of a native chief or authority, as in the trial of cases under the Bond of 1844, it remained within the province of the Judicial Assessor. The Governor was given power to regulate by Ordinance the exercise of this jurisdiction, provided that equitable regard was paid to local customs; and rules were laid down for the administration of estates of deceased persons within the protected territories. In the same year the Chief Justice and the officer commanding the newly-created Gold Coast Corps were made members of the Legislative Council, the membership being completed by the Colonial Secretary. The same persons also formed the Executive Council.[3]

First Attempt at Municipal Government

Sir Benjamin Pine made the first attempt to introduce municipal government into the Gold Coast with an Ordinance passed on 10th May, 1858. This provided for the creation of municipalities governed by an elected council headed by a mayor and having power to levy a rate in substitution for the poll tax. The council was given powers in relation to highways and markets and the creation of a police force, while the mayor was required to hold a

---

[1] This omission was remedied by an Ordinance passed on 3rd February, 1857.

[2] The two posts continued to be held by the same person, and by 1865 had ceased to be distinct: Brandford Griffith, *op. cit.*, p. 15.

[3] Royal Instructions, 28th October, 1856.

court for hearing cases arising within the limits of the town. The Ordinance was applied to Cape Coast and James Town, Accra, but was repealed on 7th January, 1861. The preamble to the repealing Ordinance[1] stated:

> " It has been found by experience that in the existing state of the said towns and of those in Her Majesty's Settlements on the Gold Coast generally, the satisfactory working of such elective municipal institutions is impracticable, particularly in consequence of the co-existence of the courts of the native kings or chiefs, from the want of a sufficient proportion of educated residents able to understand and willing to assist in their operation, from the impossibility of raising a revenue. . . . The effect of the establishment of them has been to produce serious quarrels, disturbances, and ill-will between different classes of the people. . . . With a few individual exceptions, the people of both towns earnestly desire that such municipalities should be discontinued. . . . "

Constitution of 1866

In 1865, following the tumults of the Ashanti War of 1863, when three Ashanti armies invaded the British protectorate and ravaged some of its most fertile districts, the British Government, faced with the choice of sending out a large army to assume control of Ashanti or vitually abandoning the Gold Coast, appointed another Select Committee of the House of Commons to advise on the matter. The Committee favoured the latter alternative. After reporting that, apart from the original four forts and the ceded Danish forts, a protectorate was assumed by the British over the tribes between the forts and the kingdom of Ashanti, the limits of actual British territory being " wholly indefinite and uncertain ', the Committee observed that the assumption of further posts east of the Volta had been recommended and that " the present policy inevitably leads to extension ". They went on:

> " The Dutch—the only other European power remaining on this coast besides the English—hold forts intermixed with the English, and interfering with their government. Negotiations have been entered into, without result, for better mutual relations."[2]

The Committee recommended that the Gold Coast protectorate

---

[1] No. 1 of 1861.

[2] Report from the Select Committee on Africa (Western Coast), 26th June, 1865 (No. 412), p. xi.

should only be retained " while the chiefs may be as speedily as possible made to do without it ", and that in the meantime the Gold Coast together with Lagos and Gambia should be reunited under Sierra Leone, the development of the steamship having greatly increased the speed of communications since the previous Committee had advised against such a union in 1842. All further extension of territory or assumption of government in West Africa " should be peremptorily prohibited and carefully prevented "[1]

The recommendations were soon acted upon. By a Commission dated 19th February, 1866, the Charter of 1850 was revoked and the Gold Coast, together with Sierra Leone, Lagos and the Gambia, were united under " the Government of our West Africa Settlements ". The existing Gold Coast Ordinances were however preserved, as also was the Legislative Council, although the Executive Council ceased to exist. The permanent members of the Legislative Council were to be the Administrator of the Government (who replaced the Governor), the collector of customs (who performed the duties of the Colonial Secretary) and the officer acting as magistrate.[2] The Supreme Court was also abolished in 1866 and replaced by " the Court of Civil and Criminal Justice " presided over by a chief magistrate.[3] The Order in Council of 1856 remained unrevoked and the Judicial Assessor and other magistrates continued to exercise jurisdiction outside the forts. However, the policy of restricting the extension of British territory led to a sharp rebuke from the Colonial Office when, in September, 1865, a notice was issued by the local Administration stating that all territory within a cannon shot (or five miles) of each fort belonged exclusively to Great Britain.[4]

Departure of the Dutch

Difficulty continued to be caused to the British administration by the existence on the Gold Coast of Dutch forts and settlements intermingled with those of the British. Since the Dutch declined to co-operate in the imposition of customs duties this led in particular to the practical impossibility of raising customs

---

[1] The 1865 *Report*, p. xv. A frown was directed at the Judicial Assessor of the time: " The judicial assessor does not fulfil the first intention of the office, assisting the chiefs in administering justice, but supersedes their authority by decisions according to his own sole judgment."

[2] Royal Instructions, 20th February, 1866, para. 21.

[3] Gold Coast Ordinance No. 7 of 1866.

[4] Cited Crooks, *op. cit.*, pp. 371, 374.

revenue, which otherwise would have been the most convenient and productive form of taxation. In 1860 the Dutch agreed to an exchange which would have transferred their territories east of Cape Coast to the British, and the British territories west of Cape Coast to the Dutch. Objections raised by the local population under British protection in the west to transferring their allegiance to the Dutch led to the abandonment of the scheme. It was however revived and carried through by a Convention signed on 5th March, 1867. The transfers took place, but gave rise to much unrest and to the formation of the Fanti Confederation in an attempt to preserve the unity and security of the coastal tribes. The Constitution of the Confederation, which was drawn up at Mankesim in October and November, 1871, provided an ambitious scheme for mutual defence and the development of communications, education and other services. Legislative powers (including powers of taxation) were also included. The British administration, which had not been consulted, reacted unfavourably, and the scheme came to nothing.[1]

The unrest following the exchange of territory having convinced the Dutch that their position had become untenable, a Convention was signed at the Hague on 25th February, 1871, whereby the King of the Netherlands transferred to the British Crown " all the rights of sovereignty, jurisdiction and property which he possesses on the Coast of Guinea ".[2] No payment was made for the territorial possessions, but a fair price was paid for the Dutch stores and other movables.[3] This new acquisition of territory conflicted with the policy, still in force, of not extending British power on the Gold Coast. In their instructions to the Governor of Sierra Leone, who arrived to carry out the transfer in April, 1872, the British Government stated that their objects in negotiating the treaty were " not the acquisition of territory or the extension of British power, but the maintenance of tranquillity and the promotion of peaceful commerce on the Coast ".[4] It was ironical that the inclusion in the treaty of Elmina, to which

---

[1] See Claridge, *op. cit.*, I, Ch. 32; for text of the Constitution see Sarbah, *Fanti National Constitution*, London, 1906, pp. 199–209; see also Casely Hayford, *Gold Coast Native Institutions*, London, 1903, pp. 182–193.

[2] The Dutch territories included the castle and fort at Elmina and forts at Axim, Dixcove, Sekondi, Shama and Butri—Claridge, *op. cit.*, I, 630. For text of the treaty see Crooks, *op. cit.*, p. 393.

[3] The Dutch received in return certain concessions in the island of Sumatra.

[4] Cited Claridge, *op. cit.*, I, p. 627.

the Ashantis laid strong claim, was the principal cause of the Sixth Ashanti War, which itself led to the taking over of the entire coastal area by the British and the creation in 1874 of the Gold Coast Colony.

Creation of Gold Coast Colony

The war began on 22nd January, 1873, when the main Ashanti army crossed the River Pra. It ended, after a determined assault by Sir Garnet Wolseley and an army reinforced by troops from England, with the defeat of the Ashantis and the drawing up of the Treaty of Fomena on 13th February, 1874, by which the Asantehene renounced his claim to Elmina and all other coastal territories.[1] Having at last achieved the position of sole European power on the Gold Coast, and having, at considerable cost in life and resources, at last brought about the decisive defeat of the Ashantis, the British Government, disregarding those who still pleaded for the abandonment of this troublesome region, decided that further temporizing was impossible. By a Royal Charter signed on 24th July, 1874, the Gold Coast and Lagos were separated from Sierra Leone and together constituted a separate colony under the title of the Gold Coast Colony.

2. BRITISH ASSUMPTION OF TERRITORIES, 1874–1914

During the period from 1874 to 1914 all the territories now comprised in the Republic of Ghana came under the control of the British Crown.

Constitution of 1874

The Royal Charter of 24th July, 1874, issued under the British Settlements Act, revoked the Commission of 19th February, 1866, so far as it applied to the Gold Coast and Lagos, and constituted these territories a separate colony under the title of the Gold Coast Colony. In addition to Lagos, which had been annexed by the British in 1861 so that the slave-smuggling there could be suppressed, the territory of the new colony was to comprise " all places, settlements and territories which may at any time belong to us in Western Africa " between 5° West and 2° East longitude. In providing for a Governor, Legislative Council and Executive Council, the Charter repeated with little

---

[1] For text see Claridge, *op. cit.*, II, p. 152.

B

variation the terms of the Charter of 1850.[1] The powers of the
Legislative Council now, however, derived not merely from the
Charter, but also from the Colonial Laws Validity Act, 1865. This
provided that no law made by the legislature of a colony should
be void or inoperative on the ground of repugnancy to the common
law or to any Act of the Imperial Parliament which did not apply
to the colony by express words or necessary intendment. The
Act also made it clear that Royal Instructions to the Governor
could not fetter his power to assent to legislation, and gave to the
colonial legislature full power within its jurisdiction to alter the
constitution of the legislature and to establish, reconstitute and
abolish courts of justice.

The new Charter was proclaimed at Government House, Cape
Coast, on 11th September, 1874, and on that day the former
Administrator, George Strahan, assumed office as Governor and
Commander-in-Chief.[2] On 19th March, 1877, the seat of Government was moved from Cape Coast to Accra, where it has
remained.[3] This move had been decided on as far back as 1851,
when Governor Hill obtained Lord Grey's permission for it on a
number of grounds. These included the more central position
of Accra in the British protectorate as it then existed, the need
to develop in the eastern areas educational, judicial and other
facilities (which could be better done under the eye of the
Governor), the need to subdue the tribes in the Accra region,
and the superiority of Accra over Cape Coast " in a sanitary
point of view ".[4]

The first two Ordinances made by the new colony prohibited
slave-trading and declared all persons then held in slavery to be
free. This applied both to slaves held in captivity by slave dealers
and also to those treated as slaves under customary law, though
in the latter case freedom was only conferred on persons born after
5th November, 1874.[5]

Re-establishment of Supreme Court

The Supreme Court of the Gold Coast was re-established by

---

[1] See pp. 8 *et seq. ante.*

[2] Despatch by Governor Strahan to the Earl of Carnavon, 11th
September, 1874 (Ghana National Archives, Accra).

[3] *Gold Coast Gazette,* 31st March, 1877 (notice dated 8th March).

[4] Despatch of 26th November, 1851 (Ghana National Archives, Accra).
Governor Hill remarked that Cape Coast was originally chosen only because
the Governor's personal accommodation was better there.

[5] Gold Coast Slave-dealing Abolition Ordinance, 1874 (No. 1); Gold
Coast Emancipation Ordinance, 1874 (No. 2).

the Supreme Court Ordinance, 1876, which constituted it the Supreme Court of Judicature for the Gold Coast Colony " and for the Territories thereto near or adjacent wherein Her Majesty may at any time before or after the commencement of this Ordinance have acquired powers and jurisdiction ". The court consisted of the Chief Justice and not more than four puisne judges, and it was provided that the Full Court (which was to consist of the Chief Justice and one or two puisne judges) should be a court of appeal with sittings in Accra and Lagos. A Divisional Court of the Supreme Court was required to sit in each of the three Provinces into which the area of jurisdiction was divided.[1] The Supreme Court was given the same jurisdiction, except for the Admiralty jurisdiction, as the recently-created High Court of Justice in England, and was also authorised to exercise the Lord Chancellor's powers of guardianship of infants and lunatics. The Ordinance further provided that district commissioners were to be *ex officio* Commissioners of the Supreme Court, each Commissioner exercising the powers of a judge of the Supreme Court within his own district as well as those of a bench of magistrates. A notable provision was the duty imposed on the court to promote reconciliation of differences among persons over whom it had jurisdiction, and to " encourage and facilitate the settlement in an amicable way, and without recourse to litigation, of matters in difference between them ". This duty extended not only to civil disputes but criminal matters " not amounting to felony and not aggravated in degree ". The Ordinance abolished the post of Judicial Assessor and transferred to the Supreme Court the jurisdiction formerly exercised by him in the Protectorate.[2] The Petitions of Right Ordinance, 1877 (No. 12) enabled claims against the Government to be pursued in the Supreme Court. Provision for appeals from the Supreme Court to the Privy Council was contained in an Order in Council also made in 1877.

The administration of justice in the native tribunals was regulated by the Gold Coast Native Jurisdiction Ordinance, 1883 (No. 5) (which replaced No. 8 of 1878). This Ordinance constituted native tribunals in the areas to which it was applied by proclamation. The tribunals consisted of the head chiefs of

---

[1] The Provinces came to be treated as established for general purposes, and not merely for those of the Supreme Court.

[2] For the application by the Ordinance of the rules of English law, and the difficulties which arose over the relationship between them and local customary law, see Chap. 10, *post.*

divisions, the chiefs of sub-divisions or villages, and their respective councillors. They exercised both civil and criminal jurisdiction. Land and succession cases could be tried, and also personal suits in which " the debt, damage, or demand does not exceed seven ounces of gold or twenty-five pounds sterling ".[1] Appeals lay to the Supreme Court. The Ordinance also empowered divisional chiefs to make byelaws relating to roads, water supply, fisheries, forests, mines and other matters. This included power to suppress the worship of any fetish " which it is pretended has power to protect offenders, or to injure persons giving information of the commission of offences ". Chiefs were also given certain ministerial powers as " convervators of the peace " and agents for the local administration of Ordinances. The Governor was enabled to dismiss or suspend any chief who had abused his power or was otherwise unfit for office. The Chiefs Ordinance, 1904 (No. 4), introduced the important principle of government recognition of chiefs, which still applies today.[2] Where he was satisfied that a chief had been installed or destooled in accordance with customary law, the Governor was empowered to give a certificate to that effect. The certificate was conclusive in all courts. Although introduced merely as a measure to facilitate proof of installation or destoolment, this clearly gave the Government a powerful instrument of control over chiefs, and in time it came to be used as such.

A civil police force was established by the Police Ordinance, 1894, police duties having previously been carried out mainly by military detachments.[3]

Town Councils Ordinance, 1894

Another attempt was made to establish local government in the townships with the enactment of the Town Councils Ordinance, 1894 (No. 17).[4] The Ordinance, which was applied to Accra, Cape Coast and Sekondi, provided for four of the eight members of each council to be nominated by the Governor. The remainder were to be elected by voters owning or occupying houses with

---

[1] This language is still to be found in the law relating to local courts, the successors to native tribunals, but the limit is now £G100: Courts Act, 1960 (C.A. 9), s. 98 (1) (f).

[2] See p. 178, *post.*

[3] See W. H. Gillespie, *The Gold Coast Police, 1844–1938,* Accra, 1955. The 1894 Ordinance was consolidated in 1921 and 1922, the 1922 version (No. 10) forming the basis for the present Police Service Ordinance (Cap. 37).

[4] The first attempt had been made in 1858; see p. 13, *ante.*

an annual value of £2 or more, but where the number of candidates was insufficient the Governor could nominate qualified electors to make up the number. The council was given various detailed functions and the general function of doing " such acts as may be necessary for the conservancy of the town and the preservation of the public health therein ". Power was conferred to levy a house rate up to five per cent. of the annual value. Persons using vehicles within the town limits were required to take out a wheel licence on payment of an annual fee ranging from five shillings to two pounds. Other sources of revenue included licences for spirits, auction sales and dogs, and fines for various criminal offences.

Concessions Ordinance

Towards the end of the nineteenth century efforts were made by the Gold Coast Government to deal with the growing problem of the indiscriminate granting of land concessions to expatriates. An attempt in 1894 to do this by vesting all waste lands, forests and minerals in the Crown aroused great opposition and was dropped. Even the less extreme Public Lands Bill proved unacceptable, and indeed brought about the formation of the Gold Coast Aborigines' Rights Protection Society, so the Government contented themselves with the passage in 1900 of the Concessions Ordinance (No. 14). This required details of all concessions to be notified to the Supreme Court and published in the *Gazette*. Without the leave of the court, no proceedings could be taken to enforce the concession unless it had been certified as valid by the court, which had power to modify its terms. In relation to mining, timber, rubber and other products of the soil, the area of land which could be granted to any one person or company was strictly limited. Expatriates could not engage in mining without a licence issued by the Governor. A five per cent. duty was imposed on all profits made from concessions.[1]

Constitutional Adjustments

In 1886 a charter was granted to the Royal Niger Company, which took over the administration of the British colony at Lagos. Letters Patent were accordingly issued by which, on 13th January, 1886, Lagos ceased to form part of the Gold Coast Colony. In

---

[1] For criticisms of the effectiveness of the Concessions Ordinance (which in a modified form is still in force) see Lord Hailey, *An African Survey* (1938 Edn.), p. 777.

the following year an Order in Council was made under the Foreign Jurisdiction Act empowering the Gold Coast Legislative Council to legislate for territories adjoining the Colony which had been brought under British protection.[1] The first African member of the Legislative Council, John Sarbah, was appointed in 1888.

By Royal Instructions issued on 11th March, 1895, it was provided that apart from the Governor the Executive Council should consist of the Lieutenant-Governor of the Colony (if any), the senior officer in command of regular troops in the Colony, and the Colonial Secretary, Attorney-General and Treasurer, together with such additional persons as might be appointed by royal authority. The *ex officio* members of the Legislative Council were the same as for the Executive Council, with the addition of the Chief Justice.[2] Provision was made for the royal appointment of additional persons holding offices in the Colony, who, together with the *ex officio* members, were to be styled " official members ". In addition provision was made for the royal appointment of persons not holding offices, who were to be styled " unofficial members ".

Relations with Ashanti

The time was now drawing near for the British Government to take a decisive step in the acquisition of territory. The defeat of the Ashantis in 1874 had caused a temporary break-up of the Ashanti Confederacy. It was largely a military union, and military defeat robbed it of its main purpose. However, the British still preferred to pursue a policy of non-intervention and within a few years most of the states which had thrown off allegiance to the Asantehene had rejoined the Confederacy. While favouring non-intervention, the British were prepared to extend their protection to those who wanted it, and a number of tribes from Ashanti were brought within the Colony, either by extension of its still undefined boundaries or through the emigration of the people's concerned. Things might have continued in this indecisive fashion if the Colony had not been threatened with encirclement by other European powers. On the Ivory Coast the French were extending their influence inland following the treaty with Gyaman

---

[1] Order in Council of 29th December, 1887.
[2] The Chief Justice ceased to be a member of the Legislative Council in 1911.

in 1888, while in 1885 the Germans established a settlement in Togoland.

In 1890 the British offered the Asantehene a treaty under which Ashanti would come under British protection, but this was refused. In 1896, however, a force was sent out from Britain and Kumasi was again occupied. The Asantehene, Agyeman Prempeh (Kwaku Dua III), was exiled to the Seychelles. Most of the chiefs of Ashanti accepted treaties of protection offered by the British, and a British Resident was appointed in Kumasi.[1] Treaties of friendship and protection were also made with the Kings of Dagomba (12th August, 1892) and Mamprusi (12th January, 1897), whose territories lay to the north of Ashanti.[2] In 1900 there occurred the celebrated incident in which the Governor, Sir Frederic Hodgson, demanded the Golden Stool while visiting Kumasi. At the conclusion of the Seventh Ashanti War, which immediately followed, the British Government decided to temporize no longer. On 26th September, 1901, three Orders in Council were made by which the Crown annexed Ashanti and the territories to the south which had not previously been brought within the Gold Coast Colony, and also declared a protectorate over the Northern Territories.[3] The initial decision to declare Ashanti merely a protectorate was varied in favour of annexation on the entreaty of the Chief Justice, Sir William Brandford Griffith.[4]

Constitution of 1901

The Gold Coast Order in Council, 1901, which was made under the royal prerogative, for the first time laid down the geographical boundaries of the Colony and declared annexed such of the territories included in the new boundaries as did not already form part of His Majesty's dominions. The annexed territories

---

[1] The following treaties of friendship and protection made between Queen Victoria and various Ashanti Kings are to be found in the National Archives, Accra: Sefwi (18th February, 1887); Kwahu (5th May, 1888); Attabubu (25th November, 1890); Juaben (10th February, 1896). A full list of treaties made between the British and the local chiefs is given in Appendix V to the *Gold Coast Handbook* of 1924.

[2] These treaties are also kept in the National Archives.

[3] A further Order in Council made on the same day validated legislation made in accordance with a local law which had attempted to extend the Colony to all areas in which *de facto* jurisdiction was exercised; see Brandford Griffith, *op. cit.*, pp. 21–23.

[4] See *The Far Horizon* by Sir W. Brandford Griffith, Ilfracombe, *pub.* A. H. Stockwell, 1951, pp. 176–180.

were made part and parcel of the Colony and all existing laws were applied to them. The Order came into force on 1st January, 1902, but was amended by the substitution of more precise boundaries by the Gold Coast Boundaries Order in Council, 1906.[1]

The Ashanti Order in Council, 1901, was also made under the royal prerogative and recited that the territories of Ashanti had been conquered by His Majesty's forces and that it was expedient that they should be annexed. The Order declared that they should form part of His Majesty's dominions and should be known as Ashanti. The word " colony " was not used but the effect of the Order, which came into force on 1st January, 1902, was to give Ashanti the status of a Crown colony. The administration of Ashanti was entrusted to a Chief Commissioner acting under the direction of the Governor of the Gold Coast, the latter being given power, on his own initiative and without the advice of the Gold Coast Legislative Council, to make Ordinances for the peace, order and good government of Ashanti. Ordinances so made had to be submitted to London for royal assent, disallowance or other direction. The first Ordinance was the Ashanti Administration Ordinance, 1902, which divided Ashanti into four districts, set up a Chief Commissioner's Court and district courts, regulated the functioning of native courts and applied a number of Gold Coast Ordinances to Ashanti.

The Northern Territories Order in Council, 1901, was made under the Foreign Jurisdiction Act and also came into force on 1st January, 1902. It converted the area between the eighth parallel (which formed the northern boundary of Ashanti) and the French frontier into a protectorate to be known as the Northern Territories of the Gold Coast.[2] From the standpoint of administration the position of the Northern Territories was identical to that of Ashanti—indeed the wording of the two Orders in Council after the opening paragraphs was identical. The Northern Territories Administration Ordinance, 1902, also followed the same lines as that made for Ashanti.

The Ashanti Order in Council, 1906, and the Northern Territories Order in Council, 1906, adjusted the boundary between Ashanti and the Northern Territories, bringing into Ashanti and annexing to the Crown certain areas to the north of the eighth

---

[1] This came into force on 1st January, 1907, and was not subsequently amended.

[2] The Northern Territories were not annexed until 1957; see p. 61, *post*.

parallel. They also modified in other respects the boundaries of Ashanti and the Northern Territories.

Occupation of Togoland

Within a few days after the outbreak of the First World War on 4th August, 1914, Gold Coast forces invaded the neighbouring German colony of Togoland and brought about its surrender before the month was out. This operation, carried through with the assistance of French troops from Dahomey, was completed at a cost to Gold Coast funds of approximately £60,000.[1] The main force employed was the Gold Coast Regiment, which had been created in 1901. In that year the colonial military forces in West Africa were amalgamated to form the West African Frontier Force, and the former Gold Coast Constabulary was made a unit of the new Force under the name of the Gold Coast Regiment.[2] The word Royal was added to the name of the Force in 1929.[3]

Pending the making of final arrangements for the future of Togoland at the end of the war, the British and French agreed an interim boundary line and established provisional governments to administer their respective territories.[4] The British administration continued in one form or another until Ghana became independent in 1957. The occupation of Togoland marked the close of the period of British territorial expansion in the Gold Coast. No further territories were acquired, and the Colony and its dependencies settled down to a long period of colonial government.

3. COLONIAL GOVERNMENT, 1914–1945

Sir Hugh Clifford was appointed Governor of the Colony[5] on 26th December, 1912. He immediately determined to make himself familiar with the land and its people, and spent much

---

[1] Leg. Co. Deb. (1914–15), 6.

[2] *Gold Coast Handbook* (1924), p. 350. For the earlier history of the Gold Coast military forces see *ibid.*, pp. 349–350.

[3] Ordinance No. 25 of 1929.

[4] Leg. Co. Deb. (1914–15), 5. For the later arrangements, made under the auspices of the League of Nations, see p. 28, *post*.

[5] In the remainder of this chapter " the Colony " will be used to indicate the Gold Coast Colony proper, and " the Gold Coast " to indicate the Colony plus its dependencies of Ashanti, Northern Territories and Togoland.

time in his early days travelling all over the Colony and inter-viewing chiefs and others. He found that the great development of the cocoa-producing industry since the turn of the century was causing important social changes. In an address to the Legislative Council, he said:

> " It is impossible for any thinking person to travel throughout the Gold Coast today and to examine the affairs of the Colony with any measure of sympathy without being struck with the tremendous social revolution which is in progress in our midst. This has been brought about by the phenomenal development of the cocoa industry which has been carried out by the natives themselves and which has brought with it all sorts of luxuries and has placed all sorts of things, never dreamed of by their fore-fathers, within the reach of the poorest among us."[1]

Constitution of 1916

Clifford drew the conclusion that constitutional changes were called for, and that the administration should have at its com-mand a much larger measure of advice from far more varied sources than was hitherto available. This did not mean that there was to be any relaxation of the system of Government control:

> " His Majesty's Government holds strongly, and I personally fully share the opinion, that the present stage of peaceful development of the Gold Coast still requires the maintenance of the Crown Colony system of government, which is of a paternal rather than of a democratic character."[2]

Clifford accordingly made representations to the Secretary of State for the Colonies requesting an enlargement of the Legislative Council, which then consisted of five official members and four unofficial members. The official members were the Governor himself and the Colonial Secretary, the Attorney-General, the Treasurer and the Principal Medical Officer. The unofficial members consisted of two Europeans respectively representing the merchants and the mining industry, and two Africans. One of these was T. Hutton-Mills, who represented the educated classes in the Colony, and the other was E. Mate Kole, the Konor of Eastern Krobo, who represented the chiefs and people of the Colony.[3]

The British Government accepted Clifford's view and the next

---

[1] Leg. Co. Deb. (1916–17), 16.
[2] Leg. Co. Deb. (1916–17), 19.
[3] *Ibid.*, 16–17.

step in constitutional advance was taken. On 25th September, 1916, the existing Constitution, which was established by the Letters Patent of 13th January, 1886, as amplified by Royal Instructions issued on the same date and Additional Instructions issued on subsequent dates, was revoked.[1] The new Letters Patent and Royal Instructions, which were dated 20th September, 1916, and came into force five days later, effected little alteration except the enlargement of the Legislative Council. The membership of this was increased from nine to twenty-two. The official members added were the Secretary for Native Affairs (native affairs being in Clifford's opinion the most important matters which should engage the attention of the Government), the Comptroller of Customs, the Director of Public Works and the General Manager of Railways (three technical officers whose advice was needed), and the three Provincial Commissioners, as " impartial spokesmen of the Provinces ". On the unofficial side a third European, an official of the Bank of British West Africa, was added to represent the general European interest. Also added were three paramount chiefs drawn from different parts of the Colony. These were Nana Ofori Atta (the Omanhene of Akim Abuakwa), Nana Amonoo V (the Omanhene of Anamabu) and Awame Sri II (the Fia of Awuna Ga), who were chosen to represent the peoples speaking Twi, Fanti, and Ewe respectively. Finally E. J. P. Brown and J. E. Casely Hayford were added as unofficial members to speak for the political interests of the Central Province and the Western Province respectively. At the first meeting of the new council the Governor said that the selection had been made " with a single aim, namely to obtain the best spokesmen ". He added:

> " There has been no attempt to pack this Council with Government partisans. On the contrary we desire to have on it men who will freely represent to us the feelings, wishes and needs of the communities they are appointed to represent; and we are welcoming among us today so many new members, in order that

---

[1] During the period of British rule in Ghana important constitutional changes were always made by revoking the existing Constitution, embodied in Letters Patent or an Order in Council as amplified by Royal Instructions, and substituting a new one. Thus in form the continuity of institutions such as the Governorship and the Legislative Council was broken at fairly frequent intervals. There was also the disadvantage that the detailed changes made were difficult to distinguish. The procedure was followed throughout the British Empire. For an explanation of it in detail see Wight, *British Colonial Constitutions, 1947*, Oxford, pp. 94 *et seq.*

the range of advice at the disposal of the Government may be
largely extended."[1]

Clifford regarded this enlargement of the Legislative Council
as the most important local event that occurred during his term
of office as Governor.[2] He was succeeded on 1st September, 1919,
by Sir Gordon Guggisberg, who remained in office until 1927 and
introduced many notable reforms. In the sphere of constitutional
law the most important development took place in 1926, when
provincial councils were established in the Colony and a new
Constitution came into force. Guggisberg also introduced
important changes in native administration.

The Togoland Mandate

During this period the British occupation of the western part
of the former German colony of Togoland was regularised. In
the peace treaty signed at Versailles on 28th June, 1919, Germany
renounced all rights over Togoland in favour of the Allied powers.[3]
A fortnight later, on 10th July, 1919, a Franco-British Declaration
laid down in detail the frontier between the two divisions of
Togoland and on 20th July, 1922, a mandate to administer the
part of Togoland lying to the west of this frontier was conferred
upon the British Crown under Article 22 of the Covenant of the
League of Nations.[4] Since its capture in 1914, laws had been
made for the British sphere of Togoland by proclamation. Until
1920 these proclamations were made by the officer commanding
the British forces in Togoland; thereafter they were made by the
Governor of the Gold Coast. After the British Sphere of Togoland
Order in Council, 1923, came into operation laws were made by
Ordinance as in the case of the other dependencies. The first of
these was the Administration Ordinance. The British sphere of
Togoland was divided into two sections, of which the northern
was administered as part of the Northern Territories Protectorate
and the southern as part of the Colony, this being expressly
permitted by Article 9 of the Mandate. Although the Franco-
British boundary was so drawn as to reunite tribes in the north

---

[1] Leg. Co. Deb. (1916–17), 18.
[2] Leg. Co. Deb. (1918–19), 55.
[3] *Laws of the Gold Coast* (1936), IV, p. 105.
[4] The Mandate and Declaration are set out in *Laws of the Gold Coast*
(1936), IV, pp. 88 *et seq.* and also on pp. 472 *et seq.* of the *Gold Coast Handbook*, 1924. The boundary was modified in 1929; see p. 128, *post*. For
Article 22 of the Covenant see *Laws of the Gold Coast* (1936), IV, p. 105.

who had been split between the Northern Territories and German Togoland, in the south it had the effect of dividing the Ewes into separate communities—a fact which has caused discontent down to the present day.

Attempt to improve Municipal Government

A committee was set up by Guggisberg in 1921 to consider and report upon the organisation of municipal government in the Colony. They found that the town councils in Accra, Sekondi and Cape Coast set up under the 1894 Ordinance[1] had fulfilled the purposes for which they were created but were hampered by lack of funds.[2] Complaints were made against the Ordinance because it imposed direct taxation (although feeling against this was diminishing) and because the president of each council (who was nominated by the Governor) had a casting vote which gave the Government a majority and turned the town councils into a branch of the Government. The Municipal Corporations Ordinance, 1924, which resulted from the committee's report, was designed to give autonomy to the townships, and the councillors nominated by the Government were to be limited to one-third of the total. Powers of direct taxation were not however reduced; on the contrary the maximum rate was doubled to become one-fifth of the annual value of premises. This proved the undoing of the measure. When it was proposed to apply it to Accra in 1925 a storm of protest was aroused, notwithstanding that it had been supported by the African members of the Legislative Council representing Accra, Sekondi and Cape Coast. These towns therefore remained under the 1894 Ordinance, and the 1924 Ordinance was never applied. Guggisberg described this as " the only real disappointment which I have had as your Governor ".[3] It interfered to some extent with his plans for a new, partly-elective, Legislative Council and these had to be modified slightly.

Constitution of 1925

Guggisberg had formed the view, in pursuit of the policy of indirect rule, that the native institutions required strengthening. To this end several attempts (which finally succeeded) were made

---

[1] See p. 20, *ante.*
[2] Leg. Co. Deb. (1924–25), 261.
[3] *Review of the Events of 1920–26 and the Prospects of 1927–28*, Accra, 1927, p. 14.

to pass a new Native Administration Ordinance.[1] Another step in this direction was the creation of Provincial Councils. Guggisberg saw these as:

> " . . . the breakwaters defending our native constitutions, institutions and customs against the disintegrating waves of western civilization. They are the chief means by which the nationality of the Africans of the Gold Coast will be built up out of the many scattered tribes. . . . "[2]

The Provincial Councils were created by the instrument which provided for an enlarged, partly-elected Legislative Council. This was the Gold Coast Colony (Legislative Council) Order in Council, 1925, which was made on 8th April, 1925, and came into force on 15th April in the following year.[3] It marked a considerable advance in that it gave the Colony elected representation for the first time. The new Legislative Council consisted of the Governor, together with fifteen official and fourteen unofficial members. The official members were divided into *ex officio* members, of whom there were thirteen, and nominated official members. The *ex officio* members were:

> the five senior members of the Executive Council;
> the Comptroller of Customs;
> the Director of Public Works;
> the General Manager of the Railway;
> the Commissioners of the three Provinces;
> the Surveyor-General; and
> the Director of Education.

The unofficial members consisted of the following:

> three provincial members elected by the Eastern Provincial Council;
> two provincial members elected by the Central Provincial Council;
> one provincial member elected by the Western Provincial Council;
> three municipal members elected by the voters of Accra, Cape Coast and Sekondi respectively;
> a European mercantile member elected by representatives of firms belonging to a recognised chamber of commerce;

---

[1] See p. 32, *post*.
[2] *Review of the Events of 1920–26 and the Prospects of 1927–28*, p. 23.
[3] Proclamation No. 3 of 1926.

a European mining member elected by the Gold Coast Chamber of Mines; and

three Europeans nominated by the Governor.

The Provincial Councils were established by s. 15 of the Order in Council, which provided that each Council was to consist of the persons who were recognised by the Governor as head chiefs (that is paramount chiefs) and who had their headquarters within the Province. Apart from their elective functions, the Councils were to have such other functions as might be conferred by Ordinance. In addition to these statutory functions:

> " . . . the Provincial Councils fulfil three very valuable objects: they give the head chiefs and their Councillors the opportunity of uniting for the preservation of their national institutions, of consulting together on subjects to the common welfare of their respective peoples, and, finally, of examining and advising Government on any proposed legislation affecting the people."[1]

The Eastern and Central Provincial Councils duly met and elected their representatives to the Legislative Council, but the Western Province proved a disappointment to the Governor. The Council there refused to elect a representative, the gap being filled by the Governor's nomination of Nana Ofori Atta, who would otherwise have lost his seat. Difficulty also arose from the unexpected opposition to the application of the Municipal Councils Ordinance. The Order in Council originally provided that a municipal member was only to be *elected* if the new Ordinance had been applied to his township; otherwise he was to be nominated by the Governor. This meant that the first municipal members had to be nominated; but the restriction was shortly afterwards removed by an amending Order.[2]

The constitutional changes were completed by the issue on 23rd May, 1925, of new Letters Patent and Royal Instructions, which revoked the 1916 Constitution. Apart from alterations made necessary by the new provisions for the Legislative Council, these made no change in the previous position.

---

[1] Guggisberg, *Review of the Events of 1920–26, etc.*, p. 15. The Provincial Councils came to play an important role as a link between the Government and the rural population. They frequently met in joint session, and a standing committee of the Joint Provincial Councils was later established. In 1944 it consisted of twelve paramount chiefs drawn from the three councils (Leg. Co. Deb. (1944, No. 2), 49) and was formally recognized by s. 29 of the Native Authority (Colony) Ordinance, 1944 (No. 21).

[2] The Gold Coast Colony (Legislative Council) Order in Council, 1927.

Native Administration Ordinance

In 1927, shortly before the end of Governor Guggisberg's tenure of office, the Native Administration Ordinance was passed. This was a comprehensive measure, consolidating the Native Jurisdiction Ordinance, 1883, and later Ordinances affecting chieftaincy, but also making a number of important changes. Similar Bills had been introduced into the Legislative Council by the Government in 1919 and 1922, but had been withdrawn owing to strong opposition from the unofficial members. The 1927 Bill was drawn up at meetings of paramount chiefs in 1925 and 1926 and was introduced as an unofficial member's Bill by Nana Ofori Atta. The Ordinance contained detailed provisions as to the election and destoolment of chiefs and the jurisdiction of native tribunals. It protected the office of chieftaincy by rendering it an offence to undermine or usurp the authority of a chief. It restored the position of the state councils and made clear their authority (to the exclusion of the Supreme Court) to determine constitutional disputes affecting chieftaincy. The Governor's power to depose a chief for misconduct was not reproduced, and the provisions as to recognition of installation and destoolment were modified. The Ordinance also laid down additional functions for the new Provincial Councils, which mainly concerned the settlement of inter-state disputes. The power conferred on the paramount chiefs to make byelaws was supplemented in 1931 by an amendment which enabled stool treasuries to be established, and expenditure from stool revenues to be controlled, by means of such byelaws.[1] The way was thus open for what Lord Hailey called " the most essential feature in indirect rule ",[2] but few states established treasuries and, in the absence of any power of taxation, income would in any case have remained irregular. Such power was at last given by the Native Administration Treasuries Ordinance, 1939 (No. 16), which also enabled Provincial Commissioners to order the establishment of treasuries and in default gave the Governor power to establish them himself and to control their management.

Judicial Reforms

A step towards unification of the administration of the Colony and its dependencies was taken in 1935, when for the first time

---

[1] Ordinance No. 23 of 1931.
[2] *An African Survey* (1938 Edn.), p. 471.

it became possible to legislate for the Colony, Ashanti and the Northern Territories by one Ordinance.[1] This did not alter the position under which legislation for the Colony required the advice and consent of the Legislative Council, whereas the Governor alone could legislate for the dependencies. One of the first laws to be made under this useful provision was a re-enactment of the Courts Ordinance of 1876, which was thus extended to the whole of the Gold Coast.[2] A number of changes were made in accordance with the Government's new policy that:

> " as far as it is consistent with financial needs, justice should be administered by qualified lawyers, and it is only when those qualified lawyers cannot be found that it should be administered by those not qualified."[3]

District commissioners' courts were replaced by magistrates' courts, the magistrates being lawyers where possible. District magistrates and district commissioners ceased to form part of the Supreme Court. The judges of the Supreme Courts of Nigeria, Sierra Leone and the Gambia were made *ex officio* judges of the Gold Coast Supreme Court.

Improved facilities for appeals from the Supreme Court came into being with the establishment in 1928 of the West African Court of Appeal. This meant that such appeals did not have to go direct to the Privy Council in London, although the Privy Council was not removed as a final appeal tribunal. The West African Court of Appeal consisted of the judges of the Gold Coast Supreme Court and of the other superior courts in the British colonies and protectorates in West Africa from which appeals lay. Jurisdiction was left to be regulated by the law of the individual territories, which also had to bear the expenses of the court.[4] Appeals to the Privy Council were dealt with by the West African (Appeal to Privy Council) Order in Council, 1930,[5] which gave an appeal as of right where the matter in dispute was valued at £500 or more, and an appeal by leave of the court below in other cases of general or public importance.

---

[1] The Gold Coast Ordinances Order in Council, 1934, which came into force on 1st January, 1935.

[2] Courts Ordinance, 1935 (No. 7).

[3] Leg. Co. Deb. (1935), 29.

[4] West African Court of Appeal Orders in Council, 1928–35, Consolidated (*Laws of the Gold Coast* (1936), IV, p. 190). In the Gold Coast jurisdiction was regulated by the West African Court of Appeal Ordinance, 1935 (No. 11); see *Laws of the Gold Coast* (1936), I, p. 231.

[5] *Laws of the Gold Coast* (1936), IV, p. 232.

C

Law of Sedition

In 1934 a change in the law governing sedition aroused considerable opposition. Sedition was dealt with by the Criminal Code, a comprehensive collection of penal provisions which displaced the common law (although largely reproducing its effect) and which had been in force since 1892. It did not prohibit the importation or possession of seditious matter, and the Government became alarmed when, in the early 1930s, literature began to be imported into the Gold Coast which advocated the overthrow of British rule.[1] The Bill to close these loopholes aroused protests from the African unofficial members. They did not object to being governed by the same law as prevailed in the United Kingdom, but mere possession of seditious matter was not there an offence and on this ground the opposition centred. Sir Ofori Atta (as he had by then become) said:

> " If I am intelligent enough to read a newspaper which is not good and I send it to, say, my brother the Omanhene of Winneba for him to be allured by it and I am caught, then, I have done something. But if I merely have it in my possession without making use of it, why should I be subject to the trouble and torment of going to court to defend myself? "[2]

The African unofficial members voted against the Bill, but it became law as the Criminal Code (Amendment) Ordinance, 1934 (No. 21). This was one of the rare occasions when legislation was forced through by the Government against the unanimous opposition of the African members.[3]

Restoration of the Asantehene

In the following year new constitutional provisions came into force for Ashanti and the Northern Territories. The Orders in Council of 1901 and 1906, together with the accompanying Royal Instructions, were revoked and replaced by new provisions.[4] These made little change, although the Executive Council for the Colony was deemed also to be the Executive Council for the two dependencies, and was required to be consulted by the Governor when enacting legislation. By another instrument the Chief

---

[1] *Gold Coast Gazette*, 21st February, 1934.
[2] Leg. Co. Deb. (1934), 145.
[3] Another, which occurred at the same time, concerned the Waterworks Ordinance, 1934 (No. 20): Leg. Co. Deb. (1934), 113.
[4] Ashanti Order in Council, 1934, and Royal Instructions; Northern Territories Order in Council, 1934, and Royal Instructions.

Commissioners for Ashanti and the Northern Territories were added to the Executive Council.[1] The new provisions came into force on 1st January, 1935, and coincided with the restoration of the Ashanti Confederacy and the designation of Osei Agyeman Prempeh II as the first Asantehene under the British Government, which took place on the last day of the month.[2] At the same time Native Authority and Native Courts Ordinances were passed for Ashanti,[3] and the Ashanti Confederacy Council was reconstituted.[4] A Native Authority Ordinance had been passed for the Northern Territories in 1932,[5] and a Native Courts Ordinance was passed in 1935[6]. A Native Administration Ordinance had also been passed for the southern section of British Togoland in 1932.[7]

Developments during the Second World War

Constitutional development did not cease during the Second World War. Soon after his appointment as Governor in November, 1941, Sir Alan Burns suggested to the Colonial Office that the time had come for the appointment of Africans to the Executive Council. Accordingly, in October, 1942, Sir Ofori Atta and Mr. K. A. Korsah[8] were appointed for three-year terms as unofficial members of the Executive Council.[9] Self-government for the municipalities at last arrived with the enactment in the years 1943–1945 of separate Town Council Ordinances for Accra, Kumasi, Cape Coast and Sekondi-Takoradi.[10] These introduced elected majorities on the town councils and provided for universal adult suffrage. Like Guggisberg before him, Sir Alan Burns was, as he told the Legislative Council, " very keen on the establishment of Town Councils ", as he considered that " the experience to be gained by electors and members in Town Councils where there is an elected majority, and in Native Administrations, is the best training for self-government on a larger scale ".[11] Like

---

[1] Additional Instructions dated 23rd November, 1934. By the Gold Coast Colony (Legislative Council) Amendment Order in Council, 1934, the two Chief Commissioners were excluded from the Legislative Council.
[2] See the speech of the Governor at Kumasi, *Gold Coast Gazette*, 31st January, 1935.
[3] Ordinances Nos. 1 and 2 of 1935.
[4] Ashanti Confederacy Council Order 1935 (Order No. 1).
[5] No. 2 of 1932.　　　　[6] No. 31 of 1935.　[7] No. 1 of 1932.
[8] Now Sir Arku Korsah, Chief Justice of Ghana.
[9] *Gold Coast Gazette*, 3rd October, 1942.
[10] No. 18 of 1943 (Kumasi); No. 26 of 1943 (Accra); No. 18 of 1944 (Cape Coast); No. 29 of 1945 (Sekondi-Takoradi).
[11] Leg. Co. Deb. (1944, No. 2), 81.

Guggisberg also, he was disappointed by the people's response. Out of 14,000 potential voters in Kumasi, only 828 troubled to vote in the first municipal election, and figures elsewhere were similar.[1]

Reforms were also needed in native administration. The 1927 Ordinance had been found defective, particularly in regard to native courts, and in 1944, acting on the report of the Blackall Committee, the Government secured the passing of the Native Courts (Colony) Ordinance (No. 22). This marked a revolutionary change. Instead of the old customary law tribunals, consisting of the chief sitting with his sub-chiefs, headmen, linguists and councillors, the Governor was given power to set up entirely new courts and to appoint their members as he thought fit. The new courts were divided into four grades, their jurisdiction varying accordingly. No court could be established unless the native authority's finances were sufficient to provide for the remuneration of the members of the court and its registrar. A Judicial Adviser was appointed to act as " guide, philosopher and friend " to the new courts and to review their decisions.[2] A new land court was created as a division of the Supreme Court to hear appeals from native court decisions in land cases.[3]

A large part of the Native Administration Ordinance being thus rendered obsolete, the remainder of it was replaced by the Native Authority (Colony) Ordinance, 1944 (No. 21), which also made considerable changes. The Governor was empowered to appoint one or more chiefs, native councils or other persons as a native authority for any area and to order it to be subordinate to any other native authority. The native authorities were given power to exercise a large number of functions usually regarded as falling within the province of local government, with default powers being given to the Provincial Commissioner. In an attempt to reduce stool disputes, the Governor was empowered to exclude persons from their tribal area. State Councils were allowed to retain their power to deal with stool disputes and, subject to the control of the Governor, were authorised to declare and modify rules of customary law. The sources of revenue of native authorities (including rates and also fees from the new native courts) were defined, and finance committees were required to be

---

[1] Leg. Co. Deb. (1944, No. 2), 82.
[2] *Ibid.*, 68.
[3] Ordinance No. 23 of 1944.

set up.[1] Power was given to establish native authority police. In form, if not intention, the two Ordinances marked the end of tribal administration under the old processes of customary law.

In 1943 income tax was introduced into the Gold Coast for the first time. The people's objection to direct taxation was inveterate and, as happened when an attempt was made in 1931 to bring in the tax, the Bill was opposed in the Legislative Council on the ground that there should be no taxation without full electoral representation. Conditions had altered however, and major constitutional changes were in the air. Representations for constitutional reform made by the Joint Provincial Council had been forwarded to London with the Governor's approval, and the Secretary of State was shortly to visit the Gold Coast to discuss the matter. In this atmosphere the opposition was not pressed and the Bill became law as the Income Tax Ordinance, 1943 (No. 27). Thus another source of revenue was added, but in importance it has not approached import and export duties, always the country's financial standby.

4. Attaining Nationhood, 1946–1960

Constitution of 1946

The Colony and Ashanti achieved representative government[2] with the coming into force on 29th March, 1946, of the Burns Constitution, the first of five Constitutions that were to follow in rapid succession during the ensuing fifteen years.[3] By this the operation of the Legislative Council was extended to Ashanti, the elected members were increased from eleven to eighteen, the *ex officio* members were reduced from thirteen to six, and the nominated members were increased from two to six. The elected members therefore had a majority of six over the official and nominated members.[4] This did not of course mean that the

---

[1] The Governor promised to give annual grants based on the amount raised in rates, and the amount spent on general development, by each native authority (Leg. Co. Deb. (1944, No. 2), 56).

[2] Representative government is regarded as existing when a colony has a legislative body of which at least one-half of the members are elected by inhabitants of the colony: Colonial Laws Validity Act, 1865, s. 1. The Gold Coast was the first British territory in Africa to have an elected majority of Africans in its legislature.

[3] The Orders in Council, Letters Patent and Royal Instructions making up the new Constitution were published in a supplement to the *Gold Coast Gazette* on 11th March, 1946.

[4] Gold Coast Colony and Ashanti (Legislative Council) Order in Council, 1946, ss. 4 and 5. The Governor was President of the Council but had no vote.

elected members could prevent the passage of legislation against
the wish of the Governor. The latter was given reserved powers
which enabled him, if he considered it expedient to do so in the
interests of public order, public faith or good government, to
declare effective any Bill or motion which had failed to pass the
Legislative Council. Any member who objected to the declaration
could require his objection to be forwarded to the Secretary of
State for the Colonies, who had power to revoke the declaration
or, if it related to a Bill which had received the Governor's
assent, to signify that the Bill was disallowed.[1] The legislative
powers of the Imperial Parliament and of the Crown in Council
remained unimpaired.[2]

The elected members comprised nine provincial members
elected for the Eastern and Western Provinces[3] by the Joint
Provincial Council, four Ashanti members elected by the Ashanti
Confederacy Council, and five municipal members of whom two
were elected for Accra and one each for Cape Coast, Sekondi-
Takoradi and Kumasi. The *ex officio* members were the Colonial
Secretary, the Chief Commissioners of the Colony, Ashanti and
the Northern Territories, the Attorney-General and the Financial
Secretary. Of the six nominated members three were Africans,
making a total of twenty-one African members out of thirty. The
term of office of the elected and nominated members was four
years.

The Order in Council introduced a number of features which
had become necessary owing to the representative nature of the
new Legislative Council and which in one form or another continue to apply to the present-day National Assembly. One of
these was the provision prohibiting consideration of any matter
which would dispose of public funds, or impose or alter taxation,
without the sanction of the Governor.[4] Others were provisions

---

[1] Gold Coast Colony and Ashanti (Legislative Council) Order in Council,
1946, ss. 38, 40.

[2] *Ibid.*, s. 49.

[3] The Central Province was abolished on 1st April, 1946.

[4] Section 34. See now the National Assembly Act, 1961 (Act 86), s. 18.
Section 34 of the 1946 Order in Council gave rise to some misunderstanding,
and was justified by the Governor as follows: " It is a well-recognized
principle in democratic institutions, and a long-established rule of the
British House of Commons, that financial Bills or motions can only be
considered by Parliament if they have been put forward by the Government. It would obviously be impossible for any Government to prepare
a considered Budget if financial proposals from other sources could be put
forward." (Leg. Co. Deb. (1946, No. 2) 9).

dealing with disqualification of members, voting, meetings and sessions, and prorogation and dissolution.

The transformation of the Executive Council into the present Cabinet consisting (apart from the President) of Ministers who are Members of Parliament advanced a stage in 1946 with the appointment to the Executive Council of three African members of the Legislative Council, namely Nana Tsibu Darku, Mr. C. W. Tachie-Menson and Dr. I. B. Asafu-Adjaye, one of the Ashanti members.[1]

Togoland Trusteeship

The year 1946 also saw a change in the status of British Togoland. Article 75 of the United Nations Charter, which was signed on 26th April, 1945, provided for the establishment of an international trusteeship system for the administration and supervision of certain under-developed territories, and by Article 77 of the Charter this system could be applied to territories formerly administered under mandate from the League of Nations. An agreement for the administration of British Togoland as a trust territory by the United Kingdom Government was approved by the General Assembly of the United Nations on 13th December, 1946.

The operation of this agreement was regulated by the Togoland Under United Kingdom Trusteeship Order in Council, 1949, which largely preserved the existing system of administration. A Southern Togoland Council, consisting of representatives of native authorities, was established in 1949 and empowered to elect an additional member to the Legislative Council.[2]

Disturbances of 28th February, 1948

Martin Wight remarked of colonies in the stage of constitutional development that the Gold Coast had now reached:

> " A representative legislature, deriving its strength from the popular forces behind it, tends to assert its will increasingly against the executive. There usually follows a period of extreme constitutional difficulty, marked by conflicts and deadlocks between the two powers. An irresponsible legislature confronts an immovable executive."[3]

---

[1] Leg. Co. Deb. (1946, No. 2) 7.
[2] Native Authority (Southern Section of Togoland Under United Kingdom Trusteeship) Ordinance, 1949; Gold Coast Colony and Ashanti (Legislative Council) (Amendment No. 2) Order in Council, 1949.
[3] *British Colonial Constitutions 1947*, p. 32.

A period of extreme constitutional difficulty certainly followed in the Gold Coast, but it was due less to the formal structure of the Burns Constitution than to the political movement for independence which now began to gather strength. We are here concerned only with developments in constitutional law, and it is beyond our scope to venture on the great political events of this time, which are extensively documented elsewhere. It is sufficient to say therefore that the impetus for the next step in constitutional advance came from the civil disturbances of 28th February, 1948, and succeeding days, which led to twenty-nine deaths and two hundred and thirty-seven injuries in Accra, Kumasi, Koforidua, Nsawam and Akuse.[1] An investigating commission under the chairmanship of Mr. Aiken Watson, K.C., found a large number of political, social and economic causes for these disturbances.[2] Among the political causes given were the following:

> " A feeling of political frustration among the educated Africans who saw no prospect of ever experiencing political power under existing conditions and who regarded the 1946 Constitution as mere window-dressing designed to cover but not to advance their natural aspirations."
> " A failure of the Government to realise that, with the spread of liberal ideas, increasing literacy and a closer contact with political developments in other parts of the world,[3] the star of rule through the chiefs was on the wane."

The commission found that the Burns Constitution, though well-intentioned, was conceived in the light of pre-war conditions and was out of date before it was promulgated. The Legislative Council, although predominantly African, was merely a debating chamber, while the native authorities still largely consisted of the old tribal oligarchies and gave no opportunity for the advancement of the new generation of politicians. Since (towns apart) election to the Legislative Council was by the chiefs " who naturally elect for the most part members of their own caste " almost all the African governmental authorities tended to stifle the expression of popular will and ambition. The commission concluded that a substantial measure of constitutional reform was necessary to meet the legitimate aspirations of the indigenous

---

[1] *Report of the Commission of Enquiry into Disturbances in the Gold Coast*, 1948 (Colonial No. 231), Appendix 8.

[2] The *Report*, pp. 7–8.

[3] India, Pakistan, Burma and Ceylon had recently become independent of British rule.

population, and went on to make detailed recommendations.[1]

The Coussey Committee

The British Government took the view that the recommendations of the Aiken Watson Committee should first be considered
by representatives of the public in the Gold Coast itself.[2] A
committee of forty prominent Gold Coast Africans was accordingly set up under the chairmanship of Mr. Justice Coussey and
reported on 17th August, 1949.[3] Their proposals provided for
the establishment on a fully representative basis of all bodies
responsible for the government of the Gold Coast from the smallest
local council to the central bodies where policy was determined
for the country as a whole. Local authorities were to have
elected majorities, while retaining some traditional elements.
Regional councils would be elected, while at the centre a Legislative Assembly was proposed. Nearly all the members of this
would be elected either directly or indirectly by popular vote.
The Executive Council would be reconstituted, and would become
responsible for the formulation of policy. The Governor's reserved
powers would not be capable of being used (except in emergency)
without the approval of the Executive Council or the Secretary
of State.

Constitution of 1951

The British Government, in a despatch to the Governor dated
14th October, 1949, reacted favourably to the recommendations
of the Coussey Committee, though criticising them in detail.[4] A
new Constitution was accordingly prepared, and came into force
on 1st January, 1951. The main instrument was the Gold Coast
(Constitution) Order in Council, 1950, which for the first time
applied uniform constitutional provisions to all the territories
now included in Ghana. The old Executive Council was completely
reconstituted, and the Legislative Council made way for a
Legislative Assembly consisting almost entirely of elected
Africans.[5] For the first time, elected representatives of all the

---

[1] The *Report*, pp. 27–29.
[2] Colonial No. 232, p. 7.
[3] Colonial No. 248.
[4] Colonial No. 250.
[5] The Legislative Council existed for just 100 years. For a detailed
account of its functioning see Martin Wight, *The Gold Coast Legislative
Council*.

four territories now included in Ghana met together in a law-making body.

Executive Council.—The Executive Council was designated as "the principal instrument of policy", and the Governor was required to act in accordance with its advice except where expressly empowered to act in his own discretion.[1] The Coussey Committee had recommended that the Executive Council should be collectively responsible to the Legislature, and had stated that to make the Council responsible to the Governor would not be acceptable. The British Government pointed out however that, since it was agreed that the Governor was to retain ultimate responsibility for the administration, the Council must remain responsible to him although it would also in effect be answerable to the Assembly on matters relating to the departments entrusted to the members of the Council.[2] The Executive Council consisted of the Governor as President and a number of Ministers, the first time this term had been used in Ghana.[3] There were three *ex officio* Ministers, namely the Chief Secretary, the Attorney-General and the Financial Secretary, and not less than eight representative Ministers appointed by the Governor from among the members of the Legislative Assembly and approved by that body.[4] The Legislative Assembly could bring about the dismissal of any representative Minister.[5] Acting in his discretion, the Governor could charge a Minister with the responsibility for any department or subject, and he was then styled a Minister with portfolio.[6] The Executive Council were required to elect one of their number to be Leader of Government Business in the Legislative Assembly.[7] They could also advise the Governor to appoint, from among the members of the Legislative Assembly, Ministerial Secretaries to assist the Ministers in the exercise of their duties. Each Ministry was provided with an official head, to be known as the Permanent Secretary.[8] An official was also to be appointed by the Governor as Governor's Secretary and Secretary to the Executive Council.[9]

---

[1] Gold Coast (Constitution) Order in Council, 1950, ss. 5, 6.

[2] Colonial No. 250, p. 7.

[3] Gold Coast (Constitution) Order in Council, 1950, s. 23. The wording of this section produced the effect that the Governor himself was to be styled a Minister, but this was presumably unintended.

[4] *Ibid.*, ss. 4, 7, 8.   [5] Section 9.   [6] Sections 22, 23.   [7] Section 15.

[8] Section 27. The word "Ministry" was not defined, and its meaning remained indefinite until the passing of the Civil Service Act, 1960; see pp. 180 *et seq., post.*

[9] Section 29.

Legislative Assembly.—The Legislative Assembly consisted of
the Speaker, the three *ex officio* Ministers, three representatives
of chambers of commerce, three representatives of the Chamber
of Mines, and seventy-five elected members.[1]
The elected members were classified as follows:[2]

(i) 37 *representing the Gold Coast Colony:*[3]
    (*a*) 12 territorial members:
        11 members elected by the Joint Provincial
        Council:
           3 representing the Central group of native
           authorities, 2 the Eastern Akan group, 2 the
           Ewe group, 2 the Ga-Adangme group and 2 the
           Western group;
        1 member elected by the Southern Togoland
        Council;
    (*b*) 21 rural members elected by electoral colleges chosen
        by universal suffrage;[4]
    (*c*) 4 municipal members directly elected by universal
        adult suffrage, of whom Accra returned two and
        Cape Coast and Sekondi-Kakoradi one each.

(ii) 19 *representing Ashanti:*
    (*a*) 6 territorial members elected by the Asanteman
        Council;[5]
    (*b*) 12 rural members elected by electoral colleges chosen
        by universal adult suffrage;
    (*c*) 1 municipal member directly elected by universal
        adult suffrage for Kumasi.

(iii) 19 *representing the Northern Territories.*—These were
    elected by an electoral college consisting of the members of

---

[1] Only two out of the six commercial and mining members had a vote
(s. 56).
[2] Section 40. The electoral provisions were based on the report of a select
committee of the Legislative Council (the Ewart Report).
[3] In fact this group included a member representing Southern Togoland.
The error was corrected in 1952.
[4] For the first elections the electoral law was made by an Ordinance
passed by the old Legislative Council. Power to pass the Ordinance (the
Elections (Legislative Assembly) Ordinance, 1950) was conferred by the
Gold Coast (Constitution) (Electoral Provisions) Order in Council, 1950.
[5] The names of the Ashanti Confederacy and its Council were changed
in 1950 to the traditional names of Asanteman and Asanteman Council
respectively: Ashanti Confederacy Council (Amendment) Order, 1950
(No. 147).

the Northern Territories Council and persons nominated by the six district councils.

The Governor, with the advice and consent of the Legislative Assembly, was given power to make laws for the peace, order and good government of the whole of the Gold Coast. The power was limited in various ways. No law could make persons of any racial community liable to disabilities to which persons of other such communities were not made liable. Nor could the Togoland trusteeship agreement be infringed.[1] In addition to the 1946 restriction on the introduction of financial Bills, the Governor, acting in his discretion, was given control over Bills affecting public officers or removing from his discretion the final decision of questions relating to the office of Chiefs.[2] The reserved powers of the Governor were similar to those in the previous constitution but, except in emergency, could be exercised only with the consent of the Executive Council or the Secretary of State.[3] The Crown's power of disallowance was retained.[4]

Part VI of the Order in Council provided for the administration of the Public Service, which was placed under the control of the Governor acting in his discretion. A Public Service Commission was set up to advise the Governor on appointments, promotions, discipline and other matters.[5] Control over the establishment of the Civil Service remained with the Assembly, to be exercised by voting on the Estimates.

In the general election which followed the coming into force of the new Constitution, 34 of the 38 seats open to popular vote were won by the Convention People's Party, which had been founded by Dr. Kwame Nkrumah in June, 1949. The United Gold Coast Convention, which had been founded in 1947, won three seats, and the remaining seat was won by an independent.[6] Dr. Nkrumah, who described the new Constitution as " bogus and fraudulent ", nevertheless decided to work under it as he felt it would serve as a stepping-stone to self-government.[7] He and five other C.P.P. members were appointed to the Executive Council

---

[1] Section 50. Further restrictions of the usual type were laid down in the accompanying Royal Instructions.
[2] Section 57.   [3] Section 58.   [4] Section 60.
[5] Rubin and Murray (*The Constitution and Government of Ghana* (London, 1961), p. 117) are thus mistaken in treating the Public Service Commission as established in 1957; as also in assuming that it continues to exist, it having in fact been abolished on the establishment of the Republic in 1960.
[6] *Colonial Office Report on the Gold Coast for 1951*, p. 3.
[7] Kwame Nkrumah: *I Speak of Freedom* (London, 1961), p. 23.

as representative Ministers together with a representative of Ashanti and one from the Northern Territories. The Council elected Dr. Nkrumah as Leader of Government Business.

Local Government

The recommendations of the Coussey Committee regarding local government were implemented by the Local Government Ordinance, 1951 (No. 29), which survived until its replacement by the Local Government Act, 1961 (Act 54). The Ordinance, which applied to the whole of the Gold Coast except the four municipalities, enabled the Government to set up district, urban and local councils with a chief as president. Except where it was found impracticable, one-third of the members of each urban and local council were to be traditional members appointed by State Councils or similar bodies while the remainder were to be representative members elected by adult suffrage. A similar proportion was required for the district councils, but election was by the corresponding members of the urban and local councils within the district. The councils were required generally to maintain order and good government within their areas and could be given a wide variety of detailed functions.[1] Power to levy rates was given without financial limit. Where a local authority was set up it replaced the native authority and the laws relating to the latter were repealed *pro tanto*. A Minister of Local Government was appointed to supervise the administration of the Ordinance.

A uniform law was provided for the municipalities by the Municipal Councils Ordinance, 1953 (No. 9) (now embodied in the Act of 1961), which replaced the town councils of Accra, Kumasi, Cape Coast and Sekondi/Takoradi by municipal councils. In these areas the traditional membership was made only about one-seventh of the whole, the remainder being elected by popular vote.[2]

The provisions of the Native Authority (Colony) Ordinance relating to local administration having been superseded by the Local Government Ordinance, most of the remainder were re-enacted by the State Councils (Colony and Southern Togoland)

---

[1] Section 58 of Ordinance No. 29 of 1951, which listed the detailed functions, had no less than 82 paragraphs covering such matters as agriculture, animals, buildings, education, forestry, land, famine relief, liquor, markets, public health, public order, registration of persons, roads, and trade and industry. See now the Local Government Act, 1961 (Act 54), Sch. I, which has 108 paragraphs.

[2] Accra and Kumasi have recently been raised to the status of cities.

Ordinance, 1952 (No. 8). This did not however reproduce the power to recognise chiefs and to make removal orders excluding deposed chiefs and others from specified areas.[1] In introducing the Bill, the Minister of Local Government said:

> " Local government is, I hope, now reaching a position of stabilization in the Gold Coast. Before many months have passed the position will be that, on the one hand the day-to-day matters which form the general subject of local administration will have become the concern of bodies which are largely elected by popular vote; while on the other hand customary usages and practices will still remain an important element in the social structure of the local community. . . . It is, therefore, the object of this Bill to preserve for the traditional authorities in the Colony and Togoland the powers and functions relating to these customary matters which they alone can properly exercise."[2]

The Ordinance also created the Trans-Volta Togoland Region, which consisted of the Southern Section of Togoland under United Kingdom Trusteeship together with the states of Anlo and Peki and specified Ewe divisions.

Creation of office of Prime Minister

In 1952 a number of detailed amendments were made to the Constitution. The office of Prime Minister was created in substitution for that of Leader of Government Business.[3] The Prime Minister had to be a member of the Legislative Assembly. He was proposed by the Governor and approved by the Assembly, and by virtue of his appointment was a representative member of the Executive Council or, as it was now authorised to be called, the Cabinet.[4] If the Prime Minister's office became vacant, those of the other representative Ministers would become vacant also and would thus, in accordance with British practice, be at the disposition of the incoming Prime Minister.[5] Changes were also made in the provisions regulating the election of the territorial members of the Assembly. The two members representing the

---

[1] Native Authority (Colony) Ordinance, 1944 (No. 21), ss. 15–19. The power was revived in 1959; see p. 72, *post*.

[2] Leg. Ass. Deb. (1952, No. 1), I, 233. Similar Ordinances were passed in 1952 for Ashanti (No. 4) and the Northern Territories (No. 5).

[3] Gold Coast (Constitution) (Amendment) Order in Council, 1952 (S.I. 1952 No. 455), s. 5. The office of Prime Minister existed for eight years, during the whole of which time it was held by Dr. Nkrumah. It was abolished on 1st July, 1960.

[4] *Ibid.*, s. 3.

[5] *Ibid.*, s. 8.

Ewe group in the Colony, along with the Southern Togoland member, were to be elected by an electoral college consisting of persons chosen by the traditional members of local authorities within the Trans-Volta/Togoland Region.[1] Consequential changes were made in the membership of the Joint Provincial Council.

Discussions on Constitutional Reform

In October, 1952, following a visit by the Secretary of State for the Colonies, the Prime Minister made a statement in the Assembly on constitutional reform. He said that it was clear from his discussions with the Secretary of State that if the Gold Coast were to achieve full self-government the Gold Coast Government must take the initiative and lay before the British Government proposals worked out after consultations with the chiefs and people. To enable this to be done he invited interested bodies and persons to send in their suggestions and while refraining at that stage from putting forward positive views of his own since " it would, in the opinion of the Government, be quite wrong for the preliminary discussions to be influenced by a declaration of Government policy ", he outlined some of the features of the Constitution which needed consideration. These included the presence of *ex officio* Ministers in the Cabinet, the procedure for appointing the Prime Minister and other representative Ministers, the composition of the Assembly and whether there should be a second chamber, the powers of the Governor in matters affecting chieftaincy, and the position of the Public Service.[2] The results of this invitation, together with the Government's provisional recommendations, were given in a white paper published in June, 1953.[3] Over a quarter of a million copies of the Prime Minister's statement had been distributed, and representations were submitted by 131 councils, political parties and other groups.[4] A remarkable measure of agreement was shown on the details of constitutional advance, and the Government's proposals were framed accordingly. They did not, however, support the majority opinion in favour of the creation of a second chamber of the legislature. After a four-day debate,

---

[1] Gold Coast (Constitution) (Amendment) (No. 2) Order in Council, 1952 (S.I. 1952, No. 1039), s. 8. A Trans-Volta/Togoland Council, replacing the Southern Togoland Council, was set up by Ordinance No. 16 of 1952.

[2] Leg. Ass. Deb. (1952, No. 3), 500 *et seq.*

[3] *The Government's Proposals for Constitutional Reform*, Accra, 1953.

[4] *Ibid.*, p. 5.

the Legislative Assembly approved the proposals and passed a motion authorising the Government to ask the British Government:

> " . . . to amend as a matter of urgency the Gold Coast (Constitution) Order in Council, 1950, in such a way as to provide *inter alia* that the Legislative Assembly shall be composed of members directly elected by secret ballot, and that all Members of the Cabinet shall be Members of the Assembly and directly responsible to it."[1]

The motion also, as a separate matter, authorised a request to the British Government that " as soon as the necessary constitutional and administrative arrangements for independence are made " an Act should be passed declaring the Gold Coast a sovereign and independent state within the Commonwealth. As the Prime Minister remarked in the course of the debate, " We prefer self-government with danger to servitude in tranquillity ".[2]

Constitution of 1954

The British Government accepted the proposals and on 5th May, 1954, the major part of the Gold Coast (Constitution) Order in Council, 1954 (S.I. 1954 No. 551), came into operation. This repeated many features of the previous Constitution and also for the first time in a Gold Coast Constitution included detailed provisions as to the judiciary and public finance. The principal changes were as follows.

The Executive.—The Governor ceased to be a member of the Cabinet, which was made responsible to the Assembly and consisted of not less than eight Members of the Assembly appointed on the advice of the Prime Minister. This followed British constitutional convention, which was expressly applied to the appointment and dismissal of all Ministers, including the Prime Minister.[3] The Cabinet was precluded from exercising functions in relation to defence (including internal security) and external affairs (including Togoland under United Kingdom trusteeship), which were reserved to the Governor.[4] The Governor

---

[1] Leg. Ass. Deb. (1953, No. 2), 262.
[2] Leg. Ass. Deb. (1953, No. 2), 273. The motion is known in Ghana as the Motion of Destiny.
[3] Gold Coast (Constitution) Order in Council, 1954, s. 7.
[4] *Ibid.*, ss. 5, 17. The office of Chief Secretary was abolished and the affairs of his Ministry, the Ministry of Defence and External Affairs (which was also abolished) were transferred to the Governor's department: *Gold Coast Handbook* (1954), p. 3.

had power to summon and attend a special Cabinet meeting when he thought fit.[1] Portfolios were assigned to Ministers by the Prime Minister instead of the Governor.[2] Since the Attorney-General ceased to be a Minister his responsibility for the initiation, conduct and discontinuance of prosecutions (which was put outside Ministerial control) was laid down by the Constitution.[3]

Legislative Assembly.—The Assembly consisted of the Speaker and 104 members, all elected by universal adult suffrage, as follows:

39 rural members for the Colony (other than the Trans-Volta/ Togoland Region);
13 rural members for the Trans-Volta/Togoland Region;
19 rural members for Ashanti;
26 rural members for the Northern Territories and Northern Togoland;
3 municipal members for Accra;
1 municipal member for Cape Coast;
2 municipal members for Kumasi;
1 municipal member for Sekondi-Takoradi.[4]

The restriction on the introduction of Bills affecting chieftaincy was removed, but a similar restriction was imposed in relation to Bills dealing with defence or external affairs.[5] The Governor had power to insist on the introduction of any Bill, and retained his reserved powers in cases where a Bill was not passed.[6] Express power was given to pass laws regulating the privileges of the Assembly, but these were not to exceed those enjoyed by the

---

[1] Section 13.
[2] Section 16.
[3] Section 18.
[4] Sections 24, 28. Power to provide for the elections had been granted by the Gold Coast (Constitution) (Amendment) Order in Council, 1953 (S.I. 1953 No. 1565) and had been exercised by the passing of the Electoral Provisions Ordinance, 1953 (No. 33), which is still in force.
[5] A restriction added in 1955 precluded the passing of any law enabling property to be acquired compulsorily without adequate compensation: Gold Coast Constitution (Amendment) Order in Council, 1955 (S.I. 1955 No. 1218).
[6] The Gold Coast Government had not asked for the removal of these powers, which had not been used: *The Government's Proposals for Constitutional Reform*, p. 15.

D

British House of Commons.[1] The life of the Assembly was limited to four years.[2]

Judicature.—A Judicial Service Commission was set up consisting of the Chief Justice and two other judges, the Attorney-General and the Chairman of the Public Service Commission. After 31st July, 1955, apart from the Chief Justice, who was appointed on the advice of the Prime Minister, judges and judicial officers were appointed on the advice of the Judicial Service Commission, which also had disciplinary control over judicial officers. A judge of the Supreme Court was not removable except on an address of the Assembly, carried by not less than two-thirds of the members, praying for his removal on the ground of misbehaviour or infirmity of body or mind. Interference with the Commission was made an offence punishable with imprisonment.[3]

Finance.—For the first time, details of financial procedure were inserted in the Constitution. Sections 65 and 66, which were repeated in the 1957 Constitution and thus remained in force until the inauguration of the republic, laid down the procedure for authorising and meeting expenditure, which was largely that followed for many years previously in the Gold Coast. The Minister of Finance was required to prepare annual estimates of revenue and expenditure which, when approved by the Cabinet, were to be laid before the Assembly. The expenditure estimates, except those relating to the public debt or other expenditure charged on the national assets, were to be submitted to the vote of the Assembly by means of an Appropriation Bill. Excess expenditure was to be covered by a Supplementary Appropriation Bill. The Assembly could reject any head of the estimates but could not vote to increase or reduce expenditure or to alter its destination. Expenditure could not be met unless it had been authorised by resolution of the Assembly or one of its Committees " or by any law ". Where, however, the Appropriation Bill had not become law by the beginning of the financial year, the Minister of Finance, with Cabinet approval, could authorise expenditure on any

---

[1] The power was exercised by the passing of the Legislative Assembly (Powers and Privileges) Ordinance, 1956 (No. 20). This was replaced by the National Assembly Act, 1959 (No. 78) which in turn was replaced by the National Assembly Act, 1961 (Act 86).

[2] Gold Coast (Constitution) Order in Council, 1954, s. 50 (2).

[3] See Part VII of the Gold Coast (Constitution) Order in Council, 1954.

service up to one quarter of the amount voted for that service in the previous year.[1]

Section 67 established the office of the Auditor-General, who was appointed by the Governor after consultation with the Prime Minister and was given the same security of tenure as the Judges.

The Order in Council was accompanied by the usual Letters Patent constituting the office of Governor and Commander-in-Chief of the Colony and Ashanti[2] and Royal Instructions to the Governor.[3] The latter modified the obligation of the Governor to act on the advice of his Ministers and his power to assent to Ordinances within the usual restricted classes. The general election under the new Constitution was held in June, 1954, and resulted in victory for the Government party, the C.P.P., which won 71 out of the 104 seats. 12 seats were won by the Northern People's Party and 16 by Independents, the remaining five being divided between the Togoland Congress, the Ghana Congress Party, the Moslem Association Party and the Anlo Youth Organisation.[4] The Northern People's Party was recognised as the Official Opposition, its leader being paid a salary as such.

The Questions of Federation and a Second Chamber

Later in the year a movement arose in Ashanti which posed two major constitutional questions requiring settlement before independence was achieved. Was the future Constitution to be federal or unitary? Should a second house of the legislature be established? The movement began through the dissatisfaction of the Ashanti cocoa farmers with the minimum price fixed by the Cocoa Duty and Development Funds (Amendment) Ordinance, 1954 (No. 25). Since nearly half the country's cocoa was produced in Ashanti many of the inhabitants there felt that they were entitled to a greater share in its proceeds and that this could only be obtained by a federal system under which Ashanti would have some measure of autonomy. In September, 1954, the National Liberation Movement was launched in Kumasi with the support of the Asanteman Council and nearly all the Opposition parties.

---

[1] For the alterations made to this procedure in 1960 see pp. 155 *et seq.*, *post.*

[2] L.N. 216 of 1954.

[3] L.N. 217 of 1954.

[4] *Colonial Office Report on the Gold Coast*, 1954, p. 7.

A pamphlet setting out the constitutional proposals of the Movement was published about the middle of the following year.[1] This
called for the setting up of a Constituent Assembly to draft a
federal Constitution, the argument advanced being:

> " There is not enough consciousness of national identity to
> make possible easy and at the same time democratic unitary
> government. In the absence of this consciousness the safest
> course is to ensure that not all the powers of government are
> concentrated at the centre, but that a substantial part of them
> is retained in the component territories where people have learnt
> the habits and attitudes of living together for some time."

The Government decided to appoint a select committee of the
Assembly to examine the question of a federal system of government and also the related question of an upper chamber. The
Opposition declined to participate on the ground that the matter
should have been dealt with by a Constituent Assembly. The
committee adopted Dr. Wheare's statement that:

> " Federal government exists when the powers of government
> of a community are divided substantially according to the
> principle that there is a single independent authority for the
> whole area in respect of some matters and that there are
> independent regional authorities for other matters, each set of
> authorities being co-ordinate with and not subordinate to the
> others within its own prescribed powers."[2]

Bearing this in mind the committee stated that their basis of
determining the argument was that the features of a unitary
system are simple while those of a federal system are complicated
and that " for the abandonment of the simple in favour of the
complicated, very cogent reasons should be advanced ". This
cogency was found to be lacking, and the committee felt that:

> " the cost of running many regional governments in addition
> to a central government, and many regional legislatures in
> addition to a central legislature would be huge and out of all
> proportion to any advantage federation might have."[3]

Other difficulties were the absence of sufficient skilled Africans
even to run a unitary system, and the " vexatiousness " of such

---

[1] 61. *Proposals for a Federal Constitution for an Independent Gold Coast
and Togoland by movements and parties other than the Convention People's
Party* (undated), p. 6.
[2] *Report from the Select Committee on Federal System of Government and
Second Chamber for the Gold Coast*, Accra, 1955, para. 35.
[3] *Ibid.*, para. 42.

problems as the allocation of national revenue, the subjection of the citizen to two sets of laws and two systems of taxation, and the likelihood of inter-regional jealousies.[1]

An upper chamber was also rejected, the committee adopting the arguments against it which had been advanced by the Coussey Committee. These were:

1. The probability of friction between paramount chiefs and people if the former were confined to a Second Chamber.

2. The added expenditure in setting up an additional council for chiefs and elder statesmen, involving, as it would, the journey to and stay at Accra of a great number of chiefs, with their attendants, for long sessions.

3. The stagnation in the affairs of states caused by the absence of their chiefs.

4. The effect on the number and quality of members available for the lower chamber.

5. That once a Second Chamber was established it would be extremely difficult to disestablish it should it later be found unnecessary, and the status of chiefs might be destroyed in the process.[2]

The only arguments on the other side which found favour with the select committee were that an upper house would enable emotional issues to be considered in a calmer atmosphere and that, to some extent at any rate, it might serve a useful function in revising legislation.[3] These were clearly insufficient to tip the balance, though the committee did think the question should be examined again after independence.[4] The report was adopted by the Assembly after the Opposition had staged a walk-out. At the same time the Government announced that they had decided to invite an outside constitutional expert to frame proposals for a measure of devolution to the regions.[5] The expert invited was Sir Frederick Bourne, a former Governor of East Bengal.

The controversy was exacerbated when the powers of the Asanteman Council over local constitutional matters were curtailed later in 1955 by amendments to the State Councils (Ashanti) Ordinance, 1952 (No. 4).[6] These gave an appeal to the

---

[1] The 1955 *Report*, paras. 34, 43.
[2] *Ibid.*, para. 49.
[3] *Ibid.*, paras. 61, 63, 77.
[4] *Ibid.*, para. 78.
[5] Leg. Ass. Deb. (1955, No. 2), s. 359.
[6] The amendments were made by Ordinance No. 38 of 1955.

Governor against decisions of the Asanteman Council or a State Council in all cases and not merely, as previously, in cases involving a paramount chief. This right of appeal covered cases decided since the beginning of 1954, there having been a number of destoolments of chiefs unfavourable to the National Liberation Movement. Furthermore the Governor was empowered to withdraw a case from the Asanteman Council or a State Council and decide it himself if he thought fit.[1] A similar extension of the rights of appeal was made in the south by the State Councils (Colony and Southern Togoland) (Amendment) Ordinance, 1955 (No. 37).

The Bourne proposals

In September, 1955, the constitutional adviser, Sir Frederick Bourne, arrived in the Gold Coast. He received no co-operation from the National Liberation Movement, who were incensed by the timing of the legislation curtailing the powers of the paramount chiefs in Ashanti. He therefore failed in the most important object of his mission, namely to reconcile the opposing viewpoints of Government and Opposition on the question of federation.[2] However, his detailed recommendations on regional administration pointed the way to the ultimate settlement of the controversy. They may be summarised as follows:

1. The boundaries of the Regions should be clearly defined and not subsequently altered without the consent of the local inhabitants.

2. A Regional Assembly should be established for each Region in which district councils had been set up for the whole Region, provided the majority of district councils desired it.

3. The objects of a Regional Assembly would be:
   (*a*) to afford an effective link between Regions and the central Government and thereby to remove any danger of excessive centralisation;
   (*b*) to provide for the formation and ventilation of local opinion on matters of national importance;
   (*c*) to procure the use of local knowledge and experience to ensure that legislation was devised and implemented, and projects involving expenditure in the Region

---

[1] In these matters the Governor would of course be required to act on the advice of the Cabinet.

[2] *Report of the Constitutional Adviser*, Accra, 1955, p. 1.

designed, and the required money provided, in a manner suited to the circumstances of the Region concerned.

4. Supreme legislative power would remain at the centre, but the Regional Assemblies would be given such delegated powers as were needed for them to fulfil their objects.[1]

5. A Regional Assembly should consist of all backbench members of the Legislative Assembly elected for the Region, together with an equal or greater number of members of district and municipal councils. Local residents could be co-opted.

6. No Bill affecting the traditional functions or privileges of chiefs should be passed by the Legislative Assembly unless:
   (*a*) the chiefs had been consulted, and
   (*b*) their comments had been circulated to the members of the Legislative Assembly, and considered by them on non-party lines.

7. Each Regional Assembly would consult, and receive advice from, councils of chiefs within the Region.

The Achimota Conference

The Prime Minister convened a conference to consider the Bourne Report and matters arising from it. It was hoped that this would be an all-party conference, at which the matters dividing the Government and the N.L.M. could be thrashed out. This hope was disappointed, and the opposition parties refused to join the conference or express their views to it. The conference had its first meeting at Achimota on 16th February, 1956, and found itself in broad agreement with the Bourne proposals. It was, however, felt that Regional Assemblies should be set up simultaneously in all Regions and that it should not therefore be a condition precedent that district councils had been established throughout the Region.[2] Disagreement was also expressed with the proposal that members of the Legislative Assembly should be

---

[1] Sir Frederick Bourne remarked that this " is the reverse of the system recommended in the N.L.M.'s Federal Scheme, whereby the Centre's powers are to be prescribed and all residuary powers are to rest with the units. This extreme form of Federation would, I believe, slow down development and introduce an intolerable handicap to the administration of the country ": *Report*, para. 5.

[2] There were no district councils in the Western Region and only two in the Eastern Region.

ex officio members of the Regional Assemblies. The conference recommended that a House of Chiefs should be set up in each Region, in addition to a Regional Assembly. The House of Chiefs would be empowered to advise, and initiate policy, on matters relating to African social customs and customary law, including constitutional matters affecting chieftaincy. It would also have certain delaying powers over any Bill affecting its functions. The Joint Provincial Council would function as the House of Chiefs for the Eastern and Western Regions.[1]

In a statement published in April, 1956, the Government accepted with minor variations the Bourne Report as modified by the Achimota Conference and set out their proposals for the independence of the Gold Coast under the name of Ghana.[2]   To meet the British Government's requirements that these proposals should be shown to have the support of the majority of the population before the necessary legislation was introduced, the Gold Coast Government agreed to hold a general election on the basis of the proposals.[3] The proposals were approved by the Assembly on 22nd May, 1956, after a debate in which the Opposition refused to take part.[4] The Opposition leader had stated that the proposals could be used by the Government as an election manifesto, but should not be debated in the Assembly.[5]

The Togoland Plebiscite

Meanwhile the way had been cleared for the inclusion of Togoland under United Kingdom Trusteeship in the new state of Ghana by the result of a plebiscite held earlier in the month. A considerable controversy had developed over the future constitutional status of the territory. Two main views were held. On the one hand the Gold Coast Government, supported by the Opposition and also by the British Government, wanted it to be made part of Ghana. On the other hand the Togoland Congress Party, the All-Ewe Conference, and ancillary groups desired that it should be established under separate administration as a

---

[1] *Report of the Achimota Conference*, Accra, 1956.

[2] *Constitutional Proposals for Gold Coast Independence and Statement on the Report of the Constitutional Adviser and the Report of the Achimota Conference*, Accra, 1956.

[3] Leg. Ass. Deb. (1956–57, No. 1), 3–4.

[4] *Ibid.*, 227.

[5] *Ibid.*, 65. For a defence of the Opposition's boycott of the various constitutional proceedings at this period see Leg. Ass. Deb. (Official Report—First Series, Vol. 2), pp. 92–94.

preliminary to allowing the inhabitants to choose whether (1) to federate with the Gold Coast or (2) to unite with an independent French Togoland, with the territories thus united to be federated eventually with the Gold Coast. A special mission was despatched by the United Nations Trusteeship Council in 1955 to report on the constitutional future of British and French Togoland. The mission reported that there was a clear division of opinion in British Togoland, which could only be accurately measured by a plebiscite. They recommended that this should be held, and that the questions should be:

" 1. Do you want the integration of Togoland under British administration with an independent Gold Coast?
2. Do you want the separation of Togoland under British administration from the Gold Coast and its continuance under trusteeship, pending the ultimate determination of its political future? "[1]

The plebiscite was held on 9th May, 1956, and resulted in an overall majority in favour of the first question. There were 93,095 votes (58 per cent.) in favour of integration with the Gold Coast and 67,492 votes (42 per cent.) in favour of separation in accordance with the second alternative.[2] A majority vote in favour of separation was recorded in only two of the six districts.[3] On 13th December, 1956, the General Assembly of the United Nations expressed its approval of the union of Togoland under British administration with an independent Gold Coast, and resolved that, on the date on which the Gold Coast became independent and union with the trust territory took place, the trusteeship agreement should cease to be in force, " the objectives of trusteeship having been achieved ". On 6th March, 1957, therefore, the trusteeship agreement ceased to be in force and the competence of the United Nations in respect of the former British Togoland came to an end.[4]

General Election of 1956

The Gold Coast general election was held in July, 1956, and resulted in a decisive victory for the C.P.P., although its candidates

---

[1] *Special Report on the Togoland Reunification Problem* (Trusteeship Council Official Records: Fifth Special Session, Supplement No. 2), p. 15.
[2] United Nations, *Annual Report of the Secretary-General, 1956–1957*, p. 102.
[3] *Annual Report of the Secretary-General, 1956–1957*, p. 103.
[4] *Ibid.*

were returned in only a minority of the seats in Ashanti and the Northern Territories. The state of the parties was:

> Covention People's Party—72 seats
> Northern People's Party—15 seats
> National Liberation Movement—12 seats
> Togoland Congress—2 seats
> Moslem Association Party—1 seat
> Federation of Youth Organisations—1 seat
> Independent—1 seat.[1]

Negotiations for Independence

In spite of its success in the election, the Government did not give up its attempts to secure the agreement of the opposition parties and groups to its constitutional proposals. The latter at last agreed to embark on discussions with the Government, and these began on 16th October, 1956.[2] The Government's final proposals, revised in the light of the discussions, were published as a white paper at the beginning of November.[3] After a three-day debate, they received the approval of the Legislative Assembly by 70 votes to 25.[4] Since the original proposals had received the approval of the electorate, the Government had not felt able to depart from them to any substantial degree. Some small concessions had been made, but there remained three major points, as well as a number of minor ones, on which disagreement persisted. The major opposition proposals which were rejected by the Government were as follows:

1. That there should be a Council of State, consisting of the Governor General, the four Heads of the Traditional Regions, the Prime Minister, the Leader of the Opposition and the Attorney-General. Its function would be to advise the Governor-General on the appointment and conditions of service of judges and public officers, the settlement of local constitutional disputes, and other matters. The idea was rejected by the Government as impractical, and also undemocratic since the Council would in certain fields be above the Cabinet and not answerable to the elected representatives of the people.

---

[1] Leg. Ass. Deb. (1956–57, Official Report—First Series), Vol. 1, pp. i–iv.
[2] Leg. Ass. Deb. (1956–57, Official Report—First Series), Vol. 2, p. 249.
[3] *The Government's Revised Constitutional Proposals for Gold Coast Independence*, Accra, 1956.
[4] Leg. Ass. Deb. (1956–57, Official Report—First Series), Vol. 2, p. 243.

2. That there should be a Second Chamber of Parliament, composed of members elected by the four territorial Houses of Chiefs, members appointed by the Government and members appointed on the advice of the Council of State. Although reluctant, for the reasons set out earlier,[1] to have a bicameral legislature, the Government offered to do so if the proposal for regional Houses of Chiefs was abandoned. This compromise was refused by the four territorial Councils of Chiefs.

3. That the Regions should have a measure of autonomy equivalent to that enjoyed by Northern Ireland, and that the Ashanti Region should remain undivided. The Government, supported by the territorial councils other than the Asanteman Council, believed that regional devolution should be implemented gradually and that Regional Assemblies should have powers similar to those of the London County Council. They also favoured the demand of the Brongs for a separate Region.[2]

On the day following the conclusion of the debate, the Prime Minister announced that the Government, having considered the speeches made, had decided to recommend to the British Government that the new Constitution should be based on the White Paper as approved by the Assembly.[3] The British Government had declined to do more than make the alterations in the existing Constitution which were necessary to confer Independence, with certain additional provisions (such as those relating to regional devolution) which were closely bound up with preceding political events.[4] This decision meant that the comprehensive code of fundamental rights, which both the Opposition and the Government expressed a desire to have inserted, had to be omitted from the new Constitution.[5] On the mechanics of Independence, the Government and the opposition parties and groups had agreed the following statement of principle:

> " Following the experience of the working of Parliamentary institutions, the Government believes that the advance to independence within the Commonwealth by the Gold Coast can be effected by the modification of our existing Constitution

---

[1] P. 53, *ante.*

[2] Part I of the Appendix to the White Paper sets out the proposals and objections in some detail, as also does the Prime Minister's speech in the Assembly debate (*loc. cit.,* pp. 13–70).

[3] *Loc. cit.,* p. 248.

[4] See the despatch from the Secretary of State quoted *loc. cit.,* p. 32.

[5] *Loc. cit.,* p. 31.

and by the adoption of conventions which have grown up in the United Kingdom."[1]

The statement went on to list the necessary legislative measures. Apart from a new Constitution Order in Council, Letters Patent and Royal Instructions, these included " an Act of the United Kingdom Parliament which would alter the law of the United Kingdom and confer on the Gold Coast Legislature those law-making powers which could not be conferred by Order in Council".

The Ghana Independence Act

The Ghana Independence Act, 1957[2] received the Royal Assent on 7th February, 1957. The long title described it as

> " An act to make provision for, and in connection with, the attainment by the Gold Coast of fully responsible status within the British Commonwealth of Nations."

The Act, which followed the general pattern of the Ceylon Independence Act, 1947, began by stating that the territories included in the Gold Coast were to form part of Her Majesty's dominions under the name of Ghana as from 6th March, 1957, which was the anniversary of the making of the Bond of 1844.[3] The reasons for adopting this name were given by the Prime Minister in the debate on the White Paper.[4] Dr. Nkrumah said:

> " There are many objections to continuing the name of ' Gold Coast '. It was, in the first place, not the traditional name of the country as a whole but merely the name given in the seventeenth century by the French, and afterwards by the Dutch, to the coastal strip of the present Colony. When we become independent it is most essential that no appearance is given of any one portion of the country dominating any other part and on those grounds alone it would be better to choose a name which was not closely associated with one particular region. Secondly, the name ' Gold Coast ' is only the English version of the name. It is translated by different words in each of the vernaculars of the country. There is a similar international difficulty. . . . The Government considers it very undesirable that the Gold Coast should begin its independent international life with as many names as there are languages represented in the United Nations."

---

[1] White Paper, 1, 12.

[2] Set out in Appendix A, p. 465, *post*.

[3] See p. 8, *ante*. Provision was made enabling some other date to be appointed, but was not used.

[4] Leg. Ass. Deb. (1956–57, Official Report—First Series), Vol. 2, pp. 42–44.

The name Ghana had been mooted for some years as a desirable alternative to the Gold Coast, and had been used in the title of one of the opposition parties, the Ghana Congress Party. The original suggestion for its adoption has been attributed to Dr. J. B. Danquah.[1]

In an earlier part of his speech, Dr. Nkrumah said:

> " The name ' Ghana ' is rooted deeply in ancient African history, especially in the history of the western portion of Africa known as the Western Sudan. It kindles in the imagination of modern West African youth the grandeur and the achievements of a great mediaeval civilisation which our ancestors developed many centuries before the European penetration and subsequent domination of Africa began. According to tradition the various peoples or tribal groups in the Gold Coast were originally members of the great Ghana Empire that developed in the Western Sudan during the mediaeval period. For the one thousand years that the Ghana Empire existed, it spread over a wide expanse of territory in the Western Sudan. . . . We take pride in the name, not out of romanticism but as an inspiration for the future."[2]

The effect of the opening words of the Ghana Independence Act was to place all the four territories on an equal footing as the dominions of Her Majesty in her capacity as Queen of Ghana.[3] Since neither the Northern Territories nor British Togoland previously formed part of Her Majesty's dominions, this provision had the technical effect of annexing those territories, an effect which was necessary for the creation of a unified Ghana.[4] Section 1 of the Act went on to renounce, in language derived from s. 4 of the Statute of Westminster, the legislative powers of the United Kingdom Parliament in relation to Ghana, and to confer on the Parliament of Ghana the legislative powers set out in the First Schedule.[5] The application of existing law was, however, preserved. The section also renounced the executive powers of the

---

[1] J. D. Fage, *Ghana, A Historical Interpretation*, University of Wisconsin, 1959, p. 83.

[2] Leg. Ass. Deb. (1956–57, Official Report—First Series), Vol. 2, p. 42.

[3] This title was formally established on 27th July, 1957, by the Royal Style and Titles Act, 1957 (No. 13). By this the Parliament of Ghana approved the adoption, for use in relation to Ghana, of the following style and titles: " Elizabeth the Second, Queen of Ghana and of Her other Realms and Territories, Head of the Commonwealth." The Act was repealed on the establishment of the Republic by the Constitution (Consequential Provisions) Act, 1960 (C.A. 8), s. 22.

[4] See an anonymous article in 1 J.A.L. 99, which contains a useful analysis of this and other provisions of the Independence Act.

[5] For a discussion of the First Schedule, see pp. 74, *et seq.*, *post.*

British Government in relation to Ghana, these presumably including the power of United Kingdom Ministers to advise Her Majesty on the exercise of the Royal prerogative and on the exercise of such functions as the making of Orders in Council under the British Settlements Acts and the Foreign Jurisdiction Acts.[1]

Constitution of 1957

The Ghana (Constitution) Order in Council, 1957 (S.I. 1957 No. 277; L.N. 47) the main provisions of which came into force on 6th March, 1957, embodied the new Constitution of independent Ghana, apart from the legislative powers contained in the First Schedule to the Independence Act. In many ways it repeated the provisions of the previous Constitution. The most important new features were as follows.

The Executive. The Governor was replaced by a Governor-General, whose office was created by Letters Patent dated 22nd February, 1957,[2] and who, like the Governor, was also Commander-in-Chief of the armed forces. Except where otherwise provided by law, all powers, authorities and functions vested in the Queen or the Governor-General were to be exercised in accordance with the constitutional conventions applicable to the exercise of similar powers, authorities and functions in the United Kingdom by Her Majesty.[3] The executive power of Ghana was vested in the Queen and could be exercised by the Queen or by the Governor-General as her representative.[4] In most cases, following British convention, the executive power would be exercised in accordance with advice tendered by the Queen's Ministers in Ghana, in other words the Cabinet. The previous limitations on the powers of the Cabinet were of course removed, and it was charged with the general direction and control of the Government of Ghana and made responsible to Parliament.[5] The Prime Minister was appointed by the Governor-General in his discretion, but British convention would require him to appoint the leader of the largest party in the Assembly. Other Ministers were appointed and dismissed on the advice of the Prime Minister.[6] If the Assembly passed a motion of no confidence in the Government, the Governor-General was required to dismiss

---

[1] Ghana Independence Act, 1957, s. 1 (6).
[2] L.N. 57.
[3] Ghana (Constitution) Order in Council, 1957, s. 4 (2).
[4] *Ibid.*, s. 6.
[5] *Ibid.*, s. 7 (1).
[6] Ghana (Constitution) Order in Council, 1957, s. 7 (2), (3).

the Prime Minister unless advised by him to dissolve the Assembly.[1] A minor change was that Ministerial Secretaries were renamed Parliamentary Secretaries.[2]

Parliament.—The term " Parliament " had not previously been used in relation to Ghana. The Legislative Assembly was renamed the National Assembly, and Parliament consisted of the Queen and the National Assembly, on the model of the British Constitution.[3] The number of Members remained unchanged at 104, and the existing Members retained their seats.[4] The territorial allocation of seats was not specified. Provision was, however, made for for the establishment of a delimitation commission and for the delimitation of electoral districts on the principle that each district should possess a more or less equal number of inhabitants. Voting was to be by secret ballot on the basis of adult suffrage.[5] The legislative powers were considerably enlarged, the Governor's reserved powers of course disappearing. The limitations as to laws imposing disabilities on racial grounds or providing for the compulsory acquisition of property remained,[6] and a further limitation was added to protect freedom of conscience and religion.[7] Elaborate restrictions were also placed on legislation affecting chieftaincy or regional devolution. No Bill for amending the Constitution could become law unless it had been supported by the votes of at least two-thirds of the total number of Members of Parliament, and in certain cases by two-thirds of the Regional Assemblies also.[8] This restriction had been contemplated by para. 6 of the First Schedule to the Ghana Independence Act. Subject to these restrictions, a Bill which had passed the Assembly was required to be presented to the Governor-General " who may assent thereto in Her Majesty's name or refuse such assent."[9] On

---

[1] Ghana (Constitution) Order in Council, 1957, s. 7 (4).
[2] *Ibid.*, ss. 16, 72 (2). This is of some interest, as the previous name was reverted to in 1960.
[3] *Ibid.*, s. 20.
[4] *Ibid.*, s. 73.
[5] *Ibid.*, ss. 69, 70.
[6] *Ibid.*, ss. 31 (2), 34.
[7] *Ibid.*, s. 31 (3).
[8] *Ibid.*, s. 32. Amendments in relation to the boundaries of the Regions were excepted, but these were governed by other restrictions.
[9] *Ibid.*, s. 42 (2). The British conventions which of course applied to the giving or withholding of assent, probably precludes its being withheld, and certainly precludes its being withheld otherwise than on the advice of Ministers.

receiving assent the Bill became an Act of Parliament, the term "Ordinance" being abandoned.[1] The maximum life of the Assembly was extended from four years to five.[2]

Regions and Regional Assemblies.—Ghana was divided into five Regions. The Western and Trans-Volta/Togoland Regions remained as before. The former Eastern and Accra Regions were merged into a new Eastern Region, while Ashanti was designated the Ashanti Region and the Northern Territories and Northern Togoland became the Northern Region.[3] Alterations to the areas of any Regions required the approval of the Regional Assemblies affected; and where 10,000 or more registered electors were involved, or a new Region was to be created, a referendum was required.[4]

A Regional Assembly was required to be established for each Region by Act of Parliament and to be given functions relating to local government, agriculture, education, communications, health, public works, town and country planning, housing, police and other matters.[5] Until the necessary legislation was passed, the Members of Parliament from each Region were constituted an Interim Regional Assembly, with power to advise Ministers on matters affecting the Region and to set up a Police Relations Committee with the object of encouraging good relations between the police and the public.[6] A Regional Constitutional Commission was required to be established, with a judge as chairman, to enquire into and report on the devolution to Regional Assemblies of the functions to be entrusted to them, the composition of the Assemblies, the executive, legislative, financial and advisory powers to be exercised by them, the funds required to meet their expenditure, and the form of the legislation necessary to give effect to the Commission's recommendations. As soon as practicable after the submission of the Commission's report, the Minister responsible for local government was required to introduce into the Assembly legislation to give effect to the recommendations of the Commission.[7]

The concluding story of the Regional Assemblies may be given

---

[1] *Ibid.*, s. **42** (3).
[2] *Ibid.*, s. **47** (3).
[3] *Ibid.*, s. **63** (1).
[4] *Ibid.*, s. **33**.
[5] *Ibid.*, s. **64**.
[6] *Ibid.*, ss. **85, 86.**
[7] *Ibid.*, s. **87.**

here. Notice of the appointment of the Commission, under the chairmanship of Mr. Justice Van Lare, was given in the *Ghana Gazette* on 4th June, 1957, and the Commission delivered a voluminous report, including a draft Bill of 134 clauses, on 14th April, 1958.[1] They recommended that each Assembly should consist of members directly elected by the Parliamentary electors within the Region, the number of members being twice the number of Members of Parliament representing the Region.[2] The executive functions of the Assemblies were to be of a detailed and comprehensive character, constituting a major interposition between the Government and the local authorities. Indeed many of the Minister of Local Government's functions, including the approval of local authority estimates, rates, grants, loans, contracts and byelaws, were to be transferred to the Assemblies,[3] while they were also to have numerous functions previously entrusted to local authorities.

In a White Paper giving their views on the report, the Government stated that

" it would be wasteful, cumbersome and altogether unsound, administratively, to have in the proposed local government structure another tier, in the form of Regional Assemblies."

Although obliged by the Constitution to introduce the Bill in the form drawn up by the Commission, the Government would move amendments to convert the Assemblies into merely advisory bodies.[4] This intention was carried out; and the Bill as amended became law as the Regional Assemblies Act, 1958 (No. 25) and came into operation on 3rd September, 1958.[5] The elections were held on 16th and 21st October, 1958 and, since the Opposition refused to take part, C.P.P. candidates were returned in all seats except the half-dozen won by Independents.[6] The reason for the Opposition boycott was stated in the National Assembly by Mr. J. A. Braimah as follows:

" We did not take part in the Regional Assemblies because the Government had so mutilated the Regional Assemblies

---

[1] *Report to His Excellency the Governor-General by the Regional Constitutional Commission*, Accra, 1958.

[2] *Ibid.*, paras. 24, 29. The Trans-Volta/Togoland Regional Assembly was given rather more members so that it would have enough to function efficiently (*ibid.*, paras. 30, 31).

[3] Report of the Regional Constitutional Commission, p. 226.

[4] White Paper No. 4 of 1958.

[5] L.N. 287 of 1958.

[6] *Ghana Gazette*, 27th October, 1958.

E

Bill which was drafted by the Regional Constitutional Commission that those effective powers on which we all agreed and
solemnly pledged to support had not been given to the Regional
Assemblies."[1]

The only effective act achieved by the Regional Assemblies
was the giving of approval, under s. 32 of the Constitution, to a
Bill (which is discussed below) abolishing the restrictions on the
amendment of the Constitution. Soon after this, on 14th March,
1959, the Regional Assemblies Act was repealed. All the Regional
Assemblies were dissolved and it was provided that no further
elections to them should be held.[2] In moving the second reading
of the Bill bringing this about, the Prime Minister gave his reasons
very briefly, as follows:

" the Government are convinced that Regional Assemblies are
an unnecessary complication in the machinery of Government
and constitute a waste of money and manpower."[3]

Chieftaincy.—The Constitution contained a provision stating
that " the office of Chiefs in Ghana, as existing by customary law
and usage, is hereby guaranteed."[4] A House of Chiefs was required to be established by Act of Parliament for each Region,
and was given the right to offer advice to any Minister, and to
consider any matter referred to it by a Minister or the Assembly.
It could also make a declaration of the customary law relating
to any subject in force in any part of the area of its authority.[5]
In all the Regions except Ashanti, where the Asantehene was
Head, the House of Chiefs was given power to elect the Head of
the Region.[6] Where a Bill was introduced into the Assembly
which affected the traditional functions or privileges of a chief,
the Speaker was required to refer it to the appropriate House of
Chiefs and to defer the second reading for three months so as to
give time for the House of Chiefs to make its views known.[7]

A further safeguard for Chiefs was provided by the section
relating to local constitutional disputes.[8] On the establishment
of Houses of Chiefs, provision was required to be made by Act of

---

[1] Parl. Deb., Official Report, Vol. 12, p. 18.
[2] Constitution (Amendment) Act, 1959 (No. 7), ss. 10, 11.
[3] Parl. Deb., Official Report, Vol. 14, p. 161.
[4] Ghana (Constitution) Order in Council, 1957, s. 66.
[5] *Ibid.*, s. 67. Houses of Chiefs were established by the Houses of Chiefs
Act, 1958 (No. 20).
[6] Houses of Chiefs Act, 1958 (No. 2), s. 35.
[7] Ghana (Constitution) Order in Council, 1957, s. 35.
[8] *Ibid.*, s. 68.

Parliament for the determination of such disputes by a state council (or in the case of a paramount chief in Ashanti, by a committee of the Ashanti House of Chiefs), with a final appeal through the appropriate House of Chiefs to an appeal commissioner appointed by the Judicial Service Commission.[1] This involved a reversal of the changes made in 1955, which had aroused so much controversy.[2]

Courts of Justice.—Section 54(2) of the Constitution contemplated the existence of a Court of Appeal. This was created by an Ordinance dividing the Supreme Court into the High Court of Justice and the Court of Appeal with effect from 6th March, 1957.[3] By another Ordinance, which came into force at the same time, detailed provisions were made for the jurisdiction of the new Court of Appeal, and the right of recourse to the West African Court of Appeal (which was regarded as inconsistent with independence) was abolished.[4] The jurisdiction of the Judicial Committee of the Privy Council was, for the time being, allowed to continue. Section 54 of the Constitution gave the new Justices of Appeal the same security of tenure as was enjoyed by other Supreme Court judges. In an attempt to overcome the shortage of High Court judges without dilution, an Act of the following year created the office of Commissioner of Assize and Civil Pleas.[5] The Commissioners were appointed on limited engagements and could exercise the same jurisdiction as High Court judges except that they were excluded from the most important types of case. The experiment was not found successful, and was abandoned in 1960.

Citizenship.—The arrival of independence made necessary the new concept of Ghana citizenship. Although persons born in the Colony or Ashanti were normally citizens of the United Kingdom and Colonies by virtue of the British Nationality Act, 1948, this of course ceased to be the case for persons born after independence.[6] Persons born in the former Northern Territories or British

---

[1] Effect was given to this requirement by the Houses of Chiefs Act, 1958 (No. 20). Pending the establishment of Houses of Chiefs, s. 88 of the Constitution gave an appeal direct to an appeal commissioner.

[2] See p. 53, *ante.*

[3] Courts (Amendment) Ordinance, 1957 (No. 17), s. 2. The status of the judges of other West African territories as members of the Supreme Court was abolished by s. 3.

[4] Court of Appeal Ordinance, 1957 (No. 35). See also the Courts (Amendment) Act, 1957 (No. 8).

[5] Commissioners of Assize and Civil Pleas Act, 1958 (No. 12).

[6] Ghana Independence Act, 1957, s. 2.

Togoland would also cease to enjoy the status of British protected persons.[1] Since it was felt that citizenship was essentially a matter to be decided by the new Parliament of Ghana, the Constitution did not deal with it except incidentally.[2] However the first Act to be passed by the Parliament of Ghana was the Ghana Nationality and Citizenship Act, 1957, which provided for citizenship by birth, descent, registration and naturalisation and contained transitional provisions under which persons born in Ghana before Independence, or otherwise having connections with Ghana, were granted citizenship.[3] The Act also embodied the " common form " Commonwealth clause, under which a citizen of Ghana or of any other Member of the Commonwealth was recognized in the law of Ghana as having the status of a Commonwealth citizen.[4]

Membership of the Commonwealth.—The Constitution, following the usual practice elsewhere, did not refer to Ghana's membership of the Commonwealth. On the attainment of independence Ghana became eligible for full membership, and in their constitutional proposals the Government had indicated that this would be sought. As mentioned above, the Ghana Independence Act had in its long title contemplated that Ghana would remain within the Commonwealth and this was confirmed by a statement made in the House of Commons by the British Prime Minister, Mr. Harold Macmillan, on 21st February, 1957.[5] This included the following passage:

> " I am glad to be able to say that after consultation with other Commonwealth Prime Ministers they have all agreed that Ghana shall, as from 6th March, be recognised as a Member of the Commonwealth."

Membership of the United Nations.—On 8th March, 1957—two days after independence—Ghana became a member of the United Nations Organisation.

Amendments to 1957 Constitution

During the period before the inauguration of the Republic the Constitution was subjected to numerous amendments. Many of these arose because certain of the constitutional provisions which

---

[1] Ghana Independence Act, 1957, s. 2.

[2] See the definition of " citizen of Ghana " in s. 1 (1).

[3] For an analysis of the citizenship provisions of the Independence Act see 1 J.A.L., 103 *et seq.* For an account of the present law of Ghana citizenship, see pp. 187 *et seq., post.*

[4] Ghana Nationality and Citizenship Act, 1957, Part V.

[5] U.K. Parliamentary Debates (Commons), Vol. 564, col. 605.

were regarded as necessary in the republican era, but not of sufficient importance to find their way into the republican Constitution, were re-enacted with modifications in the National Assembly Act, 1959 (No. 78) and the Ministers of Ghana Act, 1959 (No. 77). Other amendments were more substantial. The abolition of the Regional Assemblies has been described above. Before their disappearance they were used to secure the enactment of a Bill removing the restrictions on the making of amendments to the Constitution. This Bill, which became law on 18th December, 1958 as the Constitution (Repeal of Restrictions) Act, 1958 (No. 38), provided for the repeal of para. 6 of the First Schedule to the Ghana Independence Act and of ss. 32, 33 and 35 of the Constitution. In the passage of the Bill, the full procedure required by s. 32 of the Constitution was followed for the first and last time.[1] The Government had no difficulty in obtaining the required two-thirds majority in the National Assembly and, since they had a majority in each of the Regional Assemblies, these all gave the necessary approval. The reasons for the Bill were given by the Prime Minister as follows:

> " It is the belief of the Government that in a developing society such as Ghana the law must be both certain and flexible. Experience has shown that the present Constitution is defective and obscure in many respects. It is, for example, difficult to say, with certainty, whether any particular Act of Parliament may or may not indirectly amend the Constitution. . . . I wish now to inform the House, quite frankly, that my Government accepted the Constitution as drawn up in the United Kingdom with the gravest misgivings. We were, however, faced with a situation where independence might well have been delayed had we refused to accept the text which was presented to us."[2]

The Prime Minister added that the overwhelming support for the Government in the country made it unnecessary to retain the elaborate procedure of referring constitutional Bills to the Regions. Justifying the repeal of s. 35, which required Bills affecting chieftaincy to be referred to Houses of Chiefs after introduction, the Prime Minister said that the wording of the section made it difficult to determine the Bills which should in law be referred to Houses of Chiefs. He also felt that consultation

---

[1] The only previous amendment to the Constitution had been an indirect one occasioned by the establishment of the Contingencies Fund (Contingencies Fund Act, 1958 (No. 18), s. 4). This however only required a two-thirds majority in the National Assembly.

[2] Parl. Deb., Official Report, Vol. 12, p. 5.

with the chiefs was better carried out at an early stage in the drafting of a Bill. To Opposition objections that the repeals would mean that the Constitution could thereafter be amended by an ordinary Act of Parliament rushed through in one day, Mr. Kofi Baako retorted that the same position obtained in Britain.[1]

Apart from those already mentioned, the following amendments were made to the Constitution before its repeal in 1960:

1. Sections 25 and 26 (which related to disqualification for membership of the National Assembly) were amended by providing that a person should be disqualified for election to the Assembly, or, if already a member, should lose his seat, if he had been subjected to preventive detention. A member would also lose his seat if he were absent without the Speaker's consent from twenty consecutive sittings of the Assembly, or if in the course of the proceedings of the Assembly he publicly declared his intention of systematically refraining from attending its proceedings.[2]

2. The provisions relating to the resignation of Ministers and Parliamentary Secretaries were amended to counter the practice of forestalling dismissal by tendering resignation. The amendments provided that a resignation would not be effective unless accepted by the Prime Minister.[3]

3. The Judicial Service Commission established under s. 55 was dissolved. Thereafter all judges of the Supreme Court and appeal commissioners were appointed on the advice of the Prime Minister. The power to appoint and exercise disciplinary control over judicial officers became exercisable on the advice of the Chief Justice, given after consultation with the Prime Minister.[4]

4. The functions of the Public Service Commission were curtailed by bringing all foreign service posts and an additional

---

[1] Parl. Deb., Official Report, Vol. 12, p. 25.

[2] National Assembly (Disqualification) Act, 1959 (No. 16). The last two amendments were directed at the Opposition's practice of boycotting the Assembly. The amendments are now embodied in the National Assembly Act, 1961 (Act 86), ss. 1, 2.

[3] Ministerial Offices (Resignation) Act, 1959 (No. 42). The amendment relating to Ministers is now embodied in the Republican Constitution (art. 17 (c)). Parliamentary Secretaries have disappeared. Their successors, Deputy Ministers, are appointed under the President's general powers and not under express statutory provision.

[4] Constitution (Amendment) Act, 1959 (No. 7), ss. 5–7.

number of senior home service posts under the control of the Prime Minister. The latter posts included that of the Attorney-General, who was also required to act on the direction of the Prime Minister in relation to prosecutions for offences against the safety of the State.[1]

5. Section 63 was amended by the creation of the Brong-Ahafo Region, which was formed out of the northern part of the Ashanti Region and a small area taken from the Northern Region.[2] Another change was the renaming of the Trans-Volta/Togoland Region, which became the Volta Region.[3]

6. The provisions relating to Houses of Chiefs, namely ss. 63(2), 67 and 68 (except sub-s. (4)), were repealed. Certain of them had become spent or superfluous on the enactment of the Houses of Chiefs Act, 1958 (No. 20). The repeal of the remainder made it possible to restore the position under which the Government could control the final determination of local constitutional disputes. This was done by an amendment giving the Governor-General power to confirm, vary or refuse to confirm the findings of an appeal commissioner.[4]

Apart from the amendments mentioned in paragraph 6 above, a number of other changes affecting chieftaincy were made at this time. The four territorial Councils were considered to have been rendered superfluous by the establishment of Houses of Chiefs and were accordingly abolished.[5] In moving the second reading of the Bill abolishing the Joint Provincial Council, Mr. A. E. A. Ofori Atta said:

> " Hon. Members will not wish the ending of this notable institution to pass without some appreciation of the services which it has performed for the benefit, not only of the area from which its members are drawn, but of the country as a whole. The Joint Provincial Council has a long history: during its lifetime it has contributed much sound and safe advice to successive Governments, and has played a prominent part in the development of the country. I should like, Mr. Speaker, to express the gratitude of the Government, and of the country, to those members of the Council who have given so much of

---

[1] Constitution (Amendment) Act, 1959 (No. 7), ss. 3, 4, 9.
[2] Brong-Ahafo Region Act, 1959 (No. 18).
[3] Volta Region Act, 1959 (No. 47).
[4] Houses of Chiefs (Amendment) Act, 1959 (No. 8), ss. 11, 17.
[5] Councils (Northern Territories and Trans-Volta/Togoland) Dissolution Act, 1958 (No. 31); Joint Provincial Council (Dissolution) Act, 1958 (No. 51). The Asanteman Council was abolished by the Houses of Chiefs Act, 1958 (No. 20), s. 47.

their time for the benefit of their fellow-countrymen, and to express the hope and conviction that these same members although now sitting in two Houses, will continue to help and support the Government."[1]

Another change was the removal of traditional members from the local and municipal councils, making those bodies fully elective.[2] Again, the continued prevalence of stool disputes led to the passing of the Chiefs (Recognition) Act, 1959 (No. 11) (as amended by No. 48 of 1959). This restored the concept of Government recognition of chiefs, which had disappeared with the repeal of the Native Authority Ordinances.[3] It provided that no enstoolment or destoolment of a chief after 18th December, 1958 was to have any effect unless recognized by the Governor-General. It also empowered the Governor-General to direct any person not to exercise or purport to exercise the functions of a chief and not to reside within a given area, thus reviving the idea of removal orders.[4] Legislation was also passed strengthening Government control over stool lands and other stool property.[5]

During this period a number of other Acts were passed on matters usually classified under the heading of constitutional law. In the main these Acts dealt with various aspects of state security, and had important consequences for personal freedom. Since they remain part of the current law they are discussed in the chapter dealing with this subject.[6] Mention should also be made of the Bank of Ghana Ordinance, 1957 (No. 34), which established a central bank under the name of the Bank of Ghana and created the Ghana pound, at parity with sterling, as the unit of currency. The Bank was set up with the aid of the Bank of England and was seen by Dr. Nkrumah as " the foundation on which the superstructure of our economic independence would be built ".[7]

---

[1] Parl. Deb., Official Report, Vol. 12, pp. 616–617.

[2] Local Government (Amendment) Act, 1959 (No. 14), s. 2; Municipal Councils (Abolition of Traditional Members) Act, 1959 (No. 15).

[3] See p. 46, *ante.*

[4] See p. 46, *ante.*

[5] Ashanti Stool Lands Act, 1958 (No. 28); Stool Lands Control Act, 1959 (No. 79); Stool Property (Recovery and Validation) Act, 1959 (No. 31) (as amended by No. 51 of 1959).

[6] See Chap. 5, *post.* The Acts included the Emergency Powers Act, 1957 (No. 28), the Preventive Detention Act, 1958 (No. 17), the Sedition Act, 1959 (No. 64) and the Treason Act, 1959 (No. 73). Other important constitutional Acts were the Deportation Act, 1957 (No. 14) and the Immigration Act, 1957 (No. 15), which are dealt with in Chap. 4, *post.*

[7] I Speak of Freedom, p. 111.

Announcement of the Republic

On 16th December, 1959 Dr. Nkrumah announced in the course of a debate on foreign policy that his Government proposed to introduce a new Constitution in the following year. After remarking that Ghana was a monarchy with the same Head of State as the United Kingdom, he went on:

> " It is essential that we make it absolutely clear that this does not mean in any way that Ghana is dependent upon any other country whatsoever. . . . I wish to emphasise this point because our present constitutional position is often misunderstood, and responsible political leaders abroad have even suggested that our membership of the Commonwealth fetters in some way our independence. This is not so. . . . Perhaps one of the reasons for the misunderstanding arises through the fact that our present Constitution was not enacted by the Ghana Parliament but was enacted by the United Kingdom Government at the time of Ghana's independence after consultation with the Ghana Government.
>
> I am sure the whole House will agree with me that the time has now come for the people of Ghana to devise for themselves a new Constitution best suited to the needs of Ghana. The technical work on this has already commenced and various consultations in regard to it are now taking place."[1]

The Prime Minister did not at that stage disclose that it was intended to convert Ghana into a republic, but his statement was generally assumed to point to this. The means by which the republican Constitution came into existence are described in the next chapter.

---

[1] Parl. Deb., Official Report, Vol. 17, pp. 637–638.

CHAPTER 2

THE CREATION OF THE REPUBLIC

1. Legal Difficulties

Ghana was the first member of the Commonwealth to provide herself with a republican Constitution without having had the means for doing so expressly indicated by United Kingdom legislation. Both India and Pakistan, Ghana's precursors as Commonwealth republics, had been provided with Constituent Assemblies by the Indian Independence Act, 1947. Burma is in a different category, having become overnight a republic outside the Commonwealth by virtue of a treaty made between the British Government and the Provisional Government of Burma and of the provisions of the Burma Independence Act, 1947.[1] Since no Constituent Assembly had been provided for by the Ghana Independence Act it became necessary to give careful consideration to the means whereby a republican Constitution could be enacted. Not even the existence in the first place of a Constituent Assembly with unchallengeable powers had saved Pakistan from acute constitutional difficulties in trying to turn herself into a republic and it was felt that every care must be taken to avoid the possibility of doubt arising as to the validity of Ghana's new Constitution. At first it was assumed that the Constitution could be enacted by the Parliament of Ghana in the same way as an ordinary Act. It would no doubt be desirable to avoid embodying the usual enacting formula, with its reference to the Queen, in the Constitution itself but this could be done by the use of a device such as the inclusion of the Constitution in a Schedule to the Act bringing it into force. An examination of the provisions relating to the powers of the Parliament of Ghana however gave rise to doubts as to whether it would be wise to follow this course.

The powers of the Parliament of Ghana derived from the First Schedule to the Ghana Independence Act, 1957 and s. 31 of the Ghana (Constitution) Order in Council, 1957. The First Schedule

---

[1] See Halsbury's Laws (3rd Edn.), Vol. 5, p. 458.

contained six paragraphs.[1] The first three reproduced, with the same wording apart from consequential alterations, ss. 2 and 3 of the Statute of Westminster, 1931. By these it was provided that the Colonial Laws Validity Act, 1865[2] would not apply to laws made by the Parliament of Ghana, that such laws would not be inoperative on the grounds of repugnancy to the law of England or any existing or future British Act, and that the Parliament of Ghana had full power to repeal or amend British legislation forming part of the law of Ghana and to make laws having extra-territorial operation. The fourth and fifth paragraphs contained minor consequential amendments to the Merchant Shipping Act, 1894 and the Colonial Courts of Admiralty Act, 1890. The final paragraph withheld the power to alter the 1957 Constitution otherwise than in the manner specified in that Constitution. Section 31 of the 1957 Constitution stated:

" Subject to the provisions of this Order, it shall be lawful for Parliament [*sc*. the Ghana Parliament constituted by the Order] to make laws for the peace, order and good government of Ghana."

The Order contained several provisions expressly limiting the legislative power. Section 31(2) and (3) and s. 34 restricted the power to make laws imposing disabilities on racial grounds, or depriving persons of freedom of conscience or religion, or providing for compulsory acquisition of property. Sections 32 and 33 restricted the power to make laws altering the constitutional provisions, or changing regional boundaries, by requiring such laws to be passed by a special procedure. It will be seen that, whatever the political intention behind the enactment of these provisions, they were in form somewhat removed from a clear grant of full legislative sovereignty. The provisions of the First Schedule were mainly negative in form while the legislative power conferred by the 1957 Constitution was clearly limited. By using the special procedure laid down by ss. 32 and 33 of the 1957 Constitution the Ghana Parliament in 1958 removed those very sections from the Constitution, and also repealed paragraph 6 of the First Schedule to the Ghana Independence Act.[3] The other restrictions remained, although there is a strong argument for

---

[1] See Appendix A, p. 467, *post*.
[2] See p. 18, *ante*.
[3] See p. 69, *ante*.

saying that after the modification effected by the 1958 Act they could have been repealed by ordinary Act of Parliament.

It could be argued, though not very convincingly, that the words " Subject to the provisions of this Order " in s. 31 of the 1957 Constitution referred not merely to the provisions mentioned above, but also to s. 20(1), which provided:

> " . . . there shall be a Parliament in and for Ghana which shall consist of Her Majesty the Queen and the National Assembly."

The introduction of a republic of course involved the repeal, or at least the amendment, of s. 20(1). While s. 20(1) remained in the Constitution in its original form it might be said that the power to make laws was subject to its provisions and therefore did not include power to make a law removing the Queen as one of the organs of Parliament. The words " Subject to the provisions of this Order " could not be repealed (so the argument ran) since a power cannot be effective to remove its own limitations. The argument was weakened by the fact that the Order itself originally contemplated that s. 20 might be repealed, this being one of the sections included in the Third Schedule as subject to a special procedure for their amendment or repeal. This fact is perhaps not of great weight, since s. 20 contained other provisions, relating to the composition of the National Assembly, which it was clearly within the competence of the Parliament of Ghana to amend or repeal. A more convincing objection is that this construction would really have involved the proposition that the legislative power was insufficient to amend *any* provision of the 1957 Constitution—an absurdity contradicted by s. 32, which expressly contemplated such amendment.

Another possible limitation of legislative power related to the repeal of provisions contained in the Ghana Independence Act itself. A law converting Ghana into a republic could not be brought into force without the repeal of at least one provision of this, namely that part of s. 1 which states that the territories comprised in Ghana " . . . shall as from [6th March, 1957] together form part of Her Majesty's dominions ". Had the Parliament of Ghana power to effect this repeal? Paragraph 2 of the First Schedule to the Act provides that

> " . . . no law and no provision of any law made on or after [6th March, 1957] by the Parliament of Ghana shall be void or inoperative on the ground that it is repugnant to the law of

England, or to the provisions of any *existing or future* Act of the
Parliament of the United Kingdom."

This follows precisely the wording of paragraph 1(2) of the
First Schedule to the Ceylon Independence Act, 1947, which in
turn was derived from s. 2(2) of the Statute of Westminster, 1931.
Doubt exists as to whether the reference to any existing or
future Act includes a reference to the Act in which it appears.
It is tempting to say that there is no receptacle between the
present and the future which, at the moment when an Act
comes into operation, is large enough to accommodate the Act.
The Act at this moment must either be an existing Act, because
it has just come into existence, or (if it has not just come into
existence) it must be   future Act. This reasoning was not
followed by the British Parliament when it enacted the Indian
Independence Act, 1947, s. 6(2) of which prevents any law made
by the legislature of either of the new Dominions created by that
Act from being invalid on the ground that it is repugnant to
" *this* or any existing or future Act of Parliament of the United
Kingdom ". This difference in the wording of the two Independence Acts of 1947 gave rise to considerable comment, though the
general view seems to have been that it did not indicate a difference in substance. Thus Professor K. C. Wheare said:

> " In the Ceylon Act, as in the Statute of Westminster, the
> powers conferred relate to ' any existing or future Act of
> Parliament '. This raises a controversy. Does the difference in
> wording amount to anything? Does it mean that Ceylon cannot
> amend its Independence Act, just as, it has been maintained,
> the Dominions cannot amend the Statute of Westminster? Is
> the Independence Act or the Statute an ' existing ' Act of
> Parliament? If it is—and the case for this view seems sound—
> why was it thought necessary to include ' this ' in the Indian
> Independence Act? If, ' this ' was put in to resolve doubts for
> India and Pakistan, why was it not done for Ceylon also?
> Is some limitation intended upon Ceylon's legislative compe-
> tence? These questions have aroused some discussion in Ceylon.
> It may not console the people of Ceylon to know that the
> difference is probably due to nothing more than a difference of
> draftsmen."[1]

Again, Geoffrey Marshall finds the distinction " insignificant "
and goes on to remark that nothing in the legislative intention
of the United Kingdom Parliament seems to justify the conclusion that the Parliament of Ceylon is unable to legislate

---

[1] *Journal of Comparative Legislation*, 3rd Series, Vol. XXX, p. 80.

repugnantly to, or to amend, the Ceylon Independence Act.[1]

Despite these doubts the United Kingdom Parliament enacted the " repugnancy " provisions for Ghana in exactly the same terms as for Ceylon. This may be taken to indicate that Parliament thought the doubts so trivial as to be beneath notice or that it wished to indicate that there was a difference of substance between the Indian and Ceylon provisions. Either view is possible, but the former seems more likely to be correct. It had indeed been already acted on in Ghana, the Constitution (Repeal of Restrictions) Act, 1958 (No. 38) having repealed paragraph 6 of the First Schedule to the Ghana Independence Act.[2]

In the light of these difficulties there seemed to be three different methods of procedure open. These were:

1. To disregard the doubts and proceed to pass the republican Constitution as an ordinary Act of Parliament.

2. To pass an Act of Parliament under the procedure laid down by s. 1(1)(a) of the Ghana Independence Act by which the Parliament of Ghana requested and consented to the enactment by the Parliament of the United Kingdom of an Act confirming that the Parliament of Ghana had since its inception possessed full legislative power, including power to withdraw Ghana from Her Majesty's Dominions and to remove the Queen as an organ of Parliament.

3. To make the new Constitution " autochthonous " by basing it firmly on the will of the people. This could be done by the holding of a referendum on the instructions of the Cabinet and the subsequent enactment by the National Assembly, as a Constituent Assembly deriving its authority from the verdict of the people in the referendum, of the new Constitution.[3]

The second course was ruled out on political grounds. The third was felt to involve too great a danger of matters getting out of control: the referendum would not be conducted under the authority of any Act, and it might not therefore be possible to

---

[1] *Parliamentary Sovereignty and the Commonwealth,* Oxford, 1957, p. 126.

[2] The wording was changed in the Nigeria Independence Act, 1960, to read: " . . . repugnant to the law of England, or to the provisions of any Act of the Parliament of the United Kingdom, including this Act . . . " (Sch. I, para. 2).

[3] On the question of autochthony see Wheare, *Constitutional Structure of the Commonwealth,* Chap. IV; Robinson, *Constitutional Autochthony in Ghana,* the Journal of Commonwealth Political Studies, 41.

make secure provision with regard to the keeping of order during voting in the referendum and for other matters connected with it, such as the nomination of candidates.

Attention was therefore turned to the first course mentioned above. No difficulty was contemplated in securing the actual passing of the Bill by the National Assembly, but it was necessary to consider whether, in view of the doubts as to legislative capacity, the Governor-General could properly assent to the Bill. Section 42 of the 1957 Constitution provided that no Bill should become law until the Royal Assent had been given and that when a Bill had been passed by the Assembly it should be presented to the Governor-General " who may assent thereto in Her Majesty's name or refuse such assent ". By virtue of s. 4(2) of the Constitution, the functions of the Governor-General relating to assent to Bills were to be exercised in accordance with the constitutional conventions applicable to the exercise of similar functions in the United Kingdom by Her Majesty, with a saving withdrawing any action of the Governor-General from question on the ground that these conventions had not been observed.

The constitutional convention relating to the exercise of the Crown's prerogative of withholding assent to Bills seems to be established in a form which requires the withholding of assent to be done only on advice by the Queen's Ministers.[1] The convention has not had to take account of a case where the Queen has been advised to assent to a Bill which exceeds the powers of Parliament. This situation has, however, arisen in the Dominions. In South Africa, for example, the Governor-General assented to the Separate Representation of Voters Bill, 1951 and the High Court of Parliament Bill, 1952 although these Bills had not been passed by the required two-thirds majority.[2] H. J. May remarks that, notwithstanding its possible invalidity, " it is submitted that the Governor General should assent to the Bill." He goes on to add:

" . . . even where the Governor-General is required to sign a document which would create an illegality, the responsibility is not his but that of the Ministers."

Although these problems of legislative capacity required to be investigated, and caused some difficulty because of the limited

---

[1] See Jennings, *Cabinet Government* (3rd Edn.), p. 400. The learned author reviews the development of the convention and ends: " The conclusion seems to be that the Crown cannot refuse assent except on advice."
[2] H. J. May, *The South African Constitution* (3rd Edn.), p. 185.

time available for the preparation of the Constitution, they were rendered of small account by the prevailing political conditions. There might be much dispute in Ghana as to the form a new Constitution should take, but there was a unanimous view that Ghanaians were since independence free to choose their own form of government.[1] Nor was any dissenting voice to be heard from the United Kingdom, where the authorities were sympathetic to Ghana's aspirations and ready to assist their fruition. The political realities were overwhelmingly in favour of brushing aside legalistic doubts and pursuing a straightforward course. In the end the course actually followed was a combination of the first and third procedures mentioned above.

2. THE CONSTITUENT ASSEMBLY AND PLEBISCITE ACT

Under the 1957 Constitution the constitutional conventions attaching to the British Crown were expressly applied to Ghana.[2] Whether or not these conventions can be said to include the doctrine that fundamental legislation should not be enacted without a " mandate " from the electorate, this doctrine was in fact recognized as valid in Ghana. Sir Ivor Jennings has pointed out that the doctrine is not limited to the United Kingdom:

> " President de Valera declared in 1932 that the Dáil could not deal with the question of separation from the British Commonwealth of Nations because, though his Government had a mandate for removing the oath from the Constitution and for suspending the payment of the land annuities, it had no mandate to create a republic."[3]

The Ghana Government had no mandate at the beginning of 1960 to create a republic, and readily acknowledged the fact. As Mr. Ofori Atta, the Minister of Local Government, put it in the National Assembly:

---

[1] Speaking in the debate on the draft republican Constitution, Mr. J. A Braimah, who had transferred from the United Party to the C.P.P., said: " In rising to make my humble contribution to this debate, my mind automatically goes back to the Atlantic Declaration of August, 1941, which stated among other things that the signatories ' respect the right of all peoples to choose the form of government under which they will live '. In the exercise of this undoubted right, Ghana has therefore decided to choose the form of government under which her people will live and no one, in or outside this country, can quarrel with that desire." (*Proceedings of the Constituent Assembly*, 19.)

[2] By s. 4 (2).

[3] *The Law and the Constitution* (4th Edn.), p. 165.

" The present Members of Parliament were however not elected by the people for the purpose of enacting a republican constitution and the question of a republic was not an issue at the last general election. At that election, of course, certain constitutional principles were settled. The people voted for a unitary form of government and rejected a federal form of government. Nevertheless, it cannot be said that this House, as at present constituted, has a mandate from the people to adopt or make on their behalf, any particular form of republican constitution."[1]

The Government decided to seek a mandate, and took the view that the people should be asked to vote not merely on the simple question of whether Ghana should become a republic or not, but also on the broad principles to be adopted in framing the new Constitution. It was also thought desirable, assuming the people would support a change to republican status, to find a means of enabling them to choose the person they wanted as the new head of state. Furthermore there was the question on whom the mandate to enact a new Constitution was to be conferred. The United Party, who constituted the official Opposition, took the view that there should be a Constituent Assembly which would be

" . . . an entirely new body elected and appointed freely to represent all the interests of the country, i.e. the Members of Parliament, Chiefs, the University Colleges (Legon and Kumasi), the Churches, the Muslim Council, the Professional Associations, the Chambers of Commerce, the Farmers' Unions, the T.U.C., the Co-operative Societies, the Ex-servicemen's Organisations, the Ghana Women's Federation or Council and the political parties."[2]

However, in the Government's opinion, which prevailed, the existing Members of Parliament themselves were best fitted to form the Constituent Assembly:

" They were chosen by the people at the last general election to represent them in making laws for Ghana and it is therefore right that Members of Parliament and not other persons who have not been so chosen should constitute the Constituent Assembly."[3]

The Constituent Assembly and Plebiscite Bill was accordingly introduced into the National Assembly on 23rd February, 1960. Of the two main clauses, which were not altered during the passage

---

[1] Parl. Deb. Official Report, Vol. 18, col. 7 (23rd February, 1960).
[2] Parl. Deb. Official Report, Vol. 18, col. 46.
[3] *Ibid.*, col. 7 (speech of Mr. Ofori Atta).

F

of the Bill, the first (clause 2) authorised the National Assembly

" . . . to resolve itself from time to time into a Constituent Assembly with full power to enact such provisions for or in connection with the establishment of a new Constitution as it thinks fit, including provisions whereby Ghana is established as a republic."

This is believed to be unique. Although *ad hoc* Constituent Assemblies are commonly set up to make new constitutions and frequently, as in the case of India and Pakistan, to exercise the functions of an ordinary legislature at the same time, no previous example was known to the Ghana Government of an existing legislature being given this double personality. It would of course have been just as effective to confer constituent powers on the National Assembly as such but it was felt that the dignity and importance of the proceedings would be enhanced if Members of Parliament had first to resolve themselves into a Constituent Assembly.[1]

Clause 2 went on to provide that:

" a Bill for a new Constitution, any Bill containing provisions consequential on or supplemental to the new Constitution, and any other Bill passed by the Constituent Assembly under this Act shall become law notwithstanding that Her Majesty has not given Her assent thereto."

By this, s. 42 of the 1957 Constitution (which provided that no Bill should become law until the Queen's assent had been signified) was made inapplicable to Bills of the Constituent Assembly. Again the reason was more one of impression than substance, it being strongly felt that Ghanaians could not be said to be giving themselves a Constitution if what they produced had to be submitted to the Queen's representative and had to receive his assent, however freely given. This feeling was expressed by Mr. J. A. Braimah as follows:

" We all know that the Governor-General assents to Bills on behalf of Her Majesty the Queen and we all know that the Governor-General has never turned down any Bills passed by this House; besides, the Governor-General acts on the advice of the Ministers. Why then not let the people have the real thing? "[2]

Apart from removing the need for Royal Assent, this provision

---

[1] For similar reasons the Bills, order papers and minutes of the Constituent Assembly were printed on pink paper instead of the usual blue and its proceedings were separately reported.
[2] Parl. Deb. Official Report, Vol. 18, col. 31.

also served to indicate that the powers of the Constituent Assembly were not limited to enacting a Constitution, as indeed was shown by the words " or in connection with " in the opening passage of clause 2. If the powers had been so limited, argument might have arisen as to what provisions were within the scope of a Constitution and in any case it was already the intention of the Government to introduce a number of other Bills of a constitutional nature apart from the Constitution itself.

Clause 2 went on to provide that the existing law governing the National Assembly (except s. 42 of the 1957 Constitution) should apply with any necessary modifications to the Constituent Assembly, and that " subject to the provisions of any enactment made by the Constituent Assembly "—a reference to the new Constitution, which would abolish the legal existence of the old National Assembly—nothing in the Bill was to affect the working of the National Assembly as such.

Clause 3 enabled a constitutional plebiscite to be held:

> " In order, before passing a Bill for a new Constitution, to inform itself as to the wishes of the people on the form of the Constitution, or the person who is to become the new Head of the State or any other matter, the Constituent Assembly may order the holding of a plebiscite to determine such questions as the Constituent Assembly may direct."

Although power to hold a referendum already existed under the Referendum Act, 1959 (No. 10), it was felt that this should not be used for testing opinion on the republican issue. Under that Act the referendum would have had to be ordered by the Governor-General, whereas it seemed more appropriate, since the task of constitution-making was entrusted to the Constituent Assembly, to place control over the questions to be asked and other relevant matters in the hands of that body. Although the two main questions had already been chosen in principle by the Government, clause 3 allowed other questions to be put if it was later thought necessary to do so. This power did not in fact have to be used.

Clause 3 went on to give the Constituent Assembly power to make regulations governing the detailed procedure of the plebiscite. In view of recent by-election disturbances, this power was made sufficiently wide to enable public order to be maintained by the control of the movement and assembly of persons and the supply of intoxicating liquor. Power to provide for requisitioning of vehicles and buildings was also given.

Clause 4 of the Bill, which was the only one to be amended, dealt with its duration. As introduced, this provided that the Act was to be automatically repealed on the coming into operation of a Constitution enacted by the Constituent Assembly. It was amended so as to delete this repeal while taking away the right of the National Assembly to resolve itself into a Constituent Assembly once the new Constitution had come into force. One reason for the change was a technical one connected with the passing of a new Interpretation Act. The other was to enable the measure to remain on the statute book " so as to explain how Acts were enacted by the Constituent Assembly."[1] In view of the fact that the repeal of an Act does not affect its previous operation or anything done under it[2] no harm would be caused by repeal, although the Act may perhaps be allowed to remain as a historical document.

While the United Party criticised the Constituent Assembly and Plebiscite Bill on points of detail they did not press their opposition to a division at any stage. The Bill was passed on 25th February, 1960, received the Royal Assent the same day and came into operation on its publication as a supplement to the *Ghana Gazette* two days later.[3]

So that the Constituent Assembly should not find itself in procedural difficulties at its first meeting, the National Assembly passed a special motion on 29th February. This provided that the Standing Orders of the National Assembly were to apply for the purposes of the Constituent Assembly subject to certain modifications. On any day appointed for the transaction of business by the Constituent Assembly, the Speaker was required, at the conclusion of National Assembly business, to put the question " That this House do now resolve itself into a Constituent Assembly ", which was to be decided without amendment or debate. At the end of Constituent Assembly business the National Assembly was automatically to resume. The Speaker was enabled to take the chair at the Committee stage of Bills, and minor adjustments were made to the procedure for the passing of Bills.[4]

---

[1] See Parl. Deb. Official Report, Vol. 19, cols. 11 and 61.
[2] Interpretation Act, 1960 (C.A. 4), s. 8.
[3] The text of the Constituent Assembly and Plebiscite Act is given in Appendix A, p. 470, *post.*
[4] *Minutes of the National Assembly*, 29th February, 1960. The motion was later amended to allow Bills to be introduced before the prescribed period had elapsed after publication: *Minutes of the National Assembly*, 7th June, 1960.

3. THE DRAFT CONSTITUTION

The draft republican Constitution had been in preparation since the previous December, and on 6th March, 1960, the third anniversary of independence, the Prime Minister, in a broadcast to the nation, outlined his Government's proposals. He stated that the keynote of the draft Constitution was one man-one vote and the unity of Africa, namely the political union of of African countries, and that the draft Constitution was based firmly on the rule of law and left no scope for arbitrary action or for discrimination against any individual or community. The next day a Government White Paper was issued giving the text of the draft Constitution and setting out the Government's proposals in an accompanying commentary.[1] The parts of this commentary which are relevant to the Constitution as passed are described in the next chapter in the course of discussing the details of the Constitution. Two extracts only need be given here. The status of the draft Constitution was described in the opening words of the White Paper as follows:

" The draft Constitution recognises that ultimately all powers of the State come from the people, and it will be for the people and not primarily for the Constituent Assembly to determine the form of the Constitution. It is, however, the duty of the Government and of the elected representatives of the people in the Constituent Assembly to advise what is, in their view, the most suitable form for the Constitution of the Republic of Ghana. In order to enable the views of the Constituent Assembly to be expressed and made known the Government will immediately lay this White Paper before the Assembly and will ask the Assembly to endorse the draft Constitution before it is submitted to the people. If the Assembly does so the people will then be asked, in a plebiscite to be held between 19th and 26th April, 1960, whether they approve the main provisions of the draft Constitution. If this approval is given the Constituent Assembly will clearly be in duty bound to enact a Constitution along the lines of that approved by the people."[2]

This passage was elaborated at the end of the commentary, where the principles contained in the draft Constitution were summarized as follows:

" 1. That Ghana should be a sovereign unitary republic with power to surrender any part of her sovereignty to a Union of African States.

---

[1] *Government Proposals for a Republican Constitution* (W.P. No. 1/60).
[2] W. P. No. 1/60, p. 3.

2. That the Head of State and holder of the executive power should be an elected President responsible to the people.

3. That Parliament should be the sovereign legislature and should consist of the President and the National Assembly, and that the President should have a power to veto legislation and to dissolve Parliament.

4. That a President should be elected whenever there is a general election by a method which insures that he will normally be the leader of the party which is successful in the general election.

5. That there should be a Cabinet appointed by the President from among Members of Parliament to assist the President in the exercise of his executive functions.

6. That the system of courts and the security of tenure of judges should continue on present lines.

7. That the control of the armed forces and the civil service should be vested in the President."[1]

It was explained that these seven points constituted the essence of the Government's proposals. The Government would not consider itself bound to introduce a Constitution Bill which followed word for word the draft in the White Paper, since, in the light of reactions to the draft, changes of detail, arrangement and emphasis might be found desirable. However, if the people approved the proposals, the seven points would be treated as fundamental.

The constitutional proposals were received with keen interest by the world press. British comment was on the whole favourable. The *Times* expressed the view that:

" It is an ingenious constitution, avowedly aimed at efficient government during the early stages of development and expertly framed to suit Ghanaian conditions."[2]

The *Daily Mirror*, under the heading " Good Luck Ghana! ", said:

" The new Constitution puts paid to any idea that Ghana is heading for dictatorship."[3]

The Manchester *Guardian* found that:

" Altogether, the draft Constitution seems quite a promising one, and there is no reason why Ghana should not remain a welcome member of the Commonwealth under it."[4]

---

[1] W. P. No. 1/60, p. 16.
[2] Issue of 7th March, 1960.
[3] Issue of 7th March, 1960.
[4] Issue of 7th March, 1960.

The *Irish Independent* said of the proposal to couple the election of the President with that of Members of Parliament:

> " This is an arrangement without precedent and, on paper, is full of promise. It combines strong government with democracy, something which older countries have often failed to achieve."[1]

In the United States the draft Constitution was generally welcomed as marking the final emancipation of Ghana from colonial rule. The *Washington Post* commented:

> " What makes the move of special significance is that Ghana, as the first West African country to attain full independence from colonial status in 1957, is in many respects the bellwether for the continent during an exciting period."[2]

On the other hand the reception in South Africa was generally cool. The Natal *Witness* referred to " Black Bonapartism ", while the Pretoria *News* found the proposals a serious departure from British democratic principles. In France, *L'Information* described the draft Constitution as at the same time authoritarian and expansionist. All over the world, whatever the attitude adopted, great interest was shown and the press devoted much space to describing and examining in detail the blue-print for Ghana's republican future.

In Ghana itself the press reaction was predictable. The *Ghana Times* and the *Evening News*, both strong Government supporters, gave the proposals an enthusiastic welcome. The British-owned *Daily Graphic* printed the entire draft Constitution and advised those who liked the draft to accept it and those who disliked it to reject it. The *Ashanti Pioneer*, at that time an Opposition newspaper, was outspokenly critical.

The first sitting of the Constituent Assembly took place on 14th March, 1960. The Prime Minister, Dr. Nkrumah, moved

> " That the Constituent Assembly recommends to the people of Ghana the Government proposals for a republican Constitution set out in the White Paper issued on the 7th March, 1960."

His opening words were:

> " It is with joy and pride that I appear this morning, before the representatives of the people of the nation of Ghana here gathered in a Constituent Assembly, to move this motion. I do so with thankfulness to the dead and the living, who by their sweat, blood and sacrifice have made possible the victory of

---

[1] Issue of 26th March, 1960.
[2] Issue of 22nd March, 1960.

the Ghana we pronounce today. It is a great day for Ghana and the Ghanaian people, for today marks the opening of our Constituent Assembly by which the people of Ghana, for the first time in our long history, are exercising their undoubted and inalienable right to enact for themselves the Constitution by which they shall be governed."[1]

The Opposition moved an amendment to the Prime Minister's motion which, while not rejecting the Government's proposals, suggested that a Constitutional Reform Commission should be set up to enquire into them and make recommendations to the Constituent Assembly. No details were given, either in the amendment or by Opposition speakers in the ensuing debate, as to the composition or method of appointment of the proposed Commission. Indeed, in spite of the terms of their amendment, the five Opposition speakers in the two-day debate spent most of their time attacking the draft Constitution along the lines indicated by a United Party statement published a few days before.[2] This described the draft as " worse than the crudest colonial constitution of the nineteenth century." Apart from the Prime Minister and Mr. Ofori Atta (Minister of Local Government), who wound up the debate, four members of the Convention People's Party spoke. While strongly supporting the Government's proposals they did give voice to a few criticisms. Mr. J. A. Braimah thought that in the provision enabling sovereignty to be surrendered by ordinary Act of Parliament " the people will be signing a blank cheque for Parliament to use at a future date perhaps at a heavy cost." He suggested that a referendum should be necessary before sovereignty could be surrendered.[3] Mr. A. J. Dowuona-Hammond, supported by Mr. Mumuni Bawumia, expressed the view that the Chief Justice should not share the safeguards against dismissal proposed for the judges of the superior courts.[4] At the end of the debate the Opposition amendment was rejected by seventy-five votes to ten, and the Government motion was then carried without a division.

4. THE CONSTITUTIONAL PLEBISCITE

On 15th March, 1960, at the end of the debate on the constitutional proposals, the Constituent Assembly made an order for

---

[1] *Proceedings of the Constituent Assembly*, 1.
[2] *Ashanti Pioneer*, 12th March, 1960.
[3] *Proceedings of the Constituent Assembly*, 20–21.
[4] This view was later adopted in a modified form; see p. 92, *post*.

the holding of the plebiscite.[1] Voting was to take place in specified parts of Ghana on three different days so that the limited
numbers of polling staff and police available could be moved from
one place to another. Provision was included for the dates to
be changed by *Gazette* notice if necessary, and in fact this had to
be done.[2] The order provided for nominations for the office of
Head of State under the new Constitution. The candidate had
to be a citizen of Ghana who had attained the age of thirty-five,
and the nomination form had to be signed by not less than ten
Members of Parliament. As the names of the candidates could
not definitely be known until the period for nominations had
elapsed (it was thought that the Opposition might boycott the
plebiscite), the order left the actual questions to be determined
at a future time. The candidates nominated were Dr. Nkrumah
and Dr. J. B. Danquah, the doyen of the United Party.[3] When
the closing date for nominations had passed, the Constituent
Assembly made a further order directing two questions to be
submitted for the determination of the voters.[4] These were:

" 1. Do you accept the draft republican Constitution for
Ghana as set out in the White Paper issued by the Government
on 7th March, 1960?

2. Do you accept Kwame Nkrumah or Joseph Boakye
Danquah as the first President under the new Constitution? "

The White Paper had stated that the Government would propose to the Constituent Assembly that voting should be on a
parliamentary constituency basis, so that the people of Ghana
would know not only the total number of votes cast but also the
state of opinion in each constituency.[5] This was accordingly
provided for in the detailed regulations made by the Assembly to
govern voting procedure.[6] The regulations closely followed those
in force for general elections. Both the Opposition and Government parties were entitled to have polling agents present in every
polling station as a check against irregularities, and also to have a
counting agent in each constituency to witness the counting of
votes. There were four ballot boxes in each polling station, and
the voter was given two papers. One was to be put either in the

---

[1] Constitutional Plebiscite Order, 1960 (E.I. 73).
[2] *Ghana Gazette*, 30th March, 1960.
[3] *Ghana Gazette*, 21st March, 1960.
[4] Constitutional Plebiscite (Questions) Order, 1960 (E.I. 75).
[5] W.P. No. 1/60, p. 7.
[6] Constitutional Plebiscite Regulations, 1960 (E.I. 74).

box bearing the word " yes " in white on a red ground or the box bearing the word " no " in black on a white ground, indicating approval or disapproval of the draft Constitution. The other was to be put either in the box bearing the photograph of Dr. Kwame Nkrumah and the red cockerel symbol of the C.P.P. or in the box bearing the photograph of Dr. J. B. Danquah and the cocoa-tree symbol of the United Party.[1] Apart from answering the two questions posed, the votes were to serve an additional purpose. The Government had pointed out that the plebiscite would correspond very nearly to a general election. The Presidential candidates were the respective leaders of the only two political parties in the country, and voting was on a constituency basis. It would thus be possible to tell in which constituencies the Government and the Opposition had a majority. The Government had accordingly announced that if the Presidential election showed that there would be little change in the balance of parties in the Assembly if a further general election were held, they would treat this as a mandate to extend the life of the existing Assembly, which was due to be dissolved by July, 1961 at the latest.[2]

The public were informed of the holding of the plebiscite, the issues involved and the method of voting in a number of ways. Apart from the issue of the White Paper and the widespread newspaper coverage, a large number of posters were put up all over the country. Among these were posters setting out the seven points listed in the White Paper. The posters were printed in English and in nine of the vernacular languages, including Twi, Fante, Ga and Ewe.

The plebiscite was held on 19th, 23rd and 27th April, 1960, and proved a triumph for the Government. Dr. Nkrumah was elected as first President in all but two of the 104 constituencies, obtaining 1,015,740 votes as against 124,623 cast for Dr. Danquah. Only in one constituency was there a majority against the draft Constitution, which was approved by 1,009,692 votes to 131,393.[3] The great interest aroused was indicated by the fact that more than half the registered electors voted.[4]

---

[1] Constitutional Plebiscite (Symbol) Regulations, 1960 (E.I. 76).
[2] W.P. No. 1/60, p. 11.
[3] *Ghana Gazette*, 14th May, 1960.
[4] The exact proportion was calculated at 54.6%. Surprisingly, in view of its high illiteracy rate, the biggest proportion was in Ashanti, where 76% of the registered electors voted.

5. The Enactment of the Constitution

The Constitution Bill was introduced into the Constituent Assembly on 13th June, 1960. The interval of three months since the first publication of the draft Constitution had been used to make a considerable number of detailed changes designed to improve its effectiveness and to meet certain criticisms. These changes were explained in the Memorandum signed by the Prime Minister which accompanied the Bill as introduced, and were indicated by bold type in the Bill itself. The most important changes related to Parliament. The provisions of art. 20, which lays down the legislative powers of Parliament, were greatly expanded.[1] In the words of the Memorandum, it was made clear that

> " except in relation to matters reserved by the Constitution to the people, the legislative power of Parliament is supreme."

Other changes in art. 20 safeguarded the Constitution against amendment by implication, and restricted the power of Parliament to transfer its supremacy to any other body. The dignity of the National Assembly was enhanced by the insertion of a provision guaranteeing freedom of speech, debate and proceedings.[2] The franchise principle in art. 1 was strengthened by adding the requirement that votes were to be cast in freedom and secrecy. Presidential messages to the Assembly were to be read by a Minister, " to ensure that no stranger can be authorised by this provision to enter the Assembly ".[3]

A change was made in the last paragraph of the declaration of fundamental principles required to be made by the President on his assumption of office. Originally this paragraph read:

> That no person should be deprived of his property save in accordance with law, and that no law should be made by which a person is deprived of his property without adequate compensation other than a law imposing taxation or prescribing penalties for offences or giving restitution for civil wrongs or protecting health or property.

The substituted version is as follows:

---

[1] References here to article numbers are to the numbers in the Constitution as finally enacted. The text is given in Appendix A, *post*. For detailed explanations of the text see Chap. 3, *post*.

[2] Article 21 (3).

[3] Article 25 (5).

That no person should be deprived of his property save where the public interest so requires and the law so provides.[1]

Following a suggestion made by Government backbenchers,[2] the position of the Chief Justice was altered to enable him to be dismissed at will from his office of Chief Justice, though not from his judgeship.[3] As the Memorandum explained, the new version

> " assimilates the position of the Chief Justice to that of Lord Chancellor in England. The Chief Justice must be a Judge of the Supreme Court, and cannot be removed from his judgeship.[4] He may, however, be removed as Chief Justice if the President thinks fit. His capacity as Chief Justice makes him the administrative head of the Judicial Service, and in relation to such non-judicial functions it is considered that the President ought to be in a position to ensure that the Chief Justice will give his loyal co-operation."

Criticism had been aroused by a provision in the first draft which gave the President unfettered discretion to grant loans from public funds. This was met by giving the National Assembly power to require any agreement for a loan to be submitted for their ratification.[5] The opportunity was also taken to entrench the article charging the public debt on the general revenues and assets of Ghana.[6] The criticism that the Attorney-General appeared to be given power by the first draft to discontinue civil proceedings brought against the Republic was met by an amendment making it clear that this was not so.[7] Other changes that should be mentioned here were as follows. The article listing the laws of Ghana was completely altered.[8] The system of courts was

---

[1] Article 13 (1).
[2] See p. 88, *ante*.
[3] Article 44 (3).
[4] I.e., without a vote of two-thirds of the members of the National Assembly.
[5] Article 35 (2).
[6] Article 37 (2).
[7] Article 47 (2).
[8] Article 40. The original version stated that the laws comprised:
    " (a) indigenous laws and customs not being repugnant to natural justice, equity and good conscience, in so far as their application is not inconsistent with any enactment for the time being in force, and
    (b) the doctrines of common law and equity, in so far as their application is not inconsistent with such indigenous laws and customs or with any enactment for the time being in force, and
    (c) enactments for the time being in force made under powers conferred by the Constitution or previously existing."

modified—instead of a Supreme Court functioning both as a Court of Appeal and a High Court, two separate superior courts were established, namely the Supreme Court and the High Court.[1] The Supreme Court was made the final court of appeal and also given an exclusive original jurisdiction over questions as to the validity of legislation.[2] The section dealing with the Civil Service was widened to cover the Public Services generally.[3] In consequence the article establishing the Civil Service Commission was omitted, and mention was made of the police. To emphasize its civilian character, in the words of the Memorandum, the description of the police was changed from Police Force to Police Service.

Before the second reading of the Constitution Bill, which took place on the day it was introduced, the Constituent Assembly passed a procedural motion governing the Constitution Bill and all other Bills to be passed by the Constituent Assembly. This was necessary because the Ordinances Authentication Ordinance (Cap. 2) had been disapplied by s. 2(3) of the Constituent Assembly and Plebiscite Act, 1960 (No. 1). Provision had therefore to be made for such matters as the authentication, numbering and publication of Acts of the Constituent Assembly.[4] The motion was on similar lines to those subsequently laid down for Republican Acts by the Acts of Parliament Act, 1960 (C.A. 7).

The second reading debate passed off quietly. The results of the plebiscite left the Opposition little scope for objection to the Bill and they were in any case appeased to some extent by the fact that alterations had been made in the Bill to meet their criticisms. Mr. Dombo, the Leader of the Opposition, remarked:

> " I think most of the criticisms we levelled against this Constitution have been met and for that reason I say well done to the people who have redrafted it."[5]

He continued to find objectionable however the statement in art. 8(4) that the President is not obliged to follow advice tendered by any other person. This had been widely criticized as contravening the customary principle that a chief, though by forms and ceremonies appearing autocratic, was in reality bound

---

[1] Article 41.

[2] Article 42 (2).

[3] Part VIII.

[4] The text of the motion is given in *Proceedings of the Constituent Assembly*, 161.

[5] *Proceedings of the Constituent Assembly*, 178.

to act in a democratic manner, that is by consulting with his councillors before taking any action in his capacity as chief and by following the advice tendered by them.[1] To some extent the criticism appears to have been based on a misundertsanding, as illustrated by Mr. Dombo's remark that the effect of art. 8(4) is that " the President shall not take advice from anybody ".[2] All that the article does is to make plain the difference between the President's position and that formerly occupied by the Governor-General. After he has considered such advice as he is offered or seeks, the ultimate decision is the President's, taken in his own discretion. He is not, in other words, a constitutional monarch but an executive President. Even so the rule is not absolute, since it may be modified in particular cases by ordinary Act of Parliament and in practice rarely operates in full force. The tradition that the Head of State acts only on the majority opinion in Cabinet dies hard.

Two points made in the debate by Government members should be noticed here, since they led to changes in the Bill.[3] Mr. Dowuona-Hammond and Mr. Kwaku Boateng suggested that some mention of local councils should be made in the Constitution.[4] They also made another suggestion, of far greater importance, in which they were joined by Mr. Mumuni Bawumia. This was that, apart from his legislative function as an organ of Parliament, the President should be given special legislative powers of his own. Mr. Boateng put it in this way:

> " It appears that under this Constitution it is possible to have the leader of the majority party in power, who will be the President, disagreeing with Members of Parliament, and therefore when such a disagreement occurs it is likely that there may be a general election. It is also possible that this disagreement between the President and Members of Parliament may extend to members of the Cabinet, in which case it is possible that the disagreement may affect all Members of Parliament together with Ministers. When this situation arises general elections may not necessarily be the appropriate remedy. In such circumstances the country will be difficult to govern. In a rapidly developing country such a situation will produce anarchy and chaos. Further, there could be circumstances which though short of an

---

[1] *Cf.* Rattray, *Ashanti Law and Constitution*, 406. Rattray mentions that a chief on enstoolment hears the words, " We do not wish that he should act on his own initiative ": p. 82.

[2] *Proceedings of the Constituent Assembly*, 179.

[3] See arts. 51 (1) and 55.

[4] *Proceedings of the Constituent Assembly*, 182, 194.

emergency could plunge the country into political turmoil. The solution to my mind lies in some form of enabling powers for the President."[1]

Mr. Dowuona-Hammond, who at that time was Parliamentary Secretary to the Ministry of Education and Information, asked for powers enabling the President " to act, as occasion demands, by mere administrative directions which are deemed to carry the force of law ". He went on:

> " This will nip in the bud cases of espionage, insurrections or even *coups d'etat* before they rear their ugly heads to warrant declaration of a state of emergency. In a country like Ghana where some people feel they should oppose every Government measure, however wise, simply because they style themselves ' Opposition ', and where there have been instances of questionable loyalty of some Civil Servants, the long winding (*sic*) procedure of having Bills drafted, published a number of times before passing through the various stages in Parliament should be avoided. The President could by administrative action deal promptly with situations without having recourse to such procedure."[2]

In winding up the debate, the Minister of Local Government, Mr. A. E. A. Ofori Atta, answered Mr. Boateng's point in the following way:

> " The Constitution states clearly that the Government of the country is in the hands of the President and his Ministers— the Cabinet. If the Cabinet as a whole tenders its resignation to the President and he finds that because of the opposition of Members of Parliament he is unable to get other Members of Parliament to form a Cabinet, he is in duty bound to carry on the government of the country with a body of Ministers. Therefore, it is expected that if the President finds that it is impossible for him to get Ministers to help him, he should refuse to accept the resignation of his Ministers."[3]

At the end of the debate the Bill was given a second reading without a division. The committee stage was held on 24th June and a small number of amendments were made. None were opposed except the controversial addition of art. 55. Before discussing this we will mention the more important of the other amendments. Article 6 was amended to create two new Regions,

---

[1] *Proceedings of the Constituent Assembly*, 194.   [2] *Ibid.*, 182.
[3] *Ibid.*, 197–198. This is presumably only intended to apply during the period before a general election can be held. The White Paper had stated that the draft Constitution was so devised that " if the National Assembly and the President disagree the issue can be decided by a general election " (W.P. No. 1/60, p. 6).

the Upper Region and the Central Region. A new section was inserted in art. 29 to make it clear that the making of payments charged on public funds was to be automatic and not discretionary. At the same time the Minister of Finance, Mr. K. A. Gbedemah, made a statement underlining the security given to foreign investors by the provisions charging debt payments on public funds and adding a " categoric assurance " that, whatever changes might be made in the national status of Ghana as a result of steps taken to further African unification, " all financial obligations entered into by her will be fully honoured by Ghanaians and their Government ".[1] Article 51 was amended to create a new Local Government Service, although no details were given and no reference was made to the local government structure. Finally, Mr. Ofori Atta moved the insertion at the end of the Bill of a new Part headed " Special Powers for First President " and containing only art. 55. This gave the first President, during his initial period of office (which would last until some other person became President), a limited power to give directions having the force of law " whenever he considers it to be in the national interest to do so ". This was to meet an amendment put down by Mr. Mumuni Bawumia which would have added to art. 20(5) the following proviso:

> " Provided that the President may, whenever he considers it to be in the national interests to do so, give directions by regulations which shall have the force of law."[2]

Mr. Bawumia's amendment, which had much support, and which the Government were inclined to accept, would have rendered the provisions of art. 20 mutually contradictory and would have been very doubtful in its effect. Article 55 was therefore drafted to make clear the extent of the new legislative powers. It was explained by Mr. Ofori Atta on lines similar to those followed by Mr. Boateng in asking for the amendment.[3] Mr. Ofori Atta said:

> " The provision for vesting legislative power in the President is particularly very necessary during the formative period of the republican Constitution. It is possible that there may be an impasse in the legislative machinery of the State under the unamended Constitution when there is a sudden unexpected fundamental disagreement between the President and the National Assembly and if this were to occur (which God forbid) as Head of State the President should have the power to issue

---

[1] *Proceedings of the Constituent Assembly*, 359.
[2] Order Paper, 16th June, 1960.   [3] See p. 94, *ante.*

directions which have the force of law until the situation is righted to safeguard the nation against any chaos and anarchy and thereby endangering its security. . . . I have to add that the President in the exercise of these powers will always consult his Cabinet and the Central Committee of the Party."[1]

The amendment was strongly resisted by the Opposition, Mr Abayifaa Karbo being their chief spokesman. Mr. Karbo expressed disappointment at the addition of art. 55 at a stage when the Constitution as amended could be regarded " as something of a national effort which could bring the people of Ghana together and inspire them to work together ".[2] He castigated it as unnecessary, listing the numerous provisions such as the Emergency Powers Act and the Preventive Detention Act which were available to deal with the sort of situation used to justify art. 55. Nevertheless, after the only division held on the Constitution Bill, art. 55 was added to the Bill by 63 votes to 7. The third reading of the Bill was deferred as long as possible to enable such last-minute amendments as might be needed to be made. None proved necessary, and on 29th June, 1960 the Bill was read a third time and passed.[3]

6. Other Acts of the Constituent Assembly

In addition to the Constitution Bill itself, the Constituent Assembly considered eleven other Bills bearing on constitutional law. All had been prepared in the early months of 1960 and all were passed into law as Acts of the Constituent Assembly. Why, if they were constitutional in nature, were these Acts not made part of the Constitution? There were a number of reasons. In the first place, the Constitution was seen as the basic framework of government and as the fundamental law. It should therefore contain only provisions of first importance, and not be cluttered up with detail. In this way the basic structure would stand out, and be clearly perceived. Secondly, the Constitution should be worthy of respect. Respect might be lost if the Constitution concerned itself with trivialities and if it contained masses of

---

[1] *Proceedings of the Constituent Assembly*, 361–362.
[2] *Ibid.*, 362.
[3] It is suggested by Rubin and Murray (*op. cit.*, pp. 27–29) that art. 55, and the other provisions which did not appear in the draft as first published may be invalid as not having been approved in the plebiscite. This argument disregards the terms of the Constituent Assembly and Plebiscite Act. As explained at pp. 80–84, *ante*, the power to pass the Constitution was derived from this Act and not from the plebiscite, the purpose of which was to enable the Constituent Assembly to obtain information as to popular opinion.

G

ephemeral detail requiring frequent amendment. Thirdly, time was insufficient to prepare provisions on all the matters that would, on this approach, have required detailed treatment. Subjects such as elections, the regulation of the armed forces, local government and chieftaincy could hardly have been omitted, but were not dealt with in the Bills submitted to the Constituent Assembly. The subjects chosen for these Bills were ones where the law urgently needed amendment to fit it for the new era of the Republic. In the case of one Bill, which became the Courts Act, 1960 (C.A. 9), the law was consolidated principally because of the decision to alter the courts' structure and also because of the need to enact new provisions in a relatively small section of the field, namely Part F of the former Courts Ordinance (Cap. 4) (which dealt with the application of customary law and English law).[1] The Civil Service Act, 1960 (C.A. 5) was passed to implement the New Charter for the Civil Service, published by the Government as a White Paper at the same time as the proposals for a republican constitution.[2] The Judicial Service Act, 1960 (C.A. 10) was required to carry out the Government's decision to establish a new Judicial Service organised on lines similar to those of the Civil Service. The Regions of Ghana Act, 1960 (C.A. 11) replaced the provisions defining the areas of the Regions in the former Constitution. The former provisions were in any case unsatisfactory for a number of reasons. They were so drawn as to make necessary a lengthy search through previous legislation in order to ascertain the Regional boundaries, and even then some doubt remained. They had also been considerably amended, and did not of course deal with the new Upper and Central Regions.

Other Acts were needed immediately to amplify the parts of the Constitution relating to the new office of President. These were the Presidential Affairs Act, 1960 (C.A. 2), the Cabinet and Ministers Act, 1960 (C.A. 3) and the Acts of Parliament Act, 1960 (C.A. 7). The new forms of oaths made necessary by the change from Queen to President were set out in the Oaths Act, 1960 (C.A. 12). The law governing the property and contracts of the new Republic, including powers of compulsory acquisition, was set out in the State Property and Contracts Act, 1960 (C.A. 6). A Bill was prepared to regulate the procedure for civil suits by and against the Republic and to replace the Petitions of

---

[1] This is treated at some length in Part IV, *post*.   [2] W.P. No. 2/60.

Right Ordinance (Cap. 18), but this was not proceeded with.[1]

It remains to mention two Acts which bear a very close relation to the Constitution in that they affect its construction. These are the Constitution (Consequential Provisions) Act, 1960 (C.A. 8) and the Interpretation Act, 1960 (C.A. 4). As indicated above, it was desired to produce a Constitution which was clear, simple and free of extraneous detail. Nevertheless, transitional provisions were required which inevitably would be lengthy and of only fleeting importance. In the past such provisions had been included in the Constitution itself, but this was strongly felt to be undesirable. Nor was the expedient used in the Irish Constitution of authorising the Constitution to be reprinted without the transitional provisions looked on with favour. The only course was to enact the transitional provisions separately. This was done in the Consequential Provisions Act, which is not referred to in the Constitution and yet in some respects modifies its operation in the early days of the Republic. Thus, for example, art. 21(2) (which provides that Members of Parliament are to be elected on the principle of universal adult suffrage set out in art. 1) is modified, in the case of the first Republican Assembly only, by s. 1 of the Consequential Provisions Act. This states that the existing members are to be deemed to have been duly elected in pursuance of the provisions of the Constitution, although in fact they include ten women members who were elected by the National Assembly itself under the Representation of the People (Women Members) Act, 1960 (No. 8). Again, whereas art. 23(2) requires the Assembly to be dissolved not later than five years after its first sitting following the previous general election, s. 1(2) of the Consequential Provisions Act extends this period by several years in the case of the first Republican Assembly.[2] Apart from provisions of this kind, the Consequential Provisions Act included a large number of textual alterations to the existing law, and conferred power on the President to make further alterations during the first year of the Republic.[3] It also dealt with two further matters, namely the discontinuance of appeals to the Privy Council and the status of Ghana Government securities, which may conveniently be explained here.

---

[1] It was passed in the following year as the State Proceedings Act, 1961 (Act 51).

[2] This was done under a mandate taken to have been conferred in the constitutional plebiscite; see p. 90, *ante*.

[3] Constitution (Consequential Provisions) Act, 1960 (C.A. 8), s. 21. The power was exercised by L.I. 102 and 105.

The right of appeal to the Judicial Committee of the Privy
Council had long existed in Ghana.[1] In its current form the right
existed by virtue of the Ghana (Appeal to Privy Council) Order
in Council, 1957,[2] which was made at the request of the Government of Ghana on 31st July, 1957. This gave an appeal as of
right from decisions of the Ghana Court of Appeal where the
value of the matter in dispute was £500 or more, and also an
appeal by leave of the Court of Appeal in other cases where a
point of " great general or public importance or otherwise "
was involved. The Court of Appeal was required to conform with
and execute any order made on the appeal. It was felt that to
continue these appeals would not accord with Ghana's new status
and so, following the example of Canada, the Union of South
Africa, India and Pakistan, the Consequential Provisions Act
repealed the 1957 Order in Council and the other enactments
relating to such appeals. Arrangements were however made to
enable pending appeals to go forward and be decided by the
Judicial Committee.[3] The result was to make the new Supreme
Court the final court of appeal for cases in Ghana, the right to go to
the West African Court of Appeal having been abolished in 1957.[4]

Ghana Government stocks at this time enjoyed the status of
authorised trustee investments in the United Kingdom. The
Colonial Stock Act, 1900 authorised trustees to invest in colonial
stock registered in the United Kingdom if certain conditions laid
down by the Treasury were satisfied. The colony was required to
provide by legislation for the payment out of its revenues of any
sum ordered by a United Kingdom court to be paid to stockholders, and also to satisfy the Treasury that money would be
available in the United Kingdom to comply with any such order.[5]
A third condition referred to disallowance of legislation which
would be injurious to stockholders, but this was superseded for
the self-governing dominions by the Colonial Stock Act, 1934,
which stated that the third condition would be satisfied if the
government of the dominion gave a certain undertaking, and

---

[1] See pp. 19, 33, *ante.*
[2] S.I. 1957 No. 1361; L.N. 215.
[3] Constitution (Consequential Provisions) Act, 1960 (C.A. 8), s. 16.
Pending appeals were dealt with from the United Kingdom end by the
Ghana (Consequential Provision) Act, 1960, s. 2 and the Ghana (Pending
Appeals to Privy Council) Order in Council, 1960.
[4] West African Court of Appeal (Amendment) Order in Council, 1957
(S.I. 1957 No. 279; L.N. 66).
[5] Treasury Order, S.R. & O. 1900 No. 926.

continued it by an Act of Parliament of the dominion. The undertaking was that legislation of the dominion which appeared to the British Government to be injurious to stockholders or to depart from the original contract governing the stock should not be submitted for Royal Assent unless the British Government agreed. Furthermore, if attention was only drawn to such legislation after it had been passed, the dominion government must undertake to amend it when asked to do so by the British Government. This provision was applied to Ghana on the attainment of independence,[1] and the conditions were satisfied by the passing of an Ordinance which came into force at the same time as the Independence Act.[2] So that Ghana Government securities should still be authorised for trustee investment in the United Kingdom after the change to republican status, the British Government provided that the Colonial Stock Acts should continue to apply, but with modifications to fit Ghana's new status.[3] Ghana law was made to satisfy the Treasury conditions (as so modified) by various amendments to the 1957 Ordinance made by the Constitution (Consequential Provisions) Act, 1960 (C.A. 8), s. 19.

In 1961 the British Parliament effected a considerable widening of the investment powers of trustees with the passage of the Trustee Investments Act, 1961. This repealed the above-mentioned provisions of the Colonial Stock Acts and thus rendered the Ghana legislation on the subject obsolete. Trustees now have power under British law to invest in securities issued by the Ghana Government or a Ghanaian public or local authority provided they are issued and registered in the United Kingdom and do not require the holder to accept payment otherwise than in sterling.

The Interpretation Act, 1960 (C.A. 4) affects the construction of the Constitution because it applies to it, as to every other enactment, " except insofar as the contrary intention appears in the enactment ".[4] Perhaps the most important provisions in

---

[1] Ghana Independence Act, 1957, Sch. 2, para 4.
[2] Trustee Investment in Ghana Government Securities Ordinance, 1957 (No. 13).
[3] Ghana (Consequential Provision) (Colonial Stock Acts) Order in Council, 1960 (S.I. 1960 No. 969).
[4] Section 1. A useful explanation of the effect of the Interpretation Act appears at the beginning of Vol. I of the Acts of Ghana, published in the official Cumulative Binder Service. Various provisions of the Act are also dealt with elsewhere in this book.

this regard are ss. 17 and 18, which explain the meanings of the references to the common law and customary law in art. 40 of the Constitution.

In conclusion, a word should be said about the status of the Acts, other than the Constitution, which were passed by the Constituent Assembly. Except in one respect, which is discussed below, the Acts have the same status as any other Act of Parliament passed before or since, and may accordingly be repealed or amended (whether expressly or impliedly) by a later enactment. This is made clear by art. 20(6), which, subject to exceptions which relate only to the Constitution itself, states that " the power of Parliament to make laws shall be under no limitation whatsoever ". It necessarily follows that this legislative sovereignty extends to the repeal or amendment of Acts of the Constituent Assembly in the same way as it extends to the repeal or amendment of other laws. Such amendments have indeed taken place, as for example by the substitution of a new section for the original s. 1 of the Presidential Affairs Act, 1960 (C.A. 2).[3]

The exception referred to is this. We have seen above that certain provisions of the Consequential Provisions Act and the Interpretation Act modify the construction of the Constitution as opposed to providing for its working out in detail. It follows that these provisions are in effect written into the Constitution. They were made by the same body as the Constitution and came into force at the same time. They must therefore be treated as part of the Constitution and as subject to the restrictions on amendment or repeal imposed by art. 20. This is particularly important where they modify an entrenched provision. Thus an attempt to amend by ordinary Act s. 1(2) of the Consequential Provisions Act (which fixes the maximum life of the present Parliament) would be ineffective since s. 1(2) modifies an entrenched provision of the Constitution, namely art. 23(2). The correct procedure would be to hold a referendum under art. 20(2) and then, if the electors approved, modify art. 23(2) directly. Where entrenched provisions are not involved the only restriction is that imposed by the proviso to art. 20(2), which requires alterations to the Constitution to be made by an Act " expressed to be an Act to amend the Constitution and containing only provisions effecting the alteration thereof ". Let us take as an example an amendment to s. 10(2) of the Interpretation Act, which

---

[1] See the Presidential Affairs (Amendment) Act, 1960 (Act 8).

states that an enactment conferring power to do any act or thing shall be taken also to confer such additional powers as are reasonably necessary to enable the act or thing to be done. This means that a provision in the Constitution which in terms confers only primary powers—e.g., art. 39, conferring powers on the Auditor-General—actually confers these secondary powers also. An amendment which narrowed the effect of s. 10(2) would therefore narrow the effect of certain provisions of the Constitution. Because of the proviso to art. 20(2) it would not do so however unless also embodied in an additional Act satisfying the requirements of art. 20(2). It should be added that such amendments to the Interpretation Act are very unlikely to be needed. Were this not so the complications just described would be indefensible. In the case of the definitions of common law and customary law, where the possibility of future amendment of the Interpretation Act was foreseen, the complications are avoided by the opening words of art. 40, which enable the definitions to be altered without this operating as an amendment of the Constitution.

7. Inauguration of the Republic

Ghana became a republic within the Commonwealth on 1st July, 1960. In the stage of development it has now reached the Commonwealth may be defined as a group of autonomous states having equality of status and an obligation to co-operate with one another, and each recognising the Queen as the symbol of the free association of the members of the group and as such the head of the Commonwealth.[1] The White Paper containing the Government's consitutional proposals had pointed out that, in accordance with normal practice, no provision was included in the draft Constitution in regard to membership of the Commonwealth. The White Paper continued:

" It is, however, the intention of the Prime Minister to attend the Conference of Commonwealth Prime Ministers to be held in London on 3rd May, 1960. On that occasion the Prime Minister will tell the other Commonwealth Prime Ministers of the result of the plebiscite and, if the people vote in favour of the draft Constitution, will inform them that Ghana will become a republic but would wish to remain within the Commonwealth."[2]

---

[1] For a detailed examination of each element in this definition see K. C. Wheare, *The Constitutional Structure of the Commonwealth*, Oxford, 1960.
[2] W.P. No. 1/60, p. 15.

This intention was duly carried out. In view of the precedents established by India and Pakistan, no difficulty was anticipated in securing the consent of the other Commonwealth countries to Ghana's continuance as a member of the Commonwealth while renouncing allegiance to the Queen.[1] The giving of this consent was confirmed by a communique issued on 13th May, 1960 at the conclusion of the meeting of Commonwealth Prime Ministers. After referring to Ghana's intention to become a republic, the communique went on:

> " In notifying this forthcoming constitutional change, the Prime Minister of Ghana assured the meeting of his country's desire to continue her membership of the Commonwealth and her acceptance of the Queen as the symbol of the free association of its independent member nations and as such the head of the Commonwealth. The heads of delegations of the other member countries of the Commonwealth assured the Prime Minister of Ghana that the present relations between their countries and Ghana would remain unaffected by this constitutional change and they declared that their governments would accept and recognise Ghana's continued membership of the Commonwealth."[2]

In the case of Pakistan a similar declaration of the Commonwealth Prime Ministers had been subsequently ratified by a resolution of the Pakistan Assembly before the introduction into the United Kingdom Parliament of the Pakistan (Consequential Provision) Bill, which made reference to Pakistan's becoming a republic while remaining within the Commonwealth. This course was not followed in Ghana. It was felt that, since Dr. Nkrumah was President-elect at the time when he gave his assurance to the other Prime Ministers, and as President and holder of the executive power he would under the new Constitution have the sole right to decide whether or not to withdraw Ghana from the Commonwealth at any future time, his assurance would be given no greater weight by a resolution of the National Assembly. Furthermore the assent of the people of Ghana had been given to that assurance by their overwhelming support for the constitutional proposals, which, as stated above, indicated that such an assurance would be made. In spite of these considerations there would have been no objection to putting the matter to the vote of the Assembly if it had been in session at the relevant time.

---

[1] Ghana became a member of the Commonwealth on attaining independence; see p. 68, *ante*.

[2] *Commonwealth Survey*, Vol. 6, p. 452.

The Parliamentary time-table in the United Kingdom made it necessary however to introduce the Ghana (Consequential Provision) Bill on a date in May and it would have been very inconvenient to summon the Ghana Assembly before that time.

The Ghana (Consequential Provision) Act, which received the Royal Assent on 2nd June, 1960, followed in its main provisions the wording of similar Acts passed by the United Kingdom Parliament in relation to India and Pakistan. It is described in the long title as

> " An Act to make provision as to the operation of the law in relation to Ghana and persons or things in any way belonging to or connected with Ghana, in view of Ghana's becoming a Republic while remaining a member of the Commonwealth."

The principal effect of the Act is to provide by s. 1(1) that, in the territories for which the United Kingdom Parliament has power to legislate, the laws shall continue to apply in relation to Ghana as they did before the inauguration of the Republic. Power is given by s. 1(3) to amend existing laws by Order in Council so as to give effect to this object or otherwise to make provision which is expedient in view of Ghana's altered status.[1] The Act also makes detailed arrangements in s. 2 for the disposal of pending appeals to the Judicial Committee of the Privy Council.[2] It may be remarked that an incidental effect of the Act is to give formal recognition to the fact of Ghana's ceasing to form part of Her Majesty's Dominions. It thus operates as an implied repeal in British law of s. 1 of the Ghana Independence Act, 1957, which provided that Ghana was to form part of Her Majesty's Dominions. Furthermore, since it came into effect before the republican Constitution had even been introduced into the Constituent Assembly, it put an end to any lingering doubts as to the theoretical capacity of that body to enact the Constitution.[3] In what was perhaps an excess of caution, however, the judges appointed under the old Constitution were requested to submit their resignations, to take effect at midnight on 30th June, 1960. This was done, the resignations were accepted and the next day the judges were reappointed by the newly-installed President in exercise of the powers conferred by the republican Constitution.

---

[1] The power has been exercised in relation to trustee investments; see p. 101, *ante*.

[2] See p. 100, *ante*.

[3] See pp. 74 *et seq.*, *ante*.

No judge could thereafter pronounce the Constitution invalid without at the same time saying in effect that his own appointment was invalid also. He would not be a judge under the old Constitution because he had resigned. If he was not a judge under the new Constitution he was not a judge at all, and his " judgment " would be without effect.

The Governor-General, the Earl of Listowel (who had served in that office during the whole of its existence) carried out his last official act in Ghana by proroguing Parliament on 30th June, 1960. Before this was done an address of thanks to the Governor-General was moved by the Prime Minister and seconded by the Leader of the Opposition. Since this was an historic occasion we reproduce the two speeches here.

> *The Prime Minister (Dr. The Rt. Hon. Kwame Nkrumah)*: Mr. Speaker, I beg to move the following Address:
>
> " We the Speaker and Members of the National Assembly of Ghana in Parliament assembled wish to tender to Your Excellency the expression of our sincere appreciation of the devotion with which you have served Ghana.
>
> On the eve of Ghana becoming a sovereign Republic, it is fitting that we should reflect on our association with the Queen and pay our respects to Your Excellency as the last Governor-General and Commander-in-Chief.
>
> We wish Your Excellency good health and much happiness in the future."
>
> Mr. Speaker, we have adopted a republican Constitution not through any lack of affection for Her Majesty nor because of any dissatisfaction with the way in which the Office of Governor-General has been discharged.
>
> The people of Ghana have enacted for themselves a new Constitution because of our convictions that we need a form of government which will more truly interpret the aspirations and hopes of the people of Ghana and give full expression to the African personality. [*Hear, hear.*]
>
> Lord Listowel was appointed Governor-General by the Queen upon the advice of the Government of Ghana. During his tenure of office he has amply fulfilled the expectations of the Government which led them to recommend his appointment to Her Majesty.
>
> I know that the whole House will wish to join with me in expressing our thanks for the way in which he has discharged his office and will agree with me that though he may not be in Ghana, he will always be remembered by us with the warmest affection.
>
> Mr. Speaker, in the same way as the Governor-General must feel sorrow at leaving Ghana, I feel a similar sorrow in that this is the last occasion upon which I shall speak in this House as

Prime Minister and a Member of Parliament. This National Assembly has been an historic body. [*Hear, hear.*] I have known it from its beginning. In fact, I have lived in it. I have seen it carry through great constitutional changes. I myself have been a fighter within its ramparts. Indeed, it has been the foundry which has forged and moulded the new framework of our Nation.

Though, however, from midnight tonight I shall cease to be a Member of Parliament and cease to be an active participant in this august Assembly, I am certain that I shall not lose that personal and intimate connection which I have established with this House. I believe that no constitutional change can affect the personal bonds which have been established in the ten years that we have worked together in this House. I understand from the Clerk of the House that I shall be provided with a seat in the new Assembly. I shall visit you as often as is convenient.

I realise, however, from my own regrets at leaving the Assembly, how much greater a break it must be for the Governor-General both to leave Office and to depart from Ghana. Our good wishes and our goodwill go with him, and I am certain that, though he may no longer be the Governor-General of Ghana, many opportunities will occur in the future for fruitful co-operation between us. [*Hear, hear.*]

Mr. Speaker, I beg to move.

Leader of the Opposition (*Mr. S. D. Dombo*): Mr. Speaker, it is a great pleasure to me to second the Address which has been so ably moved by the Prime Minister. [*Hear, hear.*] If I may say so, Sir, it is a remarkable address moved on a historic day. It is remarkable because it is unique, in that it pays tribute to the Crown's last representative in Ghana. It is a historic day because tonight at the stroke of twelve a new Ghana will emerge—[*Hear, hear*]—a Ghana blooming with the Ghanaian personality.

A little over three years ago we won our independence. Now we seek to give more meaning to this freedom to express our innermost selves. When it came to us, independence was sweet and wonderful. Now we regard it merely as bones—dry bones into which we are about to breath life with a concerted effort. [*Hear, hear.*] Everyone knows how determined we are to help to liberate the rest of Africa. The British Prime Minister, the Right Honourable Harold Macmillan, has told the world about the wind of change blowing over this great continent. With our coming change in status we should be better able to give velocity and direction to this wind. [*Hear, hear.*]

It has been most pleasant having Lord Listowel in our midst. He was quick to learn to know us and to identify himself with our ways. In fact, we have all come to accept him as a citizen of Ghana. It is sad that in the yielding of one order to another we should lose him. He has brought this era to an end so gracefully. In a few hours' time our allegiance to the Queen will lapse but she may be assured that our respect for her person will continue, and hope that our association with Great Britain will grow and

bloom and bear fruit. It is nice to reflect on our continued association with the Queen's person and with the Crown through our membership of the great family of nations, which is affectionately known as the Commonwealth.
Question put and agreed to.
Resolved accordingly.[1]

The Governor-General then delivered a speech of farewell, in which he reviewed briefly the events of his period of office. At the end of this he read the last message to the people of Ghana from their Queen. Her Majesty pointed out that the bonds which bound the Commonwealth together could not be expressed in written constitutions or by a set and unchanging formula of relationship. The message continued:

> " I am proud that I am Head of a Commonwealth in which every nation may choose for itself the form of Government which best suits it; now that Ghana has chosen for itself a republican form of Constitution it will not affect the interest which I have always taken and shall continue to take in the welfare of its people. . . . On this last occasion when I shall have the opportunity of addressing you as your Queen, I wish to convey to the President-elect, the Members of the National Assembly and the people of Ghana, my best wishes for the future. I pray that the blessing of Almighty God may guide the destinies of the new Republic and secure peace and happiness for its people."[2]

On the following day the inauguration of the Republic was proclaimed and the President-elect, Dr. Kwame Nkrumah, assumed office as first President of the Republic by taking the oath required by art. 12 of the new Constitution.[3] This provides that the oath is to be administered by the Chief Justice but until the President-elect had assumed office by taking the oath he could not of course appoint a Chief Justice. The danger of an impasse arising from this situation had been foreseen, and the Constitution (Consequential Provisions) Act, 1960 (C.A. 8), s. 2 had provided that the oath should be administered by the person who held the office of Chief Justice immediately before the commencement of the Constitution.[4] Sir Arku Korsah accordingly

---

[1] Parl. Deb. Official Report, Vol. 19, col. 249.
[2] Parl. Deb. Official Report, Vol. 19, col. 254.
[3] *Ghana Gazette*, 1st July, 1960, 1, 2. Article 10 of the Constitution appointed Dr. Nkrumah as first President, referring to his having been chosen as such in the plebiscite.
[4] The section even guarded against the possibility that the Chief Justice might be incapacitated by illness. It stated that in his absence a Justice of Appeal should officiate.

administered the oath, and following this the new President made the solemn declaration required by art. 13.[1] During intervals between the celebrations which followed on that day the President found time to sign instruments appointing Ministers, parliamentary private secretaries, judges and others, and also an Honours Warrant establishing fifteen Republican honours and awards to replace those which had hitherto been awarded by the Queen on the advice of the Government of Ghana.[2] The President also directed a commemorative medal, to be known as the Republic Day Medal, to be given to every person serving with the armed forces or the police on 1st July, 1960.[3] An amnesty was granted by the use of the powers of mercy conferred by art. 48 of the Constitution.[4] A new table of precedence was published.[5] Finally, the President signed a proclamation summoning the National Assembly to meet the following day to commence the first session of the first Parliament of the Republic of Ghana.[6]

The sitting of the Assembly on 2nd July was solely for the purpose of the election of a Speaker and Deputy Speaker and the swearing-in of Members. At the end of the sitting the Leader of the House, Mr. Kojo Botsio, announced that the former title of Parliamentary Secretary had been changed to Parliamentary Private Secretary (it was later changed again to Ministerial Secretary). In future the Government Chief Whip would be known as the Parliamentary Secretary.[7] The formal opening of Parliament by the President took place on 4th July. In the interval since the last sitting the chamber had undergone a transformation. It had been decided to drop the concept of an official Opposition and to abolish the salaried post of Leader of the Opposition.[8] The seating of the chamber was therefore rearranged

---

[1] *Ghana Gazette*, 1st July, 1960, p. 2.

[2] *Ibid.*, pp. 3–12. The honours and awards are briefly described on p. 133, *post*. For coloured reproductions of the insignia, see the *Ghana Gazette*, 1st July, 1960, pp. 9–12.

[3] *Ibid.*, p. 13.

[4] *Ibid.*

[5] *Ibid.*

[6] *Ibid.*, p. 15.

[7] Parl Deb. Official Report, Vol. 20, col. 6.

[8] This had been announced earlier by Mr. Botsio, who said: " In our traditional ruling houses the concept of an organized opposition is unknown, and the term ' opposition ' has confused many minds and caused much misunderstanding. It is proposed that the terms ' Government side ' and ' Opposition side ' should be abolished. The party system will continue to be part of our parliamentary life and minorities in Parliament will continue to exercise their rights to freely express their views ": Parl. Deb. Official Report, Vol. 19, cols. 228–229.

so that, instead of facing benches as in the House of Commons, the benches were placed in the shape of a horseshoe. The former mace, with its insignia of the Imperial Crown, royal cypher, Tudor rose and fleur-de-lis, was replaced by a new mace. This is of silver and gilt, with Ghana's heraldic bird, the eagle, as its head. In its shaft are six traditional stools symbolising *common sharing of responsibility, the presence of God in society, lasting personality, prosperity, the presence and effect of feminine power in society, and pride*. Between the stools are embossed five *edinkra* symbols denoting *the omnipotence of God, critical examination, strength, immortality* and *justice*.[1]

A new ceremonial procedure had been devised for the opening of Parliament. The President's approach was heralded by the beating of fontomforom (traditional drums). He was received by eight linguists representing the various Regions and each carrying a distinctive stick. A libation was poured and the President then entered the chamber to the sound of mmenson (the seven traditional horns). As required by art. 25 of the Constitution, the President there delivered the sessional address, which indicated the policies proposed to be followed by his Government during the ensuing session of Parliament. This procedure is modelled on that used on the opening of Parliament in the United Kingdom, but with an interesting use of Ghanaian cultural features. It is expected to be followed on similar occasions in the future.

We conclude this chapter with a word about the honorific prefix adopted by the President. In the first few days of the Republic the prefix " His Excellency " was used, as had been the case with the Governor-General. It was soon felt however that something distinctively Ghanaian was needed. The choice fell on the vernacular term Osagyefo, meaning a warrior who, in the hour of danger, pulls his army through to victory.[2] The President is now therefore referred to as " Osagyefo the President " or simply " Osagyefo ".

---

[1] Note by the Clerk of the Assembly in the programme for the opening of Parliament, 4th July, 1960.

[2] The term is a combination of the Akan words *osa*, meaning war, and *gyefo*, meaning saviour.

CHAPTER 3

THE CONSTITUTION

The Constitution of the Republic of Ghana was passed by the Constituent Assembly on 29th June, 1960 and came into force on 1st July, 1960. Before proceeding to a detailed examination of the Constitution we might well pause to consider the formal principles on which it is drawn. In its formal aspect the Constitution is a product of modes of thought and verbal construction largely deriving from British practice. It is not therefore to be approached, like a constitution from the continent of Europe, as a collection of vague and largely unenforceable directives. Nor is it, like the constitution of the United States, a product of the days before an enactment in the English language was considered inadequate if it did not form a precise working mechanism, as free as is humanly possible from ambiguities and inconsistencies. The formal principles governing Ghana's republican Constitution may be expressed as follows:

1. It is a mechanism, and all its operative provisions are intended to have the precise effect indicated by the words used—no more and no less.

2. It is drafted on the assumption that the words used have a fixed and definite meaning and not a shifting or uncertain meaning; that they mean what they say and not what people would like them to mean; and that if they prove unsuitable they will be altered formally by Parliament and not twisted into new meanings by " interpretation ".

3. It leaves no powers unallocated: those not reserved to the people are exercisable by the authorities established by it.

4. In its original form, or as for the time being expressly amended, it overrides any inconsistent law whenever made.

5. It assumes that legitimate inferences will be drawn by the reader, but that he will not transgress the rules of logic—as by

111

drawing an inference from one provision which is inconsistent with the express words of another provision.

6. It needs to be read as a whole, and with care.

To these formal principles may be added a few words of general description. The Constitution is the basic law of the land. All the institutions of Government, of the courts and of the legislature owe their existence to it, whether directly or indirectly; all powers of the State are wielded by virtue of it. It formulates the aspirations of Ghanaians towards the unification of the continent of Africa. It states the principles on which they wish to be governed. It contains certain entrenched provisions, by which powers are reserved to the people and can only be exercised after a referendum (other provisions can be altered by ordinary Act of Parliament). Finally, it does not deal with details of the transition to republican status, apart from continuing existing laws which are not inconsistent with it. These details are contained in a separate enactment, the Constitution (Consequential Provisions) Act.

1. POWERS OF THE PEOPLE

Recognition of political sovereignty

A prominent feature of the Constitution is the emphasis given to the underlying authority of the people. This appears immediately in the Preamble, which states

> " We the people of Ghana, by our Representatives gathered in this our Constituent Assembly, in exercise of our undoubted right to appoint for ourselves the means whereby we shall be governed . . . do hereby enact and give to ourselves this Constitution."

It is taken up by the opening words of art. 1: " The powers of the State derive from the people . . ." and is driven home by the first of the fundamental principles set out in art. 13:

> " That the powers of Government spring from the will of the people and should be exercised in accordance therewith."

There is of course nothing new in this. The words " We the people . . ." have become familiar in constitutions since they were first used, under the influence of the social contract theories of John Locke[1] and Rousseau, as the opening words of the

---

[1] " For, when any number of men have, by the consent of every individual, made a community, they have made that community one body, which is only by the will and determination of the majority ": *Two Treatises on Civil Government*, Book II, §. 96.

Constitution of the United States of America in 1787.[1] The Declaration of Independence itself was made " in the Name and by Authority of the good People of these Colonies ", and of constitutions now in force, the majority explicitly recognise the sovereignty of the people.[2] Most countries are content to name the people or the nation generally, but in the case of the U.S.S.R. and the People's Democracies such expressions as " workers in cities and villages " and " the working people of town and country " are used. In the United Kingdom and other countries of the Commonwealth still owing allegiance to the Queen sovereignty is regarded as formally residing in the Crown, but the underlying power is seen to rest with the people. Thus Dicey speaks of

> " . . . the will of that power which in modern England is the true political sovereign of the State—the majority of the electors or (to use popular though not quite accurate language) the nation."[3]

This illustrates the well-known distinction between political sovereignty, the ultimate source of power in the State, which is the naked capacity for forceful action possessed by the inhabitants in the mass, and legal sovereignty, which is the power conferred by the constitutional law on certain organs of the State established under that law. The distinction is not so clear in fact as it may appear in theory. Sir Ivor Jennings has criticised Dicey's view that legal sovereignty " is a merely legal conception, and means simply the power of law-making unrestricted by any legal limit ".[4] If this is so, he remarks, " legal sovereignty is not sovereignty at all. . . . It is a legal concept ".[5] Legal sovereignty must mean more than the power to make laws. It should correspond to

---

[1] The concept appears to be indigenous to America herself. Morison and Commager record that, before any European settlement had occurred, " almost every Indian tribe called itself something equivalent to ' We the People ', and used some insulting title for its near neighbours ": *The Growth of the American Republic* (4th Edn.), Vol. I, p. 11.

Bernard Schwartz points out that " as a matter of practical reality, it was the States themselves, rather than the whole people of the United States, that formed the American Union ": *American Constitutional Law*, Cambridge University Press, 1955, p. 31.

[2] " In sixty-six nations, constituting about 71 per cent. of the total number of nations and comprehending about 80 per cent. of the world's total population this concept (*sc.* that sovereignty rests with the people) appears in existing constitutional provisions ": *Constitutions of Nations* (2nd Edn.), ed. Amos J. Peaslee, 1956, Vol. I, p. 5.

[3] *Law of the Constitution* (9th Edn.), 1939, p. 429.

[4] *Op. cit.*, p. 72.

[5] *The Law and the Constitution* (4th Edn.), 1955, p. 144.

H

the whole content of the political sovereignty inhering in the inhabitants and be vested in organs best fitted to channel popular power to work the ends desired by the people.[1] If the constitutional framework is not equipped to give effect to the popular will it is not the people who will give way in the end, but the constitutional framework.[2] The written constitution of a democratic state should be a complete formal statement by the people of the manner in which they wish the political sovereignty to find expression. By working through the procedures laid down by the constitution political sovereignty is transmuted into legal sovereignty. Legislation is one of these procedures and its product law is a manifestation of legal sovereignty the validity of which depends on its conformity or otherwise to the instrument under which it is made, namely the constitution. Where there is a well-drawn written constitution there is no difficulty in deciding whether a given proposition is or is not a law. One looks at the body by whom and the manner in which the proposition was enunciated and if these conform to the provisions in the constitution regulating legislation, the proposition, if it has not subsequently been abrogated in conformity with those provisions, is a law. The constitution may be less forthcoming about the consequences of its being a lw. It will probably leave unsaid the obvious statement that it is the duty of the courts to make orders, in cases brought before them, giving effect to the laws. It will assume that particular laws will themselves specify the persons who are to be bound by them—whether all the inhabitants or particular individuals or classes of individuals, and that laws will provide for the detailed methods of inflicting punishments ordered by the courts and otherwise carrying out court orders. A law made under a written constitution is not affected by the extent to which it is

---

[1] Again, this should not be taken too literally. There are many cases where the legal sovereign is not expected to carry out the will of the political sovereign, however clearly expressed. Thus the London *Times*, reporting in a leading article that an opinion poll had indicated an overwhelming majority of British people to be in favour both of capital punishment and corporal punishment, did not even discuss the question whether Parliament should give effect to the will of the people, but merely spoke of " the task of education still facing the reformers ": *The Times*, 22nd March, 1960.

[2] *Cf.* Aron, *France—the New Republic*, New York, 1960, p. 43: " Every time we had a crisis we made a constitution. It is a sort of permanent reaction to an event. The main quality of any constitution is to be accepted, and for more than a century and a half France never had a constitution which was generally accepted by its people."

obeyed or even by the extent to which disobedience to it is punished. Unless formally abrogated it remains a law while the constitution remains a constitution.[1]

Legislative, executive and judicial power

Since the institutions of a country cannot develop and mature if the constitutional framework is dismantled every few years, and since Ghana has, in the course of development from colonial status, of necessity undergone frequent and radical constitutional changes in the course of this century, it was all-important, having given due recognition to the real source of power, to attempt to ensure that the organs of the new republic should be well designed to achieve the smooth working of democratic government. But before popular power can be properly distributed some attempt must be made to find out what it consists of. We are discussing the people as a social group, that is a State, and our concern is with the basic methods by which civilised peoples govern themselves and regulate their relationships with other States. A basic analysis would show civilised people governing themselves first by establishing some means of laying down general rules for the ordering of individual conduct and state affairs, which they agree to enforce by their collective power, secondly by establishing some means both of finding out whether individuals have broken such of the rules of conduct as are mandatory (and punishing them if they have) and of settling disputes between individuals as to the meaning or effect of other rules of conduct, and thirdly by establishing some means of carrying into effect the rules laid down for ordering the affairs of the State. The means thus established regulate respectively the exercise of the legislative power, the judicial power and the executive power of the State. This classification of the governing powers of persons collected into a society is as old as Aristotle and is still useful as throwing light on the essential nature of civilised government.[2] The meaning of legislative power and judicial power is reasonably

---

[1] *Cf.* Jennings' note on the theory of law, *op. cit.*, pp. 302–319.

[2] Most constitutions recognise this classification, particularly those which proclaim the underlying sovereignty of the people. For example the Constitution of the Union of Burma, which was enacted in 1947, contains the following section:

" 4. All powers, legislative, executive and judicial, are derived from the people and are exercisable on their behalf by, or on the authority of, the organs of the Union or of its constituent units established by this Constitution."

clear but that of executive power is less definite. If the threefold classification is to be comprehensive (and it is usually taken to be) the executive power must be treated in a wider sense than is indicated above and made to embrace all governmental functions which are not of a legislative or judicial character, for example relationships with foreigners who are not within reach of the legislative power, and the protection of the State from attack so far as this is not provided for by the laws. This was recognised by Montesquieu, who defined the executive power as the power by which the Prince or Magistrate " makes war and peace, sends and receives ambassadors, establishes order, prevents invasions ".[1] The concept of executive power as consisting in the carrying out of laws relating to the ordering of State affairs is faulty. The laws themselves usually indicate who is to perform functions made necessary by them and no overall executive power in this sense is capable of being bestowed on any one organ of the State. The truth of this is disguised by the fact that the executive organ, or a component of it, is usually chosen by the law (having perhaps had some say in the making of it) as most suitable to be entrusted with the execution of the law. The power of administering a particular law is in general derived from the law itself, in other words from the exercise of the legislative power. This is the field of what has now come to be known as administrative law.

Distribution of powers

Having used the concepts of legislative power, judicial power and executive power as a means of indicating the content of political sovereignty, we next consider how these powers are distributed by the constitution. Montesquieu, basing himself on what he supposed to be the provisions of the British Constitution, believed that it was essential for liberty that each of the three powers should be conferred on a different organ of the State. This view was elevated by the Federal Convention of America, again on the supposition that they were following the British Constitution, into the principle that not only should the powers be possessed by different organs but that no organ should be predominant. Hence the fundamental doctrine of the American Constitution, described by the U.S. Supreme Court in the following terms:

---

[1] Cited in Jennings, *op. cit.*, p. 21.

" The fundamental necessity of maintaining each of the three general departments of government entirely free from the control or coercive influence, direct or indirect, of either of the others, has often been stressed and is hardly open to serious question. So much is implied in the very fact of the separation of the powers of these departments by the Constitution; and in the rule which recognizes their essential co-equality."[1]

In fact the separation of powers in the British Constitution is incomplete and there can be no doubt that the legislature is supreme in relation both to the executive and the judiciary. In any case, as Sir Ivor Jennings has said:

" . . . it is democracy and not merely the separation of powers that keeps Britain free."[2]

Nevertheless it is clear that all powers cannot be given to one organ of the state. As one of the Founding Fathers of the United States, James Madison, said:

" . . . . the accumulation of all powers, legislative, executive and judiciary in the same hands, whether of one, a few or many, and whether hereditary, self-appointed or elective, may justly be pronounced the very definition of tyranny."[3]

Apart from this, even where supreme power is bestowed on a democratic legislature, such a body, being essentially a deliberative assembly, is not fitted to negotiate treaties, command armies or try criminal and civil causes. The real question is not whether powers shall be divided but whether any organ of the State shall be granted supremacy, and if so which. In this matter Ghana has followed the British rather than the American model and granted supreme power to a Parliament consisting of the President and the National Assembly.[4] This power is not absolute, since the power

---

[1] *Humphrey's Executor* v. *United States* (1935) 295 U.S. 602.

[2] *Op. cit.*, p. 24.

[3] *The Federalist*, No. XLVII.

[4] Wade and Phillips in their *Constitutional Law* (4th Edn.), pp. 26 *et seq.*, pose three questions by which separation of powers can be tested. Tentative answers in relation to the Constitutions of the United States, the United Kingdom and Ghana are given below; positive answers are in most cases impossible:

	U.K.	*U.S.*	*Ghana*
1. Do the same persons or bodies form part of both the legislature and the executive?	Yes	No	Yes
2. Does the legislature control the executive?	Yes	No	Yes
3. Do the legislature and the executive exercise each other's functions?	Yes	Yes	Yes

See also Schwartz, *American Constitutional Law*, Cambridge University Press, 1955, pp. 18–22.

to repeal or alter certain entrenched provisions of the Constitution is expressly reserved to the people, but within the basic framework of the Constitution Parliament is sovereign by virtue of its possession of unlimited legislative power.[1] Provision is made for the exercise of the reserved powers of the people by the joint action of the President, the electorate and Parliament so that no gap exists in the legal means provided by the Constitution for the exercise of the political sovereignty.[2] The Constitution even provides legal means for repealing the Constitution and enacting an entirely different one in its place. (This could be done by the President ordering a referendum on the Bill for the new Constitution and, if the majority of voters in the referendum approved the Bill, by its subsequent enactment by Parliament.) The Constitution does not however follow the Burmese example and assume that all powers are either legislative, judicial or executive since there is room for argument on this and ambiguity must be avoided. Thus we find that the general power to authorise the meeting of expenditure out of national funds is conferred on the National Assembly in a way which avoids a pronouncement on the nature of this power.[3] It has the appearance of an executive power although in most countries it is exercised by an act of the parliament. In Ghana it is exercised by one organ of Parliament, namely the National Assembly.

Since it is relatively easy to decide whether a given function is or is not legislative or judicial, the tendency is to class indeterminate functions as falling within the executive power.[4] In Ghana therefore the President would exercise indeterminate functions as to which no provision was made by law. The executive power is conferred on the President and the judicial power on the courts —in both cases " subject to the provisions of the Constitution ", a phrase which enables the powers to be regulated and even curtailed by Act of Parliament as under the British Constitution, and incidentally ensures that any doubts which arise as to the detailed content of the powers can be set at rest by legislation.

---

[1] Article 20.

[2] " Unless you give a government specific powers, commensurate with its objects, it is liable on occasions of public necessity to exercise powers which have not been granted ": John Fiske, *The Critical Period of American History*, p. 207.

[3] Articles 31–33.

[4] See *Springer* v. *Phillipines Govt.* (1928), 277 U.S. 189, where the court held on this principle that the executive should exercise voting rights in Government-owned stock.

One man—one vote

The slogan one man—one vote has caught the imagination of Africa and, in a form which essays precision at the expense of succinctness, appears in art. 1 of the Constitution as the principle:

> " That, without distinction of sex, race, religion or political belief, every person who, being by law a citizen of Ghana, has attained the age of twenty-one years and is not disqualified by law on grounds of absence, infirmity of mind or criminality, shall be entitled to one vote, to be cast in freedom and secrecy."[1]

In accordance with this principle the people have the right to exercise the powers reserved to them by the Constitution and to choose their representatives in Parliament. Thus the essentially democratic nature of the Constitution is proclaimed at the outset. By an entrenched provision, not only is the underlying power of the people recognised but the guarantee of universal suffrage, through which alone that power can exert itself in an orderly and effective way, is plainly stated. Blackstone's famous dictum that " every man in England is in judgment of law party to the making of an Act of Parliament, being present thereat by his representatives ",[2] which was hardly true of England in Blackstone's time, can be applied with much greater truth to Ghana to-day.

The source of the principle of universal adult suffrage set out in art. 1 of the Constitution really lies in Africa itself, where it is seen as the passport to release from rule by white minorities. Together with the principle of African unity, it has been described by Dr. Nkrumah as " the key-note of the Constitution "[3] and is rightly regarded as one of the essentially African characteristics of it. Nevertheless nations outside Africa have also felt the force of this principle. The Bill of Rights came some way towards recognising it in 1688 by proclaiming that the election of members of Parliament ought to be free, though it was not until the complete enfranchisement of women in the nineteen-twenties that the principle was accepted in Britain to the fullest degree.

---

[1] In the draft Constitution the word " tribe " appeared after " race " in this provision, but was omitted when the Constitution Bill was introduced although retained in the corresponding paragraph of art. 13. Rubin and Murray (*op. cit.*, p. 17, repeated on p. 219) assume that the inconsistency was inadvertent, but in fact it was due to a deliberate Government decision.

[2] *Commentaries*, I, 185.

[3] *Proceedings of the Constituent Assembly*, col. 3.

No Bill of Rights was originally included in the American Constitution, which left the qualifications of electors to the House of Representatives to be determined by the varying electoral laws of the states. Even to-day there is no guarantee of universal adult suffrage although the fifteenth amendment, adopted in 1870, prohibits the denial of a vote on account of " race, color, or previous conditions of servitude ", to which a reference to sex was added by the nineteenth amendment in 1920. Perhaps the Constitution of the Italian Republic, which was brought into effect at the beginning of 1948, comes closest to the wording of art. 1.[1]

2. AFRICAN UNITY

The aim of unification

The Preamble to the Constitution states that it is enacted by the people " in sympathy with and loyalty to our fellow-countrymen of Africa " and " in the hope that we may by our actions this day help to further the development of a Union of African States ". Article 2 speaks of " the confident expectation of an early surrender of sovereignty to a union of African states and territories ". Article 13 requires the President to declare his adherence to the principle that " the union of Africa should be striven for by every lawful means and, when attained, should be faithfully preserved ". Thus is the aim of African unification, the other half of " the key-note of the Constitution ", proclaimed.

Again, we need not look beyond Africa for the source of this feature of the Constitution. As soon as the colonies began to achieve their independence they were bound to regard with dismay the curiously-drawn frontiers which threatened the Continent with " Balkanization ". The White Paper introducing the Constitution complained that

> " . . . the present frontiers of Ghana, like so many frontiers on the African continent, were drawn merely to suit the convenience of the Colonial Powers who divided Africa between them during the last century."[2]

These frontiers often divided ethnic groups in an arbitrary

---

[1] Article 48 reads: " All citizens of both sexes having attained the age of majority have the right to suffrage. The vote is personal and equal, free and secret. Exercise thereof is a civic duty. No limitation on the right to vote may be established except for civil incapacity or as a consequence of an irrevocable penal sentence or in cases of moral turpitude as determined by law."

[2] W.P. No. 1/60, p. 4.

fashion, a well-known example being that between the French and British portions of Togoland, which split the Ewe people in a way quite inconsistent with the pattern of their social and economic organisation. This is one aspect of the aim of unification; the other is perhaps more important. It is to capture the economic power and greater world influence that comes with political organisation on a continental scale. The contrast between the present standing of the United States and of the republics of South America is evidence of the immense strength that unity brings. Yet the thirteen colonies might easily have remained separate and relatively impotent. John Fiske has recorded how, in the years between the Declaration of Independence and the Federal Convention, sentiment was all in favour of preserving the self-government of the states.

> " But unless the most profound and delicate statesmanship should be forthcoming, to take this sentiment under its guidance, there was much reason to fear that the release from the common adhesion to Great Britain would end in setting up thirteen little republics, ripe for endless squabbling."[1]

Those who feel discouraged at the difficulties in the way of achieving the unification of Africa may take heart from the prophecy made by Josiah Tucker, described by Fiske as " a far-sighted man in many things " and " a liberal-minded philosopher who bore us no ill-will ":

> " As to the future grandeur of America, and its being a rising empire under one head, whether republican or monarchical, it is one of the idlest and most visionary notions that ever was conceived even by writers of romance. The mutual antipathies and clashing interests of the Americans, their difference of governments, habitudes and manners, indicate that they will have no centre of union and no common interest. They never can be united into one compact empire under any species of government whatever; a disunited people till the end of time, suspicious and distrustful of each other, they will be divided and subdivided into little commonwealths or principalities, according to natural boundaries, by great bays of the sea, and by vast rivers, lakes, and ridges of mountains."[2]

As Dean Tucker was wrong about America in the eighteenth century so may others be wrong about Africa in the twentieth. The way will not be easy, however, as the example of Europe

---

[1] *Op. cit.*, p. 57.
[2] Cited by Fiske, *op. cit.*, p. 57.

itself shows. The potential power of Europe has never been realised because it remained, and still remains, a collection of small states. The newest European constitution, that of France in 1958, does nothing to remedy this. Professor Aron has commented:

> " People favoring European unity have the feeling that the present Constitution creates obstacles in the way of any abandonment of national sovereignty. They feel that the people who drafted the Constitution are hostile to European unity."[1]

No one can say that the Constitution of Ghana puts obstacles in the way of African unity. As far as constitutions can go (which is not perhaps very far) it does everything to make unity possible. Indeed, one of the main reasons for abandoning the monarchical form of government was to bring Ghana into line with the republican status of her present and future independent neighbours in West Africa, and so facilitate the formation of the sort of loose union which is envisaged as the first step. Here the Republic of Guinea was particularly in mind. In the Preamble to its Constitution, promulgated on 12th November, 1958, Guinea too had proclaimed its aim as the unification of Africa[2] and art. 34 of the Constitution of Guinea contemplates the making with other African states of agreements of " association or community " for realising African unity. Dr. Nkrumah said in 1958 that his Government would approach the question of union " in the same spirit as that of art. 34 of the Constitution of Guinea ".[3] This was on the occasion of the National Assembly's ratification of the joint Declaration of 23rd November, 1958 made by Dr. Nkrumah and the President of Guinea, M. Sekou Touré. In this they agreed to constitute the two States as the nucleus of a Union of West African States, appealed for support from the Governments of the independent States of Africa and the leaders and peoples of the territories still under foreign rule, and invited other West African States to adhere to the Union. The contemplated nature of this Union was graphically indicated by Dr. Nkrumah earlier in his speech:

> " Inspired by our practical vision, we shall work towards the evolvement of a constitutional framework which will make it

---

[1] *France—the New Republic*, p. 51.

[2] " Il affirme sa volonté de tout mettre en oeuvre pour réaliser et consolider l'Unité dans l'Indépendance de la Patrie Africaine."

[3] Parl. Deb., 12th December, 1958, col. 392. For the text of art. 34 see p. 123, *post.*

possible for us to be as united as the hand in matters of common interest such as defence, foreign policy, monetary, financial and economic matters, while being as separate as the fingers in all purely local and domestic matters."[1]

The Ghana–Guinea Union was later augmented by the accession to it of the Republic of Mali, and the resulting association was given the name of the Union of African States (U.A.S.). In a charter drawn up in April, 1961, the Union was stated to be the nucleus of the United States of Africa and was declared open " to every State or Federation of African States which accepts its aims and objectives ". The aims were stated as follows:

" . . . to strengthen and develop ties of friendship and fraternal co-operation between the Member States politically, diplomatically, economically and culturally; to pool their resources in order to consolidate their independence and safeguard their territorial integrity; to work jointly to achieve the complete liquidation of imperialism, colonialism and neo-colonialism in Africa and the building up of African Unity;

" . . . to harmonise the domestic and foreign policy of its Members, so that their activities may prove more effective and contribute more worthily to safeguarding the peace of the world."[2]

The charter provides for regular meetings between representatives of the member states and for co-operation in the spheres of defence, diplomacy, economics and culture.[3] The Union has not yet however reached the stage of political integration and no surrender of sovereignty has occurred. It does not therefore alter any of the provisions of the Constitution or affect Ghana's position in the Commonwealth.

Surrender of sovereignty

In order to provide constitutional means for the advance towards African unification, art. 2 of the Constitution states that " the people now confer on Parliament the power to provide for the surrender of the whole or any part of the sovereignty of Ghana ". This may be compared with art. 34 of the Guinea Constitution which is as follows:—

" La République peut conclure avec tout Etat Africain les accords d'association ou de communauté, comprenant abandon partiel ou total de Souveraineté en vue de réaliser l'Unité Africaine."

---

[1] Parl. Deb., 12th December, 1958, col. 390.

[2] For the text of the charter, see *Ghana Gazette*, 1st July, 1961.

[3] For an instance of such co-operation see the Copyright Act, 1961 (Act 85), which gives favourable treatment to works of citizens of, or first published in, Guinea or Mali.

The Guinea provision is somewhat obscure. Power is vested in " the Republic " rather than in the President or the National Assembly, and in this respect art. 34 is different from any other in the Constitution and on one view may be said merely to state the obvious. Again there is a distinction between the reference to " les accords " in art. 34 and " les traités " in arts. 32 and 33 which empower the President to negotiate treaties (including treaties for the cession of territory) subject to ratification by law.

Article 2 of the Ghana Constitution attempts to avoid these difficulties by conferring the power to surrender sovereignty squarely on Parliament, which means that for certain types of surrender an ordinary Act of Parliament would suffice. If the surrender were so far-reaching as to require alteration of any entrenched provisions that do not contain a saving for art. 2—if for example the office of President were to be abolished—a referendum would be necessary. The type of union which is contemplated at least in the initial stages of unification would leave the member states with their constitutional structure intact, though with some diminution in legislative powers. It is possible to go a very long way towards complete union without repealing the constitutions of individual states, as the examples of the United States and Australia show.[1]

The White Paper introducing the draft Constitution contained the following passage:

" Apart from facilitating the entry of Ghana into a union of African states and territories, the draft Constitution is also designed to enable peoples who are at present outside Ghana but who are linked by racial, family and historical connections with Ghanaian peoples to join them in one integrated State."[2]

This is a reference to art. 5, which states:

" Until otherwise provided by law the territories of Ghana shall consist of those territories which were included in Ghana immediately before the coming into operation of the Constitution."

Where agreement had been reached for the accession of any territory to Ghana this article would enable the territory to be integrated with the Republic by ordinary Act of Parliament. By

---

[1] Section 106 of the Australian Constitution expressly preserved the constitution of each State of the Commonwealth.
[2] W.P. No. 1/60, p. 4.

the same means of course Ghanaian territory could be ceded by way of frontier adjustment or otherwise.

Apart from the case of Guinea, it is probably unique for a constitution to contemplate a surrender of sovereignty on the scale envisaged by that of Ghana. It is not unusual however for partial surrender to be provided for where this may be necessary to safeguard world peace and promote international co-operation. The Constitution of Denmark, enacted in 1953, provides for powers to be delegated to " international authorities set up by mutual agreement with other states for the promotion of international rules of law and co-operation." Uncertainty arose in France in 1954 as to whether ratification of the abortive European Defence Community Agreement would involve a surrender of sovereignty for which the Constitution of the Fourth Republic did not provide, apart from a vague statement in the Preamble that

" On condition of reciprocity, France accepts the limitations of sovereignty necessary to the organization and defence of peace."

However, beyond proclaiming the attachment of the French people to the 1946 Preamble, the 1958 Constitution did not make any provision for surrender of sovereignty either. It should be noted therefore that, apart from its primary function of facilitating African unification, art. 2 also provides the means for the sort of surrender envisaged by the Danish Constitution or involved in the European Defence Community Agreement, should the need for this ever arise. It is true that one of the paragraphs in the President's Declaration states: " That the Independence of Ghana should not be surrendered or diminished on any grounds other than the furtherance of African unity "[1] but apart from the fact that the Declaration in no way reduces the plenitude of the power conferred on Parliament by art. 2, it is submitted that the paragraph is directed to discountenancing any thought of placing Ghana once more in the hands of an alien power and does not purport to inhibit Ghana's entry into international arrangements of the type mentioned above.

3. THE UNITARY REPUBLIC

Section (1) of art. 4 proclaims that " Ghana is a sovereign

---

[1] Article 13.

unitary republic ". The only change effected by these words is the conversion of Ghana from a monarchy to a republic. Sovereignty had already been conferred by the Ghana Independence Act, 1957 and the unitary character of the State had existed since its inception.

The decision to turn the monarchy into a republic was basic. Although protests are still occasionally heard that the word " republic " has no significance other than as a description of any autonomous state,[1] it has since the American and French revolutions acquired a fairly clear meaning, though it possibly cannot be more accurately defined than as an autonomous State which is not a monarchy. Its derivation from the Latin *res publica*, " a public thing ", suggests that the crucial element is the idea of the State as existing to serve the ends of its people rather than as a possession of the monarch.

As nearly three-quarters of the world's population live in States generally described as republics, it was not surprising that Ghana decided to follow their example, although the Opposition pleaded for a form of elective monarchy.[2] A powerful factor was the desire of the Government to encourage African unification, which would, it was thought, be impeded if Ghana had a different form of Government from the other independent West African States. One of the Government supporters in the National Assembly, Mr. Braimah, put the point in this way:

> " Another reason why we must have a republican Constitution is that all the independent West African States with which we are friendly, and the majority of independent African States with whom we have mutual understanding, are republics and have Presidents with executive powers at the head of their Governments. This goes to prove that it is only the republican form of Government that suits the African."[3]

Article 4 is to some extent entrenched. Except in so far as a change from a unitary republic may be involved in a surrender of sovereignty taking place under art. 2, the power to provide a form of Government for Ghana other than that of a republic or for the form of the republic to be other than unitary is reserved to the people by s. (2) of art. 4.

---

[1] In the debate on the draft Constitution, the Leader of the Opposition said, " I have searched in vain through the recognized dictionaries and encyclopaedias and I have found that there is no one recognized definition of a republic ": *Constituent Assembly Debates*, col. 15.

[2] *Ibid.*, col. 17.

[3] *Constituent Assembly Debates*, col. 23.

Territories

Article 5 deals with the territories of the Republic. These are to remain as they were before Republic Day, but art. 5 makes it clear that Parliament has power to alter the territories by an ordinary Act. No difficulty arises in the case of an accession of territory, but it may be asked whether territory can be given up in this way. This is not likely to happen except possibly by way of boundary adjustment, where in order to achieve a more satisfactory frontier a mutual interchange of territory on a small scale may be carried out. However, even a larger surrender of territory would be legally possible by Act of Parliament. Even if such an Act were said to diminish the sovereignty of Ghana (which is in any case doubtful), power to do this is given by art. 2.

Article 5 refers, in addition to the territories comprised in Ghana immediately before the coming into operation of the Constitution, to the territorial waters as being included in the territories of Ghana. No definition is given of the expression " the territorial waters ", since this is left to be determined in accordance with international law.[1]

Frontiers

The present western and northern frontiers of Ghana were settled by agreements made towards the end of the nineteenth century between the British and French Governments. An Arrangement was signed in Paris on 12th July, 1893 which fixed the western boundary from the sea to the parallel of 9° North.[2] The remainder of the boundary with the French was fixed by a Convention signed at Paris on 14th June, 1898.[3] In this the parallel of 11° North was, with some variations, fixed as the northern boundary. The Anglo-French frontier was more precisely defined in an exchange of notes between the British Foreign Secretary and the French Ambassador which took place in London in May, 1904.[4] Beacons were later erected by a Joint Anglo-French Commission to mark the frontier as thus defined.[5]

Agreements were signed in Berlin on 1st July, 1890 and in London on 14th November, 1899, by which the boundary between

---

[1] Cf. the Territorial Waters Jurisdiction Act, 1878, s. 7. As to changes of territory see also pp.124–5, *ante.*

[2] Hertslet's *Treaties*, XIX, 228; *Gold Coast Handbook*, 1924, p. 482.

[3] *Handbook of Commercial Treaties*, Foreign Office, 1924, p. 200; *Gold Coast Handbook*, 1924, p. 507.

[4] *Gold Coast Handbook*, 1924, p. 484.

[5] A list of the beacons, with numbers, is given in *ibid.*, p. 489.

the German protectorate of Togo and the Gold Coast Colony was settled.[1] Except for its southernmost section, the present eastern frontier of Ghana is however the boundary between the former British and French sections of Togoland under United Nations Trusteeship. This boundary was fixed by the Franco-British Declaration of 10th July, 1919, as delimited and modified by the Protocol of 21st October, 1929 executed by the Commissioners appointed under the Declaration.[2]

Regions

Article 6 divides the territories of Ghana into eight Regions. This marked a change, since there were previously only six Regions. The Central Region and the Upper Region were thus created by the Constitution.[3] Article 6 nevertheless allows existing Regions to be abolished or altered in area, and new Regions to be created, by ordinary Act of Parliament. One of the Acts of the Constituent Assembly, the Regions of Ghana Act, 1960 (C.A. 11) laid down the areas of the various Regions. This was done by setting out the local authority areas comprised in each. Since these areas are defined by the executive instruments setting up the local authorities, it has become possible for the first time to ascertain the exact area of each Region. Where changes are made in local authority areas, a corresponding amendment to the Regions of Ghana Act is required to be made by legislative instrument. This ensures that the Act will always be up to date.

The Constitution is silent about the way in which the eight Regions are to be administered but the present system of administration should be briefly described here. The pre-republican system has been touched upon in the course of describing in Chapter 1 the course of Ghana's constitutional evolution. In the colonial period, when there was a threefold division of the country, each regional area was in the charge of a Chief Commissioner, who was second in authority only to the Governor and was a member of the Executive Council, the forerunner of the Cabinet. Detailed administration was in the hands of the district commissioners, who had multifarious duties

---

[1] Hertslet's *Treaties*, XVIII, p. 455; *Gold Coast Handbook*, p. 501.
[2] Togoland under United Kingdom Trusteeship Order in Council, 1949, s. 4. The text of the 1919 Declaration is given in the 1924 *Gold Coast Handbook*, p. 508.
[3] Rubin and Murray are in error in stating (*op. cit.*, p. 31) that these new Regions were created by the Regions of Ghana Act, 1960 (C.A. 11).

in relation to the supervision of native authorities, the administration of justice, education, licensing and so on.[1] Today traces of this system are still apparent. Each Region is now in the charge of a Regional Commissioner who is a Minister, though not of Cabinet rank. There is a Regional office in the principal town of each Region, which is staffed by civil servants. The old district commissioners, after a change of name to " government agents ", have disappeared and many of their functions are now exercised by local authorities, local courts, the police and other bodies. The name " district commissioner " has however returned to use with the appointment of various C.P.P. officials to posts of that name. These posts, which were first created in the Trans-Volta Togoland Region at the time of independence and now exist in every Region, started by being wholly party-political in nature. The new-style district commissioners were instructed to spread party propaganda and ensure at a local level that support for the party was maintained. At first they worked side by side with the government agents, but friction inevitably developed and the government agents were withdrawn. This has led to some of their remaining functions, in particular the supervision of local authorities, being assumed by the district commissioners. There is now at least one of these for every local authority area, and they form a link between the Regional Commissioner's office and the local councils.

Neither Regional Commissioners nor district commissioners have any statutory basis for their functions, although of course the Regional Commissioners derive their position as Ministers from the Constitution. Despite all the painstaking effort devoted in the nineteen-fifties to working out schemes of regional devolution, administration in the Regions is now conducted on an *ad hoc* basis as part of the machinery of central government.

National Flag

Article 7 describes the flag of Ghana. It is to consist of three equal horizontal stripes, the upper stripe being red, the middle stripe gold and the lower stripe green, with a black star in the centre of the gold stripe. This represented no change in the flag

---

[1] For a full list of the detailed functions, see *Report by the Commissioner on Regional Administrations*, Accra, 1951, Appendix L. The Commissioner, Sir Sydney Phillipson, observed that the list did not indicate the total duty and that the district commissioner acted as a " man of all work ", a direct authority on the spot who could deal in a commonsense way with the needs of the people: *ibid.*, pp. 117–118.

I

adopted after independence.[1] The reasons for the choice of colours have been given as follows. Red is to commemorate those who worked for independence, gold to represent the wealth of the country, linked with the old name of the Gold Coast, and green to represent the forests and farms of the country. The black star, which has five points, is described as the lodestar of African freedom.

Misuse of the flag or arms of Ghana constitutes an offence under the Flag and Arms Protection Act, 1959 (No. 61).[2] The offence is committed if the whole or any part of the design of the flag or arms is used for any purpose whatsoever without a licence granted by the Minister of the Interior. It is lawful however to display the flag without a licence from the Minister on any public holiday or any day proclaimed a festive occasion (s. 3).[3] An offender is punishable by a fine not exceeding £G100, but if the offence consists in using the design of the flag or arms upon or in connection with goods, this maximum is increased by the retail value of goods disposed of before conviction and goods not so disposed of are subject to confiscation (s. 4).

Further protection for the national flag and arms is given by s. 184 of the Criminal Code, 1960 (Act 29).[4] This makes it a misdemeanour to do any act or utter any words or publish any writing with intent to insult or bring into contempt or ridicule " the official national flag or emblem of Ghana or any representation or pictorial reproduction thereof ". As the provision dates from the time when the present flag and arms were first adopted, it is presumed that the word " emblem " refers to the arms of Ghana. An offence is punishable by imprisonment for up to three years or a fine, or both.[5]

4. THE PRESIDENT

Head of the State

The office of President is established by art. 8(1), which provides

---

[1] For an illustration of the flag as enrolled in the College of Arms, London, and also of the armorial ensigns and supporters granted by Royal Warrant on 4th March, 1957, together with a facsimile of the Warrant, see *Ghana Gazette*, 25th October, 1957.

[2] The Act came into force on 21st June, 1960; see E.I. 125 of 1960 and correction notice published in the *Ghana Gazette*, 15th July, 1960.

[3] In practice days are not proclaimed as festive occasions without also being made public holidays; see the Public Holidays Act, 1960 (Act 23).

[4] Section 184 reproduces an amendment made to the former Criminal Code by Ordinance No. 23 of 1957.

[5] Criminal Procedure Code, 1960 (Act 30), ss. 296 (4), 297 (1).

that the President shall be the Head of the State and responsible to the people. Subject to the other provisions of the Constitution, art 8(2) confers upon the President the executive power of the State.

By these provisions the Queen, acting through the person of Her Governor-General, was displaced as Head of the State and holder of the executive power by the President. The Constitution is silent as to the general content of the functions thus conferred upon the President, leaving these to be inferred from general principles. The functions of a Head of State are described by Oppenheim in the following way:

> " As a State is an abstraction from the fact that a multitude of individuals live in a country under a sovereign government, every State must have a Head as its highest organ, which represents it, within and without its borders, in the totality of its relations. . . . The Head of a State, as its chief organ and representative in the totality of its international relations, acts for his State in its international intercourse, with the consequence that all his legally relevant international acts are considered to be acts of his State. His competence to perform such acts is termed *jus repraesentationis omnimodae*. It comprises in substance chiefly: reception and mission of diplomatic agents and consuls, conclusion of international treaties, declaration of war, and conclusion of peace."[1]

These international functions are comprised in the executive power of the State, which also includes numerous other functions, many of which are spelt out in various provisions of the Constitution. The exercise of the executive power, being subject to the provisions of the Constitution, is regulated not only by such detailed provisions as those relating to the appointment of Ministers, judges and other officers, the position of the Cabinet and so on, but also to the supreme legislative powers of Parliament. Thus Parliament is free to regulate the detailed operation of the executive power, which in practice is done over almost the whole of its internal field. The regulatory provisions of the Constitution itself are mainly concerned with internal matters. So far as external relations, such as for example the negotiation of treaties, are concerned the executive power is left to be exercised in accordance with international law. Unlike many other constitutions, this one does not require Parliamentary or other consent to the conclusion of treaties. Unless therefore a treaty

---

[1] *International Law* (8th Edn.), ed. Lauterpacht, Vol. 1, p. 757.

entered into by or in the name of the President in itself provides
for ratification, no ratification will be necessary to enable the
treaty to become binding in international law. This principle is
subject to one important exception. Article 20(5) provides that
no person or body other than Parliament shall have power to
make provisions having the force of law except under authority
conferred by Act of Parliament. Although the first President is
empowered to legislate under art. 55, this power must be exercised
by legislative instrument. In the case therefore of a treaty which
cannot operate without changes in the municipal law of Ghana,
additional legislation is necessary. This follows the British rule
described by Oppenheim as follows:

> " Such treaties as affect private rights and, generally, as
> require for their enforcement by English courts a modification
> of common law or of a statute must receive Parliamentary
> assent through an enabling Act of Parliament. To that extent
> binding treaties which are part of International Law do not
> form part of the law of the land unless expressly made so by the
> legislature."[1]

This rule is also inherent in the provisions relating to the laws
of Ghana. By art. 40, the common law is included in the laws
of Ghana. The common law comprises the rules of International
Law[2] but only applies in Ghana subject to modifications contained in any enactment for the time being in force.[3]

The internal matters with respect to which the constitution
regulates the exercise of the executive power vested in the President include public finance, the discipline and regulation of the
Public Services and the Armed Forces, appointment of Ministers
and judges, summoning, prorogation and dissolution of the
National Assembly and pardons and remissions of sentence in
respect of criminal offences. All these matters are discussed
elsewhere in this chapter.

Article 8(3) provides that the President shall be the
Commander-in-Chief of the Armed Forces and the Fount of
Honour. The functions of the President as Commander-in-Chief
are explained in art. 54, and are discussed elsewhere. No
amplification is given of his functions as Fount of Honour, since
these are self-explanatory. The concept is of course borrowed
from the British Crown, and places in the hands of the President

---

[1] *Op. cit.*, p. 40.
[2] *Ibid.*, p. 39.
[3] Interpretation Act, 1960 (C.A. 4), s. 17 (5).

full control over the grant of honours and awards by the State. The functions so conferred were exercised immediately and by the the Honours Warrant, 1960 the President set up two types of honour. The first type consisted of various Orders of the Republic of Ghana, namely the Order of the Star of Ghana, the Order of the Volta and the Ghana Service Order. The second type consisted of various Presidential Awards. These were the Nkrumah Cross, the Ghana Military Cross, the Ghana Police Cross, the Kwame Nkrumah Prize, the Ghana Gallantry Medal, the Chiefs Medal, the Armed Forces Long Service and Efficiency Medal for Officers, and the Ghana Long Service and Good Conduct Medal. The Warrant went on to provide that matters relating to various Orders and Awards were to be governed by such statutes and regulations as the President might make.[1]

Article 8(4) provides that in the exercise of his functions the President shall act in his own discretion and shall not be obliged to follow advice tendered by any person. This is subject to any provision to the contrary elsewhere in the Constitution, or in any other law. This provision marks the distinction between the President and the former Governor-General. The latter was required to follow the constitutional conventions applicable to the British Crown, and could therefore act only in accordance with the advice of his Ministers. Nevertheless, the previous practice obtained such a hold that no significant difference in this regard is discernible. The President in practice always seeks the advice of his Cabinet on any matter of substance and will not be likely to exercise any of his functions in a manner not approved by the majority of his Ministers. The principle of the collective responsibility of the Cabinet has a strong hold in Ghana. This is illustrated by the following remark made by a Government spokesman in the debate on the proposals for a republican constitution:

> " It is clear from the Constitution that the President shall be assisted by a Cabinet of Members [of Parliament]. Hon. Members of the Opposition have forgotten the meaning of the words ' collective responsibility '. If they are conscious of the meaning of the words ' collective responsibility ' they will know that the President cannot allow a Bill to be brought to this House if the Cabinet have not signified their approval to it."[2]

The manner in which the President's executive powers are

---

[1] *Ghana Gazette*, 1st July, 1960, p. 5.
[2] *Proceedings of the Constituent Assembly*, col. 46.

exercisable, and the principles governing their delegation, are dealt with by the Presidential Affairs Act, 1960 (C.A. 2). This is a matter which has proved unexpectedly difficult and it may be helpful to spell out the position in the following rules:

Rule 1.—Specific functions vested in the President by the Constitution cannot be delegated and must be exercised by the President personally. Thus no one but the President can exercise, or signify the exercise of, the power to appoint and dismiss Ministers, to summon, prorogue or dissolve the National Assembly, to assent to legislation, to appoint judges, and so on. This does not apply however to a function such as the disciplinary control of civil servants which, by art. 51(2), is vested in the President " save as is otherwise provided by law " and as to which the Civil Service Act provides for delegation.[1]

Rule 2.—Rule 1 does not apply to functions which are included in the executive power of the State, and are thus vested in the President by art. 8(2), but which are not mentioned elsewhere in the Constitution. The exercise of such a function (*e.g.*, the power to make treaties) may be signified either by the President himself or under the hand of a Minister. The President may by instrument under his hand delegate such a function to a Minister or any other person.[2]

Rule 3.—The exercise of a function vested in the President by an enactment other than the Constitution may be signified either by the President himself or under the hand of a Minister. The President may by instrument under his hand delegate such a function to a Minister or any other person.[3]

Rule 4.—Rules 2 and 3 do not permit the exercise of a function to be signified under the hand of a Minister unless the Cabinet have given their approval or the President has directed that their approval is not necessary. The question whether such approval was given cannot however be raised in court proceedings.[4]

Rule 5.—The following principles apply to the delegation of a function under rule 2 or rule 3:

(*a*) the power to delegate is subject to any prohibition or

---

[1] Presidential Affairs Act, 1960 (C.A. 2), ss. 1 and 2. The original s. 1 was replaced by the Presidential Affairs (Amendment) Act, 1960 (Act 8).

[2] Constitution, art. 18 (2), proviso; Presidential Affairs Act, 1960, ss. 1 and 2.

[3] Presidential Affairs Act, 1960, ss. 1 and 2.   [4] *Ibid.*, s. 1 (2).

regulation of delegation contained in an enactment dealing with the particular function;[1]

(*b*) although the function may have been delegated it can still be exercised by the President himself if he so chooses;[2]

(*c*) a delegation may at any time be revoked by the President by instrument under his hand and, while it subsists, is subject to such directions as the President may choose to give as to the way in which it is to be exercised.[3]

Rule 6.—Where the President has, because of his absence from Ghana or any other reason, appointed a Presidential Commission under art. 18(2) of the Constitution, rule 1 does not prevent the delegation of any functions whatever to the Commission. In practice when such a Commission is set up all the President's functions are delegated to it. The above rules would then apply to the Commission in exactly the same way as they apply to the President.[4]

Legislative functions

The President takes part in the enactment of all primary legislation, that is legislation not made under delegated powers. Primary legislation is normally effected by Act of Parliament and by art. 20(1) the President is made, together with the National Assembly, a component of Parliament. No Bill passed by the National Assembly can become law unless the President gives his assent. The legislative functions of Parliament are discussed elsewhere.

In the case of the first President only, art. 55 confers additional legislative powers. This special provision applies notwithstanding anything in art. 20, s. (5) of which denies to any person or body other than Parliament the power to make provisions having the force of law except under authority conferred by Act of Parliament. Since, by virtue of s. 32 of the Interpretation Act, 1960 (C.A. 4), " Act of Parliament " includes the Constitution, art. 55 can be looked upon as conferring such authority as is referred to in art. 20(5). On this view, the two provisions are not inconsistent,

---

[1] *Ibid.*, s. 2 (1), proviso. See *e.g.*, s. 28 of the Civil Service Act, 1960 (C.A. 5), which contains precise directions as to the persons to whom the President's disciplinary powers may be delegated. These directions cannot be overridden by the use of s. 2 of the Presidential Affairs Act.

[2] This arises from the very nature of delegation; for a decision to this effect, see *Huth* v. *Clarke* (1890), 25 Q.B.D. 391. It means that although a delegation is in force the exercise of the function may nevertheless be signified either by the President himself or under the hand of a Minister.

[3] Presidential Affairs Act, 1960 (C.A. 2), s. 2 (2).

[4] As to Presidential Commissions, see p. 143, *post.*

but such inconsistency would, in view of the clear words of art. 55, in any case be immaterial.[1]

The legislative powers conferred by art. 55 are limited in a number of ways:

(1) They can only be exercised during President Nkrumah's initial period of office. This is defined by s. (5) as continuing until some other person assumes office as President. It is therefore not limited to President Nkrumah's first term. If he is re-elected in the next Presidential elections,the powers will continue to be available to him. Once he has gone out of office however, the powers will permanently cease, so that even if he returned to office after a term of office by some other President, the powers would not revive.

(2) The legislation must take the form of directions given by legislative instrument whenever the President considers it to be in the national interest to give such directions. This wording may be compared with that of art. 20(6) which, subject to various exceptions, gives unlimited legislative power to Parliament.

(3) A legislative instrument " may alter (whether expressly or by implication) any enactment other than the Constitution " but may do no more. It cannot therefore in any way affect the operation of the Constitution itself. Nor can it repeal, as opposed to altering, any other enactment. " Enactment " is defined by s. 32 of the Interpretation Act, 1960 (C.A.4) in terms which include any Act or instrument having legislative effect.

(4) The power cannot be used to impose taxation, authorise the raising of a public loan, or authorise the raising of any armed force, since these are all matters which under the Constitution can only be effected by Act of Parliament.

Article 55 is an entrenched provision while it remains operative. After the end of the first President's initial period of office it will however be spent and can then be repealed by ordinary Act of Parliament. As yet it has not been used.

---

[1] Rubin and Murray (*op. cit.*, p. 109) express doubt as to the validity of art. 55. Of the two grounds given for this doubt one is based on the curious argument that art. 55 " amends " an earlier entrenched provision, which cannot be done without a referendum. This reveals a basic misconception of the nature of a legislative enactment, which must be read as a whole and cannot be said to amend itself, although some provisions in it may override others (see p. 283, *post*). The other ground given is that art. 40 does not include instruments made under art. 55 among the laws of Ghana. Apart from the fact that art. 40 does not purport to be exhaustive, this ground is erroneous since such instruments are within art. 40(c) as made under the authority of the Constituent Assembly.

Election and assumption of office

Whenever a general election for the National Assembly is held there must at the same time be a Presidential election. This is laid down by art. 11(1), which provides that an election of a President shall be held whenever the National Assembly is dissolved or the President dies or resigns.[1] Article 11 lays down certain principles which are to govern the election of a President, but leaves the detailed regulation of the election to be provided by extrinsic law. The principles required by the Constitution to be embodied in this law are as follows:

(1) Any citizen of Ghana is to be regarded as qualified for election as President if he has attained the age of 35. The Constitution does not trouble to disqualify persons on grounds such as criminality or unsoundness of mind, resting on the assumption that no one is likely to be elected as President who posseses such obvious drawbacks.

(2) In the normal case of an election held by reason of a dissolution of the National Assembly, a contested election is to be decided by preferences given before the general election by persons subsequently returned as Members of Parliament. If however no candidate obtains more than 50% of the preferences so given, the election is to be decided by secret ballot of Members of the new Parliament.

(3) The principle of election by Members of Parliament is also to apply in a case where the election is held on the death or resignation of the President.

(4) The returning officer for the election is to be the Chief Justice.

An Act embodying these four principles and containing detailed provisions in amplification of them was passed as the first Act of the Republican Parliament. This was the Presidential Elections Act, 1960 (Act 1). The Act refers to the normal type of election held in conjunction with a general election as " a dissolution election ". Since, in the other type of case where the President has died or resigned, the election of his predecessor by vote of the Members of Parliament is likely to be for a short period only as the new President would no doubt wish to obtain a manifestation of popular support by dissolving the Assembly and holding a general election, an election held by reason of death or resignation is referred to in the Act as " an interim election ".

---

[1] Under art. 9 the President may at any time resign his office by instrument under his hand addressed to the Chief Justice.

It may of course happen that the Presidential Commission set up on the death or resignation of a President will be advised by the Cabinet to dissolve Parliament before an interim election can be held. In this event a dissolution election would follow in the normal way.

Under s. 4 of the Act a person may be nominated as a candidate in a dissolution election by two or more citizens of Ghana. The field of choice is greatly narrowed by the obligation of the nominators to declare, under heavy penalties if the declaration is false, that sufficient supporters of their candidate will be standing for election to the National Assembly to ensure that, if they were all elected, they would form a majority in the new Assembly.[1] As the law now stands this means that at least 53 supporters of the Presidential candidate must intend to stand as candidates in the general election.[2]

If more than one Presidential candidate is validly nominated, each person standing for election to the National Assembly is entitled by s. 7 to deliver to the Chief Justice a notice declaring his preference for one or other of the Presidential candidates. The consent of the candidate must be given, so as to prevent a person standing for election as a Member of Parliament on the " ticket " of a Presidential candidate who wishes some other person (no doubt of his own party) to be his official supporter in the constituency in question. Each preference so given is to be gazetted, and counts as a vote. After the results in the general election have been declared, the new Members of Parliament assemble in a place appointed by the Chief Justice to which the public have access. This need not be the usual meeting place of the Assembly—indeed, since it is the Chief Justice and not the Speaker who presides over the election, it may be considered more fitting for it to take place elsewhere, perhaps in the Supreme Court building.

The election is in two stages, although the second stage may not be necessary. The primary stage consists of the counting by the Chief Justice of the votes recorded by the new Members of Parliament in the form of preferences given before the election.

---

[1] It is submitted that Rubin and Murray (*op. cit.*, p. 101) are mistaken in concluding that the wording of s. 4(2) requires a sentence of five years' imprisonment to be imposed for a false declaration. *Cf.* the wording of s. 183(4) of the Criminal Code, 1960 (Act 29).

[2] The relevant number of seats for this purpose is at present 104, since the ten women's seats will, unless the law is altered, disappear on the next dissolution of the Assembly.

Normally there would be as many votes as there are Members of Parliament, although the lodging of preferences is not obligatory. The count must take place before the Members of Parliament and in the immediate view of such of the candidates as desire to witness it. If any candidate has obtained the votes of more than half of the number of new members, he is immediately declared by the Chief Justice elected as President and the election is over. If however, no such majority is obtained the proceedings are adjourned and when they resume the secondary stage of the election takes place. The secondary stage consists of as many ballots by the Members of Parliament, not exceeding five in all, as are necessary to secure an absolute majority for one of the candidates. The candidates need not be the same as the candidates at the primary stage. A candidate may withdraw between each ballot. This withdrawal may be at his own instance, or may be effected by the action of the majority of his nominators in substituting the name of another candidate. If a President has not been elected after five ballots, art. 11(3) of the Constitution provides that the National Assembly is deemed to be dissolved at the conclusion of the fifth ballot. This practically compels the Members of Parliament to find a President in one of the ballots, since otherwise they must face a further general election.

In the case of an interim election, the system of preferences does not of course operate. Instead of being nominated by any two citizens of Ghana however, the nomination must be by 10 or more Members of Parliament. Ballotting takes place in the same manner as in the secondary stage of a dissolution election, with the same consequences if a President is not elected after five ballots. Where the National Assembly is dissolved by the Presidential Commission before a new President has been declared elected in the interim election, no further proceedings are to be taken in that election.

The procedure outlined above did not apply to the election of the first President. President Nkrumah was chosen as President in the plebiscite held in April, 1960, and effect was given to this choice by art. 10 of the Constitution, which is in the following terms:

> " KWAME NKRUMAH is hereby appointed first President of Ghana, having been chosen as such before the enactment of the Constitution in a plebiscite conducted in accordance with the principle set out in article one of the Constitution."

Although the electoral provisions of the Constitution thus did not apply to President Nkrumah's first appointment, the provisions relating to the assumption of office of a President did of course apply.

The moment at which a President assumes office is fixed by art. 12 as the moment at which he takes his oath or affirmation of office. By virtue of art. 9, this moment marks the commencement of a term of office which, unless the President dies or resigns, will continue until the assumption of office of the person elected as President in the next following election. There may thus be a brief interval between the election of a new President and his assumption of office during which his predecessor will remain President.

The oath or affirmation of office binds the new President well and truly to exercise the functions of the high office of President of Ghana, to bear true faith and allegiance to Ghana, to preserve and defend the constitituion, and to do right to all manner of people according to law without fear or favour, affection or illwill.[1] Immediately after his assumption of office the President is required by art. 13 to make a solemn declaration before the people. The obligation to make the declaration " before the people " was taken in the case of the assumption of office of the first President to be satisfied by its being made in the State House before a gathering of some 400 leading Ghanaians and foreign visitors.

The declaration is in the following form:

> " On accepting the call of the people to the high office of President of Ghana I,   , solemnly declare my adherence to the following fundamental principles:
>
> that the powers of Government spring from the will of the people and should be exercised in accordance therewith;
>
> that freedom and justice should be honoured and maintained;
>
> that the union of Africa should be striven for by every lawful means and, when attained, should be faithfully preserved;
>
> that the independence of Ghana should not be surrendered or diminished on any ground other than the furtherance of African unity;

---

[1] The Leader of the Opposition said of this oath: " The oath which the President takes on Installation follows the customary one which is taken by a new chief in Ghana on his Installation, with just this significant difference. There is sanction attached to the chief's oath and he is liable to be destooled as soon as he does anything which is in conflict with the oath. But there is no such sanction attached to the oath to be sworn by the Head of the State ": *Proceedings of the Constituent Assembly*, col. 18.

that no person should suffer discrimination on grounds of
sex, race, tribe, religion or political belief;

that Chieftaincy in Ghana should be guaranteed and
preserved;

that every citizen of Ghana should receive his fair share of
the produce yielded by the development of the country;

that subject to such restrictions as may be necessary for
preserving public order, morality or health, no person should
be deprived of freedom of religion or speech, of the right to
move and assemble without hindrance or of the right of access
to courts of law;

that no person should be deprived of his property save where
the public interest so requires and the law so provides."

Article 13, which is an entrenched provision, is believed to be
unique. There are precedents of course for setting up directive
principles of State policy in the Constitution, as in the case of
India and Pakistan, but the President is not required by these
other Constitutions expressly to proclaim his adherence to these
principles or to enunciate them in public on his assumption of
office. What is the effect of the declaration? It clearly does not
restrict the legislative powers of Parliament, since it is not among
the limitations referred to in art. 20 and thus does not cut down the
width of the words in s. (6) of that article: " the power of Parliament to make laws shall be under no limitation whatsoever ".
Nor does art. 13 purport to restrict legislative power in any way.
It simply imposes a duty on the new President to declare his
adherence to various principles; it does not bind him to live up
to his declaration. For this reason it cannot be said to reduce
any of the powers conferred on the President, for example the
executive power of the State or the special legislative power
conferred by art. 55.

The effect of the declaration must be looked for in other
directions. In the case of any departure by the President from
the principles therein expressed, it clearly gives a strong argument
to his political opponents in resisting the departure in the National
Assembly or elsewhere and in criticising the President's conduct
whenever it comes in question on any future occasion, as for
example in a general election campaign. It may also be taken to
have some presumptive effect in relation to legislation which is
ambiguous on any point. The common law has set up various
presumptions which apply in such cases, as for example that
Parliament is presumed not to intend an Act to have retrospective
operation (except in procedural matters) unless clear words are
put in to give retrospective effect. As all legislation must be

assented to by the President, it may be that the courts will look upon his declaration as establishing similar presumptions in cases of ambiguity.

The foregoing comments on art. 13 are borne out by the decision of the Supreme Court in the leading case of *Re Akoto*.[1] The argument had been advanced that Article 13 (1) placed a limitation on the legislative powers of Parliament and that any Act which contravened the fundamental principles there set out was accordingly void. In rejecting this argument the Supreme Court said:

> " This contention . . . is based on a misconception of the intent, purpose and effect of art. 13 (1), the provisions of which are, in our view, similar to the Coronation Oath taken by the Queen of England during the Coronation Service. In the one case the President is required to make a solemn declaration, in the other the Queen is required to take a solemn oath. Neither the oath nor the declaration can be said to have a statutory effect of an enactment of Parliament. The suggestion that the declarations made by the President on assumption of office constitute a ' Bill of Rights ' in the sense in which the expression is understood under the Constitution of the United States of America is therefore untenable. . . . The contention that the legislative power of Parliament is limited by art. 13 (1) of the Constitution is . . . in direct conflict with express provisions of art. 20. . . . It will be observed that art. 13 (1) is in the form of a personal declaration by the President and is in no way part of the general law of Ghana. In the other parts of the Constitution where a duty is imposed the word ' shall ' is used, throughout the declaration the word used is ' should '. In our view the declaration merely represents the goal to which every President must pledge himself to attempt to achieve. It does not represent a legal requirement which can be enforced by the courts. . . . The declarations however impose on every President a moral obligation, and provide a political yardstick by which the conduct of the Head of State can be measured by the electorate. The people's remedy for any departure from the principles of the declaration, is through the use of the ballot box, and not through the courts."[2]

---

[1] Civil Appeal No. 42/61. The facts of the case are given at p. 224, *post*.

[2] The reasons which can be adduced for rejecting the argument are embarassingly numerous. In addition to those mentioned in the judgment, the following might also be put forward: (1) In contrast to the operative provisions of the Constitution, the paragraphs of the declaration are in general terms which could only be applied by a court in a specific instance with great difficulty. To treat them as having statutory effect would thus bring an uncertainty into the law which cannot have been intended. (2) There is no mention of legislative powers in the introductory words of art. 13 (1) and nothing to suggest them. The argument is thus based on an inference drawn in a manner inconsistent with the formal principles set out at the beginning of this chapter.

Since this decision is binding on all courts in Ghana, including the Supreme Court itself, it may well be that no more will be heard of the argument that art. 13 limits the legislative powers of Parliament.

Presidential Commissions

The Constitution makes no provision for a vice-President. In order to provide for the case where the President has died or resigned or is incapacitated or absent from Ghana, art. 18 enables a Presidential Commission to be set up. This may arise in two distinct classes of case, according to whether there is no President capable of acting or whether the President is merely temporarily incapacitated by illness or absence.

In the first case, since there is no President available, the function of setting up the Commission is entrusted to the Cabinet. In order to guard against the remote possibility of a President dismissing his Cabinet before resigning, dying or becoming incapable of acting, s. (5) enables the dismissed Cabinet to appoint a Commission and tender advice to the Commission as to the membership of the Cabinet in the first instance. A Presidential Commission appointed by the Cabinet will consist of three persons, who must execute the office of the President in accordance with the advice tendered by the Cabinet. This of course means that the Cabinet collectively exercises the powers of the President, but does so in the name of the Commission. Before appointing a Commission on the ground that the President is incapable of acting, the Cabinet must refer the question of incapacity to the Chief Justice and the Speaker.[1] The test to be applied is whether, after considering medical evidence, they are satisfied that the President is, by reason of physical or mental infirmity, unable to exercise the functions of his office. If they are so satisfied the Chief Justice and the Speaker make a joint declaration to that effect. If the President recovers his capacity the Chief Justice and the Speaker must withdraw their declaration, and as soon as it is withdrawn the President automatically resumes his functions and the Commission comes to an end.

In the other type of case the Commission is appointed not by the Cabinet but by the President himself. This may be done at any time in respect of such functions of the President as, by reason of his illness or absence from Ghana or other circumstance, cannot conveniently be exercised by him in person. " Illness "

---

[1] Rubin and Murray (*op. cit.*, p. 105) say the President himself (acting with the Speaker) determines the question, but this is clearly a slip.

here means temporary illness and does not include an illness of such gravity as to have resulted in the President's having been adjudged incapable of acting by the Chief Justice and the Speaker. The functions to be performed by a Commission appointed by the President are conferred upon the Commission by way of delegation. This delegation can of course be revoked by the President at any time, and does not prevent the President from exercising any of the delegated functions personally if he so wishes.

Section 3 of art. 18 provides that a Presidential Commission may act by any two of its members, and that if any vacancy arises by reason of the death of a member the vacancy shall be filled by the Cabinet or the President, according to which of them appointed the deceased member. There is thus no provision for the resignation or dismissal of a member, such provision being considered unnecessary in view of the close control exercised over the Commission by the Cabinet or the President, as the case may be.

Salary and allowances

Article 19 provides that the President shall receive such salary and allowances, and on retirement such pension, gratuity and other allowance, as may be determined by the National Assembly. Salaries and allowances are not to be reduced during a President's period of office, and are charged on the Consolidated Fund.

Regalia

The symbol of Presidential authority is the double-bladed sword of state, which is of solid gold and modelled on the afesa-nta, the traditional symbol of peace between tribal states. The President has a personal standard consisting of the black star and flying eagles of Ghana on a blue ground. His throne in Parliament House is carved in the form of a chief's stool and decorated with traditional symbols.

5. MINISTERS AND CABINET

The President is required by the entrenched provisions of art. 15 to appoint Ministers of Ghana from among the Members of Parliament. The appointment is made under the Presidential Seal to mark the personal nature of the President's choice. On appointment a Minister makes an oath or affirmation to serve the Republic well and truly, to support and uphold the Constitution, to give counsel and advice to the President and not to reveal secret matters (Oaths Act, 1960 (C.A. 12)). Ministers are to assist the President in his exercise of the executive power and to take charge under his direction of such Departments of State as he may assign to them. Ministries are created under the Civil Service Act, 1960 (C.A.5). Section 6 of the Act provides for the grouping of Civil Service posts into Departments. Section 7 provides that a Department or Departments may be constituted by regulations as a Ministry. Departments not included in a Ministry are known as special Departments (s.8). Section 5 of the Cabinet and Ministers Act, 1960 (C.A.3) provides that there shall be deemed to be a portfolio for each Ministry, which may be assigned by the President to a Minister or retained by the President himself. A Minister is not required by the Constitution to hold a portfolio, indeed the practice is to have a number of Ministers without portfolio as well as well as those placed in charge of Ministries. The Cabinet and Ministers Act, 1960 (C.A.3) also deals with the precedence of Ministers among themselves (s. 6) and their salaries, which are fixed by the National Assembly and charged on the Consolidated Fund (s. 7). Specific functions are frequently conferred on Ministers by statute. Where he thinks fit the President may amend any such enactment so as to transfer statutory functions from one Minister to another.[1]

Under art. 17, the President has power to dismiss a Minister at any time. The resignation of a Minister is not effective until it is accepted by the President, thus enabling the President to insist on dismissal rather than resignation where he deems it expedient to do so. If, however, the Minister is prepared to resign his seat in the National Assembly he may do so without the need for the President's acceptance, and the effect of this is that he also ceases to be a Minister. Loss of a seat in the National Assembly under any of the provisions of s. 2(2) of the National Assembly Act, 1961 (Act 86) involves loss of office as a Minister, but Ministerial office is not affected by cessation of membership of the National Assembly on a dissolution of Parliament. All Ministers automatically vacate their offices on the assumption of office of a President, thus giving the new President a completely free hand in the appointment of Ministers.

Another entrenched provision, art. 16, provides for the Cabinet. This consists of the President and not less than eight Ministers. Certain of the persons who have already been appointed Ministers are thus given a further appointment as Cabinet Ministers. This further appointment is not required to be under seal and can be revoked at any time. By itself such a revocation will not affect

---

[1] Presidential Affairs Act, 1960 (C.A. 2), s. 4. See, e.g., the Ministers' Functions (Justice) Instrument, 1961 (L.I. 154).

K

the position of the person in question as a Minister of Ghana. It follows also that if a person ceases to be a Minister he loses at the same time his Cabinet office. On the assumption of office of the first President 24 Ministers were appointed. All of these except the eight Regional Commissioners and the Minister resident in Guinea were also appointed members of the Cabinet.

Section (2) of art. 16 charges the Cabinet, subject to the powers of the President, with the general direction and control of the Government of Ghana. In practice this injunction is taken to require almost every question involving Government action to be referred to the Cabinet. All proposed Government Bills are submitted to the Cabinet for their approval, and indeed this approval is usually sought even before preparation of the Bill has begun.[1] The only matters explicitly required by the Constitution to be submitted to Cabinet are the annual, provisional and supplementary estimates of expenditure.[2] The Cabinet is also given important functions in the case of absence or incapacity of the President.[3]

6. PARLIAMENT

The Parliament of Ghana consists of the President and the National Assembly. The only function of Parliament as such is the consideration and enactment of legislation, although of course its component elements have numerous other functions. The expression " Parliament " is therefore correctly used only in relation to the President and the National Assembly acting in their joint legislative capacity. Although Parliament is created by art. 20(1), it is first mentioned in art. 1, which gives the people the right to choose their representatives in Parliament, who in this connection include the President as well as ordinary Members of Parliament, in accordance with the principle of one man-one vote established by that article.

As the creation of the Constitution, Parliament only has the powers conferred upon it by the Constitution. These powers are conferred by the provisions of art. 20. Subject to the exceptions mentioned below, this article confers on Parliament entirely and exclusively the legislative power of the State. The entirety of the power is confirmed by s. (6), which is in the following terms:

---

[1] For the functions of the Cabinet in regard to legislation, see Part III.
[2] See p. 161, *post.*   [3] See p. 143, *ante.*

" Apart from the limitations referred to in the preceding provisions of this Article, the power of Parliament to make laws shall be under no limitation whatsoever."

The exclusiveness of the power is made clear by s. (5) as follows:

" No person or body other than Parliament shall have power to make provisions having the force of law except under authority conferred by Act of Parliament."

The exclusiveness of the legislative power of Parliament is modified in the case of the first President only by the special provisions of art. 55.[1]

The legislative power of Parliament is thus unlimited except in the following respects:

1. It is not able to exercise that part of the legislative power of the State which is reserved by the Constitution to the people except by following the referendum procedure laid down by art. 20.

2. Subject to certain exceptions, Parliament cannot legislate so as permanently to divest itself of any of its powers.

3. A procedural limitation is placed on the power of Parliament to alter any of the provisions of the Constitution, whether entrenched or not.[2]

Amendment of Entrenched Provisions

The procedure for exercising powers reserved by the Constitution to the people is laid down by s. (2) of art. 20. This enables any portion of the reserved powers to be conferred on Parliament by the people. The process begins with the President himself. If it appears to him that the need has arisen for the exercise of any of the reserved powers he may order a referendum. The question posed in the referendum will be so worded that an affirmative response will operate to confer the necessary power. This power may be one that is only capable of being exercised on a single occasion or it may be a continuing and permanent power. As an example of the sort of questions that might be put in a referendum we may take a proposed amendment of art. 23(2), which requires the President to dissolve the National Assembly within five years after its first sitting in a new Parliament. If it is merely desired to alter " five years " to " seven years " in this section, the question put to the voters might be in the following form:

---

[1] See p. 135, *ante*.

[2] For the rejection by the Supreme Court of the argument that the legislative power of Parliament is limited by art. 13, see *Re Akoto*, Civil Appeal No. 42/61, p. 142, *ante*.

" Do you confer on Parliament the power to amend art. 23
of the Constitution so as to enable the National Assembly to
continue for a maximum of seven years between general
elections instead of five years as at present? "

The President may on the other hand consider that Parliament
should be given complete freedom to legislate on this matter, in
which case the question might be in the following form:

" Do you confer on Parliament the power to repeal s. (4) of
art. 23 of the Constitution, thus enabling Parliament to legislate
at any time with respect to the dissolution of the National
Assembly? "

The referendum is to be conducted in accordance with the
principle of one man-one vote set out in art. 1 of the Constitution.
This would mean in practice that the persons entitled to vote
would be the same as those having the franchise in a parliamentary election. Provisions governing the holding of a
referendum are contained in the Referendum Act, 1959 (No. 10).
If an affirmative vote is recorded by the majority of the electors
voting in the referendum Parliament will be able to exercise the
legislative power thus conferred by the people. It will not however
be obliged to exercise this power if, after further consideration,
it does not think fit to do so.

It should be noted that an Act may purport to exercise powers
reserved to the people although it does not contain any express
amendment of the Constitution. This would occur, for example,
if an Act were passed which laid down the procedure for elections
to the National Assembly but did not conform to the requirements of art. 1.

It would clearly be improper for the National Assembly to
embark on consideration of a Bill which could only be passed in
exercise of the reserved powers of the people unless it were quite
clear that, under the referendum procedure, the people had
conferred the necessary power on Parliament. If this had not
been done, proceedings on the Bill would be out of order. The
question of whether a Bill is in order or not is one for the Speaker,
and accordingly the Constitution places in his hands the function
of ensuring that the necessary powers have been given and
communicating this fact to the House. By art. 20(4), no Act
passed in exercise of a legislative power expressed by the Constitution to be reserved to the people shall take effect unless the
Speaker has certified that power to pass the Act has been conferred on Parliament under the referendum procedure. The form
of the Speaker's certificate is given in the Schedule to the Acts

of Parliament Act, 1960 (C.A. 7). This certificate is to be included in the original copies of the Act signed by the President and also in the published copies. Since the Speaker's certificate is conclusive, a heavy responsibility rests on him to ensure that it is only given in proper cases. The power to issue this certificate also, by virtue of s. 10(2) of the Interpretation Act, 1960 (C.A. 4) confers on the Speaker all such powers as are reasonably necessary to enable the certificate to be issued or are incidental to the issuing thereof. Under these auxiliary powers, the Speaker could demand the production of such evidence relating to the voting in the referendum as is necessary to enable him to decide whether the certificate should be issued or not.

The provision restricting the passing of legislation by which Parliament divests itself of its legislative powers is art. 20(3). This does not of course affect Parliament's ability to delegate any part of its powers to Ministers or other persons or bodies. Such a delegation can always be revoked and therefore does not involve a divesting of powers. If, however, an Act conferring delegated powers purported to restrict the ability of Parliament to revoke the delegation the restriction would be ineffective. So of course would an attempt to transfer legislative power, as opposed to merely delegating it.

There are two exceptions to this prohibition on divesting. The first arises because art. 20(3) is expressed to be subject to the provisions of art. 2, which authorise Parliament to provide for surrender of sovereignty. If such a surrender involved a transfer of legislative powers it could be effected by ordinary Act of Parliament without contravening art. 20(3). The second exception arises from the proviso to art. 20(3), which is in the following terms:

> " Provided that if by any amendment to the Constitution the power to repeal or alter any existing or future provision of the Constitution is reserved to the people, section (2) of this Article shall apply in relation to that provision as if the power to repeal or alter it had originally been reserved to the people."

This somewhat cumbersome provision is designed to make it possible to entrench provisions of the Constitution which are not at present entrenched or which are added in the future. For example, it might be thought expedient to entrench the provisions of art. 46, which contain safeguards for salaries and allowances of judges. Effectively to do so would involve a transfer from Parliament to the people of the power to amend art. 46 on any future occasion. It would thus amount to a divesting by Parliament of certain of its legislative powers. The proviso enables this divestment to be carried out and works in the following way. By an ordinary Act of Parliament a section would be added at the end of art. 46 saying that the power to repeal or alter the article was reserved to the people. By virtue of the proviso, the referendum procedure would thereafter be applicable in relation to art. 46 as it is applicable in relation to the existing entrenched provisions.

The third limitation on the legislative power of Parliament arises from the proviso to art. 20(2). This is in the following terms:

> " Provided that the only power to alter the Constitution (whether expressly or by implication) which is or may as aforesaid be conferred on Parliament is a power to alter it by an Act expressed to be Act to amend the Constitution and containing only provisions effecting the alteration thereof."

This provision is designed to preserve the integrity of the Constitution. Although most of the provisions of the Constitution can be amended by ordinary Act of Parliament its dignity and authority as the fundamental law of Ghana would be prejudiced if it were subject to the usual principle that a provision in a later Act which is inconsistent with another provision in an earlier Act is treated as an implied amendment of the earlier Act. The proviso displaces this principle. Even in relation to non-entrenched provisions, a later Act can only be taken as modifying the Constitution if it does so in express terms and does not include matter unconnected with the effecting of the amendment. In any other case the Constitution would prevail over the later Act.

It will be noticed that this rule applies not only to the amendment of the non-entrenched provisions, but also to powers conferred in a referendum to alter the entrenched provisions. This power must be exercised by an Act limited to effecting the alteration.

An amendment to the Constitution may take one of two forms. It may either be a verbal amendment or an overriding amendment. A verbal amendment will alter for all purposes the wording of the Constitution, whether by removing or amending certain words in it or by inserting additional words. An overriding amendment will leave the actual words of the Constitution intact but will modify their operation in some particular case. A number of such overriding provisions, temporary in their effect, are to be found in the Constitution (Consequential Provisions) Act, 1960 (C.A. 8), which came into operation at the same time as the Constitution. It should be noted that a provision will not operate as an amendment to the Constitution if the Constitution expressly contemplates that such a provision may be made. Article 6, for example, states that " *Until otherwise provided by law*, Ghana shall be divided into the following Regions. . . ." The number or names of the Regions could thus be altered by an ordinary Act of Parliament which did not refer to the Constitution, though clearly it would be more satisfactory to make a direct amendment of art. 6.

All that has been said above in relation to art. 20 is of course applicable only to that article as it stands at present. The Constitution is based firmly on the principle that there is no lacuna in the legislative powers. All that can be achieved by legislation is capable of achievement under the Constitution: where the power does not lie with Parliament it remains with the people. This means that, by using the referendum procedure laid down by art. 20, power can be given to amend any provision of that article. If, therefore, it is ever desired to impose further limitations on the powers of Parliament or to remove or change the existing limitations this can be done by amending art. 20. If for example it were desired to enable the non-entrenched provisions of the Constitution to be amended by implication where a later Act was inconsistent with it, all that would be necessary would be a referendum asking for power to repeal the proviso to art. 20(2), followed by an Act effecting the repeal.

Procedure for the Enactment of Legislation

Acts of the Republican Parliament are among the laws of Ghana mentioned in art. 40, and art. 24 provides for the passing of such Acts. A future Act begins its progress by being introduced into the National Assembly in the form of a Bill. The Constitution does not deal with proceedings in the National Assembly on Bills. These are dealt with by the National Assembly Act, 1961 (Act 86) and the Standing Orders of the Assembly. The Acts of Parliament Act, 1960 (C.A. 7) requires a Bill to be in a certain form, which must correspond to the requirements laid down for Acts by ss. 2 to 4 of that Act.

After its introduction and formal first reading, a Bill receives a second reading, when the broad principles of the Bill are debated, followed by a consideration stage at which the Bill is examined clause by clause and amendments are made if necessary. After a third reading, again usually formal, the Bill is deemed to have been passed by the National Assembly. Article 24 then requires it to be presented to the President. The method of presentation is governed by s. 5 of the Acts of Parliament Act, 1960 (C.A. 7), which requires four presentation copies on special paper to be prepared. Under art. 24 the President may do one of three things when he receives the presentation copies. He may signify his assent to the Bill, he may signify his assent to part only of the Bill and his refusal of assent to the remainder, or he may refuse assent. The power to signify partial assent would enable the President to reject an unwelcome amendment tacked on to an essential Bill without the need to reject the rest of the Bill. The power can also be used to give effect to a change of mind by the Government between the passing of the Bill and its assent.[1] The detailed procedure for signifying assent is contained in ss. 6 and 7 of the Acts of Parliament Act, 1960 (C.A. 7). Under art. 24(2) a Bill, or a part of a Bill, as the case may be, becomes an Act of Parliament on the signifying of the President's assent. This is elaborated by s. 6(3) of the Acts of Parliament Act, 1960 (C.A. 7), which states that the moment when a Bill becomes an Act is the moment when the President signs the first of the presentation copies.[2]

7. THE NATIONAL ASSEMBLY

Under art. 21 the National Assembly is to consist of the Speaker and not less than 104 Members, who are known as Members of Parliament. The Members are to be elected in the manner provided by a law framed in accordance with the principle of one man—one vote set out in art. 1. The Speaker is to be elected by the Members.[3] The number of seats in the Assembly at present is 114, that is 10 above the minimum required by art. 21. These additional 10 seats were established by the Representation of the People (Women Members) Act, 1960 (No. 8). Until the passing of this Act there were no women Members of Parliament and it was felt by the Government that this omission should be remedied before Republic Day. The Act came into operation on 13th June, 1960 and created 10 seats for women elected under the Act. The shortness of time before Republic Day precluded direct election, or even the system of indirect election by electoral

---

[1] It was used in this way when assent was given to the Casino Licensing (Amendment) Act, 1960 (Act 24).

[2] For a fuller account of the procedure, see Chapter 8, *post*.

[3] The election of Members is still governed by the Electoral Provisions Ordinance, 1953 (No. 33) and Regulations made thereunder, which are, however, in course of revision.

colleges contemplated by the Representation of the People (Women Members) Act, 1959 (No. 72) which was repealed without ever having been operated. The 1960 Act provided for the election of 10 women by the National Assembly itself, and this election duly took place on 27th June, 1960. By s. 1 of the Constitution (Consequential Provisions) Act, 1960 (C.A. 8) the National Assembly constituted under the 1957 Constitution was continued in being as the first National Assembly of the Republic and Members of Parliament in office immediately before Republic Day were deemed to have been duly elected. The Representation of the People (Women Members) Act, 1960 (No. 8) was repealed with a saving for existing women Members.[1] It follows from this that vacancies in the seats occupied by the women Members cannot be filled since there is no procedure for filling them. The Act was repealed because it could not be used for future elections without conflicting with the electoral principles laid down by the Constitution. Indeed this had already been recognised: section 6 of the Act provided that vacancies should not be filled. It is contemplated that before the next general election is held a new Representation of the People Act will be passed, probably containing provisions facilitating the election of a limited number of women.

Apart from its functions in relation to legislation and finance, which are discussed elsewhere, the main function of the National Assembly is the debating of Government policy and other matters of national importance, and the questioning of Ministers. Freedom of debate is ensured by the entrenched provision of art. 21(3) as follows:

" There shall be freedom of speech, debate and proceedings in the National Assembly and that freedom shall not be impeached or questioned in any court or place out of the Assembly."

Formal occasions for debating Government policy are provided for by art. 25. This requires the President to deliver to the Members of Parliament at the beginning of each session an address indicating the policies proposed to be followed by the Government during that session. Before the end of a session the President is required to deliver an address " indicating the manner and results of the application of the policies of the Government during the preceding period and otherwise setting forth the state of the Nation." To allow sufficient time for debate, the end-of-

---

[1] Constitution (Consequential Provisions) Act, 1960 (C.A. 8), s. 22.

session address must be delivered at least seven days before prorogation. Where it is impracticable for any reason for these Presidential addresses to be delivered in person, the President may instead send a message to the Assembly which is to be read by a Minister. The President may attend any sitting of the Assembly (art. 21(4)) and may at any time deliver an address or send a message to it.

Apart from its other functions, the National Assembly is entrusted by the Constitution with the power to bring about the dismissal of a judge of a Superior Court or the Auditor-General, and to fix the salaries and allowances of the President, the judges and the Auditor-General. Apart from the functions of the Assembly as a whole, its members are the only source from which Ministers can be appointed, and its Speaker is given, together with the Chief Justice, the function of pronouncing on the incapacity of the President.

The National Assembly continues in being from the time when it is first summoned to meet after the holding of a general election until it is dissolved by the President. The Assembly must be dissolved on the expiration of the period of five years from its first sitting after the previous general election. This requirement is imposed by the entrenched provisions of art. 23. Since the existing Assembly was kept in being as the first National Assembly of the Republic, it was necessary to indicate what should be regarded as the date of its first sitting. This is dealt with by s. 1(2) of the Constitution (Consequential Provisions) Act, 1960 (C.A. 8), which appoints the date of the first sitting after Republic Day as the relevant date. The first sitting took place on 2nd July, 1960, so that the latest date for dissolution of the present Assembly is 1st July, 1965. Although dissolution must take place before the end of the quinquennium, art. 23(3) enables the dissolved Assembly to be reconstituted if an emergency arises or exists when it stands dissolved. Two cases are possible. Either the emergency may arise after dissolution, or, when the final date for dissolution arrives, an emergency may already exist. In the latter event dissolution must still formally occur, but there need be no more than a nominal break in the sittings of the Assembly. Where an emergency arises or exists, the President may by proclamation summon an assembly of the persons who were Members of Parliament immediately before the dissolution. This is deemed to be the National Assembly until the majority of the results have been declared in the general election. Since emergency conditions may render it impracticable to conduct elections, the Constitution is silent on the question of when they must be held.

Although the National Assembly continues in being until dissolved, it does not of course sit continuously. Its period of office is divided into sessions. A session begins when the President summons the Assembly to meet by proclamation; it ends when the President prorogues the Assembly by proclamation. The entrenched provisions of art. 22 require a new session to be held once at least in every year. Although " year " when used in an enactment normally means any period of twelve months,[1] in this case a calendar year is referred to. This is apparent from the context, since art. 22(1) goes on to provide that a period of twelve months is not to elapse between the last sitting of the Assembly in one session and its first sitting in the next session.[2]

8. Public Finance

Money is the life-blood of a State, particularly of a State newly independent and straining every nerve to develop its economy. Thus we find that approximately one quarter of the articles in the Constitution are devoted to public finance. A proper financial organisation is important in a number of ways. In particular it is necessary to ensure that public revenues are all gathered in to the public purse and expended under proper safeguards, and that persons and institutions lending money to the State receive adequate security. Part V of the Constitution, which is devoted to financial provisions, concentrates almost entirely on the keeping and expenditure of public money. The raising of public money is dealt with very briefly in art. 26. This entrenched provision prohibits the imposition of taxation otherwise than under the authority of an Act of Parliament. Taxation is not defined, having its ordinary meaning of an impost of any sort. Having thus ensured Parliamentary sanction for the levying of taxation, the Constitution leaves the detailed provisions to be laid down by the ordinary law.[3]

The provisions dealing with the keeping and expenditure of public money lay down a system which differs only on points of detail from that previously in force under the Ghana (Constitution)

---

[1] Interpretation Act, 1960 (C.A. 4), s. 23 (4).

[2] For a detailed description of the working of the National Assembly, see pp. 298, *et seq., post.*

[3] By virtue of s. 32 of the Interpretation Act, 1960 (C.A. 4), the expression " Act of Parliament " includes Ordinances and Acts passed before Republic Day. Thus provisions such as the Income Tax Ordinance, 1943 (No. 27), and the Customs Ordinance (Cap. 167), continue to apply.

Order in Council, 1957. The biggest change is in the abandonment of Appropriation Acts. These had long since ceased to play any useful part in the system of Parliamentary control of expenditure, and were regarded as purely formal. Parliamentary authorisation of expenditure was actually given by resolutions approving the estimates after lengthy debate on selected heads. The Standing Orders of the National Assembly provided for the Appropriation Bill to be introduced immediately after the conclusion of the debates on the estimates. It was normally put through all its stages on one day with little debate. A similar procedure had to be followed whenever supplementary estimates were approved. Now, as explained below, the resolutions approving the estimates are all that is required. Other departures from the 1957 Constitution are mentioned in the course of the following discussion.

Article 27 of the Constitution sets up the Consolidated Fund and the Contingencies Fund, and recognises that further public funds may be provided for by law. Funds were already in being under these names, and s. 4 of the Constitution (Consequential Provisions) Act, 1960 (C.A. 8) provides for them to continue in being as the Consolidated Fund and Contingencies Fund established by art. 27. The main public fund is the Consolidated Fund, and art. 28(1) requires the produce of taxation, receipts of capital and interest in respect of public loans, and all other public revenue to be paid into the Consolidated Fund unless required or permitted by law to be paid into any other fund or account. This important provision ensures that public revenue in the widest sense will find its way into the public purse. Mention is made of receipts of capital and interest so as to make it clear that public revenue for the purposes of this article is not limited to items which under accounting practice would be treated as receipts on revenue account. Clearly this meaning would be too narrow to ensure the correct treatment of public receipts. On the other hand, public revenue does not include receipts, such for example as payments into court, which in no sense form part of the revenues of the State.[1] The effect of art. 28(1) is that public revenue must be paid into the Consolidated Fund if there is no provision having the force of law which requires or enables it to be paid into any

---

[1] In order to avoid giving an exaggerated impression of the amount of the nation's liquid assets, it may be desirable to distinguish in the Consolidated Fund accounts between revenue from taxation and revenue obtained by borrowing. At present, for example, Treasury Bill receipts are included without differentiation as Consolidated Fund revenue.

other fund or account.[1] Under s. (2) of art. 28, the President has power to direct the opening of a separate public account for any particular department, and that the revenue of the department be paid into that account. This removes the formal necessity for legislation to establish new public accounts.

Although the Constitution refers to public funds and public accounts, and actually creates the Consolidated Fund and the Contingencies Fund, this does not mean that actual physical funds are necessarily referred to. It is often difficult to reconcile legal requirements with accounting practice. The lawyer tends to think of receipts and expenditure in real terms, and legislation reflects this tendency. The accountant who is concerned in the actual management of public money seeks rather to record transactions in a way that gives a true and fair view of the financial position, and to this end similar legal requirements may be complied with in practice in a number of varying ways. In the United Kingdom the Consolidated Fund is represented by an actual cash balance in the Exchequer Account which is kept by the British Government with the Bank of England. In Ghana and some other Commonwealth countries, notably Canada, the practice continues of treating the Consolidated Fund and other public funds as merely notional. The accounts prepared by the Accountant-General at the close of each financial year include a statement which is drawn up by including in it items which by law belong to the Consolidated Fund and which represents the balance sheet of the notional Consolidated Fund; but no Consolidated Fund account is kept as such with the Bank of Ghana. What then is the Consolidated Fund? It is perhaps best to describe it as the aggregate of all balances kept by the Government at various banks (insofar as the balances represent money required by the Constitution to be paid into the Consolidated Fund) together with assets in which such balances have been invested and cash in hand at the various Government Treasuries. In fact

---

[1] The corresponding provision to art. 28 (1) in the 1957 Constitution was s. 58. This was thought to be defective in suggesting that only revenue from taxation and similar imposts was required to be paid into public funds, whereas financial control is necessary over revenue in the widest sense. Section 58 excluded from payment into the Consolidated Fund revenue " allocated to specific purposes ". This was felt to be too vague, and also to confuse the fund into which revenue is to be paid in the first instance with the purpose for which the revenue is ultimately to be used—a confusion which shows a trace of the discredited concept of earmarking the proceeds of a particular tax for expenditure on a service to which the tax is related (*e.g.*, taxes on road vehicles to be spent on maintaining roads).

the credit balance at a particular bank may contain an admixture of moneys which belong to different funds. It is apparent therefore that the Consolidated Fund is a notional entity. It may be that in time changes will be made in accounting practice in Ghana which will lead to the creation of something more like a real fund.

It may be useful to give an example of how the system works in practice. A taxpayer in Accra sends a cheque to the inspector of taxes at Accra. By virtue of art. 28(1) this is required to be paid into the Consolidated Fund. What in fact happens is that the inspector first issues a receipt and enters the amount in his cashbook. He then pays the cheque, along with the day's other cash takings, into the account of the sub-accountant, Accra, which is kept with an Accra bank. Each week he presents his cashbook and paying-in slips to the sub-accountant, Accra, who keeps the paying-in slips and issues a Treasury receipt for the relevant amount, debiting Cash and crediting Income Tax Head (Consolidated Fund). Every month the Accountant-General incorporates the account of each sub-accountant in the main Consolidated Fund account. From the point of view of the Accountant-General, the amount of the taxpayer's cheque forms part of the Consolidated Fund from the time when the Treasury receipt is issued, subsequent transactions being merely adjustments of cash balances.

It will be seen therefore that when the Constitution refers to a public fund or public account it is not necessarily referring to what the public accountant or auditor would understand by these terms. The Constitution is concerned with the keeping and expenditure of the real financial assets of the country. In constitutional terms therefore any account kept with a bank by a Government department is a public account. In so far as it represents actual financial assets, it is also a public fund.

Another example may help to make this clear. The Lotteries Act, 1958 (under which the Ghana National Lotteries are held) states that "there shall be an account to be known as the Lotteries Account". It goes on to provide that the proceeds of the sale of lottery tickets shall be paid into the Lotteries Account, and that money required for prizes and for paying ticket sellers shall be paid out of the same account. This account is kept by an official of the National Lotteries Department. There is however also a bank account kept by the same Department. The balance on the bank account represents the real financial assets of the

Lotteries Account. It is apparent, that while the Lotteries Account is a public account, because it is so described in the Act which creates it, it is also from the legal point of view a public fund, because its assets are immediately represented by a bank deposit.

It will be seen that the terms " public fund " and " public account " are more or less interchangeable. This means that, although charged expenditure is stated by the Constitution to be charged on public funds, rather than public accounts, this does not indicate any practical distinction. When therefore s. 5 of the Constitution (Consequential Provisions) Act, 1960 (C.A. 8) refers to payments required or authorised to be made out of a public fund, and charges the payments on the fund in question, it should not be taken to exclude a fund such as the Lotteries Account merely because it is described in the Lotteries Act as an account rather than a fund.

Once money has been paid into a public fund or account, it can only be withdrawn to meet expenditure in one of four ways:

(a) if the expenditure is charged by law on a public fund or on the general revenues and assets of Ghana;

(b) if the expenditure is authorised to be met out of moneys granted by the National Assembly;

(c) if the expenditure is of an urgent character and is authorised to be met out of the Contingencies Fund;

(d) if the expenditure is to be met in pursuance of an agreement by the President to grant a loan.

Article 29(1) provides that expenditure shall not be met from any public fund or public account except under a warrant issued by authority of the President.

Charged expenditure

There are certain categories of recurring expenditure which are regarded as being a first charge on the nation's resources and of such a character that no question should be entertained as to their not being met. They are thus outside the general field of expenditure which is debatable by the National Assembly and subject to the approval of that body. The Constitution itself contains a number of examples of such expenditure, and numerous others are to be found in the general law. In most cases such expenditure is declared to be charged on the Consolidated Fund. This is the position with regard to the salary and allowances of the President, the judges of the superior courts and the Auditor-General[1] and the retiring allowances of members of the Civil Service, the Judicial Service and the Police Service.[2] On the other hand, the public debt, interest thereon, sinking fund payments in respect thereof, and the costs, charges and expenses incidental to the management thereof are charged by an entrenched provision on the general revenues and assets of Ghana.[3] This distinction arises because the enactments relating to the Consolidated Fund are not entrenched and could be repealed by an ordinary Act of Parliament. In order to give the greatest possible safeguard to outside creditors of Ghana therefore, liabilities to them are charged not on a particular fund which could be abolished, but on the property of the State in whatever form it may take.

Since there were a number of existing enactments which provided for the payment of public money in circumstances where Parliamentary control was not envisaged, s. 5 of the Constitution (Consequential Provisions) Act, 1960 (C.A. 8) charged such payments on the fund out of which they are in each case directed to be made. This was done as a precaution: where in the time available such provisions could be discovered they were expressly modified.[4]

The automatic payment of charged expenditure is secured by art. 29(2), which provides that whenever a sum becomes payable which is charged by law on a public fund or on the general revenues and assets of Ghana, the President or a person authorised by him in that behalf shall cause a warrant to be issued for the purpose of enabling that sum to be paid. By virtue of s. 27 of the Interpretation Act, 1960 (C.A. 4), the use of the word " shall " in this provision is to be construed as imperative.[5]

---

[1] Articles 19, 46 (3) and 38 (4).   [2] Article 52.   [3] Article 37.

[4] As for example in the case of the Widows and Orphans (Overseas Officers) Pensions Ordinance, 1955 (No. 24); see the Constitution (Consequential Provisions) Act, 1960 (C.A. 8), Sch. II.

[5] It should be noted that " charged " is used in these provisions in its legal, and not its accounting sense. In law a charge is a form of security consisting of the right of a creditor to receive payment directly out of a specified fund or the proceeds of the realisation of specified property. In accounting terminology an account is said to be charged whenever it is debited, and the word is frequently applied to credits also. The term " statutory expenditure ", which was applied to charged expenditure by s. 59 (4) of the 1957 Constitution, was dropped in 1960 as being misleading. Expenditure is frequently provided for by statute (although it cannot actually be met without compliance with Part V of the Constitution) without being charged on a public fund or account.

Voted expenditure

Most public expenditure falls into the category of voted expenditure, that is expenditure authorised to be met out of money voted by the National Assembly. Money may be so voted either by approving estimates of expenditure, or by an extraordinary grant. Article 31 requires the President to cause to be prepared annually estimates of expenditure, other than charged expenditure, which will be required to be incurred for the public service during the following financial year. The financial year begins on 1st July.[1] These estimates, which are known as the annual estimates, are to be arranged under heads for each public service.[2] They are required to be submitted to the Cabinet, and if approved by the Cabinet are to be laid before the National Assembly.[3] Each head of the estimates is to be voted on separately. A head may be rejected by the Assembly, but no amendment is permitted. This means that, once the annual estimates have been laid before the Assembly, they cannot be altered even by the Government. If the amount specified in any head is found to be insufficient, even before the head has been approved by the Assembly, the matter can only be corrected by a supplementary estimate.

Supplementary estimates are provided for by art. 32(2). They may become necessary in one of two ways. Either it may be found that the amount specified for a particular public service in the annual estimates was insufficient, or a need may arise for expenditure on a new public service not falling under a head included in the annual estimates. Where either of these happens, the President is required to cause estimates of the additional expenditure to be prepared under the relevant heads. Again, Cabinet approval must be sought, and after it is given the supplementary estimates are to be laid before the National Assembly.

To provide for the case where it is not possible to secure the approval of the Assembly to all or any part of the annual estimates before 1st July, art. 32(1) provides for a vote on account to

---

[1] Interpretation Act, 1960 (C.A. 4), s. 32.

[2] This expression has a wider meaning than " Public Service " in Part VIII of the Constitution; it covers all services on which voted moneys are expended.

[3] Section 59 (1) of the 1957 Constitution also required estimates of charged expenditure and estimates of revenue to be submitted to the Assembly. This requirement was dropped because these estimates are not an essential part of the machinery of Parliamentary control. They are useful, and continue to be presented, but the Constitution need not concern itself with them.

L

be given. This is done by preparing estimates of expenditure which will be required for the continuance of those public services for which no vote has yet been given on the annual estimates until that vote can be taken. Again Cabinet approval is necessary, after which the estimates, which are known as provisional estimates, are to be laid before the National Assembly. Votes on account were not expressly provided for by the 1957 Constitution. Instead, s. 60(3) provided that if the Appropriation Bill had not become law by the first day of the financial year the Minister of Finance could with Cabinet approval authorise expenditure. Such a practice is contrary to the principle of Parliamentary control and in fact provision was made for votes on account by the Standing Orders of the Assembly.

An affirmative vote by the Assembly on any head of the estimates, whether annual, supplementary or provisional, is an indication that the Assembly approves the incurring of the expenditure up to the amount specified during the financial year in question in respect of the public service to which the head relates. This approval of proposed expenditure is converted by the Constitution into a grant by the Assembly. The grant is limited both as to the purpose for which it can be used and the period for which it is available. It can only be used for the service to which the relevant head relates, and it cannot be spent after the end of the financial year. The Constitution does not prescribe the manner in which the estimates are to be divided into separate heads, but assumes that normal financial practice will be followed. No provision is made as to virement or reallocation, which is the practice of expending surplus sums provided on one sub-head, item or sub-item for purposes specified in another sub-head, item or sub-item within the same head of the estimates. This practice is however clearly permissible, since the Constitution allows a head to be treated as a whole.

It should be noted that the approval of expenditure given by a vote on the estimates relates to payments and not commitments. Government accounting in Ghana is conducted on a cash basis and, so far as the Constitution is concerned, financial control is exercised at the time when payments are made. Expenditure might be said to be incurred at the time when a commitment is made, as for example on the placing of an order for goods, but the word " incurred " in art. 31 is construed as referring to actual expenditure. The Constitutional control thus operates at the later stage when payment is made for the goods which had been ordered previously. The distinction between commitments and payments matters little in the normal case where both occur in the same financial year. It becomes important however in a case where, for example, goods are ordered towards the end of one financial year and are not paid for until some time in the following year. Since the money granted by the National Assembly for the service in question in the earlier financial year is not to be used in paying for the goods, it follows that the Constitutional provisions do not directly operate to control entry into the commitment. When, however, the time for payment comes it must of course be made out of grants made by the Assembly for the following year. In theory therefore, while a commitment may, so far as the Constitution is concerned, be freely entered into where it is not to be met within the financial year in question, it is clear that when the time for payment comes in a future year it may be found that the Assembly has not authorised payment to be made. Since to refuse payment on these grounds would prejudice Ghana's reputation for meeting its liabilities, it will be seen that to incur a commitment in one year which is to be met in the next is in effect to force the Assembly to authorise payment when the time comes for considering the estimates for the following year. It is for this reason that the practice of incurring commitments of this sort is discouraged by Financial Orders and other provisions regulating the details of Government finance. The rule has its disadvantages. Even in routine matters it may well be inconvenient to be precluded from incurring commitments which are not to be met until the following financial year. Furthermore, an unexpected delay on the part of the supplier in forwarding the goods or submitting an invoice may make it impossible for payment to be made within the year in which the order was placed. Again, projects are frequently embarked upon which cannot be completed within one financial year. A major engineering work, for example, may take several years to complete and it would be absurd to suppose that contracts for carrying it out could not be placed if their duration was to exceed one year. It is for such reasons as these that the Constitution operates on a payments basis rather than on a commitments basis, leaving it for administrative instructions to lay down cases in which commitments may be entered into for payment in succeeding years.

Even so, the flavour of unconstitutionality remains wherever the Assembly's hands are tied when voting on the estimates because they include payments under past commitments. There are two ways in which this can be avoided. In the first place, art. 32 of the Constitution contemplates that estimates will be voted on before the beginning of the financial year to which they relate. This is always the case with provisional estimates, and may apply also to the annual estimates. If expenditure has already been approved for the following financial year, there can be no objection to entering into commitments before the year begins. This method may be used to avoid the disadvantages of the too rigid application of annual accounting principles. The second method, which is particularly applicable to long term commitments, is to obtain the approval of the Assembly by ordinary resolution outside the normal financial procedure. If a long term project has been approved by the Assembly, there is little force in the argument that the commitment is unconstitutional as tying the hands of the Assembly when considering future estimates. This method has been employed in relation to the various Development Plans adopted in recent years.

Article 33 embodies, for the first time in Ghana, specific provision for votes of credit and other extraordinary grants. There is thus an alternative means by which the Assembly may authorise expenditure, which can be used when estimates are inappropriate. They may be inappropriate for various reasons. In time of war or other emergency, security factors may make any disclosure of detailed plans for expenditure unwise; or a need for urgent expenditure may arise while the Assembly is sitting and there is no time to prepare detailed estimates; or it may be desirable to obtain the approval of the Assembly, by a procedure which is apart from normal financial debates, to a non-recurring item of expenditure such as the erection of a national monument or a ceremonial gift to another country. In the United Kingdom it is considered more graceful for certain grants, for example for the erection of a monument to a distinguished man, to be proposed by back-benchers rather than the Government. By using the extraordinary grant procedure this course could be followed in Ghana, provided the President's assent was signified as required by s. 18 of the National Assembly Act, 1961 (Act 86). Unless limited in time by the resolution under which it is voted, an extraordinary grant may be expended over an indefinite period. To ensure proper financial control, however, it would perhaps be wise to follow the United Kingdom practice and limit expenditure to the financial year in which the grant is given.

The grant of money effected by approval of a head of the estimates, or by a vote of credit or other extraordinary grant, is
made good when the President authorises a warrant to be issued
for the withdrawal of the relevant sums from the Consolidated
Fund or some other fund. The choice of the fund from which to
withdraw the money rests with the President, subject to any
restriction imposed by law.[1] Normally however the estimates
will indicate from which fund the expenditure is to be met.
Where they do so, the Assembly might perhaps be regarded as
having been influenced in its vote by a consideration of the fund
from which the money was proposed to be drawn and therefore it
would be unusual, if not improper, to draw it from any other fund.

Although it would be wrong, except in urgent cases dealt with
by art. 34, for expenditure to be deliberately incurred on any
public service in excess of the amount voted for that service by
the Assembly, it may be found that this amount has in some cases
been inadvertently exceeded. This may arise because the exact
position is not known until final accounts have been drawn up.
Where such an excess has occurred, the Assembly should be
asked to approve an excess vote under art. 30. Such approval
results in the amount originally granted for the service in question
being treated for accounting purposes as increased to include the
amount of the excess. This procedure is provided to enable the
final accounts for the financial year to be drawn up in a form
which does not show any unauthorised expenditure. It does not
relieve any public officer whose fault caused the excess from liability. It should be noted that an excess vote is necessary even
though the excess is discovered before the end of the financial
year in question; supplementary estimates can only be used to
authorise expenditure not yet incurred. Again this marks a change
from the 1957 Constitution, under which excess expenditure was
retrospectively authorised by the approval of a supplementary
estimate. The change is designed to make it clear to the Assembly
that unauthorised expenditure has been incurred, and also to
avoid the absurdity of " granting " money which has already been
spent.

Contingencies Fund expenditure

Cases are bound to arise from time to time where expenditure
of sums not voted by the National Assembly needs to be incurred

---

[1] *E.g.*, in relation to the Contingencies Fund by art. 34.

as a matter of urgency. If the expenditure is of a character such that it would normally require authorisation by the National Assembly, that is if it is neither charged expenditure nor the payment of a loan under art. 35, the normal procedure would be to seek the authority of the National Assembly by presenting a supplementary estimate or asking for an extraordinary grant. It may happen, however, that the National Assembly is not sitting when the need for expenditure arises and that it is not practicable to summon a meeting of the Assembly in sufficient time to obtain the necessary grant. Where this is so, the President is authorised by art. 34 to make an executive instrument under which the money required may be drawn from the Contingencies Fund.

The Contingencies Fund, which is established by art. 27[1] is fed by sums transferred from time to time from the Consolidated Fund under authority from the National Assembly given under art. 34(4). This procedure is used to ensure that an adequate balance is always available in the Contingencies Fund. However, where expenditure of any amount is met from the Contingencies Fund, a transfer of a similar amount should be made from the appropriate public fund under art. 34(3), art. 34(4) being used only to adjust the permanent balance of the fund. Although the approval of the National Assembly may be dispensed with before urgent expenditure is incurred, the opinion of the Assembly must be sought on the expenditure as soon as possible afterwards. Article 34(3) requires the executive instrument authorising expenditure, which must specify the head under which the expenditure would have been shown if it had been included in the annual estimates, to be laid before the National Assembly as soon as is practicable after the instrument is made. A Minister authorised by the President must then move a resolution authorising the transfer to the Contingencies Fund from the appropriate public fund of an amount equal to the amount of expenditure. In this way an opportunity for debate on the expenditure is ensured. Although the Assembly is of course free to reject the resolution if it thinks fit, it would be most unusual for it to do so.

Article 34 is based on the Contingencies Fund Act, 1958 (No. 18). The limit of £G1,500,000 imposed by that Act was not reproduced however, and the Fund may now have a running balance of such amount as the Assembly considers sufficient to provide for likely contingencies. Another change is that, whereas

---

[1] See p. 156, *ante*.

formerly transfers were made by Supplementary Appropriation Act, the new procedure requires a resolution the terms of which clearly indicate to the Assembly that the money has already been spent.

Public loans

Article 35 empowers the President to enter into an agreement with any person or body (including a foreign State) under which a loan is to be made to that person or body out of the public funds of Ghana. This may be contrasted with art. 36, which prohibits borrowing by the Republic except under the provisions of an Act or Ordinance. The National Assembly are given power to control the making of agreements to grant loans from public funds. By art. 35(2), the Assembly may resolve that their ratification is required before an agreement to grant a loan above an amount specified in the resolution becomes operative. Whether or not such a resolution has been passed, or applies, particulars of an agreement to grant a loan and of the borrower and the purposes for which the loan is required, are to be laid before the National Assembly as soon as practicable after the making of the agreement.

Auditing of public accounts

Safeguards against unauthorised expenditure from public funds, and other unauthorised dealings with public money, are provided by arts. 38 and 39. Article 38 establishes the office of Auditor-General, and ensures the independence of this officer by providing that, once he has been appointed by the President, he cannot be removed from office before reaching the retiring age except under a resolution of the National Assembly supported by the votes of at least two-thirds of the total number of Members of Parliament and passed on the ground of stated misbehaviour or of infirmity of body or mind. The retiring age is 55 or such higher age as may be prescribed by law. Further protection is given by s. (4), which provides that the Auditor-General's salary is to be determined by the National Assembly, is charged on the Consolidated Fund, and is not to be diminished during his term of office.

The duties and powers of the Auditor-General are specified in art. 39, which requires him to audit the accounts of all departments of State. The word " department " is here used in a wide sense and covers all branches of central government services. To enable the Auditor-General to carry out his functions, he is given a right of access at all times to any books, records, stores and other matters relating to such accounts. Thus, apart from being entitled to inspect books of accounts, vouchers and other documents, he can also check physical stores, cash in hand and other relevant matters. The Auditor-General is required to report annually to the National Assembly on the exercise of his functions and to draw attention in his report to any irregularity in the accounts audited by him. This does not of course mean that every irregularity, however trifling, must be commented on. There is, however, a clear duty to draw attention to any irregularity of a substantial character.[1]

9. LAW AND JUSTICE

Respect for principles of law and justice is manifested in several of the fundamental principles embodied in the Presidential declaration required by art. 13. Indeed more than half the principles contained in the declaration are concerned with aspects of law and justice. The second principle proclaims that freedom and justice should be honoured and maintained, the fifth that no person is to suffer discrimination on grounds of sex, race, tribe, religion or political belief, the seventh that every citizen should receive his fair share of the produce yielded by the development of the country. The two final principles enjoin respect for freedom of religion and speech, for the right to move and assemble without hindrance, for the right of access to courts of law and for the right to the protection of private property subject to the requirements of the public interest as ascertained in accordance with law. The motto of the State, which appears at the head of the Constitution and every Act of Parliament is " Freedom and Justice ".

Part VI of the Constitution contains detailed provisions relating to law and justice. The judicial power of the State is conferred by art. 41(2) on the courts of law. The power is conferred " subject to the provisions of the Constitution ", which means that the courts are to exercise it in accordance with provisions laid down by the authorities on whom legislative power is conferred by the Constitution. Since, as explained above, the legislative power is predominant in the Constitution, it must follow that the judicial power is subject to its exercise. Apart therefore from provisions such as the Courts Act, 1960 (C.A. 9) which regu-

---

[1] The duties of the Auditor-General are set out in more detail in the Public Accounts (Audit) Rules, 1959 (L.N. 103).

late the detailed exercise of judicial powers, it is also within the competence of the legislature to annul a particular judicial decision or to divert some part of the judicial power to bodies other than the courts, for example to administrative tribunals or even the National Assembly itself. These limiting words also embrace provisions in the Constitution expressly regulating the judicial power, for example those specifying the jurisdiction of the various courts. Again, the control over prosecutions for criminal offences and the powers of pardon and remission conferred by arts. 47 and 48 may be seen as curtailing the judicial powers of the courts.

Laws of Ghana

Subject to such limitations as are placed on the powers of the courts, the main function arising from possession of the judicial power of the State is of course the administration and enforcement of the laws of Ghana. Article 40 divides these laws into six categories, as follows:

  (a) the Constitution;
  (b) enactments made by or under the authority of the Republican Parliament;
  (c) enactments other than the Constitution made by or under the authority of the Constituent Assembly;
  (d) enactments in force immediately before Republic day;
  (e) the common law; and
  (f) customary law.

These six categories of laws describe the position immediately after the coming into operation of the Constitution, but the opening words of art. 40 acknowledge that any one of these categories may disappear if so provided by an enactment made after that time. As explained above, the Constitution itself could be repealed by an Act of Parliament passed after the peoples' approval had been given by referendum. If this happened, the Parliament established by this Constitution might be abolished, so that the second category of laws could also disappear. The laws in the remaining categories are all clearly subject to amendment or repeal by Acts of the Republican Parliament. It may happen, for example, that with the progress of statute law reform, all the enactments referred to in the fourth category will be replaced by Republican legislation, thus removing that category from the laws of Ghana.

The first three categories need no further comment, but some explanation must be given of the last three.[1] It is by virtue of art. 40(d) that the old laws dating from pre-Republican days are kept in force, subject of course to the modifications arising from the enactment of the Constitution and the other legislation passed by the Constituent Assembly.[2] The fifth and sixth categories, the common law and customary law, have such meanings as may be given to them by extrinsic law, since they are not defined in the Constitution itself. Definitions of these terms are contained in ss. 17 and 18 of the Interpretation Act, 1960 (C.A. 4). Section 17 confers an extended meaning on the expression " the common law ". Apart from the rules of law generally known as the common law, that is the common law as prevailing in England and in other countries which have adopted it, it also includes the doctrines of equity and any rules of customary law which may be included in the common law under any future enactment providing for the assimilation of such rules of customary law as are suitable for general application. Section 17 also brings within the ambit of the common law such of the English statues of general application as remain applicable, and contains other provisions relating to the application of the common law. Section 18 defines customary law as—

> " rules of law which by custom are applicable to particular communities in Ghana, not being rules included in the common law under any enactment providing for the assimilation of such rules of customary law as are suitable for general application."[3]

The Courts

The Constitution divides the courts of Ghana into superior and inferior courts. The superior courts, that is the Supreme Court and the High Court, are established by the entrenched provisions of art. 41. The inferior courts, apart from being incidentally referred to in arts. 41(2) and 42(2), are not dealt with by the Constitution, but are left to be set up under extrinsic law. The Courts Act, 1960 (C.A. 9) creates a system of inferior courts consisting of circuit courts, district courts, juvenile courts and local courts.

---

[1] As to the status of Constituent Assembly Acts, see p. 102, *ante.* As to instruments made by the President under art. 55, see p. 135, *ante.*

[2] These modifications may be express or implied. The difficulty raised by Rubin and Murray (*op. cit.*, p. 170) as to an old law which is inconsistent with the Constitution does not exist since a later enactment overrides an inconsistent earlier enactment.

[3] See further Part IV, *post.*

The Supreme Court is declared by art. 42(1) to be the final court of appeal, the appellate jurisdiction of the West African Court of Appeal and the Judicial Committee of the Privy Council having been abolished.[1] The Supreme Court is to have " such appellate and other jurisdiction as may be provided for by law ". Article 42(2) confers a special original jurisdiction on the Supreme Court in all matters where a question arises whether an enactment was made in excess of the powers conferred on Parliament by or under the Constitution. Article 55(4) extends this original jurisdiction to questions arising as to whether a legislative instrument made by the first President under art. 55 is *ultra vires*. If any such question arises in the High Court or an inferior court, the hearing is required to be adjourned and the question referred to the Supreme Court for decision. Such a question might be raised on one or more of the following grounds:

(1) That an Act passed in exercise of a legislative power expressed by the Constitution to be reserved to the people was not the subject of a certificate by the Speaker, given in accordance with art. 20(4), that power to pass the Act has been conferred on Parliament by the decision of a majority of the electors voting in a referendum.

(2) That the effect of an Act would be to alter the Constitution (whether expressly or by implication), but that the Act was not, as required by art. 20(2) expressed to be an Act to amend the Constitution and containing only provisions effecting the alteration thereof.

(3) That, contrary to art. 20(3), an Act purported to divest Parliament of some of its legislative powers, not being an Act authorised by art. 2.

(4) That a legislative instrument made under art. 55—
(a) purported to repeal some other enactment; or
(b) purported to repeal or alter a provision of the Constitution; or
(c) purported to have any other effect capable of being achieved only by an Act of Parliament, that is the imposition of taxation, the raising of a public loan or the raising of an armed force.[2]

---

[1] See p. 100, *ante*.
[2] Articles 26, 36 and 53.

Such constitutional questions arising in relation to Acts of Parliament must be considered by a court comprising at least three Judges of the Supreme Court.[1] No such requirement however exists in the case of questions concerning instruments made under art. 55.

Article 43 leaves the composition of superior courts in particular proceedings to be regulated by extrinsic law subject to the requirement mentioned above in relation to constitutional matters and also to a requirement that no appeal is to be decided by the Supreme Court unless the court hearing the appeal consists of at least three judges, of whom at least one is a judge of the Supreme Court. Subject to these requirements, s. 7 of the Courts Act, 1960 (C.A. 9) enables judges of the High Court and temporary judges to sit in the Supreme Court provided that the total number of judges is either three or five except in interlocutory matters where a single judge is authorised to act.

Apart from the restrictions mentioned above in constitutional matters, the High Court is to have such original and appellate jurisdiction as may be provided for by law.[2] Section 29 of the Courts Act, 1960 (C.A. 9) gives the High Court a general original jurisdiction in all matters and an appellate jurisdiction from decisions given by a circuit court in non-criminal matters.

It will be seen that, apart from the special provisions relating to *ultra vires* enactments, other constitutional questions are left to be decided by the courts in the same way as any other question of law. Article 42(2) was enacted so as to ensure that matters of vital constitutonal importance were not pronounced upon by the lower courts, with the risk of dislocation of state business during the period between the promulgation of a lower court's decision that a particular enactment was *ultra vires* and the hearing of an appeal from that decision. The provision was not necessary to bring such matters within the purview of the courts since the courts are required to administer the law and if an alleged law is beyond the powers of the body which made it it is not law and the courts must pronounce accordingly. However, even in relation to *ultra vires* enactments, the Supreme Court is not given a general power of review. It can only deal with a question of *ultra vires* if it arises in the course of proceedings (whether civil or criminal) instituted in the ordinary way. Since however all

---

[1] Article 43.
[2] Article 42 (3).

courts, including the Supreme Court itself, are bound to follow the Supreme Court's decisions, a finding in any case that an enactment was *ultra vires* would conclusively determine its status as regards all future proceedings.

This principle of *stare decisis* is laid down by art. 42(4) as follows:

> " The Supreme Court shall in principle be bound to follow its own previous decisions on questions of law, and the High Court shall be bound to follow previous decisions of the Supreme Court on such questions, but neither court shall be otherwise bound to follow the previous decisions of any court on questions of law."

It will be observed that no mention is made of inferior courts, but it is clear that inferior courts can have no greater freedom than the High Court. The High Court is not bound by its own decisions, but there is a presumption arising from the status of the inferior courts that they should follow decisions of the High Court as well as those of the Supreme Court.

Article 42(4) is intended to provide a suitable combination of certainty and flexibility in the enunciation and development of legal principles. Once the Supreme Court, as the highest court available to Ghanaians, has delivered itself of a proposition of law relevant to its decision in a particular case, that proposition is binding without modification in the High Court and the inferior courts. It is also binding in principle on the Supreme Court itself, but the use in this connection of the expression " in principle " is intended to indicate that the Supreme Court may in a particular case depart from its own previous decision if it considers that the decision was given *per incuriam* or should for any other exceptional reason not be followed. Apart from previous decisions of the Supreme Court established by the Constitution, decisions given by courts in Ghana before or after the coming into operation of the Constitution or by courts in other countries will not be binding, although no doubt many of them will be regarded as being of persuasive authority.[1]

The Judges

The appointment of judges of the superior courts is dealt with by art. 45. This provides for the judges to be appointed by the

---

[1] *Cf.* s. 17 (4) of the Interpretation Act, 1960 (C.A. 4), which provides that in deciding upon the existence or content of a rule of the common law as defined in that section the court may have regard to any exposition of that rule by a court exercising jurisdiction in any country.

President by instrument under the Public Seal. The Constitution is silent as to the qualifications necessary for appointment as a judge, but s. 8 of the Judicial Service Act, 1960 (C.A. 10) provides that no person shall be appointed as a Judge of the Supreme Court unless his standing as a legal practitioner is at least ten years. Five years' standing is required for appointment to the High Court.[1]

Unless a judge has reached retiring age or tenders his resignation to the President, he cannot be removed from office unless the National Assembly has passed a resolution for his dismissal on grounds of stated misbehaviour or infirmity of body or mind, and the resolution received the support of not less than two-thirds of the total number of Members of Parliament. The majority required thus depends on the number of Members holding seats at the relevant time, and not on the total number of Members voting. The retiring age for judges of the Supreme Court is 65, and for judges of the High Court 62. Provision is made for the extension by the President of the tenure of office of a judge for a definite period. This period must be specified in the instrument extending the tenure of office. By virtue of s. 10(1) of the Interpretation Act, 1960 (C.A. 4), which provides that where an enactment confers a power or imposes a duty the power may be exercised and the duty shall be performed from time to time as occasion requires, the President could allow two or more extensions of office. Article 45(2) requires provision to be made by law for the form and administration of the judicial oath, which must be taken by every person appointed as judge of a superior court before the exercise by him of any judicial function. This provision is made by the Oaths Act, 1960 (C.A. 12), which prescribes the form of judicial oath as follows:

> I,   , swear that I will well and truly exercise the judicial functions entrusted to me and will do right to all manner of people in accordance with the Constitution of the Republic of Ghana as by law established and in accordance with the laws and usage of the Republic of Ghana without fear or favour, affection or ill will. So help me God."

---

[1] The term " legal practitioner " was abolished by the Legal Profession Act, 1960 (Act 32), which regulates the organization and discipline of, and training for, the unified legal profession. Presumably this reference to standing as a legal practitioner should now be read as a reference to standing as a lawyer entered upon the Roll of Lawyers. Practice in the Commonwealth and elsewhere is however allowed to count towards the necessary period of standing: Judicial Service Act, 1960 (C.A. 10), s. 8 (3).

Although art. 12, in prescribing the Presidential oath, provides for the making of an affirmation in lieu of an oath, no such provision is contained in art. 45. It therefore appears that a judge is precluded from taking advantage of s. 8 of the Oaths Act, 1960 (C.A. 12), which enables any person who objects to the taking of an oath and desires to make an affirmation in lieu thereof to do so without question.

The Chief Justice

Article 44 requires the President to appoint one of the judges of the Supreme Court to be Chief Justice of Ghana. The Chief Justice is constituted President of the Supreme Court and Head of the Judicial Service. Since the Chief Justice has administrative as well as judicial functions, the appointment is made personal to the President as indicated by the fact that the instrument of appointment is required to be made under the Presidential Seal, whereas appointments of judges are made under the Public Seal. For the same reason, art. 44(3) enables the appointment of a judge as Chief Justice to be revoked at any time by the President. This revocation will not however affect the status of the Chief Justice as a judge of the Supreme Court. Since the Chief Justice is required to be also a judge of the Supreme Court, it follows that his resignation, retirement or dismissal as a judge of the Supreme Court necessarily operates as a termination of his appointment as Chief Justice.

Apart from the functions conferred on him by art. 44, the Chief Justice has various other constitutional duties. He is the returning officer for the election of the President, and is required to administer the Presidential oath or affirmation on the assumption of office of the President (arts. 11, 12). He is the person appointed to receive the resignation of a President (art. 9). He also has the delicate task, in conjunction with the Speaker, of pronouncing on any allegation that the President is, by reason of physical or mental infirmity, unable to exercise the functions of his office (art. 18(4)). The functions of the Chief Justice as Head of the Judicial Service are set out in the Judicial Service Act, 1960 (C.A. 10).

Salaries and pensions of judges

Article 46 provides for the salaries and pensions of judges of the superior courts. Salaries are to be determined by the National Assembly and no judge may suffer a diminution in salary while he remains in office. In addition to his salary as a judge of the

Supreme Court, the Chief Justice is entitled to such additional allowance as may be determined by the National Assembly. All salaries and allowances paid under art. 46 and all pensions and other retiring allowances paid in respect of service as Chief Justice or other judge of a superior court are charged on the Consolidated Fund.

The Attorney-General

Article 47 provides for the office of Attorney-General. As is generally the case throughout the Constitution, no special qualifications are required for appointment. Since the office of the Attorney-General had been non-ministerial in character, art. 47(1) expressly indicates that the person appointed may be a Minister. On the other hand, he can be a civil servant or other person. Nevertheless some political character attaches to the office, as indicated by the provision which automatically vacates it on the assumption of office of a President. Other grounds for vacation of office are revocation of appointment by the President, and acceptance by the President of the resignation of the Attorney-General. It should be noted that resignation does not become effective in this case unless and until it is accepted.

The Attorney-General's functions, which are to be exercised in accordance with any directions of the President, are declared to be responsibility for the initiation, conduct and discontinuance of civil proceedings by the Republic and prosecutions for criminal offences, and for the defence of civil proceedings brought against the Republic. Nothing is said about other functions traditionally associated with the office, for example the tendering of legal advice to the Government. The effect of art. 47(2) is *inter alia* to place under the control of the Attorney-General, subject to the President's powers, the prosecution of criminal offences. Accordingly, no prosecution can be instituted if the Attorney-General requires that it should not be, and any prosecution which has been instituted may at any time be discontinued under a *nolle prosequi* entered by the Attorney-General. This does not of course mean that the consent of the Attorney-General is required before a prosecution can be instituted. Unless the Attorney-General intervenes, such consent will not be necessary unless it is required in a particular case by extrinsic law.

Powers of Mercy

Part VI ends by conferring powers of mercy upon the President. Article 48 enables the President, in respect of any criminal offence, to grant a pardon to the offender, to order a respite of the execution of any sentence, and to remit any sentence or any penalty or forfeiture incurred by reason of the offence. Nothing is said as to the effect of the pardon, but it may be assumed to have its normal result of obliterating the conviction or, if it is granted before conviction, the liability to prosecution, and to relieve the offender of any consequences which would otherwise flow from the offence. For example, he will be relieved of the disabilities imposed by s. 1 of the National Assembly Act, 1961 (Act 86). A pardon may be granted at any time, even after the completion of a term of imprisonment.

The power to order a respite of execution applies not only to the death penalty but to other forms of punishment. It would, for example, enable a sentence of imprisonment to be deferred. Remission of sentence may be total or partial. In the latter case it will amount to a reduction of the sentence. As part of the Republic Day Amnesty, one year was remitted of every sentence of imprisonment for three years or more which was being served on 1st July, 1960. Death sentences were also remitted.[1] Where a sentence of death is remitted, art. 48(2) empowers the President to order the offender to be imprisoned until such time as the President orders his release.[2]

10. Chieftaincy

The President is required by art. 13 to declare his adherence to the principle that chieftaincy in Ghana should be guaranteed and preserved. The only other references made in the Constitution to chieftaincy are in the provisions of Part VII dealing with Houses of Chiefs. Article 49 provides that there shall be a House of Chiefs for each Region of Ghana. Since art. 6 divides Ghana into eight Regions, eight Houses of Chiefs are therefore required. As there were only six Houses of Chiefs in being on Republic Day however, s. 9 of the Constitution (Consequential Provisions) Act, 1960 (C.A. 8) contained a transitional provision which, besides continuing in being the existing Houses of Chiefs, also provided that until a separate House of Chiefs could be established for each of the Central, Northern, Upper and Western Regions, the Northern Region House of Chiefs was to function for the new Northern and Upper Regions, while the Western Region House

---

[1] *Ghana Gazette*, 1st July, 1960, p. 13.
[2] On the consideration of a petition for the exercise of his powers of mercy, the President may refer the whole case, or a particular point, to the Supreme Court: Courts Act, 1960 (C.A. 9), s. 24.

M

of Chiefs was to function for the new Central and Western Regions.

Article 50 makes it clear that, apart from the mere existence of Houses of Chiefs, all matters relating to them are to be governed by the ordinary law. It provides that a House of Chiefs shall consist of such chiefs, and shall have such functions relating to customary law and other matters, as may be provided by law. The only feature of interest in art. 50 is the reference to customary law, demonstrating the importance attached to customary law by the makers of the Constitution and indicating the role intended to be played by Houses of Chiefs in its future development.

The Chieftaincy Act

The ordinary law relating to chieftaincy was recently consolidated and is now contained in the Chieftaincy Act, 1961 (Act 81), which is divided into eight parts.

Part I.—This opens with a statement of who is a chief. He is described as an individual who has been nominated, elected and installed as a chief in accordance with customary law and who is recognized as a chief by the Minister responsible for local government. The Minister may withdraw recognition if the chief has been destooled or if the Minister considers it to be in the public interest to do so. He may also prohibit any person who is not a chief from purporting to exercise chiefly functions and may require such a person to reside outside a specified area. Four categories of chiefs are laid down:

(*a*) the Asantehene, and paramount chiefs who are not subordinate to the Asantehene;

(*b*) paramount chiefs who are subordinate to the Asantehene;

(*c*) divisional chiefs;

(*d*) Adikrofo and other chiefs not falling within the preceding categories.

It is made an offence to commit any act with intent to undermine the lawful power and authority of a chief, and the arbitral powers of chiefs are expressly preserved.

Part II.—This provides for the grouping of states, or traditional areas as they are now to be called, into divisions. There is to be a divisional council for each division, presided over by the divisional chief. The customary functions of divisional councils are preserved, and the Minister may assign other functions to them.

Part III.—The former state councils are given the name of traditional councils, and jurisdiction is conferred on them to hear and determine any cause or matter affecting chieftaincy provided that neither the Asantehene nor a paramount chief is a party to the dispute. Councils must keep accounts of revenue and expenditure, and may continue to exercise their customary functions.

Part IV.—This contains the provisions dealing with Houses of Chiefs. It lays down the composition of each House and provides for the election of members and heads. Meetings may only take place as directed by the Minister, but if a matter is referred to it by the National Assembly or any Minister the House must consider the matter and report upon it. Accounts must be kept, and annual estimates of revenue and expenditure prepared. Each House is provided with a clerk and other staff.

Part V.—This deals with the conduct of stool disputes and other proceedings affecting chieftaincy. Where a case is considered by a traditional council the decision must be given according to customary law, and customary constitutional sanctions and awards may be ordered. Enforcement is however entrusted to the ordinary courts, and an aggrieved party may appeal to a judicial commissioner appointed under the Judicial Service Act, 1960 (C.A. 10). The judicial commissioner has original jurisdiction in a case to which the Asantehene or a paramount chief is a party, and which is thus beyond the jurisdiction of the traditional council. Proceedings before a judicial commissioner are initiated by application through the appropriate House of Chiefs. The commissioner may sit alone or with assessors, and his findings must be reported to the Minister, who is required to refer the report to the President. If the findings do not appear to the President to be correct he may vary them, and his decision on the matter is conclusive.

Part VI.—Stool property is defined, and where it consists of movables its alienation is prohibited without the consent of the traditional council and the Minister.[1] Stool property cannot be seized in execution at the suit of any person. Where recognition has been withdrawn from a chief or there is a stool dispute the Minister may safeguard the stool property by ordering a local authority or public officer to take temporary possession of it.

Part VII.—This contains provisions relating to customary law, which are discussed in Chapter 11, *post.*

Part VIII.—This contains miscellaneous provisions, including the repeal or revocation of a large number of previous enactments relating to chieftaincy.

---

[1] As to alienation of land, see the Stool Lands Control Act, 1959 (No. 79).

11. PUBLIC SERVICES AND ARMED FORCES

The Public Services

Article 51 specifically constitutes four Services as Public Services of Ghana, and enables further Services to be constituted by future law as Public Services within the meaning of art. 51 without the need for amendment of the article. The four Services specifically referred to are the Civil Service, the Judicial Service, the Police Service and the Local Government Service. None of these Services were in existence under these names at the time when the Constitution came into force. In the case of two of them Constituent Assembly Acts were passed to lay down the detailed organisation of the Services in question. These are the Civil Service Act, 1960 (C.A. 5) and the Judicial Service Act, 1960 (C.A. 10). Both Acts are original in character, and attempt to provide a complete legal framework for the two Services, covering the structure of the Service (including the creation of posts), the filling of vacancies, conditions of service, misconduct and unsatisfactory service and termination of service on retirement or otherwise. As respects the other two Services, Police and Local Government, the existing law was adapted by the Constitution (Consequential Provisions) Act, 1960 (C.A. 8). The previously existing Police Force was continued in being, and deemed to be the Police Service referred to in art. 51, by s. 10 of the Act.[1] Section 11 provided that the officers and employees of local authorities were to be the members of the Local Government Service referred to in art. 51.

The Civil Service

The function of civil servants is to advise the President and his Ministers and to carry into effect Government decisions and the requirements of administrative law. The British tradition of anonymity and Ministerial responsibility is preserved:

> " In every matter of policy, civil servants must be considered to be acting in accordance with the instructions of the Minister who is responsible for the Ministry in which they are employed."[2]

Since the Civil Service is the principal organ for the execution of Government policy, some details of its structure should be given here. In most countries which follow the British pattern, the structure of the Civil Service is shrouded in mystery. Details of Civil Service posts and their disposition are normally to be

---

[1] For a description of the Police Service as at present constituted see Rubin and Murray, *op. cit.*, pp. 126–129.
[2] Kwame Nkrumah: *I Speak of Freedom*, London, 1961, p. 78.

found only in the annual estimates, where they are submerged under a great mass of information and are in any case difficult of access. This used to be the position in Ghana, but an attempt was made in 1960 to rationalise the position.

Part II of the Civil Service Act, 1960 (C.A. 5) lays down the outlines of the structure of the Civil Service, and these are filled in by the Civil Service (Structure) Regulations, 1961 (L.I. 139). The combined effect of these provisions is as follows. The Civil Service consists of persons holding posts which are Civil Service posts either because they were created by or under the Civil Service Act or because they were created in some other way, but have been designated as Civil Service posts.[1] Civil Service posts are classified in a number of different ways for different purposes. These classifications, which cut across one another to a considerable extent, are as follows:

established and unestablished posts;
general and Departmental posts;
category A, B, C and D posts;
pensionable and non-pensionable posts.

Established posts are posts which are permanent in nature and whose numbers do not fluctuate greatly. They are therefore given a fixed complement. Each description of established posts constitutes a grade, and the complement is the number of posts which have been created in the grade. Unestablished posts on the other hand have no fixed complement. Their other characteristic is that they are found only in the lower reaches of the Service.

Established posts are divided into general and Departmental posts. As this nomenclature indicates, the general posts are common to the whole of the Service, whereas the Departmental posts are only found in a particular Department. The general posts are divided into five classes. There is a head of each class, who is responsible for the posting of members of the class to the various Departments. The classes, with their heads, are as follows:

administrative class — Secretary to the Cabinet
executive class — Principal Secretary (Establishments)
personnel class — Principal Secretary (Establishments)

---

[1] Members of the Civil Service Commission, although holding posts created by the Civil Service Act, are not civil servants.

clerical class   — Principal Secretary (Establishments)
secretarial class   — Principal Secretary (Establishments)
accounting class   — Accountant-General
machine class   — Principal Secretary (Establishments)

The Civil Service is divided up into Departments. Most of the Departments are grouped into Ministries, but there are a number of Departments which either cannot appropriately be included in a Ministry or are desired to be under the President's control. These are known as special Departments and are under the direct supervision of the President. At the time of writing there are sixty-three Departments in the Civil Service. Forty-three of these are grouped into twelve Ministries. The remaining twenty are special Departments. The names of the Ministries are Agriculture, Defence, Education and Social Welfare, Finance, Foreign Affairs, Health, Information, Interior, Local Government, Trade, Transport and Communications, and Works and Housing. The special Departments, which are not comprised in any Ministry, include the Office of the President, the Establishment Office, the Auditor-General's Department, the Office of the Clerk of the National Assembly, the Office of the Civil Service Commission, and the Offices of the various Regions. Recently added as special Departments are the Budget, Labour and Lands Secretariats.

Each Department consists of the Departmental posts in the Department, together with a number of general posts which are attached to it. The headquarters of each Ministry forms a separate Department mainly consisting of administrative, executive, clerical and secretarial posts which are attached to the Department. The senior official in a Ministry is normally the Principal Secretary, who is a member of the administrative class and constitutes the official head of the Ministry. As such he is responsible to his Minister for securing the general efficiency of the Ministry. The senior officer in each Department of the Ministry is described as the official head of the Department, and is responsible to the head of Ministry for matters relating to the administration of the Department. In the case of the special Departments the Secretary to the Cabinet, who in effect is the official head of the Civil Service, takes the place of the head of Ministry. He is directly responsible to the President for securing the general efficiency of all the special Departments. The senior officer in each special Department is described as the Head of Department, and is responsible to the Secretary to the Cabinet for matters relating to the administration of the Department.

All Civil Service posts are divided into categories A, B, C and D. These categories are relevant for such matters as the filling of vacancies and the conduct of disciplinary proceedings. Category A consists of a small number of the most senior civil servants, including all the Principal Secretaries; Category B consists of civil servants in receipt of a salary of £G1,950 or above (not being in category A); category C consists of civil servants with salaries ranging from £G450 to £G1,950 and the remainder are in category D.

Although there is usually a different Minister in charge of each Ministry, this is not necessarily so. Section 5 of the Cabinet and Ministers Act, 1960 (C.A. 3) states that there shall be deemed to be a portfolio for each Ministry created under the Civil Service Act, which may be assigned by the President to a Minister or held by the President. At the time of writing all portfolios have been assigned to various Ministers.

Members of the Public Services

Article 51(2) of the Constitution vests the appointment, promotion, transfer, termination of appointment, dismissal and disciplinary control of members of the Public Services in the President. This is expressed to be " subject to the provisions of the Constitution and save as is otherwise provided by law ". Any law may therefore curtail or regulate the powers thus conferred on the President, and indeed this is done by the Civil Service Act, 1960 (C.A. 5) and the Judicial Service Act, 1960 (C.A. 10). The provisions of the Constitution referred to are those safeguarding the independence of the Auditor-General and the judges of the Supreme Court and the High Court. Article 51 is silent as to the composition of the four Public Services specified, leaving this to be established by ordinary law. It would be possible under the Civil Service Act, 1960 (C.A. 5) for the Auditor-General to be made a civil servant. In the case of the judges, s. 1 of the Judicial Service Act, 1960 (C.A. 10) makes them members of the Judicial Service, while art. 44(2) constitutes the Chief Justice as Head of the Judicial Service. By virtue of arts. 38(1) and 45(3), the holders of these offices cannot be dismissed by the President except under the authority of a vote of the National Assembly which conforms to the requirements of those sections. Nor can the President exercise disciplinary control in these cases by reductions in salary, since salaries are to be determined by the National Assembly and cannot be reduced during the term of office of a particular person (arts. 38(4) and 46).

Article 52 safeguards the pensions, gratuities and other allowances payable on retirement to members of the Civil Service, the Judicial Service and the Police Service by charging them on the Consolidated Fund and thus removing them from the field of Parliamentary Votes and executive action. Members of the Local Government Service are excluded from this provision since their retiring allowances, if given at all, would not normally be drawn from central funds.

The Armed Forces

The Armed Forces consist of the Ghana Army, as successor to the Gold Coast Regiment and the Royal West Africa Frontier Force, together with small naval and air force units.

Article 8(3) constitutes the President Commander-in-Chief of the Armed Forces and his powers as such are dealt with in art. 54. The powers are not exhaustively defined, but certain matters are specifically mentioned, others being left at large. The two matters specified are the power to commission persons as officers, and the power to order the Forces to engage in operations. These may be for the defence of Ghana, for the preservation of public order, for relief in cases of emergency or for any other purpose appearing to the Commander-in-Chief to be expedient. Section (1) is made subject to the provisions of any enactment for the time being in force, so that the powers referred to are in the nature of reserved powers available except in so far as they may be modified by law. Additional powers may of course be specified by law. The existing law relating to the Armed Forces continued to operate subject to the amendments contained in the Second Schedule to the Constitution (Consequential Provisions) Act, 1960 (C.A. 8).[1] Article 54(2), which is not made subject to the provisions of ordinary law, gives the Commander-in-Chief an overriding power to dismiss or suspend from duty any member of the Armed Forces if it appears to him expedient to do so for the security of the State.

By an entrenched provision, art. 53 prohibits the President and any other person from raising any armed force except under the authority of an Act of Parliament.

---

[1] This law has now been revised and consolidated: see the Armed Forces Act, 1962 (Act 105).

PART II

THE STATE AND THE INDIVIDUAL

SUMMARY

PAGE

CHAPTER 4. Citizens and Aliens 187

CHAPTER 5. Liberty and State Security . . . 213

CHAPTER 4

CITIZENS AND ALIENS

For a number of purposes the State treats individuals as divided into two categories: citizens of Ghana and aliens. At independence these replaced the previous categories of British subjects and aliens, the latter category having been subdivided into British protected persons and others. Although in theory the category of aliens is now subdivided into Commonwealth citizens and others, in fact the law treats all aliens alike, apart from allowing Commonwealth citizens to obtain Ghana citizenship on slightly easier conditions. Every person who is a citizen of Ghana or of any other Commonwealth country has by virtue of that citizenship the status in Ghana of a Commonwealth citizen.[1]

1. TYPES OF CITIZENSHIP

The result of the laws passed since independence is to create five types of Ghana citizenship: by birth, by descent, by marriage, by registration and by naturalisation. Citizenship by marriage does not however form part of the definitive law, being applicable only to women married before 11th May, 1957.

The first Act to be passed by the Parliament of Ghana after independence was the Ghana Nationality and Citizenship Act, 1957 (No. 1). As part of the programme of statute law reform this was recently replaced by the Ghana Nationality Act, 1961 (Act 62), which did little more than reproduce the effect of the 1957 Act with changes made necessary by the transition to republican status. It did however abrogate the provision by which Commonwealth citizens were not classified as aliens. Although the 1957 Act has been repealed it is still necessary to refer to it. To avoid duplication, and give a detailed picture of the present law of citizenship, the combined effect of the two Acts will now be considered.

What follows is an attempt to state the law with some degree

---

[1] Ghana Nationality Act, 1961 (Act 62), s. 12. This is the famous " common clause " which derives from s. 1 of the British Nationality Act, 1948 and is found in the law of most Commonwealth countries.

of precision, but a word of warning is necessary. Although the wording of the Acts of 1957 and 1961 is relatively simple, it conceals a mass of complexity. In many cases it is a formidable task to ascertain conclusively whether or not a person is a citizen of Ghana. In the case of an older person it will be necessary to consult not only the two Ghana Acts but also various Acts of the United Kingdom Parliament, such as the British Nationality Act, 1948, and the British Nationality and Status of Aliens Acts 1914 to 1943. With a person born before 1914, it may also be necessary to consider the common law rules relating to nationality. Since the citizenship of the parents is often relevant, it follows that the same sort of difficulty may arise even in the case of a person born since independence. It will be seen therefore that a full account of Ghana citizenship is beyond the scope of this chapter. All we can do here is to indicate the main outlines and caution the reader that they cannot be relied upon in every case.[1]

Four general points may be made at this stage. First, the following rules for ascertaining citizenship are of course qualified where a person has renounced or been deprived of his citizenship. Secondly, any reference to a child includes a child born out of wedlock, and references to a father, mother or parent are to be construed accordingly.[2] Thirdly, it is a general rule with regard to posthumous children that the status of the father at the birth of the child is treated as being the status which existed at the father's death.[3] Fourthly, where place of birth is relevant it should be noted that both in the law of the United Kingdom (which, as will be seen, may need to be applied to ascertain whether a person was a citizen of the United Kingdom and Colonies or a British protected person on a material date) and in the law of Ghana a person born aboard a ship or aircraft is deemed to have been born in the country in which the ship or aircraft is registered.[4] Thus, although the territories of Ghana

---

[1] More detailed information may be found in Clive Parry, *Nationality and Citizenship Laws of the Commonwealth*, London, 1957 (Vol. 1) and 1960 (Vol. 2). Where doubt exists in a particular case (whether on a question of fact or law) it can be resolved by the Minister responsible for citizenship, who has power to issue a conclusive certificate of citizenship under s. 15 of the Ghana Nationality Act, 1961 (Act 62).

[2] Ghana Nationality Act, 1961 (Act 62), s. 21. For difficulties which may arise where the *parent* is illegitimate see Parry, *op. cit.*, pp. 1246, 1254.

[3] *Cf.* Ghana Nationality Act, 1961 (Act 62), s. 13.

[4] British Nationality Act, 1948, s. 32 (5); Ghana Nationality Act, 1961 (Act 62), s. 21 (3).

include the territorial waters, a person born aboard a foreign ship in a Ghanaian port is deemed not to have been born in Ghana.

Citizenship by birth

In principle it may be said that anyone who was born in Ghana after independence, or was born before independence in any territory now included in Ghana, is a citizen of Ghana by birth unless, at the time of his birth, his father was an alien enjoying diplomatic immunity.[1] A person born before the commencement of the 1957 Act will not however be a citizen by birth unless at least one of his parents or grandparents was born in Ghana. The position is shown more precisely in the following table:

Citizens of Ghana by birth	*Exceptions*
Every person born in Ghana before 11th May, 1957 (the date of commencement of the 1957 Act).	1. A person none of whose parents or grandparents was born in Ghana. 2. A person who was not a ctiizen of the United Kingdom and Colonies or a British protected person on 10th May, 1957.

[Ghana Nationality and Citizenship Act, 1957, s. 4; Ghana Nationality Act, 1961, s.1]

Every person born in Ghana after 10th May, 1957.	A person born at a time when: (*a*) one or both of his parents possessed diplomatic immunity in Ghana, and (*b*) neither of his parents was a citizen of Ghana.

[Ghana Nationality and Citizenship Act, 1957, s. 7; Ghana Nationality Act, 1961, s. 1]

It will be observed from the above table that in order to be

---

[1] In the following discussion a reference to Ghana should, in relation to birth or residence before 6th March, 1957, be treated as a reference to any territory included in Ghana on that date (*cf.* Ghana Nationality Act, 1961 (Act 62), s. 21 (2)). Except for the word father, references to males include females (*cf.* Interpretation Act, 1960 (C.A. 4), s. 26).

certain whether a person born in Ghana before 11th May, 1957 is a citizen by birth, it is necessary to find out whether he was a citizen of the United Kingdom and Colonies or a British protected person on 10th May, 1957. This is a matter of some difficulty. An outline of the position is shown in the following table:

Persons who were citizens of the United Kingdom and Colonies on 10th May, 1957	Exceptions
Every person born in the Gold Coast Colony or Ashanti before 1st January, 1949.	A person born at a time when his father: (a) enjoyed diplomatic immunity within the dominions of the British Crown; and (b) was not a British subject.
[British Nationality Act, 1948, s. 12 (1); Status of Aliens Act, 1914, s. 1; common law.][1]	
Every person born in the Northern Territories or British Togoland before 1st January, 1949, and at a time when his father was a British subject.	None.
[British Nationality Act, 1948, s. 12 (3); British Nationality and Status of Aliens Act, 1943, s. 2; common law.][2]	
Every person born in the Gold Coast Colony or Ashanti after 31st December, 1948, and before 6th March, 1957.	A person born at a time when his father: (a) enjoyed diplomatic immunity within the United Kingdom and Colonies, and (b) was not a citizen of the United Kingdom and Colonies.
[British Nationality Act, 1948, s. 4; Ghana Independence Act, 1957, s. 2.]	

---

[1] See Parry, *op. cit.*, pp. 153 *et seq.*
[2] See *ibid.*, pp. 157 *et seq.*

Persons who were citizens of the United Kingdom and Colonies on 10th May, 1957	*Exceptions*
Every person born in the Gold Coast Colony or Ashanti after 5th March, 1957 and before 11th May, 1957, and at a time when his father was a citizen of the United Kingdom and Colonies[1].	A person born at a time when his father was a citizen of the United Kingdom and Colonies by descent only, and the conditions specified in the proviso to s. 5 of the British Nationality Act, 1948 were not satisfied.

[British Nationality Act, 1948, s. 5]

Every person born in the Northern Territories or Togoland under United Kingdom Trusteeship after 31st December, 1948 and before 11th May, 1957, and at a time when his father was a citizen of the United Kingdom and Colonies.	A person born at a time when his father was a citizen of the United Kingdom and Colonies by descent only, and the conditions specified in the proviso to s. 5 of the British Nationality Act, 1948 were not satisfied.

[British Nationality Act, 1948, s. 5]

---

[1] This is inserted here to help fill a gap which, as Dr. Parry points out (*op. cit.*, p. 1246) occurs in the Ghana transitional provisions. A person born between 6th March and 10th May, 1957 would not be a citizen of the United Kingdom and Colonies under s. 4 of the British Nationality Act, 1948, because of the changes made by s. 2 of the Ghana Independence Act, 1957. In concluding from this however that " any person born in Ghana of native parentage [between the said dates] is, apparently stateless and no person there born of any other parentage . . . between the relevent dates is a citizen of Ghana " Dr. Parry appears, with great respect, to overlook s. 5 of the 1948 Act. The fathers of most persons born at this time in what was formerly the Colony or Ashanti would still be citizens of the United Kingdom and Colonies, and the children would obtain their father's status under British law by virtue of s. 5. The present author adopts Dr. Parry's conclusion (*op. cit.*, pp. 1053, 1257) that s. 2 of the Ghana Independence Act, 1957 did not deprive existing citizens of the United Kingdom and Colonies of their status. The contrary proposition appears arguable, though its acceptance would be disastrous.

Persons who were British protected persons on 10th May, 1957	*Exceptions*
Every person born in the Northern Territories or British Togoland before 6th March, 1957.	None.

[Ghana Nationality and Citizenship Act, 1957, s. 2 (1); Ghana Independence Act, 1957, s. 2; British Nationality Act, 1948, ss. 30, 32 (1); British Protectorates, Protected States and Protected Persons Order in Council, 1949 (S.I. 1949 No. 140), ss. 5, 9]

Citizenship by descent

A person born outside Ghana may in certain circumstances be a citizen of Ghana by descent. The position differs according to whether the birth occurred before or after the commencement of the Ghana Nationality and Citizenship Act, 1957. Every person born outside Ghana before 11th May, 1957, is a citizen of Ghana by descent if:

(*a*) he was a citizen of the United Kingdom and Colonies or a British protected person on 10th May, 1957 and

(*b*) at least one of his parents was born in Ghana and was on 10th May, 1957, or at his death if it occurred before that date, a citizen of the United Kingdom and Colonies or a British protected person.[1]

Every person born outside Ghana after 10th May, 1957 is a citizen of Ghana by descent if at the time of his birth:

(*a*) his father was a citizen of Ghana otherwise than by descent; or

(*b*) his mother was a citizen of Ghana by birth.

Again it is necessary, for those born before the commencement of the 1957 Act, to consider British nationality law. The following table gives an outline of the position in relation to persons born outside Ghana:[2]

---

[1] Ghana Nationality Act, 1961 (Act 62), s. 2; Ghana Nationality and Citizenship Act, 1957 (No. 1), s. 5. On the difficulties which may arise if the parents died before the commencement of the British Nationality Act, 1948, see Parry, *op. cit.*, p. 1246.

[2] In considering the status of a *parent* either this table or the one beginning on p. 190, *ante*, may be relevant, according to whether the parent was born outside or within Ghana. Certain categories in these tables overlap, but it suffices if a person falls within any one of them. The reader is again cautioned that the tables do not purport to cover every conceivable case.

Persons who were citizens of the United Kingdom and Colonies on 10th May, 1957	*Exceptions*
Every person born before 1st January, 1949 outside Ghana but within the territory comprised on 31st December, 1948, in the United Kingdom and Colonies.	A person born at a time when his father: (*a*) enjoyed diplomatic immunity within the dominions of the British Crown; and (*b*) was not a British subject.

[British Nationality Act, 1948, s. 12 (1); Status of Aliens Act, 1914, s. 1; common law.][1]

Every person born before 1st January, 1949 outside Ghana but within the territory comprised on 31st December, 1948 in a British protectorate, protected state or trust territory, and at a time when his father was a British subject.	A person born at a time when his father satisfied none of the following conditions: (*a*) that he was born within the allegiance of the British Crown; or (*b*) that he had been granted a certificate of naturalisation; or (*c*) that he was in the service of the British Crown.

[British Nationality Act, 1948, s. 12 (3); Status of Aliens Act, 1914, s. 1; common law][2]

Every person who was born before 1st January, 1949 in a territory which was neither within the dominions of the British Crown nor under British protection, and whose father was born, or had been naturalised, in the United Kingdom and Colonies.	None.

[British Nationality Act, 1948, s. 12 (2); Status of Aliens Act, 1914, s. 1; common law]

---

[1] See Parry, *op. cit.*, pp. 153 *et seq.*
[2] See Parry, *op. cit.*, pp. 157 *et seq*

N

Persons who were citizens of the United Kingdom and Colonies on 10th May, 1957	*Exceptions*
Every person born outside Ghana before 1st January, 1949 who was a British subject immediately before that date.	A person who on 1st January, 1949 was actually or potentially a citizen of Canada, Australia, New Zealand, the Union of South Africa, Newfoundland, India, Pakistan, Southern Rhodesia or Ceylon, or was a citizen of Eire.

[British Nationality Act, 1948, ss. 12 (4), 32 (7); Status of Aliens Act, 1914, s. 1; common law]

Every person born outside Ghana but within the United Kingdom and Colonies after 31st December, 1948 and before 11th May, 1957.	A person born at a time when his father: (*a*) enjoyed diplomatic immunity within the United Kingdom and Colonies, and (*b*) was not a citizen of the United Kingdom and Colonies.

[British Nationality Act, 1948, s. 4]

Every person born outside Ghana after 31st December, 1948 and before 11th May, 1957, and at a time when his father was a citizen of the United Kingdom and Colonies.	A person born at a time when his father was a citizen of the United Kingdom and Colonies by descent only, and did not satisfy the conditions specified in the proviso to s. 5 of the British Nationality Act, 1948.

[British Nationality Act, 1948, s. 5]

Every person naturalised in the United Kingdom and Colonies before 11th May, 1957.	None.

[British Nationality Act, 1948, ss. 10, 12 (1)(b), 32 (1)]

Persons who were citizens of the United Kingdom and Colonies on 10th May, 1957	*Exceptions*
Every person registered as a citizen of the United Kingdom and Colonies under s. 6, 7, 8 or 12 (6) of the British Nationality Act, 1948 before 11th May, 1957.	None.

Persons who were British protected persons on 10th May, 1957	*Exceptions*
1. Every person born before 11th May, 1957, in a British protectorate or trust territory outside Ghana. 2. Every person born before 28th January, 1949 elsewhere than in a British protectorate or trust territory of a father who was born in a British protectorate or trust territory. 3. Every person born after 28th January, 1949[1] elsewhere than in a British protectorate or trust territory of a father who was born in a British protectorate or trust territory and was a British protected person at the time of that person's birth.	None.

[Ghana Nationality and Citizenship Act, 1957, s. 2 (1); British Nationality Act, 1948, ss. 30, 32 (1); British Protectorates Protected States and Protected Persons Order in Council, 1949 (S.I. 140), ss. 5, 9.]

Citizenship by marriage

The effect of s. 6 of the Ghana Nationality and Citizenship Act, 1957 (No. 1) (which is preserved by s. 20 of the Ghana

---

[1] This makes no provision for a person born *on* 28th January, 1949, but such seems to be the effect of the wording of s. 9 of the 1949 Order in Council.

Nationality Act, 1961 (Act 62) was to make certain women citizens of Ghana by virtue of their marriage. The provision only applies to women married before the commencement of the 1957 Act. Marriage thereafter does not confer citizenship, although, as we shall see, it may make it easier to acquire citizenship by administrative action.

Section 6 of the 1957 Act provides that a woman is a citizen of Ghana by virtue of her marriage if she satisfies the following conditions:

(a) that before 11th May, 1957 she married a man who on that date became (or but for his death would have become) a citizen of Ghana; and

(b) that on 10th May, 1957 she was by virtue of her marriage a citizen of the United Kingdom and Colonies or a British protected person (whether by registration or by operation of law).

The enactments governing the first condition have already been dealt with. The second condition will be satisfied in the following cases:

1. Where the marriage took place before 1st January, 1949 and:

(a) the woman was a British subject on 31st December, 1948, or ceased to be a British subject on or during the marriage; and

(b) the husband became (or but for his death would have become) a citizen of the United Kingdom and Colonies by virtue of the transitional provisions contained in s. 12(1)–(4) of the British Nationality Act, 1948.[1]

2. Where the woman was, before 11th May, 1957, registered as a citizen of the United Kingdom and Colonies under s. 6(2) of the British Nationality Act, 1948.

3. Where the woman was, before 11th May, 1957, registered as a British protected person under s. 11 of the British Protectorates, Protected States and Protected Persons Order in Council, 1949.

Citizenship by registration

A person who is not a citizen of Ghana by operation of law, that is in one of the ways described above, may become a citizen

---

[1] British Nationality Act, 1948, ss. 12 (5), 14.

by administrative action. Persons in certain favoured categories may become citizens by registration; others must attempt to obtain naturalisation. In either case the grant of citizenship is discretionary rather than as of right, but the qualifications required for registration are less strict.

There are four categories of persons who are qualified for registration, as follows:

1. A citizen of any Commonwealth country, or any other country which has been approved by the President for that purpose, who has attained the age of twenty-one and is not of unsound mind, and who satisfies the Minister responsible for citizenship[1] that:

(*a*) he is of good character; and

(*b*) he has sufficient knowledge of a language indigenous to and in current use in Ghana; and

(*c*) he is ordinarily resident in Ghana and has been so resident throughout the period of five years (or such shorter period as the Minister may in the special circumstances of any particular case accept) immediately preceding his application.

2. A person who was born outside Ghana after 10th May, 1957, who has attained the age of twenty-one and is not of unsound mind, and whose father or mother was, at the time of his birth, a citizen of Ghana by descent.

3. A woman (whether or not of full age and capacity) who is married to a citizen of Ghana, or who was married to a citizen of Ghana and has not since re-married.

4. A person who has not attained the age of twenty-one.

In the case of the first three categories the decision whether to grant citizenship by registration is taken by the President acting on the advice of the Cabinet. In the case of the fourth category, the decision is taken by the Minister responsible for citizenship. Only in special circumstances will a minor who is not the child of a citizen of Ghana be registered under this category.[2]

Where a person is granted citizenship by registration he

---

[1] Since independence the Minister of the Interior has been responsible for citizenship.

[2] Ghana Nationality Act, 1961 (Act 62), ss. 3, 4, 9, 21 (1), (4).

becomes a citizen on the date on which he is registered.[1] Before
he can be registered (unless he is a minor) he must take an oath
or affirmation to be faithful and bear true allegiance to the
Republic of Ghana, and to uphold the Constitution. The oath
or affirmation also embodies a renunciation of allegiance owed
to any other person or State.[2] So far the procedure has been
little used; in the period between independence and mid-1961
only ten persons were registered as citizens of Ghana.

Citizenship by Naturalisation

A person who has attained the age of twenty-one years and is
not of unsound mind may be granted a certificate of naturalisation
if he satisfies the Minister responsible for citizenship that:
  (*a*) he is of good character; and
  (*b*) he has sufficient knowledge of a language indigenous to and
       in current use in Ghana; and
  (*c*) he possesses certain residence qualifications.
The residence qualifications are somewhat complicated. There
are three conditions, all of which must be fulfilled:
  (*a*) the applicant must have resided in Ghana throughout the
       preceding twelve months. In special circumstances however
       a period of twelve months residence followed by a break
       of not more than six months may be treated as satisfying
       this condition;
  (*b*) during the period beginning eight years before the date of
       application and ending one year before that date the appli-
       cant must have resided in Ghana for periods amounting
       to at least five years. Again in special circumstances this
       condition may be relaxed. Residence in a Commonwealth
       country or other approved country may be treated as if it
       were residence in Ghana, and residence before the beginning
       of the eight-year period may be counted towards the aggre-
       gate of five years;
  (*c*) the applicant must intend to reside in Ghana if granted
       naturalisation.
The decision whether to grant a certificate of naturalisation
rests with the Minister responsible for citizenship, but no certificate may be granted without the approval of the President
acting on the advice of the Cabinet.[3]

---

[1] *Ibid.*, s. 5.
[2] *Ibid.*, ss. 3 (4), 8.
[3] Ghana Nationality Act, 1961 (Act 62), ss. 6, 7, 9, 21 (1), (4).

Where a certificate of naturalisation is granted the applicant does not become a citizen until he has taken an oath or affirmation to be faithful and bear true allegiance to the Republic of Ghana, and to uphold the Constitution. The oath or affirmation also embodies a renunciation of allegiance owed to any other person or State. When it has been taken, citizenship at once becomes effective and relates back to the date on which the certificate of naturalisation was granted.[1] Between independence and mid-1961 forty-six persons became naturalised Ghanaians.

2. LOSS OF CITIZENSHIP

Citizenship may be lost either by renunciation or deprivation.

Renunciation

A citizen of Ghana who has attained the age of twenty-one years (or is a woman of less age who has been married), who is not of unsound mind, and who is a citizen of some other country may make a declaration of renunciation of Ghana citizenship. The declaration becomes effective only when registered by the Minister responsible for citizenship, who may withhold registration if in his opinion the declaration is contrary to public policy. Subject to this overriding consideration, the Minister is obliged to register if he is satisfied that the declarant is not ordinarily resident in Ghana but in other cases may exercise his discretion.[2]

Deprivation

A person who is a citizen of Ghana by birth, descent or marriage can only be deprived of his citizenship if he voluntarily acquires citizenship of another country, but in the case of citizens by registration or naturalisation certain additional grounds for deprivation are laid down. No ground applies in the case of any person unless the Minister responsible for citizenship is satisfied that its existence means that it is not conducive to the public good that that person should continue to be a citizen. Nor can the Minister make a deprivation order without the approval of the President, acting on the advice of the Cabinet.

The full terms of the ground of deprivation applicable to all citizens are that the Minister is satisfied that the person in

---

[1] Ghana Nationality Act, 1961 (Act 62), ss. 6, 8.
[2] *Ibid.*, s. 10.

question " by a voluntary and formal act other than marriage " has acquired citizenship of another country.

Two further grounds apply only to a citizen by registration or naturalisation:

(*a*) that he has, on being so required by the Minister, failed to renounce his citizenship of any other country or to take the oath of allegiance within a specified time.[1]

(*b*) that the Minister is satisfied that the citizen obtained registration or naturalisation by means of fraud, false representation or concealment of any material 'fact.

In the case of a citizen by naturalisation, four additional grounds are laid down, namely where the Minister is satisfied that the citizen has shown himself to be disloyal to the Republic or its Government, or has traded with the enemy in time of war, or has within five years after naturalisation been sentenced to imprisonment for twelve months or more, or has been resident abroad for a continuous period of seven years without notifying his desire to retain his citizenship.[2]

No person has so far (mid-1961) been deprived of Ghana citizenship.

3. ALLEGIANCE

Until the advent of the Republic, citizens of Ghana, like other persons within Her Majesty's protection, owed allegiance to the Queen. This obligation ceased on 1st July, 1960, but the concept of allegiance was not dropped. Although historically a relationship between a monarch and his subject, and therefore in theory unsuited to a republic, allegiance had become so familiar a condition that, with a transference from the monarch to the Republic, it was retained without any enquiry into its appropriateness.[3] An oath or affirmation of allegiance to the

---

[1] Since naturalisation or registration only becomes effective when the oath of allegiance (which embodies a renunciation of foreign allegiance) is taken, this ground could operate only in rare cases.

[2] Ghana Nationality Act, 1961 (Act 62), s. 11.

[3] The concept of allegiance is of course found in the rules of customary law governing relations between chiefs. In this connection it was defined by Casely Hayford as " that *personal* relationship between the occupants of two stools whereby the inferior acknowledges the authority of the superior over him. Such acknowledgment may take the form of military or other service, and occasionally an *allegiance fee* ": *Gold Coast Native Institutions*, London, 1903, pp. 51–52.

Republic of Ghana, coupled with an undertaking to uphold the Constitution, is in one form or another required to be taken by many persons from the President downwards.[1]

Historically the relationship of allegiance connotes a duty of protection borne by the monarch coupled with a duty to be faithful, on pain of committal for treason, borne by the subject. This is still the position in the United Kingdom, but in Ghana the law of treason was in 1959 separated from the concept of allegiance to the monarch. Until then the English law of treason had applied in Ghana but the Treason Act, 1959 (No. 73) laid down entirely new provisions.[2] References to the British monarch were dropped, and the offence of treason was redefined in terms more suited to the forthcoming Republic. No reference was made to allegiance and treason can now be committed by any person, whether a citizen or alien. An alien cannot however be guilty of treason for anything done outside Ghana.[3]

What then is left of the concept of allegiance? It may be said that every person in Ghana, and every Ghana citizen elsewhere, owes a certain duty to the Republic which is the same whether or not he has actually taken an oath of allegiance.[4] This duty will be recognised by the courts in various ways, though punishment for its breach will be imposed only in accordance with specific enactments such as those relating to treason and sedition. Indirect recognition of the duty may take such forms as holding void a contract which is inconsistent with it or treating as defamatory an allegation that it has been broken. Similar indirect recognition may be given of the concomitant duty of protection owed by the Republic itself.[5] Although no longer personal to a sovereign, allegiance as an aspect of patriotic feeling still has a place in Ghana.

---

[1] See, *e.g.*, the Oaths Act, 1960 (C.A. 12), Sch. II. The list includes Ministers, judges, Members of Parliament, members of the armed forces, senior civil servants and aliens attaining citizenship by registration or naturalisation.

[2] The Act is now embodied in the Criminal Code, 1960 (Act 29), ss. 180–182.

[3] This of course may work more favourably to aliens than the previous rule, as applied in *Joyce* v. *Director of Public Prosecutions*, [1946] 1 All E.R. 186; [1946] A.C. 347.

[4] In some respects this duty may extend to a non-citizen out of Ghana if he holds a Ghana passport and thus claims the protection of the Republic. *Cf.* Foreign Enlistment Act, 1961 (Act 75), s. 1 (2), p. 209, *post*).

[5] *Cf. Glasbrook* v. *Glamorgan County Council*, [1925] A.C. 270.

4. ENTRY INTO GHANA

Entry into Ghana is regulated by the Immigration Act, 1957 (No. 15). Every person entering Ghana, whether an alien or a citizen, is required to satisfy the immigration authorities that he is entitled to do so. Certain classes of alien are described as prohibited immigrants, and may not enter except in special circumstances. These include persons who are destitute or of unsound mind, or whose entry has been declared by the Minister of the Interior to be not conducive to the public good, or who have failed to satisfy certain health requirements.[1]

In most cases an alien cannot enter Ghana without a valid passport and an entry permit. A permit to remain in Ghana may be granted at the discretion of the immigration officer and may be made subject to conditions regulating the immigrant's place of residence, type of employment and other activities. It will be valid for a limited period only. The permit is subject to revocation or variation of its conditions.[2] A person who remains in Ghana after his permit has expired, or after he has broken any of the conditions of the permit, is guilty of an offence and liable to deportation.[3] The permit may be renewed either before or after it has expired.[4]

While in Ghana an alien can only obtain employment in Government service or with an employer who is licensed to employ him. As a condition of obtaining such a licence the employer may have to guarantee the payment of the cost of repatriating the alien if his employment ceases.[5]

5. DEPORTATION

All modern states claim the right to rid themselves of undesirable aliens, and Ghana is no exception.[6] Deportation is dealt with by the Deportation Act, 1957 (No. 14), the provisions of which do

---

[1] Immigration Act, 1957 (No. 15), s. 4.
[2] *Ibid.*, s. 10(3).
[3] *Ibid.*, ss. 19, 20.
[4] *Ibid.*, s. 13.
[5] *Ibid.*, ss. 15, 16.
[6] It was not always so. In Britain for example the prerogative of the Crown to order aliens to withdraw from the realm fell into disuse after the death of Queen Elizabeth I and was only revived (in statutory form) at the time of the French Revolution. Great protests attended its revival and these have been renewed from time to time ever since. In its present form the British control of aliens dates from the First World War.

not differ in substance from those in force during the colonial regime.[1] The power to deport is restricted to aliens, although in the early days of independence two Ghanaians were deported under a special Act.[2] In this connection, as generally, Commonwealth citizens other than Ghanaians are treated as aliens.

The Government have complete discretion to order the deportation of any alien. The only necessary preliminary is a declaration by the Minister of the Interior that the alien's presence in Ghana is " not conducive to the public good ". The other grounds for deportation are a conviction for an offence punishable with imprisonment (coupled with a recommendation by the court that the offender be deported), a finding that the alien is destitute or of unsound mind or a prostitute, and a finding that the alien is a prohibited immigrant.[3] The deportation order need not be limited to the alien himself but may include his dependents, whether or not separate grounds for deportation exist in their case.[4]

An alien against whom a deportation order is made must leave Ghana and not return while the order is in force. If he does so return he is liable to imprisonment for up to five years.[5] While awaiting transportation from Ghana the alien may be kept in custody.[6] The use made since independence of the power to deport may be judged from the following figures of the number of persons subjected to deportation orders. In not all of these cases was it found possible to effect the deportation of the alien in question.

Year	No. of persons
1957	68
1958	162
1959	75
1960	54

---

[1] Replacing the Aliens Ordinance (Cap. 49) and the Immigrant British Subjects (Deportation) Ordinance (Cap. 50).
[2] Deportation (Othman Larden and Amadu Baba) Act, 1957 (No. 19).
[3] Deportation Act, 1957 (No. 14), s. 4; Immigration Act, 1957 (No. 15), s. 20.
[4] Deportation Act, 1957 (No. 14). s. 5 (3). This power does not extend to a dependant who is not himself an alien: *ibid.*, s. 3.
[5] Deportation (Amendment) Act, 1958 (No. 45), s. 2.
[6] Deportation Act, 1957 (No. 14), s. 9.

Supervision orders

Repatriation in consequence of a deportation order cannot usually be effected without the co-operation of the authorities in the country of which the alien is a citizen. Where this co-operation is not forthcoming, or the alien's nationality is in doubt, it may not be practicable to enforce the order. Difficulties of this kind led to the introduction in 1959 of supervision orders.[1]

If, on the expiration of six months from the making of a deportation order, deportation has not been effected, or if, at any earlier time, the Minister of the Interior is satisfied that deportation is for any reason impracticable or undesirable, he may make a supervision order. This suspends the operation of the deportation order, but imposes restrictions on the alien's activities in Ghana. He will probably be required to report to the police at stated intervals and to live within a specified area. His political activities may be curtailed, and he may be given directions as to his employment. Unless earlier revoked, the supervision order will remain operative for five years and then both it and the original deportation order will expire.

6. EXTRADITION

Extradition is the process by which a person who has committed a serious crime in one country, but has removed himself to another, is handed over for trial to the authorities of the country in which he committed the crime. The comity of nations prevents the police of one country from crossing the border of another to pursue and capture a criminal, even if they could do so without infringing local immigration laws. It is generally recognised to be undesirable however that a criminal should escape scot free on crossing the border of a foreign country, and while this could be met in some cases by repatriation under the deportation laws or by criminal proceedings brought by the authorities of the country of refuge there remain instances where some other procedure is needed. If, for example, a citizen of country A commits a crime in country B and then takes refuge in country C, repatriation would not enable the authorities of country B to lay hands on the criminal and a prosecution could not usually be brought in country C for an offence committed elsewhere. Accordingly the

---

[1] Deportation (Amendment) Act, 1959 (No. 65), s. 2.

practice grew in the last century of concluding bilateral extradition treaties whereby each party agreed to surrender fugitive criminals to the other if certain conditions were satisfied.

Until very recently extradition from Ghana was governed by British law, and some knowledge of this is necessary for an understanding of the present position. The law was in two parts, dealing respectively with cases where the surrender of the criminal was sought by a foreign country or a country within the Commonwealth.

Extradition Acts, 1870 to 1932

The Extradition Act, 1870[1] laid down the procedure for the surrender of fugitive criminals to foreign countries with whom extradition treaties had been made by the British Government and to which, in consequence, the Act had been applied by Order in Council. At the time of Ghana's independence there were about fifty such treaties and in most cases the extradition procedure applied throughout Her Majesty's dominions.[2] In the Gold Coast and Ashanti it applied subject to modifications contained in local Ordinances.[3] After independence the Ghana Parliament passed an Act applying the procedure to the whole of Ghana, and the local modifications of the Extradition Acts, 1870 to 1932 were made uniform.[4] The Acts themselves continued as part of the law of Ghana until 1961, when they were replaced by a consolidating and amending Act, the provisions of which are described below.

Fugitive Offenders Act, 1881

The surrender of a fugitive criminal by one British possession to another is dealt with by the Fugitive Offenders Act, 1881. The procedure is simpler than that under the Extradition Acts

---

[1] The Act and the subsequent amending Acts are set out in Vol. VI of the *Laws of the Gold Coast*, 1954, pp. 808 *et seq.*

[2] See ss. 6, 17. For a list of the foreign countries to which the Act has been applied see 9 Halsbury's Statutes (2nd Edn.) 875. For texts of treaties see S.R. & O and S.I. Revised, IX, 1 *et seq.*

[3] Extradition (Colony) Ordinance (Cap. 12); Extradition (Ashanti) Ordinance (Cap. 13). The Ordinances were made effective by the Orders in Council set out in Vol. VI of the *Laws of the Gold Coast*, 1954, pp. 829–833.

[4] Extradition Act, 1959 (No. 56). Previously extradition to foreign states from the Northern Territories or British Togoland had been dealt with by a separate procedure laid down by the Fugitive Criminals (Northern Territories) Ordinance (Cap. 14—repealed by Act No. 56 of 1959) and the Fugitive Criminals (Togoland) Ordinance (Cap. 15—repealed by Act No. 54 of 1958).

and lacks some of its safeguards, in particular that relating to
political offences.[1] A notable simplification is the procedure for
the backing of warrants. For this purpose adjacent territories
are grouped together and a warrant issued in one territory is
valid for the arrest of the criminal in any other territory within
the group if endorsed by a magistrate within the latter territory.[2]

The Fugitive Offenders Act applied directly to the Gold Coast
and Ashanti, and was extended by Order in Council to the
Northern Territories and British Togoland.[3] By the same Order
in Council all the colonies, protectorates and other territories
under British administration in West Africa were grouped together for the purpose of the backing of warrants. The Act and
Order in Council continued to apply in Ghana until superseded
in 1961.

Extradition Act, 1960

Extradition from Ghana, whether to a foreign country or a
country within the Commonwealth, is now governed by the
Extradition Act, 1960 (Act 22). This repealed the Extradition
Acts, 1870 to 1932 and the Fugitive Offenders Act, 1881 and
replaced them by a common procedure based on their provisions.
The main procedure is laid down by Part I of the Act. Part II,
which provides for the reciprocal backing of warrants, has not
yet become operative, and Part III contains miscellaneous provisions with most of which we are not here concerned.

It has not yet been practicable for Ghana to negotiate any
extradition treaties on her own account, but under international
law extradition treaties entered into by the British Government
on behalf of the territories now included in Ghana remain operative in relation to Ghana. Part I of the Act of 1960 is therefore
applied to the countries with which such treaties were in force
immediately before its commencement on 22nd April, 1961.[4] It
is also applied to those countries within the Commonwealth to
which the Fugitive Offenders Act, 1881 applied immediately
before that date.[5] In the case of these latter countries Ghana is,
until treaties can be made, yielding extradition facilities with no

---

[1] See *infra*.
[2] See Part II of the Act.
[3] West African (Fugitive Offenders) Order in Council, 1923 (see *Laws of
the Gold Coast*, 1954, VI, p. 738).
[4] Section 3 (2) (as to the treaties see p. 205, *ante*).
[5] Section 3 (1).

assurance of obtaining similar facilities in return. Where in future treaties are made by Ghana, s. 1 of the Act will enable Part I to be applied to the countries concerned by a process similar to that contained in s. 2 of the Act of 1870.

A requisition for the extradition of any person from Ghana will only be complied with if it is made by a representative of a country to which Part I of the Act applies and the following conditions are satisfied—

1. The person must be accused or convicted of having committed an extradition crime within the jurisdiction of the requisitioning country or of having counselled, procured, commanded, aided or abetted its commission or of being an accessory to its commission. Extradition crimes include homicide, abduction, rape, theft, fraud, forgery, unlawful damage, piracy, perjury, counterfeiting and offences relating to narcotic drugs.[1]

2. The crime must not be of a political character.[2]

3. It must be established that the criminal will not, without an opportunity of first returning to Ghana, be detained or tried in the requisitioning country for any offence committed before his surrender except the extradition crime in respect of which surrender is obtained.[3]

These conditions may be added to or otherwise modified by the terms of the relevant treaty. Although the wording of the Act, following that of the British Act of 1870, contemplates that such modifications will be made by the order applying the Act, in fact this has not been the practice and it is probable that the Ghana courts will follow the decision in *R*. v. *Wilson*,[4] where it was held that the order must be taken to have embodied the terms of the treaty and that the Extradition Act is only applicable so far as it can be applied consistently with those terms. This means that effect would be given to a term such as that contained in the Anglo-French treaty, under which each country is at liberty to refuse to the other the extradition of its own nationals.[5]

---

[1] See ss. 5, 6, 29, 30, Sch. I. (The list has recently been extended to include any other offence punishable on indictment: L.I. 173) The criminal need not have been physically present in the requisitioning country: *R*. v. *Godfrey*, [1923] 1 K.B. 24.

[2] See s. 2 (a). As to the scope of this restriction see *Re Kolczynski*, [1955] 1 All E.R. 31.

[3] See s. 2 (b).   [4] (1877), 3 Q.B.D. 42.

[5] *S.R. & O. and S.I. Revised*, IX, 144.

The normal procedure for obtaining extradition from Ghana is as follows. A requisition is made to the Minister of the Interior by a diplomatic representative or consular officer of the country concerned. This must give particulars of the crime and the criminal, and must state that a warrant for his arrest has been issued in the requisitioning country. If the Minister is satisfied that the necessary grounds for extradition exist, and in particular that the crime is not of a political nature, he will request the district magistrate for the area in which the criminal is believed to be located to issue a warrant for his arrest. The magistrate will only issue the warrant however on such evidence as would in his opinion justify its issue if the crime had been committed or the criminal convicted in Ghana. On the arrest of the criminal a hearing takes place before the magistrate. The ordinary rules of criminal procedure apply and evidence that the crime is of a political character or is not an extradition crime must be admitted. If the foreign warrant authorising the arrest of the criminal is produced and authenticated and if there is sufficient evidence to justify a committal for trial if the crime had been committed in Ghana, or, in the case of a convict, if the conviction is proved, the magistrate, after informing the criminal that he has fifteen days within which he may apply for an order of habeas corpus, will commit him to prison. Subject to any order made in habeas corpus proceedings the Minister will then order the criminal to be handed over to a representative of the requisitioning country. If he is not surrendered and conveyed out of Ghana within two months after his committal to prison the High Court may order his release.[1]

Where a criminal whose extradition is sought has been accused of some additional offence within the jurisdiction of Ghana or is undergoing sentence under any conviction in Ghana, he will not be surrendered until after he has been discharged, whether by acquittal or on expiration of his sentence or otherwise.[2]

Fugitives from Ghana

Where a person has committed an offence in Ghana and is taking refuge in some other country the question of his extradition by the Ghana authorities is of course determined by the

---

[1] Sections 7–12. In cases of urgency a district magistrate may issue a warrant of arrest without waiting for a request from the Minister; see s. 8 (1) (b).

[2] Section 2 (c).

law of the other country. Only one provision of the law of Ghana
is relevant in this case. Section 15 of the Extradition Act, 1960
(Act 22) provides as follows:

> " Where, in pursuance of an arrangement with any country,
> any person accused or convicted of any crime described in the
> First Schedule to this Act,[1] is surrendered by that country,
> that person shall not, until he has been restored or had an
> opportunity of returning to that country, be triable or tried for
> any offence committed prior to the surrender in Ghana other
> than such of the crimes as may be proved by the facts on which
> the surrender is grounded."

This provision is similar to that which is required to exist in a
foreign country seeking the extradition of a criminal from Ghana.[2]
It ensures that advantage will not be taken of the extradition
procedure to try a person for offences which in themselves are not
extraditable.

7. FOREIGN ENLISTMENT

The policy of neutralism in international affairs, to which
Ghana adheres, makes it important for the Government to be
able to prevent individual citizens from engaging in foreign
military activities. Until recently this matter was regulated
by British law. The Foreign Enlistment Act, 1870 applied in
Ghana and controlled among other things the enlistment of
British subjects with the armed forces of a State at war with a
country which itself was at peace with Her Majesty. The original
purpose of the Act was to enable the British Government to fulfil
its obligations under international law of non-intervention in a
war in which Britain was neutral. In recent times however this
type of control has become insufficient. Hostilities frequently
break out without a formal declaration of war, and the development of the military role of the United Nations Organization has
meant that in many cases the conduct of hostilities is no longer
in the hands of individual States. Nor does control in such a
limited form avail in cases of internal strife such as the recent
Congo disturbances. When these provisions were re-enacted in
pursuance of the statute law reform programme, their scope was
accordingly widened and the penalties made more severe.

The Foreign Enlistment Act, 1961 (Act 75) provides that the

---

[1] The First Schedule lists the crimes for which extradition from Ghana
can be obtained.

[2] See condition 3, p. 207, *ante.*

O

following are guilty of first degree felony, and thus punishable with life imprisonment:[1]

(1) A citizen of Ghana, or an alien holding a Ghana passport, who, without the President's consent, accepts or agrees to accept any commission or engagement in the military service of any other country.

(2) A citizen of Ghana, or an alien holding a Ghana passport, who induces any other person to accept or agree to accept any commission or engagement in the military service of any other country.[2]

(3) A person who leaves the Republic, or goes on board any vessel, vehicle or aircraft, for the purpose of doing an act referred to in either of the preceding paragraphs.[3]

(4) A person who induces any other person to leave the Republic or go on board any vessel, vehicle or aircraft within the Republic under a misrepresentation, with intent that he may accept or agree to accept any commission or engagement in the military service of any other country.[4]

A person in charge of a vessel, vehicle or aircraft who knowingly takes on board or engages to take on board a person proceeding on unlawful foreign enlistment is liable to imprisonment for up to ten years, and until his trial is over the vessel, vehicle or aircraft must be detained.[5] The definition of military service makes the Act applicable to—

" service in a police, army, naval or air force and any other employment whatever in connection with any military operation and any employment in secret service work or in an underground movement or as a secret agent."[6]

Although this definition is wide enough to cover international forces, the references in the substantive provisions of the Act to the military service of " any other country " indicate that enlistment with an international force will only be an offence if it is with a particular national contingent within the force.

---

[1] The maximum term of imprisonment under the Act of 1870 was two years.

[2] This applies whether or not the President's consent was given, but presumably no prosecution would be brought where there had been consent.

[3] Rather curiously, this applies even where the person is not a citizen and does not hold a Ghana passport.

[4] Sections 1–3.   [5] Section 4.   [6] Section 8.

8. Diplomatic Immunity

" As a consequence of the absolute independence of every sovereign authority and of the international comity which induces every sovereign state to respect the independence of every other sovereign state, each and every one declines to exercise by means of any of its courts, any of its territorial jurisdiction over the person of any sovereign or ambassador of any other state, or over the public property of any state which is destined to its public use, or over the property of any ambassador."[1]

This classic exposition of the acceptance by the common law of a universal principle of international law is still applicable in Ghana today. Although, as mentioned below, certain statutory extensions of these rules have been made, within their original limits the rules apply in Ghana by virtue of their being part of the common law. Certain of them are also embodied in a declaratory statute, the Diplomatic Privileges Act, 1708, which was occasioned by an affront to the Russian ambassador. This is a statute of general application, and therefore in force in Ghana, but it is of little importance since it neither defines exhaustively the nature of diplomatic privilege nor makes any extension of that privilege.[2] It does however impose penalties for certain breaches of privilege.

The privilege of a foreign diplomatic representative extends to members of his official and domestic staff and to his immediate family. The privilege may be waived, but since it is the privilege of the sovereign and not of the individual it can only be effectively waived by or on behalf of the sovereign. If a claim of diplomatic privilege is advanced in judicial proceedings the court will apply for information to the Ministry of Foreign Affairs and will accept the reply as conclusive.[3]

Commonwealth Representatives

Section 3 of the Diplomatic Immunities (Commonwealth Countries) Ordinance, 1957 (No. 22), which came into force on the date of Ghana's independence, accorded to the chief representatives of Commonwealth countries in Ghana:

" the like immunity from suit and legal process, and the like inviolability of residence, official premises and official archives as are accorded to the envoy of a foreign sovereign Power accredited to Her Majesty."

---

[1] *The Parlement Belge* (1880), 5 P.D. 197, *per* Brett, L. J. at p. 217.
[2] *The Amazone*, [1940] P. 40.
[3] *Duff Development Co.* v. *Kelantan*, [1924] A.C. 797.

Corresponding immunities were conferred by the section on members of the staffs and families of Commonwealth representatives, and a list of persons entitled to immunity was required to be published in the *Gazette* and kept up to date. The section is still in force, the reference to Her Majesty having been altered at the inauguration of the Republic to a reference to Ghana.[1] It seems likely however that the status of Ghana as an independent republic means that Commonwealth countries would in any case fall to be treated as foreign sovereign powers for the purpose of according diplomatic immunity.

International Organizations

The United Nations Organization, and a number of other international bodies of which Ghana is a member, are given immunities and privileges equivalent to those accorded to a sovereign state, both for themselves and for their officers and servants.[2]

Consular Officers

Consuls and other consular officers, being appointed primarily to facilitate commercial dealings, are not as such entitled to diplomatic immunity. However, the Consular Conventions Ordinance, 1952 (No. 32) restricts the power of the police to enter consular offices, facilitates the acquisition of land for consular purposes, and allows tax exemptions to be granted.

---

[1] Constitution (Consequential Provisions) Act, 1960 (C.A. 8), s. 23, Sch. II.

[2] Diplomatic Privileges Ordinance (Cap. 268).

CHAPTER 5

LIBERTY AND STATE SECURITY

One of the most important aspects of the relationship between the State and the individual concerns the extent to which personal freedom is curtailed in the interests of the security of the State, whether in its institutional aspect or viewed as a collection of individuals. The State demands protection for its very existence and for the orderly functioning of its institutions, such as the courts of law, the legislature and the organs of Government. It also requires that the individual shall not abuse his own liberties at the expense of the liberties of his fellow-citizens. Subject to these necessary limitations, the Constitution of the Republic of Ghana declares that freedom " should be honoured and maintained ".[1]

Although the Constitution recognises personal freedom it does not protect it by means which are enforceable by application to a court of law. Instead the British pattern is followed, with results similar to those described in a leading textbook on British constitutional law:—

> " The citizen may go where he pleases and do or say what he pleases, provided that he does not commit an offence against the criminal law or infringe the rights of others. If his legal rights are infringed by others, e.g., by trespassing upon his property or defaming his reputation, he may protect himself by the remedies provided by the law. It is in the law of crimes and of tort and contract, part of the ordinary law of the land, and not in any fundamental constitutional law, that the citizen finds protection for his political liberty, whether it is infringed by officials or by fellow-citizens. In times of emergency the executive is accorded special powers by Parliament, but there are no formal guarantees—such as are to be found in a constitutional code formally enacted—which have to be suspended."[2]

Liberty is thus not granted by the law with certain reservations, but is assumed to exist except on matters as to which the law gives other directions. These directions are embodied in the criminal law, in the civil law which regulates the rights of citizens against

---

[1] Article 13 (1).
[2] Wade and Phillips, *Constitutional Law* (6th Edn.), p. 464.

each other and against the State, and in special laws passed to meet situations of emergency. Such emergency laws are temporary in their operation—lasting from a week or two for some local disturbance to five years or longer in the case of the Preventive Detention Act, 1958 (No. 17).[1] In this chapter we shall be concerned mainly with the ways in which the State curtails individual liberty, through the criminal law and emergency laws, for the purpose of safe-guarding its existence and institutions.[2] Details of the civil law and the legal relations between individuals are beyond the scope of the present work. We shall specify the rules that curtail liberty, bearing in mind that, as mentioned above, liberty is not a state conferred by law but a natural privilege, and that the law is only concerned to lay down limitations to it where these are considered necessary.

1. FREEDOM OF THE PERSON

If one person subjects another to physical coercion which is not authorised by law he will be liable to damages in civil proceedings for assault or false imprisonment, and may also be guilty of a criminal offence. The principal cases in which physical restraint is authorised by law are as follows—

(a) arrest and detention pending trial for a criminal offence;
(b) detention in a prison, Borstal institution or similar place under a court order made on conviction for a criminal offence, or made in respect of non-payment of debt or contempt of court;
(c) detention under a deportation order, extradition order, preventive detention order or similar executive instrument;
(d) detention as a lunatic under an order of the court;[3]
(e) restraint of an infant by a parent or a person *in loco parentis.*

Arrest

The rules governing arrest for criminal offences are set out in Part I of the Criminal Procedure Code, 1960 (Act 30).[4] Except

---

[1] See pp. 220 *et. seq, post.*

[2] Offences against the safety of the State, and certain other offences, are now tried by the special criminal division of the High Court set up at the end of 1961. There is no jury and no appeal. (Act 91).

[3] Lunatic Asylums Ordinance (Cap. 79), s. 14; Courts Ordinance (Cap. 4), s. 16; Courts Act, 1960 (C.A. 9), s. 154 (3).

[4] Power to arrest in other cases is conferred by the enactment dealing with the matter in question—e.g. the National Assembly Act, 1961 (Act 86), s. 42 (arrest for contempt of Parliament)

in the cases mentioned below no person may be arrested on a criminal charge unless a warrant for that purpose has been issued by a judge or magistrate upon sworn testimony. The warrant must state shortly the offence charged and must name or describe the person against whom it is issued. This must be a specific individual; a general warrant for the arrest of any person who answers a given description cannot be issued.

Arrest without warrant.—A police officer may arrest any of the following without a warrant—

(a) a person who commits an offence in his presence or whom he suspects upon reasonable grounds of having committed a felony or misdemeanour or of being a deserter from the armed forces;

(b) a person who has escaped from lawful custody or who obstructs the police in their duty;

(c) a person who is in possession of stolen property or house-breaking tools;

(d) a person whom he reasonably believes to be about to commit a felony or misdemeanour;[1]

(e) a person whom he suspects upon reasonable grounds of having been concerned in any act committed outside Ghana which, if committed in Ghana, would have been punishable as an offence, and for which that person is liable to be arrested in Ghana;

(f) an accused person who refuses to give his true name and address.

A district magistrate may, without issuing a warrant, arrest, or order the arrest of, any person who commits an offence in his presence or of whom he knows facts which, if sworn to by someone else, would have justified him in issuing a warrant.

A private person may arrest any of the following without a warrant—

(a) a person who in his view commits a felony or misdemeanour or any offence involving the use of force or violence;

(b) a person whom he reasonably suspects of having committed a felony, provided that the felony really has been commited;

(c) a person found committing any offence involving injury to property belonging to him or his employer.

---

[1] Except at night, arrest is not justified on this ground unless there is no other practicable way of preventing the commission of the offence.

Mode of arrest.—The person making an arrest must actually touch or confine the body of the person to be arrested unless there is a submission to the custody by word or action. No more force must be used than is necessary to prevent the escape of the offender.[1] Unless caught in the act, or pursued immediately after escape from custody, the offender must be told the cause of his arrest. He may be searched and must be taken with all reasonable despatch to a police station and there charged without delay with the offence for which he was arrested.

An offender arrested by a private person must be handed over to the police without unnecessary delay. The police must then re-arrest him or, if there is no sufficient reason to believe that he has committed any offence, must at once release him.

An arrested person must be brought before a court without unnecessary delay.

Bail

An important safeguard of liberty of the person is the right, in appropriate cases, to obtain release on bail during the period between arrest on a criminal charge and the proceedings in which a court determines whether the charge is proved. A person who is held in prison before his guilt has been established is suffering punishment for an offence which he may later be found not to have committed. Such imprisonment is clearly unjust unless found to be necessary for the public safety or to prevent an accused person from escaping trial.

The constitutions of many countries contain provisions designed to ensure that bail is not fixed at an unreasonably high figure. These derive from the Bill of Rights, 1688, which stated that " excessive bail ought not to be required ". The result of requiring excessive bail is of course likely to be that the accused cannot find the necessary sureties and so is forced to remain in prison. This provision of the Bill of Rights is reproduced in Ghana in s. 96(2) of the Criminal Procedure Code, 1960 (Act 30) which states that " the amount of bail shall be fixed with due regard to the circumstances of the case and shall not be excessive ".

An application for bail may be made to a police officer at the time when the accused is charged or to any court hearing the case or to a judge of the High Court or a circuit court. The latter

---

[1] For the occasions when force is justified in arrest and other cases see the Criminal Code, 1960 (Act 29), Pt. II, Ch. 1.

may grant bail where it has been refused by a police officer or magistrate, and may reduce the amount of any excessive bail. The grant of bail is discretionary, although there are certain limitations on admission to bail otherwise than by the High Court or a circuit court. A convicted person may be admitted to bail pending the hearing of an appeal.

When bail is granted the person bailed is required to enter into a bond, with or without sureties, conditioned for his appearance before a court at the time and place mentioned in the bond. He is released as soon as the bond is executed. Alternatively, instead of executing a bond, he may be permitted to deposit a sum of money as security for his due appearance.[1]

Habeas Corpus

Where a person is unlawfully detained the mode by which he, or a person acting for him, can obtain a court order for his immediate release is by applying for a writ of *habeas corpus ad subjiciendum*. The procedure was described by Blackstone as follows:

> " The great and efficacious writ, in all manner of illegal confinement, is that of *habeas corpus ad subjiciendum*, directed to the person detaining another, and commanding him to produce the body of the prisoner, with the day and cause of his caption and detention, *ad faciendum, subjiciendum et recipiendum*, to do, submit and receive whatsoever the court or judge awarding such writ shall consider in that behalf."[2]

The value attached to the *habeas corpus* procedure is illustrated by the following words of Erskine May:

> " The writ of *habeas corpus* is unquestionably the first security of civil liberty. It brings to light the cause of every imprisonment, approves its lawfulness, or liberates the prisoner. It exacts obedience from the highest courts: Parliament itself submits to its authority. No right is more justly valued. It protects the subject from unfounded suspicions, from the aggressions of power, and from abuses in the administration of justice."[3]

Originally evolved by the common law as a means of securing the attendance of a person before a court, the *habeas corpus* procedure was fashioned into an instrument of civil liberty by two

---

[1] Criminal Procedure Code, 1960 (Act 30), ss. 15 (2), 96–107.
[2] *Commentaries*, Vol. III, § 131.
[3] *Constitutional History of England*, Vol. III, § 10.

Acts of the British Parliament. The Habeas Corpus Act, 1679, which applied only to detention in criminal cases, removed certain devices by which the issue of the writ had been delayed or frustrated, and made it issuable during court vacations. The Habeas Corpus Act, 1862 extended these provisions to other forms of detention and made a radical departure by providing that, although the return to the writ might be good on its face and show a lawful reason for the detention, the court considering the return could " examine into the truth of the facts set forth in such return " and " do therein as to justice shall appertain ". Dicey remarked that these Acts

> " . . . declare no principle and define no rights, but they are for practical purposes worth a hundred constitutional articles guaranteeing individual liberty."[1]

The common law, together with these two Acts, remains part of the law of Ghana, subject to the adaptations needed to fit republican status. Since many expositions of the subject of *habeas corpus* are to be found in writings on English constitutional law[2] it will not be further dealt with here except for a brief description of the procedure in Ghana.

Applications for a writ of *habeas corpus* are regulated by Order 59 of the Rules of the Supreme Court.[3] In term time an application is made to a judge in the High Court, but in vacation it may be made to a High Court judge anywhere. The application will usually be *ex parte*, and may either be made by the person restrained or by someone acting on his behalf. It must be accompanied by an affidavit showing that it is made at the instance of the person restrained and setting out the nature of the restraint. Unless he is prevented from doing so by the restraint, the person restrained must make this affidavit himself. Normally any relevant documents, as for example an executive instrument authorising detention, will be exhibited to the affidavit.

The application may be dealt with by the judge in various ways, although these are limited by the provision in rule 1 of

---

[1] Law of the Constitution (8th Edn.), p. 195.
[2] See, e.g., Wade and Phillips, *Constitutional Law* (6th Edn.),pp. 473–482. A detailed historical account is given by Bossman, J. in *Re Dumoga* (1961), (Misc. 19/60) although his ruling that the Act of 1816 was not in force in Ghana was reversed by the Supreme Court in *Re Akoto* (1961), (Civil Appeal No. 42/61).
[3] Laws of the Gold Coast (1954), VII, pp. 306 *et. seq.* The rules apply to the High Court also, although it is now separate from the Supreme Court.

Order 59 that no order nisi, rule nisi or summons to show cause may issue. Normally the writ of *habeas corpus* will not actually be issued even where it appears to the judge that the person restrained is entitled to his release. Instead the judge may merely order his release after considering any representations made by the other side on the hearing of the application. Refusal to obey the order will be punishable as contempt of court in the same way as refusal to comply with a writ of *habeas corpus*. If, however, the affidavit accompanying the application shows that the case is one of great urgency—as for example where the person restrained is about to be taken out of the country—the writ will issue immediately and argument as to the validity of the detention will be considered when the prisoner is brought before the court on the return to the writ.

Although the court has power to enquire into the truth of the matters stated in the return to the writ or in affidavits produced in opposition to an order for release, this power does not extend to enquiring into the reasonableness of an executive instrument ordering detention in a case where the executive authority has been empowered by statute to decide whether grounds for making the order exist.[1]

Criminal Restraint

In addition to providing for the recovery of damages in civil proceedings and for release under the *habeas corpus* procedure, the law also makes most types of unlawful restraint punishable as criminal offences. The main offences of this character are described below.

Kidnapping.—This is a second degree felony and thus punishable with imprisonment for up to ten years. It is committed by anyone who unlawfully imprisons a person and either takes him out of Ghana without his consent or detains him in Ghana in such a way as to prevent him from applying to a court for his release or as to conceal his whereabouts from those who might come to his assistance. For this purpose imprisonment has a wide meaning, and includes compelling a person to move or be carried in any particular direction.[2]

Abduction of female.—It is a misdemeanour, and thus punishable with imprisonment for up to three years, to take or detain

---

[1] *Re Akoto* (1961) (Civil Appeal No. 42/61); see p. 224, *post*.
[2] Criminal Code, 1960 (Act 29), ss. 88–90.

from the lawful possession of her parent, guardian or other protector an unmarried female under eighteen years of age.[1]

Child-stealing.—A person is guilty of a second degree felony if he unlawfully takes or detains a child under twelve years of age, with intent to deprive of the possession or control of him any person entitled thereto, or with intent to steal anything upon him or cause him any harm.[2]

Assault and battery.—Forcibly touching a person with intent to cause harm, pain, fear or anger will, unless justified, constitute a misdemeanour. The smallest amount of force will suffice, and it is not necessary to touch the body of the person provided his clothing or something else in contact with him is touched.[3] Since most forms of detention begin with an act of this kind it follows that, unless the detention is lawful, assault and battery will usually have been committed.

Slavery.—When the Gold Coast became a British colony in 1874 existing slaves were emancipated and slave-dealing was abolished.[4] The abolition of slavery was reaffirmed in 1930 by an Ordinance which declared " that slavery in any form whatsoever is unlawful " and that " the legal status of slavery does not exist ".[5] The three Ordinances containing these provisions survived until they were repealed by the Criminal Code, 1960 (Act 29), s. 318(2). The repeal was presumably effected because it was felt that those provisions of the Ordinances which were not spent were rendered unnecessary by the existence of the criminal offences mentioned above and those relating to slave-dealing which were reproduced from the previous Criminal Code. Section 314 of the Code of 1960, re-enacting s. 464 of the previous Code, makes various acts connected with slave-dealing second degree felonies.

Preventive Detention

Since the Act authorising preventive detention is expressed to be limited in its duration it might have been dealt with in the last

---

[1] Criminal Code, 1960 (Act 29), ss. 91, 92, 95.

[2] *Ibid.*, ss. 93–95.

[3] Criminal Code, 1960 (Act 29), ss. 84–87. Actual touching constitutes battery; assault is strictly the act of putting a person in fear that battery will follow.

[4] Slaves' Emancipation Ordinance (Cap. 108); Slave-Dealing Abolition Ordinance (Cap. 109).

[5] Reaffirmation of the Abolition of Slavery Ordinance (Cap. 107).

section of this chapter dealing with emergency powers. However, the Act has been in operation for most of the period since independence and there is no certainty that it will not be continued in force when the time comes for it to expire in 1963. Accordingly it will be treated here as part of the substantive law relating to freedom of the person.

The Preventive Detention Act, 1958 (No. 17) authorises the President to order the detention of any citizen of Ghana if satisfied that the order is necessary to prevent him acting in a manner prejudicial to the defence of Ghana or the relations of Ghana with other countries or the security of the State. Not later than five days from the beginning of his detention, the person detained must be informed of the grounds on which he is being detained and given an opportunity of making representations in writing to the President.[1]

The provisions dealing with the period of detention are somewhat complicated. They may be summarised as follows:

(a) the order may specify a period of detention not exceeding five years;

(b) if the person in question evades arrest and fails to comply with a notice requiring him to report to the police, his period of detention will be doubled;

(c) the prisoner may be released before his period of detention has expired, subject to recall if he does not obey stipulated conditions as to the notification of his movements;

(d) the President may at any time revoke the order or vary the specified period of detention;

(e) except as mentioned in paragraph (b) above, the prisoner cannot be detained for longer than five years, and for this purpose release subject to recall counts as detention;

(f) after final release no further preventive detention order can be mad eagainst the same person except on the ground of activities carried on after the previous order was made.[2]

The Act is limited to expire after five years, that is on 18th July, 1963. It may however be extended for a further three years by a resolution of the National Assembly. On the expiration of the Act current preventive detention orders will lapse and the prisoners will be entitled to immediate release.[3]

---

[1] Preventive Detention Act, 1958 (No. 17), s. 2.

[2] *Ibid.*, ss. 3, 4.

[3] Preventive Detention Act, 1958 (No. 17), s. 5. This is of course subject to any amending legislation that may be passed.

It is beyond our purpose to embark on the controversy which has surrounded the Preventive Detention Act. It may however assist in understanding the justification advanced for it to give extracts from Government statements explaining its enactment and use. During the passage of the Bill through Parliament, Government speakers said:

> " . . . the only persons who need be alarmed about it are those who are either attempting to organize violence, terrorism or civil war or who are acting as fifth columnists for some foreign power interested in subversion in Ghana . . . the Bill has been deliberately drafted so that the Government can deal resolutely and without delay with any attempt to subvert the State by force. The Government are determined not to be caught unprepared, as a number of other states have been, by subversion either from within or without . . . in order to preserve the due process of law, it may on occasion be unfortunately necessary to take special powers."[1]

> " The Government are seeking power to interfere with the rights of any citizen of Ghana, if that citizen is conducting himself in such a way as to interfere with the defence of Ghana, to interfere with the security of the State and with the relationship of foreign states with Ghana. The Members of the Opposition will concede the fact that it is at times necessary to adopt undemocratic methods to preserve democracy."[2]

The nature of the subversive acts feared by the Government is explained in considerable detail in a White Paper issued in 1959.[3] The Preventive Detention Act had not been brought into use immediately, but after some four months, in November 1958, a detention order was made in respect of forty-three persons. In the following month a further order was made in respect of two prominent members of the Opposition, R. R. Amponsah and M. K. Apaloo, who had been unanimously found by an independent tribunal to have been engaged in a conspiracy to carry out an act for an unlawful purpose revolutionary in character.[4]

---

[1] The Prime Minister, Dr. Kwame Nkrumah (Parl. Deb. Official Report, 14th July, 1958, col. 410).

[2] The Minister of Local Government, Mr. A. E. A. Ofori Atta (*ibid.*, 15th July, 1958, cols. 513–514).

[3] *Statement by the Government on the Report of the Commission Appointed to Enquire into the Matters Disclosed at the Trial of Captain Benjamin Awhaitey Before a Court-Martial, and the Surrounding Circumstances* (W.P. No. 10/59).

[4] *Report of the Granville Sharp Commission*, Accra, 1959. Two members of the tribunal found that the unlawful act in question was the assassination of the Prime Minister and the staging of a *coup d'etat*, but the third member, Mr. Justice Granville Sharp, dissented on this point.

The White Paper alleged that the persons detained in November were members of two secret societies, respectively known as the Zenith Seven and the Tokyo Joes, which were plotting to overthrow the Government by violence and were linked with certain members of the opposition party.[1] After a detailed description of the ramifications of the alleged plot, with supporting evidence elicited by three public tribunals of enquiry, various criminal prosecutions and other means, the White Paper concluded with the following summary of the circumstances which, in the Government's view, justified the enactment and use of the Preventive Detention Act:—

> " By no means every piece of evidence and information can be fitted into an exact place in an overall scheme. Broadly speaking, however, the overall plan is clear. It was to seek foreign support by allegations of corruption, known to those making them to be false, and to incite mob violence in Ghana by circulating forged and false documents and rumours which would set one racial group against another. Money and material for revolutionary purposes were to be sought from abroad and the help of those fundamentally opposed to African independence enlisted. The plot was to be triggered off by the use of such persons as Benjamin Awhaitey, whom it was thought could command Army support, or by the use of criminal elements such as were to be found among the ' Tokyo Joes '. The Prime Minister and other Ministers could then be assassinated without those who were in fact behind the assassination being revealed. When, in November, 1958, those associated with the first assassination plot were detained, R. R. Amponsah immediately declared that he and the Opposition generally were totally opposed to violence and the allegations made against the persons detained were a ' frame-up ' by the Government to get rid of their political opponents. At the very time he made this declaration he was, as the Granville Sharp Commission has found, himself actively engaged in another plot to assassinate the Prime Minister."[2]

The White Paper gave four instances of the difficulty of relying on criminal prosecutions rather than preventive detention in combating subversive acts of this kind:

(1) One of the tribunals of enquiry investigated 491 alleged incidents of extortion, violence and intimidation in Ashanti. Efforts were made subsequently to institute prosecutions in regard to these cases, but in fact, the lapse of time which had occurred and the reluctance of witnesses to come forward when

---

[1] W.P. No. 10/59, p. 37.
[2] *Ibid.*, p. 46.

they were not certain that they might not again be victimised at a later date, prevented any effective prosecutions and only a few convictions were obtained.[1]

(2) Two opposition members of Parliament from Togoland were prosecuted with eight others for conspiring to attack persons with armed force. The trial lasted over two months and the members of Parliament, with three others, were found guilty. The convictions were quashed on appeal on the ground of misdirection by the trial judge.[2]

(3) R. R. Amponsah was tried for sedition on a charge of making public accusations that police officers in conjunction with the Government were conniving at the printing of extra ballot papers for the rigging of elections. He was acquitted on the ground that under the law as it existed the words were not seditious.[3]

(4) Although Amponsah and Apaloo were found by the Granville Sharp Commission to have been engaged in a conspiracy to carry out an act for an unlawful purpose revolutionary in character, no such offence was to be found in the Criminal Code.[4]

Up to the end of 1960 three hundred and eighteen persons had been made the subject of preventive detention orders.[5] Two hundred and fifty-five of these cases were in 1960, when the use of the Preventive Detention Act was extended to criminal gangsters whose activities were not political.[6]

A number of abortive attempts have been made to induce the courts to declare detentions under the Preventive Detention Act illegal. The most important of these cases is *Re Akoto*, decided in 1961.[7] In November, 1959, Baffour Osei Akoto, senior linguist to the Asantehene, was detained with seven others under the Preventive Detention Act. The reason given for the detention was that it was necessary to prevent these eight persons from acting in a manner prejudicial to the security of the State and

---

[1] W.P. No. 10/59, p. 27.   [2] *Ibid.*, p. 25.

[3] *Ibid.*, p. 32. The law of sedition was altered in 1959 and it is now an offence to commit an act of this nature; see p. 228, *post*.

[4] W.P. No. 10/59, p.17.

[5] This figure is based on published orders and press releases. It is believed that no orders were made without publicity.

[6] In October, 1961 fifty persons were detained in connection with the disturbances arising from the stringent budget of that year. They included four opposition Members of Parliament and Dr. J. B. Danquah, the United Party candidate in the Presidential election of 1960 (E.I. 172 of 1961).

[7] Civil Appeal No. 42/61.

they were duly notified of the grounds upon which this reason was based.[1] An application for a writ of *habeas corpus* was refused by the High Court and on appeal this refusal was upheld by the Supreme Court. The main grounds of appeal were as follows:—

(1) The application for a writ of *habeas corpus* should not have been refused without the making of an order for a formal return.

(2) The grounds notified to the prisoners did not fall within the expression " acts prejudicial to the security of the State ".

(3) The Habeas Corpus Act, 1816 required the court to enquire into the truth of the facts given in the grounds notified to the prisoners, and it had not done so.

(4) The Minister who signed the preventive detention order had been proved to have been actuated by malice.

(5) The Preventive Detention Act was unconstitutional.

(6) The preventive detention order was contrary to the provision in the Criminal Procedure Code requiring all offences to be dealt with by judicial enquiry under the Code.

The Supreme Court rejected all these grounds of appeal. On the first ground they held that since the prisoners' own affidavit in support of their application had exhibited all the material documents there was no need to call for a formal return. On the second, third and fourth grounds they held, following *Liversidge* v. *Anderson*[2] and other English decisions, that the wording of s. 2 of the Preventive Detention Act " vests plenary discretion in the Governor-General, now President, if satisfied that such order is necessary " and that in the absence of malice, which had not been proved, the court could not therefore enquire into the truth of the facts set forth in the grounds on which each appellant had been detained. The court's reasons for rejecting the argument that the Act was unconstitutional have already been given.[3] The final ground of appeal was dismissed with the statement:

---

[1] The grounds were similar, though not identical, in each of the eight cases. In the case of Akoto himself the grounds were: " Acting in a manner prejudicial to the security of the State, in that you have encouraged the commission of acts of violence in the Ashanti or Brong-Ahafo Regions and have associated with persons who have adopted a policy of violence as a means of achieving political aims in these Regions."

[2] [1941] 3 All E.R. 338; [1942] A.C. 206.

[3] P. 142, *ante*.

P

" The mischief aimed at by the Preventive Detention Act is in respect of acts that may be committed in the future, whereas the Criminal Code (*sic*) concerns itself which acts which have in fact been committed."[1]

2. FREEDOM OF SPEECH

The declaration in art. 13 of the Constitution states:

" . . . subject to such restrictions as may be necessary for preserving public order, morality or health, no person should be deprived of freedom of . . . speech."

The word " speech " in this connection is not of course limited to ordinary oral speech but includes speech communicated through newspapers, books, letters and other written forms and by means of gramophone records, films, broadcasts, etc. The principal ways in which freedom of speech in this sense is curtailed by the law are as follows:

(a) treasonable and seditious statements, false reports and the disclosure of state secrets are punishable by the criminal law;

(b) control is exercised over the publication and importation of newspapers, books and pamphlets, and over broadcasting and the public exhibition of films;

(c) defamatory and insulting statements are both punishable by the criminal law and subject to civil proceedings;

(d) obscene publications are punishable by the criminal law.

Treasonable and Seditious Statements

Treason.—The law of treason is concerned more with substantive acts of disloyalty than with mere statements, which mostly fall under the heading of sedition. However, the definition of treason is wide enough to embrace the uttering of statements designed to further the commission of substantive acts and for convenience it is discussed here. A person is guilty of treason, and liable to suffer death, who does any of the following:

(a) prepares or endeavours to overthrow the Government by unlawful means; or

---

[1] In view of this statement it should perhaps be pointed out that ss. 22–31 of the Criminal Procedure Code, 1960 (Act 30), reproducing similar provisions in the previous Code, enable suspected persons to be required to execute a bond, with sureties, for their future good behaviour.

(b) prepares or endeavours to procure by force any alteration of the law or the policies of the Government; or

(c) prepares or endeavours to carry out by force any enterprise which usurps the executive power of the State in any matter of both a public and a general nature; or

(d) incites or assists any person to invade Ghana with armed force or unlawfully to subject any part of Ghana to attack by land, sea or air, or assists in the preparation of any such invasion or attack; or

(e) in time of war and with intent to give assistance to the enemy, does any act which is likely to give such assistance.[1]

Whether or not the mere uttering of disloyal statements, unaccompanied by other acts, amounts to treason is largely a matter of degree. A relevant factor is the intent with which the words were uttered, that is whether they were a mere expression of dissatisfaction or were seriously intended to bring about one of the objects specified in the definition of treason. In time of war the scope of treason is much enlarged, and almost any disloyal publication will be likely to fall within the fifth head of the definition.

Misprision of treason.—A person who knows of any treason and does not forthwith reveal it to the President, a Minister or a police officer is guilty of misprision of treason and liable to imprisonment for up to ten years.[2]

Treason-felony.—This is punishable with imprisonment for life. It is committed by any person who—

(a) prepares or endeavours to procure by unlawful means any alteration of the law or the policies of the Government; or

(b) prepares or endeavours to carry out by unlawful means any enterprise which usurps the executive power of the State in any matter of both a public and a general nature.[3]

The heads of this definition closely resemble the second and third heads of the definition of treason. The difference lies in the means to be used. If force is to be used the offence will be treason; if unlawful means short of force are to be used the offence will be treason-felony.[4]

---

[1] Criminal Code, 1960 (Act 29), s. 180.

[2] *Ibid.*, s. 181.

[3] *Ibid.*, s. 182.

[4] In this connection " force " includes a show of force: Criminal Code, 1960, s. 180 (2).

Sedition.—The Criminal Code renders punishable many acts connected with the uttering of spoken or written words having a seditious intention.[1] An intention is taken to be seditious if it is an intention—

(a) to advocate the desirability of overthrowing the Government by unlawful means; or

(b) to bring the Government into hatred or contempt or to excite disaffection against it; or

(c) to excite the people of Ghana to attempt to procure the alteration, otherwise than by lawful means, of any other matter in Ghana as by law established; or

(d) to bring into hatred or contempt or to excite disaffection against the administration of justice in Ghana; or

(e) to raise discontent or disaffection among the people of Ghana; or

(f) to promote feelings of ill-will or hostility between different classes of the population of Ghana; or

(g) falsely to accuse any public officer of misconduct in the exercise of his official duties, knowing the accusation to be false or reckless whether it be true or false.[2]

An intention will not however be taken to be seditious if, without advocating the overthrow of the Government by unlawful means, it points out mistakes in Government measures, or defects in the Constitution or other laws or in the administration of justice. It is also permissible to point out, with a view to their removal, any matters tending to produce feelings of ill-will or hostility between different classes of the population.[3]

False Reports

It is an offence punishable with imprisonment for up to ten years knowingly to communicate any false statement or report which is likely to injure the credit or reputation of Ghana or the Government, unless the communication is made in the National Assembly or on some other privileged occasion. A citizen of Ghana is guilty of the offence even if the act complained of was committed abroad.[4]

---

[1] Criminal Code, 1960, s. 183.

[2] *Ibid.*, s. 183 (11).

[3] *Ibid.*, s. 183 (12). Much of the definition of seditious intention derives from Sir James Stephen's *Digest of Criminal Law*, although it was remodelled in 1959, when the penalties were substantially increased (Sedition Act, 1959 (No. 64)).

[4] Criminal Code, 1960, s. 185.

The offence was introduced in 1959, following the abortive prosecution of R. R. Amponsah for sedition.[1] The Government gave the following reason for its introduction:

> " The present criminal law of Ghana in these matters [*i.e.*, relating to criminal libel] dates from the middle of the nineteenth century when press conferences and the addressing of large public meetings through loud-speaker equipment was unknown. In consequence, normally speaking, a false statement is not punishable unless it is made in writing and it is possible, for example, for all types of allegations to be made at a press conference without it being possible to charge the person concerned with criminal defamation."[2]

This statement appears to overlook s. 459 of the former Criminal Code, now reproduced as s. 208 of the present Code. By this, any person who publishes or reproduces any statement, rumour or report which is likely to cause fear and alarm to the public or to disturb the public peace, knowing or having reason to believe that the statement, rumour or report is false, is liable to imprisonment for up to three years. Knowledge of its falsity will be assumed unless the accused proves that he took reasonable measures to verify the accuracy of the statement, rumour or report.

State Secrets

State secrets are protected by the State Secrets Act, 1962 (Act 101), which replaced s. 192 of the Criminal Code. This goes wider than merely restricting freedom of disclosure and makes it an offence punishable with imprisonment up to 14 years for a person to do any of the following acts for a purpose prejudicial to the safety or interests of the Republic—

(a) to enter, approach, inspect, pass over or be in the neighbourhood of, any place which has been declared by executive instrument to be a prohibited place;

(b) to make any sketch, plan, model or note which might be useful to a foreign power;

(c) to obtain, record, publish or otherwise communicate any secret official code word or pass word, or any sketch, plan, model, article, document or information which might be useful to a foreign power;

(d) to retain any official document when he has no right to retain it, or to fail to comply with any lawful directions with regard to its return or disposal.

---

[1] See p. 224, *ante*.
[2] White Paper No. 10/59, p. 49.

Censorship and other Controls

Censorship of newspapers.—Press censorship was introduced in 1960, following increasing Government dissatisfaction with the way in which the *Ashanti Pioneer*, a newspaper supporting the Opposition, was conducted. The provision giving powers of censorship is in the following terms—

" Whenever the Present is of opinion:

(*a*) that there is in any newspaper, book or document which is published periodically a systematic publication of matter calculated to prejudice public order or safety, or the maintenance of the public services or economy of Ghana, or

(*b*) that any person is likely to publish individual documents containing such matter,

he may make an executive instrument, requiring that no future issue of the newspaper, book or document shall be published, or, as the case may be, that no document shall be published by, or by arrangement with, the said person, unless the matter contained therein has been passed for publication in accordance with the instrument."[1]

It will be noticed that this provision not only enables newspapers and similar periodicals to be censored but also allows all the writings of a particular individual to be subjected to scrutiny before publication. So far however it has only been used in the former manner, and only in relation to the *Ashanti Pioneer*. In this case a Government representative was installed in the offices of the newspaper and all copy was shown to him before being set up and printed.

Another form of censorship, which has existed for a quarter of a century, is the power of the Government to prohibit the importation of any newspaper, book or document which would be contrary to the public interest.[2] This power has been frequently used, particularly during the struggle for independence.

Registration of Newspapers.—The printers and publishers of every newspaper and news journal circulating in Ghana are required to register details of its title, editor, publisher, proprietor, printer and circulation. Annual returns must be submitted and changes notified as they occur. The names of the editor, publisher and printer must also appear on every copy sold.[3]

Censorship of Films.—No cinematograph film may be exhibited in public unless it has been passed by a Board of Control, who

---

[1] Criminal Code, 1960 (Act 29), s. 183 (2).　　[2] *Ibid.*, s. 183 (1).
[3] Book and Newspaper Registration Act, 1961 (Act 73), Part II, re-enacting an Ordinance first made in 1894.

may impose conditions requiring cuts and other modifications to be made, limiting the showing of the film to persons over sixteen, and otherwise restricting public exhibition. Posters advertising films are also subject to censorship. Exhibitors may be required to show a quota of films made by the Ghana Film Production Corporation, a Government body. Except in the case of a private residence, premises must not be used for the exhibition of films unless the premises have been licensed by the Commissioner of Police. There is no appeal against refusal of permission to exhibit or against refusal to licence premises.[1]

Control of Broadcasting.—Under a recent Act the President has " the exclusive privilege of constructing and maintaining tele-communications throughout Ghana ". The former exemption from control of private transmitters and those in ships and aircraft has thus been abolished, although provision is made for the grant of licences. No licence is now required for a radio receiver, but power to restore a licensing system is retained.[2]

Defamation

Restrictions are placed both by the criminal and the civil law on the uttering of defamatory statements. The civil law, that is the law relating to the torts of libel and slander, which are action-able in damages and subject to the grant of injunctions restraining their repetition, and the customary law rules as to defamation, are beyond the scope of this chapter.[3] The criminal rules are set out below.

Defamation of President.—Any person who, with intent to bring the President of Ghana into hatred, ridicule or contempt, publishes any defamatory or insulting matter, whether by writing, print, word of mouth or in any other manner, is liable to imprisonment for up to three years.[4]

---

[1] Cinematograph Act, 1961 (Act 76), re-enacting an Ordinance first made in 1925.

[2] Telecommunications Act, 1962 (Act 112), replacing the Wireless Telecommunication Ordinance (Cap. 216).

[3] For the rules governing the respective application of common law and customary law in cases of defamation, see Chap. 12, *post.*

[4] Criminal Code, 1960 (Act 29), s. 183A. (Added by Act 82 of 1961. The wording follows that of s. 345 of the previous Criminal Code (Cap. 9) which related to the Queen and was omitted from the original version of the Code of 1960.) If the offender is a Ghanaian citizen the offence is punishable even if committed out of Ghana (Act 93).

Defamation of National Assembly.—Defamation of the National Assembly, or of the Speaker, a Member of Parliament or an officer of the Assembly, constitutes contempt of Parliament and may be punished as such.[1]

Insult to National Flag.—Whoever does any act or utters any words or publishes any writing with intent to insult or bring into contempt or ridicule the official national flag or emblem of Ghana or any representation thereof is liable to imprisonment for up to three years.[2]

Defamation by Communal or Religious Organisation.—It is an offence for any organisation whose membership is substantially restricted to any one tribal, racial or religious community to have as one of its objects the exposure of a section of the public to hatred, contempt or ridicule on account of their community or religion. Any person concerned in the management or control of the organisation is liable to imprisonment for up to three years and it may be ordered to be wound up under the supervision of the High Court.[3]

Criminal Libel.—Criminal libel is divided into two categories, negligent libel, which is punishable by a fine not exceeding £G100, and intentional libel, which is punishable with imprisonment for up to three years.[4] The offence is committed by unlawfully publishing matter defamatory of another person in the form of written words or by any other means otherwise than solely by gestures, spoken words or other sounds. Matter is defamatory which imputes to a person any felony or misdemeanour, or misconduct in any public office, or which is likely to injure him in his occupation, calling or office, or to expose him to general hatred, contempt or ridicule. The truth of the allegation is no defence unless it is found that it was for the public benefit that the matter should be published.

The publication of a libel will not be unlawful if the publication is privileged. There are two categories of privilege, namely absolute privilege, which exists even where the matter published was not believed by the publisher to be true or where the publication was malicious, and qualified privilege, which can only exist

---

[1] See pp. 326, *et seq., post.*
[2] Criminal Code, 1960 (Act 29), s. 184. See p. 130, *ante.*
[3] Avoidance of Discrimination Act, 1957 (No. 38), ss. 3, 4, 9.
[4] Under s. 297 of the Criminal Procedure Code, 1960 (Act 30), where an offence is punishable with imprisonment the court may impose a fine instead of or in addition to the imprisonment.

where the matter was published in good faith. Examples of absolute privilege are the following—

(a) matter published in any official document or proceeding;
(b) matter published by order of the President, a Minister or the National Assembly;[1]
(c) matter published in judicial proceedings;[2]
(d) matter published by a person who is legally bound to publish it.

There are numerous instances of qualified privilege, of which the following may be singled out for mention—

(a) reports of judicial proceedings;
(b) reviews of books, plays and other items submitted to public judgment;
(c) statements made by or to persons in authority with regard to the conduct of persons under their authority;
(d) matter published for the protection of the rights or interests of the person who publishes it, or of the person to whom it is published, or of some person in whom the person to whom it is published is interested.[3]

Obscenity

A person who publishes or offers for sale any obscene book, writing or representation is liable to imprisonment for up to three years. The Criminal Code gives no definition of what is obscene and the courts would presumably be guided by the common law meaning of obscenity as it prevailed in England before the passing of the Obscene Publications Act, 1959. The test was laid down in *R.* v. *Hicklin*[4] as being " whether the tendency of the matter charged as obscene is to deprave and corrupt those whose minds are open to such immoral influences and into whose hands a publication of this sort may fall.[5] However an illustration

---

[1] *Cf.* National Assembly Act, 1961 (Act 86), ss. 20, 21, 25, 26 and 27, pp. 321 *et seq.*, *post.* These provisions to some extent duplicate those of s. 117 of the Criminal Code, 1960 (Act 29).

[2] Matter published by counsel for the defence in criminal proceedings or by counsel on either side in civil proceedings is subject only to qualified privilege.

[3] Criminal Code, 1960 (Act 29), ss. 112–119.

[4] (1867), L.R. 3 Q.B. 360, 371.

[5] *Cf.* the modern English test, under which a book or other article is deemed to be obscene " if its effect or (where the article comprises two or more distinct items) the effect of any one of its items is, if taken as a whole, such as to tend to deprave and corrupt persons who are likely, having regard to all relevant circumstances, to read, see or hear the matter contained or embodied in it ": Obscene Publications Act, 1959, s. 1 (1).

appended to the section creating the offence speaks of a publication which " is calculated unnecessarily and improperly to excite passion, or to corrupt morals ".[1] Advertisements relating to venereal disease or other complaints or infirmities connected with sexual intercourse are deemed to be obscene unless published by authority of the Ministry of Health.

Various other offences relating to obscene matter exist, including one making punishable the distribution or public exhibition of such matter. A district magistrate has power to order the destruction of obscene articles with which offences might otherwise be committed.[2]

Comment on matters which are sub judice

A person who, when proceedings are pending in any court, publishes in writing or otherwise anything concerning the proceedings or a party to them with intent to excite any popular prejudice for or against any party to the proceedings, commits a misdemeanour and is liable to imprisonment for up to three years.[3]

3. FREEDOM OF RELIGION

Freedom of religion is one of the freedoms mentioned in art. 13 of the Constitution, and it is the one freedom so mentioned that is not subject to any substantial limitation. There are no religious tests in Ghana and everyone is free to choose his own religion or to hold no religious beliefs at all.[4] Of course religion must be practised with due regard to the rights of others and to the ordinary provisions of the criminal law. It was principally this consideration which led to the restrictions on fetish worship and other customary practices imposed by the Colonial Government and still in force. Restrictions are also imposed on political activities by religious organisations. Apart from briefly describing these restrictions we need only deal here with one other matter, namely the special protection given by the criminal law to church services and other forms of religious observance.

---

[1] Criminal Code, 1960 (Act 29), s. 280. Such illustrations may be used as aids to construction: *ibid.*, s. 4 (c).

[2] *Ibid.*, ss. 280–284.   [3] *Ibid.*, s. 225.

[4] The taking of an oath without religious belief does not affect its validity, and a person who objects to taking an oath is at liberty to affirm instead (Oaths Act, 1960 (C.A. 12), ss. 7, 8). Blasphemy is not an offence. By s. 22 of the Education Act, 1961 (Act 87) admission to a school is not to be refused on account of religious persuasion, nationality, race or language, and no pupil is to be required to take part in or abstain from religious instruction or observance.

Restrictions on fetish worship, etc.

An Ordinance originally made in 1892 and still operative today gave the Governor in Council power to suppress the celebration or practice of any native custom, rite, ceremony or worship which appeared to him to involve or to tend towards the commission of crime or a breach of the peace or otherwise to be harmful.[1] Orders, which remain in force, were made under this power in relation to a large number of customs and practices.[2] The Ordinance directly suppressed the celebration of the Krobo customs and subjected any fetish priest or other person who took part in them to heavy penalties (s. 4). It also prohibited the worship or invocation of any fetish " which it is pretended or reputed, has power to protect persons in the commission of, or guilty of crime, or to injure persons giving information of the commission of crime" (s. 5).

Fetish oaths (other than those sworn before giving evidence) are unlawful and punishable with imprisonment for up to one year.[3] Local courts have jurisdiction to try a customary law offence of putting a person into fetish or swearing an unlawful oath.[4]

Political Restrictions

The Avoidance of Discrimination Act, 1957 (No. 38) was passed with the object of securing a national approach to political affairs, particularly among the opposition groups. Its aim was to prevent the formation of political parties based on communal or religious interests and to diminish communal and religious strife generally.[5] Although the following brief account is confined to matters of religion it applies equally in relation to groups having common tribal, racial or regional connections.

Defamation.—The prohibition of religious organisations having the object of defaming other groups has already been described.[6]

---

[1] Native Customs (Colony) Ordinance (Cap. 97), s. 16.

[2] See Laws of the Gold Coast, 1954, Vol. VIII, pp. 730–733.

[3] Chieftaincy Act, 1961 (Act 81), ss. 51, 65.

[4] Courts Act, 1960 (C.A. 9), s. 147.

[5] The occasion for the passing of the Act was the founding of the Ga Shifimo Kpee. This was described by the Government as " a political organisation frankly based on tribal affiliations. Its objects were in essence to drive out of Accra all those who were not of Ga origin." The formation of the United Party was claimed by the Government to be the direct result of this legislation. (White Paper No. 10/59, p. 26).

[6] P. 232, *ante.*

Elections.—No organisation established substantially for the direct or indirect benefit or advancement of the interests of any particular religious faith may organise or operate for the purposes of engaging in any Parliamentary or local government election. If it does so it may be wound up under the supervision of the High Court, and its promoters will be liable to imprisonment for up to one year.[1]

Symbols.—No political party may use any symbol or name which may be identified with any particular religious faith, and no religious organisation whose members engage in politics may permit any name or symbol associated with it to be used for a political purpose.[2]

Disturbances in churches, etc.

A person who does any of the following acts commits a criminal offence punishable by a fine not exceeding £G50—

(a) behaves irreverently or indecently in any church, chapel, mosque, or other place appropriated for religious worship;

(b) disturbs or molests any minister of religion while he is celebrating any religious rite or office in any public place, or any person assisting or attending at the celebration of such rite or office;

(c) behaves irreverently or indecently or insultingly at or near any funeral or in or near any public burial ground during the burial of a body.[3]

4. Freedom of Movement and Assembly

The declaration in art. 13 of the Constitution states:

" . . . subject to such restrictions as may be necessary for preserving public order, morality or health, no person should be deprived . . . of the right to move and assemble without hindrance."

Apart from physical restraint, which has been discussed earlier in this chapter, the main restrictions on movement and assembly are the following—

(a) the power conferred by the Public Order Act, 1961 (Act

---

[1] Avoidance of Discrimination Act, 1957 (No. 38), ss. 5, 9.

[2] *Ibid.*, ss. 6, 7.

[3] Criminal Code, 1960 (Act 29), s. 296 (11)–(13).

58) to control public meetings and processions and to impose curfews;

(b) the provisions of the Criminal Code relating to unlawful assemblies and disturbances at public meetings;

(c) the enactments governing obstruction of streets and other public places;

(d) the control over the place of residence of individuals given by s. 355 of the Criminal Procedure Code, 1960 (Act 30),[1] s. 4 of the Chieftaincy Act, 1961 (Act 81),[2] and s. 2 of the Deportation (Amendment) Act, 1959 (No. 65).[3] (Notification of place of residence is required in certain cases by ss. 395 and 399 of the Criminal Procedure Code, 1960 (Act 30)[4] and s. 3(4) of the Preventive Detention Act, 1958 (No. 17)[5]).

Control of Public Meetings and Processions

Part II of the Public Order Act, 1961 (Act 58), which provides for the control of public meetings and processions, is not universally operative but may be applied in particular localities by executive instrument as required. However the provisions now contained in Part II of the Act have been in force in all the principal towns and in most other centres of population for the past seven years or so, and the control has assumed an appearance of permanence.[6] The following account applies only to places where Part II is in force.

A meeting or procession held or formed in a public place is unlawful unless a police permit has first been obtained. In no case are the police obliged to grant a permit, and the officer considering the application must not grant it unless he is satisfied that a breach of the peace is unlikely to be caused. Where the permit is granted it may be subject to conditions regulating the time and place of the meeting, the use of music, drumming and other instruments or apparatus in the meeting or procession, the way in which it is conducted and, in the case of a procession, the

---

[1] Section 355 enables residence conditions to be imposed when an offender is put on probation.

[2] Section 4 gives power to exclude destooled Chiefs from residence in a specified area (p. 178, *ante*).

[3] Section 2 enables an undesirable alien who cannot be deported to be required to live in a specified area (p. 204, *ante*.).

[4] The sections mentioned relate to convicts released on licence or parole.

[5] Where a preventive detention order is suspended s. 3 (4) requires the released person to notify his movements.

[6] See s. 10 (2) and the Public Meetings and Processions Regulations, 1954 (L.N. 415).

time and route to be followed. Where a meeting or procession is held without a permit or the conditions of the permit are broken the police may intervene and order those taking part to disperse. Such intervention is also permissible where a breach of the peace has occurred or is likely.

The penalty for breach of the requirements of Part II of the Public Order Act, or for failure peacefully to depart on police intervention, is imprisonment for up to one year. The fine which may be imposed instead of, or in addition to, imprisonment is limited to £G100.

Unlawful Assembly

In addition to the local restrictions imposed by Part II of the Public Order Act, the Criminal Code deals generally with riot and other forms of unlawful assembly. A riot takes place when five or more persons together in any public *or private* place commence or attempt to do any of the following:

(a) to execute any common purpose with violence, and without lawful authority to use such violence for that purpose; or

(b) to execute a common purpose of obstructing or resisting the execution of any legal process or authority; or

(c) to facilitate, by force or by show of force or numbers, the commission of any crime.

Riot is punishable with imprisonment for up to three years unless offensive weapons are used, when the maximum is ten years. A person who does any act with intent to provoke a riot is also liable to imprisonment for up to three years.[1]

Apart from riot, the Criminal Code lays down as a separate offence the taking part in an unlawful assembly. The penalties are the same as for riot. The definition of unlawful assembly for this purpose is a follows:

> " When three or more persons assemble with intent to commit an offence, or being assembled with intent to carry out some common purpose, conduct themselves in such a manner as to cause persons in the neighbourhood reasonably to fear that the persons so assembled will commit a breach of the peace, or will by such assembly needlessly and without any reasonable occasion provoke other persons to commit a breach of the peace, they are an unlawful assembly. It is immaterial that the original assembling was lawful if, being assembled, they conduct themselves with a common purpose in such a manner."[2]

---

[1] Criminal Code, 1960 (Act 29), ss. 196–200.
[2] Criminal Code, 1960 (Act 29), ss. 201, 202.

Disturbance of Lawful Assembly

There are two offences of disturbing a lawful meeting or other assembly, each punishable with imprisonment for up to three years. The first arises where a person unlawfully and with violence obstructs or disturbs the assembly, or with violence disperses or attempts to disperse it. The other is committed by any person present at the assembly who uses threatening, abusive or insulting words or behaviour with intent to provoke a breach of the peace or in a way that is likely to lead to a breach of the peace.[1]

Obstruction of Streets, etc.

Freedom of movement and assembly does not of course carry any right to trespass on private property for the purpose of holding meetings or processions, and for this purpose most land in public ownership ranks as private property. Nor can the exercise of freedom of movement by one group of persons be allowed to interfere with the free movement of others. In any human society each person's freedom must be bounded by the freedom of his fellows.

Free passage along highways is protected by s. 296 of the Criminal Code, paragraph (16) of which renders any person who, by obstructing any public way, wilfully prevents or hinders the free passage of any other person or of any vehicle liable to a fine of £G50. Paragraph (21) of the same section imposes a similar penalty or any person who—

" . . . assembles with other persons in any public place, or in any open space near a public place, for any idle, vicious, or disorderly purpose, or otherwise than in the regular performance or in pursuance of some lawful calling or object, to the annoyance or obstruction of any passenger or person frequenting such public place or of any person living in the neighbourhood thereof, and does not move away when required by a constable."

Power to regulate the movement of pedestrians and other traffic is conferred upon local authorities and police officers.[2]

Curfews

Power to impose a curfew is conferred by Part III of the Public Order Act, 1961 (Act 58). If the Minister of the Interior is satisfied that it is necessary in the interests of public order or the

---

[1] Criminal Code, 1960 (Act 29), ss. 204, 207. *Cf.* s. 298 (acts tending to disturb the peace in a public place) .

[2] Local Government Act, 1961 (Act 54), s. 47 and Sch. I, para. 62; Police Force Ordinance (Cap. 37), s. 54 (1), (2).

maintenance of the public peace, he may, by executive instrument, impose a curfew in such places as may be specified in the instrument. Where a curfew is in force no person who is not entitled to exemption may be out of doors within the prescribed hours (usually hours of darkness) without a permit. The penalty for disobedience is imprisonment for up to one year. The fine which may be imposed instead of, or in addition to, imprisonment is limited to £G100.

The power to impose curfews has been little used. Since independence only four curfew orders have been made, in Kpandu (1957), parts of Accra (1958), Wamfie (1958) and Sekondi/Takoradi (1961). All were revoked soon after they were made.

5. Freedom of Association

Although freedom of association is not mentioned in the Constitution it is one of the natural freedoms which usually finds a place in discussions of constitutional law. It has two aspects: one concerning the types of association prohibited or regulated by the law and the other relating to the cases in which membership of a particular organisation is made more or less compulsory.

The following types of association are prohibited in Ghana—
(a) associations formed to further a criminal conspiracy;
(b) trade unions which do not conform to the enactments regulating industrial relations;
(c) associations which contravene the Avoidance of Discrimination Act, 1957 (No. 38).[1]

Conspiracy

The offence of criminal conspiracy is defined in the following way—

> " If two or more persons agree or act together with a common purpose for or in committing or abetting a crime, whether with or without any previous consort or deliberation, each of them is guilty of conspiracy to commit or abet that crime, as the case may be."[3]

This definition is considerably narrower than the common law meaning of criminal conspiracy, which it supersedes. There must be an actual crime in contemplation, that is " any act punishable

---

[1] See p. 232, *ante.*
[2] Criminal Code, 1960 (Act 29), s. 23 (1).

by death or imprisonment or fine ",[1] whereas the common law, as still applying in England, also punishes agreements concerning acts which, though immoral or otherwise unlawful, are not criminal if done only by one person.

The punishment for conspiracy differs according to whether the contemplated crime is actually committed or not. If it is, the penalty is the same as for the crime itself. If it is not, the conspirators are punishable to the same extent as if they had abetted the crime.[2] In practice the distinction is unimportant since, except in the case of capital offences (where it is punishable with life imprisonment) abetment of a crime is punishable in the same way as the crime itself.[3]

Tortious conspiracy.—A person who suffers loss from the action of persons in association may have a common law remedy in damages. The tort of conspiracy was defined by Sir Percy Winfield as follows:

> " When two or more persons combine for the purpose of inflicting upon another person an injury which is unlawful in itself, or which is rendered unlawful by the mode in which it is inflicted, and in either case the other person suffers damage, they commit the tort of conspiracy."[4]

Unlawful training.—If three or more persons meet or are together for the purposes of military training or exercise without the permission of the President, or of some officer or person authorised by law to give such permission, each of them is guilty of a misdemeanour and liable to imprisonment for up to three years.[5]

Unlawful oaths.—A person is guilty of a misdemeanour and liable to imprisonment for up to three years if he takes, or adminsters, or attempts or offers to administer to any other person, any oath or engagement to commit or abet any crime, or to conceal a design to commit any crime, or to prevent the discovery of any crime, or to conceal the existence, purposes or proceedings of any association of persons associated for any treasonable or seditious purpose.[6]

---

[1] Criminal Code, 1960 (Act 29), s. 1.
[2] *Ibid.*, s. 24.
[3] *Ibid.*, s. 20.
[4] *A Text-book of the Law of Tort* (4th Edn.), p. 428.
[5] Criminal Code, 1960 (Act 29), s. 189.
[6] *Ibid.*, s. 191.

Q

Trade Unions

The T.U.C.—The representative of the trade union movement in Ghana is the Trades Union Congress, which in its present form was established by statute in 1958 and which, through its close connection with the ruling Convention People's Party, has great influence in all matters concerning industrial relations.[1] The T.U.C. is a body corporate consisting of three members drawn from each of the sixteen trade unions affiliated to it. The unions are affiliated by statute, and the effect of the relevant enactments is that all unions must be affiliated. The statutory functions of the T.U.C. include " the efficient organisation, management, working and disciplinary control " of the affiliated unions. The leading post is that of Secretary-General, the holder of which, although not a member of Parliament, has been officially styled Minister Plenipotentiary and Ambassador Extraordinary.[2] The funds of the T.U.C. come from dues which must be deducted by employers from wages and salaries and paid by them direct to the T.U.C., who have power to fix the amount.[3]

Closed Shop.—The principle of the " closed shop " or " union shop " became almost universal in 1960, when it was enacted that no worker of a class covered by a collective bargaining certificate could be kept in any employment for more than a month unless he belonged to the appropriate union. Breach of this requirement by an employer constitutes an unfair labour practice.[4] Most civil servants are required by law to belong to a trade union.[5] With certain exceptions, no person may be given employment unless he is registered at a public employment centre.[6]

Position of Trade Unions.—An association cannot lawfully function as a trade union unless it has been registered under the Trade Unions Ordinance (Cap. 91). Registration cannot be

---

[1] The T.U.C. has been described by a Government spokesman as " an integral part of the Convention People's Party "—*Parl. Deb. Official Report*, Vol. 22, col. 218 (23rd Feb., 1961).

[2] *Ibid.*, cols. 226–227.

[3] Industrial Relations Act, 1958 (No. 56), Part I and s. 40, as amended by Act 7 (1960).

[4] *Ibid.*, ss. 16, 31. Unfair labour practices also include interference by employers in trade union affairs, failure to give facilities to trade union officials and acts by an employee intended to cause a serious interference with the business of his employer. They are dealt with by a tribunal, who may order an unfair practice to cease on pain of committal as for contempt of court (*ibid.*, Part V).

[5] Civil Service Act, 1960 (C.A. 5), s. 24; Civil Service (Interim) Regulations, 1960 (L.I. 47), reg. 43.

[6] Labour Registration Act, 1960 (Act 9), s. 6.

effected without the consent of the Minister responsible for labour. A registered trade union is a body corporate and has a similar protection in law to that enjoyed by unions in England. It purposes are not, by reason merely that they are in restraint of trade, to be deemed unlawful so as to render a member liable to criminal prosecution for conspiracy or otherwise, or so as to render void or voidable any agreement or trust.[1] Nor is any combination to do an act in contemplation or furtherance of a trade dispute indictable or actionable as a conspiracy unless the act would be unlawful if done by one individual.[2] Peaceful picketing is made lawful, and an act done in contemplation or furtherance of a trade dispute is not actionable as an interference with contractual relations.[3] No action in tort can be brought against a trade union in respect of any act committed in contemplation or furtherance of a trade dispute.[4]

Exceptions to the above immunities exist in the case of illegal strikes and lockouts, that is those which have objects other than or in addition to a trade dispute and are calculated to coerce the Government either directly or by inflicting hardship upon the community.[5] A strike or lockout is also unlawful where compulsory arbitration has been directed or the employees are not of a class specified in a collective bargaining certificate.[6] It is an offence for an employee maliciously to break a contract of service when the probable consequence is to interefere with the supply of an essential public service or to endanger life or property.[7]

Except in relation to workers paid at a rate of £G680 a year or more, it is in general an offence for any person other than a trade union official to engage in collective bargaining on behalf of employees.[8]

Co-operative Societies

The Government's recent policy has been to expand and develop the use of co-operative societies in all fields of industry, including agriculture and retail supply. For this purpose the National Co-operative Council was established in December,

---

[1] Trade Unions Ordinance (Cap. 91), ss. 3, 4, 9, 10, 11, 14.

[2] Conspiracy and Protection of Property (Trade Disputes) Ordinance (Cap. 90), s. 3.

[3] *Ibid.*, ss. 7–9.   [4] *Ibid.*, s. 10.   [5] *Ibid.*, ss. 6, 11.

[6] Industrial Relations Act, 1958 (No. 56), ss. 28, 29. In this case an offender is liable to imprisonment for up to one year, although it is not an offence for an individual merely to stop work (*ibid.*, s. 30).

[7] Conspiracy and Protection of Property (Trade Disputes) Ordinance (Cap. 90), ss. 4, 5.

[8] Industrial Relations (Amendment) Act, 1959 (No. 43), s. 5.

1959 as the body responsible for co-ordinating the activities of the co-operative sector of the country's economy. Consumers' co-operatives are also receiving Government support.[1] The position is fluid, and the necessary modifications to the law are still in the preparatory stage at the time of writing. Co-operatives remain subject to the Co-operative Societies Ordinance (Cap. 190), which confers the benefits of corporate status on a registered society, but as this Ordinance is likely to be repealed shortly it will not be considered here.

6. FREEDOM OF PROPERTY

The final paragraph of the declaration contained in art. 13 of the Constitution states—

" that no person should be deprived of his property save where the public interest so requires and the law so provides."

All countries find it necessary to interfere to a considerable exten₁ with the individual's freedom to retain and use his property. The following principles find acceptance in Ghana as in most other countries:

(a) all citizens must contribute a fair proportion of their property in payment of taxes, rates, duties and other imposts necessary to provide the public revenue;

(b) if private property is needed for a public purpose it may be acquired compulsorily on payment of fair compensation;

(c) development of land and the use of buildings will be so controlled as to conform to the requirements of good planning, the proper use of natural resources and the preservation of public health;

(d) the regulation of the national economy may call for measures affecting private property, such as those relating to imports and exports, and exchange control;

(e) an individual must not use his property in such a way as to injure his neighbour: *sic utere tuo ut alienum non laedas*.

The laws which carry these principles into operation and otherwise affect rights of property are numerous and extensive. Those relating to the public revenue have been described in Chapter 3.[2] Others of major importance will be briefly discussed here.

---

[1] *Parl. Deb. Official Report*, Vol. 22, col. 193 (23rd February, 1961).

[2] Pp. 155, *et seq.*, *ante*. See also the Compulsory Savings Act, 1961 (Act 70), which introduced a system of compulsory savings by the purchase of bonds issued by the Bank of Ghana, and the Income Tax (Amendment) Act, 1962 (Act 110), an extraordinary provision which gives the Commissioner of Income Tax *carte blanche* to raise unchallengeable assessments for income tax in past years.

Compulsory Acquisition

The main provisions relating to the compulsory acquisition of land and other property are contained in Part I of the State Property and Contracts Act, 1960 (C.A. 6). If the owner cannot be persuaded to agree to sell the property required, the following procedure is laid down for compulsory acquisition:

(a) the President, or someone acting on his behalf, declares by a notice in the *Gazette* that the property is required for the public service;

(b) copies of the notice are served on the owner, affixed on the property, and published in three consecutive issues of a newspaper circulating in the district where the property is situated;

(c) within three months from the publication of the declaration persons having an interest in the property must notify the Chief Lands Officer;

(d) at any time after the date of the declaration the Chief Lands Officer is entitled to receive from the High Court a certificate of title vesting the property in the President and his successors in defeasance of all prior rights;

(e) compensation must be paid at a figure which will include not only the full market value of the property but also any loss by way of severence, injurious affection or disturbance and the cost to the owner of survey and valuation fees. Disputes as to the amount of compensation or the ownership of the property are determined by the High Court with an appeal to the Supreme Court.[1]

Land can only be acquired by this procedure where its use is required for some public purpose. There are two methods however by which the procedure is adapted for application in other cases. The first is used where the Government considers that it would be in the national interest for certain land to be developed by a private industrial undertaking but the company concerned is unable to obtain the land for itself. An executive instrument is made declaring the land an industrial area and this has the same effect as a declaration that it is required for the public service. When the land has been acquired however it is permissible for

---

[1] State Property and Contracts Act, 1960 (C.A. 6), ss. 4 (1), (4), 8 (1), 9, 10, 14.

the Government to grant a lease of it to the industrial developer.[1] The other method of adapting the procedure is by making it available to statutory corporations and other semi-public bodies by the inclusion of appropriate provisions in their instruments of incorporation.[2] In the case of land required by local authorities the President may direct that the procedure shall apply if he is satisfied that the purpose for which the land is required is of public benefit or importance.[3]

Planning Laws

Planning of land development and use is regulated in Ghana by methods similar to those employed in the United Kingdom, that is by public health powers vested in local authorities and by town and country planning laws.

Local authorities are given detailed and extensive powers to make building regulations, but these can only be exercised with Ministerial approval. Among the subjects covered are the construction of buildings and other structures, the execution of work on existing buildings and structures, the making of streets and the provision of sanitary facilities.[4]

Town and country planning legislation was introduced into Ghana in 1945. Control is exercised only within areas designated as planning areas. Within such areas development or change of use of land is only permissible if it conforms to a planning scheme for the area or is done with the consent of the appropriate Minister, who may however exclude certain activities within the area from control. Breach of the restrictions is punishable by a fine of £G10 together with £G1 for every day during which the offence continues.[5]

The need to prevent soil erosion and safeguard the timber industry has also led to extensive legislation giving power to designate private lands as forest reserves and imposing restrictions on the destruction of trees.[6]

---

[1] State Property and Contracts Act, 1960 (C.A. 6), ss. 5, 6.

[2] See, *e.g.*, the University of Ghana Act, 1961 (Act 79), s. 12 (2).

[3] Local Government Act, 1961 (Act 54), s. 73. Section 19 of the Education Act, 1961 (Act 87) enables the Minister of Education to close, or to take over on payment of such compensation as he thinks fit, any private school.

[4] Local Government Act, 1961 (Act 54), s. 58.

[5] Town and Country Planning Ordinance (Cap. 84), ss. 9, 10 as amended by Act No. 30 of 1958 and Act 33 (1960).

[6] The principal legislation is the Forests Ordinance (Cap. 157), which dates from 1927.

Economic Controls

Imports and Exports.—The power to prohibit the importation, carriage coastwise or exportation of any goods whatsoever, which was formerly exercisable by the Governor in Council, has now passed to the Minister of Finance. In addition to this completely general control, restrictions are imposed on a large number of specified articles.[1]

Concessions.—The need to protect the local inhabitants from exploitation by mining and other interests led to the passing of the Concessions Ordinance in 1900.[2] The present version of the Ordinance applies to the whole of Ghana except the Northern and Upper Regions.[3] It restricts the grant, by any person of African birth entitled to land under customary law, of any right in the land or the minerals, timber or other produce of the land. Notice of concessions must be filed with the High Court, who must certify whether the concession is valid or invalid. In determining validity the court is guided by a number of factors, including adequacy of consideration, whether customary rights are protected, and whether the appropriate Minister is satisfied that the concession will be properly worked. If necessary the court may modify the terms of the concession. Certain small concessions are excluded from control. Without the consent of the President no one person or company may hold mining concessions exceeding twenty square miles in total area. A similar limit applies in the case of rights to collect rubber, or other products except timber. Miners and prospectors also require a licence from the Government for their activities.[4]

Exchange Control.—As in the United Kingdom, it has been found necessary in Ghana to perpetuate the wartime system of exchange control. Indeed the system was extended in 1961 to regulate transactions within as well as outside the sterling area.[5] Among the requirements imposed are the following—

---

[1] Customs Ordinance (Cap. 167), ss. 41–43. Some of the restricted articles are specified in other enactments, e.g. the Pharmacy and Drugs Act, 1961 (Act 64), ss. 43–46 (narcotics and other drugs).

[2] See p. 21, *ante.*

[3] In these Regions control over land transactions was exercised under the Land and Native Rights Ordinance (Cap. 147). The Ordinance was repealed by the State Property and Contracts Act, 1960 (C.A. 6), s. 19 of which enables similar control to be exercised by regulations.

[4] Concessions Ordinance (Cap. 136).

[5] Exchange Control Act, 1961 (Act 71).

(a) Ghana residents may be made to surrender holdings of gold or external currency on payment of an equivalent sum in Ghana pounds;

(b) the purchase or sale by Ghana residents of gold and external currencies is restricted;

(c) payments and transfers of securities to external residents are restricted, and goods may not be exported (with exceptions) unless payment of their full value has been made to a Ghana resident.

Other Controls.—Numerous other enactments directly or indirectly affect freedom of property on economic grounds. These include the Rent Control Ordinance, 1952 (No. 2), the Control of Prices Act, 1962 (Act 113) and the Labour Ordinance (Cap. 89) (which provides for a minimum rate of remuneration for most workers). The Farm Lands (Protection) Act, 1962 (Act 107) extinguishes the title of a person who buys land for farming but does not farm it within eight years.

Protection of Rights of Property

A reasonable amount of self-help is permitted to a person defending his property from unlawful interference. Such force as is reasonably necessary may be used to repel or eject trespassers, to recover goods wrongly detained, or to overcome any obstruction or resistance to the exercise of any other legal right.[1]

Search warrants.—In general a magistrate's warrant is required before premises can lawfully be entered and searched without the consent of the occupier. Where however a police officer has reasonable cause to believe that the premises contain property which has been stolen or dishonestly received he may search for and seize the property without a warrant, though unless he is of senior rank himself he will require a written authorisation from his superior.[2] A search warrant may be granted if the magistrate is satisfied by evidence given on oath that the premises contain any article that relates to the commission of an offence for which the offender may be arrested without warrant, or which is likely to be used to inflict personal injury. Articles seized under a search

---

[1] Criminal Code, 1960 (Act 29), s. 39.

[2] Criminal Procedure Code, 1960 (Act 30), s. 94. Special powers of entry and search without warrant are conferred by other enactments, *e.g.*, Pharmacy and Drugs Act, 1961 (Act 64), ss. 50–53; Akpeteshi Act, 1961 (Act 77), s. 3.

warrant must be brought before a magistrate, who may order them to be detained until the conclusion of court proceedings.[1]

Offences.—Offences against rights of property are laid down by Part III of the Criminal Code, 1960 (Act 29). They are too numerous to summarize here, but include stealing, fraudulent breach of trust, defrauding by false pretences, receiving stolen property, robbery, extortion, unlawful entry, forgery and unlawful damage.

Civil remedies.—These are provided by the common law rules relating to the torts of trespass, detinue and conversion. Infringement of rights in " intellectual property " is dealt with by statute.[2]

Compensation for riot damage.—The Riot Damages Ordinance (Cap. 46), which was passed in 1950, gives a right to compensation where any house, shop or other building has been damaged or destroyed, or any property or article has been damaged, stolen or destroyed, by any persons riotously or unlawfully assembled together. Entitlement to, and the amount of compensation is assessed by a special commissioner without appeal to the courts. The inhabitants of the riot area may be ordered to contribute to the cost of paying compensation.

Stool property.—Property which belongs to a stool or skin is protected by Part VI of the Chieftaincy Act, 1961 (Act 81).[3]

7. REMEDIES AGAINST THE STATE

Civil proceedings against the Republic are regulated by the State Proceedings Act, 1961 (Act 51), which replaced the former procedure by way of petition of right. Other remedies are provided by the writ of habeas corpus[4] and the orders of mandamus, certiorari and prohibition. Certain limitations are placed on the bringing of civil actions against public officers and other authorities. Criminal prosecutions may be brought in the same way as against private individuals or bodies.

---

[1] Criminal Procedure Code, 1960 (Act 30), ss. 88, 91.
[2] Copyright Act, 1961 (Act 85); Patents Registration Ordinance (Cap. 179); Trade Marks Ordinances (Caps. 180, 181); United Kingdom Designs (Protection) Ordinance (Cap. 182); Merchandise Marks Ordinance (Cap. 178).
[3] See p. 179, *ante.*
[5] Pp. 217 *et seq.*

State Proceedings Act

The Act, which is modelled on the Crown Proceedings Act, 1947 of the United Kingdom, is designed to ensure

> " . . . that, subject to the necessity for obtaining the Attorney-General's *fiat* for an action against the Republic, the liability of the Republic shall, so far as practicable, be based on the same principles as govern the liability of private persons."[1]

The principal differences between the civil liability of the Republic and that of private persons are as follows—

(1) No action may be brought against the Republic without the *fiat* of the Attorney-General.[2] This rule does not differ in substance from that obtaining under the previous law.[3] It was explained in the Memorandum to the Bill in the following terms—

> " The purpose of the *fiat* is to prevent frivolous or vexatious claims being made against the Republic. At present the *fiat* is granted by a Minister on the advice of the Attorney-General, but under Article 47 of the Constitution the Attorney-General is, subject to the directions of the President, responsible for the defence of civil proceedings brought against the Republic, and it therefore seems appropriate that he should be the person to grant the *fiat*."

(2) The Act does not enable an action to be brought by any public officer or member of the armed forces in respect of his salary or pension, or in respect of damages for wrongful dismissal.[4]

(3) No action can be brought against the Republic in respect of a tort committed by a person executing judicial process.[5]

(4) Limitations are placed on the right of members of the armed forces to sue for injury suffered on account of their service.[6]

(5) The court cannot grant an injunction or make an order for specific performance against the Republic, nor can it order the recovery of land or chattels, or entertain any

---

[1] Memorandum to the State Proceedings Bill (13th April, 1961).
[2] Section 1 (1).
[3] See Petitions of Right Ordinance (Cap. 18), ss. 4, 6.
[4] Section 2. A civil servant on contract may sue to enforce the terms of the contract: Civil Service Act, 1960 (C.A. 5), s. 41.
[5] Section 3 (2).
[6] Section 8.

proceedings *in rem* against the Republic. Instead the court may make an order declaratory of the rights of the parties.[1]

(6) The Act does not affect the special provisions as to liability contained in the enactments relating to the postal, telegraph and railway services. Thus the Republic is not liable for the loss, mis-delivery or delay of, or damage to, any postal article in course of transmission by post, or for any loss suffered by reason of an error or failure in relation to a telegram; and restrictions are placed on liability for loss or injury suffered on the railways, which are State-owned and run as a Government department.[2]

Where the Republic is to be sued the action may be brought against the Attorney-General, or any officer authorised in that behalf by him.[3] If the plaintiff is successful the court's order is embodied in a certificate which is served on the Accountant-General or, if the order does not require the payment of money, on the Attorney-General. Where the certificate is served on the Accountant-General he must pay the amount specified to the person entitled or his solicitor.[4]

The Act also deals with actions brought *by* the Republic but its provisions in this respect are merely procedural, being de-designed to place the Republic in the same position as a private person in securing the enforcement of its civil rights.

Civil proceedings by or against the President are subject to the same rules as govern actions to which the Republic is a party.[5]

Limitation of Actions

Special time limits are laid down for the bringing of actions against certain public authorities.

Public Officers Act, 1962 (Act 114).[6]—This provides that an action against any *person* " for any act done in pursuance or execution or intended execution of any enactment or of any public duty or authority, or in respect of any alleged neglect or default

---

[1] Sections 13 (1), 19.
[2] Section 25 (1). See the Post Office Ordinance (Cap. 214), s. 8; the Telecommunications Act, 1962 (Act 112), s. 10; the Railways Ordinance (Cap. 233), Part III.
[3] Section 10 (2).
[4] Section 15. The Act does not charge the payment on any public fund. It must therefore be paid out of moneys granted by the National Assembly.
[5] Presidential Affairs Act, 1960 (C.A. 2), s. 9 (as amended by Act 103).
[6] Re-enacting the Public Officers (Liabilities) Ordinance (Cap. 26) and the Public Officers' Protection Ordinance (Cap. 27).

in the execution of any such ordinance, duty or authority " must be brought within three months after the occurrence of the act, neglect or default complained of, or in the case of a continuance of injury or damage, within three months after it has ceased. Since the word " person " includes an incorporated or unincorporated body of persons,[1] this stringent requirement has an application wider than is suggested by the title of the Ordinance, although it does not apply to an action brought against a local authority.[2]

Local authorities.—The provision limiting the period within which actions may be brought against local authorities uses the same wording as the Ordinance just mentioned, but instead of three months, the period of limitation is twelve months.[3]

Railways.—Where a cause of action arises in connection with the operation of the railways, proceedings must be instituted within six months after the cause of action arose. No action can be commenced unless a month's notice in writing has first been given to the railway administration.[4]

Mandamus, Certiorari and Prohibition

These remedies, originally evolved in England as prerogative writs, continue to be available in Ghana. They will only be mentioned briefly here since full accounts are available in textbooks on British constitutional law.[5] Mandamus is used to compel public officers and other authorities to perform functions imposed on them by law for the benefit of individuals. The applicant for an order of mandamus must be one of the class intended to benefit and must have no other means open to him of compelling the performance of the functions. Certiorari is used to bring before the High Court a decision of an inferior court or other tribunal so that the High Court may enquire into the decision and, if it proves defective through want of jurisdiction, breach of the rules of natural justice or other cause, quash it. Prohibition is used to restrain an inferior court, or any other body having a judicial or quasi-judicial function, from proceeding in a manner which exceeds its jurisdiction.

---

[1] Interpretation Act, 1960 (C.A. 4), s. 32 (1).
[2] *Tsiboe* v. *Kumasi Municiapl Council*, [1959] G.L.R. 253.
[3] Local Government Act, 1961 (Act 54), s. 133.
[4] Railways Ordinance (Cap. 233), s. 90.
[5] See, *e.g.*, Wade and Phillips, *Constitutional Law* (6th Edn.), pp. 622–635.

Applications for orders of mandamus, certiorari or prohibition are regulated by Order 59 of the Rules of the Supreme Court.[1] No application can be made unless leave has been obtained from the High Court or, in vacation, a judge in chambers. Leave to apply for an order of certiorari will not be granted unless asked for within six months of the decision complained of.

8. EMERGENCY POWERS

The safeguards for individual liberty described in the previous sections of this chapter are subject to temporary suspension in time of national emergency. The Emergency Powers Act, 1961 (Act 56)[2] enables almost any temporary laws to be made by the Government in dealing with a critical situation. It does not however allow any provision of the Constitution to be suspended or permit the trial of civilians by military courts. Apart from this Act there are certain other provisions, relating mainly to the control of arms and explosives, which fall within the scope of this section.

Emergency Powers Act

The Act distinguishes between a general emergency, such as would exist if the country were at war or were in the throes of widespread disturbance, and a local emergency. The definition of emergency, which applies whether the conditions are general or local, states that the term includes—

" (a) any emergency arising out of any action taken or immediately threatened whether in or outside Ghana by any person or persons and from its nature or scale likely to be prejudicial in Ghana to the public safety or public order or public health, or to deprive any substantial portion of the community of the essentials of life, or to interfere in any way with Government services;

(b) any emergency arising out of an event due to natural causes with or without human intervention."[3]

The Act is brought into play by the proclamation of a state of emergency by the President acting with the approval of the Cabinet. The proclamation may delcare the emergency to exist

---

[1] Laws of the Gold Coast (1954), Vol. VII, pp. 306 *et seq.*

[2] Reproducing with modifications provisions first enacted in the Colonial period.

[3] Section 11. Since the definition is inclusive it presumably does not rule out other types of emergency.

in the whole of Ghana or only in a specified area. The only legal effect of the proclamation is to bring into operation a sweeping power to make regulations to deal with the emergency. This power is expressed in a general provision, followed by a number of limited provisions dealing with specific matters. The general provision emplowers the President, on the making of a proclamation of emergency, to make, by legislative instrument and with the approval of the Cabinet—

> " such regulations as he may consider necessary or expedient for securing the public safety, the defence of Ghana, the maintenance of public order, the efficient prosecution of any war in which the Republic may be engaged, and for maintaining supplies and services essential to the community in the whole or any part of Ghana."[1]

The limited provisions, which are without prejudice to the general provision, enable regulations to be made in the same way for such matters as the detention of persons or the restriction of their movements, the requisitioning of property, the suspension or amendment of any law other than the Constitution or the Emergency Powers Act itself, and the imposition of penalties for breach of the regulations not exceeding imprisonment for five years or a fine of £G500 or both.[2] Where the state of emergency exists only in a part of Ghana, the emergency regulations apply only in that part.[3]

A proclamation of emergency must at once be communicated to the National Assembly. If however the Assembly is not sitting the position varies according to whether the emergency is general or local. If it is general, the Assembly must be summoned to meet within ten days. If it is local this is not necessary but the Assembly must be informed of the emergency as soon as it meets.[4] Emergency regulations must be laid before the Assembly after being made.[5]

As an illustration of the way in which the procedure works we may take the situation which arose in September 1961 following the " austerity budget ", which increased taxation, introduced purchase tax and property tax and provided for the deduction from wages and salaries at source of income tax and an amount in

---

[1] Section 3 (1).
[2] Section 3 (2).
[3] Section 3 (3).
[4] Section 2.
[5] Section 5.

respect of compulsory savings. The budget was followed by a strike of railway and dock workers accompanied by civil disturbances centred at Takoradi, Ghana's leading port. The President was absent from Ghana at the time but the Presidential Commission declared a state of emergency limited to Sekondi-Takoradi and all land in the country vested in the railways and harbours administration.[1] On the same day a comprehensive set of regulations was made.[2] These imposed heavy penalties for such acts as the publication of disturbing reports, incitement to disaffection, sabotage and looting. They gave power to control processions and meetings, the wearing of uniforms and emblems, and the movement of traffic. They also authorised the requisitioning of property, the entry and search of premises, and the detention or removal of trouble-makers.[3] Various executive instruments were made under the regulations. These prohibited public meetings and processions in the emergency area and dealt with looting, traffic control and requisitioning.[4] In addition two executive instruments were made under the ordinary law. One imposed a curfew in Sekondi/Takoradi between 6 p.m. and 6 a.m. and the other restored the censorship of the *Ashanti Pioneer* newspaper which had been lifted a few months previously.[5] The state of emergency was revoked by the President on his return to Ghana after having been in force for nine days.

Control of Arms, Ammunition and Explosives

Part I of the Public Order Act, 1961 (Act 58) enables the Minister of the Interior, if he is satisfied that it is necessary for the maintenance of public order or the preservation of the public peace, to make an executive instrument prohibiting or restricting the possession or carrying of arms, ammunition or explosives in any specified part of Ghana. A police constable may arrest without warrant any person whom he suspects on reasonable grounds of possessing or carrying arms in contravention of the instrument. A magistrate may authorise premises to be searched for prohibited articles, which if found are liable to forfeiture.

---

[1] L.I. 143.

[2] Emergency Regulations, 1961 (L.I. 144).

[3] It is interesting to observe that although, by virtue of s. 3 (3) of the Emergency Powers Act, the regulations only applied in the emergency area, their wording was entirely general and seemed to indicate an intention that some provisions at least (*e.g.*, those relating to disturbing reports) should apply throughout Ghana.

[4] E.I. 150–154 of 1961.

[5] E.I. 155 and 156 of 1961.

The possession of arms in Kumasi has been prohibited under these provisions since 1955, and they are currently operative in other parts of the Ashanti Region.

Permanent control over the movement, possession and carrying of arms and ammunition and the movement and storage of explosives is conferred by other enactments.[1] The carrying of an offensive weapon in a public place without lawful authority constitutes an offence under the Criminal Code, 1960 (Act 29), s. 206.

---

[1] Arms and Ammunition Ordinance (Cap. 253); Explosives Ordinance (Cap. 254).

PART III

LAW-MAKING UNDER THE REPUBLIC

SUMMARY

		PAGE
CHAPTER 6.	Modes of Legislation	259
CHAPTER 7.	Legislative Functionaries . . .	298
CHAPTER 8.	Legislative Methods: Acts of Parliament .	350
CHAPTER 9.	Legislative Methods: Statutory Instruments	381

CHAPTER 6

MODES OF LEGISLATION

Legislation may be understood either as the process of law-making or as the product of that process. In this Part we are concerned with both these meanings. It is proposed to discuss the various types of legislation provided for by the Republican Constitution, the functionaries who are concerned with producing the laws and the detailed methods by which laws come into existence. We take the Constitution as it exists and deal with normal legislation. The special case of constitutional amendment and the exercise of the reserved powers of the people has already been discussed.[1]

1. ACTS OF PARLIAMENT

Ghana has inherited the British system under which supreme legislative authority is conferred on Parliament. Subject only to the Constitution which created it, Parliament, consisting of the President and the National Assembly, has complete power to make and unmake law. It does so through the medium of an Act of Parliament, which is literally an *act* done by Parliament in the exercise of its constitutional functions. This, when it comes into force, affects the existing body of law by altering certain of its provisions or by adding new ones. It may operate not only on other Acts of Parliament but on any element in the existing law, such as an Ordinance of the former Gold Coast Colony, a statutory instrument, a rule of customary law, an English statute of general application and so on.[2] It always supersedes an earlier law which is inconsistent with it, whether it mentions the earlier law or not.

A law is usually understood to be a general rule of conduct which is laid down by the legislature and which the inhabitants of the country must obey. Thus, for example, s. 20 of the National Assembly Act, 1961 (Act 86)[3] states:

---

[1] See pp. 147, *et seq.*, *ante.*
[2] For an explanation of the various elements in the laws of Ghana, see pp. 169, *et seq.*, *ante.*
[3] The section is also embodied in art. 21 (3) of the Constitution.

" There shall be freedom of speech, debate and proceedings in the Assembly and that freedom shall not be impeached or questioned in any court or place out of the Assembly."

This lays down an express rule of conduct, which applies to everyone. Breach of the rule is a contempt of Parliament and is punishable accordingly.[1] This may be regarded as a classic example of a law, but in fact Acts of Parliament seldom take this form. A general rule is more often laid down by implication than in express terms. Thus in the Criminal Code rules of conduct are laid down not, as one might expect, in the form " No person shall commit fraudulent breach of trust ", but in the form " Whoever commits fraudulent breach of trust shall be guilty of a misdemeanour ".[2] Again, a rule frequently applies not to the community generally but only to one section of it. An example of this is s. 23 of the Civil Service Act, 1960 (C.A. 5), which states that " A Civil Servant holding a category A post shall not take part in any activity on behalf of a trade union . . ." These matters apart, many Acts of Parliament—perhaps the majority— do not lay down rules of conduct at all, or only do so incidentally. They are concerned instead with such things as establishing, and laying down the structure and functions of, public corporations and other bodies,[3] specifying the legal rights of individuals in civil matters,[4] conferring executive powers on Ministers and other functionaries of the State,[5] and so on. An Act may even deal specifically with an isolated matter in a way which has nothing of the general law-giving quality about it at all, as by indemnifying an individual against a particular legal claim or ordering the deportation of named persons.[6] The field within which Acts of Parliament may operate is infinitely various but every Act has the characteristic that persons affected by it are expected to conduct themselves in accordance with its provisions. If they do not they run the risk of sanctions being imposed against them—usually by the courts. They may be subjected to a fine or imprisonment where a criminal offence is involved. In other cases they may fail to obtain some right or advantage which

---

[1] See the National Assembly Act, 1961 (Act 86), ss. 28, 45.

[2] Criminal Code, 1960 (Act 29), s. 128.

[3] See, *e.g.*, the Ghana Holding Corporation Act, 1958 (No. 45).

[4] See, *e.g.*, the Contracts Act, 1960 (Act 25).

[5] See, *e.g.*, the State Property and Contracts Act, 1960 (C.A. 6).

[6] See, *e.g.*, the Kumasi Municipal Council (Validation of Powers) Act, 1959 (No. 86), the Deportation (Indemnity) Act, 1958 (No. 47) and the Deportation (Othman Larden and Amadu Baba) Act, 1957 (No. 19).

compliance with the law would have secured. If they purport to exercise statutory powers but do not observe the conditions laid down they may find their acts ineffective. If they fail to carry out a duty imposed upon them they may be made the subject of an injunction issued by the court. If they meddle unlawfully with the property of others, or deal improperly with their own, they may be required to pay damages, or forfeit their property. These are all personal sanctions, but there is often a higher interest at stake. Legislation is the instrument by which many of the Government's policies are implemented. If the requirements and procedures laid down by Act of Parliament are not loyally observed national efficiency and progress inevitably suffer. The nation pays a penalty even where the individual escapes.

The term " Act of Parliament " came into use when Ghana was first provided with a Parliament on obtaining independence in 1957. It has of course long been employed in the United Kingdom and elsewhere in the Commonwealth to describe supreme legislative enactments. Its current use in Ghana is referable to art. 24(2) of the Constitution. This provides that a Bill passed by the National Assembly shall become an Act of Parliament when the President signifies his assent to it. It tells us that, again following the British practice, an Act of the Parliament of Ghana starts its life as a Bill. The form of Bills, and the procedure for their introduction and passage through the Assembly, are not dealt with in the Constitution, but are regulated by the National Assembly Act, 1961 (Act 86), the Acts of Parliament Act, 1960 (C.A. 7) and the Standing Orders of the National Assembly. These are described in detail in Chapter 8 of this book, but some of the salient features may be given here. The form of a Bill closely resembles that of an Act. Indeed the Bill is so drawn that it is capable of operating as an Act as soon as assent is given and with no alteration except in the formal words at the beginning. It contains a short title, followed by a long title indicating its scope and purpose. After the enacting formula the body of the Bill appears. In most cases this is divided up into clauses, and clauses of any length are usually further divided into subsections. At the end of the Bill one or more schedules may appear. Any member of Parliament has the right, on obtaining the leave of the Assembly, to introduce a Bill. The invariable practice in Ghana, however, has been for the Government only to introduce Bills. Before it can be presented for the President's assent a Bill must pass through various stages. These are the first reading (which is formal), the second reading (at which the main principles of the Bill are debated), the consideration stage (at which the Bill is examined clause by clause, and amendments made where necessary) and finally the third reading.

Although a Bill goes through three " readings " this does not mean that the Bill is read aloud in the Assembly. Since a printed copy is available for each member reading aloud is not necessary.[1] The significance of the three readings, together with the consideration stage, is that they provide several opportunities for Members to weigh up the merits of the Bill and to suggest improvements. Whether these opportunities are taken or not depends on the alertness and interest shown by Members, and also, it must be said, on the timetable laid down by the Business Committee. There is a tendency in Ghana for Bills to be put through all their stages at one time—a process which rules out the possibility of errors being corrected, and improvements made, through the perspicacity of Members.

A Bill is taken to have been passed by the Assembly if, but only if, it has been read three times and has passed through the consideration stage.[2] If opinions differ about whether a Bill should pass any stage the decision is taken by holding a division, the question being decided by a simple majority of votes cast. When a Bill has been passed by the Assembly it must be presented to the President, who may assent to the whole or a part of it or refuse assent. When the President signifies his assent the Bill, or the part to which assent is given, as the case may be, becomes an Act of Parliament. Acts of the Republican Parliament are numbered consecutively from Act 1, the numbering not being started again at the beginning of a year.

2. STATUTORY INSTRUMENTS

The will of Parliament is expressed by Acts of Parliament but it is not possible to include in an Act all the matters of detail which will need attention if the legislative purpose is to be achieved. There are a number of reasons for this. Most countries which use the Parliamentary system have found that, under the circum-

---

[1] A person is not qualified for election as a Member of Parliament unless he is able to read the English language with a degree of proficiency sufficient to enable him to take an active part in the proceedings of the Assembly. A person prevented from reading by blindness or other physical cause is not however disqualified. (National Assembly Act, 1961 (Act 86), s. 1 (1)).

[2] Standing Order No. 68.

stances of today, when it is generally accepted that legislation should regulate almost every aspect of a nation's social and economic life, Parliament has neither the time nor the capacity to concern itself with all the ramifications of its enactments. Furthermore the conditions upon which legislation operates are often in a state of change, necessitating frequent adjustments to the law which, where they are not substantial, it would be unnecessarily rigid to call upon Parliament to make itself. Again, particularly in the administrative field, the legislative purpose may call for day-to-day decisions to be taken by Ministers, civil servants and others. These decisions, which are often executive rather than legislative in character, may require expert knowledge which Parliament does not possess. Whether this is so or not, they can usually only be taken on the facts of particular cases as they arise, and thus cannot be taken by Parliament itself. These factors are commonly experienced, and have everywhere led to the delegation of Parliamentary powers. In Ghana they are felt also, but one point of difference should be noted. It can hardly be said that the National Assembly has no time to consider more detailed legislation than it does at present. In fact, owing to the disinclination of many Members to join in debate and the lack of use made of the opportunities offered by Parliamentary procedure (for example the right of back-benchers to put down amendments and to introduce Bills of their own), the House often finds itself with nothing to do. On the other hand, to balance this factor, the Government frequently requires important legislation to be prepared so quickly that there is not time to do more than set out the broad outlines in the Act and leave the details to be filled in later under delegated powers. This may have an incidental advantage. If the Act is properly drafted, the legislative scheme is easier to grasp when it is not obscured by masses of detail.

In Ghana delegated powers have a history as old as the Colonial regime itself. Indeed, in Colonial times all the Governor's powers were delegated to him by the Crown and were exercised in the form of Ordinances, Orders of the Governor in Council, proclamations and so on.[1] After the setting up of the Parliament of Ghana in 1957, Acts of Parliament provided for the delegation of a wide variety of powers. These ranged from power to make

---

[1] See Chapter 1, *ante*. Ordinances frequently provided for further delegation; indeed it was common to include in an Ordinance a wide power to make regulations for carrying it into effect, though this was often reserved to the Governor himself.

rules or regulations which were legislative in character and of a general and lasting importance to power to make an order or other instrument of an executive and personal character, such as a deportation order or an instrument of appointment to an office. Despite their differing character and importance almost all these instruments were described as " delegated legislation ", numbered in one series and bound up together in one annual volume. In some cases, however, an important power, as for example to bring an Act into operation, would be exercisable not by a formal instrument but by a notice published in the *Gazette*. This system, or lack of it, led to difficulties. It was troublesome to hunt up important regulations in a volume containing masses of ephemeral executive orders. It was worse to find that no scheme of noting up the regulations or otherwise presenting them in their current form existed. Nor could such a scheme be made practicable until the wheat was first separated from the chaff.[1] Towards the end of 1959 it was therefore decided to reform the entire system of subordinate legislation. Since the reform was based to some extent upon similar reforms carried out in the United Kingdom it is necessary to say a word about these first.

Until 1893 there was no general control over the form and publication of delegated legislation in the United Kingdom. In that year however, following complaints of difficulties caused by the growing volume of such legislation and the failure to make it sufficiently known to the public, the Rules Publication Act, 1893 was passed. This required all statutory rules to be numbered in one series and published by the Queen's Printer, and applied to rules, regulations or byelaws which were made under an Act of Parliament and which related to procedure in courts of justice or were made by Her Majesty in Council or a Government department. Thereafter, until 1947, annual volumes of these instruments, under the name of " Statutory Rules and Orders ", were published by the Stationery Office. The definition of " statutory rules " in the Rules Publication Act was found to be too narrow and in 1946 the Act was replaced by the Statutory Instruments Act. By this the new term " statutory instrument " was applied

---

[1] The 1958 volume of subsidiary legislation contains 419 legal notifications (as they were then called). Of these only 84 were, under the system later adopted, " wheat ", that is legislative instruments. The remaining 355 were " chaff ", or executive instruments. In 1960, the first year in which the new system operated, 92 legislative instruments were made as against 273 executive instruments.

to orders, rules, regulations and other subordinate legislation made by a Minister under a power conferred by that or any future Act if the Act in question stated that the power was exercisable by statutory instrument.[1] This means that, when an Act conferring power to make subordinate legislation is being enacted in the United Kingdom it is for Parliament (or in practice the department concerned) to decide whether an instrument by which this power is exercised is likely to be sufficiently important to be published in the numbered series of statutory instruments.

In Ghana it was decided to adopt the term " statutory instrument " but to widen its meaning by including in it all instruments made under statutory powers, drawing a distinction between statutory instruments which were legislative in character and those which were executive. Although in many cases it is obvious whether an instrument is legislative or executive, there is a wide borderland in which this is very much a matter of opinion. As mentioned above, the British Statutory Instruments Regulations state that instruments made under statutory powers earlier than 1948 are to be treated as statutory instruments if they are " of a legislative and not an executive character ". In order to decide whether to look in the statutory instruments series for an instrument made under a pre-1948 power it is therefore necessary to make up one's mind whether the instrument is likely to be legislative in character. This is often a matter of considerable difficulty, and in Ghana it was found possible to attain greater precision by expressly stating which powers under existing legislation were powers to make instruments of a legislative character. The great complexity and bulk of British statute law made this course impracticable in the United Kingdom, but in Ghana the chance was seized while the body of statute law was still relatively small. The importance of the distinction between the two types of instrument in Ghana lies mainly in the method of publication. Legislative instruments, which are usually general in application and permanent in nature, and are often subject to amendment, are published in a convenient form in the cumulative binder service, which incorporates amendments as they are made.[2] Executive instruments are published

---

[1] Statutory Instruments Act, 1946, s. 1. The term also includes Orders in Council, and instruments of a legislative character made under Acts passed before 1948 (Statutory Instruments Regulations, 1947 (S.I. No. 1), reg. 2).

[2] This is discussed in detail at pp. 291, *et seq., post.*

separately and amendments (which are infrequent) are not incorporated.

The new system was introduced by the Statutory Instruments Act, 1959 (No. 52). Section 3 of the Act provides that an instrument made (whether directly or indirectly) under a power conferred by an enactment shall be known as a statutory instrument. The term thus covers not only delegated legislation but also what is sometimes known as sub-delegated legislation, that is instruments made under powers contained in other subordinate legislation. The word " enactment " has a special meaning here, the effect of which is to bring within the description " statutory instrument " all past and future instruments made (whether directly or indirectly) under any Act, Ordinance or Order of Her Majesty in Council. Since it might have been said that an Act of Parliament was itself made under an enactment in this sense, provisions laying down the legislative powers of Parliament were expressly excluded.[1] It will be seen that the definition of statutory instrument is so wide that it covers the most trivial documents, for example a driving licence or a letter of appointment to a post. It also covers documents issued by or under the authority of a court of law. It was considered impracticable to attempt to exclude such things as these, but, for reasons which will appear, the width of the definition does not matter in practice.

The Act next proceeds to define a legislative instrument. This is done differently in relation to existing powers and powers to be contained in future Acts. In relation to existing powers the Attorney-General was enabled by s. 4(1) to make a declaration to the effect that statutory instruments made under specified enactments " are legislative in character and of sufficient importance to justify separate publication ". This is the only indication given by the Act of the nature of legislative instruments, but further light may be obtained from the explanatory note at the beginning of Volume 1 of the cumulative binder service. This begins as follows:

> " Legislative instruments form the most important body of delegated legislation in Ghana. They consist of those statutory instruments (*i.e.*, instruments made under statutory powers) which are legislative in character and are of general importance either because they amend or otherwise affect Ordinances and Acts of Parliament or because they embody rules, regulations or similar provisions of continuing public concern.

---

[1] Statutory Instruments Act, 1959 (No. 52), s. 2.

The order embodying the Attorney-General's declaration was made some three months after the passing of the Statutory Instruments Act.[1] During this period the entire statute book, consisting of the four volumes of the 1951 edition of the Ordinances, the two volumes of the 1952–1954 supplement and the five subsequent annual volumes, was read through to pick out the provisions which should be treated as conferring power to make legislative instruments. This was done by one person so as to produce uniformity of treatment. The resulting order specified four hundred and eleven empowering provisions, of which two hundred and forty-four conferred power to make regulations. Other descriptions of the delegated legislation in question included orders, rules, declarations, notices, notifications, resolutions, instruments, proclamations and byelaws. The use of such terms as these is not affected by the new arrangements, and a set of rules or regulations, for example, may continue to be described as such although embodied in a legislative instrument.

The other half of the definition of a legislative instrument dealt with future Acts. This was a much simpler matter. It would be left to the draftsman of the Act to decide, when drawing a provision conferring power to make statutory instruments, whether the power was of such a nature that the instruments should be legislative. Thus s. 4(2) of the Statutory Instruments Act states that, in addition to those made under powers specified in the Attorney-General's declaration, instruments made " under powers expressed to be exercisable by legislative instrument " shall be known as legislative instruments. The first use of this formula occurs in s. 4 itself, which begins " The Attorney-General may *by legislative instrument* declare . . ." Deciding whether a power should be exercisable by legislative instrument or not is to some extent one of " feel ", but draftsmen have been advised that the following should normally be legislative instruments—

    (a) instruments which amend Acts, Ordinances, or other legislative instruments;

    (b) rules and regulations which are " permanent " and either general or, although local, of national importance;

    (c) instruments made under powers contained in consolidation Acts reproducing any of the enactments specified in the Attorney-General's declaration;

---

[1] Statutory Instruments Order, 1960 (L.I. 9).

(d) instruments bringing an Act into operation;

(e) instruments which are otherwise legislative rather than executive in their effect and of national importance—not being merely temporary.

In exceptional cases even temporary instruments may, because of their great importance, be classed as legislative. Thus for example regulations made when a state of emergency has been declared under the Emergency Powers Act, 1961 (Act 56)[1] are treated as legislative because they are likely to contain drastic provisions, including provisions modifying Acts of Parliament. Legislative instruments are required by s. 4(3) of the Statutory Instruments Act to be published by the Government Printer. If the instrument itself is not published in the *Gazette*, a notice of its publication must be inserted in the *Gazette* as early as possible. In fact legislative instruments are published in a separate series.[2] They are numbered consecutively from L.I. 1, the numbering not being started again at the beginning of a year.

Section 5 of the Act provides that statutory instruments other than legislative instruments or instruments of a judicial character are to be known as executive instruments. As mentioned above, court orders, being made under statutory powers, are within the definition of a statutory instrument. It would be misleading to describe them as executive instruments however, and hence they are excluded. Also excluded as being of a judicial character are a small number of instruments which more closely resemble delegated legislation, as for example declarations under s. 9 of the Stool Lands Boundaries Settlement Ordinance (Cap. 139).

The Act does not require executive instruments to be published, but such a requirement is sometimes included in the enactment which empowers a particular executive instrument to be made. In practice executive instruments of any importance are usually published—most of them in the executive instruments series which is published by the Government Printer and numbered from E.I. 1 onwards, starting afresh at the beginning of each year. Some instruments which are strictly executive instruments are however for greater convenience published in the *Gazette* itself or in one of the three Official Bulletins.

A power to make a statutory instrument normally implies a power to amend or revoke the instrument once made.[3] This is

---

[1] See p. 253, *ante*.   [2] See p. 295, *post.*

[3] The term " revoke " is applied to statutory instruments, " repeal " being used only of Acts.

laid down by s. 14(1) of the Statutory Instruments Act, which applies unless the context of the empowering enactment otherwise requires. The amendment or revocation must be done by the same authority as has power to make original instruments and must be exercised in the same manner.[1] A power to make, amend or revoke an instrument may be exercised from time to time, as occasion requires.[2]

The Statutory Instruments Act concludes by empowering the Attorney-General, by legislative instrument, to amend any existing enactment conferring power to make statutory instruments so as to bring it into line with the new arrangements, or to make such other provision as appears expedient for the purposes of the Statutory Instruments Act.[3] It was contemplated that the amending powers would be used to make textual amendments in all the enactments specified in the Attorney-General's declaration. However, many of these enactments have, under the statute law reform programme begun early in 1960, been repealed and re-enacted with appropriation modifications. Since this programme is expected to continue until the entire pre-Republican statute law has been re-enacted in modern form the amending powers are not likely to be used. The power to make " such other provision as appears expedient " has been used to lay down rules as to the form of statutory instruments. These rules, together with provisions of the Statutory Instruments Act which govern the making of instruments, are described in Chapter 9.

3. Other Modes of Legislation

It may be thought that since art. 20 of the Constitution provides that so much of the legislative power of the State as is not reserved by the Constitution to the people is conferred on Parliament there can be no room for modes of legislation other than those already discussed. This is true in the sense that Parliament is the only sovereign legislature, whose powers are superior to all others and whose enactments, if duly made, can override any existing laws. Nevertheless there are other bodies whose actions can change the law in various ways. These are as follows—

---

[1] Note that where the power to make original instruments has been transferred since the instrument which is to be amended or revoked was made, it is the transferee authority who has power to amend or revoke, and not the authority who made the instrument.

[2] Interpretation Act, 1960 (C.A. 4), s. 10.

[3] Statutory Instruments Act, 1959 (No. 52), s. 17.

(a) The courts, by their pronouncements on what the law is;
(b) The first President, by the exercise of his special powers under art. 55 of the Constitution; and
(c) chiefs and other customary bodies, by declarations and modifications of customary law.

The courts

There is a long-standing controversy over whether courts which follow the British tradition exercise a legislative or merely declaratory function in making pronouncements about the rules of common law and equity. The matter has been discussed at length by a number of writers and it is not proposed to embark upon it here.[1] What is certain however is that the courts in Ghana have been given a freedom to choose between different lines of development of common law and equity which in effect confers upon them something very like legislative power.[2] Again, within the field of statute law, this quasi-legislative power exists. Suppose a particular enactment to be ambiguous. Before the courts have pronounced upon it, the law on this topic may be one thing or it may be the other—no one knows. If then the High Court adopt one interpretation and reject the other they have to some extent played a law-making role. There is now authority for saying that the enactment is not ambiguous but has a definite meaning. Now suppose that the same point comes before the Supreme Court, who overrule the previous decision and pronounce in favour of the other interpretation. It is possible to argue that the law has not changed, but has only at last been properly enunciated. Nevertheless the practical effect is the same as if Parliament had passed an Act stating that, for the avoidance of doubt, the second interpretation was declared to be the correct one. Since every court is bound by art. 42(4) of the Constitution to follow the Supreme Court's decision it has on such a matter as this the same effect as an Act of Parliament. Nor is the principle restricted to ambiguities—it applies whenever Parliament has failed to make its intention clear or has deliberately left the detailed working out of its intention to the courts. In the United Kingdom a celebrated example of the latter occurred in the Workmen's

---

[1] See, *e.g.*, Salmond, *Jurisprudence* (11th edn.), pp. 163–164. The learned author concludes by rejecting the declaratory theory in relation to common law and equity: " We must admit openly that precedents make law as well as declare it."

[2] This is discussed more fully at p. 173, *ante*.

Compensation Act, 1906, which gave a right to compensation where a workman was injured in an accident " arising out of and in the course of his employment ". These simple words were found to conceal great difficulties and in the spate of litigation which followed over the next forty years the British courts worked out for themselves the detailed rules which might have been embodied in the Act in the first place. Another well-known example of Parliament's leaving it to the courts to make law was to be found in s. 15 of the Road Traffic Act, 1930,[1] which required the court to impose disqualification on a person driving when not insured unless there were " special reasons " for not doing so. Here also the British courts worked out rules for determining what is a " special reason "—as for example that it must be a reason special to the circumstances of the particular offence and not applicable to the offender whenever he may have been driving. Sir Carleton Allen, in discussing this legislative function of the courts, has said with reference to their reaction when faced with a *casus omissus* in a statute:

> " In innumerable instances the fate of the *casus omissus* lies entirely in the hands of the judges, and in no real sense depends on the will of the legislator. The courts lay down a rule exactly because the legislature has not done so, and has not intended to do so. Judges must and do carry out the express will of the legislature as faithfully as they can; but there is a very wide margin in almost every statute where the courts cannot be said to be following any will except their own . . . It is in the process of filling in these gaps, more than anywhere else, that the common law may be called, with some plausibility, ' judge-made law '. To assert, as is sometimes done, that judges do not in fact cement these interstices in statutes is to run counter to a thousand instances.[2]

Legislative powers of first President

The special legislative powers of the first President have been described in Chapter 3 and little more need be said about them here.[3] The powers are exercisable by legislative instrument and thus are subject to such of the provisions of the Statutory Instruments Act, 1959 (No. 52) as are not inconsistent with art. 55 of the Constitution. Since the powers are conferred directly by the Constitution, however, and since they enable the first President to modify Acts of Parliament at any time he thinks fit, they

---

[1] Repealed by the Road Traffic Act, 1960.
[2] *Law in the Making* (6th edn.), p. 484.
[3] See 135 *et seq., ante.*

can hardly be looked upon as powers to make delegated or sub-ordinate legislation. Legislative instruments made under art. 55 must be looked on as a form of primary legislation. Whether they will come to form an important body of primary legislation cannot as yet be foreseen. At the time of writing, nearly two years after the passing of the Constitution, no such instruments have been made.

Declarations and modifications of customary law

Customary law is stated by art. 40 of the Constitution to form part of the laws of Ghana. Modes of altering customary law are therefore modes of legislation. Customary law is subject to altera-tion not only by the modes already discussed but also by the action of chiefs and other authorities exercising the functions which custom gives them. These functions have been modified and regulated by statute to some extent and are of little importance today. They are discussed further in Chapter 11.

4. Interpretation

When the legislature has expressed its will by means of an Act or statutory instrument it is the duty of everyone concerned to conduct himself accordingly. This cannot be done unless the meaning and effect of the enactment is clear. In Ghana, as in the United Kingdom, the preparation of Bills and the more important statutory instruments is entrusted to a professional draftsman, and great reliance is placed on his skill and attention to detail. So important is the role of the draftsman in translating Govern-ment policy into legislation fitted to carry it out that considerable space will be devoted to it in the following chapters. Before de-scribing in detail the ways in which legislation is prepared how-ever, we should say something about the rules governing its interpretation.

Ghana has followed the modern practice of equipping itself with an Interpretation Act to shorten and clarify Acts and statutory instruments.[1] The Interpretation Act is the shadowy companion of each Act and statutory instrument, having the same effect as if expressly written into it. For this reason no one

---

[1] The practice began with the passing in the United Kingdom of Lord Brougham's Act in 1850. Its title was " An Act for shortening the language used in Acts of Parliament."

who has occasion to consult legislation should fail to consider the Interpretation Act; without this he will have only part of the story. Also to be borne in mind are the rules of construction which have been worked out by the courts but have not found their way into the Interpretation Act because they are not sufficiently precise in their application to be capable of statement in legislative form.

The Interpretation Act

Ghana has been equipped with a statute laying down rules of interpretation since the establishment of the Gold Coast Colony.[1] The purpose of such a statute is to lay down once and for all definitions and rules of interpretation which apply generally and would otherwise have to be set out afresh or otherwise provided for in every new Act or statutory instrument. Thus for example the earliest of all interpretations statutes, Lord Brougham's Act of 1850, introduced in s. 4 the rule (which has been repeated in interpretation statutes ever since) that:

> " . . . in all Acts words importing the masculine gender shall be deemed and taken to include females, and the singular to include the plural, and the plural the singular, unless the contrary as to gender and number is expressly provided."

Previously it had been considered necessary either to include such a provision in each separate Act or to use such tedious locutions as

> " . . . if any person or persons shall be summoned as a witness or witnesses . . . and shall neglect or refuse to appear at the time and place to be for that purpose appointed, without a reasonable excuse for such his, her or their neglect or refusal . . . "[2]

Ghana's present interpretation statute is the Interpretation Act, 1960 (C.A. 4). This Act, which was passed by the Constituent Assembly, marked a fresh start in Ghana. The previous Act, the Interpretation Act, 1957 (No. 29), had been the latest in a series of revisions of the 1876 Ordinance. The present Act was drafted anew. Some of its provisions were drawn from similar enactments in the United Kingdom, Canada, Northern Ireland and the Irish Republic; others were original. Unlike many interpretation statutes this one confines itself to matters of interpretation;

---

[1] The first of these was the Interpretation Ordinance, 1876 (No. 3).
[2] Land Tax Redemption Act, 1802, s. 191.

S

provisions governing the form, citation, etc., of Acts and statutory instruments are contained elsewhere.[1] Nevertheless the Act has a fairly wide scope. It not only applies to statutes, that is the Constitution, Acts and Ordinances, but also to statutory instruments. It not only lays down rules of construction and the meanings of common terms but also defines the content of a statute or instrument, namely what does and what does not form part of it. It deals with such important matters as the meaning of " common law " and " customary law " and the countries recognized as members of the Commonwealth.

The Act begins by stating that, with one important exception, each provision of the Act applies to every *enactment* being:

(a) the Constitution, an Act (including the Interpretation Act itself) of the Constituent Assembly or the Republican Parliament;

(b) a legislative measure continued in force by the Constitution, or

(c) an instrument made (directly or indirectly) under any such enactment.[2]

It will be noticed that the various laws specified here are only covered if they are *enactments*. The term " enactment " is defined in s. 32(1) and since it is a term which is frequently used, not only throughout the Interpretation Act itself but in legislation generally, we must examine it in detail. The term is defined as " an Act or statutory instrument or any provision of an Act or statutory instrument ". It may thus be used interchangeably to mean an entire piece of legislation or any portion of it. This makes the term extremely flexible and useful. The reference in the definition to an Act is elaborated by a separate definition which is also given in s. 32(1). This states that " Act " or " Act of Parliament " means the Constitution, an Act of the Constituent Assembly or of Parliament, or any legislative measure of an authority formerly exercising power to make laws for the territory or any part of the territory comprised in the Republic, but does not include an English statute of general application.[3] Returning to the opening words of the Act, we now see that, with the important exception already mentioned, each provision of the Act

---

[1] See the Acts of Parliament Act, 1960 (C.A. 7) and the Statutory Instruments Act, 1959 (No. 52).

[2] Interpretation Act, 1960 (C.A. 4), s. 1. For the relationship of the Act to the Constitution, see p. 99, *ante*.

[3] As to statutes of general application, see pp. 395, *et seq.*, *post*.

applies to all written law in force in Ghana (whenever made) except the English statutes of general application, which are governed by Lord Brougham's Act and any interpretation provisions they may themselves contain.[1] The important exception referred to lies in the concluding words of s. 1, which state that the Act applies to an enactment " except insofar as the contrary intention appears in the enactment ". When reading the Interpretation Act it is essential to bear this exception in mind since it only appears in this one place and is not, as is frequently the case with interpretation statutes, repeated wherever it applies. A contrary intention may occasionally be expressed in terms which actually refer to the Interpretation Act but will more usually be implied, as by the insertion of a different definition of a term defined by the Interpretation Act or the use of language which indicates that a term is to have its natural meaning or that a rule of construction is not to apply.[2]

Having indicated the way in which the Interpretation Act applies, we will now describe its most important provisions, except those that are dealt with elsewhere in this book. Five of its sections (ss. 5 to 9) deal with the effect that one enactment may have upon another by way of repeal, revocation or amendment.

(1) *Repeals*.[3]—A repeal may be effected either by the statement that the enactment in question " is hereby repealed " or by a statement of similar purport, *e.g.* that the enactment shall cease to have effect. For the sake of uniformity the former is preferred. Apart from the Interpretation Act and any savings contained in the repealing enactment, an enactment which is repealed " must be considered (except as to transactions past and closed) as if it had never existed ".[4] The Interpretation Act modifies this in the following ways—

    (a) the repeal does not revive anything not in force or existing when it takes effect;[5]

---

[1] In the case of enactments made in Ghana before the Republic " Act " and " Act of Parliament " retain the misleadingly wide meaning given to them by the Interpretation Act, 1957 (No. 29); see the Interpretation Act, 1960 (C.A. 4), s. 32 (2).

[2] *Cf.* the definitions of " enactment " and " instrument " in the Statutory Instruments Act, 1959 (No. 52), s. 2.

[3] What is said here about repeals applies equally to the revocation of statutory instruments and, where appropriate, to cases where an enactment expires, lapses or otherwise ceases to have effect (*cf.* Interpretation Act, 1960 (C.A. 4), s. 8 (2)).

[4] *Per* Lord Tenterden in *Surtees* v. *Ellison* (1829), 9 B. & C. 750, at p. 752.

[5] Interpretation Act, 1960 (C.A. 4), s. 8 (1) (a).

(b) the repeal does not affect the previous operation of the repealed enactment, or anything duly done or suffered under it, or any right or liability acquired or incurred under it;[1]

(c) where another enactment is substituted for the repealed enactment by way of amendment, revision or consolidation, certain things such as appointments, legal proceedings and documents continue to be effective under the new enactment, and any reference to the repealed enactment is taken to refer to the new enactment.[2]

(2) *Amendments.*—Amendments may be verbal or indirect. A verbal amendment occurs when the actual wording of the enactment is altered by repealing certain words in it or substituting different words. An indirect amendment consists in a modification of the effect of an enactment without an alteration in its wording. An example will show the distinction.

Original enactment. (Section 10 of the Animals Act).—" No person shall slaughter any cow or sheep without a licence from the Minister."

Verbal amendment.—" After the word ' cow ' in section 10 of the Animals Act there is hereby inserted the word ' pig '."

Indirect amendment.—" Section 10 of the Animals Act shall apply in relation to pigs as it applies in relation to cows and sheep."

An amendment may be even more indirect than this. If, for example, it were desired to abolish the need for a licence for the slaughter of cows this could be achieved by saying " Notwithstanding anything in any enactment, a licence from the Minister shall no longer be required for the slaughter of a cow." Verbal amendments are always to be preferred to indirect amendments because, provided the statute-book is kept in an up-to-date form, they give the reader the whole story. In the case of the above example, a noted-up version of the Animals Act or one which, as in Ghana, is reprinted as amendments occur, will show at a glance that a licence is needed for the slaughter of pigs as well as cows and sheep, whereas the indirect amendment might

---

[1] Interpretation Act, 1960, ss. 6 (3), 7, 8 (1).

[2] *Ibid.*, ss. 6 (2), 9. Note that there is no saving for statutory instruments made under the repealed enactment. It was felt that these would need careful scrutiny and should not be kept alive automatically.

easily be missed. The only disadvantage of the verbal amendment in the above example is that it does not tell Members of Parliament and others who are interested in the Bill containing the amendment what its real effect is. This disadvantage can be got round by describing in the amendment itself what section 10 of the Animals Act does, so that the amendment would read:

> " After the word ' cow ' in section 10 of the Animals Act (which prohibits the slaughter of cows and sheep without a licence from the Minister) there is hereby inserted the word ' pig '."

Since arguments have been advanced in English courts to the effect that descriptive words such as these may be used as guides to the meaning of the enactment to which they refer, s. 5 of the Interpretation Act makes it clear that they are for convenience of reference only and are not to be used as an aid to construction. In many cases it is not possible to cram into a few words the full effect of a section, and as the memorandum to the Interpretation Bill remarked:

> " . . . if such descriptive words were to be regarded as aids to interpretation the result would be that their use would have to be discontinued."[1]

The Interpretation Act also has something to say about the case where an enactment refers to another enactment which has been or is later amended. Section 6(1) provides that the reference is to be construed as referring to the enactment

> " . . . as for the time being amended by any provision, including a provision contained in the enactment in which the reference is made or in a later enactment."

As this is a matter of some difficulty and importance a full explanation will be attempted here. Take the case of an Act (let us call it the Disqualification Act) which imposes a disqualification on " any person who has contravened section 10 of the Animals Act ". Suppose that at the time when the Disqualification Act was passed s. 10 had already been amended by the verbal amendment given above. Does the disqualification extend to a person who slaughters a pig without a licence? Before the enactment of s. 6(1) of the Interpretation Act the matter would have

---

[1] This memorandum, which contains a useful summary of the Act, is reprinted at the beginning of Vol. I of the cumulative binder service of Acts of Ghana.

been in doubt unless the point had been dealt with, as was commonly done, by referring to s. 10 of the Animals Act " as subsequently amended ". Even this would not help however if, after the passing of the Disqualification Act, s. 10 were further amended by adding a reference to horses. Would a person who thereafter slaughtered a horse without a licence be liable to disqualification? It will be seen that s. 6(1) takes care of this possibility too, and also the third possibility of an amendment being made to s. 10 of the Animals Act by the Disqualification Act itself. A reference to another enactment is thus made self-modifying, a point to be borne in mind particularly where indirect amendments have been made.

The Interpretation Act next proceeds to perform the useful function of spelling out the consequences of conferring certain functions.[1] In particular, power to appoint a person to an office is stated to carry with it power to remove, suspend, reappoint or reinstate him and power to appoint a substitute.[2] Again, the consequences of authorising or requiring the service of documents are spelt out in great detail, thus avoiding frequent repetition of the procedure for effecting service.[3]

The Act begins its general treatment of the interpretation of enactments by acknowledging that its own provisions may not be enough. Section 19 empowers the court to turn for help—

" . . . to any text-book or other work of reference, to the report of any commission of inquiry into the state of the law, to any memorandum published by authority in reference to the enactment or to the Bill for the enactment and to any papers laid before the National Assembly in reference to it, but not to the debates in the Assembly."

This marks a considerable increase in the sources made available to the court. In includes such things as Government White Papers and the memorandum of objects and reasons published on the front of every Bill. In relation to textbooks it removes the argument that the author must be an established authority (or must even be dead) before the court can consider what he has to say. It does not of course interfere with the rule that where the words of an enactment are clear effect must be given to them. Nor does it prevent the court from attaching what weight it things fit

---

[1] Interpretation Act, 1960 (C.A. 4), ss. 10, 12, 14 and 15.
[2] *Ibid.*, s. 12.
[3] *Ibid.*, s. 13.

to the sources named. The exclusion of references to debates in the Assembly was explained in the memorandum to the Interpretation Bill as follows:

> " There are two cogent reasons for their exclusion: first, it would not be conducive to the respect which one organ of State owes to another that its deliberations should be open to discussion in Court; and, secondly, it would greatly interfere with the freedom of debate if members had to speak in the knowledge that every remark might be subject to judicial analysis."

A third reason might be added, namely that the extempore answer of a Minister pressed to explain a provision in a Bill is not always a reliable guide to its meaning.

The Act goes on to deal with a number of miscellaneous matters, most of which do not require special comment. The Republic, like the Crown before it, is not bound by an enactment except under express terms or necessary implication.[1] References to time, distance and age are explained.[2] Male words are made to include females and the singular to include the plural, and vice versa.[3] " Shall " and " may " are stated to mean what they say.[4] Recognized abbreviations, such as " the United Kingdom " are authorised.[5] Finally a list of forty-nine definitions is given.[6] The tests adopted in deciding whether to include a particular term in this list were stated by the memorandum to the Bill to be—

> " . . . first, whether the term is capable of being given a settled meaning; secondly, whether the term is generally employed in the same sense; thirdly, whether it has already been defined generally in some other enactment; and fourthly, whether its meaning is so obvious as not to require definition."

It should be mentioned that in the third of these reasons " defined " has a rather wide meaning. The case referred to is rather one where a universal *name* has been assigned by another enactment. If for example a statutory corporation is set up under a particular name—say the Bank of Ghana—it has that name for all purposes and it would be otiose to include in the Interpretation Act or any individual interpretation section a provision to the effect that " Bank of Ghana " means the body corporate established by the Bank of Ghana Ordinance.

---

[1] Interpretation Act, 1960 (C.A. 4), s. 20.
[2] *Ibid.*, ss. 22–25.
[3] *Ibid.*, s. 26.
[4] *Ibid.*, s. 27.
[5] *Ibid.*, s. 30.
[6] *Ibid.*, s. 32.

Judicial rules of interpretation

The courts of Ghana have hitherto followed the rules of statutory interpretation laid down by British courts, and legislation is drafted on the assumption that they will continue to do so. Since very full accounts of these rules are available elsewhere we will do no more than mention briefly some of the more important of them.[1] The antiquity of many is shown by their being embodied in Latin maxims.

The golden rule.—The golden rule of statutory interpretation is that where the words used in an enactment are clear and unambiguous effect must be given to them. This is so even though the court thinks that the result is unjust or otherwise unsatisfactory. Where Parliament has used plain language it is not for the court to argue that it could not have meant what it has said. The rule is salutory. Apart from preventing interference by the judiciary with the sovereign power of Parliament, it tends in the long run to keep up the quality of the law. If the clear words of a statute produce injustice or absurdity it is for Parliament to alter them—if it chooses, as it normally will. The alteration can then be done in a thoroughgoing way, in which the words of the Act are corrected to meet all cases and for all to see. An attempt by the court to mitigate hardship by putting a gloss on the Act can only produce uncertainty as to how far the gloss extends; hard cases make bad law. In England this is small comfort to the person whose misfortune has brought the point to light, since retrospective amendments are frowned upon—especially where they effect a reversal of a court decision. In Ghana however the law is frequently altered with retrospective effect, occasionally even to the advantage of a litigant who has been unsuccessful in court proceedings.[2]

Ut res magis valeat quam pereat (it is better that a thing should have effect than be made void).—Parliament cannot be taken to have stultified itself by enacting a nullity. If therefore there is a choice between two interpretations, but one of them will render

---

[1] The leading authority is *Maxwell on The Interpretation of Statutes* (10th Edn.), one of the editors of which was until lately a judge of the Supreme Court of Ghana. See also *Craies on Statute Law* (5th Edn.).

[2] See, *e.g.*, Kumasi Municipal Council (Validation of Powers) Act, 1959 (No. 86). Here the unsuccessful litigant was a municipal corporation, the other party being a private individual: see *Tsiboe* v. *Kumasi Municipal Council* 1959 G.L.R. 253. The case is not cited here as an example of the retropsective amendment of an unjust law, but rather to show that such an amendment would be feasible in Ghana.

the enactment ineffective, the other must be adopted. Even if, on a literal interpretation, only the construction which would render the enactment ineffectual is open, the words used can seldom be regarded as so clear that the golden rule is to be applied. In such a case it is the duty of the Court to strive to give effect to the underlying intention.[1]

Penal provisions.—If two or more constructions are equally open, the Court should prefer a construction which does not impose a penalty over one which does. If persons are to be penalized by the law it is only fair and reasonable that the conditions under which the penalty is to be incurred should be plainly stated.

Ejusdem generis (of the same kind).—Where a string of terms all of the same kind is followed by a wider term not expressly limited to that kind, the final term is, under the *ejusdem generis* rule, taken to be so limited by implication. Thus in the expression " any orange, lime, paw-paw, banana or other article " the word article would be taken to be limited to an article of the same genus as the preceding words, namely fruit. There must be at least two preceding words: in a reference to " any banana or other article " the word article would not be taken as restricted to fruit under this rule, although in certain contexts the *noscitur a sociis* rule might be held to apply. There must also be a genus: if the preceding words are widely dissimilar the final word will not be taken to be limited by them. Because of the uncertainty of its application, the draftsman should not deliberately rely on the *ejusdem generis* rule—in the first example given above " or other article " should be replaced by " or similar article ", or better still " or other fruit ".[2]

Noscitur a sociis (a thing is known from its associates).—This is similar to the *ejusdem generis* rule but is wider in scope. Where words or phrases capable of analogous meanings are associated, they take colour from each other and this may exclude meanings which would be possible if the words or phrases stood alone. Thus, where a power was given to " break up the soil and pavement of roads, highways, footways, commons, streets, lanes,

---

[1] Where the court's sympathies are against this intention it may not strive very hard, as occurred in *Cornish Mutual Assurance Co., Ltd.* v. *Inland Revenue Commissioners*, [1926] A.C. 281.

[2] The *ejusdem generis* rule was disapplied by s. 35 of the Interpretation Act, 1957 (No. 29), but this section was omitted from the 1960 Act.

alleys, passages and public places " the court held, " construing the word ' footway ' from the company in which it is found " that the power was limited to paved footways in towns and did not extend to a field footpath.[1]

Expressio unius est exclusio alterius (to mention one thing is to exclude another).[2]—This is a most important rule, of frequent application. If a reference is wide enough to cover a number of different things, but the enactment goes on to mention only some of them, the others are by implication excluded. Thus an enactment may refer to a man " and his issue ". If this stands alone it may be uncertain whether " issue " is limited to children or includes all descendants, and also whether illegitimate issue are covered. If, however, the phrase is followed by the words " including his legitimate grandsons " the *expressio unius* rule indicates that all descendants other than children and legitimate grandsons are excluded, though whether the children must be legitimate to qualify remains in doubt. The rule may lead to danger where unnecessary references are made. Suppose there are three separate sections in an Act which deal with the supply of drugs. Section 1 says that no person shall sell any drug from premises which have not been registered under the Act. Section 2 says that no person shall sell a poison except on prescription, Section 3 says that no person shall sell a narcotic without a licence from the Minister. These three sections are mutually independent, and it is clear that a licence from the Minister under s. 3 to sell a narcotic which also happens to be a poison cannot authorise it to be sold from unregistered premises, or without a prescription. But if, in a way which frequently happens, the draftsman has ended s. 3 with the words " Provided that nothing in this section shall affect the requirements of *section two* of this Act " doubt immediately arises. What about s. 1? If the Minister has granted a licence, can a narcotic be sold on prescription from *any* premises, whether registered or not? The *expressio unius* rule indicates that it can, but the court, treating the rule with the caution that is often necessary, would probably hold this to be contrary to the intention of the Act.

Generalia specialibus non derogant (general provisions do not derogate from particular ones).—It frequently happens that an enactment lays down a general rule in terms wide enough to

---

[1] *Scales* v. *Pickering* (1828), 4 Bing, 448.

[2] Another version is: *expressum facit cessare tacitum* (where some things only are mentioned the ones not mentioned are taken to be excluded).

cover a particular case for which a special rule has already been provided. If the special rule is not repealed it may be held to remain unaffected by the later enactment. Thus a Bills of Sale Act requiring registration of agreements creating a charge over movable property has been held not to supersede provisions in a Companies Act providing in detail for the special case of the registration of debentures issued by a limited company, although such debentures would be agreements of the type mentioned in the Bills of Sale Act.[1]

An Act is to be construed as a whole.—This is an important rule, since it is easy, by taking a particular provision of an Act in isolation, to obtain a wrong impression of its true effect. The dangers of taking passages out of their context are well known in other fields, and they apply just as much to legislation. Even where an Act is properly drawn it still must be read as a whole. Indeed, a well-drawn Act consists of an interlocking structure, each provision of which has its part to play. Warnings will often be there to guide the reader, as for example that an apparently categorical statement in one place is subject to exceptions laid down elsewhere in the Act, but such warnings cannot always be provided. Where an Act is defective, the rule is even more important, since a statement in one place may be countered by what appears to be an inconsistent statement elsewhere, and the reader must then try to arrive at the intention of the legislature by construing the Act as a whole. It should be stressed, however, that this does not enable express words to be evaded because they conflict with an *implication* which might otherwise be drawn from elsewhere: *expressum facit cessare tacitum.* Where two provisions of an Act are contradictory, and the contradiction cannot be resolved by construing the Act as a whole, the earlier provision gives way to that which appears later in the Act: " the known rule is that the last must prevail ".[2]

It was formerly common practice to provide in an Act that it should be read as one with an earlier Act or Acts. This practice has fallen into disfavour because it tends to produce intolerable complexities.[3] Where it has been followed the result is that every provision of each Act must be construed as if contained in a single

---

[1] *Re Standard Manufacturing Co.,* [1891] 1 Ch. 627.
[2] *Wood* v. *Riley* (1867), L.R. 3 C.P. 26.
[3] These were particularly acute in the case of the nineteenth century public health legislation in England.

Act except where some inconsistency requires it to be assumed that the later Act has modified the earlier.[1] In Ghana a statutory instrument is normally to be construed as one with the Act under which it is made.[2] This does not permit the instrument to over-ride the Act, unless of course the Act authorises it to do so.[3] The main purpose of the rule is to avoid the need to repeat in the instrument interpretation provisions contained in the Act.

5. PUBLICATION OF LAWS

The duty to act in accordance with law requires for its observance that the law should be readily available in its most up to date form. This brings us to the subject of how laws are published. The system of publication was changed on the inauguration of the Republic, but since many pre-republican laws remain in force the system developed in Colonial days is of present importance as well as historical interest.

The Colonial system

Throughout the Colonial period primary laws made in Ghana took the form of Ordinances, and a threefold system was developed to make the Ordinances available to those who needed to refer to them. The first stage was the publication in the *Gazette* of the text of each Ordinance as it was made. The second stage was the publication soon after the end of each year of a bound volume containing the Ordinances made in that year. The third stage was the publication every few years of a collected edition, printed in England, of the Ordinances currently in force. Subsidiary legislation, Imperial Acts applying to the Gold Coast, Imperial Orders in Council, Letters Patent and other relevant instruments were treated in much the same way, the collected editions including these as well as the Ordinances. Ten of these collected editions were published in the century preceding the attainment of independence, the years of publication being 1860, 1874, 1887, 1898, 1903, 1910, 1920, 1928, 1937 and 1954–1956. As the number of volumes required grew from one in 1860 to eleven in 1954–1956 so the method of treatment grew more elaborate, and special Ordinances were passed to enable the form of the law to be

---

[1] *Phillips* v. *Parnaby* [1934] 2 K.B. 299.
[2] Interpretation Act, 1960 (C.A. 4), s. 21.
[3] Statutory Instruments Act, 1959 (No. 52), s. 7.

revised and to make the resulting edition the authorised statute book.[1] The table on p. 286 gives an outline of the position.

Factors such as the humidity of the climate and the voraciousness of paper-loving insects mean a short life for books in Ghana, and not even the National Archives in Accra possess a complete set of editions of Gold Coast laws. The table has been compiled from the materials available and is believed to be complete, although it is possible that further collected editions were published in the nineteenth century and have since been lost sight of.

The editions of 1860 and 1874 were merely collections in chronological order of the Ordinances and other laws in the form in which they were made, the 1874 edition containing also the texts of various treaties made with local Chiefs. In the 1887 edition, the first of the three prepared by Sir William Brandford Griffith, certain improvements were made. An Ordinance was passed which repealed a number of spent and obsolete enactments and thus enabled them to be omitted from the collected edition.[2] Although the remaining Ordinances were printed in chronological order as passed, footnotes were included to show where amendments had been made. It must have been apparent however that this was not enough, and before work was begun on the next edition an Ordinance was passed appointing Sir William Brandford Griffith a Commissioner for the purpose of preparing a revised edition and authorising him to do anything relating to form and method which might be necessary for the perfecting of the new edition.[3] In particular he was authorised to omit spent enactments, to consolidate Ordinances *in pari materia*, to alter the arrangement of Ordinances, and to add short titles and marginal notes. On being approved by the Governor the edition so prepared was to constitute " the sole and only proper Statute Book of the Gold Coast Colony up to the date of the latest of the Ordinances contained therein ".

The 1898 edition, which was prepared under this Ordinance, did not perhaps exploit the powers given as fully as it might have done. Apart from the incorporation of amending Ordinances in the principal Ordinances affected by them, the method remained

---

[1] Between 1894 and 1954 no less than twenty-eight Ordinances were passed with respect to these collected editions, as well as a number of others which repealed spent Ordinances or otherwise provided for statute law revision.

[2] Statute Law Revision Ordinance, 1886 (No. 1).

[3] Reprint of Statutes Ordinance, 1896 (No. 14).

Collected Editions of Gold Coast Laws

No. of volumes	Title	Containing law in force at	Published	Extent	Statutory authority	Prepared by
1	Ordinances of the Forts and Settlements on the Gold Coast	31st Dec., 1859	1860	H.M.'s jurisdiction	—	—
1	Ordinances of the Gold Coast Colony	31st Dec., 1870	1874	Colony	—	Algernon Montagu
1	Laws of the Gold Coast Colony	7th April, 1887	1887	Colony	—	Sir William Brandford Griffith, *Chief Justice of The Gold Coast Colony*
2	Ordinances of the Gold Coast Colony	June, 1898	1898	Colony	Reprint of Statutes Ordinance, 1896 (No. 14)[1]	Sir William Brandford Griffith, *Chief Justice of The Gold Coast Colony*
2	Ordinances of the Gold Coast Colony	31st March, 1903	1903	Gold Coast	Reprint of Statutes Ordinance, 1903 (No. 4)	
3 / 1	Ordinances of the Gold Coast Colony / Ordinances of Ashanti/Ordinances of the Northern Territories	31st Dec., 1909	1910	Gold Coast	Reprint of Statutes Ordinance, 1909 (No. 16)	F. H. Gough, *a Puisne Judge of the Colony*
3 / 1 / 1	Laws of the Gold Coast Colony 1920 / Laws of Ashanti 1920 / Laws of the Northern Territories of the Gold Coast 1920	31st Dec., 1919	1920	Gold Coast	Revised Edition of the Laws Ordinance, 1920 (No. 16)[2]	Sir Donald Kingdon, *Attorney-General of the Colony*
3 / 2	Laws of the Gold Coast Colony 1928 / Laws of Ashanti, British Togoland and Northern Territories 1928	1st Jan., 1928	1928	Gold Coast and British Togoland	Revised Edition of the Laws Ordinance, 1928 (No. 12)[3]	E. G. Smith, *a Puisne Judge of the Colony*
4	Laws of the Gold Coast (including Togoland under British Mandate) 1936	1st Sept., 1936	1937	Gold Coast and British Togoland	Revised Edition of the Laws (Gold Coast) Ordinance, 1936 (No. 24)[4]	Sir Leslie M'Carthy, *Solicitor-General of the Gold Coast*
5	Laws of the Gold Coast (1951)[5]	31st Dec., 1951	1954	Gold Coast and British Togoland	Revised Edition of the Laws Ordinance 1951 (No. 36)[6]	Sir Percy McElwaine
4	Laws of the Gold Coast (1954)[6]	31st Dec., 1954	1956			Sir Patrick Branigan, *Attorney-General of the Gold Coast*
2	Laws of the Gold Coast Supplement 1952–1954[7]		1955			

[1] As amended by Ordinances No. 17 of 1897 and No. 13 of 1898.

[2] This was the Colony Ordinance; similar Ordinances were passed for Ashanti (No. 8 of 1920) and the Northern Territories (No. 5 of 1920).

[3] As amended by Ordinance No. 26 of 1929. This was the Colony Ordinance; similar Ordinances were passed for Ashanti (No. 2 of 1928 as amended by No. 21 of 1929 British Togoland (No. 1 of 1928) and the Northern Territories (No. 1 of 1928).

[4] As amended by Ordinances Nos. 8 and 29 of 1937. The Togoland Ordinance was No. 30 of 1936, as amended by Ordinance No. 16 of 1937.

[5] Volumes I to V of the 1951–54 Edition, containing Ordinances only. [6] Volumes VI to IX of the 1951–54 Edition, containing subsidiary legislation, etc.

[7] Containing the Ordinances of 1952–1954, the Income Tax Ordinance, 1943 and a chronological table of Ordinances from 1852...

much as before and the Ordinances continued to be arranged in chronological order. This was also true of the two following editions, made under similar powers. In 1920 however Sir Donald Kingdon introduced a new method, following a recommendation made in a circular from the Secretary of State.[1] The Ordinances of the Colony were arranged under twenty-four Titles, each Ordinance being given a chapter number in place of its original number. The Titles were as follows, the figures in brackets indicating the number of chapters in each—

1. Legislation (4).
2. Abolition of Slavery (2).
3. Administration of Justice (11).
4. Public Officers (13).
5. Police and Prisons (6).
6. Political Prisoners (7).
7. Military Affairs (5).
8. Posts and Telegraphs (5).
9. Medical and Sanitary Affairs (12).
10. Local Government (1).
11. Religion and Education (4).
12. Marriage (6).
13. Labour (3).
14. Native Affairs (5).
15. Land (7).
16. Mines (3).
17. Forestry and Agriculture (4).
18. Animals (2).
19. Ways and Communications (11).
20. Finance (22).
21. Trade and Customs (24).
22. Regulation and Control of Various Matters (17).
23. Immigration (5).
24. War (18).

The arrangement of Titles, and of chapters within them, was designed to bring as close together as possible subjects of a similar nature and matters continually being dealt with by the same individuals. Another change made in this edition was the separation of the Colony subsidiary legislation from the Ordinances from which it derived. The first two volumes contained the

---

[1] Circular Dispatch dated 18th September, 1915.

Ordinances under chapter numbers from 1 to 197 and the third contained subsidiary legislation as well as Imperial statutes, Orders in Council, etc. Each item of subsidiary legislation was made easy to find by being grouped under the same chapter number as the Ordinance giving power to make it, a useful system which continued to be employed in the subsequent editions. In the volumes for Ashanti and the Northern Territories the Ordinances continued to be arranged in chronological order, since Sir Donald Kingdon considered that the fact that a large part of the law in force consisted of applied Ordinances of the Colony precluded arrangement under Titles.[1]

In the 1928 edition the grouping of Ordinances under Titles was, " by special request of His Excellency the Governor ", abandoned in favour of an alphabetical order according to the short title of each Ordinance.[2] Short titles which began with a word which was not indicative of the subject-matter, and would thus have been difficult to find in the alphabetical arrangement, were suitably altered.[3] The alphabetical arrangement was not limited to the Colony, but applied to the three so-called dependencies as well, and the chronological order was finally abandoned. The number of chapters of the Colony Ordinances remained almost the same at 190. In addition there were 24 chapters of Ashanti Ordinances, four chapters of British Togoland Ordinances and 22 chapters of Northern Territories Ordinances.

The system of Titles was restored in the 1936 edition and the new power to legislate in one Ordinance for the Colony, Ashanti and the Northern Territories[4] enabled the edition to take for the first time the form of a single statute-book covering all four territories.[5] The Titles were in the main similar to those used in the 1920 edition, although they appeared in a different order. The Titles Political Prisoners, Regulation and Control of Various Matters, and War disappeared. New Titles were Electricity and Water, Administration (relating only to the dependencies), Books and Publications, and Miscellaneous (ranging from Oaths

---

[1] See the preface to these volumes.

[2] Preface to the 1928 Edition, p. vii. The Governor was Sir Alexander Slater, who had succeeded Guggisberg the year before.

[3] *E.g.* the short title " British and Colonial Probates Ordinance " was changed to " Probates (British and Colonial) Ordinance ".

[4] See pp. 32–33, *ante.*

[5] By virtue of the British Sphere of Togoland Order in Council, 1923 the laws of the Colony applied in general to the southern section of British Togoland, and the laws of the Northern Territories applied in general to the northern section of British Togoland.

to Girl Guides). Another change was the omission of certain Ordinances, which were listed in the Schedule to the Revised Edition of the Laws (Gold Coast) Ordinance, 1936 (No. 24). These were described as being " obsolescent or of a temporary nature or being under revision or being Ordinances the carrying into effect the provisions of which is doubtful ". Their omission did not affect whatever force and validity they had.[1] Although the 1936 edition was thus able to be produced in only four volumes, the problem of obsolescence caused by the increasing bulk of current legislation was becoming more acute. It was little use having the revised laws in four volumes if within a few years as many more volumes had also to be handled in order to ascertain the state of the law. To meet this problem a system of cumulative annual supplements was embarked upon in 1938.[2] Ordinances enacted after 1st September, 1936 which amended chapters of the 1936 edition were arranged in the supplement in the order of those chapter numbers. Other Ordinances so enacted were given in chronological order, incorporating any amendments subsequently made to them. Subsidiary legislation was treated in the same way. In order therefore to find out if an enactment included in the 1936 edition had been amended or repealed, it was only necessary to look in one place in the latest cumulative supplement. Unfortunately shortage of staff due to war conditions led to the suspension of the scheme in 1940 after only two annual supplements had been produced.[3] It was never revived.

When the last Colonial revision was undertaken in 1951 the bulk of statute law had greatly increased, and the task was the most formidable that had faced any editor of the Gold Coast laws. The Revised Edition of the Laws Ordinance, 1951 (No. 36) therefore authorised the editor, Sir Percy McElwaine (a former Chief Justice of the Straits Settlements), to omit a considerable number of Ordinances, which nevertheless retained their validity.[4] Provision was also made for further omissions, and also amendments and additions, to be authorised by the legislature and

---

[1] Revised Edition of the Laws (Gold Coast) Ordinance, 1936 (No. 24), s. 5.

[2] Revised Edition of the Laws (Annual Supplements) Ordinance, 1938 (No. 37).

[3] The suspension was imposed by Regulations, (No. 20 of 1940) and continued at the end of the war by Ordinance No. 3 of 1946.

[4] See the Schedule to the Ordinance which, as amended, is printed at pp. xv to xvii of Vol. I of the 1951 edition. Further entries were made by Ordinance No. 35 of 1954.

T

reflected in the revised edition.[1] These steps did not prevent the edition from reaching the unprecedented size of nine volumes, with two more being added by way of supplement.[2] The Ordinances themselves were contained in five volumes and were again arranged under Titles. The number of chapters increased from 221 to 272, and the number of Titles from 26 to 30. The new Titles were Town Planning and Housing, Liquor Trade, Enquiries, Statistics and Valuation, and Arms, Explosive (*sic*) and Inflammatory Substances. The order of the remaining Titles was virtually unchanged. The system of Titles was deprived of much of what value it possessed by the failure to follow the previous practice of listing all the Titles at the beginning of the first volume.

Although containing the law as in force at the end of 1951, the volumes containing the Ordinances were not published until 1954, by which time much of the law had been altered. To prevent the subsidiary legislation volumes from falling even further behind, an Ordinance was passed to enable these to include instruments made up to the end of 1954,[3] but even so they were not published until 1956. The work was completed by a two-volume supplement which contained the Ordinances passed in 1952–1954 and also the consolidated edition of the Income Tax Ordinance, 1943 which had been prepared under separate statutory authority.[4] Those Ordinances which amended chapters included in the five volumes published in 1954 were set out under the appropriate chapter numbers after the Income Tax Ordinance at the beginning of the supplement; the remainder were given in chronological order. Subsidiary legislation under Ordinances passed in 1952–1954 was included in Volume VI of the main work.

In concluding this brief survey of the Colonial system of publishing laws some mention should be made of indexing and noting-up. The practice varied, but it was usual to supplement each

---

[1] Revised Edition of the Laws Ordinance, 1951, (No. 36) s. 6. The procedure was used to effect a considerable tidying-up of the statute book—see the Revised Edition of the Laws (Miscellaneous Provisions) Ordinance, 1952 (No. 52).

[2] The figures exaggerate the real increase, since not only were the 1951 volumes smaller than those of 1936 but heavier paper was used.

[3] Revised Edition of the Laws (Amendment) Ordinance, 1954 (No. 35), s. 2.

[4] Income Tax (Amendment) Ordinance, 1952 (No. 18), s. 50. The supplement itself was authorised by the Revised Edition of the Ordinances (1952–1954 Supplement) Ordinance, 1954 (No. 36).

collected edition by a full subject-matter index and also a chronological table showing every Ordinance and its subsequent fate—
repeal, absorption into a chapter of a revised edition, omission
or otherwise. Sometimes the index was published separately, as
in the case of the 1936 and 1951–1954 editions, and sometimes it
was given at the end of a volume. In the case of the 1951–1954
edition not only was a full index published separately, but an
alphabetical list of Ordinances was given at the end of every
volume. In each annual volume of Ordinances published thereafter a cumulative index arranged in alphabetical order of short
titles was printed at the end of the volume. Noting-up was provided for by the issue, at intervals of a few months, of noting-up
instructions. These set out, in order of chapter numbers of the
latest collected edition followed by subsequent legislation in
chronological order, the textual amendments made to Ordinances
and, after Independence, to Acts of the Parliament of Ghana.
The instructions enabled minor amendments to be noted in manuscript on the enactment affected, while larger amendments were
cut out of the noting-up booklet and pasted in at the appropriate
place in the bound volume. No noting-up service was provided
for subsidiary legislation.

The present system
When the constitutional legislation was being prepared in the
early months of 1960 it became necessary to consider the question
of replacing the 1951–1954 edition of the laws. More than three
hundred Ordinances and Acts had been enacted since the end of
1954, together with nearly two thousand items of subsidiary
legislation. In all, the local enactments were distributed among
twenty-one volumes, and the absence of an up-to-date comprehensive index made the task of finding out the law on any point
increasingly troublesome. In addition there was the problem of the
application of British statutes. As explained elsewhere in this
book, there were in force in Ghana British statutes of three
types, namely the statutes of general application in force in
England on 24th July, 1874, the Imperial Acts which had applied
to the Gold Coast by express provision or necessary intendment,
and the statutes (governing such matters as divorce, merchant
shipping and registered designs) which were applied by local
enactments. Although some statutes of the first two types were
set out in Vol. VI of the 1951–1954 edition, there was in existence
no comprehensive list of the British statutes in force in Ghana,

and the texts of most of them were available only in British collections where they had to be read with such modifications as were necessary to fit Ghanaian conditions. Other relevant factors were that the form and much of the content of the Colonial legislation had been rendered obsolete by the actual and proposed changes in the constitutional system, and that legislation was expected to continue for some years at the high rate necessary to implement the Government's plans for social and economic development.

What was to be done? Attention was first turned to the possibility of continuing the Colonial system and publishing a revised edition of the laws as soon as possible after the inauguration of the Republic. Weighty reasons were however advanced against this, some of a general nature and others arising out of Ghana's situation at the time. These reasons may be summarized as follows—

1. The system of producing sets of bound volumes every few years is too rigid when the law is constantly changing. The edition is out of date before it is published and can only maintain its usefulness by means of the noter-up system, which is troublesome to operate, highly susceptible to error by the clerk entering the amendments, and produces after a time volumes made difficult to read by the presence of innumerable manuscript corrections and pasted-in bits of paper.[1] Even with noting-up there are many laws which are new and cannot be incorporated into the main volumes.

2. The system is theoretically unsatisfactory because it means that the laws change their identity every few years, being rearranged and renumbered, and frequently given new titles, new sidenotes and even new wording. The original enactment by Parliament is lost sight of, and Parliament can have no real control over the new form it assumes. Furthermore the risk of accidental omissions and other errors is considerable.

3. The system involves a great upheaval, with all the law being put in a different place and all existing volumes (with, it

---

[1] In the Objects and Reasons for the Revised Edition of the Laws Bill, 1951 the comment was made that " where the amendments of the Laws since the [last] revision have been incorporated in the main volumes of the Laws the books have become very cumbersome and dilapidated."

may be, the user's annotations) being superseded overnight. Law reports, textbooks, contracts and other documents referring to particular enactments immediately become difficult to follow.

4. The system involves the engagement of a Commissioner and other extra staff, since the work is too great over a short period to be absorbed by the Government's normal legal staff. Apart from the difficulty of finding suitable people, this adds (if not substantially) to the already heavy cost of printing and binding sets of a dozen or so large volumes.[1]

The conclusion reached was that while the Colonial system of publishing laws no doubt had its merits when the enacted law was small in quantity and relatively static (and when what was required was two or three volumes which the district commissioner could slip into his bag when going on trek) the system had outlived its usefulness in Ghana. A new one had therefore to be devised. It was decided to get round the first of the objections noted above by having loose-leaf binders and issuing replacement pages incorporating amendments as they were made. It would have been ideal to make a fresh start by publishing in this form a completely new set of laws, including a re-enactment of such of the British statutes as were still required, but this would have been an immense task calling for a large staff and was rejected as impracticable. Instead, it was decided to achieve the same results by degrees. Early in 1960 a statute law revision branch was set up within the Attorney-General's Department and a programme of consolidation of the Ghanaian and relevant British statute law was embarked upon. The resulting laws have been put through, as they became ready, in the form of ordinary Acts of Parliament, along with Acts in the current legislative programme. When complete, the law reform programme is expected to supersede, by Acts of the Republican Parliament, all local Ordinances and Acts which came into force before 1st July, 1960 and all British statutes applying to Ghana.

The cumulative binder service of Acts and legislative instruments was inaugurated on 1st July, 1960.[2] The binders are as

---

[1] The total cost of the 1951–1954 edition was approximately £37,000, only a small proportion of which was recovered from sales.

[2] For an explanation of the division of subsidiary legislation into executive and legislative instruments see pp. 265 *et seq.*, *ante*.

stout as could be obtained, and heavy paper is used to reduce the risk of tearing—a notorious disadvantage of loose-leaf systems. The first volume of the Acts of Ghana, for which red binders are used, contains a note explaining the system, followed by an alphabetical table of Acts included in the binder and a note on the Interpretation Act, 1960. The Acts begin with the Constitution (which is printed on grey paper so that it can be easily distinguished) and the eleven other Acts of the Constituent Assembly. In accordance with a resolution of the Constituent Assembly, all the Acts passed by it were numbered, in accordance with the order in which they were passed, by the insertion in the original copies of the letters C.A. followed by the appropriate numeral.[1] In the published copies, however, this numeral was, as required by the resolution, omitted in the case of the Constitution. As the fundamental law, the Constitution did not need a reference number and would have appeared slightly undignified if given one.

After the Acts of the Constituent Assembly, the first volume continues with Acts of the Republican Parliament in chronological order. By s. 7 of the Acts of Parliament Act, 1960 (C.A. 7), these Acts are required to be numbered consecutively from the establishment of the Republic, and the numbering is not to begin afresh at the commencement of a calendar year, a new Parliament or any other period. The object of this is to enable an Act to be referred to simply as, for example " Act 29 ", rather as the corresponding chapter of the Laws of the Gold Coast (the Criminal Code) used to be referred to as " Cap. 9 ". As Acts are passed they are issued to subscribers by the Government Printer for insertion in the binder. As soon as possible after the end of each meeting of the National Assembly, that is about once a quarter, replacement pages are issued. These incorporate amendments made to Acts already in the binder, note repeals and keep the alphabetical table up to date. Amendments and repeals of pre-Republican Acts and Ordinances continue to be dealt with by the noter-up service. Acts are no longer published in the *Gazette*, or as supplements to the *Gazette*. Notice of their enactment is given in the *Gazette* however, and separate bound copies of each Act are available from the Government Printer. Although the binder service presents the law in up-to-date form, it may

---

[1] The text of the resolution is given in *Proceedings of the Constituent Assembly*, col. 161.

occasionally be necessary to refer to the original text of an Act which has been amended or repealed. To provide for this a limited number of annual bound volumes of Acts will continue to be published.

The binder service of legislative instruments, for which black binders are used, operates in much the same manner. Volume I begins with an explanatory note and is followed by a key to Acts and Ordinances and an alphabetical table of instruments included in the binder. The key lists enactments under which legislative instruments have been made since the beginning of 1960. The list begins with chapters of the 1951–1954 edition and continues with subsequent Acts and Ordinances in chronological order. Thus to find whether a legislative instrument has been made under s. 3 of the Wild Animals Preservation Ordinance (Cap. 246) one looks under Cap. 246 in the key and sees that L.I. 8 has been made under it. The key does not help with subsidiary legislation made before 1960, but as time goes on and the older instruments are gradually superseded it will come to present a more complete picture. After this preliminary matter the volume continues with the legislative instruments made since the beginning of 1960. Like the Acts, these are numbered consecutively without a break at the end of the year or at any other time. The numbers do not of course correspond with the numbers of the Acts under which the instruments are made—this useful feature of the Colonial system is hardly possible with the type of loose-leaf system now used. What is said above as to the issue of new material and replacement pages, the giving of notice in the *Gazette*, and the publication of bound copies and annual volumes applies to legislative instruments as it does to Acts.

It remains to consider executive instruments. These are published in a separate series, and their numbering starts afresh at the beginning of each year. There is no binder service and the instruments are issued as they are made, being notified in the *Gazette*.[1] Bound annual volumes of executive instruments are also published.

---

[1] A number of enactments require statutory instruments to be published in the *Gazette*. To enable uniformity of treatment to be given, the Official Publications Act, 1959 (No. 85) was passed. Section 2 of the Act states that the publication by the Government Printer of any Act, instrument, or other document otherwise than in the *Gazette* shall, if *notice* of the publication thereof is given in the *Gazette*, have the like effect as if the document had been published in the *Gazette*. The section does not apply to the publication of Bills.

The new system of publication of laws depends for its success on efficient indexing, particularly while so much of the older law remains concurrently in force. Previous indexes have perhaps tended to concentrate too much on the divisions laid down by the arrangement of chapters in the latest collected edition, and to give insufficient cross-references. We may take as an example of this the treatment of the administration of estates of deceased persons in the comprehensive index to the 1951–1954 edition, which ran to 232 pages. There were five relevant Ordinances, namely the Probates (British and Colonial) Ordinance (Cap. 21), the Administration of Estates by Consular Officers Ordinance (Cap. 22), the Administration (Foreign Employment) Ordinance (Cap. 23), the Appropriation of Lapsed Personalty Ordinance (Cap. 24) and the Probate Exemption Ordinance (Cap. 25). On looking up " Administration of Estates " in the index however one finds a reference to Cap. 22 only. On looking up " Probate " one finds references only to Caps. 21 and 25, and so on. In fact the index, in spite of its length, was really designed only to show the arrangement of material within each Ordinance, a thing which might perhaps have been more conveniently done by printing an arrangement of sections at the beginning of each Ordinance in the main volumes. Nor did the arrangement of Ordinances under Titles help very much. As mentioned above, the 1951–1954 edition did not set out in one place what the Titltes were, so that they could be gathered only by looking at the beginning of five different volumes. Apart from this, it is notoriously difficult to arrange laws under really helpful Titles. The first four of the Ordinances mentioned above were printed under the Title " Justice ", but the fifth was printed in a different volume under the Title " Public Officers ". These problems can be met only by having an index which lists all the relevant law under a heading such as " Administration of Estates " and contains cross-references to this heading under words such as " Probate " which are likely to be looked up by a reader in search of information on the subject. A further essential is that the index should always be kept up to date.

In an attempt to satisfy these requirements an index of all Acts and Ordinances in force on 31st March, 1961 was prepared by the statute law revision branch and published in June, 1961. This was issued in a bound volume, which also contained a chronological table of chapters in the 1951–1954 edition and subsequent Ordinances and Acts, showing repeals and the headings under which live enactments were dealt with in the index. It is proposed to reissue the volume as soon as possible in a loose-leaf binder, which will be kept up-to-date in the same way as the binder service of Acts and legislative instruments. In time it is hoped to produce a similar index for legislative instruments.

CHAPTER 7

LEGISLATIVE FUNCTIONARIES

In this chapter we consider the various bodies and persons who take part in the processes of legislation by Act of Parliament or statutory instrument. These processes can be divided into the formal and the informal. The formal are those laid down by constitutional law as being essential for the making of valid and effectual legislation, such as the passing of a Bill by the National Assembly and the signifying of Presidential assent. The informal processes are those which go on behind the scenes, such as the taking of policy decisions on the content of the new law, and the processes of drafting. Some functionaries take part in both types of process; others in only one. Thus, while the President has a formal part to play in giving his assent to Bills passed by the Assembly and also an informal part in deciding on legislative policy, the part of Parliamentary Counsel and other Civil Servants is played entirely behind the scenes. The manner in which these functions are exercised will be described in the following chapters. Here we are only concerned to name the functionaries, to state their role in law-making, and to explain how they are organized to carry it out.

1. PARLIAMENT

Parliament, as the legislature of Ghana, is the first body we must consider. Its constituent elements are the President and the National Assembly, and the provisions of the Constitution by which they are established and regulated have been described in CHAPTER 3. We need say no more here about the formal legislative functions of the President, although his informal role will be discussed in the next section in connection with the Cabinet. It may however be useful to examine rather more fully the way in which the National Assembly is organized to carry out its law-making role.

PARLIAMENT HOUSE

The National Assembly meets in Parliament House, which is situated next to the Supreme Court in Accra. The building was erected as a memorial to King George V and was originally used for general purposes. When the Legislative Assembly was set up in 1951 it required new premises, since the Supreme Court accommodation which had been used by the former Legislative Council was too small. For a time the building was shared by the Accra Municipal Council and the Assembly, but this arrangement proved inconvenient and the building was taken over by the Assembly and enlarged.

The Chamber

The Chamber was rearranged and refurbished at the time of the inauguration of the Republic. It is divided into the Officers' Area and the Members' Area. The Officers' Area, at the north end of the Chamber, contains the Chair, which is occupied by the Speaker or other person presiding, and the Table, at which the Clerks sit, and which stands just below the dais supporting the Chair. The Chair was a gift from the House of Commons at the time of Ghana's independence in 1957. The whole of the Officers' Area, which is carpeted in gold, is raised above the level of the blue-carpeted Members' Area. The benches for the Members are arranged in a horseshoe with the Chair and Table at the open end. For the convenience of members a table is placed in the middle of the horseshoe. On this stand the two dispatch boxes from which front-bench members are entitled to address the House. Unlike that in the House of Commons, the seating is extensive enough to accommodate all the members. When the President comes to address the House however the middle portion of the horseshoe is removed to make a passage for his procession. The consequent crowding in the remaining benches heightens the excitement of the occasion. Openings on either side of the Chamber lead to the two division lobbies, the Ayes lobby being on the south-west and the Noes lobby on the south-east. The Chamber is equipped with sufficient microphones for every member to be within reach of one. On all four sides of the Chamber there are galleries for distinguished visitors and the public generally, although strictly these form part of the precincts of the Assembly and not of the Chamber itself.

The Precincts

The precincts of the Assembly are " the offices of the Assembly and the galleries and places provided for the use or accommodation of strangers ". While the Assembly is sitting, and subject to any exceptions made by direction of the Speaker, the precincts include the entire building and also its courtyard and garden.[1] Apart from the Chamber itself, Parliament House contains a number of offices and other rooms. The rooms used by members generally are the library, the reading room (which contains a bar) and the members' common room. There are also a Ministers' common room, a room reserved for the President, and separate offices for the Speaker, the Deputy Speaker, the Parliamentary Secretary, and each of the Clerks.[2]

MEMBERS, OFFICERS AND STRANGERS

We now consider the various persons who have duties in the Assembly or may otherwise be found within its precincts. These persons may be divided into three categories: members, officers and strangers. The only person who does not fit into this classification is the President who, although not a Member of Parliament, has the right under art. 21(4) of the Constitution to attend any sitting of the Assembly, but not to join in debates. He also normally attends to deliver the Sessional Addresses and Sessional Reports required by art. 25, and to open Parliament at the beginning of each session. Under art. 21(1) the Assembly proper consists of the Speaker and not less than 104 Members of Parliament. Officers of the Assembly other than the Speaker are provided for by or under the National Assembly Act, 1961 (Act 86).

The Speaker

The Speaker is held in great respect as the spokesman of the Assembly and the person who presides over its deliberations and maintains order in the Chamber and precincts. In a sense he embodies the dignity and authority of Parliament and for this reason is accorded privileges and immunities not enjoyed by any other officer. Unlike the Speaker of the House of Commons, Ghana's Speaker is not a Member of Parliament. He may be a

---

[1] National Assembly Act, 1961 (Act 86), s. 46.
[2] A new block is to be built shortly which will contain a dining room and kitchens as well as a new library, reading room and meeting rooms.

Member when elected as Speaker, but if so his seat thereupon becomes vacant and a by-election must be held. The Speaker is elected by the Members and a candidate for the office may be any person not being of ministerial rank or a public officer. The election must be held before the despatch of any other business at the first sitting of the Assembly after the office has become vacant, and if contested is decided by ballot. As soon as possible after his election the Speaker-elect must come to the Assembly and take the oath of allegiance and the official oath. These are administered by the Clerk of the Assembly, who acts as presiding officer until they have been taken. The Speaker holds office until the first sitting of the Assembly after a dissolution, unless he resigns or dies, or is unfortunate enough to incur a vote of no confidence supported by at least two-thirds of the total number of Members. The Speaker is entitled to a salary and various allowances, the payment of which is charged on the Consolidated Fund.[1] Like the Members, he is entitled to a gratuity after every five years' service.[2] He wears no special dress in the Assembly, appearing either in *kente* or lounge suit.

The symbol of the Speaker's authority is the Mace.[3] This stands upright before the Table during all sittings of the Assembly except during the Consideration Stage of Bills, when it is tilted towards the Chair.[4] The standing Mace was explained by Mr. Kojo Botsio when Leader of the House as " giving the effect of a traditional Kyiame's stick ".[5]

The Deputy Speaker

Since the Speaker cannot be present throughout all the sittings of the Assembly, the National Assembly Act provides for a Deputy Speaker. The Deputy Speaker is elected by the Members in the same way as the Speaker. A candidate for the office must however be a Member himself, not being of ministerial rank, and he retains his seat after election. He holds office only for the session, and a further election must be held at the beginning of a new session. If he is appointed to ministerial rank, or loses his

---

[1] The present salary is £G2,500; allowances total £G1,740. (The Ghana pound is at parity with sterling.)

[2] See p. 303, *post.*

[3] For a description of the new Mace, see p. 110, *ante.*

[4] Standing Order 19.

[5] *Parl. Deb. Official Report*, Vol. 19, col. 228 (28th June, 1960).

seat otherwise than by reason of a dissolution, the Deputy Speaker automatically forfeits his office. Apart from resignation or death, he may also lose his office if a vote of no confidence in him is passed by a simple majority.[1]

Section 11 of the National Assembly Act requires the Deputy Speaker to exercise all the Speaker's obligatory functions in the case where the office of Speaker is vacant. In other cases the Deputy Speaker may be empowered by the Speaker or by Standing Orders to perform any functions conferred by law on the Speaker—unless of course the law in question forbids this. Most Standing Orders referring to the Speaker apply equally to the Deputy Speaker when he is presiding.[2] The Member holding the office of Deputy Speaker is entitled to an increased salary and allowances, the payment of which is charged on the Consolidated Fund.[3]

Members of Parliament

The present membership is 114, of whom all but twelve belong to the Government party, the C.P.P. The remainder belong to the United Party. All except ten of the Members are men representing the one hundred and four electoral districts established by the Electoral Provisions Ordinance, 1953 (No. 33).[4] The remainder are women elected by a special procedure in 1960.[5] There is no law reserving the electoral districts to men but in fact women have not been successful in being chosen as candidates —hence the special procedure, which ensured at least some feminine representation.

To be qualified for election as a Member, a person must be a citizen of Ghana who has attained the age of twenty-five and who can speak and read the English language sufficiently well to enable him to take an active part in the proceedings of the Assembly.[6] The President, the Speaker and all Civil Servants and other public officers are disqualified from membership, as also are persons who are of unsound mind or who have incurred certain

---

[1] National Assembly Act, 1961 (Act 86), s. 11; Standing Order 3.

[2] Standing Orders 1, 7 (4).

[3] The present salary is £G1,500; allowances total £G1,318.

[4] The electoral districts are set out in the Schedule to the Ordinance, as amended by L.I. 19.

[5] See p. 152, *ante.* For the principle of universal adult suffrage laid down by the Constitution see p. 119, *ante.*

[6] National Assembly Act, 1961 (Act 86), s. 1 (1).   Blindness or other physical cause preventing reading does not disqualify.

criminal disabilities.[1] After his election a Member must, before taking part in the proceedings of the Assembly, take the oath of allegiance and the oath of a Member of Parliament.[2] A Member retains his seat until the Assembly is dissolved and a general election is held, unless the seat for some reason becomes vacant earlier. There are a number of ways in which this can happen. The Member may resign or die, or become subject to one of the factors mentioned above which disqualify a person for election. Or the Member may lose his seat by being expelled for grossly improper conduct or by declaring in the Assembly his intention of boycotting its proceedings or by being absent without leave for twenty consecutive sittings.[3] A Member is entitled to a salary and allowances, and, whenever he completes a period of five years' service, to a gratuity.[4] The first gratuity amounts to one-fifth of his salary and basic allowance during the five-year period. For subsequent gratuities the proportion is reduced to one-tenth. In the case of Ministers, and also the Speaker and Deputy Speaker, the proportion is one-sixth for each gratuity.

Staff of the Assembly

Apart from the Speaker and Deputy Speaker, the Assembly's most important officer is the Clerk of the National Assembly, whose office is created by statute[5] and who is in charge of the staffing and administration of Parliament House as well as having the heavy burden of dealing with matters of procedure.[6] The department of the Clerk forms part of the Civil Service. To assist the Clerk there are a Deputy Clerk and two assistant Clerks. While on duty at the Table the Clerk wears a plain black gown except on ceremonial occasions, when he wears a black gown decorated with *edinkra* symbols in gold.

An officer closely connected with the Speaker is the Marshal,

---

[1] National Assembly Act, 1961 (Act 86) s. 1 (2).

[2] *Ibid.*, s. 4; Standing Orders 4 and 5. The form of oath is set out in the First Schedule to the Oaths Act, 1960 (C.A. 12). Affirmation is permitted: *ibid.*, s. 8.

[3] National Assembly Act, 1961 (Act 86), s. 2.

[4] *Ibid.*, ss. 5–8. At present the salary for members who do not hold ministerial office is £G1,200; allowances total £G600. Members also receive certain free travel, postal and telephone facilities.

[5] National Assembly Act, 1961 (Act 86), s. 13.

[6] The Clerk also has duties in connection with Ghana's membership of the Inter-Parliamentary Union and the Commonwealth Parliamentary Association.

formerly known by the title of his British equivalent, the Serjeant at Arms. The Marshal is appointed by the Speaker and has the duty of bearing the Mace before the Speaker when he enters and leaves the Chamber, and of attending upon the Speaker during the proceedings of the Assembly. If serious disorder arises it is the Marshal's duty to carry out the Speaker's directions for dealing with it. There is an Assistant Marshal, also appointed by the Speaker.[1]

A staff of fifteen is employed to take a complete verbatim record of all the proceedings of the Assembly and to prepare this for publication in the Official Report, or *Hansard*, as it is familiarly known. Other staff include eight ushers for attending on members and other employees. About a dozen policemen under a superintendent are on duty at Parliament House when the Assembly is sitting. All the staff, including the police on duty, are under the orders of the Speaker and come within the definition of officers of the Assembly.[2]

Strangers

All persons other than the President, the Speaker, the Members and officers are strangers to the Assembly and can only enter the precincts by authority of the Speaker (which may be exercised through the Clerk). Admission tickets bearing the signature of the Clerk are normally issued without question to strangers wishing to enter the public galleries. The House can of course order strangers to withdraw whenever it pleases, and the Speaker has a similar discretion. Strangers are forbidden, without express permission from the Speaker, to take briefcases or cameras into the Chamber, or to draw or write in the Chamber. While the Assembly is sitting no Member may take a stranger into those parts of Parliament House which are reserved for Members.[3]

PARLIAMENTS, SESSIONS, MEETINGS AND SITTINGS

Parliamentary time is divided up into Parliaments, sessions, meetings and sittings. A Parliament extends approximately from one general election to the next—normally about five years. A session usually lasts just under a year and consists of four meetings. A sitting almost invariably begins and ends on the same day, although

---

[1] Standing Order 20.
[2] National Assembly Act, 1961 (Act 86), s. 46.
[3] Standing Order 99.

the Assembly is said to be "sitting" or "in session" from the beginning to the end of a meeting. Between meetings the Assembly stands adjourned. Between one session and the next the Assembly is in recess. The Parliamentary quinquennium is illustrated by the diagram on p. 306, which shows the normal position although, since the only things fixed by law are the maximum life of a Parliament and the fact that there must be a new session in every year, the details may vary from time to time.

Parliaments

A Parliament begins when the President by proclamation first summons the Assembly to meet after a general election and performs the ceremony of opening Parliament.[1] It ends when the President by proclamation dissolves the Assembly.[2] The Assembly must be dissolved not more than five years after its first sitting following the previous general election.[3] Within two months after dissolution a general election must be held.[4]

Sessions

A session begins when the President by proclamation summons the Assembly to meet and performs the ceremony of opening Parliament. It ends when the President by proclamation prorogues the Assembly or dissolves the Assembly without having first prorogued it.[5] Article 22(1) of the Constitution requires there to be a new session once at least in every calendar year, and that twelve months shall not elapse between the end of one session and the beginning of the next. The effect of prorogation, or of course dissolution, is to terminate all pending proceedings in Parliament. Unfinished business, such as Bills in progress or the proceedings of select committees, is automatically quashed, and must be begun all over again (if desired) in the next session. The system of sessions thus gives the Assembly a fresh start every year and avoids the perpetuation of stale business. Normally a session runs from early in July to late in the following June.

---

[1] As to the beginning of the first Parliament of the Republic, see p. 154, *ante*.

[2] Constitution, art. 23 (1).

[3] *Ibid.*, art. 23 (2). For the power to recall a dissolved Assembly during an emergency see p. 154, *ante*.

[4] National Assembly Act, 1961 (Act 86), s. 3 (1).

[5] *Ibid.*, s. 46.

U

THE PARLIAMENTARY QUINQUENNIUM

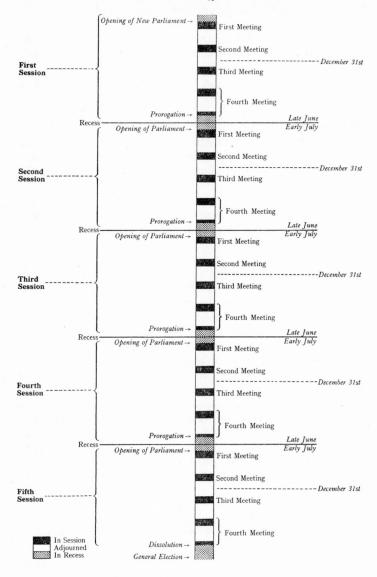

First Session

Recess

Second Session

Recess

Third Session

Recess

Fourth Session

Recess

Fifth Session

Opening of New Parliament →   First Meeting

Second Meeting

------------------------------------ *December 31st*

Third Meeting

} Fourth Meeting

Prorogation →   *Late June*

Opening of Parliament →   *Early July*

First Meeting

Second Meeting

-------------------------------- *December 31st*

Third Meeting

} Fourth Meeting

Prorogation →   *Late June*

Opening of Parliament →   *Early July*

First Meeting

Second Meeting

-------------------------------- *December 31st*

Third Meeting

} Fourth Meeting

Prorogation →   *Late June*

Opening of Parliament →   *Early July*

First Meeting

Second Meeting

-------------------------------- *December 31st*

Third Meeting

} Fourth Meeting

Prorogation →   *Late June*

Opening of Parliament →   *Early July*

First Meeting

Second Meeting

-------------------------------- *December 31st*

Third Meeting

} Fourth Meeting

In Session
Adjourned
In Recess

Dissolution →
General Election →

Meetings

A meeting begins when the Assembly meets at the beginning of a session or after a break during which it has stood adjourned *sine die*, that is without having fixed a date for its next sitting. In the latter case the Speaker fixes the date for the beginning of the new meeting, after consulting the Government.[1] Normally there are four meetings in a year, each lasting from four to six weeks. The last meeting of the session falls into two parts, the members being recalled a week before the end of the session to receive and debate the President's sessional report.

Sittings

A sitting is a period during which the Assembly sits continuously without adjournment. Unless the Assembly for some special reason decides otherwise, sittings begin at 4 p.m. and go on until shortly after 8 p.m. During a meeting the House sits on all days of the week except Saturdays and Sundays, although it sometimes takes a break when business is insufficient to keep it occupied.[2] Unless it otherwise orders, the Assembly automatically adjourns at the conclusion of business until 4 p.m. on the next sitting day.[3]

ARRANGEMENT OF BUSINESS

To secure the smooth and orderly despatch of the Assembly's business, various rules of practice and procedure have been adopted by analogy with those worked out over the course of centuries by the House of Commons. Much of the remainder of this discussion of the way in which the Assembly is organized for law-making will consist of a description of these rules, which also apply of course to the Assembly's other functions of debating matters of national and international importance, criticizing the activities of Government and authorising expenditure. Before considering how business is conducted, we must examine the way in which items of business are chosen and arranged.

The Business Committee

Standing Order 96 requires a select committee of members, known as the Business Committee, to be set up at the beginning

---

[1] Standing Order 8 (2). In cases of urgency the President may fix the date (Standing Order 12 (3)).

[2] A new system has now been introduced of continuous sittings for the first month of every quarter, and it is hoped to avoid such breaks in future.

[3] Standing Order 9.

of the session with the function of determining the business of each day and the order in which it shall be taken. The committee consists of the Leader of the House as chairman, two other Ministers, the Parliamentary Secretary, a Deputy Minister and three back-bench Members. It enjoys the unique privilege of deciding matters for itself, and does not, like other select committees, merely make recommendations to the Assembly. Nevertheless the determinations of the Business Committee are subject to certain limitations. They must give way to the Speaker's ruling as to what matters may properly be introduced into the Assembly. They must conform to Standing Order 22(1), which gives Government business precedence over private Members' business on all days except Fridays. They must whenever possible conform to the order of items laid down by Standing Order 21, which is described below. On each Friday the chairman of the Business Committee is required to make a statement in the House of the business arranged for the succeeding week.[1]

Order of Business

The normal order of business, as laid down by Standing Order 21, is as follows. The line marks the commencement of public business, and divides formal matters from those on which debate may arise.

Taking of oaths by new Members.
Presidential addresses and messages.
Speaker's announcements.
Election of Deputy Speaker.
Presentation of papers and petitions.
Questions to Ministers.
Statements by Ministers.
Complaints of contempt of Parliament.
Personal statements.
Presentation of Government Bills.

Motions for the introduction of Bills.
Motions on definite matters of urgent public importance.
Bills and substantive motions.
Half Hour motions.

It will be obvious that not all of these items occur on any one day;

---

[1] Standing Order 23.

indeed some of them occur only very rarely. Most of the important items are discussed in detail elsewhere in this book: we will say a word about the remainder here.

Papers.—Statutory instruments, annual reports of statutory bodies, and other documents of a similar nature are sometimes required by law to be laid before the Assembly. In addition to these, other papers may be presented to the Assembly by the Speaker, a Minister or the chairman of a select committee. Normally copies must be distributed to Members, and the person presenting a paper is entitled to make a short explanatory statement.[1]

Petitions.—Anyone who can persuade a Member to act for him is entitled to present a petition to the Assembly praying for the redress of grievances or otherwise. The petition must be in a certain form and must not offend against the privileges of the Assembly. The Member presenting the petition is entitled to move that it be read, printed or referred to a select committee, and may make a short speech in doing so. Further debate is not allowed.[2]

Questions.—As in the House of Commons, question time is an important and lively feature of the Parliamentary day. Any Member may question a Minister about public affairs with which the Minister is officially connected, or proceedings pending in the Assembly, or any matter of administration for which the Minister is responsible. Questions relating to matters under the control of a statutory body must be restricted to those matters for which a Minister is made responsible by law or which affect the general policy of the body. Questions on the day-to-day administration of a statutory body may only be asked if the Speaker considers them to be of sufficient public importance.[3] Five days' notice of intention to ask a question must be given, and if he requires an oral answer the Member must indicate this by marking his question with an asterisk. Not more than four questions requiring oral answer may be asked by a Member at any one sitting, and numerous restrictions are imposed on the form and content of questions in order to prevent abuse of this valuable facility.[4]

---

[1] Standing Order 27. As to the laying of statutory instruments, see p. 388, *post.*
[2] Standing Order 27.
[3] Standing Order 28.
[4] Standing Orders 29–31.

Immediate debate on the answer given to a question is not allowed, although supplementary questions are permissible.[1] A Member who is dissatisfied with the answer to a question may give notice that he intends to raise the matter on a Half Hour motion.[2]

Urgent motions.—At the time appointed under Standing Order 21 any Member may move that leave be given to make a motion on a definite matter of urgent public importance. The Member must have informed the Speaker of his intention to move before the commencement of the sitting, and the Member can move only if the Speaker is satisfied that the matter is urgent, of publc importance, and in order. If the Member is allowed to move, and the House grants leave, the main debate on the matter in question stands over until the remaining business for that day has been disposed of.[3]

Half Hour motions.—Private Members are entitled to ballot for the privilege of moving a motion, on any subject they choose for which the Government are responsible, during the last half hour of the sitting. At the conclusion of the debate the question is put without a division and the House then rises for the day.[4] Until the changes in 1960, the debate arose on the motion for the adjournment of the Assembly, following House of Commons practice. Now a substantive motion, beginning with such words as " That this House notes . . .", is debated, it having been felt to be somewhat artificial to debate substantive matters on procedural motions.[5]

Order Paper, Minutes, etc.

One of the duties of the Clerk of the Assembly is to supervise the preparation of Agendas, Order Papers and Minutes. At least two weeks before the commencement of a meeting, the Clerk is required to send to each member the Agenda for the meeting, which lists the items of business received but does not show when they will be taken. Whenever necessary a supplementary Agenda is to be circulated.[6] Before each sitting commences the

---

[1] Standing Order 32.
[2] This notice may be given orally: Standing Order 36 (6).
[3] Standing Order 10.
[4] Standing Order 9.
[5] For the same reason a corresponding change was made in relation to urgent motions.
[6] Standing Order 13.

Clerk must circulate the Order Paper, which sets out the order of business to be taken at the sitting, as arranged by the Business Committee. At the same time a provisional Order Paper, showing the business which has been arranged for the following sitting, is sent out.[1] On the day following a sitting the Minutes for that sitting are circulated. These show the names of the Members who attend and specify the decisions taken at the sitting.[2] The Clerk also keeps the Order Book, in which he enters all matters intended for discussion in the Assembly.[3] All records and other documents of the Assembly are in the custody of the Clerk, and are open to inspection by Members.[4]

PROCEEDINGS IN THE ASSEMBLY

Standing Orders

Proceedings in the Assembly are regulated in detail by Standing Orders made under s. 14 of the National Assembly Act. This section empowers the Assembly to make Standing Orders " for the regulation and orderly conduct of proceedings and the despatch of business ". Any Standing Order may be suspended with the consent of the Speaker and the majority of Members present.[5] In cases of doubt Standing Orders are to be interpreted by the Speaker as he thinks fit, and where any matter is not provided for by Standing Orders the Speaker has power to determine it.[6]

Standing Order 97 requires a sessional select committee known as the Standing Orders Committee to be constituted under the chairmanship of the Speaker with the function of reporting to the Assembly on any proposal for the amendment of Standing Orders which may be referred to it. By Standing Order 41, when a motion for the amendment of Standing Orders has been proposed and seconded in the House it stands referred to the Standing Orders Committee and further proceedings on it in the House are suspended until the Committee has reported.

Commencement of Sitting

At the time appointed for the commencement of a sitting,

---

[1] Standing Order 14.
[2] Standing Order 17. Copies of the Official Report are also circulated under Standing Order 18.
[3] Standing Order 15.
[4] Standing Order 16.
[5] Standing Order 100.
[6] Standing Orders 101 and 102.

normally 4 p.m., the Speaker's procession enters the Chamber. This consists of the Assistant Marshal, then the Marshal bearing the Mace, and finally the Speaker himself. After the Speaker has taken his seat and the Mace has been placed in its standing position before the Table, prayers are read by the Clerk. The prayers, which were specially composed for the Republican Parliament, run as follows:

" Almighty God, we humbly beseech Thee to look with favour upon this Parliament of the Republic of Ghana. Grant that it may perform its high duty as in Thy sight. Give Divine guidance to the President of the Republic; endow Members of Parliament with discernment and vision, integrity and courage, and that through the labours of government this land and people may be well and truly served, and Thy good purposes for the common human life be realised in our midst.   Amen."

" O God, grant us a vision of our country, fair as it might be: a country of righteousness, where none shall wrong his neighbour; a country of plenty, where evil and poverty shall be done away; a country of brotherhood, where all success shall be founded on service, and honour shall be given to the deserving; a country of peace, where government shall rest on the will of the people and the love for the common good. Bless the efforts of those who struggle to make this vision a living reality. Inspire and strengthen our people that they may give time, thought and sacrifice to speed the day of the coming beauty of Ghana and the total liberation of Africa.   Amen."

The Speaker (or his Deputy) remain in the Chair throughout the proceedings of the Assembly, the practice of having a Committee of the whole House presided over by the Deputy Chairman for certain types of proceedings having been abandoned in 1960. As the Leader of the House, Mr. Kojo Botsio, pointed out in announcing this change, the practice of the House resolving itself into Committee was a device of the House of Commons originally used to get rid of the Speaker who in the seventeenth century was regarded as a King's man and therefore mistrusted.[1]

Quorum

The Assembly cannot proceed to business unless the Speaker is satisfied that a quorum is present, and no business except that of adjournment may be transacted at any time if objection is taken by a Member that a quorum is not present. The quorum is twenty-five.[2] The Assembly follows the House of Commons

---

[1] *Parl. Deb. Official Report*, Vol. 19, col. 229.
[2] National Assembly Act, 1961 (No. 86), s. 16.

practice whereby, if objection is taken to the insufficiency of members, the Speaker orders a " count ". If after ten minutes sufficient members have not entered the Chamber to form a quorum the Speaker must adjourn.[1] Where objection is not made to the lack of a quorum the proceedings, once having started, must continue. This arrangement, though perhaps illogical, is convenient since it allows Members to be elsewhere in the Assembly precincts without incurring the risk of an undesired adjournment.

Motions

Proceedings in the public business are conducted by means of motions, and after the commencement of public business there must always be some motion before the House or the proceedings will be out of order. Except in certain cases, mostly of a formal character, 24 hours' notice must be given of Government motions and 48 hours' notice of motions by private Members.[2] All notices are submitted to the Speaker, who may direct the wording to be amended before the motion is printed in the Order Paper. Where the Speaker considers that a motion is so out of order that it cannot be cured by amendment he may direct it to be returned to the member who submitted it.[3] A motion may fall into this category where a private Member seeks to encroach upon the financial initiative of the Government,[4] or where the motion infringes Standing Order 74. This requires the President's consent to be signified to any Bill or motion by a private Member which seeks to alter the conditions of service of public officers. It also prohibits the Assembly from proceeding on any Bill or motion which, in the opinion of the Speaker, relates to or affects any matter the responsibility for which is vested in the Attorney-General by art. 47 of the Constitution.

A motion moved by a private Member must normally be seconded by another Member before it can be debated . Government motions need not be seconded.[5] When a motion has been moved, and if necessary seconded, the Speaker throws it open for debate by *proposing the question*. Special rules are laid down by Standing Orders for the form of proposing the question in the

---

[1] Standing Order 11.
[2] Standing Orders 35, 37.
[3] Standing Order 36.
[4] See p. 38, *ante*.
[5] Standing Order 38.

complicated cases that may arise when amendments are moved
to a motion or even, it may be, where a Member seeks to amend
an amendment.[1] A Member who has proposed a motion may
withdraw it, but if the motion has been seconded he may do so
only by leave of the majority of members present.[2]

Rules of Order and Debate

Standing Orders put the Speaker firmly in charge of proceedings
in the Assembly and make him responsible for the observance of
order and of the rules of debate. His decision on any point of
order is not open to appeal and cannot be reviewed by the Assembly except on a substantive motion made after due notice.[3]
When the Speaker rises to address the House any Member then
standing must immediately resume his seat, and silence must be
observed.[4]

All proceedings are conducted in English.[5] In debate, members
must address the Speaker and not each other.[6] Nor must one
Member refer to another by name, but by such words as " The
honourable Minister for Finance ", " the honourable Member for
Accra Central " or " the honourable Lady who has just spoken ".[7]
These latter rules help to avoid personal abuse and invective, and
to keep down the temperature of debates. A Member shows that
he wishes to speak by rising in his place; he should not begin his
speech until the Speaker calls on him by name.[8] The speech must
be relevant to the question before the House and must not contain offensive, blasphemous or unbecoming words, or impute
improper motives to other Members, or make personal allusions.
Prejudicial references must not be made to any matter on which
a judicial decision is pending. Except on a substantive motion
for that purpose, no matter already decided in the current session
may be reopened and no criticism of the conduct of the Speaker,
other Members or any judge may be made.[9] Consideration of a
Bill which has been introduced may not be anticipated by debate

---

[1] Standing Order 40.
[2] Standing Order 39.
[3] Standing Order 50.
[4] Standing Order 49.
[5] Standing Order 6.
[6] Standing Order 42 (1).
[7] Standing Order 42 (3)–(5). The style *honourable* is used only in the
Assembly except in the case of the Speaker and Ministers, of whom it is
used generally.
[8] Standing Order 42 (1), (2).
[9] Standing Orders 44, 45.

on the subject with which the Bill is concerned.[1] A Member may not read his speech, although he is permitted to refresh his memory by reference to notes.[2] Except on the Consideration stage of Bills, a Member is not normally entitled to make more than one speech on the same question.[3]

With two exceptions, a Member who is in the course of a speech must not be interrupted by other Members.[4] The first exception arises when, as frequently happens, the Member speaking makes some remark which one of his hearers does not understand or which he pretends not to understand. An interruption for the purpose of elucidation is then permitted if two conditions are satisfied. The first is that the Member making the speech chooses to give way and resumes his seat, and the second is that the Speaker calls upon the Member wishing to interrupt, who will have risen to his feet to indicate his intention. The other exceptional case is where the Member who is speaking has, in the opinion of another Member, transgressed the rules of order. If the other Member rises to his feet and says " Mr. Speaker, on a point of order . . .", the Member who is speaking must give way and resume his seat while the point of order is put and dealt with by the Speaker. Since an interruption on a point of order compels the person who is speaking to give way it is tempting to make such interruptions where in fact no point of order exists, and this is often done. Although considerable latitude is allowed, such tactics, if carried too far, constitute an abuse of procedure and in the long run are unfair to other Members. Although interruptions are strictly out of order except in these two cases, it must not be supposed that they do not occur. Debates are usually punctuated by cheers, counter-cheers and exclamations from Members. Provided these do not seriously interfere with the ability of a Member to continue his speech, the Speaker does not normally intervene. Indeed, such manifestations of feeling are part of the atmosphere of debate.

The Speaker, and indeed the Assembly itself, possesses wide powers to deal with disturbance and disorder. In the case of general disturbance the only remedy, if the Speaker's requests for order are not heeded, is to adjourn the proceedings. The

---

[1] Standing Order 47.
[2] Standing Order 42 (10).
[3] Standing Order 42 (6), (7).
[4] Standing Order 43. A third exception, which does not arise in practice, is on a claim to apply the closure; see p. 317, *post*.

Speaker has power to adjourn without question put if he thinks it necessary to do so.[1] In the case of disorder by an individual Member a number of courses are open, depending on the degree of gravity of the offence. These may be summarized as follows:

1. A Member who deviates from Standing Orders may be immediately called to order by the Speaker, or by another Member rising to a point of order.[2]

2. If a Member persists in irrelevance, or tedious repetition either of his own arguments or of those previously advanced during the debate, the Speaker, having called the attention of the House to his conduct, may direct him to discontinue his speech.[3]

3. If a Member uses objectionable words, and on being called to order fails to retract or explain the words and offer an apology to the Speaker's satisfaction, any other Member may, with the consent of the Speaker, move that he be no longer heard. The question on the motion is put forthwith, without amendment or debate.[4]

4. If the conduct of a Member is grossly disorderly the Speaker may order him to withdraw immediately from the Assembly for the remainder of the sitting. He must thereupon leave the precincts—if necessary being ejected by the Marshal.[5]

5. Where the case is more serious still the Speaker may " name " the Member. The senior Minister present must then move an immediate motion to the effect that the Member is guilty of contempt of Parliament. If the motion, which cannot be debated or amended, is carried the Member is immediately suspended and must leave the precincts.[6] He may also be subjected to any of the other penalties laid down for contempt of Parliament.[7]

Apart from these five ways of dealing with a disorderly Member, the Assembly has an inherent power to control its own proceedings

---

[1] Standing Order 51 (11).
[2] Standing Order 51 (1).
[3] Standing Order 51 (2).
[4] Standing Order 46.
[5] Standing Order 51 (3), (10); National Assembly Act, 1961 (Act 86), s. 36.
[6] Standing Order 51 (3)–(6). For the period of suspension see p. 330, *post*.
[7] See pp. 330 *et seq.*, *post*.

within the limitations imposed by law. It can thus, if it chooses, proceed against a Member who offends against Standing Orders, or in some other way, in whatever manner it thinks fit.[1]

Termination of Debate

To guard against filibustering, Standing Orders enable a debate to be brought to an end before all the Members who wish to take part have delivered their speeches. This procedure, known as the closure, is brought into effect when a Member (who would normally be the Parliamentary Secretary) interrupts the proceedings by claiming to move that " the question be now put ". The Speaker must allow the motion unless he thinks it is " an abuse of the rules of the Assembly or an infringement of the rights of the minority ". Where the motion is allowed no debate or amendment is permissible, and the Assembly must decide forthwith whether to apply the closure. If the matter is pressed to a division, the closure is not applied unless at least fifty members have voted for it.[2]

When all the Members who wish to address the House on the question before it have finished their speeches, or when the closure has been applied, the Speaker *puts the question*. He does this by saying: " The question is that . . . As many as are in favour say *aye* [a pause for the voices of the Ayes], as many as are not say *no*. The Speaker assesses the relative strengths of the voices and then, if it seems that the motion is carried, says " I think the Ayes have it; the Ayes have it ". If the motion appears lost the Speaker says " I think the Noes have it; the Noes have it ". Except in certain special cases, questions in the Assembly are decided by simple majority.[3] The Speaker himself has no vote, but if the Deputy Speaker or any other Member is in the Chair he is entitled to an original vote but not a casting vote.[4] Where votes are equal the motion is lost.[5]

If any Member desires to do so, he may challenge the Speaker's declaration that the Ayes (or Noes) have it, and claim a division. The following events then ensue, unless the Speaker considers the claim for a division to be merely frivolous.[6]

---

[1] Standing Order 51 (8).
[2] Standing Order 48. As yet the procedure has not been used.
[3] National Assembly Act, 1961 (No. 86), s. 17. Larger majorities are required for the removal from office of judges, etc.; see p. 174, *ante*.
[4] National Assembly Act, 1961 (Act 86), s. 16 (2).
[5] Standing Order 54 (9).
[6] Standing Orders 53, 54.

1. The Speaker calls out " Clear the lobbies! " and the ushers make sure that no one is within either of the division lobbies.

2. The division bells ring for one minute to warn Members who are within the precincts to come into the Chamber.

3. The Speaker puts the question and declares the result in the same manner as before. Only if he is again challenged does he order a division to be held, thus giving an opportunity for the division to be called off if Members have had second thoughts about it.[1]

4. Where he orders a division to be held the Speaker at the same time names two Members from among the Ayes and two from among the Noes to act as tellers. The tellers are allowed to vote.

5. Members who wish to vote for the motion file in through the entrance door of the Ayes lobby, while those opposing enter the Noes lobby. A Member is not obliged to vote, but if he does so must vote according to his voice.

6. As Members leave the lobbies their names are recorded by the division clerks and they are counted by the tellers. The entrance doors are locked five minutes after the division has been ordered.

7. The tellers come to the Table and give the voting figures to the Clerk. The Clerk writes down the figures and reports them to the Speaker, who then announces the result of the division.

Effect of irregularities in procedure

The rules of procedure are designed to enable the Assembly to carry out its business speedily and efficiently. Breaches of the rules are the concern of the Assembly alone, and cannot be relied on to support an argument by outside persons that its proceedings have been thereby invalidated. Nor does the fact that by-elections are pending, or even that a stranger has taken part in the proceedings, affect the validity of anything done by the Assembly.[2]

---

[1] If the Speaker considers that a division is unnecessary he may, instead of putting the question again, call upon Members to rise to their feet and be counted: Standing Order 54 (6).

[2] National Assembly Act, 1961 (Act 86), s. 19.

Select Committees

Almost all important Parliamentary business is carried on at sittings of the full Assembly. Provision is made however for particular matters to be referred to small committees of Members, known as select committees. There are no standing committees, such as exist at Westminster for examining the details of Bills. Select committees are of two types, sessional and *ad hoc*.

Sessional select committees

Standing Orders require the Speaker, at the beginning of each session of Parliament, to nominate the members of the five permanent committees known as sessional select committees. These are the Committee of Privileges, the House Committee, the Public Accounts Committee, the Business Committee and the Standing Orders Committee. Two of these have already been discussed.[1] A third, the House Committee, which is meant to advise the Speaker on " all matters connected with the comfort and convenience of Members "[2] in fact never meets. In an Assembly as intimate as that of Ghana, Members are able to express their views on the amenities provided for them in less formal ways than through a select committee.

Committee of Privileges.—This consists of the Leader of the House as chairman, one other Minister, the Parliamentary Secretary and seven back-benchers. Its duty is to enquire into any complaint of contempt of Parliament or any matter of privilege which may be referred to it.[3] Only one such reference has been made.[4]

Public Accounts Committee.—This and the Business Committee are the most active of sessional select committees. The Committee meets frequently and issues two reports a year. It consists entirely of back-benchers and elects its own chairman, normally a member of the minority party. The duty of the Committee is to examine the accounts which show how money granted by the Assembly to meet national expenditure has been spent, and also to examine any accounts of a statutory corporation which have

---

[1] The Business Committee (p. 307, *ante*) and the Standing Orders Committee (p. 311, *ante*).
[2] Standing Order 94.
[3] Standing Order 93.
[4] *The Adama Case* in 1958, which is described at p. 327, *post*.

been laid before the Assembly.[1] The Auditor-General or one of his senior staff is always in attendance at meetings of the Committee. Where accounts reveal matters which require looking into, the Committee, which has power to send for persons, papers and records and to examine witnesses on oath, carries out the necessary investigation either itself or by appointing a sub-committee.[2] The reports of the Committee, which are presented to the Assembly and published, are brief and to the point. As an example of the subjects dealt with, we may take the first report for 1960–61. This described investigations, and contained recommendations, relating to the purchase of stationery by the Cocoa Marketing Board, an alleged over-payment of compensation for the Achiasi-Kotoku railway, maintenance allowances to the staff of the Ghana Library Board, disposal of deteriorated foodstuffs by the Ghana Agricultural Development Corporation and the handling by the Corporation of a loan scheme for farmers, valuation of assets of the Cocoa Marketing Board, methods of increasing railway passenger traffic, excessive railway overtime working, and the method of purchase of locomotives and rolling stock.[3]

Ad hoc select committees

If the Assembly considers it necessary to do so, it may at any time set up an *ad hoc* select committee to examine and report on whatever matter is entrusted to it by the Assembly. The committee is appointed on a motion made after notice. It consists of such number of Members as the Assembly may determine, and has power to elect its own chairman.[4] *Ad hoc* select committees are very rare. One which has already been mentioned is the committee set up in 1955 to examine the question of a federal system of Government and a second chamber.[5]

Procedure of select committees

Standing Orders lay down rules of procedure which apply to all select committees, whether sessional or *ad hoc*. The members of the committee must be drawn from the various parties in accordance with their relative strengths in the House, and no person

---

[1] Standing Order 95.
[2] Standing Orders 83 and 84.
[3] *First Report from the Public Accounts Committee of the National Assembly for the year 1960–61*, Accra, 1961.
[4] Standing Order 77.
[5] See p. 52, *ante*.

other than a member of the committee or an officer having duties in connection with the committee may attend its meetings unless the committee has decided to sit in public. With the exception of the House Committee and the Standing Orders Committee, every select committee has power to send for persons, papers and records, and to examine witnesses on oath. The Speaker may issue a warrant for the arrest of a witness who fails to attend.[1] The draft report of the committee is considered formally paragraph by paragraph; amendments may be moved and the committee may divide. The report is presented to the Assembly by the chairman of the committee and the Assembly may accept or reject it as it thinks fit.[2]

Parliamentary Privilege

To enable it to function effectively the National Assembly enjoys certain privileges conferred upon it by the Constitution and the National Assembly Act. Such privileges are common to most legislative bodies, and in relation to the two Houses of the British Parliament are explained by Erskine May as follows:

> The privileges of Parliament are rights which are absolutely necessary for the due execution of its powers. They are enjoyed by individual Members, because the House cannot perform its functions without unimpeded use of the services of its Members; and by each House for the protection of its Members and the vindication of its own authority and dignity. . . . The Commons, in their reasons offered at a conference with the Lords in the controversy arising from the case of *Shirley* v. *Fagg*, in asserting that privilege of Parliament belongs to every Member of the House of Commons, declared " that the reason of that Privilege is, that the Members of the House of Commons may freely attend the public affairs of that House, without disturbance or interruption ". The earliest occasion on which this reason was given was in the Commons Petition to Henry IV in 1404.[3]

In Ghana certain privileges are conferred on the Assembly generally; others on individual Members or officers. All are

---

[1] Standing Order 52; National Assembly Act, 1961 (Act 86), s. 14 (2).
[2] The procedure of select committees is dealt with by Standing Orders 75–92.
[3] *The Law, Privileges, Proceedings and Usage of Parliament* (15th Edn.), pp. 40–42.
X

designed to ensure that Members come to and from the proceedings of the Assembly without hindrance, that those proceedings function in freedom from outside interference, and that the dignity and authority of the Assembly are preserved. Breach of privilege in most cases constitutes contempt of Parliament, and is punishable by the Assembly itself and also, when committed by strangers, by the courts administering the criminal law.

The principal statement of Parliamentary privilege is contained in the Constitution itself:

> " There shall be freedom of speech, debate and proceedings in the National Assembly and that freedom shall not be impeached or questioned in any court or place out of the Assembly."[1]

" Freedom of speech is a privilege essential to every free council or legislature."[2] " There could be no assured government by the people, or any part of the people, unless their representatives had unquestioned possession of this privilege."[3] These quotations show the importance that has been attached to this general principle of Parliamentary freedom. Since the principle is taken from the Bill of Rights (although it had been recognized long before) it may be assumed that it will be treated in Ghana as having much the same effect as in England. By analogy with the English position, as described by Erskine May, the following rules may be drawn from it. Some aspects of them, as will appear, have been separately stated in the National Assembly Act.

1. The principle extends not only to everything done in the full Assembly or a committee in the course of Parliamentary business, whether by Members or officers, or by strangers concerned in such business, e.g. as witnesses, but also things done outside the Assembly for the purposes of its business—as for example the action of a Member in sending to the Clerk written notice of a question to be asked in the Assembly. This does not mean that every act done even in the Chamber itself will be protected. For example, a slanderous conversation carried on between two Members while a debate was in progress, or an assault by a Member upon an usher, might well be held to fall outside the scope of proceedings in Parliament.

---

[1] Article 21 (3). The wording is adapted from the 9th Article of the Bill of Rights. It is repeated in Part IV of the National Assembly Act, 1961 (Act 86), which is thus made comprehensive.

[2] Erskine May, *op. cit.*, p. 46.

[3] White, *The English Constitution*, p. 440.

2. The principle gives the Assembly complete and exclusive control over the subjects chosen for debate, legislation and other business and over the procedure adopted for dealing with those subjects. The Assembly, in the words of Erskine May, " is not responsible to any external authority for following the rules it lays down for itself, but may depart from them at its own discretion ".[1]

3. In respect of an act to which the principle extends, no person may be questioned about the act in court or elsewhere, or be proceeded against for having done the act, whether by civil or criminal proceedings, or be intimidated, molested or treated in any discriminatory or prejudicial manner by reason of the doing of the act. In particular therefore, a Member may, again in the words of Erskine May, " state whatever he thinks fit in debate, however offensive it may be to the feelings, or injurious to the character, of individuals; and he is protected by his privilege from any action for libel, as well as from any other question or molestation ".[2] The most important aspects of this rule are made explicit by s. 21 of the National Assembly Act, which provides that, without prejudice to the general principle of freedom of debate, no civil or criminal proceedings shall be instituted against a Member in any court or place out of the Assembly by reason of anything said by him in the Assembly or any of its committees, or any matter or thing brought by him before the Assembly or a committee by petition, Bill, motion or otherwise.

4. The previous rule does not prevent the Assembly itself, in exercise of the power to control its own proceedings, from taking action against a Member or other person who abuses his privileges. Privileges are given not for the benefit of individuals but for the benefit of the Assembly as a whole. We have seen how misbehaviour in debate is dealt with by the Speaker, and when we come to consider contempt of Parliament and the punishment of offences it will appear that the Assembly possesses ample powers to punish abuse of privilege. Another way in which a Member may offend the Assembly itself is by entering into an engagement which is designed, or tends, to restrict his own freedom of speech. Every Member is under

---

[1] *Op. cit.*, p. 60.
[2] *Op. cit.*, p. 51.

a duty to the Assembly to safeguard Parliamentary freedom so far as lies within his power. He is clearly in breach of this duty if he fetters his own freedom. The House of Commons resolved in 1947 that:

> " It is inconsistent with the dignity of the House, with the duty of a Member to his constituents, and with the maintenance of the privilege of freedom of speech, for any Member of this House to enter into any contractual agreement with an outside body controlling or limiting the Member's complete independence and freedom of action in Parliament or stipulating that he shall act in any way as the representative of such outside body in regard to any matters to be transacted in Parliament; the duty of a Member being to his constituents and to the country as a whole, rather than to any particular section thereof."[1]

5. The Assembly has the right to exclude strangers from its proceedings whenever it thinks fit. This right, which enables the Assembly to prevent strangers from disturbing its proceedings or attempting to influence debate from the galleries, and to go into secret session when necessary, has already been discussed.[2]

Particular privileges

In addition to the general statement of Parliamentary privilege laid down by the Constitution and explained in the five rules suggested above, the National Assembly Act confers a number of particular privileges which will now be discussed.

It would hamper the Assembly in carrying on its proceedings, as well as prejudicing its dignity, if the courts were permitted to subject Members and officers to judicial process at times when their services were required by the Assembly. For this reason the National Assembly Act confers certain privileges by restricting the normal powers of the courts in relation to the service and execution of process and the summoning of persons as witnesses, jurymen or assessors.

Immunity from service of process and arrest.—No civil or criminal process can be served on, or executed in relation to, the Speaker or any Member while he is on his way to, attending at or returning from any proceedings of the Assembly.[3] Thus, for

---

[1] Erskine May, *op. cit.*, p. 50.
[2] See p. 304, *ante.*
[3] National Assembly Act, 1961 (Act 86), s. 22 (a).

example, a Member who is on his way to the Assembly cannot be served with a writ or arrested under a warrant issued by a court. In criminal matters however the Speaker has power to waive Parliamentary privilege where he thinks it proper to do so and to give consent to the service of a summons on a Member, or the execution of a warrant for his arrest, or otherwise.[1] In addition to these restrictions, the Act also prohibits altogether the service or execution of civil or criminal process within the precincts of the Assembly at a time when the House is sitting, or through the Speaker, Deputy Speaker or any officer.[2]

Immunity from witness summons.—While attending the Assembly the Speaker, Members and officers are immune from any requirement to attend as a witness elsewhere. The immunity ceases when the Assembly is not sitting.[3]

Immunity from jury service.—The Speaker, Members and officers are at all times exempt from service as jurymen or assessors.[4]

The particular privileges mentioned above are personal to Members and officers. We now turn to various privileges which may be claimed by strangers as well.

Immunity for acts authorised by Assembly.—No person can be under any civil or criminal liability in respect of an act or omission ordered or authorised, in accordance with law, by the Assembly or a committee, or by the Speaker, a Member or officer.[5] Where the act is authorised by an individual the immunity exists only if the act is in some way connected with the business of the Assembly. A certificate by the Speaker is conclusive evidence of the ordering or authorising of the act.

Immunity for publication of proceedings.—No person can be under any civil or criminal liability in respect of the publication of the text or a summary of any report, paper, minutes, votes or proceedings of the Assembly unless it is shown that the publication was effected maliciously or otherwise in want of good faith.[6] This rule is subject to the provisions relating to contempt of Parliament, which, as we shall see, make it an offence to publish

---

[1] National Assembly Act, 1961 (Act 86), proviso to s. 22.
[2] *Ibid.*, s. 22 (b), (c).
[3] *Ibid.*, s. 23.
[4] *Ibid.*, s. 24.
[5] *Ibid.*, s. 25.
[6] *Ibid.*, s. 26.

certain evidence or documents in defiance of an order of the Assembly. The immunity is primarily directed against outsiders, and not the Assembly itself. Erskine May remarks:

" . . . the publication, whether by order of the House or not, of a fair and faithful account of a debate . . . is protected by the same principle as that which protects fair reports of proceedings in courts of justice, namely, that the advantage to the public negatives the presumption of malice and outweighs any disadvantage to individuals."[1]

If the publication is by order of the House protection will be given by the preceding rule, and even proof of malice will not destroy the immunity.

Privilege of witnesses.—Witnesses before the Assembly or a select committee are entitled to the same privilege as witnesses before a court of law; and except in criminal proceedings for perjury an answer given by such a witness is not admissible in evidence against him in any other proceedings. Evidence on matters of state cannot be demanded by the Assembly from public officers except with the President's consent.[2]

Contempt of Parliament

The National Assembly Act contains a number of sections specifying the acts which constitute contempt of Parliament. It might be thought that contempt of Parliament would be simply the obverse of Parliamentary privilege, or in other words that those acts which infringed privilege, and only those acts, would constitute contempt. The position is not as simple as this, however. Indeed Erskine May treats breach of privilege and contempt as two different things.[3] In Ghana the matter is treated entirely under the heading of contempt, but this embraces a number of matters which are not included in the Part of the National Assembly Act dealing with privilege, as for example disobedience to the orders of the Assembly and defamation of Members. Similarly, not every act which went against a particular privilege would constitute contempt. Thus service of a writ on a Member in ignorance of the fact that he was on his way to Parliament House might well be held not to amount to contempt,

---

[1] *Op. cit.*, p. 54.
[2] National Assembly Act, 1961 (Act 86), s. 27.
[3] *Op. cit.*, p. 41.

although it would clearly infringe the member's immunity from service of process. In general, the scope of contempt is wider than that of privilege, though in both the constitutional law is concerned with the same object, namely to safeguard the efficiency and dignity of the Assembly.

General definition of contempt

Part V of the National Assembly Act begins by stating that any act or omission which impedes or tends to impede the Assembly in the exercise of its functions, or affronts the dignity of the Assembly, is a contempt of Parliament.[1] Although the Act goes on to specify particular types of contempt this is not to be taken to limit the generality of the opening definition, which applies to Members, officers and strangers alike. No case has yet arisen under this general definition, but mention may perhaps be made here of the only case of breach of privilege (or contempt of Parliament, as it is now called) upon which proceedings have ever been brought in the National Assembly. This was the *Adama Case*, which occurred in 1958, at a time when Parliamentary privilege was governed by an Ordinance which contained no general definition of breach of privilege.[2] Mr. Adama, who was then the Opposition Chief Whip, announced in debate that he had received a secret Cabinet paper which recorded a decision that the Northern Territories should be left undeveloped and educationally backward so as to preserve the supply of " hewers of wood and drawers of water ". When challenged he said that he had got the document in his pocket, but later denied this and said he would produce it on another occasion. Some three weeks later he did so, and read it out to the Assembly. The following day the Assembly resolved to refer the matter to the Committee of Privileges and ordered the Committee to report whether the document was genuine or false and whether Mr. Adama had committed a breach of privilege. In the Committee's report, which was accepted by the House, it was found that the document was a false and fabricated one, that Mr. Adama knew it to be so when he referred to it in debate, and that by using it in the House in the way he did he committed a breach of the privileges of the House. No punishment was inflicted since Mr. Adama craved the indulgence of the House and rendered an

---

[1] National Assembly Act, 1961 (Act 86), s. 28.
[2] Legislative Assembly (Powers and Privileges) Ordinance, 1956 (No. 20).

unqualified apology, which Members accepted without dissent. The interesting feature about this case is that no specific provision of the Powers and Privileges Ordinance was relied on—indeed, as Mr. Adama himself pointed out, it would have been difficult to find one that fitted the case. The Assembly never went beyond its undoubted power to refer what it thought fit to one of its own Committees and to debate the Committee's report. The stage of imposing punishment, at which difficulties might have been encountered, was never reached. If a similar case arose under the present law there would be no difficulty in bringing it within the general definition of contempt. To address arguments to the House based on a " Cabinet paper " which the speaker knew to be false and fabricated would clearly tend to impede the Assembly in the exercise of its functions and might well be held to affront its dignity. In addition, the production of a false document has been included among the particular contempts.[1]

Particular contempts

The particular contempts specified by the National Assembly Act are not easy to classify. Some relate only to acts done by Members, or by strangers; others may be committed by anyone. The seriousness of the contempt may range from the grave, such as an assault on the Speaker while in the Chair, to the trivial, such as the entry of a stranger into the precincts in technical disobedience of Standing Orders. No classification is ideal, but the Act divides particular contempts into five categories: interference with Members and officers, interference with proceedings, inducing false or incomplete evidence, disobedience to the orders of the Assembly, and defamation of the Assembly. Of these, the first four are concerned more with the earlier part of the general definition of contempt, namely impeding the exercise of the Assembly's functions, while the fifth is related to the later part of the definition and protects the dignity of Parliament.

Interference with Members and officers.—If *any person* assaults, obstructs, molests or insults the Speaker or a Member within the precincts of the Assembly, or while the Speaker or Member is on his way to or returning from the proceedings of the Assembly, he is guilty of contempt. The same rule applies in relation to the

---

[1] The record of the various proceedings in the *Adama Case* will be found in *Nat. Ass. Deb. Official Report* Vol. 11, cols. 1397–1403, 1420–24, 1969–72, 2042–78; Vol. 16, cols 1423–38.

officers of the Assembly except that no contempt arises unless the offender was aware, or had reasonable grounds for believing, that the person in question was an officer.[1] It is contempt for *any person* to endeavour, by means of bribery, fraud or the infliction or threatened infliction of violence, restraint or spiritual injury, to influence a Member in the exercise of his functions, or to inflict violence, restraint or spiritual or temporal injury on a Member by reason of anything he has done or failed to do in connection with Parliamentary business. If a *Member* accepts a bribe or other benefit, or procures a benefit for himself or anyone else, in return for an undertaking to vote in a particular way, or otherwise to carry out his Parliamentary functions in a certain manner, the Member is himself guilty of contempt.[2]

Interference with proceedings.—There are three offences under this heading. It is contempt for *any person* to create or join in a disturbance (whether within or outside the precincts) which interrupts or is likely to interrupt the proceedings of the Assembly. It is contempt for a *stranger* to sit or vote in the Assembly. It is contempt for a *Member* persistently to obstruct the proceedings of the Assembly, whether or not in contravention of Standing Orders.[3]

Inducing false or incomplete evidence.—The Assembly itself does not in practice hear evidence, but the need to do so sometimes arises with select committees, particularly the Public Accounts Committee. Accordingly the giving of false evidence, the production of a false document, the suborning of witnesses, and similar offences are specified as contempts when done by *any person*.[4]

Disobedience to the Assembly's orders.—It is contempt for *any person* to disobey without reasonable excuse an order made by the Assembly or a select committee to attend before it or produce a document or answer a question, or to publish evidence or documents in contravention of the Assembly's order prohibiting such publication.[5] It is contempt for a *Member* to disobey an order given in accordance with Standing Orders by the person

---

[1] National Assembly Act, 1961 (Act 86), s. 29 (1).
[2] *Ibid.*, s. 29 (2).
[3] *Ibid.*, s. 30.
[4] *Ibid.*, s. 31.
[5] *Ibid.*, s. 32.

presiding at a meeting of the Assembly or a committee.[1] It is
contempt for a *stranger* to enter or remain within the precincts
in contravention of an order of the Assembly or to behave within
the precincts otherwise than in accordance with Standing Orders
or an order given thereunder.[2]

Defamation of Assembly.—It is contempt for *any person* to make
a statement or otherwise publish any matter which falsely or
scandalously defames either the Assembly as a whole or the
Speaker or an individual Member or officer in his capacity as such,
or which contains a gross or scandalous misrepresentation of any
proceedings of the Assembly.[3]

PUNISHMENT OF OFFENCES

Members

The National Assembly Act specifies four different penalties for
offending Members, not all of which are limited to cases of contempt of Parliament. In ascending order of gravity the penalties
are: exclusion, reprimand, suspension and expulsion. Unlike
a stranger, a Member who is guilty of contempt is not liable to
criminal proceedings unless his act also consistutes a criminal
offence under the general law.

Exclusion.—A Member whose conduct is grossly disorderly
may be excluded from the precincts for the remainder of the day's
sitting.[4]

Reprimand.—Where a Member has been found guilty of contempt by the Assembly he may be directed by the Assembly to
be reprimanded in his place by the Speaker.[5]

Suspension.—The suspension of a Member " named " for disorder has already been mentioned.[6] Suspension is not limited to
disorderly conduct, but may be imposed by the Assembly in any
case of contempt. The period of suspension may be anything up
to nine months, but where a Member is " named " Standing
Orders lay down the period which is to apply unless the Assembly
otherwise orders. If the Member has not previously been

---

[1] National Assembly Act, 1961 (Act 86), s. 33.
[2] *Ibid.*, s. 34.
[3] *Ibid.*, s. 35.
[4] *Ibid.*, s. 36.
[5] *Ibid.*, s. 37.
[6] See p. 316, *ante*.

" named " during the session the period is five sitting days. If he has been " named " once before, the period is extended to ten sitting days. If he has been " named " more than once before, the period is twenty sitting days. For the period of his suspension a Member forfeits his salary and allowances as a Member and the period does not count towards entitlement to a gratuity.[1]

Expulsion.—A Member may be expelled if he has been found by the Assembly to have been guilty of conduct which, whether or not it amounts to contempt, is so grossly improper as to indicate that he is unfit to remain a Member. At least seven days' notice must be given of a motion for expulsion, and the votes of at least two-thirds of the total number of Members are required.[2]

Officers

Where an officer other than the Speaker or Deputy Speaker has been found by the Assembly to be guilty of contempt the action which may be taken by the Assembly itself is narrowly limited. Since the officer will normally be a civil servant the appropriate punishment will be by way of disciplinary proceedings under the Civil Service Act, 1960 (C.A. 5). Accordingly the National Assembly Act merely provides that the Assembly may order the finding of contempt to be reported to the Civil Service Commission. The Assembly may also suspend the officer from duty pending the conclusion of disciplinary proceedings. While suspended he must not enter the precincts.[3] No special provision is made for misconduct by the Speaker or Deputy Speaker. The only remedy the Assembly would have against an offending Speaker would be to dismiss him: the Deputy Speaker is subject to the same penalties as any other Member.

Strangers

As might be expected, the severest penalties are reserved for strangers. In ascending order, they are as follows: exclusion, reprimand, detention for one day, criminal prosecution. In addition, a stranger who is trespassing may, like a Member who has been suspended or excluded, or an officer who has been suspended, be removed from the precincts by the Marshal or any

---

[1] National Assembly Act, 1961 (Act 86), ss. 6 (4), 38; Standing Order 51 (5).
[2] National Assembly Act, 1961 (Act 86), s. 39.
[3] *Ibid.*, s. 40.

other officer, who is entitled to use such force as is reasonably necessary.

Exclusion.—When a stranger has been found by the Assembly to be guilty of contempt, the Assembly may order him not to enter the precincts for a period not exceeding nine months.[1] Although in many cases this would hardly amount to any punishment at all, there are some people, such as lobby correspondents of newspapers or news agencies, who might suffer from being denied access to Parliament House.

Reprimand.—A stranger found guilty of contempt may be ordered by the Assembly to appear at the bar of the House and be reprimanded by the Speaker.[2]

Arrest and detention.—Any officer may, without warrant or order, arrest a stranger whom he sees misbehaving in a way which amounts to contempt, or whom he reasonably suspects to have been guilty of such misbehaviour. The arrest must be reported to the Speaker, who may order the stranger to be detained for the remainder of the day's sitting or handed over to the police to await criminal prosecution.[3]

Criminal prosecution.—Whether or not any proceedings have been taken against him by the Assembly itself, a stranger who has committed a contempt of Parliament is liable to criminal prosecution. If found guilty by the court he may be sentenced to imprisonment for up to one year or fined up to £G100, or both.[4] Certain contempts, notably bribery and perjury, constitute offences under the Criminal Code and may be prosecuted accordingly, whether committed by strangers or by Members or officers.

2. THE CABINET

The Cabinet is the body which, as part of its constitutional function of exercising general direction and control over the government of the country, decides what legislative proposals are to be introduced into the National Assembly or carried into

---

[1] National Assembly Act, 1961 (Act 86), s. 41.
[2] *Ibid.*, s. 43.
[3] *Ibid.*, s. 42.
[4] *Ibid.*, s. 45.

effect by statutory instrument. As the opportunities available for the introduction of private Members' Bills are not used, the Cabinet in practice entirely controls the introduction of Bills. Since 1951, when the Assembly was first established, the present Government has enjoyed a substantial Parliamentary majority. This has meant that a Cabinet decision to introduce a Bill has, with a few exceptions, been equivalent to a decision to pass the Bill into law. Cabinet Ministers are also leading Members of the Assembly, and are responsible for explaining during the passage of a Bill the Cabinet's object in promoting it. There is thus a close link between the two bodies, and while Members of Parliament speak their minds freely on the Bills put before them, and have wide opportunities for reshaping and even rejecting Government Bills, it is true to say that in Ghana as in many other democracies it is the decisions of the Cabinet that provide the motive power for legislative action.

The way in which the Cabinet carries out its various and important functions in the legislative process will be explained in the course of the two following chapters. Here we will merely describe briefly its composition, legislative role and general organization. The provisions of the Constitution which provide for the existence of the Cabinet have already been described.[1] They are amplified by Part I of the Cabinet and Ministers Act, 1960 (C.A. 3). At the time of writing, one year after the inauguration of the Republic, the Cabinet consists of the President and fifteen Members, and normally meets twice a week on Tuesdays and Fridays. Meetings are called by the President or, in his absence, by a Cabinet Minister authorised by the President for that purpose.[2] The President is required to attend and preside at Cabinet meetings whenever practicable. When the President is not at the meeting a Cabinet Minister authorised by him to do so is required to take the chair.[3] At present the Cabinet meets in the President's headquarters at Flagstaff House, Accra; the Cabinet table and chairs are an exact replica of those used at 10, Downing Street—a gift from the British Government at the inauguration of the Republic. Cabinet meetings are not limited to Members of the Cabinet, and other persons holding office in the Government or the Convention Peoples Party are frequently

---

[1] See pp. 144 *et seq.*, *ante.*
[2] Cabinet and Ministers Act, 1960 (C.A. 3), s. 1. In practice Cabinet meetings are rarely if ever held in the absence of the President.
[3] *Ibid.*, s. 2.

invited to attend and voice their opinions.[1] This is expressly recognized by s. 3 of the Cabinet and Ministers Act, which states:

" . . . any proceedings of the Cabinet shall be valid notwithstanding that some person who was not entitled to do so sat or voted in the Cabinet or otherwise took part in the proceedings."

The section goes on to provide that the quorum is to be five although, as in the case of the National Assembly, this does not become operative unless attention is drawn to the lack of a quorum. Cabinet decisions are by simple majority, the President or other person presiding having a casting vote as well as his original vote.[2]

The Cabinet does not usually decide to embark on legislation unless a memorandum advocating this has been laid before it by a Minister after consultation with his advisers, with the Law Officers, and with interested bodies and persons outside. It sometimes happens however that a discussion will arise in Cabinet about some matter which has not previously been considered in the context of legislation. This may be one of the many non-legislative subjects on the agenda or may be something raised in the spontaneous discussions which frequently occur. These spot decisions, taken without advice and background information, are often difficult to implement. They happen frequently enough to justify the statement that the Cabinet has a twofold role as a legislative functionary. On the one hand it takes decisions about legislative proposals initiated elsewhere; on the other it initiates such proposals itself and commands their execution. As will be seen, the Cabinet not only decides on the principles of new legislation but also on the detailed drafts by which it is to be carried into effect and on the timing, amendment and, where necessary, withdrawal of Bills.

Cabinet Secretariat

The Cabinet and Ministers Act provides that the Secretary to the Cabinet, who is the administrative head of the civil service, is to have charge of the Cabinet office. He is required, in accordance

---

[1] In addition to the actual members of the Cabinet, the following are invariably notified of the agenda and invited to attend: the Regional Commissioners, the Minister Resident in Guinea, the Guinea and Mali Resident Ministers in Ghana, the Executive Director of the Development Secretariat, and the General Secretaries of the T.U.C. and Ghana Farmers Council.

[2] Cabinet and Ministers Act, 1960 (C.A. 3), s. 3 (3), (4). In practice voting does not occur.

with such instructions as may be given to him by the President, to arrange the business for, and keep the minutes of, meetings of the Cabinet, and convey the decisions of the Cabinet as soon as is practicable to the appropriate person or authority.[1] In practice these duties are delegated to an official known as the Deputy Secretary to the Cabinet, who acts as head of the Cabinet Secretariat. He is assisted by the Clerk to the Cabinet, who relieves him of much routine work and acts as a " progress chaser " to ensure that effect is given to Cabinet decisions. Apart from the Assistant Secretary, who is subordinate to the Clerk, the remainder of the Cabinet Secretariat consists of the usual secretarial and clerical staff.

Legislation committee

There are a number of standing committees of the Cabinet which handle matters such as delegation of the President's powers, preparation of Government speeches, civil service establishments and so on. The only one which is concerned with our present subject is the Legislation Committee. The chairman of the Committee is the Minister for Parliamentary Affairs and Leader of the House. The other members at present are the Minister of Justice, the Minister of Foreign Affairs and the Minister of Transport and Communications. The meetings of the Committee, which are also attended by Parliamentary Counsel and members of the President's office, normally take place about one month before the beginning of a meeting of the National Assembly. The Committee considers a draft legislative programme for the Assembly meeting and the two following meetings and, in the light of comments from Parliamentary Counsel as to the drafting progress of the various Bills, approves the programme with such revision as may be necessary. The draft programme is compiled from returns submitted by the Ministries and special Departments in response to a request circulated by the President's Office about two months before each meeting of the National Assembly. When approved by the Legislation Committee, the programme is submitted to the full Cabinet, who usually pass it without discussion.

The work of the Legislation Committee is unfortunately hampered by factors such as the suddenness with which legislative

---

[1] Cabinet and Ministers Act, 1960 (C.A. 3), s. 4.

proposals are often decided upon and put through, the departmental delays caused by congestion of work and reorganization, and the frequent visits abroad of the President, in whose absence major decisions are rarely taken. The result is that the carefully-planned programme for the next meeting often bears little relation to what in fact occurs.

3. DEPARTMENTAL MINISTERS

Apart from their legislative functions as Members of Parliament and members of the Cabinet, Ministers who are in charge of Government departments have certain additional duties. Besides their general responsibility in relation to legislation dealing with subjects assigned to them by the President, such Ministers may be regarded as having the following specific functions.

(1) Initiation of proposals

An alert Minister, who has a real interest in the subjects within his portfolio, will often have his own projects for legislation. Before laying them before his Cabinet colleagues he will probably wish to set the officials in his Ministry to work on investigating the background details of the project, seeking expert advice from outside the Ministry, framing appropriate legislative proposals and so on. When this work has been done and discussed with the Minister he may decide to seek Cabinet approval in principle with a view to having a Bill drafted or he may reach the conclusion that the proposal should not after all be proceeded with.

(2) Adjudicating on proposals submitted by officials

As pointed out in the next section, administrative civil servants will sometimes come across a need for legislative action and will seek the agreement of their Minister to approaching the Cabinet. Again, as mentioned in Section 5 of this chapter, Parliamentary Counsel, besides drafting legislation, also have occasion to propose it. Proposals at the official level cannot reach the Cabinet without the intervention of a Minister—or of course the President himself. The departmental Minister will thus often be called upon to decide whether to agree to submit a memorandum to the Cabinet asking for the necessary approval.

(3) Ensuring that Cabinet decisions are implemented

It is the duty of a Minister, once the Cabinet has ordered legislation to be prepared on a matter within his portfolio, to ensure that his officials do what is required to comply with the order, and to give them such assistance as lies within his power.

4. ADMINISTRATIVE OFFICIALS

Officials in the administrative class of the civil service, and their counterparts in statutory corporations and other public bodies, have an important part to play in the processes of legislation.[1] Their functions may be summarized as gathering information, shaping policy, advising Ministers and instructing Parliamentary Counsel.[2]

In the course of their day-to-day work in supervising the workings of the executive government, administrative officials come across many instances which reveal defects in the law or show the need for novel departures. This is particularly so where the law in question is recently enacted, as is the case with a great deal of Ghana's law in these early days of the Republic. On the other hand defects are equally likely to exist in old law designed for the quite different circumstances of a Crown Colony. As such instances accumulate in the files of the Ministry it is likely that legislative action will be proposed from one quarter or another. If no one else suggests it, the Principal Secretary or Head of Department may himself raise the matter with his Minister. In any event the background information thus collected will be invaluable in helping to produce effective new law.

Another aspect of the need for information arises in the case where it is desired to set up a branch of law or a statutory system which is quite new to Ghana. An independent state needs to provide for matters, such as a central bank, a currency system, a law of nationality and citizenship, and a national defence organization, which in the case of a dependency are the responsibility of the ruling power. Moreover the rulers of Ghana have ideas of their own to carry out, as for example the development of co-operative enterprises, and the creation of a great hydro-electric and aluminium smelting project on the Volta River. In

---

[1] For details of the administrative class, and of the civil service organization generally, see pp. 180 *et seq., ante.*

[2] Parliamentary Counsel, whose main function is the drafting of legislation, are described in the next section, p. 339, *post.*

Y

all such cases legislation is necessary, and the administrative official may need to go far beyond Ghana in his search for useful information. Other countries may be asked about their own experiences in similar matters; international bodies such as the specialist organizations of the United Nations may be consulted, and so on. Occasionally it may be necessary to appoint a commission of enquiry to carry out a thorough investigation,[1] but in most cases it falls upon the administrative officer to organize the accumulation of facts upon which a sound legislative structure can be built.

The crucial role of the administrator is in the shaping of policy. The need for this arises as soon as a legislative project comes under discussion. If it first comes under discussion at the official level some suggestions as to the policy to be followed must be worked out for submission to the Minister. If the Minister raises the matter himself he will need the assistance of his officials in settling the outlines of policy which are to be laid before the Cabinet in seeking approval in principle. If the Cabinet decides to legislate on its own initiative it will not do more than state briefly the policy to be followed, leaving it to the departmental officials, in consultation with their Minister, to hammer out the details.

In the normal case, where Cabinet approval in principle has been sought and obtained, the shaping of policy then enters on another, more detailed, stage with the need to prepare drafting instructions. It is now that the main outlines should be filled in, so that Parliamentary Counsel can be presented with a complete picture of what is wanted. Where the Cabinet has decided to legislate on its own initiative the two stages are combined, since the draftsman must be instructed as soon as possible thereafter.[2]

Throughout all stages of legislation the administrative official needs to be quick-thinking and assiduous. He should be always ready with sound and well-informed advice whenever his Minister needs it. He may, if he is alert, be able to prevent the taking of ill-considered decisions, or at least secure a necessary modification in them. This role does not come easily to Ghanaians, who are not accustomed to dispute (however tactfully) with their superiors and whose natural courtesy inclines them to agree

---

[1] Commissions of enquiry are described in Section 6 of this chapter, p. 346, *post*.

[2] Drafting instructions are dealt with more fully in the next chapter, p. 365, *post*.

with whatever is said. It is important that both Ministers and their subordinates should appreciate how essential it is that legislative decisions should not be taken without full advice and information and that the official who insists on proffering useful, though perhaps unpalatable, advice is discharging his duty far better than he who tells his Minister only what he wants to hear.

5. PARLIAMENTARY COUNSEL

The drafting of all Government Bills and of the more important legislative instruments is carried out by specialist lawyers known as Parliamentary Counsel.[1] The Parliamentary Counsel Branch of the Attorney-General's Department was set up in 1957 and re-replaced the system under which legislative drafting was not treated as a specialised subject but was entrusted to a Government lawyer temporarily holding the post of Legal Draftsman in the course of his career in the legal service of the Colonial Government. The advent of independence called for a heavy programme of legislation, and the Government decided to follow the pattern of the Parliamentary Counsel Office in Westminster and encourage a limited number of lawyers to devote themselves to Parliamentary drafting. There are now about half a dozen draftsmen in the Parliamentary Counsel Branch.

In the case of a new country like Ghana, which relies exclusively on the enactment of statutes for remodelling its system of laws, it is difficult to exaggerate the importance of the draftsman's role in legal development. Almost invariably he is the sole lawyer concerned with working out the details of a legislative project, and the burden of producing a sound Bill, well adapted to carry out Government policy and yet fitting harmoniously into the framework of an evolving jurisprudence, rests almost entirely on him.

Furthermore his work is not, before it passes into law, subjected to the close and expert scrutiny which is brought to bear on legislative proposals in countries with a longer experience of Parliamentary government. The importance which thus attaches to the draftsman is not widely understood; perhaps because, in

---

[1] An exception exists in the case of Bills relating to income tax, which have always been drafted in the Income Tax Department.

Ghana as elsewhere, there is a tendency to underrate statute law.[1]

Nor is very much known about the way the draftsman goes about his task. A detailed exposition of drafting technique is beyond the scope of this book but it may be helpful to give here a brief account of some of the more important aspects.

Drafting technique

It is necessary that there be rules to govern the drafting of legislation. Without these there would be such a lack of consistency in the law as seriously to impair its effect. Moreover many words would be needed to convey a meaning which, by the use of some drafting convention, can often be briefly expressed.

As the American draftsman, Reed Dickerson, has pointed out:

> " Suitable standards and conventions not only save the draftsman's time, but the time of private citizens, administrative officials and the courts. (It is safe to say that the lack of these things costs the government and the public many millions of dollars annually.) More important, they improve the quality of the end product as a vehicle for carrying out the legislative will. Sound legislative approaches, consistence, and clearness are tools for eliminating errors of substance or omission that would otherwise remain hidden until after enactment."[2]

With the introduction of a Republic in Ghana, the opportunity arose of laying down new rules for the drafting of legislation which it was hoped would promote its maximum efficiency. These are dealt with elsewhere in this Part and here we need only mention the necessity, in construing the new legislation, of bearing these rules in mind. The draftsman will have relied upon them and his meaning cannot be understood unless the reader consults them also.

As we shall see in the two following chapters, the draftsman is given instructions as to the changes in the law which, as a matter of policy, are required to be made. It is his task to discover how the policy can be implemented in the way which will best fit the existing framework of the law. The change of law must leave

---

[1] Professor G. W. Paton has remarked on this tendency in English legal education. In his view " not enough emphasis is placed on the technique of drafting statutes " and " only the fullest knowledge of the technique of drafting and interpretation of statutes will succeed in retaining some consistency in English law as a whole ": *A Text-book of Jurisprudence* (2nd Edn.), p. 195.

[2] *Legislative Drafting*, p. 6.

no loose ends elsewhere to cause trouble later nor must it conflict unintentionally with legal principles that are intended to remain undisturbed. It is a job of dovetailing. All this means that a good deal of research and hard thinking is required of the draftsman. It may often have to be done against the clock, since legislation in Ghana is usually required very quickly and the belief is widely held outside the Parliamentary Counsel Branch that the interval between taking a policy decision and producing a Bill should normally be a matter of days, if not hours, whereas in many cases it ought to be a matter of months.[1] So far as he can in the time allowed him, the draftsman will prepare the ground thoroughly before beginning his draft, and will act upon the principle of taking nothing he is told about the legal background for granted. He will check every reference by going to the source, and never merely accept what he is told by those instructing him as to the effect of any provision of the existing law, or rely entirely on his own memory. The good draftsman has the sort of memory that warns him that a particular point needs consideration and gives him some idea of where to look it up. Sometimes a provision in a Bill will make necessary an extensive search of the Statute Book to make sure that no consequential amendments have been overlooked. Occasionally it may even be necessary for the draftsman to go right through the Statute Book for this purpose. An obvious example is the enactment of the Constitution, which called for consequential amendments in almost every Ordinance and Act, but the need may arise in ordinary legislation.[2]

The drafting of legislation is a task that calls for the highest degree of accuracy.[3] In construing a legal enactment, every word counts—at least if proper rules of drafting have been observed and no unnecessary words included. If, as is nearly always the case, a Bill involves some amendment of existing law and is not an entirely fresh departure, it is necessary before drafting is begun to study the law which is to be altered. No Act should ever be

---

[1] " . . . there is for each bill an irreducible period for preparation . . . as the time is cut down, the quality deteriorates, so that ultimately the point is reached where no bill fit for introduction can be produced ": Driedger, *The Composition of Legislation*, Ottawa, 1957, p. xvi.

[2] As in the case of the Statutory Instruments Order, 1960 (L.I. 9); see p. 267, *ante.*

[3] " Bill drafting must have the accuracy of engineering, for it is law engineering; it must have the detail and consistency of architecture, for it is law architecture ": cited Reed Dickerson, *Legislative Drafting*, p. 11.

amended unless it has been carefully examined from beginning
to end. This is necessary because any change nearly always involves consequential alterations elsewhere in the Act. It may
well involve consequential amendments also in other Acts. It is
the duty of the departmental official who prepares instructions
for the draftsman to indicate the places in which amendments of
this sort will be required, but the draftsman cannot rely on this
and must make his own researches.

Apart from accurately informing himself as to the existing law,
the draftsman must of course display accuracy in his Bill. He
must be accurate in relying on definitions contained in the Interpretation Act, and on those he inserts in his Bill. It is not
uncommon to find an expression defined in the Bill itself which
is not accurately employed. A provision in a Bill may sometimes
depart from a definition in using a particular term, but it must
be done deliberately and in a manner which clearly shows that a
departure is being made.

An attention to accuracy is needed at all stages of the preparation and passing of a Bill. It is rarely wise to include in a first
draft of a Bill any provision whose accuracy is suspect. It may
be tempting to put something down with the intention of checking
on it later, but a later opportunity may not arise or the draftsman may forget that the draft was provisional. Whenever an
alteration is made in a draft care has to be taken to see that
consequential alterations are made. These may be no more than
the renumbering of clauses and section references, or they may
involve substantial alterations all through the Bill. A thorough
final check of the accuracy of a Bill also has to be made after its
publication in the *Gazette* and before the blue copies are printed
for distribution to Members of Parliament. By Standing Order
58(1) it is permissible, with the consent of the Clerk of the National
Assembly, to make minor alterations in the published text
before the Bill is introduced. If a Bill is amended during its
passage through the Assembly, accuracy is again called for in
making sure that all consequential amendments are effected.

Accuracy is again essential where a statutory instrument is
being drafted. It is the first duty of the draftsman of a statutory
instrument to ensure that it does not exceed the power under
which it is made. Accordingly the most careful scrutiny of the
empowering Act must be made. Care has to be taken to recite
in the instrument the occurrence of any events which are a
necessary pre-requisite to the exercise of the power. Thus the

enabling Act may say " If the Minister is satisfied that a state of emergency exists he may, by executive instrument. . . ." The executive instrument will begin by reciting that the Minister is satisfied that a state of emergency exists. The instrument will also employ the same terminology as the enabling Act.[1]

Accuracy (and indeed industry) is also needed in the marking and checking of proofs. Although Ghana is the fortunate possessor of an excellent Government Printing Department, misprints cannot be entirely avoided and it is the responsibility of the draftsman as well as the printer to check proofs with meticulous accuracy. To have to ask the Cabinet to approve the introduction of an amending Bill because, say, a line of type has dropped out unobserved is to confess a failure which every self-respecting draftsman would wish to avoid—even at the cost of much time spent in the pedestrian task of proof-reading.[2]

Alertness is also needed in drafting. If he is not alert, the draftsman may assume that because he has been instructed to prepare a Bill which will effect a particular change in the law he must therefore proceed to prepare the Bill in every case. It frequently happens, however, either that no Bill is necessary because the desired purpose is already provided for by the existing law or that the instructions for the Bill are misconceived because it would be simpler and more satisfactory to achieve the desired result in some other way—perhaps by some slight modification of an existing enactment or procedure instead of the setting up of an entirely new system. It is sometimes said that one of the disadvantages of statute law as compared with other forms is that its growth is inorganic. Whereas customary law or common law is developed gradually by the working out and extension of established principles, statute law is a crude system of disconnected provisions. If the draftsman is alert, he can on occasion take some of the force out of this criticism by producing the desired result through a modification or development of an existing and familiar statutory provision—a process which has something of the organic about it.

Another aspect of the need for alertness lies in the field of

---

[1] For an example of this see s. 4 (1) of the Statutory Instruments Act, 1959 (No. 52) and para. 2 of the Statutory Instruments Order, 1960 (L.I. 9).

[2] " Except for uncontrollable time limitations, the other principal reason why most proposed Bills are insufficiently revised is either a distaste for detail or simple laziness. If a lawyer lacks the will to overcome these difficulties he will never be a first-rate draftsman ": Reed Dickerson, *Legislative Drafting*, p. 41.

policy. The draftsman ought not to be concerned with policy as such, but he is concerned, and has a duty, to see that the policy decision is effected in a way that will be workable. He should therefore be alert to observe flaws in the policy scheme which may interfere with its smooth working when transformed into law. For this he also needs some degree of imagination. By visualising what a scheme will mean in terms of real life when it comes to be put into operation, the draftsman may be able to suggest improvements and to point out defects. For example, he may be instructed to prepare a Deportation Bill which includes a provision that any ship or aircraft leaving the country may be required to include among its passengers the alien who is to be deported. If the draftsman tries to visualise the circumstances in which the deportation may take place and the countries to which persons may be deported, he will realise that it may in some cases be necessary to deport a person to a neighbouring country, and to do so by the use of a land vehicle. He will thus be able to suggest the addition of this form of transport to those mentioned in his instructions. As Sir Courtenay Ilbert has said:

> If a parliamentary draftsman is to do his work well, he must be something more than a mere draftsman. He must have constructive imagination, the power to visualize things in the concrete, and to foresee whether and how a paper scheme will work out in practice.[1]

There is also room for subtlety in the art of drafting. No enactment can deal in express terms with every situation in which it may fall to be applied. For one thing, no one can envisage at a time when legislation is being prepared all the possible combinations of future circumstances. For another, even if such foresight were possible, an enactment which tried to deal expressly with all combinations of events would be so long and complicated as to be unendurable. This problem is one of the most difficult facing the draftsman. He can meet it by producing a draft which, although its terms are short and simple, yet by the use of subtlety contains the key to determine a very large number of possible combinations of circumstance.

A manifestation of subtlety by the draftsman is in the use of implications. This needs to be frequent, both to avoid length and unwieldiness in the draft and also to avoid stating propositions which are obvious and yet may need to be confirmed in some way.

---

[1] *Legislative Methods and Forms*, p. 240.

Thus, in a Bill setting up a new office, the draftsman, in defining the circumstances in which the office may become vacant, will want to avoid providing expressly that a vacancy shall arise on the death of the office-holder, since this is so obvious as to make a formal statement of it absurd. He may on the other hand feel reluctant to leave the matter entirely without mention. A simple solution is to bring it in in a provision relating to the method by which the vacancy is to be filled.[1]

Implications are of great importance in drafting and both the draftsmen and the reader should constantly watch for them. To take one example, a statement that " No person shall supply a poison in a container which does not bear the prescribed label " contains an implication that everyone is free to supply poison in a container which does bear the prescribed label. This implication may be cut down by other provisions. Elsewhere the Act may state that no person who is not a pharmacist shall supply any poison. These two provisions taken together carry by implication the proposition that every pharmacist is free to supply poisons if they are in correctly-labelled containers. To add this proposition expressly is neither necessary nor desirable, since legislation proceeds on the principle that a man may do as he chooses except where the law forbids him.

Other functions of Parliamentary Counsel

The functions of Parliamentary Counsel are not limited to the actual preparation of legislation but extend to the initiation of proposals for legislation on matters of peculiarly legal concern. In the course of their duties Parliamentary Counsel inevitably come across cases where some defect in the law calls for legislation, or where heavy amendment of enactments dealing with a particular subject has made their consolidation desirable. Furthermore when, as at the present time, a programme of statute law reform is under way, Parliamentary Counsel will need to put forward the necessary Bills.

The functions of Parliamentary Counsel also include the giving of advice to Government departments, the police and other public bodies on the meaning and effect of the law in force. Because of the absence of departmental lawyers many requests for legal advice are received by the Attorney-General's Department. Where these relate to the construction of Acts or statutory

---

[1] See, *e.g.*, ss. 2 and 3 (2) of the National Assembly Act, 1961 (Act 86).

instruments they are generally referred to the draftsman of the legislation in question, following the practice instituted in England when the Parliamentary Counsel Office was established in 1869.[1] This is done notwithstanding Lord Halsbury's well-known dictum

> " . . . in construing a statute I believe the worst person to construe it is the person who is responsible for its drafting."[2]

As Sir Courtenay Ilbert has pointed out

> " . . . the Parliamentary Counsel can often, from his knowledge of the history and intention of an enactment, give a clue to its true construction."[3]

It is obvious that no one can know the structure and mechanism of an Act so well as its author. If a doubt arises he is often able to point to the provisions which will resolve it.

Parliamentary Counsel also have a close relationship with the Clerk of the National Assembly, whom they are often called upon to advise on matters of Parliamentary procedure. Among their other miscellaneous functions is that of supervising the publication of Acts and statutory instruments and the maintenance of the binder service.[4]

6. COMMISSIONS OF ENQUIRY

Before concluding this discussion of legislative functionaries, we must give some account of commissions of enquiry. The Commissions of Enquiry Ordinance (Cap. 249) empowers the President to appoint one or more commissioners to enquire into any matter in which any enquiry would, in the opinion of the President, be for the public welfare. Although not limited to matters requiring legislative action—and indeed frequently used for other purposes—the Ordinance has proved very useful in tackling complicated problems of law reform. Recently, for

---

[1] Ilbert, *Legislative Methods and Forms*, 1901, p. 93.

[2] *Hilder* v. *Dexter*, [1902] A.C. 474, at p. 477. The remark was made in explanation of Lord Halsbury's refraining from delivering a judgment in a case concerning a statute largely drafted by him. Although it may be undesirable that a draftsman should deliver judgment on his own work in court this does not of course mean that his advice as to construction is necessarily without value.

[3] *Op. cit.*, p. 94.

[4] See pp. 291 *et seq.*, *ante*.

example, commissions have been set up to investigate such matters as company law, inheritance and insolvency.[1]

In its usual form, the commission begins by reciting the powers under which it is made and the opinion of the President that an enquiry " into the matters hereinafter mentioned " would be for the public welfare. It then names the commissioners, states the quorum and sets out the terms of reference. After appointing the chairman the commission may then give directions as to the way in which the commissioners' task is to be carried out. In the case of the Insolvency Commission for example, the terms of reference were—

(a) to consider and make recommendations regarding the better protection by law of creditors and debtors in cases of involvency; and

(b) to consider what legislation is desirable for the purpose of the administration of the assets of insolvent persons, estates, firms and companies and of related matters, and to make detailed recommendations thereon.

The directions to the commissioners required them " to take into account the need for encouraging African enterprise in Ghana and the encouragement of foreign investment " and also to consult with the company law commissioner, whose final report was still pending.

The commission usually ends by appointing a secretary, fixing the time and place of the first meeting, stating whether meetings are to be in public or private, requiring the Commissioner of Police to place constables at the disposal of the commissioners, and finally instructing the commissioners, in reporting their conclusions, to embody a full statement of their reasons. After it has been issued by or in the name of the President, the commission must be published in the *Gazette* and takes effect from the date of publication.[2]

Before embarking on his duties, each commissioner makes an oath or affirmation to the effect that he will faithfully, fully, impartially and to the best of his ability discharge the trust and perform the duties devolving on him by virtue of the commission.[3] The times and places of meetings other than the first

---

[1] See *Ghana Gazette*, 25th August, 1958 (company law) 23rd May, 1959 (inheritance) and 6th February, 1960 (insolvency).

[2] Commissions of Enquiry Ordinance (Cap. 249), s. 16.

[3] *Ibid.*, s. 5.

are normally left to the discretion of the commissioners, as is the decision on whether meetings should be in public or private. Commissioners have the same powers as the Supreme Court to summon witnesses and examine them on oath, and also to call for the production of books, plans and documents.[1] A witness who gives false evidence commits perjury.[2]

As an example of the way commissions of enquiry operate as legislative functionaries we may take the Insolvency Commission, whose terms of reference have been given above. The commission consisted of the secretary of the Bank of Ghana as chairman, a Kumasi business man (who was also President of the Kumasi branch of the Ghana Chamber of Commerce), and an expert in company law and administration seconded from the Board of Trade in London. A Senior State Attorney from the Attorney-General's Department was appointed as secretary. No bankruptcy or insolvency law existed in Ghana, so the commission had a clear field. It was decided that the major part of their recommendations, relating to the insolvency of individuals, should be presented in the form of an annotated draft Bill. This would enable greater precision to be obtained and would avoid the lengthy delay that otherwise would necessarily ensue between the delivery of their report and the enactment of the resulting law. Since none of the commissioners was experienced in the drafting of legislation, Parliamentary Counsel was attached to the commission for this purpose.

The commission was appointed on 20th January, 1960 and its appointment took effect on 3rd February. The first meeting was held on 18th February and an opening statement was read by one of the commissioners. This outlined some of the main questions with which the enquiry would be concerned and on which the commissioners would appreciate advice, which could be given at the meetings of the commission or in the form of memoranda. The statement then set out the principal objectives of insolvency legislation and gave the commissioners' tentative views on some of the more important points.[3]

The commission held 33 meetings in towns all over Ghana. It met 27 organizations and other bodies and a total of 184 persons, as well as receiving a quantity of written memoranda.

---

[1] *Ibid.*, ss. 10, 12.
[2] *Ibid.*, s. 11.
[3] *Opening Statement by the Commissioners appointed to enquire into the insolvency law of Ghana*, Accra, 18th February, 1960.

After considering, with the aid of a bankruptcy expert from the United Kingdom, all the evidence received, the commissioners set about the task of deciding upon the content of the draft Bill. They reached the conclusion that this should be novel in its terms and approach and, apart from incidental borrowings, should not be copied from the law of any other country. The commission's draft proposals, consisting of a brief introduction and an annotated draft Bill, were published on 15th April, 1961.[1] Following this the commissioners again embarked on a tour of the country, in the course of which 19 further meetings were held. After considering the comments received on the draft Bill and making appropriate amendments, the commissioners presented their final report to the President on 31st August, 1961.[2]

---

[1] *Draft Proposals of the Commissioners appointed to enquire into the insolvency law of Ghana*, Accra, 15th April, 1961.

[2] *Report of the Commissioners appointed to enquire into the insolvency law of Ghana*, Accra, 31st August, 1961.

CHAPTER 8

LEGISLATIVE METHODS: ACTS OF PARLIAMENT

Having described the nature of an Act of Parliament and the functionaries who are concerned with its enactment, we now turn to the detailed methods used to turn a legislative proposal into an operative Act. In order that these may be understood it is necessary first to explain the structure of what begins life as a draft Bill and, if it survives the hazards of Parliamentary procedure, ends as an Act of Parliament. We shall not only describe the component parts of a Bill or Act but also give some account of the way in which it is, or should be, drafted. The importance of this is not limited to the draftsman himself: any person who looks at a Bill or Act will understand it better if he knows something of drafting methods.

1. THE STRUCTURE OF A BILL

As is recognized by the Acts of Parliament Act, the structure of a Bill corresponds closely with that of an Act, and a description of the one virtually describes the other.[1] Such differences as there are will appear in the course of this chapter.

Short Title

Every Bill is required to bear at the head a short title, the citation of which, when the Bill has become an Act, is sufficient to identify the Act.[2] The short title almost always ends with the word " Act " followed by the year in which assent is given. Only in the case of codifying Acts is this practice occasionally departed from, as for example with the Criminal Code, 1960 (Act 29).

The short title is intended to serve two purposes. One is to indicate at a glance the subject-matter of the Bill, and later the Act. The other is to provide a brief name by which the Bill or Act can be referred to. The first purpose requires that the short

---

[1] See Acts of Parliament Act, 1960 (C.A. 7), s. 1.
[2] *Ibid.*, ss. 2, 12.

title should be as descriptive as possible; the second that it should be as short as possible. It will be apparent that these two purposes may compete. If, for example, a Bill dealt with Ministers, the Cabinet, Government Departments and Ministerial Secretaries, a fully descriptive short title might be The Cabinet, Ministers, Government Departments and Ministerial Secretaries Act. But it would be intolerable to have to write all this out in order to refer to it, and a briefer title must therefore be chosen, for example, the Ministers of Ghana Act. This is not chosen merely by picking out one only of the matters with which the Bill is concerned. Ministers will be found to be connected with each of the four matters referred to previously. They form the Cabinet, the Government Department is a Minister's Department and Ministerial Secretaries are appointed to assist Ministers. The art of choosing an appropriate short title lies in selecting what is the predominant purpose of a Bill. If it proves impossible to discover one predominant purpose this may indicate that the subject-matter should be divided among two or more separate Bills.[1]

A number of different short titles may be equally appropriate for the same Bill, but some consistency should be used in choosing titles for Bills dealing with the same subject-matter. For example, if there is already an Act entitled The Representation of the People Act, a further Act on the same subject should be given a similar title and not called for example The Electoral Provisions Act, although in other respects the latter might be equally suitable.

A word should be said about Consolidation Acts. It was the custom towards the end of the last century in England always to use the word " consolidation " in the short title of a Consolidation Act, e.g. The Customs Consolidation Act, 1876. This practice adds to the length of the short title, and it is now considered to serve no useful purpose. In any case consistency requires that it should either be used for all Consolidation Acts or none.

Where an Act makes minor amendments in a major Act, it is sometimes thought desirable to include the word " amendment " in the short title. Thus an Act amending a Courts Act which contains the bulk of the statutory provisions relating to courts might be called the Courts (Amendment) Act. Since however most Acts which do not consolidate existing Acts will

---

[1] *Cf.* Standing Order **57** (1): " Matters having no proper relation to each other shall not be provided by the same Bill."

be found to amend them, there is much to be said for omitting
the word amendment in the short title. Nor is it necessary to
include the name of the Act which is being amended.[1]

Where a Bill contains provisions on a large number of minor
points within one subject, it is sometimes useful to use the words
" miscellaneous provisions " in the short title. This indicates that
the Bill is not concerned with major amendments of the law.

Long title

The short title is required to be followed by a long title describing the provisions of the Bill.[2] The Interpretation Act
provides that the long title is to be treated as forming " part of
an Act intended to assist in explaining the purport and object of
the Act ".[3] Although useful, it is relatively unimportant except
in relation to the restriction of debate and of the putting down
of amendments to the Bill. This brings us to the doctrine of
scope.

Every Bill has its own scope, and an amendment to a Bill
which is beyond its scope is out of order. It is a matter for the
Speaker or other person presiding at proceedings of the National
Assembly on the Bill to determine what the scope is if the question
should arise. In doing this, he will be guided by the long title.
It is important therefore that the long title should adequately
embrace everything contained in the Bill when it is introduced.
If there is no desire on the part of the promoters of the Bill to
restrict debate and the moving of amendments, the long title
can be brief and comprehensive. If on the other hand such restrictions are desired, it may be necessary to have an elaborate
long title. An example may help to make this clear. A Bill is
required to do two things. One, to establish a new system of
retirement pensions for the police and two, to set up a new police
promotions board. If it is desired to restrict debate and the
moving of amendments to these two points, the long title of the
Bill might run as follows:

> " An Act to provide, in relation to the Police Service, for the
> establishment of a new system of retirement pensions and for the
> setting up of a promotions board."

---

[1] An awful warning of what this practice may lead to is furnished by the
British Act whose short title was "the Artizans Dwellings Act, (1868)
Amendment Act, (1879) Amendment Act, 1880".

[2] Acts of Parliament Act, 1960 (C.A. 7), s. 2.

[3] Interpretation Act, 1960 (C.A. 4), s. 2.

If, on the other hand, it is proposed that debate shall be free to range over the whole subject of the police, it will be enough to have a long title in such terms as

" An Act to make further provision with respect to the Police Service."

This illustrates how the long title determines the scope of a Bill. In the first example given above, the scope of the Bill is restricted to the two questions of retirement pensions and promotions. In the second example, the scope is the Police Service as a whole.

There are limits, however, to the way in which the scope can be restricted by the long title. If a Bill were intended to deal not only with police pensions and promotions, but also with the provision of marriage quarters, the payment of compensation for injury and the stoppage of pay for indiscipline, the scope could not be limited to these five matters by listing them in the long title. A Bill such as this would clearly throw the whole of the police organisation under discussion. It may be said that the scope of a Bill containing one or two specific matters can be restricted in this way, but that more than two specific matters will be likely to lead to a decision that the scope is thrown open to the whole field of the Bill.[1]

It should be emphasised that an amendment will not necessarily be out of order because it is not within the wording of the long title. In the example given above of the Police Bill dealing with five different subjects it would be quite in order to put down an amendment to deal with, e.g., recruitment. But if the long title had been drawn in restrictive terms it would be necessary, if the amendment were accepted, to amend the long title accordingly.

Strictly speaking, a Bill is out of order if it is introduced with a long title insufficient to cover the whole of its contents.[2] For this reason use is sometimes made of " sweeping up words " such as " and for matters connected therewith ". The use of such words is to be discouraged, however, as is the use of any words in the Bill which are not strictly necessary. A long title will not be construed narrowly with the purpose of holding a Bill to be out of order, and it will happen but rarely, if ever, that the provisions

---

[1] Since private Members rarely use their right to move amendments the doctrine of scope has not yet assumed much importance in Ghana.

[2] See Standing Order 57(2): " No Bill shall contain anything foreign to what its Long Title imports."

z

of the long title are held not wide enough to cover the inclusion of ancillary provisions.

Preamble

A preamble was often used in former times to explain the reasons and objects of the legislation. Its place is now partly taken by the explanatory memorandum which is affixed to the front of a Bill. The advantage of this is that it does not form part of the Bill and therefore no possibility can arise of inconsistency between the objects stated in the preamble and the provisions of the Bill. Such inconsistency formerly arose not infrequently and was the subject of a troublesome line of authority.

Nevertheless the preamble is not entirely obsolete, and it was thought worth while to include in the Interpretation Act the statement that the preamble forms " part of an Act intended to assist in explaining the purport and object of the Act ".[1] It is still used to add dignity to a Bill of great constitutional importance, as for example in the Constitution and the Acts of the Constituent Assembly, and its use may assist considerably in the drafting of other types of Bill, particularly where the Bill is not readily comprehensible unless some pre-existing state of affairs can be assumed to be known by the reader. Such an assumption cannot easily be made where the Bill is dealing with some matter of mainly private concern, e.g., is altering the constitution of a body such as the Red Cross or the St. John Ambulance Brigade. Suppose, for example, it is desired to extend the powers of the St. John Ambulance Brigade. The following alternatives may be open to the draftsman—

(1) To use a preamble and start the Bill as follows—

" Whereas, by a charter of incorporation made on the 18th day of February, 1956, the St. John Ambulance Brigade was empowered to expend money for any purpose connected with the relief of persons suffering an injury:

And whereas it is expedient to empower the said Brigade to expend money for other purposes:

Now therefore be it enacted etc.

The charter of incorporation of the Brigade is hereby amended as follows, that is to say, for the words " the relief of persons suffering an injury " there shall be substituted the words " the relief of persons suffering any injury, illness or other disability ".

---

[1] Interpretation Act, 1960 (C.A. 4), s. 2.

(2) To dispense with a preamble, and express the operative provisions of the Bill as follows—

> " The charter of incorporation of the St. John Ambulance Brigade (which at present limits expenditure of money by the Brigade to expenditure for the relief of persons suffering an injury) is hereby amended by the substitution, for the words " persons suffering from an injury" of the words " persons suffering any injury, illness or other disability ".

The first method has the advantage of telling the reader exactly what is being done, but the second method is shorter and, in view of the advent of the explanatory memorandum, just as effective.[1] Since consistency is important, enabling those who look at Bills to know what to expect, it seems that the preamble should be reserved for the rare occasion when a Bill of constitutional magnitude is in question, or where the necessary statement of preliminary facts is lengthy and complex; and that the explanatory memorandum should ordinarily be regarded as taking its place.

Enacting formula

The enacting formula, couched in the imperative mood, is what gives effect to the legislative provisions. Formerly every section of a British Act required to be prefaced by words of enactment, but the current rule is that the enacting formula at the beginning governs all the provisions. Section 3 of the Acts of Parliament Act requires the provisions of every Act to be prefaced by the words " *Be it enacted by the President and the National Assembly in this present Parliament assembled as follows—* . . ." These words extend " to all sections of the Act and to any Schedules and other provisions contained therein ". Unlike the case in the United Kingdom, where a special formula is used for Bills imposing taxation or making good Parliamentary grants the enacting formula used in Ghana is invariable, although where there is a preamble the words " Nowtherefore " are inserted before " be it enacted ".

Clauses

After the preliminary features described above come the substantive provisions of the Bill. Where a Bill contains more than

---

[1] The second example incidentally illustrates the use of descriptive words where another enactment is mentioned and it is desired to show its purport. Such words " are intended for convenience of reference only and do not form part of the enactment ": Interpretation Act, 1960 (C.A. 4), s. 5.

one substantive provision it is required to be divided into numbered clauses, which on enactment become sections.[1] Bills vary
in size from the one-clause Bill, which has only a single thing to
say, to the major Bill containing hundreds of clauses and designed
to regulate a whole branch of the law.[2]

One of the first arts of the draftsman is to be able to divide his
material into appropriate clauses. He needs to take plenty of
elbow-room, and begin a fresh clause as each new aspect of the
subject comes to be dealt with. This rule would only need to be
departed from if it were expedient for political reasons, in assisting the passage of the Bill, to keep down the number of clauses.[3]
The draftsman engaged in consolidation should bear in mind that
an Act which he is consolidating may have been drafted with such
political reasons in mind, and may therefore have a smaller
number of sections, each containing more material, than is really
desirable. In consolidation of course there is no reason why the
clauses should not be taken apart so that the reader gets a clearer
view. Amendments made during the passage of a Bill may also
have distorted the structure, and this again can be corrected in
consolidation.

Except where the material to be embodied in a clause is short,
it will be necessary to divide the clause into subsections.[4] Each
subsection, or, where the clause is not divided into subsections,
the clause itself, should read as one sentence. It is not generally
desirable to include successive sentences within one subsection,
since it becomes difficult to identify a particular sentence when
reference needs to be made to it. If it is thought necessary to do
so, as where an expression used in a subsection needs to be defined, the second sentence should be inserted as a new paragraph.
Where an expression requiring definition is used only once in a
Bill the definition should be placed as a separate paragraph in the
subsection in which the expression is used. If it is used several

---

[1] Acts of Parliament Act, 1960 (C.A. 7), s. 4. *Cf.* Standing Order 56.

[2] Until 1960, in Ghana as in the United Kingdom and elsewhere it was
impossible to have a genuine " one-clause Bill " since it was always necessary to have a clause conferring a short title. This pointless requirement was
done away with by ss. 2 and 12 of the Acts of Parliament Act, 1960 (C.A. 7).

[3] This consideration, which often arises at Westminster—where debate
on " clause stand part ", particularly in committee of the whole House, is
sometimes protracted—has scarcely yet arisen in Ghana.

[4] Section 4 of the Acts of Parliament Act, 1960 (C.A. 7) requires that
" if a section contains more than one enactment it shall be divided into
subsections ". The term " subsection " is used both for clauses and sections.

times, but only in one clause, the definition should be placed as a subsection at the end of the clause or, if the clause is difficult to understand unless the definition has first been read, at the beginning. Where the term is used throughout the Bill, either it is defined in the first place where it occurs and a reference to the definition is inserted in the interpretation clause at the end of the Bill, or, if the meaning of the term is fairly self-evident and it is defined merely to avoid doubt, the definition appears only in the interpretation clause.

The draftsman should try to avoid producing clauses or subsections consisting of many lines of uniform print. Such blocks of print make understanding difficult, and can easily be avoided by the use of paragraphs. Paragraphs are numbered (a), (b), (c) and so on. If sub-paragraphs are required they are numbered (i), (ii), (iii) and so on. A subsection should not break immediately into a paragraph: introductory words are needed. Where paragraphs are used, care should be taken not to leave the reader waiting too long for the verb and the substance of the provision. There can be no doubt which of the two following variations is to be preferred—

> " 1. A person who is—
>   (a) a Member of Parliament, or
>   (b) a practising barrister, or
>   (c) a Judge or officer of the Supreme Court, or
>   (d) a local court magistrate,
>   shall not be liable for jury service."

> " 2. A person shall not be liable for jury service if he is—
>   (a) A Member of Parliament, or
>   (b) a practising barrister, or
>   (c) a Judge or officer of the Supreme Court, or
>   (d) a local court magistrate."

A clause can often be rendered more easily comprehensible by the use of the proviso. This enables a general statement to be made followed by words reducing its generality in particular cases. The use of the proviso should be restricted to cutting down the generality of the immediately preceding proposition. Thus a proviso to a subsection should not cut down the generality of words not found in that subsection. A common infringement of this rule is found in a proviso such as the following—

> " A person guilty of driving without due care shall be liable to a fine of fifty pounds:
> Provided that nothing in this Act shall render a person liable to be punished twice for the same offence."

Where the exception can be expressed very shortly, it may be of advantage, instead of using a proviso, simply to continue the sentence with the words " so however that . . ." If the proviso is to contain more than one excepting provision, it should be arranged in paragraphs.

The proviso is sometimes criticized by writers on drafting technique, but it has its uses and in Ghana, as in the United Kingdom, it is used frequently. It comes into its own when a general principle is to be laid down with relatively minor excep- tions. Often it is much clearer and simpler to state the general principle first and then follow it with the list of exceptions in the form of a proviso. When the correct modern use of the proviso is properly understood and applied this method has no defect in substance, whatever formal objections may be levelled on his- torical or grammatical grounds.[1] Suppose the intention is to require all holders of foreign currency (with certain limited excep- tions) to offer it for exchange to the Bank of Ghana. One could draft in this way:

> " Every person in possession of foreign currency, other than a banker, or a person whose holding is of the value of £G10 or less, or who holds the currency on behalf of some other person, or with the consent of the Bank of Ghana, shall within the pre- scribed period offer it to the Bank of Ghana for exchange into Ghana currency."

It is surely better however to express the proposition like this:

> " Every person in possession of foreign currency shall within the prescribed period offer it to the Bank of Ghana for exchange into Ghana currency:
> Provided that this requirement does not apply to—
> (a) a banker,
> (b) a person whose holding is of the value of £G10 or less,
> (c) a person who holds on behalf of some other person, or
> (d) a person who holds with the consent of the Bank of Ghana."

Here it is easy to take in the general statement and then, warned by the words " Provided that ", to register one by one the various exceptions.

It frequently happens that the complete expression of a single proposition requires the inclusion of a considerable amount of detail. Thus to lay down what types of persons are disqualified

---

[1] Elmer Driedger criticizes the use of the proviso through an entire chapter: see *The Composition of Legislation*, Chap. XI. The examples he gives, and succeeds in demolishing, are all however examples of its *misuse*.

for election to the National Assembly it was necessary to mention a number of different cases, some of them complex.[1] This could not be done within the ambit of an ordinary subsection, and yet the details were too important to be relegated to a Schedule. The solution to such difficulties lies in the use of a table set out at the end of the subsection.[2]

Arrangement and grouping of clauses

A well-drawn Bill is a well-arranged Bill. The draftsman will have worked out a logical and orderly scheme and the reader will be taken through the subject-matter in a clear, connected fashion. After careful examination by the draftsman most legislative projects will be found to be divisible into a number of distinct compartments[3] and, once the policy is clear to him, it is his prime duty to work out what these compartments are and in what order they should be presented. In the case of major Bills the clauses will be so grouped as to form separate Parts. Smaller Bills, or Parts within a major Bill, may have the clauses arranged in groups, each with a descriptive cross-heading. Where the Bill contains only a few clauses neither method of sub-division will be needed.

It is often easier to divide the subject-matter into compartments than to work out the order in which these should be presented. Sometimes, as with " miscellaneous provisions " Bills, the compartments will bear little relation to one another and their order does not matter. Usually, however, there is a connecting thread. The only general principle is that the reader should be able to start at the beginning of the Bill and progress by logical steps to

---

[1] The most complex was the following—

" A person who has been convicted in Ghana of an offence which involved dishonesty, not being a person—
- (a) who has been granted a free pardon in respect of the said offence, or
- (b) whose imprisonment for the said offence terminated more than five years previously, or
- (c) who, not having been sentenced to imprisonment for the said offence, was convicted more than five years previously."

[2] National Assembly Act, 1961 (Act 86), s. 1 (2). Note how the need for repeating the table in relation to unseating of members is avoided by the wording of s. 2 (2) (a) and compare the corresponding provisions (ss. 25 and 26) of the Ghana (Constitution) Order in Council, 1957 (L.N. 47). For other examples of the use of tables see Civil Service Act, 1960 (C.A. 5), s. 28; Judicial Service Act, 1960 (C.A. 10), s. 8; Pharmacy and Drugs Act, 1961 (Act 64), s. 41.

[3] In what follows " compartment " is used as a neutral word which may refer to a Part of a major Bill, or to a group of clauses within a smaller Bill or within a Part, or to a clause.

the end. He should not be subjected to puzzles, as by coming across an expression such as " the Minister " which clearly needs definition but is not defined in the place where it first occurs. Nor should he be misled, as by reading a succession of clauses imposing severe restrictions only to find at the end of the Bill a clause providing for wholesale exemptions from them.

Often a chronological order will be most suitable. Where some form of procedure is being laid down it is best to start with the initiation of the procedure, then deal one by one with the successive stages, and close with the way in which the procedure may be terminated. Two examples may be given: the Criminal Procedure Code, 1960 (Act 30) and the draft Bill recommended by the recent Insolvency Commission.[1] The Criminal Procedure Code begins by dealing with the arrest of an offender and then successively provides for the place of trial, the initiation of proceedings, the conduct of the trial, the punishments which may be imposed, the execution of sentences, the bringing of appeals and the release of convicts. In the case of the draft Insolvency Bill the task of arrangement was complicated by the fact that, while there are of course successive stages in insolvency proceedings there are also many functions connected with the administration of an insolvent's affairs and the distribution of his assets which may be exercised during two or more stages. Also there are a number of special cases to be dealt with, such as those where the debtor is dead or is of unsound mind, or a private arrangement with creditors is made, or the debtor undergoes successive insolvencies. Where such complications exist it may be impossible to produce an arrangement which is satisfactory in all respects. The draft Insolvency Bill, consisting of seventy-eight clauses, was divided into seven Parts. The first Part set the stage by creating the office of Official Trustee and providing for the new administrative machinery that would be needed. The second Part, comprising seven groups of clauses arranged under cross-headings, dealt successively with the entire course of the formal insolvency proceedings, beginning with the initiation of proceedings by petition and ending with the discharge of the debtor and the mode of terminating proceedings. The chronological arrangement had to be interrupted in the middle by a group of clauses laying down the general duties and disabilities of the debtor. In the third Part, directing the mode of administration and distribution of

---

[1] See p. 349, *ante*.

the debtor's property, a chronological order was inappropriate and the Part was divided into three groups. The first specified the various ways in which assets of the debtor could pass to the Official Trustee, the second laid down the various duties of the Official Trustee in the administration, and the third described in chronological order the methods by which assets would pass from the Official Trustee. Subsequent Parts were concerned with arrangements with creditors apart from insolvency proceedings, modifications of the earlier provisions in special cases, administration of the estates of deceased insolvents, and supplemental provisions. Most Bills of any size require supplemental provisions dealing with such matters as interpretation, the making of regulations, repeals and commencement. These machinery clauses are now put at the end of the Bill so that the more important matters may come first, the former practice of putting them at the beginning having been abandoned in 1960. This was a reversion to the principle advocated by the earliest of the British Parliamentary Counsel, Lord Thring, who said

> The Bill should be clear and should state at the very commencement the important principle of the measure and the greatest pains should be taken to separate the material from the comparatively immaterial provisions."[1]

Titles given to Parts of Bills, and cross-headings separating groups of clauses, " are intended for convenience of reference only and do not form part of the enactment ".[2]

Sidenotes

Every clause is required by Standing Order 56 to have annexed in the margin a sidenote giving a short indication of its contents. It is not, however, correct to give sidenotes to subsections of a clause, since these are distracting and take away from the unity of the clause as expressed in its sidenote. The sidenote does not form part of the Bill. It is for convenience of reference only and is not to be used as an aid to construction.[3] It should be so worded as to provide a very brief but comprehensive description of the contents of the clause, and it is a good practice to compose the sidenote as soon as the clause is drafted, if not before. Difficulty in finding a suitable sidenote may indicate that too much

---

[1] *Practical Legislation* (John Murray) 1902, p. 8.
[2] Interpretation Act, 1960 (C.A. 4), s. 4.
[3] *Ibid.*

has been put into one clause. If amendments made during the passage of the Bill affect the correctness of the sidenote, it is suitably altered by the Clerk after consulting the draftsman. To avoid confusion the same sidenote should not be used for more than one clause of the Bill.

Where clauses have been divided up into groups the sidenote will be worded on the assumption that the relevant cross-heading has been read. For example, the Presidential Elections Act, 1960 (Act 1) consists of fourteen sections divided into six groups by cross-headings. One cross-heading reads " Dissolution Elections " and the sidenote of the first section in it is " Preferences ". Some draftsmen might have preferred not to use cross-headings but the sidenote would then have had to be expanded to read " Preferences in dissolution elections ".

It is a mistake to try and make the sidenote a precis of the effect of the clause. It should be in telegraphic form, omitting as many verbs as is consonant with its making sense. Where the clause is very short, every effort should be made to keep down the length of the sidenote. There have been cases where the sidenote has been longer than the clause! Apart from its absurdity, this leads to a distracting gap between one clause and the next, since the sidenote may take up several more lines of print than the clause. The greatest care must be taken to ensure that the sidenote is not in any way inconsistent with the clause, since this can only cause confusion.

Schedules

Schedules contain matter which because of its length cannot be conveniently embodied in the clauses of the Bill and which is of relatively minor importance. Matter of major importance should only be included in a Schedule in special cases, as for example, where an Act is to be passed to confirm a treaty. The body of the Act will be very brief and the treaty will be contained in a Schedule to it.

Where a Bill contains repeals exceeding two or three in number it is the practice to include a Schedule of repeals. This Schedule should be comprehensive, that is it should include all repeals effected by the Bill even if some have been included in the body of the Bill already. This will have been done if the repeals are of such importance that it is necessary to place them in a prominent position. Where this double repeal is to be effected, it is the practice in England to say in the body of the Bill that the enactment in question shall " cease to have effect ", and then repeal it by means of the repeal Schedule. The repeal Schedule should not contain any repeal that is not either consequential on some provision in the Bill or of minor importance, *e.g.* the repeal of a spent enactment. It is the practice to place the repeal Schedule at the end of the Schedules. Where numerous amendments are made to other enactments they are often embodied in a Schedule. Again, these may repeat amendments already made in the body of the Bill and should in any case be consequential or minor.

It was formerly the practice in England to include in a Schedule any forms required to be used in the administration of an Act. This practice has become obsolete: it is much better to give power to prescribe forms by statutory instrument, since this enables alterations to be readily made and keeps down the bulk of the Statute Book.

Similar principles are used in the drafting of Schedules to those mentioned above for clauses. The subdivisions of a Schedule are known as paragraphs, and a lengthy Schedule may be arranged in Parts or in groups of paragraphs under cross-headings. A Schedule is made effective by an appropriate reference to it in one of the clauses, although if such a reference were accidentally omitted the Schedule could not be ignored since it forms part of the Bill.[1]

Punctuation

Punctuation forms part of a Bill or Act and may be used as an aid to its construction.[2]

2. Preparation of Bills

In the discussion of legislative functionaries in the previous chapter, we have touched upon various aspects of the initiation and preparation of Parliamentary Bills. We will now describe the process in chronological order, taking first a typical departmental Bill and then mentioning some of the differences that may arise in the case of other types of Bill. The stage before introduction into Parliament may be subdivided as follows:

    (a) initiation of the legislative proposal;

    (b) obtaining Cabinet approval in principle;

    (c) preparation of drafting instructions;

---

[1] Acts of Parliament Act, 1960 (C.A. 7), s. 3.
[2] Interpretation Act, 1960 (C.A. 4), s. 3.

(d) settlement of draft Bill;
(e) obtaining Cabinet approval of draft Bill and consent to introduction;
(f) publication of draft Bill.

Initiation of the legislative proposal

There are numerous ways in which a decision to legislate may originate, but the beginnings will usually be found within one particular Ministry or Department. The Minister may start the ball rolling on his own initiative, or he may be prompted by someone else—perhaps the President or a fellow Minister, or some departmental official. Occasionally the initiative will come from representations made by some person or body outside the circle of Government altogether. However this may be, responsibility for the Bill must be assumed by some Minister. The matter is governed by administrative instructions issued under the Civil Service Act, which provide that where proposals for legislation are initiated within a Ministry they are the responsibility of the Minister holding the portfolio for the Ministry, but that where they are initiated within a special Department they are the responsibility of the Minister for Presidential Affairs, who must be approached by the Head of Department with a view to obtaining his decision as to whether the legislation is necessary. In either case interested persons and bodies are to be consulted wherever possible.[1]

Cabinet approval in principle

Having decided that new or amending legislation by Act of Parliament is necessary, the Minister must seek the approval of his Cabinet colleagues to the principles of the proposed legislation. This is done by the submission of a memorandum prepared by the administrative official in charge of the project. This sets out the principles of the policy intended to be carried into effect by the proposed Bill and the reasons why it is considered necessary, but should not enter on the detailed changes in existing law which will be needed. A draft of the memorandum is required to be sent in advance to the Attorney-General's department so that Parliamentary Counsel may advise on whether an Act of Parliament is in fact necessary in order to achieve the objects desired,

---

[1] *Administrative Instructions on the Preparation of Legislation*, Accra, 1961, para. 1 (1), (2).

and on other legal aspects of the proposal.[1] The memorandum must state the recommended priority of the Bill, for which purpose there are four categories providing respectively for introduction at the current meeting, the next meeting, the next but one, or some later time.[2] If the Cabinet approve the Bill in principle, they will normally adopt the Minister's view as to its priority, and the Bill will then take its appropriate place in the legislative programme, subject to such recommendations as may later be made by the Legislation Committee.[3] Administrative instructions provide:

> " Legislation which is not included in the programme may be introduced during the Meeting, with the approval of the Cabinet, if the need should arise, but this should as far as possible be avoided, since in such cases there is seldom time for full consideration of the drafting of the Bill. Hasty and ill-considered legislation is likely to contain errors which may interfere with its intended working and bring the law into disrepute."[4]

Drafting instructions

Where Cabinet approval in principle is given, the Cabinet Office notify the Department concerned and also the Attorney-General's Department. It is then the duty of the head of the Ministry or Department responsible for the Bill to prepare drafting instructions for Parliamentary Counsel. Much will depend on the thoroughness with which this is done. In the words of Lord Thring,

> " The sum of the whole matter is this, that to prepare a good Bill the draftsman must receive sufficient instructions, but they will necessarily be short, and he must exercise a very large discretion in filling up the gaps."[5]

Drafting instructions are required to contain full details of the policy intended to be carried into effect by the Bill and must refer to the enactments (if any) proposed to be repealed or amended. The priority as fixed by the Cabinet must also be stated.[6] It is important that no attempt be made to present the instructions

---

[1] *Administrative Instructions on the Preparation of Legislation*, para. 1 (4).
[2] *Ibid.*, para. 1 (3).
[3] See p. 335, *ante.*
[4] *Administrative Instructions on the Preparation of Legislation*, para. 4 (2).
[5] *Practical Legislation*, John Murray, 1902, p. 8.
[6] *Administrative Instructions on the Preparation of Legislation*, para. 3 (1).

in the form of draft clauses, since the draftsman will best understand what he has to do if the policy is described in ordinary language.[1] Drafting instructions are required to be accompanied by any relevant memoranda, reports of committees, and other material which may be useful to the draftsman.[2]

Settlement of draft Bill

With a Bill of any complexity, the process of settling the draft for submission to Cabinet will fall into two stages: the period before and the period after the production of the first draft. On the initial reading of his instructions the draftsman, coming to the subject with a fresh mind, will form some valuable first impressions. A particular proposal may strike him as unworkable or unnecessary, or it may be inconsistent with something elsewhere in the instructions or in conflict with established legal principles. There may be omissions or obscurities which he cannot clear up himself. A complicated scheme may be suggested for achieving an object which could be gained more simply. A proposal may affect the work of another Department, which apparently has not been consulted. The draftsman will do well to note down these first impressions immediately, and after further consideration of the instructions and any accompanying material he will decide whether he can proceed with the preparation of the Bill or whether he must ask for additional information. In the latter case a letter or telephone call may elicit what is required, but more often a meeting with officials of the instructing Ministry and other persons concerned will be necessary. This may last an hour or two, or, in extreme cases, may go on for several days while the details of the Bill are hammered out in discussion. The draftsman should always resist pressure to begin drafting before the policy is clear and definite. He may be asked to provide alternative drafts to help those in charge of policy to make up their minds, but wherever possible such requests should be refused. They are usually an excuse for procrastination, since it is nearly always much easier to decide between alternative lines of policy when they are expressed in ordinary language rather than the more formal phrases demanded by the law.

Having elicited the information he requires from those instructing him and having made a thorough examination of all

---

[1] See Driedger, *op. cit.*, pp. xvi–xvii.
[2] *Administrative Instructions on the Preparation of Legislation*, para. 3 (2).

existing laws which will be affected by the proposed Bill or otherwise have a bearing on it, the draftsman is in a position to begin work on the draft. With all but the simplest Bills it is first necessary to draw up a scheme of arrangement. The principles governing the arrangement of a Bill have been discussed in the previous section of this chapter, and here we need hardly do more than emphasize the crucial importance of working out, in advance of actual drafting, a proper legislative structure. The draftsman must decide whether the Bill is to be divided into Parts, and if so, the subject-matter of each Part. He must work out the approximate order of the clauses, and the material to be contained in each. The result will resemble the Arrangement of Clauses which will subsequently appear at the beginning of the Bill, although in some cases it may be helpful to present it in the form of Heads of a Bill.[1] The scheme of arrangement will normally be for the sole use of the draftsman, but if its preparation throws up problems not seen earlier, it may form a useful basis for further discussion with instructing officials.

When he embarks on actual drafting, the draftsman will often have second thoughts about his scheme of arrangement. He should not regard it as sacrosanct, but make adjustments as they appear necessary. He may in some cases be forced to the conclusion that his original arrangement is so defective that it should be scrapped. He should not hesitate to scrap it and work out another one—it will be much more difficult to do so once the first draft of the Bill has been completed.

The first draft is normally printed by the Government Printer on the instructions of Parliamentary Counsel, who sends copies to the Ministry concerned and any other interested body. Since the draft is confidential, it will not normally be sent to persons outside the public service. There has been a tendency to assume that when a legislative proposal has been " put into legal language " by Parliamentary Counsel it can be accepted without examination. The new administrative instructions frown upon this facile view:

> " It is the duty of all persons to whom a draft Bill is sent to scrutinise the Bill with care to make sure that it gives effect to the policy desired. It should not be assumed that, because a Bill has been drafted by Parliamentary Counsel, it does not require scrutiny in this way. It may happen that there has been

---

[1] For the meaning of this expression, and many others used in legislation, see the glossary set out in Appendix B, p. 491, *post.*

some misunderstanding over the legislative intent, or there may be other reasons calling for corrections in the draft."[1]

Scrutiny of the first draft, both by instructing officials and the draftsman himself, will usually bring to light points on which some amendment is needed. Any formal errors arising from typing and printing will also have to be put right. With simple Bills these matters can be dealt with by corrections to the proof when it is returned for the printing of Cabinet copies. In other cases it may be necessary to hold further meetings to discuss the draft and work out the necessary changes. Where a major Bill is concerned, the process may have to be repeated through several successive drafts—perhaps amounting to a dozen or more. Alterations to the text of the draft Bill must in no circumstances be made otherwise than by Parliamentary Counsel.[2]

Cabinet approval of draft Bill

When the form of the Bill has been agreed between the Ministry concerned and Parliamentary Counsel, the Minister responsible will submit it to the Cabinet for final approval and seek permission to introduce the Bill into the National Assembly.[3]

In most cases a draft of the explanatory memorandum required by Standing Order 55 to appear on the front of the Bill will be submitted to Cabinet at the same time. Although the memorandum is the responsibility of the sponsoring Minister, he often likes to obtain the approval of his colleagues to its wording. The memorandum is drafted by the appropriate administrative official, but Parliamentary Counsel should be consulted to ensure that it correctly describes the contents of the Bill.[4]

Publication of draft Bill

When the Cabinet have given permission for the introduction of a Bill, the draft is normally published as a supplement to the following Friday's *Gazette* so that Standing Order 58 may be complied with.[5] It is the duty of the sponsoring Ministry to arrange for this, although Parliamentary Counsel has the responsibility of checking the proof of the *Gazette* copy.[6] Administrative instructions point out:

---

[1] *Administrative Instructions on the Preparation of Legislation*, para. 5 (3).
[2] *Ibid.*
[3] *Ibid.*, para. 7 (1).
[4] *Ibid.*, para. 6.
[5] See p. 371, *post.*
[6] *Administrative Instructions on the Preparation of Legislation*, para. 8 (2).

" It is sometimes the case that a Bill prepared at the instance of one Ministry and designed for a particular purpose affects other Ministries, or is one to which an amendment could be moved to deal with minor points with which other Ministries are concerned. It is important therefore that all Ministries should study Bills published in the *Gazette*, as well as paying careful attention to the legislative programme generally."[1]

Special cases

The procedure outlined above is sometimes departed from in various respects. The types of Bill which most often give rise to these departures are mentioned below. In addition it must be pointed out that the desire of the Government for extreme haste in legislation often makes it difficult to conform to all aspects of the procedure.

Cabinet Bills.—As mentioned in the previous chapter, the Cabinet sometimes orders legislation to be prepared on its own initiative and without previous consideration.[2] Where this happens much of the normal procedure is by-passed. There will be no memorandum seeking approval in principle, and there are unlikely to be any drafting instructions beyond the sentence or two recording the Cabinet decision in the minutes. The first draft will probably be the final draft, and as often as not the Bill will not be published, but will be introduced on a certificate of urgency and passed through all its stages in one day.

Law Reform Bills.—Consolidation Bills, Bills re-enacting English statutes of general application and other law reform Bills originate in the Attorney-General's Department. Approval in principle is not sought for individual Bills, since the Cabinet has given general approval to the law reform programme. No drafting instructions are prepared; the draftsman, as it were, instructs himself. The draft is, however, sent out to interested departments, who may see an opportunity for making reforms they have long sought and put forward appropriate suggestions. Since these Bills are of peculiarly legal interest, consultations often take place with the judges, the Bar Council, and the Law School.

Committee Bills.—Ghana is familiar with the practice of appointing an expert committee to advise on the content of a Bill

---

[1] *Administrative Instructions on the Preparation of Legislation*, para. 8 (4).
[2] See p. 334, *ante*.

AA

required to deal with a specialised subject. The degree of formality varies. Sometimes a commission of enquiry is set up with all the ceremony described in the previous chapter.[1] In other cases a working-party of officials is convened, or an expert from abroad is obtained to examine the problem and tender his advice. Almost always Cabinet approval will have been obtained before the committee begins work, and the committee tends to occupy the role of the administrative officials in the process of Bill-preparation. It instructs the draftsman, criticizes his draft and works out with him the details of the Bill which is to be included in its report. Alternatively the committee omits any draft legislation from its report but makes recommendations which, if the report is adopted, will later form the basis for drafting instructions. In rare cases the committee may draft a Bill itself, but unless Parliamentary Counsel is a member of the committee this is to be discouraged, since the result, even if well done, is likely to be out of line with normal drafting practice in Ghana, and to require extensive revision by Parliamentary Counsel before it can be enacted.

3. THE PASSAGE OF A BILL

The National Assembly is left to decide for itself the procedure for the introduction, consideration, amendment and passing of Parliamentary Bills. The procedure is laid down by the Standing Orders made by the Assembly under s. 14 of the National Assembly Act, 1961 (Act 86). In theory, Bills are divided for the purpose of their passage through the Assembly into two categories, public Bills and private Bills; and the category of public Bills is subdivided into Government Bills, private Member's Bills and hybrid Bills. In practice all Bills are Government Bills. The various types may be defined as follows:

Public Bill.—Any Bill which is not a private Bill.

Private Bill.—A Bill which is introduced by a private Member and of which the *sole* purpose is " to affect or benefit some particular person, association or corporate body ".[2]

Government Bill.—A Bill introduced by a Minister, a Ministerial Secretary or the Parliamentary Secretary.

---

[1] See p. 346, *ante.*
[2] See Standing Order 69.

Private Member's Bill.—A public Bill (not being a hybrid Bill) which is introduced by a private Member.

Hybrid Bill.—A Bill which is introduced by a private Member and of which the purpose is in part the same as that of a private Bill, but which also has some public purpose.

Standing Order 69 requires additional publicity to be given to a private or hybrid Bill before introduction and provides that after second reading it shall stand referred to a select committee, before whom any person affected may appear and make representations. In other respects the procedure for such Bills is the same as for a private Member's Bill, and they will not be further referred to here.[1]

Introduction of Bills

Leave of the Assembly is required for the introduction of a private Member's Bill, but Government Bills are introduced without leave.[2] Except where the Government introduce a Bill on a certificate of urgency, no Bill can be introduced and no motion for leave to introduce a Bill can be made unless certain requirements as to publication have been satisfied.

Publication.—The text of the Bill must have been published as a supplement to an ordinary issue of the *Gazette* within a specified period.[3] The period normally begins with the termination of the previous meeting of the Assembly and ends seven days before the day on which the Bill is to be introduced or the motion made for leave to introduce. To allow for the case where a meeting begins shortly after the end of the previous meeting it is permissible to treat the period as beginning one month before the date of introduction or motion. The text of the Bill as introduced need not be exactly the same as the published text—variations are permitted if, in the opinion of the Clerk of the Assembly, they are merely of a trival or drafting character.[4]

Certificate of Urgency.—Every Government finds it necessary occasionally to pass legislation without taking time to give advance publicity. In Ghana this could be done merely by suspending the relevant Standing Order, but the Assembly has preferred

---

[1] The British procedure requiring Government Bills which affect particular individuals or bodies to be treated as hybrid is not followed in Ghana.

[2] Standing Order 58 (3).

[3] Ordinary issues of the *Gazette* are published weekly on Fridays.

[4] Standing Order 58 (1).

to lay down a special procedure. The President signs a certificate to the effect that the Bill is required to be passed into law without delay. The certificate is sent to the Speaker (who lays it before the Assembly) and operates to dispense with the need for prior publication of the Bill. It also enables the Bill to be passed through all its stages in one day. Administrative instructions sound the following warning:

> " It is emphasized that this procedure for the introduction of a Bill is for use in emergency only and is to be avoided as much as possible. In order to achieve its purpose of giving effect to Government policies, legislation needs to be prepared with care and due consideration. Apart from its other drawbacks, legislation put through in haste and without adequate publicity is likely to prove defective."[1]

Nevertheless approximately half the Bills put through in the first year of the Republic were introduced under a certificate of urgency.

Memorandum.—Standing Order 55 requires every Bill to be accompanied by a memorandum explaining the main features of the Bill. This is signed by the Minister or other Member introducing the Bill and printed at the front of it. The memorandum should state the effect of the principal provisions and give reasons for the proposal to enact them. In Colonial times it was known as the statement of objects and reasons and appeared at the back of the Bill.

Mode of Introduction.—At the stage in the day's business set aside for the presentation of Bills, the Speaker calls successively each Member in whose name a Bill stands on the order paper. As each Member's name is called he rises in his place and bows to the Chair, whereupon the Clerk of the Assembly reads aloud the long title of the Bill. This ceremony constitutes both the introduction and first reading of the Bill. Copies of the Bill printed on blue paper are then circulated among the members, and if the Bill has not already been published in the *Gazette* it must be so published unless it is to be put through all its stages on that day.[2]

Second reading

The proceedings on second reading provide the House with its

---

[1] *Administrative Instructions on the Preparation of Legislation*, para. 9 (3).
[2] Standing Order 58 (5), (6).

first opportunity to get to grips with the Bill. The Member in charge of the Bill moves that it " be now read a second time " and delivers a speech explaining the purpose of the Bill.[1] Members are then free to debate " the principle and general merits " of the Bill, but at this stage they are not allowed to move amendments to it.[2] They may, however, move to amend the motion for second reading if they do not wish the Bill to proceed further. There are two ways of doing this. The first is to seek to amend the motion so that it reads " That the . . . Bill be rejected ". The other is to move a " reasoned amendment " to substitute words stating " the object and motive on which the opposition to the Bill is based ". These words must be strictly relevant to the Bill and not deal with its details.[3] If an amendment in either form is agreed to by the House, or if the original motion for second reading is lost, proceedings on the Bill lapse.

The second reading is the most important stage of a Bill's progress. If it is agreed to, the House is taken to have accepted the main policy of the Bill, though not its details. Although there remains another opportunity for rejecting the Bill, in practice further examination by the House will be directed to ensuring that the clauses of the Bill are apt to carry its policy into effect.

Detailed consideration of the Bill by the Assembly normally follows the second reading, but Standing Orders allow for the Bill to be referred at this stage to a select committee. This would allow a complex Bill to be examined in detail by a small number of Members who were specially interested in the subject or peculiarly qualified to discuss it. Since, however, the procedure is not used, it will not be further discussed here.[4]

Consideration stage

Where a Bill has been read a second time and has not been referred to a select committee, it is required to pass through the consideration stage in the Assembly. Until the advent of the Republic this was known as the committee stage, the Bill being referred to a committee of the whole House. Except where the Bill was introduced under a certificate of urgency, forty-eight

---

[1] In the case of a private Member's bill the motion must be seconded.
[2] Standing Order 59 (1).
[3] Standing Order 59 (3). For an illustration of a reasoned amendment see Appendix B, p. 495, *post*.
[4] For details of the procedure see Standing Orders 60, 63 and 65.

hours (excluding days when the Assembly is not sitting) must elapse between second reading and consideration.[1]

The purpose of the consideration stage is to enable the House to scrutinise each individual clause and other provision, to amend it if necessary, and to decide whether it shall form part of the Bill. New clauses and schedules may also be added. What members are not allowed to do is re-open discussion on the principle of the Bill.[2] The informality associated with the old committee stage remains, and Members may speak more than once to any question.[3]

The consideration stage begins with the first clause; the long title and any preamble are deferred to the end. The Clerk of the Assembly reads out the number of the clause and the sidenote, and members may then move amendments and discuss the details of the clause. If no one wishes to do either of these things, the Clerk proceeds to read the number and sidenote of the next clause, and so on until a clause is reached on which some Member rises to speak. When this happens the Speaker puts the motion, on the previous clauses not yet agreed to, " That clauses . . . to . . . [or it may merely be " clause . . ."] stand part of the Bill ". Where necessary, clauses may be taken in an order different from that in which they are arranged in the Bill.

An amendment may consist of the deletion of words in the Bill, or the insertion of further words, or the substitution of one set of words for another. In the case of substitution, two separate questions arise, namely whether the words proposed to be left out should stand part of the Bill and if not, whether the new words should be inserted. It is not in order to move an amendment to delete a whole clause: the correct procedure is to vote against the motion that the clause stand part of the Bill. A motion may be made to insert a new clause, and this will be considered when the existing clauses have been disposed of or, if more convenient, at the place where it is proposed to insert the new clause. A new clause is treated as if it were a newly-introduced Bill. It is given a formal first reading by the Clerk calling out the sidenote, immediately followed by a second reading, the consideration of any amendments proposed to it, and then the motion that it be added to the Bill. After the clauses have been considered, the same procedure is gone through with the Schedules, if any.

---

[1] Standing Order 61 (1).
[2] Standing Order 61 (2).
[3] Standing Order 42 (6).

Finally the House deals with any preambles and then the long title, which may require amendment to make it fit changes made in the body of the Bill.[1]

Third reading

Not less than twenty-four hours after the completion of the consideration stage (excluding any day on which the Assembly is not sitting) the Member in charge of the Bill may move that the Bill " be now read a third time ". No interval is necessary where the Bill was introduced under a certificate of urgency. The proceedings on third reading are usually formal and no amendments to the Bill may be moved. If last-minute amendments are thought necessary, they can be made after the passage of a motion, at any time before a Member rises to move the third reading, that the Bill, or the relevant portion of it, do pass through a second consideration stage.

The motion to give the Bill a third reading is subject to the same type of amendment as is described above in the case of second reading. In practice, however, such amendments are rarely moved, and the practice is for Bills to be given a third reading without debate. Where the motion for third reading is agreed to, the Clerk reads out the long title and the Bill is then deemed to have been read the third time and passed.[2]

Withdrawal of Bills

Either before the commencement of public business or at the commencement of any stage of a Bill, the Member in charge of a Bill may make a motion without notice for its withdrawal.[3] The same result can be achieved by refraining from moving the second or third reading, and the Bill will then lapse at the end of the session. A Government Bill will not be withdrawn, and major amendments will not be made to it, without the approval of the Cabinet. Where sudden opposition arises in the House, however, the Minister in charge of a Bill may on his own initiative move that proceedings on the Bill be suspended, and in such cases it sometimes happens that the proceedings are not resumed.

4. THE PRESIDENT'S ASSENT

The procedure which is to be followed when a Bill has been passed by the National Assembly is laid down by the Acts of

---

[1] The procedure on consideration is regulated by Standing Order 62.
[2] Standing Order 66.
[3] Standing Order 67.

Parliament Act, 1960 (C.A. 7). The Clerk of the Assembly is required to send the text of the Bill as passed to the Government Printer, who must print four copies " on vellum or on paper of enduring quality ".[1] These are known as presentation copies, since they are to be presented to the President for his assent. The only change made in printing is the substitution for the words " A Bill " at the beginning, of the words " Act of the Parliament of the Republic of Ghana ". The printer also inserts at the end of the presentation copies the formulas for authentication and assent which are mentioned below.

When the Clerk receives the presentation copies from the printer he is required to make a careful comparison of them with the text of the Bill, and if he finds them to be correct he must sign on each a statement to that effect in the prescribed form, and insert the date of authentication.[2] In the case of a Bill which contained an amendment to any entrenched provision of the Constitution, the Clerk would at this stage have to submit the presentation copies to the Speaker so that he could certify that power to pass the Bill had been conferred on Parliament in the manner provided by art. 20(2) of the Constitution.[3]

The Clerk next takes the four presentation copies to the President's office for assent. Except in cases of urgency he usually waits to do this until he has two or three Bills which can be dealt with at the same time. There is no ceremony of assent, as there is in the case of the Royal Assent to Bills in the United Kingdom Parliament.[4] Ghana continues the tradition of informality inaugurated in the days of the Governor-General. The Clerk waits

---

[1] Acts of Parliament Act, 1960 (C.A. 7), s. 5 (1).
[2] *Ibid.*, s. 5 (2). The form is set out in Part I of the Schedule to the Act.
[3] Acts of Parliament Act, 1960 (C.A. 7), s. 5 (3).
[4] Sir Courtenay Ilbert described the British ceremony as follows: " The ceremony dates from Plantagenet times, and takes place in the House of Lords. The King is represented by Lords' Commissioners, who sit in front of the throne, on a row of arm-chairs, arrayed in scarlet robes and little cocked hats. . . . At the bar of the House stands the Speaker of the House of Commons, who has been summoned from that House. Behind him stand such Members of the House of Commons as have followed him through the lobbies. A Clerk of the House of Lords reads out, in a sonorous voice, the Commission which authorizes the assent to be given. The Clerk of the Crown at one side of the table reads out the title of each Bill. The Clerk of the Parliaments on the other side, making profound obeisances, pronounces the Norman-French formula by which the King's assent is signified: ' Little Peddlington Electricity Supply Act '. ' Le Roy le veult.' Between the two voices six centuries lie ": *Parliament*, p. 75.

(sometimes for quite a long time) until the President has a few moments free. He then enters the President's room and hands the presentation copies to one of the President's staff, who impresses the Presidential seal on each. On the signing by the President of the Statement of Assent on the first of the four copies the Bill becomes an Act.[1] Immediately after the signing, and the insertion by the President of the date of assent, the Clerk inserts the number of the Act in words at the beginning.[2] The same procedure is then followed with the remaining three copies.

The President is of course entitled to refuse assent to the whole or any portion of a Bill.[3] Total refusal has not yet occurred, and is unlikely unless on a sudden change of Government policy after the Assembly has passed a Bill. There has, however, been one instance of partial refusal. In 1959 the Government decided to encourage the tourist industry by enabling licences to be granted to casino operators. As an experiment a licence was granted in June, 1960 for the opening of " Casino Africa " in Accra's leading hotel, the Ambassador. In the Government's view the experiment was not a success and after a few months the licence was revoked. There being some doubt as to whether any of the grounds for revocation specified in the enabling Act were satisfied, the Government later introduced a Bill, which was passed by the Assembly, to correct this.[4] The Bill as passed contained two clauses only. The first added as a ground for revoking a casino licence the case where the Minister was satisfied that it was in the public interest to do so. The second made the Bill retrospective to July 1, 1960, thus validating the revocation of the licence of " Casino Africa ". After the Bill was passed the Government had second thoughts however, and assent was given only to clause 1 and refused to clause 2.[5]

In the case of partial assent a special form of Statement of Assent is used,[6] and the Clerk is required to make in each presentation copy " such deletions, and such amendments of figures, punctuation and grammar " as may be necessary for the purpose of the conversion into an Act of the part of the Bill which has

---

[1] Acts of Parliament Act, 1960 (C.A. 7), s. 6 (3).
[2] *Ibid.*, s. 7 (2). Occasionally the delay in obtaining access to the President is so great that the Clerk has to leave the presentation copies to be signed later, having first numbered them.
[3] See pp. 151–2, *ante*.
[4] Parl. Deb. Official Report, Vol. 21, cols. 152–163.
[5] Casino Licensing (Amendment) Act, 1960 (Act 24).
[6] Acts of Parliament Act, 1960 (C.A. 7), Schedule, Part IV.

received assent.[1] The Bill is thereafter deemed to have been passed as so altered.[2]

The Act is now in its complete and final form, and takes its place in the series of Acts of the Republican Parliament. The numbering of these runs consecutively from the first Republican Act, which was the Presidential Elections Act, 1960. It does not begin afresh at the commencement of a calendar year, a new Parliament or any other period.[3] This means that for ordinary purposes an Act can be referred to simply as " Act 46 " just as an Ordinance in the collected edition of the Laws of the Gold Coast can be referred to simply as " Cap. 46 "—a matter of some convenience, particularly where the short title is not as short as it might be.

Where the procedure outlined above purports to have been followed in relation to presentation copies of an Act, the copies are deemed to be the original copies of the Act and are conclusive evidence of the terms of the Act, its number and the date of assent.[4] The President retains one of the original copies. Two others are placed in the custody of the Chief Justice and the Speaker respectively, while the fourth is deposited in the national archives.[5]

Publication

The final stage is the publication of the Act. The responsibility for this is placed upon the Government Printer, who must publish as soon as may be after the President's assent has been signified. The Act is not published exactly in the form taken by the original copies. It would be wasteful and distracting to reproduce in every published copy the authentication statement and the Statement of Assent. These are accordingly authorised to be omitted. The date of assent, which normally indicates the commencement of the Act, cannot however be omitted without causing inconvenience. It is therefore inserted by the Government Printer after the long title. In the case of an Act amending the entrenched

---

[1] The draftsman should be consulted before these changes are made.

[2] Acts of Parliament Act, 1960 (C.A. 7), s. 6 (2).

[3] Acts of Parliament Act, 1960 (C.A. 7), s. 7 (1).

[4] *Ibid.*, s. 8 (1). In case it is thought odd to refer to something as an " original copy " it should be pointed out that an Act has an existence apart from any document setting out its terms, which is necessarily only a copy of the Act. An Act is not repealed by destroying all existing copies of it.

[5] *Ibid.*, s. 8 (2).

provisions of the Constitution, the Speaker's certificate is also required to be included.[1] The published copies are *prima facie* evidence of the terms of the Act, its number and the date of assent.[2]

Commencement

An Act comes into force at midnight on the day of assent, unless the Act itself otherwise provides.[3] It will otherwise provide where for some reason it is desired to make the Act retrospective or where the time is not ripe for it to be brought into operation.[4] Retrospective Acts are generally frowned upon as tending to contravene the rule of law, but they are not uncommon in Ghana. From a technical standpoint it is rarely necessary to deem an Act to have come into force at some earlier date, since the desired result can often be more satisfactorily obtained by dealing expressly with the past cases. A legislative scheme designed to be acted on in the future by persons already aware of its provisions will not always fit past cases where persons were necessarily acting in ignorance of them.

There is one way in which people can be made to act in accordance with new legislation before it has been enacted. This is by making it retrospective to the date of publication of the Bill. In the case for example of the Exchange Control Act, 1961 (Act 71), which extended Ghana's exchange control restrictions to countries within the sterling area, there was an awkward problem of timing. It was thought desirable to enable banks, commercial concerns and other persons affected to study the new scheme generally for a period before it was enacted. Yet there were certain transactions brought under control by it which, if not restricted as soon as it was known about, would inevitably be carried out in large numbers to the detriment of Ghana's currency reserves. The solution was to publish the Bill with a clause giving its commencement as the date of publication, and to include in the memorandum a warning of the consequences of carrying out the forbidden transactions after that date.

Where an Act is passed but the time is not yet ripe for it to come into operation, there are two ways of providing for its

---

[1] Acts of Parliament Act, 1960 (C.A. 7), s. 9.
[2] *Ibid.*, s. 10.
[3] *Ibid.*, s. 11 (1).
[4] Although the following discussion is in terms of Acts as a whole, what is said applies equally to portions of Acts.

commencement. Either a definite date may be specified in the Act or the Act may empower the President or a Minister to bring it into force by legislative instrument.[1] The second method is more flexible but occasionally leads to an enactment being left high and dry because after some time has elapsed it no longer seems suitable or even because no one has remembered to do anything about it.[2]

---

[1] It may be asked how such a power can be effectively given by an Act which *ex hypothesi* has not come into operation. Section 11 (2) of the Acts of Parliament Act, 1960 (C.A. 7) makes the power effective and avoids refined arguments of the type which have given some trouble in England.

[2] The former was the fate of the Road Transport Licensing Ordinance (Cap. 230), originally enacted in 1946 and still inoperative but unrepealed. Total forgetfulness occurred over the Spirits (Distillation and Licensing) Act, 1959 (No. 80); and s. 9 of the Akpeteshi Act, 1961 (Act 77) is perhaps worth quoting in full as showing the trouble that can be caused by spirits:—

" 9. (1) In consequence of the provisions of this Act the following enactments are hereby repealed—

    (a) the Excise (Amendment) Ordinance, 1957 (No. 38) (which shall be deemed not to have amended the Excise Ordinance 1953 (No. 31));

    (b) the Excise (Amendment) Act, 1958 (No. 5) (which shall be deemed never to have had any effect at all); and

    (c) the Spirits (Distillation and Licensing) Act, 1959 (No. 80) (which was never brought into operation).

(2) The Excise (Spirits) Regulations, 1958 (L.N. 13 of 1959) are hereby revoked and shall be deemed never to have been made."

CHAPTER 9

LEGISLATIVE METHODS: STATUTORY INSTRUMENTS

The nature of statutory instruments, and their division into legislative and executive instruments, have been described in Chapter 6.[1] We will now explain the way in which a statutory instrument is made and comes into force, beginning, as in the case of Acts of Parliament in the previous chapter, with an account of its structure. The structure will be the same whether the instrument is legislative or executive.

1. THE STRUCTURE OF A STATUTORY INSTRUMENT

Short title

Every statutory instrument is required to bear at the head a short title, but must not include any other provision conferring a short title.[2] As with Acts, the former practice of including a paragraph conferring a short title in the body of each instrument was abandoned in 1960. It is sufficient for all purposes to cite an instrument by its short title.[3] If, as has occasionally happened, a mistake is found to have been made in the short title the authority by whom the instrument was made may by notice in the *Gazette* correct the title, which must thereafter be cited in its corrected form.[4]

Much of what has been said in the previous chapter about the short title of a Bill[5] applies *mutatis mutandis* to statutory instruments, and it is only necessary to add that the ending of the short title varies according to the nature of the instrument. If the instrument is in the form of regulations, rules or byelaws, or is an order, the title will be framed accordingly. In other cases the word instrument may be used. Usually, but not always, the title ends with the year in which the instrument is made.

---

[1] See pp. 262 *et seq., ante.*
[2] Statutory Instruments Rules, 1960 (L.I. 39), r. 2.
[3] Statutory Instruments Act, 1959 (No. 52), s. 15 (1).
[4] *Ibid.*, s. 15 (2).
[5] See pp. 350 *et seq., ante.*

Unlike an Act of Parliament, a statutory instrument does not contain a long title.

Recital

Very often a power to make a statutory instrument can only be exercised if certain findings of fact have first been made. Thus a deportation order can only be made in respect of a person if he is found to be an alien and has been convicted of one of a specified class of offences or has been declared by the President to be a person whose presence in Ghana is not conducive to the public good. In such cases the instrument should begin with a recital stating that the necessary facts have been found.[1] This will help to counter any argument that the instrument was made in excess of the enabling power.

Apart from recitals of this type it may occasionally be useful to employ a recital in cases similar to those where a preamble is included in a Bill.[2]

Introductory words

Every statutory instrument must state the powers under which it is made. It is obviously necessary to give the reader particulars of the enabling Act, and the Statutory Instruments Rules lay down a common formula for this purpose.[3] To illustrate this we may take the introductory words of the Rules themselves—

" IN EXERCISE of the powers conferred on the Attorney-General by section 17 of the Statutory Instruments Act, 1959 (No. 52), these rules are made this 6th day of July, 1960."

It will be noticed that the introductory words convey the following information—

(i) the name of the enabling enactment;
(ii) the name of the authority on whom power to make the instrument is conferred;[4]
(iii) the date on which the instrument is made.

Where the power is exercisable by the named authority only with the approval or consent, or after consultation with, some other authority the introductory words embody the statement that the approval or consent has been given or that the consultation has taken place, as the case may be.

---

[1] Statutory Instruments Rules, 1960 (L.I. 39), r. 4.
[2] See p. 354, *ante*.
[3] Statutory Instruments Rules, 1960 (L.I. 39), r. 3.
[4] This must correspond exactly with the name as given in the enabling enactment: Statutory Instruments Rules, 1960 (L.I. 39), rule 3 (2).

Body of the instrument

Where an instrument contains two or more substantive provisions the body of it is divided up in much the same way as that of an Act of Parliament. A subdivision is not known as a section however, but as a regulation, rule, article or paragraph, or otherwise according to the nature of the instrument. For convenience, the word paragraph will be used here to refer to a subdivision of this kind.[1]

With the exception of the material relating to the passage of a Bill through Parliament, all that is said in the previous chapter with regard to clauses of a Bill applies in substance to the paragraphs of a statutory instrument.[2] It is unnecessary to repeat it here, but mention should perhaps be made of the express rule that, as with Bills, " formal provisions relating to interpretation, commencement or other matters should normally be placed at the end of the instrument ".[3]

Sidenotes

It is laid down that where a statutory instrument contains two or more paragraphs each should be numbered and given a sidenote briefly describing it. Sidenotes may, however, be dispensed with where there are only two or three short paragraphs.[4] Again, the provisions of the previous chapter relating to sidenotes of clauses apply with necessary modifications to statutory instruments, and will not be repeated here.[5]

Schedules

Schedules may be annexed to statutory instruments in the same way as to Bills.[6] Whereas, however, forms are nowadays seldom scheduled to a Bill they are frequently scheduled to statutory instruments. Indeed, the sole purpose of a statutory instrument may be to prescribe forms for use in the administration of the principal Act.

Punctuation

Punctuation forms part of a statutory instrument and may be used as an aid to its construction.[7]

---

[1] *Cf.* r. 10 of the Statutory Instruments Rules, 1960 (L.I. 39).
[2] See pp. 355, *et seq.*, *ante.*
[3] Statutory Instruments Rules, 1960 (L.I. 39), r. 8 (1).
[4] *Ibid.*, r. 5.
[5] See p. 361, *ante.*
[6] See p. 362, *ante.*
[7] Interpretation Act, 1960 (C.A. 4), s. 3.

Signature

A statutory instrument is made when it is signed by or on behalf of the authority having power to make it. The signature and description of the person making it must appear at the end of the instrument, that is after any Schedules that may be annexed to it.[1] The description may differ from that given in the enabling Act. If, for example, power to make an order is conferred on " the Minister responsible for Town and Country Planning " and responsibility for this subject is for the time being vested in the Minister of Works and Housing, the signature will be followed by the words " Minister of Works and Housing ".[2]

Special rules as to signature are laid down where power to make a statutory instrument is vested in the President or a Presidential Commission.[3]

2. PREPARATION OF STATUTORY INSTRUMENTS

Statutory instruments differ widely in their nature and there is no uniform procedure governing their preparation. The procedure will differ according to whether Cabinet approval is necessary or not, whether the instrument is to be drafted within the responsible department or by Parliamentary Counsel, and so on. Some instruments are of such importance that they are prepared in much the same way as Parliamentary Bills. Others are in common form and their actual preparation takes little time and trouble, although the political decisions on which they are based may be taken at Cabinet level.[4]

Initiation

The decision to make a statutory instrument is normally taken by the authority who has power to make it, although in some cases the Cabinet will order it to be made. Administrative instructions lay down that where it is proposed to make a statutory instrument it is the responsibility of the Minister concerned, subject to any directions given by the President, to decide whether Cabinet

---

[1] Statutory Instruments Rules, 1960 (L.I. 39), r. 9 (1).
[2] See Example D annexed to r. 9 (1) of the Statutory Instruments Rules, 1960 (L.I. 39) and *cf.* Example A annexed to r. 3.
[3] See *ibid.*, r. 9 (2)–(4) as amended by L.I. 73.
[4] An example of the former type is the Exchange Control Regulations, 1961 (L.I. 133), which were drafted in parallel with the parent Act. Many executive instruments, such as deportation, preventive detention and destoolment orders, are examples of the latter.

approval for the making of the instrument is necessary. Where Cabinet approval is considered necessary a memorandum asking for this must be submitted by the Minister to the Cabinet.[1]

Drafting

Legislative instruments are drafted by, or under the supervision of, Parliamentary Counsel. Except in cases of special difficulty, executive instruments are drafted by an administrative official within the appropriate Ministry or special Department.

Subject to any directions given by the Cabinet or the Minister responsible, it is for the official head of the Ministry or special department to decide whether a legislative instrument is to be drafted by Parliamentary Counsel. If it is, drafting instructions must be prepared in the same way as for a Bill and the details of the draft instrument will be worked out in similar fashion.[2] Where a legislative instrument has not been drafted by Parliamentary Counsel it must be submitted in draft to the Attorney-General's department, so that its validity and form may be checked before it is made.[3]

The principles governing the drafting of statutory instruments are for the most part the same as those governing the drafting of Bills. The subordinate nature of a statutory instrument gives rise to certain special rules however, apart from those mentioned in describing the structure of the instrument.

(1) Special care is needed to ensure that the instrument is not drafted in terms which go wider than the power conferred by the enabling Act. An *ultra vires* instrument is void in so far as it exceeds the power under which it purports to have been made.

(2) An enactment conferring power to make a statutory instrument is not to be taken to authorise the inclusion in the instrument of any provision amending, repealing or conflicting with any Act or Ordinance, except as may be expressly stated in the enactment conferring the said power.[4]

(3) A statutory instrument is to be construed as one with the Act under which it was made.[5] This rule makes it unnecessary

---

[1] *Administrative Instructions on the Preparation of Legislation*, para. 13.
[2] *Ibid.*, para. 14 (2). See pp. 365 *et seq., ante.*
[3] *Ibid.*, para. 14 (3).
[4] Statutory Instruments Act, 1959 (No. 52), s. 7.
[5] Interpretation Act, 1960 (C.A. 4), s. 21.

BB

to repeat in the instrument definitions contained in the Act.

(4) A single statutory instrument may be made by one authority under two or more separate powers, or by two or more authorities jointly under one or more separate powers vested in each of them. The powers must however be all of the same type, that is they must either all refer to legislative instruments or all refer to executive instruments, though it matters not if one power refers say to rules and another to regulations.[1]

(5) Even where the enabling Act does not confer power to create criminal offences, a statutory instrument may include penal provisions so long as the penalty imposed for any offence does not exceed a fine of £G100 or imprisonment for twelve months or both.[2]

3. MAKING OF STATUTORY INSTRUMENTS

There is no parallel in the case of statutory instruments to the complicated Parliamentary procedure by which a Bill becomes an Act. Indeed, except in certain rare cases which are described below, the National Assembly has nothing to do with the making of statutory instruments. It has played its part by examining and passing the Act which authorises the instrument to be made, and in doing so has agreed to delegate a portion of its legislative power to some other authority. The only point of similarity is that both an Act and a statutory instrument are brought into existence by the signing of a document.

As mentioned in the previous section, a statutory instrument is made when it is signed by or on behalf of the authority having power to make it, although it does not necessarily come into force immediately. The instrument may even be made before the commencement of the enabling Act. Section 6 of the Statutory Instruments Act provides:

" . . . a statutory instrument may be made under an enactment contained in any Act at any time after the passing of the Act notwithstanding that the said enactment has not come into operation."[3]

---

[1] Statutory Instruments Act, 1959 (No. 52), s. 8.
[2] *Ibid.*, s. 9.
[3] The reference to " passing " here refers to the giving of Presidential assent: a Bill is passed when it is given a third reading; an Act is passed at the moment when it comes into existence.

The purpose of this is to allow an Act which needs to be supplemented by delegated legislation to be brought into force at the same time as the necessary statutory instruments and not before. An instrument cannot actually come into operation before the enabling Act has done so.[1]

Publication

All legislative instruments are required to be published. In the case of executive instruments publication is at the discretion of the authority by whom the instrument is made, unless specific directions as to publication are given in the enabling Act.[2] Failure to publish a legislative instrument, or to comply with any specific directions as to the publication of an executive instrument, does not invalidate the instrument but the National Assembly may at any time resolve that the instrument shall be deemed never to have come into operation or shall be deemed to be revoked.[3]

Commencement

Where a statutory instrument is silent about the date of its commencement the position differs according to whether it is legislative or executive. Subject to an exception mentioned below, if it is executive in character the instrument will come into operation on the date on which it is is made, but if it is legislative its commencement will be deferred until notice of its publication has been given in the *Gazette*. This is to ensure that the more important instruments will not come into force until persons affected have had an opportunity to study them. The date of *Gazette* notification is given at the end of the published copy of each legislative instrument. The exception mentioned arises where a statutory instrument is made in advance of the commencement of the enabling Act. Here the instrument will not become operative until the date on which the Act does so.

Where a statutory instrument specifies a date for its commencement (whether before or after the date on which it is made) it will come into force on that date provided it is not earlier than the commencement of the enabling Act. If it is, the instrument will not become operative until the date on which the Act does so.

---

[1] Statutory Instruments Act, 1959 (No. 52), s. 13 (1).
[2] For mode of publication see p. 295, *ante*.
[3] Statutory Instruments Act, 1959 (No. 52), s. 16.

No person can be deemed to be guilty of an offence under a retrospective statutory instrument in respect of anything done or omitted to be done before the instrument was made.[1]

The National Assembly

As mentioned above, the National Assembly rarely takes any active part in the working of the procedure governing statutory instruments. The ways in which the Assembly may be involved in this procedure are set out below.

Laying before Assembly.—Some enabling Acts require a statutory instrument to be laid before the Assembly after being made so that members may be informed of its contents. In practice most instruments are so laid, whether required to be or not.[2] Where such a requirement exists the instrument must be laid at least seven days before it is to come into operation unless a Minister notifies the Speaker that urgency renders this impracticable.[3] Failure to comply with this procedure does not affect the validity of the instrument, but renders it subject to revocation by the Assembly.[4]

Annulment.—So as to give the Assembly control over the way in which a delegated power is exercised, the enabling Act sometimes declares any instrument made under it to be subject to annulment by the Assembly. This formula brings s. 11 of the Statutory Instruments Act into play. The instrument is required to be laid before the Assembly after being made and if within twenty days the Assembly resolves that it be annulled it is deemed to be revoked, but without prejudice to the making of a further instrument.[5]

Confirmation.—Occasionally an instrument requires confirmation by the Assembly. Thus if an order varying customs duties is not confirmed by the Assembly it ceases to have effect after a certain interval.[6]

---

[1] Statutory Instruments Act, 1959, s. 13. No commencement provision is to be inserted in a statutory instrument unless the instrument is to come into operation at a different time from that provided by this section: Statutory Instruments Rules, 1960 (L.I. 39), r. 8 (2).

[2] For the procedure as to the laying of papers see p. 309, *ante.*

[3] Statutory Instruments Act, 1959 (No. 52), s. 10. The days must normally be sitting days, although a break of up to three days is allowed: *ibid.*, s. 12.

[4] *Ibid.*, s. 16.

[5] *Ibid.*, s. 11. Again s. 12 specifies sitting days, subject to a break of up to three days.

[6] Customs Ordinance (Cap. 167), ss. 11, 12.

PART IV

COMMON LAW AND
CUSTOMARY LAW

SUMMARY

		PAGE
CHAPTER 10.	The Reception and Continuance of English Law	391
CHAPTER 11.	Customary Law	408
CHAPTER 12.	Internal Conflict of Laws	436

CHAPTER 10

THE RECEPTION AND CONTINUANCE OF ENGLISH LAW

1. The Position Before Republic Day

English law was formally introduced into Ghana on the setting up of the Gold Coast Colony in 1874 although it had been administered there to some extent since the time of the Foreign Jurisdiction Act, 1843 and the Bond of 1844, and unofficially even earlier.[1] Except as respects the native courts and local courts, the relative application of English law and customary law was principally regulated during the period before Republic Day by the provisions of Part F of the Courts Ordinance (Cap. 4).[2] It is necessary to set out the terms of certain of these provisions here.[3]

Part F.—Law in Force in Courts

83. How far the law of England in force.—Subject to the terms of this or any other Ordinance, the common law, the doctrines of equity, and the statutes of general application which were *in force in England on the 24th day of July, 1874*, shall be in force *within the jurisdiction of the Courts*.

* * * *

85. Rules as to the application of Imperial laws.—*All Imperial laws* declared to extend or apply to the jurisdiction of the Courts shall be in force so far only as *the limits of the local jurisdiction and local circumstances permit* . . .

86. Law and equity to be concurrently administered.—In every civil cause or matter which shall come in dependence in any of the Courts, law and equity shall be administered concurrently; and such Courts in the exercise of the jurisdiction vested in them by this Ordinance shall have power to grant, and shall grant, either absolutely or on such reasonable terms

---

[1] See Chapter 1, *ante*.
[2] Part F is given in full in Appendix C, p. 498, *post*.
[3] The italics indicate passages which have given rise to particular difficulty.

and conditions as shall seem just, all such remedies or relief whatsoever, interlocutory, or final, as any of the parties thereto may appear to be entitled to in respect of any and every legal or equitable claim or defence properly brought forward by them respectively, or which shall appear in such cause or matter; so that as far as possible all matters in controversy between the said parties respectively may be completely and finally determined, and all multiplicity of legal proceedings concerning any of such matters avoided; and in all matters in which there is any conflict or variance between the rules of equity and the rules of the common law with reference to the same matter, the rules of equity shall prevail."

The title of this Part of the Courts Ordinance indicates a somewhat curious attitude to law. It was not regarded, as is normally the case, as prevailing generally, but as " in force in courts ". " Court " was defined in s. 2 of the Courts Ordinance in terms which excluded the Native Tribunals, the Native Courts and the local courts. Did this mean that English law was not " in force within the jurisdiction " of these inferior tribunals? Or, since the territorial jurisdiction of the High Court covered the whole of Ghana, was s. 83 to be read as applying English law to the whole of Ghana also? A strong case could be made in favour of the former view. The enactments governing the inferior tribunals contained no reference to English law, and s. 83 had remained virtually unchanged since the days when no other tribunal but a court within the meaning of the Courts Ordinance had jurisdiction to apply English law. However, s. 15 of the Local Courts Act, 1958 (No. 23), following the provisions of s. 15 of the Native Courts (Colony) Ordinance (Cap. 98), required a local court to administer any law " binding between the parties ", and s. 10 (vi) conferred jurisdiction in personal suits where the " debt, damage or demand " did not exceed fifty pounds without the restriction to customary law claims which applied to the other types of jurisdiction conferred by s. 10. It appears therefore that one should take the view that s. 83 in effect applied English law throughout Ghana, though the point that it did not remained open right up to Republic Day.

What was the English law which applied by virtue of s. 83, subject to the savings for customary law which were set out in s. 87 of the Courts Ordinance[1]? In the first place, no law applied if it was inconsistent with any Ordinance, which expression

---

[1] Section 87 (1) is set out, and its terms analysed, in the following chapter.

included an Act of Parliament and, it seems, " any order, proclamation, rule, regulation or bye-law duly made under the authority
of an Act, Ordinance, Order of Her Majesty in Council or any
other legislative enactment applicable to and in force in Ghana ".[1]
Thus the common law rules of criminal liability were almost entirely excluded by s. 11 of the Criminal Code (Cap. 9). Secondly,
and subject to the limitation just referred to, the English law
applied was " the common law, the doctrines of equity, and the
statutes of general application which were in force in England on
the 24th day of July, 1874 ". This description gave rise to considerable difficulty on two points. The first was as to whether the
date specified applied to the common law and equity as well as
to the statutes of general application. Dr. Allott's view is that
it did.

> " Whilst it is possible to read (and the punctuation suggests
> that reading) section 83 as applying the limiting date solely
> to the statutes, it is submitted that by necessary intendment
> the date should govern the rules of common law and equity
> applicable as well. Had the intention of the legislature been
> different, the relevant words might have followed those of
> section 17 of the Courts Ordinance, which provided that the
> Gold Coast Supreme Court was to exercise matrimonial juris-
> diction ' in conformity with the law and practice for the time
> being in force in England.' "[2]

The opposite view was, however, more generally held. Dr.
Allott's argument by analogy with s. 17 is, with respect, un-
convincing since the English matrimonial jurisdiction is entirely
based on statute law and s. 17 intended to apply current English
law whether the statutes in question were of general application
or not and regardless of when they came into force. Nor can it
be accepted that there was any grammatical ambiguity in the
wording of s. 83, quite apart from the placing of the commas.
It would be necessary to insert " the rules of " before " the
common law " in order to make the plural verb extend beyond
the statutes. Again, the reading " the common law . . . which
were in force " would lead to difficulties in the case of common
law rules which had been superseded or modified by statutes
which were in force in England in 1874 but were not of general
application. Where a rule had been superseded neither the rule
nor the statute replacing it would be in force in Ghana and where

---

[1] Interpretation Act, 1957 (No. 29), s. 3.
[2] *Essays in African Law*, Butterworths, 1960, p. 31.

the rule had been merely modified it would be difficult to say in what form the rule, bereft of its modifying statute, could be said to have been in force in England in 1874. More serious perhaps than these arguments was the point that Dr. Allott's view appears to run counter to the line of judicial authority on s. 83 and similar provisions in other territories, as he himself points out,[1] and that, whatever view one takes of the theory that the common law exists *in nubibus*, whence it is garnered by the judges, the fact remains that it is unnatural to speak of the common law as in force at a particular date and that judgments are invariably given in the form of expositions of existing principles rather than as instances of quasi-legislative action.

Presumably no difference was intended by the fact that s. 85 referred to " Imperial laws " whereas s. 87 referred to " English law ".[2] Both sections probably applied not only to the law brought in by s. 83 but also to the English adjectival, lunacy, infancy and matrimonial laws applied by ss. 15 to 17. Section 85 can scarcely have governed an Imperial Act applying *proprio vigore* to any territory now included in Ghana. More serious problems arose on the second italicized phrase in the opening passage of s. 85. In the first place did this passage apply to common law and equity as well as statute law? Apparently it did, and it would be illogical if it did not, but later references in the section to " verbal alterations " and " any such statute " suggest the exclusion of unwritten law.[3] More baffling is the reference in s. 87(1) to " a strict adherence to the rules of English law ", since the purpose of s. 85 must have been to remove the necessity for such strict adherence. It is far from clear how far it went in this direction: the reference to the limits of the local jurisdiction was meaningless after independence if it was not before; " local circumstances " seem to allow for practically any alteration the

---

[1] *Op. cit*, p. 33. In *Obeng* v. *Ampofo* (1958) (Civil Appeal No. 53/57—unreported) the Ghana Court of Appeal in its judgment, delivered by Ollennu, J., cited House of Lords and Privy Council decisions on the common law decided in 1878 and 1922 respectively and added " each of which is binding on this Court ".

[2] See p. 408, *post.*

[3] An exactly opposite point arose on similar provisions in British Honduras, where the common law was stated to be in force only as far as suitable to local conditions but the same qualification was not expressly applied to statute law. Lord Hobhouse remarked in the Judicial Committee of the Privy Council that the qualification must be implied " because it would be absurd to suppose that common law is to prevail in the Colony only if suitable, and that laws abrogating it are to prevail whether suitable or not ": *Jex* v. *McKinney* (1889), L.R. 14 App. Cas. 77, at p. 81.

court thinks fit to make. Dr. Allott considered that the most important relevant local circumstances were:

> " that the population of Ghana consists of Africans leading a way of life partly or entirely foreign to that of England, and that customary law and Islamic law are recognised and applied in a wide variety of cases, thus excluding the English law which would otherwise have been applicable."[1]

The latter circumstance was however provided for by s. 87, while, with respect, the former is so vague as to give unlimited scope but very little guidance.

Statutes of general application

The other point which caused difficulty in connection with s. 83 was the reference to " statutes of general application ". This difficulty is of course common to most British territories in Africa and, under various guises, elsewhere. In Ghana the problems appear to have been more theoretical than practical. Most of the decisions on the applicability of English law concern land transactions and other cases where the parties were taken to have agreed to be governed by English law. Here there has been little trouble in treating the whole corpus of relevant law as applying, although the different principles of land tenure prevailing in Ghana and England have cause occasional awkwardness. Where English law was not imported by agreement, the courts have only rarely found it necessary to decide whether to apply statutes of general application.[2] Occasionally the decision has not been altogether easy to reach, as in *Inspector-General of Police* v. *Morlai Kamara*,[3] where the West African Court of Appeal held that s. 11 of the Summary Jurisdiction Act, 1848, requiring a summary prosecution to be brought within six months of the offence, did not apply in the Gold Coast, although it was a statute of general application, since it did not fit in with local circumstances and was, on the true construction of the relevant local Ordinances, superseded by them. Redwar, in his book *Comments on Some Ordinances of the Gold Coast Colony* pointed out that " statute of general application " did not mean the same thing

---

[1] *Op. cit.*, p. 206.
[2] This is in line with experience elsewhere. In Alberta, Canada, it has only been necessary to list one English statute, the Divorce and Matrimonial Causes Act, 1857, as applying locally: Revised Statutes of Alberta, Appendix B.
[3] (1934), 2 W.A.C.A. 185.

as " public general Act " but must inevitably be narrower in scope.[1] He cited *Jex* v. *McKinney*[2] in which the Judicial Committee of the Privy Council held that the Statute of Mortmain could not be taken to have been applied in British Honduras since " it was framed for reasons affecting the land and society of England and not for reasons applying to a new colony ". The expression " statutes of general application " was not used in the British Honduras legislation applying English law, but the Judicial Committee has tended to disregard distinctions in wording on this point and approach the matter, in whatever territory it arose, as a broad question of whether English statutes could suitably be applied, either as they stood or subject to modifications. The power to modify contained in such provisions as s. 85 of the Ghana Courts Ordinance disposed of difficulties such as were graphically described by Lord Cranworth in *Whicker* v. *Hume*:[3]

> " The Act says ' all the laws adapted to the situation of the colony '. Who is to decide whether they are adapted or not? That is a very difficult question. But with regard to this Statute of Mortmain, ordinarily so called, I cannot have the least doubt that that cannot be regarded as applicable to the colonies. One thing that the Act requires is, that the deed is to be enrolled in Chancery within six months. When that statute was passed I believe people would have thought it very chimerical to imagine that they could get from the antipodes to this country and back again to the antipodes in six months. It might possibly have been done, but it would have been thought a remarkably good voyage; and to suppose that an Act of Parliament is to be held in force which requires something so difficult to be performed, as applied to those distant colonies, seems to me very chimerical. But, besides that, there is the exception in favour of the Universities and Colleges of Eton and Winchester. It is absurd to suppose that any enactment of this sort could be meant to apply to those distant possessions of the Crown. And more particularly there is no evidence whatever that the evil which that statute was meant to remedy, namely the increase of the disherison of heirs by giving property to charitable uses, was at all an evil which was felt or likely to be felt in the colonies."

It cannot be said that the West African cases reveal a consistent pattern of treatment in relation to the expression " statutes of general application ". Judges have sometimes been driven to

---

[1] Pp. 8 *et seq.*; *see also* Allott, *op. cit.* pp. 9–10.
[2] (1889), L.R. 14 App. Cas. 77.
[3] (1858), L.R. 7 H.L. 124 at p. 161.

say that they found the expression meaningless[1] or to utter such remarks as " I am not prepared at present to say precisely what it means; my present view is that it means the Public General Statutes, excluding those which are inapplicable in a Colony ".[2] Perhaps the most helpful test was that cited in *A.-G. v. Holt*:[3]

> " Two preliminary questions can . . . be put by way of a rough, but not infallible, test, *viz.:* (1) By what courts is the statute applied in England; and (2) to what classes of the community in England does it apply? If on [the date of reception] an Act of Parliament were applied by all civil or criminal courts, as the case may be, to all classes of the community, there is a strong likelihood that it is in force within the jurisdiction. If, on the other hand, it were applied only by certain courts (e.g., a statute regulating procedure), or only to certain classes of the community (e.g., an Act regulating a particular trade), the probability is that it would not be held to be locally applicable."

On the whole, however, the reported cases indicate that the judges in West Africa decided whether or not to apply English statutes on an *ad hoc* basis, in accordance with what seemed to them appropriate in the proceedings before them. A handful of statutes came to be recognised as applicable where a matter was not governed by customary law, as for example the Limitation Acts, the Statute of Frauds, and the Wills Act, 1837. On the other hand the Bankruptcy Acts have not been treated as applying. They require special courts, officials and procedures not provided in the Colonial territories except where a local bankruptcy law has been enacted, and are not of course the type of provisions that can be held to be imported by agreement of the parties.[4]

Although the importing, by means of such provisions as s. 83 of the Courts Ordinance, of British statutes of general application may not have given rise to much practical difficulty, it is clearly unsatisfactory. No one can be sure what the law really is; it cannot be taught properly; and a fog of doubt hangs over the country's jurisprudence. The area of the problem becomes smaller, as time passes, with the encroachment of local enactments on the field of English law. Many countries have not, however, been content to let the matter be resolved in this way and have taken more energetic steps. Attempts to clarify the position by

---

[1] E.g. Macleod, J., in *Des Bordes* v. *Des Bordes*, Sarbah, F.C.L. 267.

[2] *Per* Hutchinson, C.J. in *Fisher* v. *Swanikier* (1889), Redwar 137.

[3] (1910), 2 N.L.R. 1.

[4] See Elias, *Groundwork of Nigerian Law*, pp. 19–20. As to the Habeas Corpus Acts, see pp. 217 *et seq., ante*.

publishing authoritative lists of the statutes which apply have
not met with much success. In British Honduras, where it is
enacted that " the common law of England and all Acts in abro-
gation or derogation or in any way declaratory of the common
law " passed before 1st January, 1899 shall extend to the colony
" so far only as the jurisdiction of the Court and local circumstances reasonably permit and render such extension suitable and
appropriate ", an attempt was made in 1887 to provide an authoritative list of the Imperial Acts extending to the colony.
Two hundred and ninety-two Acts were included in that list,
which formed an appendix to the volume of Consolidated Laws
of the Colony. At the next revision of the laws in 1914 the list
was omitted by the Commissioner on the ground that it was incomplete and included Acts the applicability of which was open
to serious argument. It has not since been replaced.[1] In Ghana
the reverse method was employed, and a list of British statutes
which did *not* apply was first published as long ago as 1893 and
subsequently revised.[2]

Perhaps the most elaborate attempt to clarify the position
as to the application of British statutes was that undertaken
by Sir Leo Cussen in the Australian State of Victoria in 1922.
Under an Act of George IV, " all laws and statutes in force within
the realm of England " at the time of the passing of the Act in
1828 were in force in Victoria " so far as the same can be applied "
and subject of course to later legislation applying in Victoria.
The Imperial Acts Application Act, 1922, of the State of Victoria
was described by its long title as:

> " An Act to declare that certain Enactments of the Parlia-
> ment of England and of the Parliament of Great Britain and
> of the Parliament of the United Kingdom of Great Britain and
> Ireland in force at the time of the passing of the Act 9 George
> IV c. LXXXIII shall not apply in Victoria and to transcribe
> or consolidate other Enactments of such Parliaments and for
> other purposes."

The scheme of the Imperial Acts Application Act, 1922 is
complex. It can be summarized in the following way—[3]

---

[1] Preface to the Laws of British Honduras (1954), p. iii. The collected
edition of Laws of New Zealand contains a long list of Imperial Statutes
" apparently in force in New Zealand, either by enactment, or by adoption,
or by implication " though the list is admitted to be incomplete.

[2] Statute Law Revision Ordinance (Cap. 3 in 1951 Revised Edition).

[3] This summary has been worked out with the aid of the Explanatory
Paper which accompanied the Bill for the 1922 Act.

1. A number of English Acts of particular importance in Victoria were reproduced in Part III of the Act in consolidated form, that is as new, independent enactments. These included provisions relating to the administration of estates, the writ of certiorari, charitable trusts, lotteries and gaming, marriage, and unlawful oaths.

2. Other Acts which had been judicially held to be in force in Victoria or which were probably in force there, but which either could not be conveniently consolidated or were out of harmony with current conditions, were enumerated in the First Schedule. The provisions of these which remained relevant were transcribed in Part II of the Act, the remainder being repealed with savings. The transcribed provisions included a number dealing with criminal law, judicial procedure and real property as well as parts of 13 Eliz. I c.5 (avoiding gifts in defraud of creditors) and 31 Chas. II c.2 and 56 Geo. III c.100 (habeas corpus). Unlike the consolidated enactments, the transcribed enactments were not given any greater effect than they had before. Transcription was merely for convenience of reference, and the enactments continued to have " such force and effect, if any, as they had at the commencement of this Act ".[1]

3. Other Acts were dealt with by simply being enumerated in the Second Schedule. These, which included the Bill of Rights, the Petitition of Right, and enactments relating to treason and piracy, were Acts which were difficult to consolidate or transcribe, or which dealt with matters mainly beyond the domain of the Parliament of Victoria or which were only applicable to Victoria by virtue of post-1828 Imperial legislation. Such of these Acts as already applied in Victoria were kept in force so far as they were in force in England on 31st December, 1921.[2]

4. All other pre-1828 English Acts were repealed with elaborate savings, including savings for enactments which—

" (a) by express words apply to the dominions or other possessions of the Crown and which on their proper construction are applicable to Victoria as being included in such dominions or other possessions;

---

[1] Section 4.
[2] Section 6.

(*b*) by necessary intendment either as involving matters of Imperial concern or otherwise are applicable to Victoria."[1]

The Act thus cleared up some of the difficulties surrounding the application of English statute law while leaving others undisturbed. It was most successful with regard to the consolidated provisions, most of which were in 1928 absorbed in new consolidation Acts dealing comprehensively with the subjects in question. These could hardly have been prepared without the preliminary work accomplished by the Act. Even in the large field where the question of applicability was left unresolved by the Act, the work of transcription and enumeration was no doubt of great assistance.

Coming nearer home, we find that Western Nigeria in 1958 inaugurated an ambitious scheme, under the control of Sir John Verity as Commissioner for Laws Revision of the Western Region, for replacing by separate Acts such of the English statutes of general application as it was expedient to retain and repealing the remainder so far as power to do so lay with the Region. 1st January, 1900 was the official date of reception of English law so far as Western Nigeria was concerned, and the relevant English statutes in force on that date were gathered into twenty-one laws as follows—

Administration of Estates Law, 1959 (No. 23)
Apportionment Law, 1958 (No. 26).
Bills of Sale Law, 1958 (No. 47).
Carriers Law, 1958 (No. 30).
Contracts Law, 1958 (No. 22).
Defamation Law, 1958 (No. 42).
Habeas Corpus Law, 1958 (No. 24).
Infants Law, 1958 (No. 25).
Innkeepers Law, 1958 (No. 20).
Landlord and Tenant Law, 1958 (No. 32).
Limitation Law, 1959 (No. 7).
Married Women's Property Law, 1958 (No. 21).
Mercantile Agents Law, 1958 (No. 27).
Partnership Law, 1958 (No. 44).
Prescription Law, 1958 (No. 23).
Property and Conveyancing Law, 1959 (No. 21).
Sale of Goods Law, 1958 (No. 43).

---

[1] Sections 5, 7.

Statutory Declarations Law, 1958 (No. 31).
Torts Law, 1958 (No. 41).
Trustee Law, 1959 (No. 8).
Wills Law, 1958 (No. 28).

The enterprise was completed by the Law of England (Application) Law, 1959 (No. 9), which provides that, " subject to the provisions of any written law, the Common Law of England and the doctrines of Equity observed by Her Majesty's High Court of Justice in England shall be in force throughout the Region "[1] and goes on to state that, subject to savings in respect of accrued rights and liabilities, " no Imperial Act hitherto in force within the Region shall have any force or effect therein ".[2] Imperial Acts which apply to the Region by express words or by necessary intendment, or which relate to any matter in respect of which the exclusive power to enact laws is conferred on the Federal Legislature are not affected.[3] This was much more radical than the Victorian scheme and went as far as was possible for a unit in a Federation not then independent of the United Kingdom. A complete removal of the need to refer to English statutes can hardly be achieved until the territory in question has achieved independence. Indeed republican status may well be necessary before it is practicable to repeal every Imperial statute.

Common law and equity

Section 86 of the Courts Ordinance, which regulated the relative application of rules of English common law and equity, was derived from the Supreme Court of Judicature Act, 1873.[4] Sections 24 and 25 of that Act laid down in great detail the new arrangements for the fusion of law and equity in England but at that time the authorities in the Gold Coast were content to pick out one or two of these provisions and leave the rest. Section 86 of the Courts Ordinance accordingly consisted, amalgamated in one sentence, of the opening words of s. 24 followed by para. (7) of that section and ending with para. (11) of s. 25. No harm seems to have come from the omissions. There was in Ghana no

---

[1] Section 3.
[2] Section 4.
[3] Sections 6, 7.
[4] This Act has sometimes been treated as one of the statutes of general application referred to in s. 83 of the Courts Ordinance. In fact, however, most of its provisions did not come into force until 2nd November, 1874, some months after the date of reception specified in s. 83.

CC

specialisation comparable to that between Chancery and common law counsel in England, and Professor Hanbury's remarks on the present position in England have been more or less true of Ghana since 1876:

> "The vast majority of practitioners must be prepared to meet points of equity, mixed up with points of law, in the same case, and they will be faced with the necessity of pooling together the sum of the resources of the two systems, and arriving at a composite result. In such a process it is neither serviceable nor rational to ascribe each component to its historical antecedent and to label it as a matter of equity or of law."[1]

2. THE PRESENT POSITION

Basic decisions

When preparatory work was begun on the new Constitution, one of the many factors to be considered was the future structure of the courts in Ghana. It was decided to replace the old Supreme Court, consisting of the Court of Appeal and the High Court, by two separate Courts to be known as the Supreme Court and the High Court respectively. It was also decided to abolish the Commissioners of Assize and Civil Pleas, who had been appointed under an Act passed in 1958[2] and replace both them and the Senior Magistrates by Circuit Judges; and furthermore to abolish the Lands Division of the Supreme Court, and to make various other changes in the system of courts. The Courts Ordinance had already been heavily amended, and it was clear that the new proposals could not be carried through except by enacting a new Courts Act. This immediately raised the problem of replacing Part F of the Courts Ordinance and various other provisions relating to the application of English law and customary law. The current revision of the Courts Ordinance dated from 1951, when the struggle for independence had barely begun, and its outlook was firmly colonial. This was nowhere more apparent than in Part F, with its references to "Imperial laws" and "natives". It might have been possible to reproduce these provisions in the new Courts Act without any other alteration than the substitution for such out-of-date expressions of their modern equivalents. But the difficulty went much deeper than this. The whole language of the Ordinance was antiquated and, more important, the provisions in question were so defective that

---

[1] *Modern Equity* (7th edn.), p. 20.
[2] The Commissioners of Assize and Civil Pleas Act, 1958 (No. 12).

it was unthinkable to shirk the task of putting in their place entirely fresh ones. Accordingly, although the time available for consideration and consultation was extremely short, the attempt was made to match the new Constitution by new provisions regulating the application in Ghana of English law and customary law.

The first question of course was whether English law should be retained at all. It was tempting to say that, with the disappearance of the last formal link with the English Crown the formal links with English law should be severed also. Consideration was given to a suggestion that English law should cease to apply and be replaced by a discretion given to the courts to decide any case which was not governed by statute or customary law in accordance with the principles of " justice, equity and good conscience ". This seemed, however, too great a burden to thrust suddenly upon the courts and also to be likely to lead to an undesirable amount of uncertainty as to the content of the law, at any rate in the early stages. It was felt particularly that persons having commercial interests in Ghana, or contemplating investing in the country, might be perturbed at a sudden withdrawal of the substratum of English law.

It was also necessary to consider the future of customary law. Probably all civilised countries have begun with a miscellaneous collection of unwritten customary laws applying to particular tribes, communities or areas within the country. With the passage of centuries, these customary laws become, through the intervention of the courts, uniform and thoroughly developed. Incidental variations are ironed out with the passage of time; customs that do not fit the general pattern of the people fall into disuse, and in the end a common system of law prevails. This process is probably superior to the process whereby a foreign system of law is received into another country and made a part of its legal system. Its great disadvantage from the point of view of Ghana today is the length of time needed for its accomplishment. Ghana cannot wait for centuries, or even for decades, before having a developed system of unenacted law. This should not mean, however, that Ghana's own indigenous law is to be scrapped. The best solution therefore appeared to be to begin the Republic by retaining English law, but devising some system by which those princples of customary law which are suitable for general application could be brought into the common law by a quicker means than is accorded by the traditional method. The new legislation is framed to enable this to happen.

Continuance of English law

Article 40 of the Constitution states that the common law and customary law are comprised in the laws of Ghana. This is subject to the provisions of any enactment made after the coming into operation of the Constitution, so that an Act of Parliament could provide, if the occasion should ever arise, that the common law should no longer form part of the laws of Ghana. This could of course be done without amending the Constitution.

The Constitution contains no definition of either the common law or customary law. This represents a change from the draft Constitution published on 7th March, 1960.[1] Article 39 of that draft included in the laws of Ghana " indigenous laws and customs not being repugnant to natural justice, equity and good conscience, in so far as their application is not inconsistent with any enactment for the time being in force " and " the doctrines of common law and equity, in so far as their application is not inconsistent with such indigenous laws and customs or with any enactment for the time being in force ". Between the publication of the Constitution Bill, it became clear that it was unwise to insert in the Constitution definitions of these terms and accordingly the definitions were deleted. The meaning of the expression " the common law " as found in art. 40 of the Constitution is laid down by s. 17 of the Interpretation Act, 1960 (C.A. 4). This is in the following terms:

" **17. The common law.**—(1) The common law, as comprised in the laws of Ghana, consists, in addition to the rules of law generally known as the common law, of the rules generally known as the doctrines of equity and of rules of customary law included in the common law under any enactment providing for the assimilation of such rules of customary law as are suitable for general application.

(2) In the case of inconsistency, an assimilated rule shall prevail over any other rule, and a rule of equity shall prevail over any rule other than an assimilated rule.

(3) While any of the statutes of general application continue to apply by virtue of the Courts Act, 1960 (C.A. 9), they shall be treated as if they formed part of the common law, as defined in subsection (1), prevailing over any rule thereof other than an assimilated rule.

(4) In deciding upon the existence or content of a rule of the common law, as so defined, the Court may have regard to any

---

exposition of that rule by a court exercising jurisdiction in any country.

(5) A reference in an enactment to the common law shall be construed as a reference to it as affected by any enactment for the time being in force."

Subsection (1) of s. 17 refers to " the rules of law generally known as the common law " and " the rules generally known as the doctrines of equity ".

The rules are not described as " English ", but this probably does not represent any departure from the effect of s. 83 of the old Courts Ordinance. Although the contents of s. 83, and the side-note to that section, suggest that English common law and equity were referred to, on the preferred interpretation[1] the words " in force in England " did not apply to the references to the common law and equity, although it is true it was to English decisions on common law and equity that the courts in Ghana looked. Indeed, as we have seen, they regarded themselves as bound by decisions of the House of Lords and the Privy Council in England.[2] It was considered inexpedient to refer expressly to English law in these provisions describing the unenacted laws of Ghana. Furthermore, although common law and equity originated in England they have of course been received by the law of many other countries. Wherever territories have been ceded to or settled or conquered by the British, common law and equity have found a foothold which has not easily been dislodged. Nearly two hundred years after the American War of Independence, common law and equity still flourish in most of the states of the U.S.A. It is this concept of common law and equity as a world-wide system of law that is now imported into the laws of Ghana. This is emphasized by sub-s. (4) of s. 17 of the Interpretation Act, 1960 (C.A. 4), which enables the courts to seek guidance on any doubtful point on the common law or equity from decisions of courts in any country. The freedom of the courts to depart from decisions of the House of Lords and Privy Council, and other English courts, is made plain by art. 42(4) of the Constitution. Although no doubt the courts in Ghana will continue to seek guidance from the principles of English law in which their judges and legal practitioners have been nurtured, they are now free to take their own view of the correctness of

---

[1] See p. 393, *ante.*
[2] See p. 394, *ante.*

English decisions on doubtful points. Where, therefore, the court in Ghana considers that a wrong turning has been taken by the judges in England, as, perhaps, in relation to the doctrine of common employment, they are at liberty to review the principles of law in question and, if they think fit, interpret them differently.

Just as it was not practicable to jettison the rules of English common law and equity, so it was not felt to be possible to jettison the English statutes of general application also applied by s. 83 of the old Courts Ordinance. At the same time the need was realised for replacing the statutes of general application as soon as possible by Acts of the Ghana Parliament setting out in modern language, and with suitable modifications, such of these statutes as required to be retained. Work has already begun on the task, and it is expected that it will be accomplished within two or three years. For this reason, the statutes of general application were kept in force by a saving provision at the end of the Courts Act, 1960 (C.A. 9)[1] rather than by a substantive provision in s. 17 of the Interpretation Act, 1960. Section 154(4) of the Courts Act, 1960 contains a proviso having a similar effect to s. 85 of the old Courts Ordinance. This proviso states that the statutes of general application " shall be subject to such modifications as may be requisite to enable them to be conveniently applied in Ghana ". These modifications are of course to be made by the court in applying a particular statute.

Section 17(1) of the Interpretation Act, 1960 also contemplates the inclusion in the common law, as comprised in the laws of Ghana, of rules of customary law which are suitable for general application, and sub-s. (5) makes it clear that rules of common law and equity, statutes of general application and assimilated rules of customary law all apply subject to any enactment for the time being in force. " Enactment " is defined by s. 32(1) of the Interpretation Act, 1960 as meaning " an Act or statutory instrument or any provision of any Act or statutory instrument ". " Act " is defined as meaning " the Constitution, an Act of the Constituent Assembly or of Parliament, or any legislative measure of an authority formerly exercising power to make laws for the territory or any part of the territory comprised in the Republic, but does not include a statute of general application continuing to apply by virtue of section 154 of the Courts Act, 1960 ". A statutory instrument is an instrument made under a power con-

---

[1] Section 154 (4).

ferred by an Act, not being a power of legislation conferred on Parliament.[1] Subsection (2) of s. 17 of the Interpretation Act, 1960 states that in the case of inconsistency, an assimilated rule shall prevail over any other rule, and the rules of equity shall prevail over any rule other than an assimilated rule.[2]

Thus we see that as used in Ghana from now on, the expression " the common law " has an extended meaning.[3] This extended meaning is not altogether an innovation. The common law is sometimes used to include equity in a context where it is desired to draw a distinction between unwritten or unenacted law and statute law.[4] Although the statutes of general application are not of course unwritten, they are treated in Ghana in the same way as the unwritten laws originally developed by the English courts. Customary laws, which may now be imported into the common law, are also of course largely unwritten. It may be thought therefore, that it is not straining language too far to give an extended meaning to the expression " the common law " particularly as it is hoped that in a short time it will become truly " the common law of Ghana ".[5] The order of priority among the various elements now included in the common law works out as follows:

1. Assimilated rules of customary law.
2. Statutes of general application.
3. The doctrines of equity.
4. The rules of common law in the narrow sense.

All these are subject to the provisions of any enactment, and as the statutes of general application are replaced it will be necessary to look at each replacing Act to see how far it modifies the application of the other elements in the common law. Replacing Acts so far passed include the Contracts Act, 1960 (Act 25), the Lotteries and Betting Act, 1960 (Act 31), the Bills of Lading Act, 1961 (Act 42), the Bills of Exchange Act, 1961 (Act 55), and the Administration of Estates Act, 1961 (Act 63).

---

[1] Statutory Instruments Act, 1959 (No. 52), ss. 2, 3.

[2] As to the procedure for assimilating customary rules into the common law,see p. 429, *post*. As yet there are no assimilated rules.

[3] Section 32 (1) of the Interpretation Act, 1960 provides that in any enactment the expression " the common law " is to be construed in accordance with s. 17 of that Act.

[4] See Salmond, *Jurisprudence* (11th edn.), p. 96.

[5] The use of the expression is criticized by Rubin and Murray (*op. cit.*, p. 171), but their suggested alternative, "the national law" is so wide as to include Acts of Parliament and statutory instruments, and does not import the required reference to the English substratum.

CHAPTER 11

CUSTOMARY LAW

1. Section 87(1) of the Courts Ordinance[1]

Until the changes made on 1st July, 1960, the application of customary law in Ghana was mainly governed by s. 87(1) of the Courts Ordinance. This was in the following terms, the italics indicating passages of particular difficulty:

> " 87. **Application of native laws.**—(1) Nothing in this Ordinance shall *deprive* the Courts of the right to observe and enforce the observance, or shall deprive *any person* of the benefit, of any native law or custom *existing* in Ghana, such law or custom not being repugnant to natural justice, equity and good conscience, nor incompatible either directly or by necessary implication with any Ordinance for the time being in force.
>
> Such laws and customs shall be deemed applicable in causes and matters where the parties thereto are *natives*, and particularly, but without derogation from their application in other cases, in causes and matters relating to *the tenure and transfer of real and personal property*, and to *inheritance and testamentary dispositions* and also in causes and matters between natives and non-natives where it may appear to the Court that substantial injustice would be caused by a *strict* adherence to the rules of English law.
>
> No party shall be entitled to *claim the benefit* of any local law or custom, if it shall appear either from *express* contract or from the nature of the transactions out of which any suit or question may have arisen, that such party *agreed* that his *obligations* in connection with such transactions should be regulated *exclusively* by English law; and in cases where no *express* rule is applicable to any matter in controversy, the Court shall be governed by the principles of justice, equity, and good conscience."

Treating s. 83 of the Courts Ordinance as applying English law throughout Ghana, we must take s. 87(1) as primarily laying down exceptions to its application. Thus it is implied by the second

---

[1] The bearing of s. 87 (1) on problems of internal conflict of laws is discussed in the next chapter, pp. 436, *et seq.*, *post*.

paragraph that English law would normally apply where the parties include both " natives " and " non-natives ", and s.87(1) appears to have no application at all where all the parties are "non-natives ".[1] Although framed in this way, as an excepting or saving provision, s. 87 (1) was nevertheless of the greatest general importance. By its means the application of customary law was preserved and thus the English law brought in by s. 83 and other provisions of the Ordinance was displaced for the great majority of the inhabitants in favour of their own indigenous systems of law. The true position might perhaps have been better expressed by putting the emphasis the other way, as was originally done in the Order in Council of 3rd September, 1844.[2] Nevertheless it was true in 1876, when the Courts Ordinance was first promulgated, and it is more obviously true in the expanded commercial and industrial situation in Ghana today, that the common law, with its higher degree of development and its doctrine of applicability to any circumstances[3] is likely to be a more effective " background law " then could be provided by any form of customary law.[4] The courts have therefore always fallen back on English law to deal with cases, even between Africans, where the relevant customary law was silent, or was unknown or not proved.[5]

Section 87(1) cut down the application of customary law in two ways. As with the English law applied by s. 83, customary law had to give place to any Ordinance (including, after Independence,

---

[1] *Sed quaere:* a " native " who was not a party could be " deprived of the benefit " of a right under customary law by a judgment in an action between non-natives unless s. 87 (1) is taken to prevent this; *cf. Nelson* v. *Nelson* (1951), 13 W.A.C.A. 284 (p. 438, *post*)—in an action between the " non-native " second and third defendants the court would surely not have made an order in disregard of the customary law rights of the Nelson family.

[2] Judges, etc., shall " observe until further order such of the local customs . . . as may be compatible with the principles of the law of England, and, in default of such customs, shall proceed in all things, as nearly as may be, according to the said law of England "—cited Redwar, *Comments on some Ordinances of the Gold Coast Colony* (London 1909), p. 61. At the time when Redwar wrote, the spirit of this early provision appears still to have been prevalent. He put forward five rules as embodying the principles later contained in section 87 (1) (ib., pp. 59–65) but rule 2, to the effect that in mixed cases English law is only made applicable by the contract of the parties, and rule 3, to the effect that even where such a contract exists in mixed cases customary law applies if English law would cause substantial injustice, appear plainly contrary to the wording of the section.

[3] *In novo casu, novum remedium apponendum est:* 2 Co. Inst. 3.

[4] *See* Allott, *op. cit.*, p. 7.

[5] *Morris* v. *Monrovia* (1930), 1 W.A.C.A. 70 is a good example.

any Act of Parliament) which was inconsistent with its application. A custom might be prohibited altogether by Ordinance, as with the Krobo customs,[1] or might on certain facts be expressly displaced in favour of English law, as in the case of succession to the property of persons married under the Marriage Ordinance (Cap. 127), s. 48. Again, custom might be excluded " by necessary implication " arising from an Ordinance.[2] The other factor which might limit the application of customary law was repugnancy to " natural justice, equity and good conscience ".[3] This time-hallowed expression, originally imported from British India, has been widely used in colonial Africa and generally regarded as a tautology, little attempt having been made to apportion separate meanings to the three concepts embedded in it.[4] In some territories, such as Tanganyika, repugnancy is by reference to " justice and morality ", which more effectively indicates the two main elements involved.

An example of a rule of customary law which was " outlawed " on the ground of repugnancy to natural justice, equity and good conscience is that of *panyarring* or *adwo*, which, where a person failed to pay a debt, enabled a member of his family or even in some cases, a stranger, to be kidnapped and held until the debt was paid—usually under coercion from the near relatives of the seized one.[5] The denial of this remedy, coupled with the continued recognition[6] of the custom whereby family property could not be seized for the debt of a member of the family, worked injustice in some cases, although imprisonment for debt remained a sanction in all cases until 1934 and still remains where the debtor has been guilty of misconduct.[7]

Another example of such repugnancy is found in the Nigerian case of *Edet* v. *Nyon Essien*.[8] Here the appellant had entered into a customary law marriage with Inyang when she was still a child, paying dowry to her parents. Later Inyang went through

---

[1] Native Customs (Colony) Ordinance (Cap. 97), s. 4. Many other customs were suppressed by orders made under the Ordinance; see *Laws of the Gold Coast* (1954), vol. VIII, p. 730.
[2] E.g., the Native Administration Treasuries Ordinance (Cap. 96).
[3] *Cf.* the curious phrase " repugnant to the laws of Ghana " used in the definition of customary law contained in the Local Courts Act, 1958 (No. 23) and the Houses of Chiefs Act, 1958 (No. 20).
[4] But see Allott, *op. cit.*, pp. 197–201.
[5] See Rattray, *Ashanti Law and Constitution*, Oxford, 1929, p. 370.
[6] But see Sarbah, F.L.R. 179.
[7] See Meek, *Land Law and Custom in the Colonies* (Oxford, 1946), p. 181.
[8] (1932), 11 N.L.R. 47.

a similar ceremony with the respondent, who also paid dowry. The relevant customary law contained a rule under which children born to Inyang and the respondent could, until such time as the dowry paid by the appellant was returned, be claimed by the appellant. The court held that this rule was void as being repugnant to natural justice, equity and good conscience.

When rules repugnant either to enacted law or to justice, equity and good conscience had been laid aside what remained? The Courts Ordinance gave no guidance as to the nature of the customary law to be applied other than by describing it in s. 87(1) as " any native law or custom existing in Ghana ".[1] This at least seemed to make it clear that customs which had fallen into disuse were not to be enforced, but even here there was a doubt. Did " existing " mean existing at the date when the Courts Ordinance came into operation or existing at the date when the proceedings in question arose? If a custom had fallen into disuse between those dates was it to be recognized in the proceedings? It might be thought that, since a statute is taken to be always speaking, " existing " meant existing when the matter in question arose. However it seems that the courts in Ghana have taken the opposite view.[2] As Lord Merrivale once remarked in pronouncing upon a dispute over the same expression, " the use of words in the English tongue is not so rigidly governed by rule as to render impossible either of the alternative constructions ".[3] Nevertheless it is respectfully submitted that the former is the correct interpretation. The practice of periodically revising the Ordinances meant that the date of commencement of the current Courts Ordinance was purely fortuitous and no one could found any principle of policy upon it. On the other hand a policy that a customary law was to be enforced if it was existing at the time a particular dispute arose and not otherwise would clearly be fair and reasonable. There is in addition the further argument that, where a date of reference was considered important, as with the English statutes of general application applied by s. 83

---

[1] *Cf.* the definitions, each in identical terms, in the Local Courts Act, 1958 (No. 23) and the Houses of Chiefs Act, 1958 (No. 20): "'customary law' means any uncodified rule or rules having the force of law and not repugnant to the laws of Ghana, whereby rights and correlative duties fortified by established usage have been acquired or imposed, and includes any declaration of customary law published from time to time in the *Gazette* ".

[2] See cases cited in Report of Korsah Commission on Native Courts (1961), p. 16.

[3] *The Yuri Maru*, [1927] A.C. 906, at p. 910.

of the Courts Ordinance, the date was inserted in the 1876 Ordinance and not altered in subsequent revisions .

A further question was whether a custom had not only to be presently existing but also to have been in existence for any particular length of time. An early attempt was made to import the English rule that a custom is not enforceable as law unless it dates from time immemorial. In *Welbeck* v. *Brown*[1] two of the three judges of the Supreme Court of the Gold Coast laid down that this rule applied. The third, Macleod, J., declined to support them. The Chief Justice of the time took the most extreme view, holding that, since the mode of disinheriting a nephew by cutting an " ekal " had given place to disinheritance by merely driving him away from the family house, the custom of disinheritance could not be recognized. The old mode was not admissible because it was not " existing " and the new mode was not admissible because it did not date from " a time to which the memory of man runneth not to the contrary ". Smallman Smith, J., took the view that the essence of the custom was disinheritance and that the mode by which this was accomplished might be varied without impugning the validity of the custom. The Korsah Commission commented in 1951:

> " This case has been described as ' probably bad law ' and does not seem to have been relied on in later cases . . . Whatever the theoretical force of *Welbeck* v. *Brown* however, in practice antiquity appears to matter little in the Supreme Court."[2]

The Judicial Committee of the Privy Council has recognized customs in Nigeria which have only grown up since the arrival there of Europeans.[3]

When we come to consider the detailed provisions of s. 87(1) regulating the application of customary law as limited in the manner referred to above, immediate difficulty is encountered. We may pass over the inelegance of the first use of " deprive " in s. 87(1). Since the courts are statutory creations they can of course only have such jurisdiction as statute confers, and jurisdiction to administer customary law was not, except incidentally, conferred elsewhere than in this section. The opening words

---

[1] (1884), Sarbah F.C.L. 185.
[2] *Loc. cit.*
[3] *Oshodi* v. *Brimah Balogun* (1936), 4 W.A.C.A. 1; see also *Golightly* v. *Ashrifi* (1955), 14 W.A.C.A. 676.

must therefore be read in the reverse sense, as conferring jurisdiction. The inelegance is particularly unfortunate since the
second use of " deprive " must presumably be taken to mean what
it says. It is remarkable that here the section prohibits " any
person " and not simply a " native " from being deprived of
the benefit of customary law. Should this be taken in the same
way as a " conferring " provision, entitling " non-natives " to
the benefit of customary law? Certainly a " non-native " in an
action with a " native " might receive the benefit of customary
law in a " substantial injustice " case under the second paragraph
of s. 87(1). Furthermore a " non-native " may under customary
law, acquire rights (and liabilities) if that law permits of its application to him. An obvious example of this is a customary marriage
entered into by a European with an African and recognized as
valid by the customary law in question. If " any person " is
taken literally neither party should be deprived of the benefit of
the customary law relating to the marriage but in *Savage* v.
Macfoy[1] the Supreme Court of Nigeria, construing a provision
with similar wording to that of s. 87(1), declined to uphold a
mixed marriage of this sort, the Chief Justice remarking:

> " It has been urged upon the court that the words ' any
> person ' means all persons whomsoever, and that consequently
> Europeans can validly contract marriages in this Colony
> according to native custom. On reading the section in its
> entirety, this proposition does not appear to be in accordance
> with the canons of interpretation or in accordance with the law
> of the Colony. If that reading of the section is correct, what was
> the necessity for special provision as to transactions between
> Europeans and natives? "

It is far from clear who were " natives " within the meaning of
s. 87(1). The term was defined in s. 2 of the Courts Ordinance as
follows:

> " Native means a person of African descent: Provided that
> the expression shall not include any person who does not belong
> to a class of persons who have ordinarily been subject to Native
> Tribunals."

The question of African descent in itself provides innumerable
problems in cases of mixed blood, but the proviso to this definition defies elucidation and appears to have been entirely ignored.
In *Brown* v. *Miller*[2] the Supreme Court held that a Jamaican

---

[1] (1909) Renner's Reports 504.
[2] (1921) Full Court Judgments 1920–1921, 50.

woman, presumably of African descent, who had lived in the
Gold Coast for more than sixty years was not a " native " although
certain Native Tribunals had accepted her as such. This was
under a provision which defined " native " as " any person who
is under native customary law or under any Ordinance a member
of a native community of the Colony, Ashanti or the Northern
Territories ".[1] The court laid down that before a stranger could
be treated as a member of a native community he must have committed himself to the adoption of membership of the community
by " definite and unmistakable signs and acts " such as the payment of stool levies and debts, and participation in stool ceremonies. This throws some light on the proviso cited above, but
the question of when a person was to be taken to have joined or
left a particular " class of persons " and the meaning of " subject
to Native Tribunals " in days when Native Tribunals had ceased
to enjoy statutory recognition remained obscure. No definition
of " Native Tribunal " was given and, even if the proviso had
been otherwise comprehensible, it was uncertain whether Native
Tribunals in other parts of Africa were included. In *Morris* v.
Monrovia[2] both parties were members of the Kroo tribe of
Liberia and had settled in the Gold Coast. They were clearly of
African descent, but the court understandably made no attempt
to grapple with the problem of whether they were prevented by
the proviso from being treated as " natives ".[3]

2. THE PRESENT MEANING OF " CUSTOMARY LAW "

As stated above[4] the definition of customary law included in
the original draft Constitution was dropped. The problems of
defining customary law are well known. A number of different
definitions have been attempted in Ghana and elsewhere and all
of them have been open to criticism.[5] In spite of the difficulties
attending any definition, the practical problem is small, since the
courts know perfectly well what customary law is and tend to
ignore verbal subtleties in any definition they encounter. It
was tempting therefore to follow the example of the Courts
Ordinance and provide no definition at all. This despite Dr.

---

[1] Dr. Allott has collected at least a dozen different definitions of " native "
or " African " in the law of Ghana: *op. cit.* p. 168.

[2] (1930), 1 W.A.C.A. 70.

[3] Further problems arising on s. 87(1) are discussed in the following
chapter, pp. 436 *et seq. post.*

[4] *Ante*, p. 92.

[5] See Allott, *op. cit.*, p. 165.

Allott's remark that " refusal to define what the courts are to administer is understandable, but must be stigmatized as cowardly ".[1] However, although the courts know well enough what customary law is, it was thought desirable to make it clear that customary law as comprised in the laws of Ghana was limited to customs applicable to particular communities in Ghana, thus excluding other forms of African customary law where the peoples who were subject to them were not represented in sufficient numbers in Ghana to be described as a community. At the same time it was desirable to state that any rule of customary law assimilated into the common law as being suitable for general application would be withdrawn from the body of customary law. Accordingly, a definition of sorts was inserted in the Interpretation Act, 1960 (C.A.4.) in the following terms:

" 18.—(1) Customary law, as comprised in the laws of Ghana, consists of rules of law which by custom are applicable to particular communities in Ghana, not being rules included in the common law under any enactment providing for the assimilation of such rules of customary law as are suitable for general application."

This definition is intended to avoid the difficulties which have arisen over the word " existing " in s. 87 of the old Courts Ordinance.[2] Since s. 18 will be always speaking, the court in any particular case will have to decide whether, at the time when the dispute before it arose, the rules in question were by custom applicable. There are many theoretical difficulties about this, notably as to the point at which a custom becomes "a rule of law", but it is not expected that any practical trouble will be caused. By virtue of s. 67(1) of the Courts Act, 1960, (C.A.9) any question as to the existence or content of a rule of customary law is made a question of law and not of fact. Thus it may be expected that the court will hold that once a pronouncement has been made by the Supreme Court or the High Court on the existence or content of a particular rule that pronouncement will be regarded as having the same authority as a similar pronouncement about the common law would have. Unless, therefore, the rule is subsequently altered under statutory authority it would no doubt normally be treated as firmly established as part of the laws of Ghana. The courts are left to determine how far subsequent variation in the

[1] *Op. cit.* p. 164.
[2] See p. 411, *ante.*

practical application of the rule will be recognized as changing the law. If the courts in Ghana choose to follow the early example of the English courts they will no doubt tend to discourage the recognition of such variations.[1]

Section 18(2) of the Interpretation Act, 1960 (C.A.4) contains a similar provision to that made with reference to the common law by s. 17(5), namely, that references in enactments to a customary law are to be construed as references to it as affected by an enactment for the time being in force. This reproduces the effect of s. 87(1) of the Courts Ordinance.

It will be observed that another provision of s. 87(1), namely that a customary law will not be enforced if it is repugnant to natural justice, equity, and good conscience has not been reproduced. It was considered unfitting to the dignity of the indigenous laws of the people of Ghana to suggest that this repugnancy might continue to exist. For over one hundred years, customary laws which were considered to be repugnant to natural justice, equity and good conscience have not been enforced because the law forbade their enforcement. It seems reasonable to assume therefore that such customary laws as remain will not offend in this respect.

3. Ascertainment of Customary Law

One of the chief difficulties associated with customary law in Ghana concerns the means by which the existence and content of a customary law rule is capable of being established in court. Before the changes made on 1st July, 1960, the leading authority on the subject was *Angu* v. *Attah*, a Privy Council case decided in 1919. The judgment in this case contained the following passage:

> " The land law in the Gold Coast Colony is based on native customs. As is the case with all customary law, it has to be proved in the first instance by calling witnesses acquainted with the native customs until the customs have, by frequent proof in the Courts, become so notorious that the Courts take judicial notice of them."[2]

---

[1] See pp. 424–5, *post*.
[2] P.C. (1874–1928) 43, at p. 44; this was followed by the Privy Council in *Amissah* v. *Krabah* (1931), 2 W.A.C.A. 30.

Customary law as a question of fact

The rule that the ascertainment of customary law was to be regarded as a question of fact in cases where judicial notice could not be taken of it had become firmly established, although the suggestion in the passage cited above that the question would only be decided by calling expert witnesses was incorrect, since other methods have frequently been relied on. The methods available before Republic Day in such cases may be summarized as follows:

(a) the calling of expert witnesses by the parties or by the court;

(b) reliance by the court on its own expert knowledge;

(c) reliance by the court on the expert knowledge of assessors;

(d) reference of the question to a local court or native court;

(e) consultation of textbooks and other works of authority.

These methods are discussed more fully below. Two or more might of course be used in determining a single question.[1]

Calling of expert witnesses.—This was of frequent occurrence. The following are instances of the type of witness employed: a linguist to the Asantehene, on the custom in Ashanti as to the property of an ahinkwa of a chief,[2] the parties to an action themselves, on the custom to be applied in the proceedings,[3] a clergyman familiar with the customary law in question,[4] kings and chiefs,[5] the Ga Manche, on Ga customary marriage,[6] a Paramount Chief, on the Akran custom as to self-acquired property,[7] European merchants and solicitors with knowledge of customary law.[8] (See also Allott, *Essays in African Law*, p. 77.)

Although uncontradicted, the evidence of expert witnesses might be rejected if it ran counter to established opinion as evidenced by textbooks and judicial observations.[9]

Section 87(2) of the Courts Ordinance provided:

" In deciding questions of native law and custom the court . . . may call to its assistance chiefs or other persons whom the

---

[1] See, *e.g. Owoo* v. *Owoo* (1945), 11 W.A.C.A. 81 at p. 83.
[2] *Kweku Kodieh* v. *Kwami Affram* (1930), 1 W.A.C.A. 12.
[3] *Balogun* v. *Balogun* (1935), 2 W.A.C.A. 287.
[4] *Ibid.*
[5] *Mensah* v. *Toku* (1887), Sarbah's Fanti Law Reports, p. 42.
[6] *Re The Marriage Ordinance* (1934) Div. Court, 1931–37, 69.
[7] *Yamuah IV* v. *Sekyi* (1936), 3 W.A.C.A. 57.
[8] *Okai* v. *Quist* (1895), Renner's Reports 122.
[9] See *Golightly* v. *Ashrifi* (1955), 14 W.A.C.A. 676 at p. 681.

court considers to have special knowledge of native law and custom."

This vaguely-worded provision was inserted in 1951 in place of the more precise, though more limited, wording of s. 74(2) of the former Courts Ordinance, which enabled persons with special knowledge to be called as witnesses[1] " on the application of any party " and empowered the court to require them to give evidence on oath. Since the court had power under s. 90 of the Courts Ordinance to call its own expert witnesses the alteration does not appear to have been necessary for this purpose and its only effect was to introduce uncertainty as to what was covered by the phrase " may call to its assistance ". Had the assistance to be given in open court? Could the expert be served with a subpoena? Could he be cross-examined? Was what he said " evidence "? No judicial answer appears to have been given to these and other questions. In its original form the provision described the experts as referees,[2] whose opinions were to be treated as evidence, and went on to say, "the court shall presume the correctness of such evidence ". This was assumed to mean that the evidence was to be treated as conclusive, even though conflicting evidence was produced by the parties.[3] See also the Supreme Court (Civil Procedure) Rules, Order 37A, as to the appointment of a court expert. Judging from r. 11 of the Order, this was not intended to apply to proof of customary law but there seems no reason why it should not.

Expert knowledge of the court.—In former times, when judges of the Supreme Court were all non-Africans, only the Native Tribunals, composed mainly of chiefs and headmen, possessed expert knowledge of customary law. By the time of the inauguration of the Republic the position was quite different. A judge of the Supreme Court might himself, as a member of the African community to which a customary law in question before him applied, be expert in that law, whereas a local court magistrate might be a person with little if any knowledge of customary law. This reflected the healthy tendency towards the removal of the principle that the higher courts were restricted to applying

---

[1] They are referred to as " referees " in s. 25 (5); Allott treats them as assessors (*op. cit.*, p. 78).

[2] Hence the reference to referees in s. 25 (5), in which the necessary consequential amendment was not made.

[3] *Kudwo Toku* v. *Kofi Ama*, Sarbah's Fanti Law Reports, 58 at p. 61.

English law while the lower courts were restricted to applying customary law. It suggests that the modification of the rule in *Angu* v. *Attah*, namely that it did not apply " to Native Courts of which the members are versed in their own native customary law ", which was recognized in *Ababio II* v. *Nsemfoo*[1] should be regarded as extending to the higher courts.[2] As M'Carthy, J. pointed out in *Ababio II* v. *Nsemfoo*, this did not of course mean that expert evidence could not also be called. A judge might also seek information from a fellow-judge on a point of customary law.

The weight to be attached to a finding of a lower court based on its own knowledge of customary law is illustrated by *Amoabimaa* v. *Badu*.[3] The case arose out of a dispute between members of the Yego clan of Nyakrom, which had farmed land in common for several generations until disagreements led to the division of the land between the several family groups. One of the families later sought to challenge this division and alleged that they retained rights over the former common land. The Native Court, of its own knowledge, held that the division had taken place according to the custom of " cutting ekar " and could not be upset. On appeal, the learned judge of the Land Court held that the lands of a family stool cannot revert to one branch of a family and that the finding on customary law by the Native Court was wrong. On a further appeal to the West African Court of Appeal the court held that the learned judge of the Land Court should not have interfered with the finding of the Native Court, which was expert in native custom, and reversed his decision. See also *Akumanyi* v. *Pepra*,[4] where the Supreme Court declined to reverse a finding of a Native Court, apparently based on its own knowledge, although it was said to be contrary to customary law as stated in Sarbah's *Fanti Customary Laws*. Compare *Vanderpuye* v. *Botchway*,[5] where the setting aside by a Divisional Court of a decision of the Ga Native Court was upheld.

Assessors.—Section 25 of the Courts Ordinance provided that if a question of customary law was involved in a case before a Land Court deriving jurisdiction under the Ordinance it must be tried with the aid of an assessor or assessors. The decision of the case rested with the Land Judge alone, but any dissent by an

---

[1] (1947) 12 W.A.C.A. 127.
[2] But see Allott, *op. cit.*, p. 91.
[3] (1956), 1 W.A.L. 227.
[4] (1956), 2 W.A.L. 112.
[5] (1951), 13 W.A.C.A. 164.

assessor had to be recorded. It was ruled by the West African Court of Appeal[1] that the result of any consultation by a Land Court with an assessor on a material point of customary law should be announced in open court before judgment, when it could presumably be challenged, but the assessor held an uneasy position as a judge who had no responsibility for the judgment and a witness who could not be cross-examined, and was a relic of times when British judges were in need of the sort of general assistance he could provide as to African habits, customs, modes of thought, and language.[2]

Reference to a local or native court.—Section 89 of the Courts Ordinance enabled the High Court or a Magistrate's Court, when trying a civil case, to refer a question " as to the right of any native " under customary law to a competent Local Court or Native Court for determination. The court could accept or reject this determination, or could " deal therewith in such manner as justice and the circumstances of the case shall appear to it to require ". Under the similar provisions of the previous Courts Ordinance (s. 76) a Divisional Court in 1945 referred to the Ga State Council certain questions relating to an alleged six-cloth marriage.[3] The determination of all the questions except one was accepted by the learned judge, the remaining one being " neither accepted nor rejected ". This reference was only possible because the definition of " Native Courts " in the previous Ordinance included a tribunal exercising jurisdiction under the Native Administration (Colony) Ordinance. After 1951 State Councils ceased to be available under s. 89 as a source of reference on points of customary law. Strangely, the Houses of Chiefs Act, 1958 (No. 20) did not provide for reference by the courts to Houses of Chiefs.

Works of Authority.—Section 87(2) of the Courts Ordinance provided:

> " In deciding questions of native law and custom the Court may give effect to any book or manuscript recognized in Ghana as a legal authority. . . ."

Thus works such as Sarbah's *Fanti Customary Laws* (1904) and Redwar's *Comments on some Ordinances of the Gold Coast Colony*

---

[1] *Acquah III* v. *Ababio* (1948), 12 W.A.C.A. 343.
[2] See also Allott, *op. cit.*, pp. 78–81, and *Nelson* v. *Nelson* (1951), 13 W.A.C.A. 248 at p. 249.
[3] *Sackeyfio* v. *Ayichoe Tagoe* (1945), 11 W.A.C.A. 73.

(1909) have frequently been relied on by the courts, even in the absence of any supporting evidence.[1] The existence of this provision illustrates the confusion surrounding the treatment of customary law. Where judicial notice could not be taken of a rule of customary law its existence and content was a question of fact. Yet the most extreme form of hearsay evidence, namely the view expressed on another occasion by some dead (or even living) author on the very fact to be found by the court was, by a statutory rule, made the basis on which the court could found its decision. This paradox is well illustrated by *Adedibu* v. *Adewoyin*.[2] In this Nigerian case the trial judge referred to a document described as " Mr. Ward Price's Memorandum of Land Tenure in the Yoruba Province ", which had not been tendered as evidence. The Nigerian provision equivalent to s. 87(2) refers to " any book or manuscript recognized by natives as a legal authority " and the West African Court of Appeal, possibly basing itself on the fact that in Nigeria this provision appears in the Evidence Ordinance, held that the Memorandum should not have been relied on since it was neither tendered in evidence nor proved to be recognized by natives as a legal authority. This decision did not reflect the practice in Ghana, where the court did not normally require the book or manuscript to be tendered in evidence and would usually decide if it was authoritative by taking judicial notice of whether it was generally accepted or not.[3] Perhaps the most rational way to deal with this method of proof would have been to treat the author of the textbook or other work as if he were an expert witness, but allow his evidence to be given in the form of his published work if he could not be called in person. This would involve something on the lines of s. 60 of the Indian Evidence Act, which is in force in certain parts of East Africa:

---

[1] See *e.g.*, *Nelson* v. *Nelson* (1951), 13 W.A.C.A. 248, at p. 251; and for an example of a proposition by Sarbah frequently followed by the Courts see *Kwainoo* v. *Ampong* (1953) 14 W.A.C.A. 250.

[2] (1951), 13 W.A.C.A. 191.

[3] Compare the common law rule as to proof of foreign law: the court will not refer independently to textbooks, but will insist on the testimony of expert witnesses. (Phipson's *Law of Evidence* (9th edn.), p. 405). In former times customary law was treated as being on all fours with foreign law (see *Hughes* v. *Davies* (1909), Renner 550) but this later came to be regarded as erroneous. See Sarbah, *Fanti Customary Laws*, London, 1904, p. 18.

" The opinions of experts expressed in any treatise commonly offered for sale, and the grounds on which such opinions are held, may be proved by the production of such treatises, if the author is dead or cannot be found, or has become incapable of giving evidence, or cannot be called as a witness without an amount of delay or expense which the court regards as unreasonable."[1]

It is clear that each of the five different methods of establishing customary law in Ghana in cases where judicial notice was not taken of the rule in question depended on a consideration by the court of the views of persons (who might include the court itself) possessing expert knowledge of the rule. It is relevant to observe therefore that, with some exceptions, the superior courts in Ghana seem to have paid little attention to the qualifications of persons alleged to possess expert knowledge. If anyone was put forward as an expert, particularly if his views were uncontradicted, it seems that the court usually accepted him at face value. This practice had its dangers, since inaccurate opinions might in this way receive the seal of judicial authority and in time pass into the realm of judicially-noticed law. As Griffith, C.J., remarked in *Yerenchi* v. *Akuffo* as long ago as 1905:

" . . . it is a serious thing either to refuse to accept a native custom, which may have existed for ages, or to put the judicial hall-mark upon a native custom, and I think that before the court holds one way or another the evidence in favour of or against any such custom should be more than merely preponderating."[2]

Judicial notice of customary law

In accordance with the second branch of the rule in *Angu* v. *Attah*, judicial notice was taken of the existence and content of a rule of customary law when it had become notorious by frequent proof in the courts. There are two aspects to this. Certain rules have become so well known that the judges would recognize them without reference to previous authority. The rule that no title to land can be acquired under customary law by lapse of time is in this category.[3] So also are the following: the liability of a " caretaker " to account for property received by him;[4]

---

[1] Cited [1958] 2 J.A.L. 8.
[2] Cited by Ollennu, J., in *Kwaku* v. *Addo* (1957) 2 W.A.L. 306.
[3] See, *e.g. Adu* v. *Kuma* (1937), 3 W.A.C.A. 240; *Dadzie* v. *Kojo* (1940), 6 W.A.C.A. 139; *Owoo* v. *Owoo* (1945), 11 W.A.C.A. 81 at p. 84; *Fiscian* v. *Nelson* (1946), 12 W.A.C.A. 21; *Cofie* v. *Ashong* (1956), 1 W.A.L. 82 at p. 86.
[4] *Nelson* v. *Nelson* (1932), 1 W.A.C.A. 215; *Ruttmern* v. *Ruttmern* (1937), 3 W.A.C.A. 178.

the absence of liability to account in the case of a chief or head of a family;[1] descent to nephew on the maternal side in cases of intestacy;[2] forfeiture in case of letting by a grantee of land to a stranger;[3] the right of a chief's successor to take up residence in the Ahinfie;[4] samansiw or nuncupative will;[5] inventory in dispute as to stool property.[6] On the other hand, in the case of many alleged rules of customary law the court would carry out an examination of previous decisions before taking judicial notice. Unfortunately, judges did not always make it clear whether they were taking judicial notice or treating previous decisions in the same way as they treat text-books, and the answer has to be inferred (often with difficulty) from the judgment.[7] Recent cases where judicial notice has apparently been taken in this way include the following: *Acquah III* v. *Ababio*[8] (right of Stool in relation to chief's private property); *Wellington* v. *Papafio*[9] (rights of children under Ga customary law); *Eze* v. *Igiligbe*[10] (communal nature of land tenure); *Amarfio* v. *Ayoakor*[11] (intestacy in Ga customary law). Earlier cases include *Quayson* v. *Abba*[12] (the custom of sarvie); *Tawiah* v. *Kwa Mensah*[13] (destoolment); and *Angu* v. *Attah* itself (tribute in relation to stool lands).

Authority on the number and type of previous decisions required to enable judicial notice to be taken is scanty. In *Larinde* v. *Afiko*[14] the West African Court of Appeal held that the trial judge was wrong in treating an alleged customary law relating to land in the Awori District of Lagos as established by a single decision in 1892. Nevertheless single decisions appear to have been relied on when reinforced by textbooks or expert evidence.[15]

---

[1] *Abude* v. *Onano* (1946), 12 W.A.C.A. 102 at p. 104.
[2] *Mensah Larkai* v. *Amorkor* (1933), 1 W.A.C.A. 323 at p. 327; *Ekem* v. *Nerba* (1947), 12 W.A.C.A. 258; *Nelson* v. *Nelson, supra.*
[3] *Bassey* v. *Eteta* (1938), 4 W.A.C.A. 153 at p. 155.
[4] *Quansah* v. *Yankum II* (1949), 12 W.A.C.A. 435.
[5] *Nelson* v. *Nelson* (1951), 13 W.A.C.A. 248 at p. 249.
[6] *Kojo* v. *Anane* (1956), 1 W.A.L. 131.
[7] See, *e.g.*, *Owiredu* v. *Moshie* (1952), 14 W.A.C.A. 11; and *cf.* the advice given to judges by the Privy Council in *Amissah* v. *Krabah*, cited *Allott, op. cit.*, p. 91.
[8] (1948), 12 W.A.C.A. 343.
[9] (1952) 14 W.A.C.A. 49 at p. 51.
[10] (1952) 14 W.A.C.A. 61.
[11] (1954) 14 W.A.C.A. 554 at p. 556.
[12] (1934) Div. Court, 1931–37, 50 at p. 54–5.
[13] (1934) Div. Court, 1931–37, 65 at p. 68.
[14] (1940), 6 W.A.C.A. 108.
[15] As in *Owiredu* v. *Moshie* (1952) 14 W.A.C.A. 11.

In *Kwaku* v. *Addo*[1] Ollennu, J. held that, as the cases he had consulted on the customary law rules of defamation left the content of the rules in doubt, he could not take judicial notice of them.

It appears that the " notoriety " required for judicial notice was not the sort of factual notoriety that enables the court to take judicial notice of, say, the geographical location of Ghana on the West Coast of Africa, but rather legal notoriety. The question of how many people affected by the rule under consideration were aware of the previous judicial decisions which recognise it was thus irrelevant. In Ghana as in England every citizen is presumed to know the law and this is not a presumption that can be displaced by rebutting evidence.

One of the most important and difficult questions arising in relation to judicial notice of a rule of customary law was whether any alteration of the rule would be accepted by the court after judicial notice had been taken of it. This alteration might come about through a ruling by a State Council or chief, or by virtue of a declaration made by a House of Chiefs under s. 16 of the Houses of Chiefs Acts, 1958 (No. 20)[2] or simply through the changed behaviour of the persons who are subject to the rule. Was the rule to be applied by the courts in the form in which it had received " the judicial hall-mark " or the form in which it was observed in practice? Reference to English law affords little help on this. It is usually assumed that once a custom has received judicial notice it becomes part of the common law and cannot be altered except by legislation, but authority is difficult to find. Sir John Salmond, referring to usage rather than custom and citing *Edie* v. *East India Co.*[3] and *Goodwin* v. *Robarts*,[4] said:

> " When a general usage has once been received by judicial recognition into the body of the common law, so that it has now its immediate source in judicial precedent as a rule of case law, it appears that the law so constituted cannot be altered by the growth of any later usage in conflict with it. . . . If any rule of law so established is to be excluded or modified in any particular case, it must be done by express agreement of the parties, and not by reliance on any new usage which derogates from the law so constituted."[5]

---

[1] (1957), 2 W.A.L. 306.
[2] See now the Chieftaincy Act, 1961 (Act 81), s. 59, p. 429, *post*.
[3] (1761), 2 Burr. 1216.
[4] (1875), L.R. 10 Ex. 357.
[5] Jurisprudence (11th edn.), p. 240.

In *Goodwin* v. *Robarts*[1] a very strong Court of Exchequer Chamber (Cockburn, L.J., Mellor, Lush, Brett and Lindley, J.J.) said:

" We must by no means be understood as saying that mercantile usage, however extensive, should be allowed to prevail if contrary to positive law, including in the latter such usages as, having been made the subject of legal decision, and having been sanctioned and adopted by the courts have become, by such adoption, part of the common law. . . . And we quite agree that this would apply quite as strongly to an attempt to set up a new usage against one which has become settled and adopted by the common law as to one in conflict with the more ancient rules of the common law itself."[2]

We are here in the realm of commerce, where an established usage, while it cannot be modified by later usage, can in a particular case be adjusted by agreement to suit the parties. It is submitted that the customary law of Ghana is more akin to the general and local customs of England, which were absorbed by the common law in accordance with rules, e.g., those requiring the custom to date from time immemorial and to be " reasonable ", which do not apply in Ghana.[3] Accordingly little assistance is to be obtained on this question from English law.

Turning to decisions on the law of Ghana we may observe that in *Angu* v. *Attah*[4] the Privy Council expressed the view:

" In the Gold Coast Colony the principal customs as to the tenure of land have now reached the stage at which the Courts recognize them, and the law has become as it were crystallised."

This suggests that contrary custom could not be proved after " crystallization " had occurred, and there do not appear to be any decisions to contradict this suggestion. In *Aryeh* v. *Dawuda*[5] the West African Court of Appeal appeared to countenance the production of evidence of a custom displacing the ordinary rule as to descent of property through the female line, but this was probably on the ground not that the general rule might have been modified but that it might not have applied to the parties in question. In *Golightly* v. *Ashrifi*[6] the West African Court of

---

[1] (1875), L.R. 10 Ex. 357.
[2] *Cf. Diamond Alkali Corpn.* v. *FI. Bourgeois*, [1921] 3 K.B. 443 at p. 458.
[3] *Welbeck* v. *Brown*, Sarbah F.C.L. 185, where the test of time immemorial was applied, is now regarded as wrongly decided: see Korsah Report (1951), p. 16. See also Sarbah F.C.L. p. 16. The test of reasonableness is perhaps not very different from that of repugnancy.
[4] (1956), 1 W.A.L.R. 128.
[5] (1944), 10 W.A.C.A. 188.
[6] (1955), 14 W.A.C.A. 676.

Appeal laid down that the customary law applied " must not be the native law or custom or usage of ancient times, but existing native law or custom ".

This was not said with specific reference to judicially-noticed law and was perhaps merely a recognition of the fact that customs may change and develop in practice. Section 87(1) of the Courts Ordinance did however refer to " native law or custom *existing* in Ghana ". The view of the courts towards well-established rules of customary law appears to be accurately indicated by this statement in the judgment of Lingley, J. in *Kuma* v. *Kofi*.[1]

> " It is established law that a pledgor can redeem his land after any lapse of time. However much one may feel that, with changing conditions, there ought to be some limitation of this doctrine it is a well established principle and it is not open to this court to depart from that principle."

Mention should be made of the view that the crystallization or otherwise of judicially-noticed custom may be determined by the wording of statutory definitions. The Korsah Commission stated in 1951:

> " This freedom to change is preserved in the Colony and Southern Togoland, where customary law is defined as a body of rules ' which obtains and is fortified by established native usage '. The same words occurred in the 1924 Ashanti Ordinance, but were later dropped."[2]

These words continued to be used until 1960, however. They appeared in the definitions of customary law contained in the Local Courts Act, 1958 (No. 23) and the Houses of Chiefs Act, 1958 (No. 20). The Commission went on to draw the conclusion that the absence from the Courts Ordinance of any definition of customary law produced " the seeds of divergence between the Supreme Court and the Native Courts in some territories " and expressed the view that the definition " avoids the petrifying effect of judicial precedent ".[3]

The new provisions

Section 67 of the Courts Act, 1960 (C.A. 9) lays down new provisions relating to the ascertainment of customary law. Subsection (1) provides:

---

[1] 1 W.A.L.R. 130.
[2] Report, p. 16.
[3] Dr. Allott takes a similar view: *op. cit.*, pp. 89–90.

" any question as to the existence or content of a rule of customary law is a question of law for the court and not a question of fact."

It might be thought that, since customary law is stated by the Constitution to be one of the components of the laws of Ghana, sub-s. (1) is unnecessary. It has been inserted to emphasize the true characteristics of customary law and to show that the old conception that a customary law rule relied on by a party in any proceedings had to be proved by evidence and was therefore to be treated as a question of fact has been abandoned. Since almost all the judges and magistrates in Ghana are now and will continue to be Ghanaians, there is no obstacle in the way of asserting the proposition that the courts are to be taken to have judicial knowledge of customary law as they are taken to have judicial knowledge of any other of the laws of Ghana. Since the meaning of customary law is confined to law applicable to Ghanaian communities[1] the courts here will not be expected to have judicial knowledge of customary laws prevailing in other parts of Africa.

Although the general proposition that the courts have judicial knowledge of Ghanaian customary law is now tenable, it was nevertheless recognized that some special procedure might still necessary to enable the court to satisfy itself as to the existence or content of lesser-known rules. Even after hearing legal arguments put forward on behalf of the parties and consulting such reported cases, textbooks and other sources as may be appropriate, the court may still occasionally find itself in doubt. Where this happens, s. 67 provides for a form of judicial enquiry to be held to clear up the doubts. This enquiry will not be separate from the proceedings in question, but will form part of them although it may be necessary for the proceedings to be adjourned to enable experts to be called to give their opinion. Indeed, sub-s. (2) requires an adjournment in such cases, although the period of the adjournment is not specified and serious delay is not likely to be caused.

The court is given considerable freedom in the methods used at the enquiry, and sub-s. (3) confers on the court the same power to compel experts to attend the enquiry as exists in relation to the attendance and testimony of witnesses. This means that Part IV of the Courts Act will apply for the purpose of these

---

[1] Interpretation Act, 1960 (C.A. 4), s. 18 (1).

enquiries,[1] but the court is given a discretion to modify the provisions relating to witnesses in any way that may appear to it to be necessary. An example of the sort of modification that is envisaged concerns the requirement in s. 73 that persons are to be examined on oath or affirmation. It may be appropriate to require an expert to give his opinion on oath where it is based on historical facts known to him personally. Where, however, his statements at the enquiry are limited to pure questions of opinion an oath or affirmation may not be appropriate, although there seems no reason why he should not be asked to swear or affirm that his opinion is genuinely held if this course seems to the court to be appropriate.

The proviso to s. 67(3) modifies the normal freedom of parties to call such witnesses as they think fit. Paragraph (*a*) of the proviso requires the parties to the action to submit to the court the names of person they desire to be heard at the enquiry. The court will wish to satisfy itself that such persons are unbiased and competent to pronounce upon the matter in issue.

Paragraph (*b*) of the proviso allows the court to consider written statements of opinion from such bodies as Houses of Chiefs and State Councils[2] without making it necessary to summon any person before the enquiry to deliver the opinion of the body.

It is contemplated that the procedure laid down by s. 67 will help to elucidate and place on record the detailed rules of the customary laws of Ghana. Its success will depend on the attitude of the courts. If the courts adopt the view that their decisions, particularly judgments which are likely to be reported, should be as clear and precise as possible in the enunciation of rules of customary law, it may be expected that within a short time a strong body of authority will be built up which will go far to clear away the obscurities which still surround much of the customary law.

4. PART VII OF THE CHIEFTAINCY ACT

Part VII of the Chieftaincy Act, 1961 (Act 81) contains important provisions relating to the declaration, alteration and assimilation of rules of customary law. Similar provisions as to the declaration and alteration of such rules have existed for many years but, except in relation to constitutional matters, little use

---

[1] Sections 113–117 in the case of local courts.
[2] Now known as Traditional Councils

has been made of them.[1] The new provisions are given in full in an appendix to this book[2] but they will be briefly summarized here.

Each traditional council is authorised to consider the customary law in force within its area and, if the law is uncertain or it is considered desirable that it should be modified, or assimilated by the common law, the council must make representations to the appropriate House of Chiefs. Each House of Chiefs has power to draw up a draft declaration of a customary law rule, or a draft statement of desirable alterations to such a rule, but this has no effect unless confirmed by the Minister of Justice, who may modify the draft. Where the rule applies in more than one Region the draft must be prepared by a joint committee of the Houses of Chiefs for each region affected.

The procedure for the assimilation of a rule of customary law by the common law is as follows. The Minister convenes a joint committee of all Houses of Chiefs. If, after hearing representations and investigating the matter, the joint committee think the rule should be assimilated they draw up a draft declaration setting out the rule, with such modifications as they may consider desirable. If, after consulting the Chief Justice, the Minister finds the draft acceptable, either as submitted or with modifications, he may declare the rule assimilated. The rule then becomes part of the common law and may be referred to as a common law rule of customary origin. It becomes applicable to every issue within its scope whether that issue would, if assimilation had not taken place, have been determined according to the common law or any system of customary law. In applying it the court may have regard to textbooks explaining the rule and are to treat it generally in the same way as any other common law rule.[3]

5. LOCAL COURTS

Jurisdiction under the Local Courts Act, 1958

Apart from cases arising under statute and personal suits where the debt, damage or demand did not exceed fifty pounds,

---

[1] Recent constitutional declarations are embodied in the Declaration of Customary Law (Akwapim State) Order, 1960 (L.I. 32) and the Declaration of Customary Law (Dagomba State) Order, 1960 (L.I. 59).

[2] See Appendix C, p. 502, *post*.

[3] For the priority of an assimilated rule over statutes of general application and over the rules of equity and common law in the narrow sense see p. 407, *ante*.

the jurisdiction of the local courts under the Local Courts Act, 1958 (No. 23) was limited to actions in which the law applicable was customary law. The question of the applicability of English law scarcely arose therefore—indeed, as mentioned previously[1] it was possible to argue that English law had no application in local courts at all. If it could be applied in the " fifty pound cases " it was only as " law binding between the parties ". Since local courts had unrestricted jurisdiction as to persons[2] it was theoretically possible for, say, one Englishman to sue another for a debt of fifty pounds in a local court, though no question of conflict of laws would arise in such a case. There was not even the guidance provided by s. 87(1) of the Courts Ordinance to tell the court what should govern the relative application of English law and customary law in cases where Africans were involved, although the proviso to s. 15 (*b*) appears to have produced the result that English law might in certain circumstances be applied in cases where some or all of the parties were Africans. This proviso, which followed the wording of the last paragraph of s. 87(1), can only be given any meaning if it is read not as a proviso but as an enlarging provision, enabling the court to apply not only the law prevailing within its jurisdiction and the law binding between the parties, but also, if the parties to a suit all gave their consent, some other law which the parties had expressly or by implication agreed should govern the transaction.

Dr. Allott discusses the meaning of the expression " the law prevailing within the jurisdiction of the court "[3] and suggests that it could mean either (i) " found " or " existing ", or (ii) " dominant " in the area. The only reported case Dr. Allott has discovered, a Nigerian decision arising under criminal law, helps little if at all in the context of civil proceedings in Ghana.

The expression " the law binding between the parties " merely begs the question in a case where inter-customary law conflict arises. Where the court could discover what this law was it would prefer it to the law prevailing within its jurisdiction.[4]

Section 24 of the Local Courts Act, 1958 provided that, subject to the Act and any regulations made under it, the procedure and practice of local courts was to be regulated by customary law.[5]

---

[1] *Ante*, p. 392.
[2] Section 8 (1).
[3] *Op. cit.*, p. 160.
[4] See the remarks on *Ghamson* v. *Wobill*, p. 447, *post*.
[5] This is still the case; see now the Courts Act, 1960 (C.A.9), s. 103.

One important effect of this provision was to free local courts from the rules of evidence prescribed by English law.

" There are no strict rules of evidence in Native customary procedure, the tendency being to admit all that materially throws light on the controversy."[1]

Present jurisdiction

The Local Courts Act, 1958 (C.A.9) was repealed and re-enacted with some modifications by the Courts Act, 1960 (No. 23). The provisions relating to local courts are contained in Part VI of the 1960 Act and the changes relevant to the subject under discussion are as follows:

1. Section 15 of the 1958 Act, which laid down the types of law to be administered in the local courts was not reproduced. Subject to the considerable restrictions on its civil jurisdiction imposed by s. 98 of the 1960 Act, a local court must now apply in civil proceedings the general law of the land.

2. Section 25 of the 1958 Act, by which in any land or other cause in which it appeared to the local court magistrate that an exceptionally difficult question of customary law was involved the magistrate could apply to the Minister of Local Government for the aid of an assessor was not reproduced. Such difficulties are now to be dealt with by the methods laid down in s. 67 of the 1960 Act.[2]

3. The special definition of customary law[3] was dropped.

The first change was made in accordance with the firm decision to break away from the conception that different laws were in force in different courts. It was considered that the proper way to delimit the powers of inferior courts was by curtailing their jurisdiction. If this is done it seems unnecessary and inelegant to go further and require the courts to ignore certain elements of the general law. The civil jurisdiction laid down by s. 10 of the 1958 Act was altered in certain respects by s. 98 of the 1960 Act, but it remains true that for most civil matters the local court has no jurisdiction unless the law applicable is customary law. The exception is " personal suits where the debt, damage or demand

---

[1] *Per* Coussey P., *Asenso* v. *Nkyidwuo* (1956), 1 W.A.L.R. 243 at p. 247·
[2] See p. 426, *ante.*
[3] Set out in note 1 on p. 411, *ante.*

does not exceed £G100 "—a limit increased from £G50 in the 1958 Act. Section 98(2) introduces a restriction on jurisdiction in land matters by providing that where it appears that the subject matter of a suit relating to the ownership, possession or occupation of land exceeds £G200 the local court shall not exercise jurisdiction except with the consent of the parties.

It can be seen therefore that the repeal of s. 15 of the 1958 Act does more to promote clarity and obviate juridical anomaly than it does to bring about practical change. The local courts remain chiefly concerned with customary law, though no longer under a duty to restrict themselves, except in certain obscurely-defined cases, to the law " prevailing " within the jurisdiction."[1] This concentration on customary law will be necessary while the magistrates continue to be non-lawyers and the representation of litigants by legal practitioners continues to be forbidden[2]. In time, however, magistrates may become sufficiently expert to be given wider jurisdiction. Provision is made for magistrates to be given general advice and assistance by a Senior Local Courts Adviser, who must be a legal practitioner of three years' standing, and four Local Courts Advisers with knowledge of law and judicial process. The functions of these advisers include the provision of courses of instruction for local court magistrates.[3] There is also the safeguard provided by the powers of control possessed by District Magistrates, who are legally qualified and who can review decisions of local court magistrates and vary them as justice may require.[4]

The second change mentioned above was made in the interests of uniformity and because the system of assessors is thought to have outlasted its usefulness. The possibilities of delay in the requirement to make an application to the Minister were also a factor in the decision. Although s. 67 will apply to local courts the procedure adopted will no doubt be much simpler than in the case of the superior courts. In most cases it is likely to amount to little more than an informal discussion between the magistrate and persons tendering opinions. The magistrate will have more

---

[1] In land cases, however, the court of trial must still generally be the court whose area of jurisdiction includes the land in question: Courts Act, 1960 (C.A.9), s. 102.

[2] *Ibid.*, s. 104.

[3] *Ibid.*, s. 144. The Minister responsible for Justice is given power by s. 138 (2) to require magistrates to attend courses of instruction in law and procedure.

[4] *Ibid.*, ss. 134–7.

control than under the old law over the persons allowed to put forward opinions. He will have a clear right to exclude any person whom, after preliminary questioning, he regards as unreliable on ground of bias or ignorance.

Customary procedure

Since detailed rules as to the procedure and practice of local courts were laid down by the Local Courts Act, 1958 (No. 23) and the Local Courts Procedure Regulations, 1959,[1] little scope was left for customary procedure. The custom of commencing proceedings by swearing an oath on the defendant was however preserved, though subject to statutory modification. Rattray gives an example of the operation of this custom as follows:

> " Two men were quarrelling and they began to abuse each other; one slapped the other; he asked, ' Why did you slap me? ' The other replied ' You abused me.' The other man retorted ' I speak the great forbidden name that I did not abuse you.' The second man accepted this challenge."[2]

The proceedings which followed were primarily an enquiry into the breaking of taboo constituted by the invocation of " the great forbidden name ", although the merits of the dispute would be investigated. The loser might suffer penal sanctions, even death; or his transgression in swearing the oath might be forgiven by the chief or other person hearing the case. Under the statutory provisions any person swearing an oath recognised by customary law as lawful upon or against any person is required to report the occurrence to the registrar of the local court having jurisdiction over the subject matter in dispute, and the report is deemed to institute a cause to determine the dispute.[3] The oaths which are lawful for this purpose are limited by the Regulations to

> " the state or local oath or oaths recognised in each state (as distinct from fetish or religious oaths) in use in the area of jurisdiction of the respective local courts."[4]

The fetish or religious oath thus excluded is defined as

---

[1] These regulations continue to apply by virtue of s. 143 (4) of the Courts Act, 1960 (C.A.9).

[2] *Ashanti Law and Constitution*, p. 379; Rattray's Akan phrases are not reproduced.

[3] Local Courts Act, 1958 (No. 23), s. 28 (1); reproduced in Courts Act, 1960 (C.A.9), s. 106 (1).

[4] Local Courts Procedure Regulations, 1959, regs. 34, 36.

EE

" an oath reputed to belong to a fetish or some deity and which the swearer believes has some ominous effect on, or influence over, persons on whom or against whom it is sworn."[1]

Examples of such oaths given by Dr. Danquah are the fetish oath (Duabo) and the chief's personal oath (Brepo or Nhyira).[2] An attempt to commence proceedings by swearing an excluded oath is made an offence punishable by a fine not exceeding five pounds.[3] The offence can be tried by a local court[4] as also can the customary law offence of recklessly, unlawfully or frivolously swearing an oath.[5] The Regulations also contain the following definition:

" ' State or local oath ' means some expression or word adopted and regarded by a state as a taboo which depicts some disaster or tragic event in the history of that state and the mention of which has been prohibited by the state and which mention necessitates investigation of the matter in respect of which it is sworn. It may be either the name of the place or of the day on which such an event or disaster took place. It may also refer to some victory which was achieved by the state at some considerable or immense loss to it."[6]

The state oath of Akim Abuakwa is " Wukuda ne Kwanyako " or " Ntankesee Nmiensa ". This is explained by Dr. Danquah as follows:

" Kwanyako is the name of a town in Tanti, and Wukuda is the Akan word for Wednesday, Ne means and. The two names were consecrated as the National Oath of Akyem Abuakwa because of some tragic event which befell the State whilst an occupant of the Paramount Stool of Akyem Abuakwa (the Ofori Stool) and his people were engaged in terrific warfare at Kwanyako on a Wednesday. Wednesday is a consecrated holiday in Akyem Abuakwa and no ordinary work connected with the state is done on this day. There is a special celebration

---

[1] Local Courts Procedure Regulations, 1959, reg. 2.

[2] *Akan Laws and Customs*, London, 1928, pp. 69–78.

[3] Local Courts Act, 1958 (No. 23), s. 28 (4); see now the Courts Act, 1960 (C.A.9), s. 106 (4).

[4] Local Courts Act, 1958 (No. 23), s. 11, Sched. I, Part I, para. 9; see now the Courts Act, 1960 (C.A.9), ss. 99 and 146 (h).

[5] Local Courts Act, 1958 (No. 23), s. 11, Sched. I, Part II; see now the Courts Act, 1960 (C.A.9), ss. 99, 147. The other customary law offences triable by a local court are those of putting any person into fetish and of possessing any poisonous, noxious or offensive thing with intent to use it to endanger or destroy human life or to hurt, aggrieve or annoy any person. The maximum penalty for all three customary law offences is a fine of £G25 or three months' imprisonment, or both.

[6] Regulation 2.

held every six weeks on a Wednesday, called ' Awukudae ' in commemoration of the event. The National Oath is also called ' Ntankesee Mmiensa ' or the three great oaths, owing to the fact that besides the Kwanyako incident, two other fatal events have happened to the Ofori Stool on Wednesdays."[1]

Any person upon or against whom a lawful oath has been sworn, whether he responds to the oath or from religious conviction or other reason refuses or fails to respond to the oath, is required to report or surrender himself to the local court having jurisdiction over the subject matter in dispute, and this constitutes an appearance in answer to the cause instituted.[2] Further modification of the customary law rules relating to the commencement of proceedings by oath-taking is contained in the provisions prohibiting any chief or other person from forgiving or punishing the swearer or holding any arbitration in respect of the oath[3] and providing that failure to report the fact that an oath has been sworn shall not be punishable and that the losing party in an oath case shall not be automatically fined for swearing the oath.[4]

---

[1] *Op. cit.*, p. 78. See the following pages thereof for an explanation of the procedure.

[2] Courts Act, 1960 (C.A.9), s. 106 (2).

[3] *Ibid.*, s. 107.

[4] Local Courts Procedure Regulations, 1959, regs. 37 (b), 38. As to oath procedure in a cause or matter affecting chieftaincy, see the Chieftaincy Act, 1961 (Act 81), s. 50.

CHAPTER 12

INTERNAL CONFLICT OF LAWS

1. The Position Before Republic Day

Section 87(1) of the Courts Ordinance[1]

The second paragraph of s. 87(1) of the Courts Ordinance, read with the third, produced the result that in proceedings where all the parties were " natives " customary law always applied unless the parties had agreed that English law should apply. No guidance was given for determining which of two or more conflicting customary laws applied, and therefore the courts had to try to work out rules for themselves. The second paragraph singles out for mention causes or matters relating to the tenure and transfer of real and personal property and to inheritance and testamentary dispositions.[2] These are no doubt among the most important elements of customary law but there seems no reason why any particular elements should have been referred to and the courts have not treated them as having by virtue of this provision a claim to special emphasis.

The second paragraph went on to provide that in mixed cases, that is where one party was a " native " and the other a " non-native ", English law was to be applied unless strict adherence to it would cause a substantial injustice. The point that strict adherence was in any case rendered unnecessary by s. 85 has been mentioned above.[3] A further point is that applying English law may be unjust to one party while applying customary law may be unjust to the other. This was very nearly the position in *Koney* v. *Union Trading Co. Ltd.*[4] Koney, an educated African carpenter, had bought a sawing machine from the defendants and claimed damages for breach of contract on the ground that it was not fit for its purpose. Nine years had passed between the alleged breach and the issue of the writ, and the defendants pleaded the Statute of Limitations. The Divisional Court held that to apply the

---

[1] For text of this see Appendix C, p. 499, *post.*
[2] Formerly a reference to marriage was included: see Ordinance No. 4 of 1876, s. 19.
[3] See p. 394, *ante.*
[4] (1934), 2 W.A.C.A. 188.

Statute would cause substantial injustice to the plaintiff. This was reversed by the West African Court of Appeal, Graham Paul, J., remarking:

> " In considering whether a case of substantial injustice is made out by one party to a suit the court must not lose sight altogether of the interests of the other party. Substantial justice or injustice in a suit to a party in that suit cannot be done without reference to the claims to justice of the other party."[1]

The Appeal Court held that no injustice above that always involved in applying the Statute of Limitations would be caused to the plaintiff, but pointed the way out of the dilemma posed above by ruling that the onus rested on the party alleging that the application of English law would be unjust to prove it.[2] This onus was held to have been discharged in *Nelson* v. *Nelson*[3] where the result of applying English law would have been to substitute a right to an undivided share in land for the customary right to use and occupy the land and to control its alienation.

The opening words in the last paragraph of s. 87(1) suggested that customary law was not applicable unless a party claimed the benefit of it, and this was supported by the 1954 revision of the Supreme Court (Civil Procedure) Rules, Order 19, r. 31 of which ran as follows:

> " In all cases in which the party pleading relies upon a native law or custom, the native law or custom relied upon shall be stated in the pleading with sufficient particulars to show the nature and effect of the native law or custom in question and the geographical area and the tribe or tribes to which it relates."

Where the existence of a customary law fell to be treated as a question of fact this rule was in accordance with the principle that facts must be pleaded if they are to be given in evidence, but where judicial notice was to be taken of the customary law the rule was in conflict with another principle of pleading, namely that law is not to be pleaded.[4] The question that concerns us now however is whether failure to " claim the benefit " altered the law to be applied. Since English law applied where s. 87 did not bring in customary law it seems that a failure to plead a customary

---

[1] (1934), 2 W.A.C.A., at p. 196.
[2] *Ibid.*, at p. 194.
[3] (1951), 13 W.A.C.A. 248.
[4] Dr. Danquah contented that the rule did not apply where the custom was one of " general application "; see *Kwaku* v. *Addo* (1957), 2 W.A.L.R. 306, at p. 309.

law would, if leave to amend were not asked for and given, have required the court to apply English law. The reports do not indicate that this sort of logic was employed however,[1] and the results of applying it would frequently have been grotesque.

The last paragraph of s. 87(1) went on to provide that customary law, though otherwise applicable, was not to be applied if the parties had agreed to the exclusive application of English law. This again bristles with difficulties, but before these are discussed one point should be emphasized, and that is the application of the principle *nemo dat quod non habet*. If a person subject to customary law acquires a right by a procedure based on English law, but does so with the aid of property in which other persons subject to customary law have an interest, the *content* of the right acquired by him will, unless the other interested persons otherwise agree, fall to be determined according to customary law; and he can thereafter only deal with the right *as so determined*, even though he deals with it by a procedure again based on English law. This rule is illustrated by the important case of *Nelson* v. *Nelson*,[2] in which the facts were as follows:

> Self-acquired land was left by a death-bed disposition to N for himself and all the other children of the deceased who constituted his family. Part of the land was later acquired by the Government and with the compensation money N acquired Blackacre in his own name by a conveyance in English form. By a similar conveyance, executed without the consent of the family, N purported to convey Blackacre to a limited company.

Under English substantive law as applied by s. 83, the conveyance of the legal title in Blackacre to N by the method used would have vested in him the power to convey a good legal title to anyone else by the same means. English substantive law did not apply, however, because N and his family were all subject to customary law and the family were held not to have agreed to the displacement of that law. Under customary law land bought with the compensation money was subject to the same family rights as the original land acquired by the Government, and since one of those rights was a right to decide whether or not the land should be alientated, N possessed no power to convey Blackacre without the consent of the family, and the purported conveyance to the limited company was therefore void. It made

---

[1] See *Bonsi* v. *Adjena* (1940) 5 W.A.C.A. 241.
[2] (1951) 13 W.A.C.A. 248.

no difference that this conveyance was in English form because no one, under any law, can exercise a power he has not got.[1] The following difficulties might arise in considering whether customary law had been displaced by agreement.

1. *In mixed cases did the agreement provision override the " substantial injustice " provision in the second paragraph of s. 87(1)?*

The two provisions are inconsistent, but the positive opening to the third paragraph, and its relative position in the section, indicated that it was to prevail. In 1951 it was referred to by the court in *Nelson* v. *Nelson* as a " proviso "[2] and there treated as conclusive, Verity, Ag. P., remarking that if the parties " agreed or must from the nature of the transaction be taken to have agreed that their obligations are to be regulated by English law, then the question as to what law is applicable has been determined by their conduct."[3] In mixed cases the question of agreement to apply English law could only arise if it were first found that the application of English law would cause substantial injustice, since otherwise it would apply anyway.[4] Not the least odd feature of these provisions is therefore that the courts in a mixed case were in certain circumstances under a statutory duty to perpetrate a substantial justice.

2. *Did the reference to an express contract exclude implied contracts?*

The distinction appears to be between an agreement which specifically refers to English law and a transaction which of its very nature imports English law without expressly referring to it. In *Ferguson* v. *Duncan*,[5] Windsor-Aubrey, J., said of this provision:

> " Counsel for the appellant particularly stresses the words ' express ' and ' exclusive ' [*sic*] though to my mind the weight to be attached to the first-mentioned word should not be over-stressed since it refers only to one particular form of contract and is not applicable to all transactions."

---

[1] Cf. *Enimil* v. *Tuakyi* (1950), 13 W.A.C.A. 8, in which it was held that, in a sale of land under a power contained in a mortgage, the purchaser could only acquire " the right, title and interest under native law of the original judgment debtor "; and see the passage from the judgment in *Andoh* v. *Franklin* (1952) cited Allott, *op. cit.*, p. 263, and *Villars* v. *Baffoe* (1909), Renner's Reports 549.

[2] As indeed it had been until inexplicably altered in the 1936 revision.

[3] (1951), 13 W.A.C.A. 248, at p. 249.

[4] *Koney* v. *U.T.C.* (1934), 2 W.A.C.A. 188.

[5] (1953), 14 W.A.C.A. 316, at p. 317.

The answer to the question is therefore no, although it should be mentioned that the willingness of the courts to find an agreement to be bound by English law on relatively slight evidence and their unwillingness to distinguish between the phrase " express contract " and " the nature of the transactions " made it seldom necessary to enter into nice points about implied contracts. For example, in *Kwesi-Johnson* v. *Effie*[1] the evidence of a contract for the sale of land between two " astute, intelligent and sophisticated Africans " consisted of a receipt for part of the purchase price of the land in question " as specified in, and in pursuance of the terms of the conveyance to be prepared in this behalf " together with a receipt, given two days after the first receipt, for £3 " Tirama ", which the purchaser was proved to have paid unwillingly. The West African Court of Appeal found that " in these circumstances . . . the payment of the ' Tirama ' loses its significance " and that the purchaser did not consider the transaction a binding sale. Basing itself on the fact that the first receipt referred to a conveyance, which forms no part of a sale by customary law, the court held that the parties had intended that the transaction should be regulated exclusively by English law, though without deciding whether this was because of express contract or the nature of the transactions. This attitude of the courts also made it unnecessary to raise awkward questions about whether the English law of contract had first to be applied to discover whether an " express contract " in binding form had been entered into.

3. *With whom must the agreement be made? Was a unilateral " agreement " excluded?*

The " party " referred to is clearly a party in a suit before the court, and it would seem that his agreement to be bound by English law could only operate if, and so far as, it was made with another party to the suit or a person through whom another party to the suit claimed. If it was made with anyone else it would be *res inter alios acta*. In *Amuakwa* v. *Anyan*[2] it was held that the plaintiff was not precluded from claiming the benefit of customary law by the fact that he had agreed with the other parties to the transaction in question that it should be regulated by English law since none of those parties was before the court and there was no privity of contract between the plaintiff and the defendant.

---

[1] (1953), 14 W.A.C.A. 254.
[2] (1936), 3 W.A.C.A. 22.

This was a strong decision, since the plaintiff based his claim on the allegation that the other parties to the transaction were agents of the defendant—in other words that there *was* privity of contract. Was the person whose agreement was alleged to have displaced customary law required to be a party to the transaction as well as a party to the suit? Again, *Nelson* v. *Nelson*[1] comes to our aid. The court held that even if the members of N's family could be said to have agreed to his purchase of Blackacre by a conveyance in English form they were not strictly speaking parties to the transaction and accordingly their agreement did not displace customary law. The principle was therefore that a person who was not a party to the transaction could not be taken to have agreed that it should be governed by English law on the basis of an implication drawn from the nature of the transaction, but that if by a collateral contract he had expressly agreed that English law should apply the other parties to that contract could hold him to his agreement.

As to the second question, that of " unilateral " agreements, it is clear that the first limb of the provision under discussion could not operate. There must be at least two parties to a contract, which is a *vinculum juris* binding two or more persons together. It is less certain however whether it was impossible for a person unilaterally to embark on a transaction which by its nature indicted his " agreement " (with the world in general?) that it should be regulated by English law. Indeed the courts recognized that this could be done in certain cases, subject of course to the rule *nemo dat quod non habet*, discussed above. In *Villars* v. *Baffoe*[2] it was held that the plaintiff, by taking out letters of administration in English form, had " elected " to be bound by English law, although this could not affect the rights of other persons in the family property.[3]

4. *Was it significant that the agreement was required to relate only to* obligations?

It is typical of the extraordinary language of this part of the Courts Ordinance that the paragraph under discussion reads " No party shall be entitled to claim the benefit . . . if . . . such party agreed that his *obligations* should be regulated by English law." It is tempting to infer some subtlety based on the

---

[1] (1951), 13 W.A.C.A. 248, at p. 250.
[2] (1909), Renner's Reports 549.
[3] But see *Solomon* v. *Allotey* (1938), 4 W.A.C.A. 91.

principle that no one can take a benefit without taking the
obligations that go with it, but the truth seems to be that this is
just one more verbal infelicity. In a case, therefore, where the
obligation was all with one party, as where goods to be delivered
on a future occasion were bought for cash, the other party might
still it seems be precluded from claiming the benefit of customary
law by this provision. Furthermore the courts assumed that
benefits and obligations could not be treated differently—they
must both go one way or the other.

5. *What weight was to be given to the word " exclusively "?*
The courts have attached some importance to this word. In
Ferguson v. *Duncan*,[1] Windsor-Aubrey, J. said:

> " The word ' exclusive ' [*sic*], however, applies to all forms of
> contract. In other words, as I understand the position, native
> law and custom are not ousted even when the parties had no
> clear conception in their minds and contemplated a mixture of
> English law and native law and custom."

On the other hand Dr. Allott observes:

> " At times it appears as though learned judges have overlooked
> the presence of this or similar terms, and have failed to inquire
> whether the essence or the whole of the contract was pure English
> law, contenting themselves instead with the bare assertion that
> ' English law applies '."[2]

In *Ferguson* v. *Duncan* the original transaction was a simple loan
of money evidenced by an ordinary receipt bearing a twopenny
stamp. A receipt of this kind " is not technical in form and is
exceedingly common even amongst almost illiterate Africans "[3]
and the court therefore declined to infer from it an agreement to
be bound exclusively by English law even though the loan was
secured after an interval of four years by a mortgage in English
form.

This decision was attacked by Adumua-Bossman, J., in a full
and closely-reasoned judgment delivered in *Cobbina Ackon* v.
Solomon.[4] This was an appeal to a Divisional Court from a
judgment of the District Magistrate, Cape Coast. The plaintiff
had claimed the sum of £68 9s. 2d. as due under two I.O.U.s

[1] (1953), 14 W.A.C.A. 316, at p. 317.
[2] *Op. cit.*, p. 250; see also pp. 251–2.
[3] (1953), 14 W.A.C.A. 316, at p. 318.
[4] Civil Appeal No. 6/1959 (unreported).

given by the defendant in Hamburg while both parties were on a visit to Europe in 1925. The I.O.U. was in the following form:

> " I owe Mr. J. B. Cobbina Ackon the sum of Fifty-five pounds one and two pence (£55 1s. 2d.) being amount received from him.
>
> > (*Sgd.*) J. S. Solomon.
> > Hamburg—27/2/25."

The second was similar except that it included a reference to goods supplied. Both parties were " natives " and the learned magistrate had rejected the defendant's plea that the I.O.U.s demonstrated an intention that English law should exclusively apply and that the claim was therefore barred under the Statute of Limitations. In his view the effect of *Ferguson* v. *Duncan* was to place an onus on the defendant to satisfy the court in a dispute between two " natives " that customary law had been displaced by English law. There is certainly a dictum to that effect in the judgment of Windsor-Aubrey, J., but, as the learned judge in the instant case pointed out, the dictum seems to be based on a misunderstanding of *Koney* v. *U.T.C.*[1] In the view of Adumua-Bossman, J., no such onus existed, except perhaps where evidence had already been brought to show that the transaction was one recognized by customary law and that some customary requirements, e.g. the presence of witnesses, had been observed. The learned judge was also inclined to doubt the likelihood of parties to a simple transaction such as an ordinary loan of money contemplating a mixture of English and customary law. In any case, he went on:

> " . . . it is submitted that even if the parties have not a clear conception in their minds, their language and/or utterances and actions will operate to make the contract fall on one side or the other of the line, i.e. indicate that from a legal point of view the contract between the parties is a customary one or else an English one."

It is respectfully submitted that this approach is more satisfactory than one based on onus of proof. In a civil action, as opposed to a criminal prosecution, it is for the court to pronounce judgment according to the balance of probabilities as gathered from the evidence as a whole. Although, as the hearing progresses, one party may pile up the probabilities in his favour and thus in a sense place an onus on the other to bring rebutting evidence, this

---

[1] See p. 436, *ante*.

is not an onus in law, such as rests upon the prosecution from the beginning of a criminal trial. In the instant case, having regard to the fact that the transaction was entered into by eduated Africans in a European country by the use of an I.O.U., a well-known form of English commercial document, and to the total absence of any evidence that customary procedure was employed, the learned judge had no hesitation in allowing the appeal.[1] The decision is also interesting by reason of the way in which the learned judge dealt with the position of written documents in relation to customary transactions. Apart from possible recent modifications, writing is of course unknown to customary law. Where it has been employed by the parties to a transaction it tends to show therefore that English law was intended to govern the matter unless the writing is only a memorandum of a transaction already completed in accordance with customary law procedure, that is, in the words of the learned judge, unless the situation is one

> " . . . in which contractual rights and obligations brought into existence by forms and/or methods and in accordance with concepts of customary law are afterwards merely reduced to writing for their better and safer preservation."[2]

6. What of a contract whereby the parties agree that, say, French law shall apply?

In accordance with the maxim *modus et conventio vincunt legem*, it is a common law rule that, subject to overriding considerations such as those of public policy, the parties to a contract may agree that it shall be regulated by whatever system of law they choose. The provision under discussion displaced customary law only where *English* law was agreed on, however. Did this mean that an express agreement between " natives " that French law should apply was nugatory, leaving customary law undisplaced? Or could one interpret the agreement as applying the common law doctrine referred to above, and reach French law by way of English law? No guidance seems obtainable from reported decisions but it is submitted that the latter view produces the more sensible result, though by an interpretation that perhaps falls little short of sophistry.

---

[1] This result could also have been arrived at on the ground that the documents were not stamped, but the learned judge declined to " decide the appeal on that minor point and shirk determination of the much more important point of law ".

[2] *Cf. Kwamina Aradzie* v. *Kobina Yandor* F.C. 1922, p. 91; *Teye Norh* v. *Gbedemah* F.C. 1926–29, p. 395.

The final point to be considered in this analysis of s. 87(1) is the meaning to be attached to the words " in cases where no express rule is applicable to any matter in controversy, the court shall be governed by the principles of justice, equity and good conscience ". It must be noticed that this was not in terms a provision for coming to the rescue of the court where it was doubtful whether customary law or English law applied or, if it was clear that customary law applied, where there was a conflict between two or more varieties of customary law. On the contrary, the court had first to decide which system of law applied and then fill in any gaps in that system with the aid of the principle here set forth. If English law applied there could of course be no such gaps since the common law is all-pervasive, although the court may have to " develop " it slightly to meet new circumstances. If customary law applied there were not likely to be any " express rules " to cover the matter in question anyway, since customary law is largely unwritten. Perhaps, however, the word " express ", like so many words in these provisions, should not be taken to mean what it says. In theory, therefore the words under discussion should be treated as providing a method by which the judges could fill out the gaps in customary law by decisions which, under the doctrine of *stare decisis*, would have a quasi-legislative effect. There seems no evidence that the courts so regarded them, however. In *Okai* v. *Quist*[1] Brandford Griffith, C.J., held, on a claim under a continuing oral guarantee, that although detailed evidence of customary law relating to guarantees had been given this merely showed that continuing guarantees were not known to customary law and " that being so the rules of English law must apply and the guarantee should have been in writing ".

There are many other instances where gaps in particular customary rules have been supplied from the resources of common law and equity. Thus, in the absence of customary rules of *res judicata* and other forms of estoppel, the English law on these matters has been universally applied, though rather because it has become an accepted practice to do so than by reason of a appeal to " justice, equity and good conscience ".[2] This recourse to English law rather than the court's independent view of what

---

[1] (1895), Renner's Reports 123.
[2] Redwar urged, surely rightly, that " equity " in this phrase was not equivalent to Equity in the technical sense used in England, but had its popular meaning: *op. cit.*, p. 63.

the particular case demanded is well displayed in *Abbey* v. *Ollenu*[1] where two distinct English doctrines, *res judicata* and equitable acquiescence were in question. Nor has the application of such doctrines in customary law cases been limited to filling gaps in customary law. Indeed it might well be said that more often than not their application cuts across the customary law rule rather than supplementing it. In *Ado* v. *Wusu*,[2] a land case governed by customary law, in which the defendant and his predecessors had been in occupation for over two hundred years and the defendant claimed to have carried out improvements on the land in the belief that he owned it, the West African Court of Appeal was apparently prepared to apply some form of estoppel if the facts had justified it notwithstanding that, as the court pointed out:

> " The native custom in such a case is clear and undoubted, namely that the ultimate ownership remains in the original owner for all time. . . . Further the native custom as to the resting place of the ultimate ownership would be well known to the defendant and his people, but they could not be expected to reply on the English doctrine of estoppel to defeat the undisputed ownership of the plaintiff. According to native ideas there would be no question of the ultimate ownership in the land having passed."

Nor can this practice of the courts be explained on the ground that the customary law in question is repugnant to natural justice, equity and good conscience within the meaning of the first paragraph of s. 87(1). The courts have not advanced this as the reason for applying the doctrines under discussion and in any case its application would have required the whole rule, e.g. that title to land cannot be acquired by prescription, to be rejected *in toto* if it were found repugnant, and not to be toned down by occasional modifications drawn from English law.

Inter-customary law conflicts

As stated previously, no guidance was provided by the Courts Ordinance for determining conflicts between various customary laws. In theory each law should contain its own rules for settling conflicts with other customary laws but, apart from the difficulty that these rules might well be inconsistent, it is doubtful how far they exist. If, in a case where customary law applied, it were

---

[1] (1954) 14 W.A.C.A. 567.
[2] (1940), 5 W.A.C.A. 24.

proved to the court, or the court were able to take judicial notice, that the customary laws in question did contain rules for settling conflict of laws, and that those rules were not mutually inconsistent, the court would no doubt have applied them without further question. For many years, however, the courts regarded " native law " as more or less uniform in the Gold Coast and no developed theory of internal conflict of laws is discernible from the earlier cases. In more recent times, and particularly with the advent of African judges, differences in customary laws have been more readily recognized by the courts, but the various laws canvassed may well give the same result in a particular case, so that the court is not required to decide between them.[1] Even where this is not so there is a tendency to settle conflicts by the light of reason rather than on evidence of rules embodied in customary law. This is well illustrated by *Ghamson* v. *Wobill*,[2] in which the facts were as follows:

> Essie Osuomba, who was subject to Fanti law, was entitled to a house in Winneba, where Efutu law is in force. Essie Osuomba died. Under Efutu law the house would pass to her daughter Essie Kuma, but under Fanti law it would pass to Kwesi Kra, the head of her family. On the assumption that it had passed to their mother, Essie Kuma, and on her death to them, Mary and John Danquah sold the house by deed to Wobill, an Efutu. Wobill sued for possession and Kwesi Kra claimed to have the deed of sale set aside.

The trial judge made an heroic attempt to lay down a general rule for land cases by applying Efutu law as the *lex situs*. The West African Court of Appeal, however, turned for assistance to s. 15 of the Native Courts (Colony) Ordinance (Cap. 98) on the argument that the Supreme Court ought to apply the same law as would be applied in a native court if the case were heard there. Section 15 required the native court to apply the customary law prevailing within its own jurisdiction and, with equal emphasis, the provisions of any law binding between the parties. The court gave its opinion (not apparently based on evidence) that the law binding between the parties was Fanti:

> " We are of opinion that, although Fanti law would not ordinarily be binding between Wobill, an Efutu, and Kwesi Kra, a Fanti, it is in this case because Wobill's claim depends on the issue as to succession, and he claims through the Danquahs who are in this respect subject to Fanti customary law."

---

[1] As in *Annan* v. *Bin* (1947), 12 W.A.C.A. 177.
[2] (1947), 12 W.A.C.A. 181.

The law prevailing in the Winneba area was of course Efutu, so matters did not seem much further advanced. However, by calling in aid the provision corresponding to the first paragraph of s. 87(1) of the Courts Ordinance whereby no person is to be deprived of the benefit of customary law, the court held that the law " binding between the parties " was to be preferred.[1] Accordingly the appeal succeeded and the sale to Wobill was set aside. It is curious that the superior courts should have held themselves to be governed by provisions designed for inferior courts, but it would be even more curious if on the same facts a different law were to be applied in the one than in the other.

It is rare for a customary law other than the *lex situs* to be applied in land cases because those interested in the land are usually local people subject to the local customs. Even when theys are not, there appears to be a presumption that the *lex situs* applies, which is only displaced by clear evidence of some other law. Thus in *Ekem* v. *Nerba*[2] the court were prepared, even in the light of *Ghamson* v. *Wobill,* to apply the *lex situs* to land at Cape Coast owned by a Nigerian in the absence of evidence of the identity and content of his own tribal law. See however *Weytingh* v. *Bessaboro*[3] where a claim to trace title by customary law from a Dutch settler who had cleared bush land 180 years previously was rejected on the ground that " native law is inapplicable, inasmuch as the original owner was a European " and that there was no evidence of the relevant Dutch law. The courts have been prepared to accept a mere allegation in the pleadings as to the applicability and effect of personal customary law where the allegation is not disputed by the other side. This occurred in *Okaikor* v. *Opare*[4] where the court accepted that the Tema custom of the deceased owner of land in Accra entitled his children to succeed to the land. This may not have affected the result, however, since the plaintiff, the sister of the deceased, had performed the Ga custom of " Tako mli mfo ", thus abrogating her right to participate in his estate.

Apart from these land cases, judical authority on inter-customary law conflicts appears to be practically non-existent. In Nigeria attempts have been made to lay down statutory rules[5].

---

[1] The Nigerian courts have reached a similar conclusion: see *Osuagwu* v. *Soldier* (1959), N.R.N.L.R. 39, cited Allott, *op. cit.,* pp. 163–164.

[2] (1947), 12 W.A.C.A. 258.

[3] (1906), Renner's Reports 428.

[4] (1956), 1 W.A.L. 275.

[5] See Allott, *op. cit.,* pp. 161–163.

2. THE APPLICATION OF LAW RULES

It having been decided that the common law and customary law were to be treated as separate elements of the laws of Ghana, the most difficult question of all had to be tackled. What rules were to govern the question of whether the common law or customary law applied in a particular case? The imperfections already discussed[1] of the rules laid down by s. 87 of the Courts Ordinance made it necessary to formulate new rules. This was a task of immense difficulty, and only time will show whether the result is any more successful than was the old s. 87. The method used was to examine as many reported decisions of the West African Court of Appeal and other tribunals exercising jurisdiction over the territories now included in Ghana as was possible in the time available, and to attempt to extract from them certain principles. It is significant that the decisions fall into a fairly clear plattern which is not to be discovered from reading s. 87. The result of this research is now embodied in s. 66 of the Courts Act, 1960 (C.A.9). This section may appear complex at first sight, but the rules it embodies are essentially simple. Particular cases are singled out to be dealt with in accordance with principles which on the whole will not be found to differ significantly from those discernible from the reported cases. There is then a residual rule to cover the cases not dealt with by the earlier rules. Under this rule, which does represent a new departure, the common law will apply unless the plaintiff is subject to a system of customary law and claims to have the issue determined according to that system. Subsection (1) of s. 66 is in the following terms:

" 66. **Application of common law and customary law.**—
(1) Subject to the provisions of any enactment other than this subsection, in deciding whether an issue arising in civil proceedings is to be determined according to the common law or customary law and, if the issue is to be determined according to customary law, in deciding which system of customary law is applicable, the court shall be guided by the following rules, in which references to the personal law of a person are references to the system of customary law to which he is subject or, if he is not shown to be subject to customary law, are references to the common law:—

Rule 1.—Where two persons have the same personal law one of them cannot, by dealing in a manner regulated by some other law with property in which the other has a present or

---

expectant interest, alter or affect that interest to an extent which would not in the circumstances be open to him under his personal law.

Rule 2.—Subject to Rule 1, where an issue arises out of a transaction the parties to which have agreed, or may from the form or nature of the transaction be taken to have agreed, that such an issue should be determined according to the common law or any system of customary law, effect should be given to the agreement.

In this rule ' transaction ' includes a marriage and an agreement or arrangement to marry.

Rule 3.—Subject to Rule 1, where an issue arises out of any unilateral disposition and it appears from the form or nature of the disposition or otherwise that the person effecting the disposition intended that such an issue should be determined according to the common law or any system of customary law, effect should be given to the intention.

Rule 4.—Subject to the foregoing rules, where an issue relates to entitlement to land on the death of the owner or otherwise relates to title to land—

(a) if all the parties to the proceedings who claim to be entitled to the land or a right relating thereto trace their claims from one person who is subject to customary law, or from one family or other group of persons all subject to the same customary law, the issue should be determined according to that law;

(b) if the said parties trace their claims from different persons, or families or other groups of persons, who are all subject to the same customary law, the issue should be determined according to that law;

(c) in any other case, the issue should be determined according to the law of the place in which the land is situated.

Rule 5.—Subject to Rules 1 to 3, where an issue relates to the devolution of the property (other than land) of a person on his death it should be determined according to his personal law.

Rule 6.—Subject to the foregoing rules, an issue should be determined according to the common law unless the plaintiff is subject to any system of customary law and claims to have the issue determined according to that system, when it should be so determined.

The opening words of the subsection make it clear that the guidance it gives is subject to the provisions of any other enactment which is inconsistent with it. It goes on to provide that civil proceedings only are being dealt with. No problem arises in the case of criminal proceedings because all criminal offences, with the exception of a small number of customary law offences, are statutory in the sense that they are laid down by enactments comprised in the laws of Ghana. They therefore do not fall within the common law and so can raise no problem of its application. The rules in sub-s. (1) apply in two categories of case. In the first place they apply where it is necessary for the court to decide whether the common law or customary law should govern a particular issue. In the second place, they apply where it is necessary for the court to decide which of two or more different customary law systems are to apply.

It should be noted that the subsection applies to *issues* and not to cases as a whole. Where a number of different issues arise in one case it may well happen that some issues fall to be decided under the common law, while others are governed by customary law. For example in a transaction relating to property, where the transaction has been carried out by a form of conveyance drawn from English law, it may be necessary to determine whether the person entering into the transaction was the owner of the property in question by applying customary law. If it is established that under customary law he was the owner, it may then be necessary to apply the common law in order to determine the effect of the transaction. Or, to take a case that is unfortunately not uncommon in Ghana, it may happen that A has executed a conveyance of land, say in English form, to B and has later purported to convey the same land, say by customary formalities, to C. Litigation may arise in a number of ways. B and C may each apply to the Court for a declaration of title. Of, if B has gone into possession, C may sue for trespass and an eviction order. Or C may not dispute B's title but sue A for damages. Whatever the form of the litigation the issues are likely to be the same. First, did the conveyance to B confer a good title? If there is no preliminary question as to A's right to convey at all, this first issue will probably fall to be decided, in accordance with Rule 2, under the common law. If for some reason the conveyance to B is found to have been ineffective, so that A remained the owner of the land at the time of the later conveyance to C, the quite separate issue may arise of whether the conveyance to C conferred a good title. The rules will then be applied over again to this further issue. In the vast majority of cases it will no doubt be clear that the common law or a particular customary law system applies throughout, but the point that this subsection deals with issues separately should be kept in mind as the rules will fail in their purpose if they are sought to be applied always to cases as a whole.

The opening words of sub-s. (1) provide that the court shall be *guided* by the following rules. This wording is intended to show that the rules are laying down principles rather than rigid instructions. There may well be cases where the rules will not fit exactly as they stand. For example, rule 6, with its reference to " the plaintiff " would not fit a case where there were joint plantiffs each subject to a different system of customary law. It is thought that such cases will be rare, and that the rules are as comprehensive as it was possible to make them without excessive complication. Nevertheless, in a case where the rules do not fit exactly, the court, in being guided by the principles they lay down, should find no difficulty in extending them by analogy.

The opening words of sub-s. (1) end with a definition of " personal law ". This expression is only used in rules 1 and 5, but the same concept, of a person being " subject to " customary law, is also employed in rules 4 and 6. It is appreciated that the courts may at times experience difficulty in deciding whether a person is subject to customary law, and if so which system of law applies to him. The principles governing this matter are bound to vary from system to system. They are an integral part of customary law and thus are not suitable for incorporation in rules of this kind. Problems may of course arise which are difficult of solution by the court, as for example where it is alleged that one person is subject to two or more systems of customary law. Even so, some guidance may be obtainable from the rules. For example, it may be alleged that a Fanti woman who has married an Ewe is subject to both Fanti and Ewe customary law. Reference to rule 2 may, however, show that the woman remains subject to Fanti customary law except that, on matters arising out of the marriage she is to be taken to have agreed that Ewe customary law should apply. If, where it becomes relevant to discover whether a person is subject to customary law, he is not *shown* to be subject to customary law, his personal law will be the common law.[1] This contains very interesting possibilities. If, with the spread of industrialisation and urbanisation in Ghana, the courts tend to adopt the view that customary law ties are being severed by more and more Ghanaians, there is an opening here for accelerating the demise of customary law as such and bringing more and more

---

[1] See Example A, p. 458, *post.*

people under the aegis of the common law as strengthened by the assimilation of rules of customary law found suitable for general application.

Rule 1.—This rule reproduces the effect of the principle *nemo dat quod non habet* as applied by the courts in relation to customary law.[1] It thus codifies a principle already recognized. Its main application is of course in relation to family property. It makes it clear that a member of a family cannot, by using a form appropriate to the common law or some other system of law than that to which the family is subject, convey an interest in family property greater than it would be possible for him to convey in similar circumstances under his family law. Thus, if under his family law, the consent of the other members of the family would be necessary to enable him to convey property vested in him, he cannot, by a conveyance in, say, English form, dispose of the property without their consent. Nor could he, by a will in English form bequeath property which he could not dispose of under customary law forms. It should be noted, however, that if an absolute disposition is possible under customary law, as by samansiw in relation to self-acquired property, a similar disposition can be made under an English form of will without contravening rule 1.[2]

Rule 2.—This is based on the third paragraph of s. 87(1) of the Courts Ordinance. It attempts, however, to avoid the difficulties that arise on that paragraph. The reference to " express contract " becomes a reference to the agreement of the parties. There is thus no problem of whether " contract " is to be given its technical common law meaning, so that consideration and other elements must be present. Nor does it matter whether the agreement is express or implied. In considering whether there is any implied agreement, both the form and the nature of the transaction are relevant. The rule goes beyond s. 87(1) in contemplating an agreement that a particular system of customary law should apply. This widens its effect considerably, since it thus covers any transaction which manifests an intention to be bound by customary law even where that law is the law to which the parties entering into the transaction are themselves subject. In other words the rule is not limited to the case where the parties agree to adopt some other law than that which would normally

---

[1] See p. 438, *ante.*

[2] See Examples B, C and I, pp. 459, 462, *post,* and of *Kwan* v. *Nyieni* (1959) G.L.R. 67.

apply to them—it covers all transactions entered into under their own law as long as that law has left its mark on the transaction in some way. Since the word " transaction " is expressed to include a marriage and an agreement or arrangement to marry, this means that, by entering into a marriage or an agreement or arrangement to marry in accordance with the forms of a particular system of customary law, any persons in Ghana, including Europeans, can enter into a customary marriage, no matter what their personal law may be.[1]

Rule 3.—This applies the principle expressed in rule 2 to unilateral dispositions. It thus represents another extension of the wording of the third paragraph of s. 87(1) of the Courts Ordinance. Subject to the principle laid down in rule 1, there seems no reason why a person who chooses to execute, say, a deed of gift in English form should not be free to do so. The same applies to the making of a will in English form. Subject to the principle that no greater disposition of property can be made than would be possible under the customary law of the testator, a disposition by a will which manifests the intention that the disposition should be governed by the common law will, under this rule, be construed accordingly by the court.[2]

Rule 4.—Since most litigation in Ghana appears to involve questions of title to land, rule 4 is of considerable importance. It applies where an issue relates to entitlement to land on the death of the owner or otherwise relates to title to land, but it is subject to the provisions of rules 1, 2 and 3. Subject to the effect of these earlier rules, rule 4 is simple. If all the parties to the proceedings trace their claim to the land from a person or persons who are all subject to the same customary law, the question of title is to be determined according to that customary law. In any other case it is to be determined according to the *lex situs*. This probably reproduces the effect of the law previously existing.[3] The problems that remain, such as that of deciding in certain cases what is the law of the place in which the land is situated, have always been present.[4] It should be less difficult to determine

---

[1] See Examples B, C, D and E, pp. 459–60, *post*.
[2] See Example I, (p. 462 *post*.), and *Bickersteth* v. *Shanu*, [1936] A.C. 290.
[3] See pp. 447–8, *ante*.
[4] Section 59 of the Chieftaincy Act, 1961 (Act 81) provides for the making of a written declaration by a House of Chiefs of what in its opinion is the customary law relating to any subject in force in any part of the area of its authority; see p. 429, *ante*.

which system of customary law prevails in the limited area in which the land is situated than it was formerly to decide on the law prevailing within the jurisdiction of the court.[1]

Rule 4 is only likely to be affected in its operation by the earlier rules in a case where a transaction has taken place manifesting an intention that questions of title to the land should be determined according to some other system of law than that which would fall to be applied under rule 4. If under rule 4 the law to be applied is Fanti customary law, but the parties in the action are the vendor and purchaser under a conveyance in English form, the issue would normally fall to be decided, in accordance with rule 2, according to the common law. Complications may arise if the parties to the action include other persons besides the vendor and the purchaser. The agreement to be bound by the common law, which is to be inferred from the making of a conveyance in English form, will not of course bind persons who were not parties to the conveyance and do not claim through those parties. Rule 1 may well provide the answer in a case of this sort. If the vendor executed the conveyance without having obtained the consents necessary under customary law rule 1 would produce the result that no title passed under the conveyance. The purchaser would then, apart from overriding statutory provisions such as those contained in the Land Development (Protection of Purchasers) Act, 1960 (Act 2), be left with a remedy restricted to an award of damages for breach of contract against the vendor.

Rule 4 refers to the tracing of claims. This concept should not give rise to any difficulty. It is for the court to satisfy itself, on the evidence and the implications to be drawn from the evidence, whether there is a common predecessor, as in *Ghamson* v. *Wobill*[2] or whether the origins of the claim to title are different as in *Owusu* v. *Mantse of Labadi*.[3]

" Land " in rule 4 has the meaning assigned to it by s. 32 of the Interpretation Act, 1960 (C.A.4) so that it includes "land covered by water, any house, building or structure whatsoever, and any estate interest or right in, to or over land or water ". Although the application of rule 4 is not in terms limited to land in Ghana, such a limitation is imposed by sub-s. (3) (*a*) of s. 66 since it is a rule of private international law that questions of title to land in

---

[1] See p. 430, *ante.*
[2] See p. 447, *ante.*
[3] (1933), 1 W.A.C.A. 278.

a foreign country are to be determined according to the *lex situs*.[1]

Rule 5.—This is the rule which will principally regulate the application of law in cases concerning the devolution of the movable property of a person on his death. Subject to rules 1 to 3, such questions are to be determined according to the personal law of the deceased. By virtue of the opening provisions of the subsection, where the deceased was subject to customary law the effect of this rule will be that the system of customary law to which he was subject will determine questions as to the devolution of his movable property. If he was not subject to customary law, the common law will fall to be applied.[2] If the deceased was subject to customary law but has made a will in English form, or in a form prescribed by any other system of law than his own customary law, rule 3 will probably, subject to the restrictions contained in rule 1, displace rule 4 with the result that questions of devolution of movable property will be governed not by the personal law of the deceased but by the law which, by the form used for his will, he indicated should apply. Rule 2 is seldom likely to be relevant in this connection, but there may be cases where, for example, by marrying under a system of customary law other than his own, a man is to be taken to have agreed to the devolution of his movable property on death in accordance with the system of law under which the marriage was performed.[3]

Rule 6.—Apart from torts, there are not likely to be many cases in which rule 6 will fall to be applied. The effect of the rule is that the common law will apply in any case not governed by the previous rules unless the plaintiff is subject to any system of customary law and claims to have the issue determined according to that system. In matters such as tort and quasi-contract, therefore, the well-developed rules of the common law will always be available to a plaintiff. On the other hand, if a person has suffered a wrong for which his own system of customary law gives what he regards as an adequate remedy, he is free to pursue that remedy even against a person who is not subject to that system of customary law or indeed any other system of customary law. This means that foreigners in Ghana cannot, within this field,

---

[1] See Examples D to I and L, pp. 460 *et seq.*, *post*.
[2] That is the rules laid down in the Statute of Distribution, 1670, which were extended to cover land as well as personalty by s. 105 (2) of the Administration of Estates Act, 1961 (Act 63).
[3] See Example I, p. 462, *post*.

be allowed to plead ignorance of customary law. This is in accordance with the new treatment of customary law as an integral part of the laws of Ghana, and is a logical consequence of the new rule that questions as to the existence or content of rules of customary law are matters of law and not fact.[1] The rule will have some application in contract cases where no agreement can be inferred from the conduct of the parties manifesting an intention to be bound by a particular system of law. Thus, for example, in the case of a simple debt where there is nothing to show what the parties' intention was, rule 6 would mean that the common law of contract would apply unless the plaintiff chose to proceed under his customary law. Where the plaintiff is not a member of a Ghanaian community, but is subject to the customary law of a community in some other part of Africa, he will not be able to claim to have the case decided under his own system of customary law unless he can show an agreement by the other party to be bound by this system or can, under the rules of private international law which are included in the common law, claim to have the case decided by his own law.[2]

Subsection (2) of s. 66 of the Courts Act, 1960 (C.A.9) originally provided as follows:

> " (2) Where under this section customary law is applicable in any proceedings but a relevant rule of customary law has been assimilated by the common law under any enactment such as is mentioned in section 18 (1) of the Interpretation Act, 1960, that rule shall nevertheless apply in those proceedings, but in the form in which it has been so assimilated."

This subsection was considered necessary to preserve the effectiveness of the Application of Law Rules once the process of assimilation has begun. When, however, the procedure for assimilation was laid down by Part VII of the Chieftaincy Act, 1961 (Act 81), it was provided that any assimilated rule should apply to every issue within its scope whether that issue would, if assimilation had not taken place, have been determined according to the common law or any system of customary law.[3] This removed the need for sub-s. (2) of s. 66, which was accordingly repealed.[4]

Subsection (3) of section 66 provides that certain common law rules are to apply to certain issues notwithstanding that under

---

[1] Courts Act, 1960 (C.A.9.), s. 67 (1).
[2] See Examples J and K, p. 462–3, *post.*
[3] Chieftaincy Act, 1961 (Act 81), s. 63 (2).
[4] *Ibid.,* s. 69 (1).

the earlier provisions of the section customary law may be applicable. It is in the following terms:

" (3) Notwithstanding anything contained in the foregoing provisions of this section, but subject to the provisions of any other enactment—
 (a) the rules of the common law relating to private international law shall apply in any proceedings in which an issue concerning the application of law prevailing in any country outside Ghana is raised;
 (b) the rules of estoppel and such other of the rules generally known as the common law and the rules generally known as the doctrines of equity as have heretofore been treated as applicable in all proceedings in Ghana shall continue to be so treated."

The rules of private international law, or external conflict of laws, form a developed system of rules for deciding issues concerning the application of foreign law. For obvious reasons they have no counterpart in customary law, which is not based on national territorial divisions.[1]

Paragraph (b) of the subsection is designed to permit the continuance of the practice whereby the courts made use of such doctrines as *res judicata*, equitable estoppel and other forms of estoppel to modify the application of certain customary law rules.[2] It should be noted that the reference to the common law in para. (b) means the common law in the narrower sense, the wording following that used in s. 17(1) of the Interpretation Act, 1960 (C.A.4).

Examples of the operation of the application of law rules

Example A. A, whose mother was a slave girl from the Northern Territories bought by a member of a family in Akim Abuakwa, died leaving a will. In order to determine questions of the succession to A's property it was necessary to decide what was A's personal law within the meaning of this section. The court was satisfied that by the Akim Abuakwa customary law the child of a slave woman is considered to be a member of the father's family, and thus subject to the customary law of that family. It was not known to what customary law A's mother had originally been subject.

Question: How was A's personal law to be determined?

---

[1] See Example K, p. 463, *post*.
[2] See pp. 445–446, *ante*.

Answer: Section 66(1) provides that if a person is not shown to be subject to customary law his personal law is the common law. Since, under the customary law of the area and family in which A was born and brought up, he was subject to that law, this was sufficient to establish that law as his personal law notwithstanding that a different result might have been indicated by the personal law of his mother if it had been known.[1]

Example B. A was entitled, together with other members of his family, to an undivided interest under X customary law in certain family property. In the mistaken belief that under X customary law A enjoyed an undivided half share as a tenant in common, which he was free to dispose of, B Ltd. took a mortgage of the property in English form, granted by A without the consent of his family. Under a power contained in the mortgage B Ltd. sold the property to C.

Question: Is the issue whether C obtained a good title to be determined by X customary law or the common law?

Answer: Since A and the other members of his family have the same personal law (X customary law) and each have an interest in the family property, rule 1 must be consulted. This indicates that, assuming A to be unable under X customary law to mortgage the property without the consent of his family, he cannot do so by means of a mortgage under English law. The preliminary issue as to whether the mortgage to B Ltd. was valid must therefore be determined according to X customary law. If the mortgage were found to be valid the issue of whether C obtained a good title under the sale would, in accordance with rule 2, be determined according to the common law.[2]

Example C. A, who was the head of a family subject to X customary law and was acting with the consent of the family, put B, a member of the family, into possession of certain family land with authority to let it and recoup from the rent money owed to him by A. B granted a yearly lease of the land in English form to C Ltd., who subsequently, at the instigation of A, ceased paying rent to B on the ground that the family and not B were their landlords.

---

[1] Based on *Santeng* v. *Darkwa* (1940), 6 W.A.C.A. 52; *cf. Bassil* v. *Honger* (1954), 14 W.A.C.A. 569.
[2] Based on *Olowu* v. *Desalu* (1955), 14 W.A.C.A. 662.

Question: Is the issue of the right of C Ltd. to deny B's title and pay their rent to the family to be determined according to the common law or X customary law?

Answer: The issue clearly arises out of a transaction (the lease) which from its form or nature indicates that the parties agreed that such an issue as this should be determined by the common law. Subject to rule 1 therefore, rule 2 applies with the result that the issue is determined according to the common law, under which a lessee cannot dispute his lessor's title. Is this affected by rule 1? The answer is no, because the arrangement with C Ltd. could in substance, and in the circumstances (i.e. the agreement of the family), have equally well been carried out by a customary law procedure. Note however that in an action by the family against B for an account of the rents received by him, rule 2 would not apply since this would not be an issue covered by the implied agreement between B and C Ltd.[1]

Example D. A, by a deed of gift in English form, transferred buildings to B, C and D, " their heirs and assigns ". As the survivor of the three joint tenants, D, who was subject to X customary law, ultimately became solely entitled to the premises and later died intestate. Her daughter E claimed to succeed under the common law but other members of the family claimed under X customary law.

Question: Was the devolution of the property on D's death subject to the common law, i.e. English rules of intestacy, or X customary law?

Answer: Rules 2 and 4 have to be considered here. Although under rule 2 the common law would have applied for determining any question as to D's title (which in fact was undisputed), it does not apply to the question of the devolution of D's property, which is too remote from the original deed of gift to be said to arise in connection with it. The parties all trace their claims from D and rule 4 (*a*) therefore produces the result that the question of devolution falls to be determined by X customary law.[2]

Example E. A, who was subject to X customary law, was the holder of a mortgage made in English form. A died.

Question: Is the issue of the devolution of A's interest as

---

[1] Based on *Amokwandoh* v. *U.A.C.* (1932), 1 W.A.C.A. 179.
[2] Based on *Fynn* v. *Gardiner* (1953), 14 W.A.C.A. 260.

mortgagee to be determined by X customary law or the common law?

Answer: Since there is no issue as to A's title as mortgagee rule 2 has no application. Since A's interest was personalty, being principally a right to the money secured by the mortgage, rule 4 has no application. Rule 5 therefore applies, and the issue of devolution is governed by A's personal law, namely X customary law.[1]

Example F. A, who was subject to X customary law, owned a house in an area in which Z customary law prevailed. Under X customary law the house would pass on A's death to B but under Z customary law it would pass to C. On the assumption that the house had passed to C, and then on C's death to D, D purported to sell the house to E, who was subject to Z customary law.

Question: In a dispute between B and E, is the title to the land to be ascertained according to X or Z customary law?

Answer: Since both B and E trace their claims from A, who was subject to X customary law, that law applies in accordance with para. (*a*) of rule 4.[2]

Example G. A and B each claim title to land in an area in which X customary law applies, and each traces his claim from C, a Nigerian. It does not appear from the evidence to what part of Nigeria C belonged or to what law he was subject.

Question: By what law is the issue of title to be determined?

Answer: Although the claims are traced from one person, it is not established that that person is subject to customary law within the meaning of s. 18 of the Interpretation Act, 1960 (C.A. 4), that is a customary law applicable to a particular community in Ghana. Accordingly, under para. (*c*) of rule 4, the issue should be determined according to X customary law as being the law of the place in which the land is situated.[3]

Example H. A dispute arises as to who is entitled to the compensation money for land compulsorily acquired. The land is in an area in which X customary law prevails. The Manche of

[1] Based on *Wellington* v. *Papafio* (1952), 14 W.A.C.A. 49.
[2] Based on *Ghamson* v. *Wobill*; see p. 447, *ante*.
[3] Based on *Ekem* v. *Nerba*; see p. 448, *ante*.

X claims the money under X customary law on the ground that the X people acquired the land by conquest 150 years previously. A, who is in occupation of the land, claims the money on the ground that the land was settled by his ancestor, who was subject to Z customary law, 100 years ago.

Question: Is the title to the land, and therefore to the compensation money, to be ascertained according to X or Z customary law?

Answer: Since the parties trace their claims from persons subject to different customary laws, para. (*c*) of rule 4 applies and the issue should be determined according to X customary law as being the law of the place in which the land is situated.[1]

Example I. A, who was subject to X customary law, died leaving a will in English form by which he disposed of certain land and chattels. In order to apply the will it was necessary to decide as a preliminary issue which of the property in question was family property.

Question: Should this issue be determined according to the common law or X customary law?

Answer: The will was a unilateral disposition within the meaning of rule 3, but apart from the fact that rule 1 prevents effect being given to a disposition made by an English law procedure which exceeds the powers of disposition possessed under customary law, the preliminary issue can hardly be said to arise " out of " the testamentary disposition and in any case is not an issue which the testator could, by reason of his having made a will in English form, be taken to have intended to be governed by the common law. Accordingly, subject to rule 1, rule 4 will apply in relation to the land and rule 5 in relation to the chattels, producing the result that the issue is to be determined according to X customary law.

Example J. A utters before witnesses a slander against B, who is subject to X customary law.[2]

Question: Are the issues of whether B has any remedy against

---

[1] Based on a slight variation of the facts in *Owusu* v. *Manche of Labadi* (1933), 1 W.A.C.A. 278. Note that the application of any of these rules may be affected by statutory provisions—e.g. s. 14 of the State Property and Contracts Act, 1960 (C.A. 6), which raises a presumption in favour of the person in possession.

[2] Based on *Mensah* v. *Takyiampong* (1940) 6 W.A.C.A. 188.

A, and if so what that remedy is, to be determined according to the common law or X customary law?

Answer: Since none of the earlier rules is relevant, the matter falls to be determined according to rule 6. The common law will therefore apply unless B claims to have the issue determined according to X customary law.[1]

Example K. A and B, members of a Liberian tribe, lived for many years as man and wife, although unmarried, in a part of Ghana subject to X customary law. During that time B persuaded A to build a house for them and, to assist him to do this, handed over to him a sum of money belonging to her. On A's death B sought to recover this money from his estate.

Question: By what law is the question of B's right to recover the money to be determined?

Answer: Since none of the earlier rules is relevant, rule 6 falls to be applied. The common law will therefore govern the matter unless B claims to have the issue determined according to the customary law of her Liberian people. This will not however fall within the meaning of customary law as used in rule 6 unless enough of those people have settled in Ghana to constitute a community there.[2] If this has not occurred, the only way in which B can secure that her own customary law applies is by showing that it is applicable under the common law rules of private international law.[3]

Example L. A sold Blackacre to B by a procedure conforming to X customary law, which prevailed in the area in which Blackacre was situated. C, in a subsequent action against A, obtained a declaration that he was entitled to land which included Blackacre, but did not inform B, who in ignorance of the declaration and to the knowledge of C, proceeded to erect a house on Blackacre. C sued B for possession of Blackacre and the house. All the parties and their predecessors were subject to X customary law.

Question: By what law is the question of the right to possession of Blackacre to be determined?

---

[1] *Cf. Kwaku* v. *Addo* (1957), 2 W.A.L. 306.
[2] Interpretation Act, 1960 (C.A. 4), s. 18 (1).
[3] Courts Act, 1960 (C.A. 9), s. 66 (3) (*a*). This example is based on *Morris* v. *Monrovia* (1930), 1 W.A.C.A. 70.

Answer: Under rule 4, X customary law clearly applies, and under that law C will succeed. C however has been guilty of equitable fraud in standing by while B erected the house and, if the court considers that the application of rule 4 as it stands would produce a substantial injustice it may, under the power conferred by sub-s. (3) (*b*) of s. 66, apply the doctrine of equitable estoppel. The rule described by Fry, J., in *Willmott* v. *Barber*[1] will thus operate to prevent C from succeeding in dispossessing B.[2]

---

[1] (1880), 15 Ch.D. at p. 105.
[2] Based on *Abbey* v. *Ollenu* (1954), 14 W.A.C.A. 567. Again, other statutory provisions must be watched; on these facts the High Court would probably be asked to exercise its powers under the Land Development (Protection of Purchasers) Act, 1960 (Act 2) if the land were in an area to which the Act applied.

APPENDICES

SUMMARY

		PAGE
APPENDIX A.	Constitutional enactments	467
	Ghana Independence Act, 1957	467
	Constituent Assembly and Plebiscite Act, 1960 . .	472
	Constitution of the Republic of Ghana	473
APPENDIX B.	Glossary of terms used in legislation . .	491
APPENDIX C.	Enactments relating to the application of common law and customary law	498
	Courts Ordinance (Cap. 4), Part F	498
	Courts Act, 1960 (C.A. 9), ss. 66, 67	500
	Chieftaincy Act, 1961 (Act 81), ss. 58–64 . . .	502

Note. In Appendices A and C the sidenotes, which in the official print would appear in the margins, have here, for the convenience of book production, been set in bold type at the beginning of their sections.

APPENDIX A

CONSTITUTIONAL ENACTMENTS

THE GHANA INDEPENDENCE ACT, 1957
(5 & 6 Eliz. 2 c. 6)

An Act to make provision for, and in connection with, the attainment by the Gold Coast of fully responsible status within the British Commonwealth of Nations   [7th February 1957]

1. Provision for the fully responsible status of the Gold Coast under the name of Ghana.—The territories included immediately before the appointed day in the Gold Coast as defined in and for the purposes of the Gold Coast (Constitution) Order in Council, 1954, shall as from that day together form part of Her Majesty's dominions under the name of Ghana, and—

(a) no Act of the Parliament of the United Kingdom passed on or after the appointed day shall extend, or be deemed to extend, to Ghana as part of the law of Ghana, unless it is expressly declared in that Act that the Parliament of Ghana has requested, and consented to, the enactment thereof;

(b) as from the appointed day, Her Majesty's Government in the United Kingdom shall have no responsibility for the government of Ghana or any part thereof;

(c) as from the appointed day, the provisions of the First Schedule to this Act shall have effect with respect to the legislative powers of Ghana:

Provided that nothing in this section other than paragraphs (a) to (c) thereof shall affect the operation in any of the territories aforesaid of any enactments, or any other instrument having the effect of law, passed or made with respect thereto before the appointed day.

2. Consequential modification of British Nationality Act.— As from the appointed day, the British Nationality Act, 1948, shall have effect—

(a) with the substitution in subsection (3) of section one thereof (which provides for persons to be British subjects or Commonwealth citizens by virtue of citizenship of certain countries) for the words " and Ceylon " of the words " Ceylon and Ghana ";

(b) as if in the British Protectorates, Protected States and Protected Persons Order in Council, 1949, the words " Northern Territories of the Gold Coast " in the First Schedule thereto and the words " Togoland under United Kingdom Trusteeship " in the Third Schedule thereto were omitted:

Provided that a person who, immediately before the appointed day, was for the purposes of the said Act and Order in Council a British protected person by virtue of his connection with either of the territories mentioned in paragraph (*b*) of this section shall not cease to be such a British protected person for any of those purposes by reason of anything contained in the foregoing provisions of this Act, but shall so cease upon his becoming a citizen of Ghana under any law of the Parliament of Ghana making provision for such citezenship.

3. Consequential modifications with respect to development schemes, etc.—(1) No scheme shall be made on or after the appointed day under the Colonial Development and Welfare Acts, 1940 to 1955, wholly or partly for the benefit of Ghana.

(2) Any scheme in force under the said Acts immediately before the appointed day which was made solely for the benefit of Ghana or any part thereof shall cease to have effect on that day without prejudice to the making of payments in pursuance of that scheme on or after that day in respect of any period falling before that day; and, so far as practicable, no part of any sums paid out of moneys provided by Parliament for the purposes of any other scheme made under those Acts before that day shall be employed in respect of any period falling on or after that day for the benefit of Ghana.

(3) Nothing in the two foregoing subsections shall restrict the making of, or the employment of sums paid out of moneys provided by Parliament for the purposes of, any scheme under the said Acts with respect to a body established for the joint benefit of Ghana and one or more of the following territories, that is to say, the Federation or any Region of Nigeria, Sierra Leone and the Gambia, in a case where Ghana has undertaken to bear a reasonable share of the cost of the scheme.

(4) [*Repealed by Overseas Resources Development Act, 1958.*]

4. Consequential modification of other enactments.—(1) Notwithstanding anything in the Interpretation Act, 1889, the expression " colony " in any Act of Parliament of the United Kingdom passed on or after the appointed day shall not include Ghana or any part thereof.

(2) As from the appointed day, the expression " colony " in the Army Act, 1955, and the Air Force Act, 1955, shall not include Ghana or any part thereof, and in the definitions of " Commonwealth force " in subsection (1) of section two hundred and twenty-five and subsection (1) of section two hundred and twenty-three respectively of those Acts . . . for the words " or Ceylon " there shall be substituted the words " Ceylon or Ghana ".

(3) Any Order in Council made on or after the appointed day under the Army Act, 1955, or the Air Force Act, 1955, providing for that Act to continue in force beyond the date on which it would otherwise expire shall not operate to continue that Act in force beyond that date as part of the law of Ghana.

(4) As from the appointed day, the provisions specified in the Second Schedule to this Act shall have effect subject to the amendments respectively specified in that Schedule, and Her Majesty may by Order in Council, which shall be subject to annulment in pursuance of a resolution of either House of Parliament, make such further adaptations in any Act of the Parliament of the United Kingdom passed before this Act, or in any instrument having effect under any such Act, as appear to her necessary in consequence of section one of this Act; and any Order in Council made under this subsection may be varied or revoked by a subsequent Order in Council so made and, though made after the appointed day, may be made so as to have effect from that day:

Provided that this subsection shall not extend to Ghana as part of the law thereof.

Note. The words omitted in sub-s. (2) were repealed by the Naval Discipline Act, 1957.

5. Short title and appointed day.—(1) This Act may be cited as the Ghana Independence Act, 1957.

(2) In this Act, the expression " the appointed day " means the sixth day of March, nineteen hundred and fifty-seven, unless before that date Her Majesty has by Order in Council appointed some other day to be the appointed day for the purposes of this Act.

SCHEDULES

Section 1   FIRST SCHEDULE

LEGISLATIVE POWERS OF GHANA

1. The Colonial Laws Validity Act, 1865, shall not apply to any law made on or after the appointed day by the Parliament of Ghana.

2. No law and no provision of any law made on or after the appointed day by the Parliament of Ghana shall be void or inoperative on the ground that it is repugnant to the law of England, or to the provisions of any existing or future Act of the Parliament of the United Kingdom, or to any order, rule or regulation made under any such Act, and the powers of the Parliament of Ghana shall include the power to repeal or amend any such Act, order, rule or regulation in so far as it is part of the law of Ghana.

3. The Parliament of Ghana shall have full power to make laws having extra-territorial operation.

4. Without prejudice to the generality of the foregoing provisions of this Schedule, sections seven hundred and thirty-five and seven hundred and thirty-six of the Merchant Shipping Act, 1894, shall be construed as though reference therein to the legislature of a British possession did not include reference to the Parliament of Ghana.

5. Without prejudice to the generality of the foregoing provisions of this Schedule, section four of the Colonial Courts of Admiralty Act, 1890 (which requires certain laws to be reserved for the signification of Her Majesty's pleasure, or to contain a suspending clause) and so much of section seven of that Act as requires the approval of Her Majesty in Council to any rules of court for regulating the practice and procedure of a Colonial Court of Admiralty shall cease to have effect in Ghana.

6. Notwithstanding anything in the foregoing provisions of this Schedule, the constitutional provisions shall not be repealed, amended or modified otherwise than in such manner as may be specified in those provisions.

In this paragraph, the expression " the constitutional provisions " means the provisions for the time being in force on or at any time after the appointed day of the Gold Coast (Constitution) Orders in Council, 1954 to 1956, and of any other Order in Council made before that day, or any law, or instrument made under a law, of the Parliament of Ghana made on or after that day, which amends, modifies, re-enacts with or without amendment or modification, or makes different provision in lieu of, any of the provisions of any such Order in Council or of any such law or instrument previously made.

Section 4   SECOND SCHEDULE

AMENDMENTS NOT AFFECTING LAW OF GHANA

Diplomatic immunities

1. In section four hundred and sixty-one of the Income Tax Act, 1952 (which relates to exemption from income tax in the case of certain Commonwealth representatives and their staffs) for the words " or Ceylon " in both places where they occur there shall be substituted the words " Ceylon or Ghana ".

2. In subsection (6) of section one of the Diplomatic Immunities (Commonwealth Countries and Republic of Ireland) Act, 1952, after the word " Ceylon " there shall be inserted the word " Ghana "; and the proviso to subsection (1) of that section shall not apply in relation to Ghana until a law of the Parliament of Ghana making provision for citizenship of Ghana has come into force.

Financial

3. As respects goods imported after such date as Her Majesty may by Order in Council appoint . . . section two of the Isle of Man (Customs) Act, 1932 (which relate to imperial preference other than colonial preference) shall apply to Ghana.

Note. The words omitted were repealed by the Import Duties Act, 1958.

4. In the Colonial Stock Act, 1934 (which extends the stocks which may be treated as trustee securities), the expression " Dominion " shall include Ghana. . . .

Note. The words omitted were deleted by the Ghana (Consequential Provision) (Colonial Stock Acts) Order in Council, 1960.

Visiting forces

5. In the Visiting Forces (British Commonwealth) Act, 1933, section four (which deals with attachment and mutual powers of command) and the definition of " visiting force " for the purposes of that Act which is contained in section eight thereof shall apply in relation to forces raised in Ghana as they apply in relation to forces raised in Dominions within the meaning of the Statute of Westminster, 1931.

6. In the Visiting Forces Act, 1952—
   (*a*) in subsection (1) of section one (which specifies the countries to which that Act applies) for the words " or Ceylon " there shall be substituted the words " Ceylon or Ghana ";
   (*b*) in paragraph (*a*) of subsection (1) of section ten the expression " colony " shall not include Ghana or any part thereof;

and, until express provision with respect to Ghana is made by an Order in Council under section eight of that Act (which relates to the application to visiting forces of law relating to home forces), any such Order for the time being in force shall be deemed to apply to visiting forces of Ghana.

Ships and aircraft

7. In subsection (2) of section four hundred and twenty-seven of the Merchant Shipping Act, 1894, as substituted by section two of the Merchant Shipping (Safety Convention) Act, 1949, for the words " or Ceylon " there shall be substituted the words " Ceylon or Ghana ".

8. In the proviso to subsection (2) of section six of the Merchant Shipping Act, 1948, for the words " or Ceylon " there shall be substituted the words " Ceylon or Ghana ".

9. [*Repealed by Emergency Laws Repeal Act*, 1959.]

10. The Ships and Aircraft (Transfer Restriction) Act, 1939, shall not apply to any ship by reason only of its being registered in, or licensed under the law of, Ghana; and the penal provisions of that Act shall not apply to persons in Ghana (but without prejudice to the operation with respect to any ship to which that Act does apply of the provisions thereof relating to the forfeiture of ships).

Note. Para. 10 is repealed as from 1st January, 1965 by the Emergency Laws Repeal Act, 1959.

11. In the Whaling Industry (Regulation) Act, 1934, the expression " British ship to which this Act applies " shall not include a British ship registered in Ghana.

Copyright

12.—(1) If on or after the appointed day the Parliament of Ghana repeals or amends the Copyright Act, 1911, in so far as it forms part of the law of Ghana or of any part of Ghana, the following provisions of this paragraph shall have effect.

(2) Any provision of the said Act in force at the date of the repeal or amendment as part of the law of the United Kingdom shall no longer apply in relation to, or to any part of, Ghana, whether as part of Her Majesty's dominions to which that Act extends or by virtue of section twenty-eight of that Act:

Provided that—

(a) this sub-paragraph shall not prejudicially affect any legal rights existing at the time of the repeal or amendment;

(b) Ghana shall be included in the expression " self-governing dominion " for the purposes of subsection (2) of section twenty-five and subsection (3) of section twenty-six of that Act (which relate to reciprocity with self-governing dominions having their own copyright law), and the said subsection (2) shall have effect in relation to Ghana as if that Act, so far as it remains part of the law of Ghana or of any part of Ghana, had been passed by the Parliament of Ghana;

(c) this sub-paragraph shall not apply to any provision of that Act which continues to have effect as part of the law of the United Kingdom by virtue only of paragraph 40 of the Seventh Schedule to the Copyright Act, 1956.

(3) If at the date of the repeal or amendment any provision of the Copyright Act, 1956, has come into operation but does not extend to all parts of Ghana by virtue of an Order in Council made before the appointed day under section thirty-one of that Act and has not been applied in the case of

Ghana by an Order in Council made on or after that day under section thirty-two of that Act, any reference in that provision to countries to which that provision extends shall, notwithstanding anything in sub-paragraph (2) of paragraph 39 of the Seventh Schedule to that Act, not be construed as if that provision extended to Ghana or any part thereof.

THE CONSTITUENT ASSEMBLY AND PLEBISCITE ACT, 1960

(Ghana No. 1 of 1960)

Assented to in Her Majesty's Name and on Her Majesty's behalf this 25th day of February, 1960.

LISTOWEL
Governor-General

An Act to provide for a Constituent Assembly and for the holding of a Plebiscite on matters relating to the establishment of a new Constitution. [27th February, 1960]

1. Short title.—This Act may be cited as the Constituent Assembly and Plebiscite Act, 1960.

2. Constituent Assembly.—(1) The National Assembly is hereby authorised to resove itself from time to time into a Constituent Assembly with full power to enact such provisions for or in connection with the establishment of a new Constitution as it thinks fit, including provisions whereby Ghana is established as a Republic.

(2) A Bill for a new Constitution, any Bill containing provisions consequential on or supplemental to the new Constitution, and any other Bill passed by the Constituent Assembly under this Act shall become law notwithstanding that her Majesty has not given Her assent thereto.

(3) Subject to any necessary modifications, the National Assembly Act, 1959, the Standing Orders of the National Assembly and all other provisions relating to the National Assembly, other than the provisions contained in section 42 of the Ghana (Constitution) Order in Council, 1957 (which provides for assent to Bills) and in the Ordinances Authentication Ordinance shall apply in relation to the Constituent Assembly as they apply to the National Assembly.

(4) Subject to the provisions of any enactment made by the Constituent Assembly, nothing in this Act shall affect any law relating to the National Assembly as such or the exercise by the National Assembly as such of its functions under any law.

3. Plebiscite.—(1) In order, before passing a Bill for a new Constitution, to inform itself as to the wishes of the people on the form of the Constitution, or the person who is to become the new Head of the State or any other matter, the Constituent Assembly may order the holding of a Plebiscite to determine such questions as the Constituent Assembly may direct.

(2) The Constituent Assembly may make regulations containing such requirements, prohibitions and other provisions as it thinks expedient for or in connection with the holding of a Plebiscite under this section, including provisions giving power, for the purpose of maintaining public order, to control the movement and assembly of persons, to restrict the supply of intoxicating liquor and to use temporarily without the consent of the owner thereof any vehicle or building.

4. Duration of powers.—On the coming into operation of a Constitution enacted by the Constituent Assembly, the power of the National Assembly to resolve itself into a Constituent Assembly shall cease.

THE CONSTITUTION OF THE REPUBLIC OF GHANA

ARRANGEMENT OF ARTICLES

Article   PAGE

PART I—POWERS OF THE PEOPLE

1. Powers of the people 476
2. Realisation of African unity 476
3. Powers of the people entrenched 476

PART II—THE REPUBLIC

4. Declaration of Republic 476
5. Territories 476
6. Regions 477
7. National Flag 477

PART III—THE PRESIDENT AND HIS MINISTERS
Head of the State

8. Head of the State 477
9. Term of office 477

First President

10. First President 477

474 *Appendix A*

Article   PAGE

Election of President and Assumption of Office

11. Election of President 477
12. Assumption of office 478
13. Declaration of fundamental principles 478

Official Seals

14. Official Seals 479

Ministers and Cabinet

15. Appointment of Ministers. 479
16. The Cabinet 479
17. Tenure of office of Ministers 479

Supplemental Provisions as to President

18. Presidential Commissions 479
19. Salary and allowances of President 480

PART IV—PARLIAMENT

20. The Sovereign Parliament 481
21. The National Assembly 481
22. Sessions of the Assembly 482
23. Dissolution of the Assembly 482
24. Legislation 482
25. Presidential addresses and messages 482

PART V—PUBLIC REVENUE AND EXPENDITURE
Taxation

26. Restriction on taxation 483

Custody of Public Money

27. Public funds 483
28. Public revenue 483
29. Payments out of public funds 483
30. Excess expenditure 484

Moneys granted by Vote of the National Assembly

31. Moneys granted on the annual estimates 484
32. Moneys granted on provisional and supplementary estimates 484
33. Extraordinary grants 485

Expenditure out of Contingencies Fund

34. Expenditure out of Contingencies Fund 485

Public Loans

35. Granting of loans 485
36. Raising of loans 486
37. The public debt 486

Audit of Public Accounts

38. The Auditor-General 486
39. Duty to audit and report 486

Article   PAGE

PART VI—LAW AND JUSTICE
Laws of Ghana

40. Laws of Ghana 486

Superior and Inferior Courts

41. Superior and inferior courts 487

Provisions as to Superior Courts

42. Jurisdiction 487
43. Composition of courts 487

Judges of the Superior Courts

44. Chief Justice 487
45. Judges 488
46. Salaries and pensions 488

Attorney-General

47. Attorney-General 488

President's powers of mercy

48. President's powers of mercy 489

PART VII—HOUSES OF CHIEFS

49. Houses of Chiefs 489
50. Composition and functions 489

PART VIII—THE PUBLIC SERVICES

51. The Public Services 489
52. Retiring allowances 489

PART IX—THE ARMED FORCES

53. Prohibition of irregular forces 489
54. Powers of Commander-in-Chief 489

PART X—SPECIAL POWERS FOR FIRST PRESIDENT

55. Special powers for first President 490

WE THE PEOPLE OF GHANA, by our Representatives gathered in this our Constituent Assembly,

IN EXERCISE of our undoubted right to appoint for ourselves the means whereby we shall be governed,

IN SYMPATHY with and loyalty to our fellow-countrymen of Africa,

IN THE HOPE that we may by our actions this day help to further the development of a Union of African States, and

IN A SPIRIT of friendship and peace with all other peoples of the World,

DO HEREBY ENACT and give to ourselves this Constitution.

This Constitution is enacted on this twenty-ninth day of June, 1960 and shall come into operation on the first day of July, 1960.

PART I

POWERS OF THE PEOPLE

1. Powers of the people.—The powers of the State derive from the people, by whom certain of those powers are now conferred on the institutions established by this Constitution and who shall have the right to exercise the remainder of those powers, and to choose their representatives in the Parliament now established, in accordance with the following principle—

That, without distinction of sex, race, religion or political belief, every person who, being by law a citizen of Ghana, has attained the age of twenty-one years and is not disqualified by law on grounds of absence, infirmity of mind or criminality, shall be entitled to one vote, to be cast in freedom and secrecy.

2. Realisation of African unity.—In the confident expectation of an early surrender of sovereignty to a union of African states and territories, the people now confer on Parliament the power to provide for the surrender of the whole or any part of the sovereignty of Ghana.

3. Powers of the people entrenched.—The power to repeal or alter this Part of the Constitution is reserved to the people.

PART II

THE REPUBLIC

4. Declaration of Republic.—(1) Ghana is a sovereign unitary Republic.

(2) Subject to the provisions of Article Two of the Constitution, the power to provide a form of government for Ghana other than that of a republic or for the form of the Republic to be other than unitary is reserved to the people.

5. Territories.—Until otherwise provided by law, the territories of Ghana shall consist of those territories which were comprised in Ghana immediately before the coming into operation of the Constitution, including the territorial waters.

6. Regions.—Until otherwise provided by law, Ghana shall be divided into the following Regions, which shall respectively comprise such territories as may be provided for by law, that is to say, the Ashanti Region, the Brong-Ahafo Region, the Central Region, the Eastern Region, the Northern Region, the Upper Region, the Volta Region, and the Western Region.

7. National Flag.—The Flag of Ghana shall consist of three equal horizontal stripes, the upper stripe being red, the middle stripe gold and the lower stripe green, with a black star in the centre of the gold stripe.

PART III

THE PRESIDENT AND HIS MINISTERS

Head of the State

8. Head of the State.—(1) There shall be a President of Ghana, who shall be the Head of the State and responsible to the people.

(2) Subject to the provisions of the Constitution, the executive power of the State is conferred upon the President.

(3) The President shall be the Commander-in-Chief of the Armed Forces and the Fount of Honour.

(4) Except as may be otherwise provided by law, in the exercise of his functions the President shall act in his own discretion and shall not be obliged to follow advice tendered by any other person.

(5) The power to repeal or alter this Article is reserved to the people.

9. Term of office.—The term of office of the President shall begin with his assumption of office and end with the assumption of office of the person elected as President in the next following election, so however that the President may at any time resign his office by instrument under his hand addressed to the Chief Justice.

First President

10. First President.—KWAME NKRUMAH is hereby appointed first President of Ghana, having been chosen as such before the enactment of the Constitution in a Plebiscite conducted in accordance with the principle set out in Article One of the Constitution.

Election of President and Assumption of Office

11. Election of President.—(1) An election of a President shall be held whenever one of the following events occurs, that is to say—

(*a*) the National Assembly is dissolved, or
(*b*) the President dies, or
(*c*) the President resigns his office.

(2) Provision shall be made by law for regulating the election of a President, and shall be so made in accordance with the following principles—

(*a*) any citizen of Ghana shall be qualified for election as President if he has attained the age of thirty-five years;

(*b*) the returning officer for the election shall be the Chief Justice;

(*c*) if contested, an election held by reason of a dissolution of the National Assembly shall be decided by preferences given before the General Election by persons subsequently returned as Members of Parliament, or, if no candidate for election as President obtains more than one-half of the preferences so given, by secret ballot of the Members of the new Parliament;

(*d*) if contested, an election held by reason of the death or resignation of the President shall be decided by secret ballot of the Members of Parliament.

(3) If an election is to be decided by balloting among the Members of Parliament and a President has not been declared elected after five ballots the National Assembly shall be deemed to be dissolved at the conclusion of the fifth ballot.

(4) Where a person has been declared by the Chief Justice to be elected as President his election shall not be questioned in any court.

12. Assumption of office.—(1) The President shall assume office by taking an oath in the following form, which shall be administered before the people by the Chief Justice—

I................do solemnly swear that I will well and truly exercise the functions of the high office of President of Ghana, that I will bear true faith and allegiance to Ghana, that I will preserve and defend the Constitution, and that I will do right to all manner of people according to law without fear or favour, affection or ill-will. So help me God.

(2) Instead of taking an oath the President may if he thinks fit make an affirmation, which shall be in the like form with the substitution of *affirm* for *swear* and the omission of the concluding sentence.

13. Declaration of fundamental principles.—(1) Immediately after his assumption of office the President shall make the following solemn declaration before the people—

On accepting the call of the people to the high office of President of Ghana I................solemnly declare my adherence to the following fundamental principles—

That the powers of Government spring from the will of the people and should be exercised in accordance therewith.

That freedom and justice should be honoured and maintained.

That the union of Africa should be striven for by every lawful means and, when attained, should be faithfully preserved.

That the Independence of Ghana should not be surrendered or diminished on any grounds other than the furtherance of African unity.

That no person should suffer discrimination on grounds of sex, race, tribe, religion or political belief.

That Chieftaincy in Ghana should be guaranteed and preserved.
That every citizen of Ghana should receive his fair share of the produce yielded by the development of the country.
  That subject to such restrictions as may be necessary for preserving public order, morality or health, no person should be deprived of freedom of religion or speech, of the right to move and assemble without hindrance or of the right of access to courts of law.
  That no person should be deprived of his property save where the public interest so requires and the law so provides.

(2) The power to repeal this Article, or to alter its provisions otherwise than by the addition of further paragraphs to the declaration, is reserved to the people.

Official Seals

14. Official seals.—There shall be a Public Seal and a Presidential Seal, the use and custody of which shall be regulated by law.

Ministers and Cabinet

15. Appointment of Ministers.—(1) The President shall from time to time appoint by instrument under the Presidential Seal persons from among the Members of Parliament, who shall be styled Ministers of Ghana, to assist him in his exercise of the executive power and to take charge under his direction of such departments of State as he may assign to them.

(2) The power to repeal or alter this Article is reserved to the people.

16. The Cabinet.—(1) There shall be a Cabinet consisting of the President and not less than eight Ministers of Ghana appointed as members of the Cabinet by the President.

(2) Subject to the powers of the President, the Cabinet is charged with the general direction and control of the Government of Ghana.

(3) The appointment of a Minister as a member of the Cabinet may at any time be revoked by the President.

(4) The power to repeal or alter this Article is reserved to the people.

17. Tenure of office of Ministers.—The office of a Minister of Ghana shall become vacant—
- (a) if the President removes him from office by instrument under the Presidential Seal; or
- (b) if he ceases to be a Member of Parliament otherwise than by reason of a dissolution; or
- (c) on the acceptance by the President of his resignation from office; or
- (d) immediately before the assumption of office of a President.

Supplemental provisions as to President

18. Presidential commissions.—(1) The office of the President shall be executed, in accordance with advice tendered by the Cabinet, by a Presidential Commission consisting of three persons appointed by the Cabinet—

    (a) during an interval between the death or resignation of a President and the assumption of office by his successor; and

    (b) whenever the President is adjudged incapable of acting.

(2) Any functions of the President which, by reason of the illness of the President or his absence from Ghana or any other circumstance cannot conveniently be exercised by him in person, may, so long as he is not adjudged incapable of acting, be delegated by the President to a Presidential Commission consisting of three persons appointed by him:

    Provided that nothing in this section shall be taken to prejudice the power of the President, at any time when he is not adjudged incapable of acting, to delegate any exercise of the executive power to some other person.

(3) A Presidential Commission may act by any two of its members, and if any vacancy arises by reason of the death of a member the vacancy shall be filled by the Cabinet or by the President, according to which of them appointed the deceased member.

(4) The President shall be deemed to be adjudged incapable of acting if the Chief Justice and the Speaker—

    (a) have jointly declared that, after considering medical evidence, they are satisfied that the President is, by reason of physical or mental infirmity, unable to exercise the functions of his office, and

    (b) have not subsequently withdrawn the declaration on the ground that the President has recovered his capacity.

(5) If, at the time when a Presidential Commission falls to be appointed under section (1) of this Article, the number of Ministers in the Cabinet is less than eight or there are no Ministers in the Cabinet, then, for the purpose of the appointment of a Presidential Commission and the tendering of advice to the Commission as to the membership of the Cabinet in the first instance, one or more persons shall be deemed to be included in the Cabinet as follows:—

    The person or persons who last ceased to be in the Cabinet shall be deemed to be included and, if the number remains less than eight, the person or persons who before him or them last ceased to be in the Cabinet shall also be deemed to be included, and so on until the number is not less than eight.

    Persons shall be deemed to be included whether or not they are still Ministers, and persons who ceased to be members of the Cabinet on the same day shall be treated as having ceased to be members at the same time whether or not the fact that they are all deemed to be included raises the number above eight.

19. Salary and allowances of President.—(1) The President shall receive such salary and allowances, and on retirement such pension, gratuity and other allowance, as may be determined by the National Assembly.

(2) The salary and allowances of the President shall not be reduced during his period of office.

(3) Salaries and allowances payable under this Article are hereby charged on the Consolidated Fund.

PART IV

PARLIAMENT

20. The Sovereign Parliament.—(1) There shall be a Parliament consisting of the President and the National Assembly.

(2) So much of the legislative power of the State as is not reserved by the Constitution to the people is conferred on Parliament; and any portion of the remainder of the legislative power of the State may be conferred on Parliament at any future time by the decision of a majority of the electors voting in a referendum ordered by the President and conducted in accordance with the principle set out in Article One of the Constitution:
Provided that the only power to alter the Constitution (whether expressly or by implication) which is or may as aforesaid be conferred on Parliament is a power to alter it by an Act expressed to be an Act to amend the Constitution and containing only provisions effecting the alteration thereof.

(3) Subject to the provisions of Article Two of the Constitution, Parliament cannot divest itself of any of its legislative powers:
Provided that if by any amendment to the Constitution the power to repeal or alter any existing or future provision of the Constitution is reserved to the people, section (2) of this Article shall apply in relation to that provision as if the power to repeal or alter it had originally been reserved to the people.

(4) No Act passed in exercise of a legislative power expressed by the Constitution to be reserved to the people shall take effect unless the Speaker has certified that power to pass the Act has been conferred on Parliament in the manner provided by section (2) of this Article; and a certificate so given shall be conclusive.

(5) No person or body other than Parliament shall have power to make provisions having the force of law except under authority conferred by Act of Parliament.

(6) Apart from the limitations referred to in the preceding provisions of this Article, the power of Parliament to make laws shall be under no limitation whatsoever.

(7) The power to repeal or alter this Article is reserved to the people.

21. The National Assembly.—(1) The National Assembly shall consist of the Speaker and not less than one hundred and four Members, to be known as Members of Parliament.

(2) The Members shall be elected in the manner provided by a law framed in accordance with the principle set out in Article One of the Constitution, and the Speaker shall be elected by the Members.
HH

(3) There shall be freedom of speech, debate and proceedings in the National Assembly and that freedom shall not be impeached or questioned in any court or place out of the Assembly.

(4) The President may attend any sitting of the National Assembly.

(5) The power to repeal or alter this Article is reserved to the people.

22. Sessions of the Assembly.—(1) There shall be a new session of the National Assembly once at least in every year, so that a period of twelve months shall not elapse between the last sitting of the Assembly in one session and the first sitting thereof in the next session.

(2) The President may at any time by proclamation summon or prorogue the National Assembly.

(3) The power to repeal or alter this Article is reserved to the people.

23. Dissolution of the Assembly.—(1) The President may at any time by proclamation dissolve the National Assembly.

(2) The President shall in any case dissolve the National Assembly on the expiration of the period of five years from the first sitting of the Assembly after the previous General Election.

(3) If an emergency arises or exists when the National Assembly stands dissolved, the President may by proclamation summon an assembly of the persons who were Members of Parliament immediately before the dissolution and, until the majority of results have been declared in the General Election following the dissolution, the assembly shall be deemed to be the National Assembly.

(4) The power to repeal or alter this Article is reserved to the people.

24. Legislation.—(1) Every Bill passed by the National Assembly shall be presented to the President who shall—
  (*a*) signify his assent to the Bill, or
  (*b*) signify his assent to a part only of the Bill and his refusal of assent to the remainder, or
  (*c*) signify his refusal of assent to the Bill.

(2) On the signifying by the President of his assent to a Bill passed by the National Assembly or to a part thereof, the Bill or that part thereof, as the case may be, shall become an Act of Parliament.

25. Presidential Addresses and Messages.—(1) At the beginning of each session of the National Assembly the President shall deliver to the Members of Parliament an address indicating the policies proposed to be followed by the Government during that session.

(2) At least seven days before each prorogation of the National Assembly the President shall deliver to the Members of Parliament an address indicating the manner and results of the application of the policies of the Government during the preceding period and otherwise setting forth the state of the Nation.

(3) If circumstances render it impracticable for the President himself to deliver any such address, he may instead send a message to the National Assembly embodying the address.

(4) In addition to delivering any address or sending any message under the preceding provisions of this Article, the President may at any time deliver an address to the Members of Parliament or send a message to the National Assembly.

(5) Every message sent by the President to the National Assembly shall be read to the Members of Parliament by a Minister.

PART V

PUBLIC REVENUE AND EXPENDITURE

Taxation

26. Restriction on taxation.—(1) No taxation shall be imposed otherwise than under the authority of an Act of Parliament.

(2) The power to repeal or alter this Article is reserved to the people.

Custody of Public Money

27. Public funds.—There shall be a Consolidated Fund and a Contingencies Fund, together with such other public funds as may be provided for by law.

28. Public revenue.—(1) The produce of taxation, receipts of capital and interest in respect of public loans, and all other public revenue shall be paid into the Consolidated Fund unless required or permitted by law to be paid into any other fund or account.

(2) The President may, in relation to any department of State, direct that a separate public account be established for the department and that the revenue of the department be paid into that account.

29. Payments out of public funds.—(1) Expenditure shall not be met from any public fund or public account except under a warrant issued by authority of the President.

(2) Whenever a sum becomes payable which is charged by law on a public fund or on the general revenues and assets of Ghana, the President or a person authorised by him in that behalf shall cause a warrant to be issued for the purpose of enabling that sum to be paid.

(3) A warrant may be issued by authority of the President for the purpose of enabling public money to be applied—

    (*a*) as part of moneys granted for the public service by a vote of the National Assembly under this Part of the Constitution, or

    (*b*) in defraying, in the manner provided by Article Thirty-four of the Constitution, urgent expenditure authorised under that Article, or

    (*c*) in performance of an agreement to grant a loan made under Article Thirty-five of the Constitution.

30. Excess expenditure.—Where—

(a) money is drawn out of a public fund or public account for the purpose of being applied as part of moneys granted for a particular public service by a vote of the National Assembly, but

(b) the money so drawn proves to be in excess of the amount granted for that service,

particulars of the excess shall be laid before the National Assembly and, if the National Assembly so resolve, the amount originally granted for the service in question shall be treated for accounting purposes as increased to include the amount of the excess.

Moneys granted by Vote of the National Assembly

31. Moneys granted on the annual estimates.—(1) The President shall cause to be prepared annually under heads for each public service estimates of expenditure, other than expenditure charged by law on a public fund or on the general revenues and assets of Ghana, which will be required to be incurred for the public services during the following financial year; and, when approved by the Cabinet, the estimates so prepared (which shall be known as " the annual estimates ") shall be laid before the National Assembly.

(2) Each head of the annual estimates shall be submitted to the vote of the National Assembly but no amendment of the estimates shall be moved.

(3) A vote of the National Assembly approving a head of the annual estimates shall constitute a grant by the Assembly of moneys not exceeding the amount specified in that head to be applied within the financial year in question for the service to which the head relates.

32. Moneys granted on provisional and supplementary estimates.—(1) If it appears that the vote of the National Assembly on any heads of the annual estimates will not be taken before the commencement of the financial year to which they relate, the President shall cause to be prepared under those heads estimates of the expenditure which will be required for the continuance of the public services in question until the said vote is taken; and, when approved by the Cabinet, the estimates so prepared (which shall be known as " provisional estimates ") shall be laid before the National Assembly.

(2) If, after the National Assembly has voted upon the annual estimates for any financial year, it appears that the moneys granted in respect of any heads thereof are likely to be insufficient or that expenditure is likely to be incurred in that year on a public service falling under a head not included in the annual estimates, the President shall cause to be prepared under the relevant heads estimates of the additional expenditure; and, when approved by the Cabinet, the estimates so prepared (which shall be known as " supplementary estimates ") shall be laid before the National Assembly.

(3) Sections (2) and (3) of Article Thirty-one of the Constitution shall apply in relation to provisional and supplementary estimates as they apply in relation to the annual estimates:

Provided that, where an item of expenditure is included both in provisional estimates and in the annual estimates, a grant in respect of that item shall not by virtue of this section be taken to have been made more than once.

33. Extraordinary grants.—In addition to granting moneys on estimates of expenditure the National Assembly may, if satisfied that it is necessary in the public interest to do so, make any extraordinary grant of money for the public service, including a grant on a vote of credit, that is a grant of money to be used for a purpose which, for reasons of national security or by reason of the indefinite character of the service in question, cannot be described in detailed estimates.

Expenditure out of Contingencies Fund

34. Expenditure out of Contingencies Fund.—(1) Where in the opinion of the President—

(a) money is urgently required to be expended for a public service, and

(b) the payment thereof would exceed the amount granted by the National Assembly for that service or the service is one for which no amount has been so granted, and

(c) it is not practicable to summon a meeting of the National Assembly in sufficient time to obtain the necessary grant,

the President may by executive instrument authorise the money required to be drawn from the Contingencies Fund.

(2) An executive instrument made under this Article shall specify the head under which the expenditure in question would have been shown if it had been included in the annual estimates.

(3) As soon as is practicable after an executive instrument has been made under this Article—

(a) the instrument shall be laid before the National Assembly, and

(b) a resolution authorising the transfer to the Contingencies Fund from a public fund specified in the resolution of an amount equal to the amount of the expenditure to which the instrument relates shall be moved in the National Assembly by a Minister authorised in that behalf by the President.

(4) In addition to sums transferred under section (3) of this Article, the National Assembly may from time to time authorise the transfer from the Consolidated Fund to the Contingencies Fund of sums required to maintain an adequate balance therein.

Public Loans

35. Granting of loans.—(1) The President may on behalf of the Republic enter into an agreement for the granting of a loan out of any public fund or public account if he thinks it expedient in the public interest so to do.

(2) If the National Assembly so resolve, agreements entered into under this Article for amounts exceeding the amount specified in the Assembly's resolution shall not become operative unless ratified by the Assembly.

(3) As soon as is practicable after an agreement has been entered into under this Article, particulars of the agreement, and of the borrower and the purpose for which the loan is required, shall be laid before the National Assembly.

36. Raising of loans.—No loan shall be raised for the purposes of the Republic otherwise than under the authority of an Act of Parliament.

37. The public debt.—(1) The public debt, interest thereon, sinking fund payments in respect thereof, and the costs, charges and expenses incidental to the management thereof are hereby charged on the general revenues and assets of Ghana.

(2) The power to repeal or alter this Article is reserved to the people.

Audit of Public Accounts

38. The Auditor-General.—(1) There shall be an Auditor-General, who shall be appointed by the President and who shall not be removable except by the President in pursuance of a resolution of the National Assembly supported by the votes of at least two-thirds of the total number of Members of Parliament and passed on the ground of stated misbehaviour or of infirmity of body or mind.

(2) The Auditor-General shall retire from office on attaining the age of fifty-five years or such higher age as may be prescribed by law.

(3) The Auditor-General may resign his office by writing under his hand addressed to the President.

(4) The salary of the Auditor-General shall be determined by the National Assembly, is hereby charged on the Consolidated Fund and shall not be diminished during his term of office.

39. Duty to audit and report.—(1) The accounts of all departments of State shall be audited by the Auditor-General who, with his deputies, shall at all times be entitled to have access to all books, records, stores and other matters relating to such accounts.

(2) The Auditor-General shall report annually to the National Assembly on the exercise of his functions under section (1) of this Article, and shall in his report draw attention to irregularities in the accounts audited by him.

PART VI

LAW AND JUSTICE

Laws of Ghana

40. Laws of Ghana.—Except as may be otherwise provided by an enactment made after the coming into operation of the Constitution, the laws of Ghana comprise the following—
 (*a*) the Constitution,
 (*b*) enactments made by or under the authority of the Parliament established by the Constitution,

(c) enactments other than the Constitution made by or under the authority of the Constituent Assembly,

(d) enactments in force immediately before the coming into operation of the Constitution,

(e) the common law, and

(f) customary law.

Superior and Inferior Courts

41. Superior and inferior courts.—(1) There shall be a Supreme Court and a High Court, which shall be the superior courts of Ghana.

(2) Subject to the provisions of the Constitution, the judicial power of the State is conferred on the Supreme Court and the High Court, and on such inferior courts as may be provided for by law.

(3) The power to repeal or alter this Article is reserved to the people.

Provisions as to Superior Courts

42. Jurisdiction.—(1) The Supreme Court shall be the final court of appeal, with such appellate and other jurisdiction as may be provided for by law.

(2) The Supreme Court shall have original jurisdiction in all matters where a question arises whether an enactment was made in excess of the powers conferred on Parliament by or under the Constitution, and if any such question arises in the High Court or an inferior court, the hearing shall be adjourned and the question referred to the Supreme Court for decision.

(3) Subject to section (2) of this Article, the High Court shall have such original and appellate jurisdiction as may be provided for by law.

(4) The Supreme Court shall in principle be bound to follow its own previous decisions on questions of law, and the High Court shall be bound to follow previous decisions of the Supreme Court on such questions, but neither court shall be otherwise bound to follow the previous decisions of any court on questions of law.

43. Composition of courts.—Provision shall be made by law for the composition of superior courts in particular proceedings:

Provided that no appeal shall be decided by the Supreme Court unless the court hearing the appeal consists of at least three Judges, of whom at least one is a Judge of the Supreme Court; and no question whether an enactment was made in excess of the powers conferred on Parliament by or under the Constitution shall be decided by the Supreme Court unless the court considering the question comprises at least three Judges of the Supreme Court.

Judges of the Superior Courts

44. Chief Justice.—(1) The President shall by instrument under the Presidential Seal appoint one of the Judges of the Supreme Court to be Chief Justice of Ghana.

(2) The Chief Justice shall be President of the Supreme Court and Head of the Judicial Service.

(3) The appointment of a Judge as Chief Justice may at any time be revoked by the President by instrument under the Presidential Seal.

45. Judges.—(1) The Judges of the superior courts shall be appointed by the President by instrument under the Public Seal.

(2) Provision shall be made by law for the form and administration of the judicial oath, which shall be taken by every person appointed as Judge of a superior court before the exercise by him of any judicial function.

(3) Subject to the following provisions of this Article, no person shall be removed from office as a Judge of the Supreme Court or a Judge of the High Court except by the President in pursuance of a resolution of the National Assembly supported by the votes of not less than two-thirds of the Members of Parliament and passed on the grounds of stated misbehaviour or infirmity of body or mind.

(4) Unless the President by instrument under his hand extends the tenure of office of the Judge for a definite period specified in the instrument, a Judge of the Supreme Court shall retire from office on attaining the age of sixty-five years and a Judge of the High Court shall retire from office on attaining the age of sixty-two years.

(5) A Judge of a superior court may resign his office by writing under his hand addressed to the President.

(6) The power to repeal or alter this Article is reserved to the people

46. Salaries and pensions.—(1) The salary of a Judge of a superior court shall be determined by the National Assembly and shall not be diminished while he remains in office.

(2) The Chief Justice shall be entitled to such additional allowance as may be determined by the National Assembly.

(3) All salaries and allowances paid under this Article and all pensions and other retiring allowances paid in respect of service as Chief Justice or other Judge of a superior court are hereby charged on the Consolidated Fund.

Attorney-General

47. Attorney-General.—(1) There shall be an Attorney-General, who shall be a Minister of Ghana or other person appointed by the President.

(2) Subject to the directions of the President, there shall be vested in the Attorney-General responsibility for the initiation, conduct and discontinuance of civil proceedings by the Republic and prosecutions for criminal offences, and for the defence of civil proceedings brought against the Republic.

(3) The office of the Attorney-General shall become vacant—

(*a*) if his appointment is revoked by the President; or
(*b*) on the acceptance by the President of his resignation from office; or
(*c*) immediately before the assumption of office of a President.

President's powers of mercy

48. President's powers of mercy.—(1) The President shall have power, in respect of any criminal offence—

   (*a*) to grant a pardon to the offender, or

   (*b*) to order a respite of the execution of any sentence passed on the offender, or

   (*c*) to remit any sentence so passed or any penalty or forfeiture incurred by reason of the offence.

(2) Where the President remits a sentence of death he may order the offender to be imprisoned until such time as the President orders his release.

Part VII

Houses of Chiefs

49. Houses of Chiefs.—There shall be a House of Chiefs for each Region of Ghana.

50. Composition and functions.—A House of Chiefs shall consist of such Chiefs, and shall have such functions relating to customary law and other matters, as may be provided by law.

Part VIII

The Public Services

51. The Public Services.—(1) The Public Services of Ghana shall consist of the Civil Service, the Judicial Service, the Police Service, the Local Government Service, and such other Public Services as may be provided for by law.

(2) Subject to the provisions of the Constitution and save as is otherwise provided by law, the appointment, promotion, transfer, termination of appointment, dismissal and disciplinary control of members of the Public Services is vested in the President.

52. Retiring allowances.—All pensions, gratuities and other allowances payable on retirement to members of the Civil Service, the Judicial Service and the Police Service are hereby charged on the Consolidated Fund.

Part IX

The Armed Forces

53. Prohibition of irregular forces.—(1) Neither the President nor any other person shall raise any armed force except under the authority of an Act of Parliament.

(2) The power to repeal or alter this Article is reserved to the people.

54. Powers of Commander-in-Chief.—(1) Subject to the provisions of any enactment for the time being in force, the powers of the President as Commander-in-Chief of the Armed Forces shall include the power to commission persons as officers in the said Forces and to order any of the said Forces to engage in operations for the defence of Ghana, for the preservation of public order, for relief in cases of emergency or for any other purpose appearing to the Commander-in-Chief to be expedient.

(2) The Commander-in-Chief shall have power, in a case where it appears to him expedient to do so for the security of the State, to dismiss a member of the Armed Forces or to order a member of the Armed Forces not to exercise any authority vested in him as a member thereof until the Commander-in-Chief otherwise directs; and a purported exercise of authority in contravention of such an order shall be ineffective.

Part X

Special Powers for First President

55. Special powers for first President.—(1) Notwithstanding anything in Article Twenty of the Constitution, the person appointed as first President of Ghana shall have, during his initial period of office, the powers conferred on him by this Article.

(2) The first President may, whenever he considers it to be in the national interest to do so, give directions by legislative instrument.

(3) An instrument made under this Article may alter (whether expressly or by implication) any enactment other than the Constitution.

(4) Section (2) of Article Forty-two of the Constitution shall apply in relation to the powers conferred by this Article as it applies in relation to the powers conferred on Parliament.

(5) For the purposes of this Article the first President's initial period of office shall be taken to continue until some other person assumes office as President.

(6) The power to repeal or alter this Article during the first President's initial period of office is reserved to the people.

APPENDIX B

GLOSSARY OF TERMS USED IN LEGISLATION

Note. The use of italics indicates that the term italicized is itself defined in the glossary.

Act. A law made by *Parliament* which comes into being on the signifying of *assent* to a *Bill passed* by the National Assembly.

Amendment. (1) A *motion* to alter the wording of a *Bill*, or insert a new provision, made on the *Consideration Stage* or *third reading* of the Bill. (2) An alteration or addition made to an *enactment* after it has become law. (3) A motion to alter the wording of another motion. Cf. *reasoned amendment; verbal amendment*.

Article. A subdivision equivalent to a *section* or *paragraph* but slightly more dignified. The subdivisions of the Constitution and of instruments of incorporation, for example, are described as Articles.

Assent. The agreement of the President to a *Bill* or part of a Bill *passed* by the National Assembly. It is signified by the affixing of the President's signature and seal to the *original copies* of the Bill.

Bill. A provision or set of provisions *introduced* into the National Assembly by a Member of Parliament with a view to its becoming an *Act*.

Business Committee. A *Sessional select committee* charged with the function of determining the business of each sitting day and the order in which, subject to S.O. 22, it is to be taken.

Byelaws. Provisions having a local or otherwise limited application made by a local authority, statutory corporation or similar body.

Certificate of Urgency. A certificate signed by the President which enables a *Bill* to be *introduced* without prior publication in the Gazette or distribution to Members and permits the *Second Reading, Consideration Stage* and *Third Reading* of the Bill all to be taken on the same day.

Chapter. Each *Ordinance* was treated as a separate chapter (frequently shortened to " Cap.") of what was officially described as " the Statute Book of the Gold Coast ", which was last published collectively as the Laws of the Gold Coast (1951).

Clause. One of the numbered subdivisions of a *Bill*. When the Bill becomes an *Act* each clause becomes a *section*.

Codify. To codify is to embody the unwritten law on a particular subject, together with any relevant statutory provisions, in one *Act* known as a Code.

Examples: the Criminal Code, 1960 (Act 29) and the Criminal Procedure Code, 1960 (Act 30).

Collective Title. When an *Act* is passed supplementing a previous Act or Acts on the same subject but not consisting merely of *verbal amendments*, it may be convenient to provide for a collective title to enable both or all the Acts to be cited together.

Examples: " The XYZ Acts, 1960 and 1962 (where there are two); " The XYZ Acts, 1960 to 1965 " (where there are three or more).

Commencement. The time at which an *Act* comes into operation. Unless the Act otherwise provides, this is the expiration of the day on which the President's *assent* is signified.

Consideration Stage. The stage following the *second reading* of a Bill, at which the Bill is examined *clause* by clause. Until 1960 it was known as the Committee Stage.

Consolidate. To consolidate is to collect together in one Act a number of different *enactments* on the same subject, the enactments consolidated being thereupon repealed.

Construction. The process of ascertaining the meaning of an *enactment*.

Cross-Heading. A title in italics indicating the subject-matter of a *fasciculus* within a *Bill, Act* or *statutory instrument* or within a *Part* of a Bill, Act or statutory instrument.

Enacting Formula. The words placed at the beginning of an *Act* which operate to enact it. The formula runs: Be it enacted by the President and the National Assembly in this present Parliament assembled as follows:—

Enactment. (1) An *Act* or *statutory instrument* taken as a whole. (2) Any separate provision of an Act or statutory instrument.

Executive Instrument. A *statutory instrument* which is neither a *legislative instrument* nor an instrument of a judicial character.

Extent. The areas within which an *enactment* has the force of law. If nothing to the contrary is said in the enactment its extent will be taken to be the whole of Ghana.

Example: " This Act extends to the Accra District only."

Fasciculus. A group of *clauses, sections,* etc. which deal with a particular subject-matter and, while not sufficiently distinct to constitute a separate *Part*, fall naturally under one *cross-heading*.

First Reading. A purely formal stage immediately following the *introduction* of a *Bill*. No debate is permitted or motion put.

Gloss. An *amendment* which refers to another provision but, while altering its effect, does not alter its actual wording.
> Example: " The ABC Act, 1961 shall apply to spirits manufactured in Ghana as it applies to imported spirits."

Government Bill. A *Bill introduced* by a Minister.

Head. A sub-division of a sub-paragraph and the smallest unit into which an enactment can be divided.
> Example: " Head (A) of sub-paragraph (i) of paragraph (*a*) of subsection (1) of section one of the principal Act is hereby repealed." (Note: this is the art of drafting *in extremis*; heads in a Bill or Act can hardly ever be necessary—it is different with a statutory instrument, where the largest unit is usually a paragraph).

Heads of a Bill. A document reducing a legislative proposal into numbered paragraphs roughly arranged in the way a Bill to give effect to that proposal might be arranged, but with no attempt to draft them as clauses of a Bill.

Introduction. The process by which a *Bill* begins its progress through the National Assembly. Leave of the Assembly is required except in the case of Government Bills. (Cf. *Presentation*).

Legislative Instrument. A *statutory instrument* which is made under an *enactment* specified in the Schedule to the Statutory Instruments Order, 1960 (L.I. 9) or under a power expressed to be exercisable by legislative instrument.

Long Title. The words following the *short title* of an *Act* which concisely describe the provisions of the Act.

Marginal Note. See *Sidenote*.

Meeting. A period of more or less continuous *Sittings* of the Assembly. It comes to an end if the Assembly is adjourned *sine die* or at the conclusion of a *Session*.

Memorandum. A statement signed by the Minister or other Member introducing a *Bill* which explains its main features. It is required by Standing Orders to appear on the front of every Bill when introduced.

Motion. A proposition submitted by a Member for the decision of the National Assembly. In relation to *Bills* it may be for leave to *introduce* or *withdraw* a Bill, for the *Second* or *Third Reading* of the Bill, for reference of the Bill to a *Select Committee* and so on.

Order. A *statutory instrument*, usually requiring some particular act to be done, after which the effect of the order will be spent. It may however have a continuing effect. (Cf. *rules* and *regulations*.)

Order-Paper. A paper circulated to Members before each *Sitting* setting out the business to be taken at that Sitting.

Ordinance. A law made before Independence by the Legislative Assembly, the Legislative Council or the Governor.

Original Copies. The copies of an *Act* which are signed and sealed by the President to signify his *assent* to the Act.

Paragraph. (1) A sub-division of a *section, clause* or *article*.
(2) A division of a *statutory instrument* corresponding to a section in an *Act*.

Parliament. The supreme legislative body, consisting of the President and the National Assembly.

Part. A group of *clauses, sections*, etc., dealing with a distinct and severable division of the subject-matter of a *Bill, Act*, etc. Usually only employed where the Bill, Act, etc. is lengthy.

Passing. A *Bill* is deemed to be passed when a *third reading* is given. It is then submitted to the President, but remains a Bill until *assent* is signified. Occasionally an *Act* is said to have been passed, although the only correct verb to use in relation to the creation of an Act is the somewhat obvious one " enacted ".

Petition. An application to the National Assembly presented through a Member, who may describe its contents, etc., and (if he thinks fit) move that it be read, printed or referred to a *Select Committee*. No debate is permitted.

Preamble. Introductory words to an *Act* or *statutory instrument* which begin "Whereas . . ." and go on to state the circumstances which made the enactment necessary or the powers under which it was made or otherwise give relevant information (Cf. recital).
Example: The Acts of the Constituent Assembly.

Presentation. Virtually the same as *Introduction*. A *Bill* is presented by the Member who is introducing it rising in his place when called by the Speaker and bowing to the Chair, whereupon the Clerk reads aloud the *Long Title*.

Private Bill. A *Bill* intended to affect or benefit some particular person, associate or corporate body. A special procedure applies unless it is a *Government Bill*.

Private Member's Bill. A *Bill introduced* by a Member who is not a Minister or other member of the Government.

Proclamation. A formal announcement, usually by or on behalf of the Head of State. In former times made by the Governor or Governor-General; now by the President. When made under statutory powers, which it now invariably is, it is classed as a *statutory instrument*.

Provisional Order-Paper. A paper circulated to Members setting out the business provisionally fixed for a Sitting after the next Sitting.

Proviso. A provision starting " Provided that . . ." which is placed at the end of a *section, clause*, etc., and cuts down the width of the preceding words.

> Example: " No person shall give medical attention unless he is a registered medical practioner:
>
> Provided that this section shall not prevent any person from administering first aid in case of accident."

Reasoned Amendment. An *amendment* to a *motion* which includes words explaining why the amendment is proposed.

> Example: Original motion—" That the ABC Bill be now read a second time."
>
> Reasoned amendment—" Leave out from ' That ' to the end and insert ' this House declines to give a second reading to a Bill which fails to provide a remedy for RST or UVW and is otherwise inadequate to deal with the problems of ABC.' "

Recital. Equivalent to a *preamble* but placed at the beginning of an individual *clause, section*, etc., or at the beginning of a *statutory instrument*.

Regulations. Provisions contained in a *statutory instrument* which regulate in detail some administrative procedure or other activity governed by *statute*.

Repeal. The process by which an *Act* or *Ordinance* ceases to exist, (Cf. *revocation*).

Repugnancy. An enactment is said to be repugnant to another enactment if its provisions are inconsistent with those of the other. Subject to the rule *generalia specialibus non derogant*, a later enactment which is repugnant to an earlier impliedly amends the earlier to the extent of the repugnancy.

Revocation. The process by which a *statutory instrument* ceases to exist. (Cf. *repeal*.)

Rules. Provisions similar to *regulations* but usually relating to a court or other tribunal.

Schedule. Provisions contained at the end of an *Act* or *statutory instrument* which deal with matters which are not of first importance and are too detailed to be set out in the body of the Act or instrument or, as with treaties, agreements, letters, etc., are required to be reproduced verbatim. (Cf. *table*.)

Second Reading. The stage following the *first reading* of a *Bill* at which the principles of the Bill rather than the details of its wording are debated. No *amendments* to the Bill can be moved.

Section. See *clause*. In the Constitution subdivision of Articles are described as sections.

Select Committee. A Committee of Members of Parliament appointed by the Assembly and so constituted as to ensure, so far as possible, that the balance of parties in the Assembly is reflected in the Committee. (Cf. sessional select committee.)

Session. The period between the first sitting of the National Assembly after Prorogation or Dissolution and its last sitting before the next Prorogation or before Dissolution if it occurs earlier.

Sessional Select Committee. A *select committee* set up at the beginning of each *Session* and remaining in being throughout the Session—e.g. the *Business Committee*.

Short Title. The description, ending with the word " Act " and the calendar year in which the President's assent is given, by which an *Act* may be cited and which appears at the head of the Act.

Sidenote. A brief description of the contents of a *section, paragraph*, etc., which is printed in the margin.

Sitting. A period during which the National Assembly is sitting continuously without adjournment.

Spent. An *enactment* is spent when, through lapse of time or alteration of circumstances, it has ceased to be capable of having any operation.

Standing Orders. Provisions of a semi-permanent character made by the National Assembly for regulating the conduct of their proceedings.

Statute. Another term for an *Act* or *Ordinance*.

Statutes. Provisions such as those regulating the award, investiture, wearing, etc., of Orders of the Republic of Ghana, or regulating the internal government of a university.

Statutory Instrument. An instrument made (whether directly or indirectly) under a power conferred by an *Act* or *Ordinance*.

Sub-Clause. A subdivision of a *clause*. (Cf. *subsection*).

Subsection. When a *Bill* becomes an *Act* each *sub-clause* becomes a subsection. The term is frequently applied to clauses as well as sections.

Table. Where it is convenient to set out a number of provisions in tabular form but they are too important to be relegated to a *Schedule* they may be inserted in the form of table at the end of a *section* or *subsection*.
　　Examples: National Assembly Act, 1961 (Act 86), s. 1; Civil Service Act, 1960 (C.A. 5,) s. 28.

Table of Comparison. A table provided at the beginning of a *Consolidation Bill* showing the enactments consolidated and their place in the Bill.

Third Reading. The final stage of the passage of a *Bill*.

Verbal Amendment. An *amendment* which makes a direct change, by substitution or omission, in the wording of a *Bill, enactment,* etc., as opposed to a change by way of *gloss* or *repugnancy.*

Warrant. A document by which the President's pleasure is made known.
Example: the Honours Warrant, 1960.

APPENDIX C

ENACTMENTS RELATING TO THE APPLICATION OF COMMON LAW AND CUSTOMARY LAW

THE COURTS ORDINANCE
(Cap. 4)[1]

*   *   *   *

PART F.—LAW IN FORCE IN COURTS

83. How far the law of England in force.—Subject to the terms of this or any other Ordinance, the common law, the doctrines of equity, and the statutes of general application which were in force in England on the 24th day of July, 1874, shall be in force within the jurisdiction of the Courts.

84. Practice and procedure.—The jurisdiction by this Ordinance vested in the Courts shall be exercised (so far as regards procedure and practice) in the manner provided by this Ordinance and the Criminal Procedure Code, or by such Rules and Orders of Court as may be made pursuant to this Ordinance.

85. Rules as to the application of Imperial laws.—All Imperial laws declared to extend or apply to the jurisiction of the Courts shall be in force so far only as the limits of the local jurisdiction and local circumstances permit, and subject to any existing or future ordinances of the Colonial Legislature; and for the purpose of facilitating the application of the said Imperial laws, it shall be lawful for the said Courts to construe the same with such verbal alterations, not affecting the substance, as may be necessary to render the same applicable to the matter before the Court; and every Judge, or person exercising judicial powers, Magistrate or officer of the Supreme Court having or exercising functions of the like kind, or analogous to the functions of any Judge or officer referred to in any such law, shall be deemed to be within the meaning of the enactments thereof relating to such last-mentioned Judge or officer; and whenever the Great Seal or any other seal is mentioned in any such statute it shall be read as if the seal of the Supreme Court or the seal of a Magistrate's Court were substituted therefor: and in matters of practice all documents may be written on ordinary paper, notwithstanding any practice or directions as to printing or engrossing on vellum, parchment, or otherwise.

---

[1] Repealed by the Courts Act, 1960 (C.A. 9).

86. Law and equity to be concurrently administered.—In every civil cause or matter which shall come in dependence in any of the Courts, law and equity shall be administered concurrently; and such Courts in the exercise of the jurisdiction vested in them by this Ordinance shall have power to grant, and shall grant, either absolutely or on such reasonable terms and conditions as shall seem just, all such remedies or relief whatsoever, interlocutory, or final, as any of the parties thereto may appear to be entitled to in respect of any and every legal or equitable claim or defence properly brought forward by them respectively, or which shall appear in such cause or matter; so that as far as possible all matters in controversy between the said parties respectively may be completely and finally determined, and all multiplicity of legal proceedings concerning any of such matters avoided; and in all matters in which there is any conflict or variance between the rules of equity and the rules of the common law with reference to the same matter, the rules of equity shall prevail.

87. Application of native laws.—(1) Nothing in this Ordinance shall deprive the Courts of the right to observe and enforce the observance, or shall deprive any person of the benefit, of any native law or custom existing in the Gold Coast, such law or custom not being repugnant to natural justice, equity, and good conscience, nor incompatible either directly or by necessary implication with any ordinance for the time being in force.

Such laws and customs shall be deemed applicable in causes and matters where the parties thereto are natives, and particularly, but without derogating from their application in other cases, in causes and matters relating to the tenure and transfer of real and personal property, and to inheritance and testamentary dispositions, and also in causes and matters between natives and non-natives where it may appear to the Court that substantial injustice would be done to either party by a strict adherence to the rules of English law.

No party shall be entitled to claim the benefit of any local law or custom, if it shall appear either from express contract or from the nature of the transactions out of which any suit or question may have arisen, that such party agreed that his obligations in connection with such transactions should be regulated exclusively by English law; and in cases where no express rule is applicable to any matter in controversy, the Court shall be governed by the principles of justice, equity, and good conscience.

(2) In deciding questions of native law and custom the Court may give effect to any book or manuscript recognized in the Gold Coast as a legal authority and may call to its assistance Chiefs or other persons whom the Court considers to have special knowledge of native law and custom.

(*Subsection substituted by* 39 *of* 1951, *s.* 29).

88. The Supreme Court and Magistrates' Courts not to entertain causes and matters relating to elections and constitutional relations of Chiefs.—The Supreme Court and Magistrates'

Courts shall not have jurisdiction to entertain either as of first instance or on appeal any civil cause or civil matter instituted for—

(1) the trial of any question relating to the election, installation, deposition, or abdication of any Paramount Chief, Head Chief, or Chief;

(2) the recovery or delivery up of Stool property in connection with any such election, installation, deposition, or abdication;

(3) the trial of any question touching the political or constitutional relations subsisting according to native law and custom between two or more Chiefs, or between a Paramount Chief and a Chief, or between a Head Chief and a Chief.

89. Reference to Native Court of questions involving native and custom.—If and whenever in any civil cause or matter before the Supreme Court or a Magistrate's Court a question arises as to the rights of any native under native law and custom, such Court may, if it shall deem it expedient or convenient so to do and notwithstanding that any party to such civil cause or matter may be a non-native, refer such question to a competent Native Court for determination. Upon such reference being made, the question shall as soon as possible be enquired of, tried, and determined accordingly by such Native Court; and the Native Court shall thereupon report its decision on such question to the Court which referred the same. No appeal shall lie from such decision; but it shall be competent to such Court in whole or in part to adopt or reject such decision, or to deal therewith in such manner as justice and the circumstances of the case shall appear to it to require, and to give such judgment and make such orders as to it shall seem lawful and just; and the Court shall also have the same powers with respect to such reports and decisions of the Native Court as it has with respect to the proceedings and report in writing of a referee under Order 38 of the Second Schedule to this Ordinance.

THE COURTS ACT, 1960

(C.A. 9)

* * * *

PART III—COMMON LAW AND CUSTOMARY LAW

66. Application of common law and customary law.—(1) Subject to the provisions of any enactment other than this subsection, in deciding whether an issue arising in civil proceedings is to be determined according to the common law or customary law and, if the issue is to be determined according to customary law, in deciding which system of customary law is applicable, the court shall be guided by the following rules, in which references to the personal law of a person are references to the system of customary law to which he is subject or, if he is not shown to be subject to customary law, are references to the common law:—

Rule 1. Where two persons have the same personal law one of them cannot, by dealing in a manner regulated by some other law with property in which the other has a present or expectant interest, alter or affect that interest to an extent which would not in the circumstances be open to him under his personal law.

Rule 2. Subject to Rule 1, where an issue arises out of a transaction the parties to which have agreed, or may from the form or nature of the transaction be taken to have agreed, that such an issue should be determined according to the common law or any system of customary law effect should be given to the agreement.

In this rule " transaction " includes a marriage and an agreement or arrangement to marry.

Rule 3. Subject to Rule 1, where an issue arises out of any unilateral disposition and it appears from the form or nature of the disposition or otherwise that the person effecting the disposition intended that such an issue should be determined according to the common law or any system of customary law effect should be given to the intention.

Rule 4. Subject to the foregoing rules, where an issue relates to entitlement to land on the death of the owner or otherwise relates to title to land—

(a) if all the parties to the proceedings who claim to be entitled to the land or a right relating thereto trace their claims from one person who is subject to customary law, or from one family or other group of persons all subject to the same customary law, the issue should be determined according to that law;

(b) if the said parties trace their claims from different persons, or families or other groups of persons, who are all subject to the same customary law, the issue should be determined according to that law;

(c) in any other case, the issue should be determined according to the law of the place in which the land is situated.

Rule 5. Subject to Rules 1 to 3, where an issue relates to the devolution of the property (other than land) of a person on his death it should be determined according to his personal law.

Rule 6. Subject to the foregoing rules, an issue should be determined according to the common law unless the plaintiff is subject to any system of customary law and claims to have the issue determined according to that system, when it should be so determined.

(2) Where under this section customary law is applicable in any proceedings but a relevant rule of customary law has been assimilated by the common law under any enactment such as is mentioned in section 18 (1) of the Interpretation Act, 1960, that rule shall nevertheless apply in those proceedings, but in the form in which it has been so assimilated.

(3) Notwithstanding anything contained in the foregoing provisions of this section, but subject to the provisions of any other enactment—

(a) the rules of the common law relating to private international law shall apply in any proceedings in which an issue concerning the application of law prevailing in any country outside Ghana is raised;

(b) the rules of estoppel and such other of the rules generally known as the common law and the rules generally known as the doctrines of equity as have heretofore been treated as applicable in all proceedings in Ghana shall continue to be so treated.

67. Ascertainment of customary law.—(1) Any question as to the existence or content of a rule of customary law is a question of law for the Court and not a question of fact.

(2) If the Court entertains any doubt as to the existence or content of a rule of customary law relevant in any proceedings after considering such submissions thereon as may be made by or on behalf of the parties and consulting such reported cases, textbooks and other sources as may be appropriate, the court shall adjourn the proceedings to enable an inquiry to take place under the next subsection.

(3) The inquiry shall be held as part of the proceedings in such manner as the Court considers expedient, and the provisions of this Act relating to the attendance and testimony of witnesses shall apply for the purpose of the tendering of opinions to the Court at the inquiry, but shall apply subject to such modifications as may appear to the Court to be necessary:

Provided that—

(a) the decision as to the persons who are to be heard at the inquiry shall be one for the Court, after hearing such submissions thereon as may be made by or on behalf of the parties;

(b) the Court may request a House of Chiefs, State Council or other body possessing knowledge of the customary law in question to state its opinion, which may be laid before the inquiry in written form.

THE CHIEFTAINCY ACT, 1961
(Act 81)

*　　　*　　　*　　　*

PART VIII—CUSTOMARY LAW

58. Function of Traditional Councils.—A Traditional Council may consider the customary law in force within its area; and if the law is uncertain or it is considered desirable that it should be modified, or assimilated by the common law, the Council shall make representations to the House of Chiefs having jurisdiction over the area.

59. Declarations of customary law.—(1) A House of Chiefs may, either after receiving representations from a Traditional Council or on its own initiative, and shall if so required by the Minister[1], draft a declaration of what in its opinion is the customary law relating to any subject in force in its area or any part thereof.

(2) A draft prepared under the preceding subsection shall be submittedt o the Minister, and if the Minister is satisfied that the draft, either as submitted or with such modifications as he considers necessary, is a correct statement of the customary law rule in question, he shall make a legislative instrument embodying the draft, or the draft as so modified, as the case may be, and providing that the rule shall have effect within the area in question in the form set out therein.

60. Alterations of customary law.—(1) A House of Chiefs may, either after receiving representations from a Traditional Council or on its own initiative, and shall if so required by the Minister, draft a statement of the alterations it thinks desirable in any rule of customary law in force in its area or any part thereof.

(2) A draft prepared under the preceding subsection shall be submitted to the Minister and if the Minister is satisfied that effect should be given to the draft, either as submitted or with such modifications as he considers necessary, he shall make a legislative instrument embodying the draft, or the draft as so modified, as the case may be, and a statement of the rule as so modified, and providing that the rule shall have effect within the area in question in the form set out therein.

61. Houses of Chiefs affected by same rule of customary law.—(1) Where a question affecting the customary law is common to more than one House of Chiefs there shall be a joint committee of the Houses affected.

(2) The joint committee mentioned in the preceding subsection shall be made up of a committee of each House set up for the purpose.

(3) The joint committee under this section shall have the same authority as if the question before it were before a House of Chiefs, and this Part of this Act shall apply accordingly.

62. Assimilation of customary law.—(1) The Minister may, either after receiving representations from a House of Chiefs or on his own initiative, convene a joint committee of all Houses of Chiefs to consider whether a rule of customary law should be assimilated by the common law.

(2) If, after considering such evidence and representations as may be submitted to them and carrying out such investigations as they think fit, the joint committee are of opinion that the rule should be assimilated by the common law, they shall draft a declaration describing the rule, with such modifications as they may consider desirable.

(3) A draft prepared under the preceding subsection shall be submitted to the Minister and if, after consulting the Chief Justice, the Minister is satisfied that effect should be given to the draft, either

[1] I.e. the Minister of Justice: L.I. 177.

as submitted or with such modifications as he considers necessary, he shall make a legislative instrument embodying the draft, or the draft as so modified, as the case may be, and declaring the rule to be assimilated in that form.

63. Effect of assimilation.—(1) Where a rule is declared to be assimilated under subsection (3) of the preceding section it shall become part of the common law and may be referred to as a common law rule of customary origin.

(2) A common law rule of customary origin shall apply to every issue within its scope whether that issue would, if assimilation had not taken place, have been determined according to the common law or any system of customary law.

(3) Where an issue falls to be determined by a combination of two or more rules, nothing in this Part shall prevent any rule of common law or customary law which is not within the scope of a relevant common law rule of customary origin from being applied, in accordance with section 66 of the Courts Act, 1960 (C.A. 9) in combination with the said rule of customary origin.

(4) Subject to the provisions of this Part, in applying a common law rule of customary origin the court may have regard to such textbooks and other sources indicating the content of the rule as would be available if it had not been assimilated, and shall treat the rule in the same way as any other common law rule.

(5) Nothing in this section shall be taken to modify the provisions of sections 17 and 18 of the Interpretation Act, 1960 (C.A. 4) (which explain the meaning of the expressions the common law and customary law).

64. Power to include transitional provisions.—A legislative instrument made under this Part of this Act may contain such transitional provisions as the Minister may consider necessary in relation to cases pending at the date when the instrument is made or otherwise.

INDEX

A

ABDUCTION
female, of, 219

ACCOUNT
public—
auditing—
of, 167, 486
meaning, 158–9
withdrawal from, 159

ACCRA
establishment of seat of government at, 18

ACHIMOTA CONFERENCE, 55

ACT OF PARLIAMENT. *See also*
LEGISLATION
amendment of, 276–8, 341–2, 343
British—
application of, 391 *et seq.*
in force in colony of Ghana, 291
commencement, 379
content of, 260
courts bound by words of, 280
definition, 274, 491
terms, of, 356–7
drafting of, 340–5, 356–63, 365–
70
enacting formula, 355
first use of term in Ghana, 261
form, 261
indexing, 296
interpretation, 356–7
courts, by. *See* INTERPRETA-
TION OF ENACTMENTS
long title, 352–4, 493
numbering of, 262, 294, 378
original copies, 378
Parts, division into, 359–61
preamble, 354–5, 494
presentation copies, 376
procedure for enactment, 151,
261, 482
publication of, 291–5, 346, 378
punctuation, 363
purpose of, 259–61
repeal of, 275

ACT OF PARLAMENT—*contd.*
replacing English statutes, 407
retrospective, 379
saving of, 276
Schedules, 362
sections—
arrangement and grouping,
359–61
division into, 355–9
paragraphs, division into, 357
provisos, 357
sidenotes, 361–2
subsections, division into, 356
short title—
consistency, 351
Consolidation Acts, of, 351
purpose of, 350–1
statute law revision, 293
structure of, 350 *et seq.*

ACTS
Constituent Assembly, of, status
of, 102–3

ADVERTISEMENTS
obscene, 234

AFFIRMATION
judge, by, 175
President, by, 140, 478
right of, 175, 234, 478

AFRICA
Balkanization of, 120
unification of, 120 *et seq.*, 476

ALIENS
categories of, 187
Commonwealth citizens, 187
deportation of, 202–4
employment of, 202
entry into Ghana by, 202
extradition of, 204–8
passport, necessity for, 202
prohibited immigrants, 202
repatriation of, 204
supervision orders, 204
treason by, 201

ALLEGIANCE
concept of, 200–1

AMBASSADORS
diplomatic immunity, 211

AMMUNITION
control of, 256
emergency, in, 255

AMNESTY
Republic Day, 177

ANNUAL ESTIMATES, 161 *et seq.*,
484

APPEAL
Court of, provisions under 1957
Constitution, 66
Privy Council, to, 33
repeal of provisions as to, 99,
105
West African Court of—
abolition of right of recourse to,
67
composition, 33
establishment, 33

ARMED FORCES
Commander-in-Chief of, 184, 489
provisions relating to, 184, 489

ARMS
control of, 256
emergency, in, 255

ARREST
mode of, 216
rules governing, 214
warrant for, 215
warrant, without—
district magistrate, by, 215
emergency, in, 255
police officer, by, 215
private person, by, 215, 216
search warrant in case of, 248

ASSAULT
definition, 220

ASHANTI
achievement of representative
government, 1946, 37
annexation, 22–3, 24
boundaries of, 24
chiefs, curtailing of power, 53–4
defeat of, 1874, 17
Executive Council, 34
Legislative Assembly, membership, 43
National Liberation Movement,
51
restoration of Confederacy, 34–5
status of, 24
treaties with, 5, 6

ASSEMBLY
Constituent. *See* CONSTITUENT
ASSEMBLY
freedom of, 236–40
lawful, disturbance of, 239
National. *See* NATIONAL
ASSEMBLY
unlawful—
damage by, compensation, 249
definition, 238
obstruction by, 239
riot, 238

ASSENT
definition, 491
Presidential, 152, 375–8, 482

ASSOCIATION
freedom of, 240

ATTORNEY-GENERAL
appointment, 176, 488
functions, 176, 488

AUDIT
public accounts, of, 167, 486

AUDITOR-GENERAL
powers and duties of, 167, 183,
486

B

BAIL
release on, 216–7

BATTERY, 220

BILL
amendment of, 353, 374–5
assent of President, 152, 262,
375–8, 482, 491

BILL—*contd.*
Cabinet—
  approval by, 146
  ordered by, procedure, 369
certificate of urgency, 371
clauses—
  arrangement and grouping,
    359–61
  definition, 492
  division into, 355–9
  paragraphs, division into, 357
  provisos, 357
  sidenotes, 361–2
  subsections, division into, 356
Commission of Enquiry, drafted
    by, 348
Committee to advise on, 369
consideration of, 373
consolidation, drafting of, 369
definition, 491
  terms, of, 356–7
draft—
  Cabinet approval of, 368
  first draft, 366–8
  publication of, 368
  settlement of, 366
drafting of, 339 *et seq.*, 340–5,
    356–63
  instructions as to, 365
enacting formula, 355
explanatory memorandum, 368,
    372, 493
first reading, definition, 493
form, 261, 350 *et seq.*
Government, 261, 370
hybrid, 371
interpretation, 356–7
introduction of, 261, 371, 372
  Cabinet, by, 333
law reform, drafting of, 369
legislative proposal, initiation of,
    364
long title, 493, 352–4
motion, definition, 493
partial assent of President, 377
Parts, division into, 359–61
passage of, 370–8
passing of, 262, 482, 494
preamble, 354–5
preparation of, 363–70
presentation copies, 376
private, 370
Private Members', 371
procedure, 151, 261–2, 363 *et seq.*,
    370 *et seq.*
proposed, Cabinet approval, 364
public, 370
publication, 371

BILL—*contd.*
punctuation, 363
rejection of, 373
Schedules, 362
scope of, 352–4
second reading, 372
short title, 350–1
structure of, 261, 350 *et seq.*
third reading, 375
urgent, passage of, 371
withdrawal of, 375

BLASPHEMY
not an offence, 234

BOOK
censorship, 230
importation of, prohibition, 230
obscene, publication or sale of,
    233

BOURNE REPORT, 54–6

BROADCASTING
control of, 231

BUILDINGS
control of use of, 244, 246

BUSINESS COMMITTEE
definition, 491

C

CABINET
Constitution of 1954, under, 48
    1957, under, 62
Republic of Ghana, of—
  appointment of Presidential
    Commission by, 479–80
  approval of proposed legisla-
    tion, 364
  Bills, approval by, 146
    introduction of, 333
  Clerk to, 335
  collective responsibility of, 133
  committees, 335
  composition, 145, 333, 479
  draft Bill, approval of, 368

CABINET—*contd.*
  Republic of Ghana, of
  functions, 146, 332–4, 479
  implementation of decisions,
    337
  Legislation Committee, 335
  legislative role, 334
  meetings, 333–4
  power of, 333
  Presidential Commissioner
    appointed by, 143
  procedure as to legislation, 369
  proposals by departmental
    Ministers to, 336
  quorum, 334
  Secretariat, 334

CENSORSHIP
  films, of, 230
  newspapers, of, 230, 255
  publications, of, 230

CENTRAL REGION
  creation of, 96

CERTIORARI
  order of, 249, 252

CHIEF JUSTICE
  Gold Coast, of, 12
  Republic of Ghana, of—
    appointment of, 175, 487
    duties and functions, 175, 487
    salary and allowances, 176,
      183 488
    status of, 92

CHIEFTAINCY
  divisions, 178
  Houses of Chiefs. *See under*
    CHIEFS
  jurisdiction over matters affect-
    ing, 178
  law relating to, 178–9, 489,
    502–4
  Ordinances affecting, consolida-
    tion, 1927...32
  preservation of, 177, 489
  protection of stool property, 249
  provisions under 1957 Constitu-
    tion, 66

CHIEFS
  Asantahene, 178, 179
  categories, 178
  control of, 20
  definition, 178
  destooled, 178
  divisional, 178
  Government recognition of, 20,
    72
  Houses of, 177–8, 489
    declaration, alteration and
      assimilation of customary
      law by, 429, 502–4
    Joint Committee of, 503
    provisions under 1957 Con-
      stitution, 66
    recommendations of Achimota
      Conference, 56
    statutory provisions, 179, 489
  Legislative Assembly of, 12
  paramount, 178
  powers of, 178, 489
  provisions of Native Administra-
    tion Ordinance, 1927, as to,
    32

CHILD-STEALING, 220

CHURCH
  irreverent behaviour in, 236

CITIZEN. *See also* CITIZENSHIP
  Commonwealth, status of, 187
  entry into Ghana by, 202

CITIZENSHIP
  birth, by, 189–92
  descent, by, 192–5
  loss of—
    deprivation, by, 199–200
    renunciation, by, 199
  marriage, by, 195–6
  naturalisation, by, 198–9
  provisions of 1957 Constitution as
    to, 67
  registration, by, 196–8
  rules for ascertaining, 188
  types of, 187

CIVIL PROCEEDINGS
  public authorities, against, 249
  state, against, 250

CIVIL SERVICE
administrative class—
legislative functions, 337
information gathering, 337–9
policy shaping, 338
Constitution of 1951, under, 44
Departments—
grouping into, 145, 182
special, 145
legislation as to, 98
Ministries, 182, 183
organisation of, 180 *et seq.*, 489
pensions, safeguarding of, 184,
489
posts—
categories, 183
Departmental, 182
established, 181
general, classes of, 181
unestablished, 181
structure, 180 *et seq.*

CLOSED SHOP
principle of, 242

COMMANDER-IN-CHIEF
Armed Forces, of, 184, 489

COMMISSION OF ENQUIRY
composition of, 346–7
drafting of Bill by, 348
legislative functions of, 348–9
operation of, 347–9

COMMON LAW
application under Courts Act,
1960—
agreement, by, 450, 453, 501
cases in which customary law
also applies, 451, 500–2
estoppel, rules of, 458, 502
intention, importance of, 450,
454, 455, 501
land, title to, cases of, 455,
458 *et seq.*, 501
private international law, to,
458, 463, 502
rules, 449–64, 501
examples of operation of,
458–64
tort and contract, cases of, 456
unilateral disposition, issue
arising from, 450, 454, 501
assimilation of customary law by,
403, 404, 406, 428–9, 457,
501, 502, 503–4

COMMON LAW—*contd.*
assimilation of rules by, 406, 407,
457, 501
conflict with customary law,
Courts Act, 1960, under, 449
et seq., 459, 460, 462, 463,
500–2
custom receiving judicial notice
as part of, 424
elements of, 407
English—
application of, 391 *et seq.*, 401
" background law," as, 409
retention of principles, 404–6
See also ENGLISH LAW
exclusion of rules as to criminal
liability, 393
extended meaning of, 407
inclusion in laws of Ghana, 132
meaning, 170, 404
rules as to application of, 449–64,
501

COMMONWEALTH
citizens, status in Ghana, 187
definition, 103
membership of, 68
representatives, diplomatic immunity of, 211

COMPANY OF MERCHANTS, 4

COMPENSATION
compulsorily acquired land, for
245
damage to property, for, 249

COMPULSORY ACQUISITION
property, of, 244, 245

CONCESSIONS
restrictions on grant of, 247

CONFLICT OF LAWS
customary and common law,
between, rules as to, 449 *et
seq.*, 459, 460, 462, 463
customary and English law,
between, 436–46
customary laws, between—
before Republic Day, 446–8
Courts Act, 1960, under, 449
et seq., 458, 459, 461, 462, 463
external, application of common
law, 458

CONSOLIDATED FUND
  definition, 157
  expenditure charged from, 158–9
  notional nature of, 157
  payments into, 156, 483
  setting up of, 156, 483
  withdrawal from, 159, 165, 483

CONSPIRACY
  criminal—
    definition, 240
    punishment, 241
  tortious, 241
    unlawful oaths, 241
      training, 241

CONSTITUENT ASSEMBLY
  Acts of, procedure, 93
  application of Standing Orders of
    National Assembly to, 84
  consolidation of enactments by,
    98
  creation of, 81, 472
  first sitting of, 87
  legislation of, 91 *et seq.*, 97 *et seq.*,
    472
  powers of, 83, 472

CONSTITUTION
  1850, of, 8
  1866, of, 14
  1874, of, 17
  1901, of, 23
  1916, of, 26
  1925, of, 29
  1946, of, 37
  1951, of, 41
  1954, of, 48
  1957, of, 62
    amendment of, 68–72
  financial provisions, continua-
    tion of, 155 *et seq.*
  federal, proposals as to, 1954, 51
  Republic of Ghana, of—
    amendment to, 150–1
    African unity, provisions to
      facilitate, 120 *et seq.*, 123 *et
      seq.*, 476
    approval of, 90
    description, 112 *et seq.*
    draft, 85 *et seq.*
      plebiscite on, 88–90
      reception of, 86–8
      summary of, 85–6
    enactment of, 91 *et seq.*
    entrenched provisions of, 147
      et seq., 376, 476, 479, 481,
      482, 483, 486, 487, 488, 490

CONSTITUTION—*contd.*
  Republic of Ghana, of
    entrenchment of provisions of,
      149
    establishment of, 472
    evolution of, 3 *et seq.*
    financial provisions, 155 *et seq.*,
      483 *et seq.*
    integrity of, preservation of,
      150
    means of enactment, 74
      repealing, 118, 476
    power to alter, 481
    powers of the people, 112, 476
      reserved by, 147 *et seq.*
    principles, 111 *et seq.*
    publication, 294
    regulatory provisions, 131
    text of, 473 *et seq.*
    transitional provisions, 99

CONTEMPT
  Parliament, of. *See under* PAR-
    LIAMENT

CONTINGENCIES FUND
  expenditure from, 165–7, 485
  payments into, 166, 485
  setting up of, 156, 483
  withdrawal from, 159, 485

CONTRACTS
  legislation as to, 98

CO-OPERATIVE SOCIETIES,
  243–4

COUNCIL
  divisional, 178
  executive. *See* EXECUTIVE
    COUNCIL
  legislative. *See* LEGISLATIVE
    COUNCIL
  traditional, 179
    consideration of customary law
      by, 429, 502–4

COURTS
  Court of Appeal, provisions under
    1957 Constitution, 66
  High Court. *See* HIGH COURT
  local. *See* LOCAL COURT
  native, Gold Coast Colony, in,
    reform of, 1944, 36
  provisions as to—
    1954 Constitution, under, 50
    1957 Constitution, under, 66

COURTS—*contd.*
Republic of Ghana, in—
consolidation of legislation as
to, 98
divisions of, 170, 487
inferior, establishment, 170, 487
interpretation of enactments
by, 270, 280–4
jurisdiction, customary law, to
administer, 412–3
legislative power of, 270
power conferred on, 168, 487
statute, bound by, 280
structure of, 402
superior, jurisdiction, 487
revision of Courts Ordinance, 402
Supreme Court. *See* SUPREME
COURT

COUSSEY COMMITTEE, 41

CREDIT
votes of, 164

CRIMINAL CONSPIRACY
definition, 240
punishment, 240

CRIMINAL LIBEL. *See* LIBEL

CROWN
land, grants of, Royal Charter of
1850, under, 11
resumption of government of
Gold Coast by, 1843, 6, 7
vesting of possessions in, 1821...5

CURFEW
power to impose, 240, 255

CUSTOM. *See also* CUSTOMARY
LAW
existing, meaning of, 411, 412
judicial notice of, 422–6
local, observation of, 8
native, restrictions on, 235
repugnant, 235, 410, 411, 416

CUSTOMARY LAW
African countries other than
Ghana, of, application, 461,
463
alteration of, 272, 428–9, 503
application before Republic
Day—
agreement to apply English
law, 438–44, 498–500

CUSTOMARY LAW—*contd.*
application before Republic
Day—
agreement to apply foreign
law, 444
benefit of—
must be claimed, 436, 437
persons entitled to, 413
decision by courts as to, 445,
499
English law, displacement by,
409, 410, 438–44, 498–500
exceptions, 408
" existing " law, meaning of,
411, 412, 426
exclusion of English law by,
391 *et seq.*
failure to plead, 437–8
interrelation with English law,
391, 408 *et seq.*, 436 *et seq.*,
498–500
jurisdiction to administer,
412–3
limitations, 409 *et seq.*
mixed cases, in, 436
" native " cases, in, 436
non-natives entitled to benefit
of, 413
pleading of, 436, 437
where no express rule applicable, 445
application under Courts Act,
1960—
agreement of both parties,
450, 453, 501
cases in which common law
also applies, 451, 502
intention, importance of, 450,
454, 455, 501
land, title to, cases of, 450,
454, 458 *et seq.*, 501
lex situs, determination of, 454,
501
movable property, devolution
of, 450, 456, 501
rules, 449–64, 501
examples of operation of,
458–64
unilateral disposition, issue
arising from, 450, 454,
501
ascertainment of, 416 *et seq.*
assessors, 419
system superseded, 431, 432
expert knowledge of court, 418
witnesses, 417
reference to local court, 420
works of authority, 420

CUSTOMARY LAW—*contd.*
  assimilated rules, 406, 407, 457, 501
  assimilation into common law, 403, 404, 406, 428–9, 457, 501, 502, 503–4
  Chieftaincy Act, 1961, provisions of, 428, 502
  conflict of laws—
    common law, with, 449 *et seq.*, 459, 460, 462, 463, 500–2
    customary laws, between—
      before Republic Day, 446–8
      Courts Act, 1960, under, 449 *et seq.*, 458, 459, 461, 462, 463, 501, 500–3
    English law, with, 436–46
  declaration of, 28–9, 502, 503–4
  definition, 170, 411, 414–6
  development of, 403
  early observation of, 8
  gaps filled by application of English law, 445
  ignorance no excuse, 456–7
  judicial enquiry into, 427–8
      knowledge now expected, 427
      notice of, 422–6
  oath recognised by, 433–5
  offences triable by local court, 433, 434
  Ordinance, displacement by, 410
  provisions of Constitution as to, 178, 489
  question of fact, as, 417
      law, as, 426–8, 457
  recording of, 428
  repugnancy to natural justice, equity and good con-science, 410, 416
  rules as to application of, 449–64, 501
      of, declaration, alteration and assimilation, 428–9, 502–4
  traditional council, consideration by, 429, 502–4
  written documents, 444

D

DEBATE
  Parliamentary—
    formal occasions for, 153
    freedom of speech in, 322–4
    procedure, 313–8
    report of, privileged, 325–6
    rules as to, 314–7
    termination of, 317

DEFAMATION
  civil law, under, 231
  criminal law, under, 231–3
    libel, 232
  community, by, 232
  insult to national flag or emblem, 232
  organisation, by, 232
  President, of, 231

DELEGATION
  parliamentary powers, of, 263

DEPORTATION
  provisions as to, 202–4

DETENTION
  preventive. *See* PREVENTIVE DETENTION

DETINUE
  civil remedies, 249

DIPLOMATIC IMMUNITY
  Commonwealth representatives, of, 211
  consular officers, of, extent of, 212
  international organisations, of, 212
  judicial proceedings, in, 211
  principles of, 211

DISTRICT COMMISSIONERS, 129

DISTRICT MAGISTRATE
  arrest without warrant by, 215
  power to review decisions of local court, 432

DIVISIONAL COUNCILS, 178–9

DRAFTSMAN
  parliamentary—
    importance of, 339
    instructions to, 365
    interpretation of enactment by, 346
    role of, 272
    statutory instrument, drafting of, 385
    technique of drafting, 340–5, 356–63, 366–8
    See also BILL

DUTCH
  departure of, 15
  relations of British with, 14, 15

E

ELECTION
general, 1956, of, 57
independence proposals, on, 56
municipal, Gold Coast Colony, in,
20, 35
parliamentary, 152, 302, 481
Presidential, 477–8
interim, 138, 139
procedure, 137 *et seq.*, 477

ELECTORATE
mandate from, 80

EMERGENCY
ammunition, control of, 255
arms, control of, 255
arrest without warrant in, 255
definition, 253
explosives, control of, 255
general, 254
laws, 214, 219–26, 253–6
local, 254
powers, 253–6
preventive detention, 219–26
procedure in, 254–5
radio stations, control of, 256
regulations, 254, 255
state of, proclamation, 253, 254

ENACTMENT. *See* ACT OF PARLIA-
MENT; STATUTORY INSTRUMENT
definition, 274, 492

ENGLISH LAW
Acts not applying, list of, 398
application of—
agreement of both parties to,
438–44, 499
evidence of, 439–44
implied, 439, 499
onus of proof, 443
rights acquired by customary
law, 438
when mixture of English
and customary law con-
templated, 442
with whom made, 440
writing, employment of, as,
evidence of, 444
customary law displaced by
agreement, 438–44, 499
decision by court as to, 445, 499
gaps in customary law, to fill,
445–6

KK

ENGLISH LAW—*contd.*
application of—
land transactions, 395
mixed cases, in, 436, 439
provisions regulating, 391 *et
seq.*, 403
unilateral agreement to, 440–1
when inconsistent with Ordinance, 392
" background law," as, 409
common law and equity, relative
application of, 391, 401
continuation of, 403, 404–6
customary law—
displacement by, 408–9
interrelation with, 391, 408 *et
seq.*, 436 *et seq.*, 498–500
estoppel, application in customary
law cases, 446
formal introduction of, 391
limitations on application, 391 *et
seq.*
local court, application in, 430
principles, retention of, 402 *et seq.*
res judicata, application in customary law cases, 446
" statutes of general application," 395–401, 406

ENLISTMENT
foreign, prohibition of, 209

ENQUIRY
Commission of. *See* COMMISSION
OF ENQUIRY

EQUITY
administration of, 391
application of, 401
retention of principles, 404–6
rules of, application of, 458

ESTIMATES
annual, 161 *et seq.*, 484
Constitution of 1954, under, 50
expenditure in excess of, 165, 484
provisions of Constitution as to,
484
supplementary, 161, 484
voting on, 162, 484

EXCHANGE CONTROL
restrictions, 247

EXECUTION
respite of, 177, 489

EXECUTIVE COUNCIL
Gold Coast Colony, of, 22
Gold Coast, of—
appointment of Africans to, 35, 39
Ashanti and Northern Territories represented on, 34
Constitution of 1850, under—
composition and conduct, 10, 13
establishment, 9, 10
reconstitution, 1951...41, 42

EXECUTIVE POWER
concept of, 115 *et seq.*, 118
exercise of, regulation, 131
functions of, 116

EXPENDITURE
annual estimates of, 161 *et seq.*, 484
approval of, 161 *et seq.*, 483 *et seq.*
charged, how met, 158–9
commitments, basis of payment, 162–3
credit, votes of, 164
Contingencies Fund, from, 165, 485
exceeding estimate, 165, 484
extraordinary grants, 164, 485
recurring, categories of, 159
unauthorised, 165
voted, 161 *et seq.*, 483 *et seq.*

EXPLOSIVES
control of, 256
emergency, in, 255

EXPORTS
prohibitions on, 247

EXTRADITION
conditions, 207
criminal, of, 204–8
extraditable offences, 207
former provisions as to, 205–6
fugitives from Ghana, of, 209–10
political crimes, for, 207
procedure, 208
treaties, 205, 206

F

FALSE REPORT
communication of, 228

FANTI BOND, 8

FANTI CONFEDERATION, 16

FETISH
oath belonging to, 433, 434
worship, restrictions on, 234, 235

FILMS
censorship of, 230
licensed premises, 231

FINANCE
Consolidated Fund. *See* CONSOLIDATED FUND
Constitution of 1954, under, 50
Contingencies Fund. *See* CONTINGENCIES FUND
economic controls, 247
exchange control, 247
expenditure. *See* EXPENDITURE
introduction of Income Tax, 37
provisions of Constitution as to, 483–6
public, 155 *et seq.*, 483 *et seq.*
Public Accounts Committee, 320
separate public accounts, 157

FLAG
National, 129, 477
insult to, 232

FOREIGN ENLISTMENT
prohibition of, 209

FOREST RESERVES
designation of land as, 246

FREEDOM
assembly, of, 236–40
association, of, 240–4
individual, of, 213 *et seq.*
movement, of, 236–40
physical, authorised exceptions, 214
property, of, 244–9
religion, of, 234–6
speech, of, 226–34
Parliament, in, 322–4

FRONTIERS
Republic of Ghana, of, establishment of, 127–8, 476

FUND
Consolidated. *See* CONSOLIDATED FUND
Contingencies. *See* CONTINGEN-CIES FUND
public—
custody of, 483
meaning, 158–9
payment out of, 159, 165, 483
withdrawal from, 159, 165, 483

FUNERAL
irreverent behaviour at, 236

G

GHANA. *See also* ASHANTI; GOLD COAST; GOLD COAST COLONY; NORTHERN TER-RITORIES; TOGOLAND
independence. *See* INDEPENDENCE
name—
adoption of, 3, 60
origin of, 3, 61
origins and development, 3 *et seq.*
Republic of—
announcement of, 73
civil liability of, 250
civil proceedings against, 249–53
by, 251
Commonwealth status of, 467 *et seq.*
Constitution. *See under* CON-STITUTION
constitutional development, 3 *et seq.*
creation, 74 *et seq.*
declaration, 476
entry into, 202
financial obligations, 96
flag of, 129, 477
frontiers, 127, 476
geographical position, 3
inauguration, 103
mandate to create, 80 *et seq.*
National Assembly. *See* NATIONAL ASSEMBLY
Parliament. *See* PARLIAMENT
people, powers of, 112, 476
power to surrender sovereignty, 123, 476
President of. *See* PRESIDENT
Regions, division into, 128, 477
territories of, 127, 476
unitary character of, 125 *et seq.*, 476

GHANA-GUINEA UNION
formation of, 122–3

GOLD COAST. *See also* GOLD COAST COLONY
Chief Justice of, 12
constitutional difficulties, 1948...39–40
reform, discussions on 1952...47–8
definition, 25
establishment of laws, etc., in, 7
Executive Council. *See* EXECUTIVE COUNCIL
government of—
before 1821, 4
1821–1874, 4 *et seq.*
1874–1914, 17–25
1914–1945, 25–37
1946–1960, 37–73
Governor of—
establishment of, 1850...9
legislative powers—
under 1946 Constitution, 38
1951 Constitution, 44
powers—
under 1850 Royal Charter, 11
1950 Constitution, 49
independence. *See* INDEPEND-ENCE
judicial reform, 1935, 34
laws of, collected editions of, 285–90
Legislative Assembly, establish-ment of, 1951, 41, 43
Legislative Council—
Constitution of 1850, under—
composition and conduct of, 9–10, 13
establishment of, 9
Ordinances, 10
Constitution of 1866, under, 15
Constitution of 1916, under, 26–8
Constitution of 1946, under—
membership, 38
representative government, achievement of, 37
Supreme Court—
Courts Ordinance, 1935, under, appeal from, 33
establishment, 1850, 12
jurisdiction under 1853 Ordin-ance, 12–13

GOLD COAST COLONY
  achievement of representative
    government, 1946, 37
  chiefs, control over, 20
  creation of, 17
  definition, 25
  establishment of police force, 20
  Executive Council—
    appointment of Africans to, 35
    composition, 22
    establishment, 17
  extent of, 17
  geographical boundaries of, 23
  Governor, 17
  judicial reform, 1935, 34
  Legislative Council—
    appointment of first African
      member, 22
    composition, 1925, 30
    enlargement, 1916, 26–8
      1925, 30
    establishment, 17
    powers, 18, 22
  local government, attempts to
    establish, 20
  municipal government—
    proposals to improve, 1921, 29
    self-government for municip-
      alities, 35
  Provincial Councils—
    creation of, 30, 31
    functions, 31, 32
  Royal Charter, 18
  Supreme Court of—
    composition, 19
    establishment of, 18
    jurisdiction, 18

GOVERNMENT
  federal, proposals as to, 1954, 51
  form of, right to choose, 80
  offences against, emergency
    powers, 219–26
  people, by, 112, 476

GOVERNOR
  Gold Coast Colony, of, 17
  Gold Coast, of—
    establishment, 1850...9
    legislative powers—
      under 1946 Constitution, 38
        1951 Constitution, 44
    powers—
      under 1850 Royal Charter, 11
        1954 Constitution, 49

GOVERNOR-GENERAL
  address of thanks to, 106
  creation of office of, 1957, 62
  proroguing of Parliament by, 106

H

HABEAS CORPUS
  Acts, in force in Ghana, 399
  writ of, 217–9, 249
    application for, 218
      refusal under Preventive De-
        tention Act, 225

HANSARD, 304

HIGH COURT
  Republic of Ghana, of—
    appeal from, 171
    appellate jurisdiction, 172, 487
    customary law, reference to
      lower court, 420
    establishment of, 93, 170, 487
    judges—
      appointment, 173–4, 488
      judicial oath, 174, 488
      pensions, 175–6, 184, 488
      removal from office, 174,
        183, 488
      retirement, 174, 488
      salaries, 175–6, 183, 488
    original jurisdiction, 172, 487
    precedent, when bound by,
      173, 487

HIGHWAY
  obstruction of, 239

HONOURS
  grant of, 132–3, 477

HOUSE OF LORDS
  decisions of, binding effect of, 405

I

IMMIGRANT
  entry permit, 202
  prohibited, 202

IMPORTATION
  books and newspapers, of, pro-
    hibition, 230
  powers of prohibition, 230, 247

INCOME TAX
introduction into Gold Coast, 37

INDEPENDENCE
election on issue of, 56
negotiations for, 58
Opposition proposals, 58–9
passing of Ghana Independence
Act, 60

INTERNATIONAL AFFAIRS
neutralism in, 209

INTERPRETATION OF ENACT-
MENTS
Act of 1960—
application, 274–5
contents of, 274–9
amendments, 276–8
constitution, applied to, 101
draftsman, by, 345–6
" golden rule," 280
judicial, 270, 273, 280–4
construction of Act as whole,
283
eiusdem generis, 281
*expressio unius est exclusio
alterius*, 282
*generalia specialibus non dero-
gant*, 282
noscitur a sociis, 281
penal provisions, of, 281
rules of, 280–4
ut res magis valeat quam pereat,
280
miscellaneous provisions as to,
278–9
necessity for, 272–3
Parliamentary counsel, by, 345–6

J

JUDGES
Chief Justice. *See* CHIEF JUSTICE
superior courts, of—
appointment, 173–4, 488
oath to be taken by, 174, 488
pensions, 175–6, 184, 488
qualifications, 174
removal from office, 174, 183,
488
retirement, 174, 488
salaries, 175–6, 183, 488

JUDICIAL OATH, 174, 488

JUDICIAL POWER
conferred on courts of law, 168,
487
limitations on, 169
subordinate to legislative power,
168

JUDICIAL SERVICE
legislation as to, 98
organisation of, 180, 489

JURY
service, immunity of Members of
Parliament, 325

JUSTICE
principles of, 168 *et seq.*

K

KIDNAPPING, 8, 219, 410

L

LAGOS
administration by Royal Niger
Company, 21
annexation of, 17
separation from Gold Coast
Colony, 21
union with Gold Coast, 17

LAND
acquisition of, 244, 245
concessions, limitations on, Gold
Coast Colony, in, 21
conflict of laws in relation to,
449 *et seq.*
development of, 244, 246
right in, restrictions on concessions, 247
title to, customary law, application of, 450, 454, 458 *et seq.*
transactions, application of
English law, 395

LAW
administration of, 169 *et seq.*, 391
categories of, 169, 486
common. *See* COMMON LAW
customary. *See* CUSTOMARY LAW
definition, 259
enforcement of, 169 *et seq.*
English. *See* ENGLISH LAW
personal, determination of, 449,
450, 452, 453, 456, 458 *et
seq.*
principles of, 168 *et seq.*
provisions of Constitution, 168 *et
seq.*, 486
See also LEGISLATION

LAWS
colonial, collected editions of, 285–90
conflict of. *See* CONFLICT OF LAWS
publication of, 284–97
Republic of Ghana, of, publication, 291–7

LEGISLATION
Act of Parliament. *See* ACT OF PARLIAMENT
amendment of, 341–2, 343
authentication of, 93
British, in force in Colony of Ghana, 291
civil servants, role of, 337
Cabinet, role of, 334–5
colonial, superseding of, 293
courts, by, 270
delegated. *See under* SUBORDIN-ATE, *infra*
drafting of, 340–5, 356–63, 365–70
formal, definition, 298
informal, definition, 298
initiation of, 364
interpretation. *See* INTERPRETA-TION OF ENACTMENTS
legislative functionaries, 298 *et seq.*
meaning, 259
Ministers, role of, 336–7
President, by, 271
procedure for enactment of, 151, 482
proposed—
Cabinet approval, 364
memorandum on, 364
publication, 284–97
retrospective, 280, 379
statute law revision, 293
sub-delegated, 266
subordinate—
Colonial, publication, 289, 290
emergency, in, 268
history, 263–4
necessity for, 263
power to make regulations, 267
reform of system, 264
See also STATUTORY INSTRU-MENT
validity of, jurisdiction over, 93

LEGISLATIVE ASSEMBLY
Constitution of 1954, under, 49
Gold Coast, of—
election to, 46

LEGISLATIVE ASSEMBLY
—*contd.*
Gold Coast, of—
establishment of, 1951, 41
membership, 43
proposals as to reform, 1952, 47–8
native chiefs, of, 11–12
renaming of as National Assembly, 63

LEGISLATIVE COUNCIL
Constitution of 1850, under—
composition and conduct of, 9–10, 13
establishment, 9
Ordinances of, 10
Constitution of 1866, under—
composition, 15
Constitution of 1916, under—
enlargement, 26–8
Constitution of 1946, under—
membership, 38
Gold Coast Colony, of—
appointment of first African member, 22
composition, 30
enlargement of, 1916, 26–8
1925, 30
extension to Ashanti, 1946, 37
powers, 18, 22

LEGISLATIVE POWER
concept of, 115 *et seq.*
function of, 116
limitations on, 147, 481
Parliament, invested in, 146, 481
predominance over judicial power, 168
reserved, 147 *et seq.*

LIBEL
criminal—
intentional, 232
negligent, 232
privilege, defence of, 232–3
publication of, privilege, defence of, 232–3

LIMITATION OF ACTIONS
public authorities, against, 251
railways, against, 252

LOAN
public—
agreement to make, 167, 485
raising of, 486
restrictions on, 92, 486

LOCAL AUTHORITIES
limitation of actions, 252

LOCAL COURT
advice available to, 432
customary law offences triable by,
432, 433, 434
procedure, 433–5
decision of, review of, 432
jurisdiction—
Courts Act, 1960, under, 431–3
Local Courts Act, 1958, under—
customary law, application
of, 430
English law, application of,
430
limitations on, 429–30
procedure, 431, 432, 433

LOCAL GOVERNMENT
Gold Coast Colony, in, 20, 29
attempts to establish, 20
Ordinance of 1951, provisions
of, 45

LOCAL GOVERNMENT
SERVICE
organisation of, 180, 489

LOCKOUTS, 243

LOTTERIES ACCOUNT
nature of, 159

M

MACE
bearing of, 304
symbol of Speaker's authority,
301

MAGISTRATE
local court, of, instruction of, 432

MANDAMUS
order of, 249, 252

MARRIAGE
customary law, under, 450, 454

MARSHAL
National Assembly, of, 304

MEETING
public, control of, 237

MERCHANTS
Committee of, 4 *et seq.*
Company of, 4

MERCY
powers of, 176, 489

MILITARY TRAINING
unlawful, 241

MINING
concessions, restrictions, on 21,
247
licence for, 247

MINISTERS
appointment, 144, 479
departmental—
assignment of duties to, 183
functions of, 336
implementation of Cabinet
decisions by, 337
proposals to Cabinet by, 336
dismissal of, 145
loss of office, 145
resignation of, 145
tenure of office, 479

MINISTRIES
creation of, 145
grouping into, 182

MISPRISION OF TREASON, 227

MOVEMENT
freedom of, 236–40

MUNICIPAL COUNCILS
Gold Coast Colony, in, 20,

MUNICIPAL GOVERNMENT
Gold Coast Colony, in, 20
introduction of, 13
proposals for improvement, 1921
...29

MUNICIPALITIES
Gold Coast, in, creation of, 13

N

NATIONAL ASSEMBLY. *See also*
PARLIAMENT
agenda, preparation of, 310
business—
arrangement of, 307–11
Business Committee, 307
order of, 308
Cabinet. *See* CABINET
categories of persons, 300
Clerk of, 303
Deputy, 303
duties, 310, 312
composition of, 152, 300, 481
contempt. *See under* PARLIAMENT
debates—
formal occasions for, 153
freedom of speech in, 322–4
procedure, 313–8
report of, privilege, 325–6
termination of, 317
defamation of, 232, 330
disobedience of orders of, 329
dissolution, 154, 305, 482
dissolved, reconstitution in emergency, 154, 482
disturbance in, 315–7
division, 317–8
election of Members, 152, 481
first sitting of, 154
freedom of debate, 153
functions, 154
other than legislative, 153, 154
Legislative Assembly renamed as,
63
Marshal—
appointment and duties, 304
Assistant, 304
meeting, definition, 493
Member of Parliament. *See under*
PARLIAMENT
motions in, 310, 313
number of seats, 152, 481
officers of, 300–304
contempt by, punishment,
331
interference with, 328–9
parliamentary privileges, 324–6
Order Papers, preparation of, 310
papers laid before, 309
Parliamentary Counsel. *See* PAR-
LIAMENTARY COUNSEL
parties, 303
petition to, 309, 494
Presidential address, 153, 482
privileges. *See* PARLIAMENTARY
PRIVILEGE

NATIONAL ASSEMBLY—*contd.*
proceedings in, 311–21
record of, 304, 325
proclamation summoning, 109
prorogation, 482
questions in, 309
quorum, 312
rules of order and debate, 314–7
secret session, 304
select committees. *See* SELECT
COMMITTEE
sessions of, 155, 304, 305, 306,
482
sittings, duration, 304, 306, 307,
311–2
Speaker. *See* SPEAKER
Standing Orders, 311
Committee, 311
statutory instruments laid before,
388
strangers in, 304
offences by, 329, 330, 331–2
women members, 152, 302

NATIVE
authorities, Gold Coast Colony,
in, 36
definition, 413
tribunals, administration of
justice in, 19

NATURALISATION
citizenship by, 198–9

NEUTRALISM
policy of, 209

NEWSPAPER
censorship of, 230, 255
importation of, prohibition, 230
registration of, 230

NKRUMAH, KWAME
assumption of office as first
President by, 108, 478
election as President, 139, 477
legislative powers of, 135–6, 271
special powers as first President,
135–6, 271, 490

NORTHERN TERRITORIES
establishment of protectorate, 24
Executive Council, 34
Legislative Assembly, membership of, 44

O

OATH
 allegiance, of, 200
 customary law, under, 433–5
 form of, legislation as to, 98
 judicial, 174, 488
 objection to, 234
 Presidential, 140, 478
 taking without religious belief,
  234
 unlawful, 241

OBSCENE PUBLICATIONS
 advertisements, 234
 definition, 233
 offences as to, 233–4

OBSTRUCTION
 streets, of, 239

OFFENCES AGAINST THE
  PERSON, 219–20

OFFENDER
 arrest of, 214–6
 search of, 216

OFFICIAL SECRETS
 offences concerning, 229

ORDER. *See also* STATUTORY
  INSTRUMENT
 definition, 493

ORDINANCES
 collected editions of, 285–90
  table of, 286
 definition, 392–3, 494
 drawing up of, 10
 exclusion of English law by, 392
 indexing of, 290, 296
 publication of, 284–91

P

PANYARRING
 outlawing of, 8, 410

PARDON
 power to grant, 176, 489

PARLIAMENT. *See also* NATIONAL
  ASSEMBLY
 Act of. *See* ACT OF PARLIAMENT
 Cabinet. *See* CABINET
 Chamber, 299
 constituent elements, 146, 298,
  481
 Constitution of 1957, under, 63–4
 Counsel. *See* PARLIAMENTARY
  COUNSEL
 contempt of—
  breach of privilege, 322, 326,
   327
  categories, 328
  defamation of Assembly, 232,
   330
  definition, 326, 327
  disobedience of Assembly's
   orders, 329
  false document, production of,
   327, 328, 329
   evidence, giving of, 329
  freedom of debate, breach of
   rule as to, 260
  interference with Members,
   officers or proceedings,
   328, 329
  officers, by, punishment, 331
  punishment, 330–2
  strangers, by, 329, 330, 331–2
 debate. *See* DEBATE
 delegation of powers, 263
 dissolution, 154, 305, 482
 draftsman. *See* DRAFTSMAN
 duration, 304, 305, 306
 formal opening of, 109
 function of, 146, 481
 House, 299
 legislative power—
  exclusively invested in, 146,
   481
  limitations on, 147, 149, 150,
   481
 meeting, duration of, 306, 307
 Member of—
  arrest of, 324
  bribery of, 329
  contempt by, 328–9, 330, 331
  defamation of, 232, 330
  disobedience by, 329
  disorderly, 315–7, 330
  election, 152, 302–3, 481
  exclusion of, 330
  expulsion, 331
  freedom of speech, 322–4
  immunities, 324–6
  interference with, 328
  loss of seat, 303

PARLIAMENT—*contd.*
Member of—
motions moved by, 310, 313
reprimand of, 330
suspension, 316, 330
petitions presented by, 309
privileges. *See* PARLIAMENT-
ARY PRIVILEGE
procedure by, 313 *et seq.*
punishment of, 330
qualifications, 262, 302
questions by, 309
rules of order and debate, 314–7
salary and allowances, 303
service of process on, 324
women, 152, 302
Order in Council bestowing
powers on, 74 *et seq.*
parties, 302
powers of, 74–5, 481
derivation, 74
restrictions on, 75
precincts, 300
President. *See* PRESIDENT
privilege. *See* PARLIAMENTARY
PRIVILEGE
publication of proceedings, 304,
325
reserved powers conferred on, 147
session, duration of, 155, 304, 305,
306, 482
sitting, duration of, 304, 306, 307,
311–2
Speaker. *See* SPEAKER
surrender of sovereignty, powers
as to, 149, 476

PARLIAMENTARY COUNSEL
advice by, 345–6, 364–5
drafting instructions to, 365
draftsman—
importance of, 339
technique of drafting, 340–5,
356–63, 365–70
functions, 340–6
interpretation of statutes by,
345–6
legislation—
initiation of proposals for, 336,
345
preparation of, 340–5
statutory instruments, drafting
of, 385

PARLIAMENTARY PRIVILEGE
abuse of, 323
arrest, restrictions on, 324
breach of, 322, 326

PARLIAMENTARY PRIVILEGE
—*contd.*
freedom of speech, 322–4
immunities—
acts authorised by Assembly,
325
jury service, 325
publication of proceedings, 325
witness summons, 325
process, service of, restrictions
on, 324
reasons for, 321–2
waiving of, 325
witnesses before Assembly, of,
326

PASSPORT
necessity for, 202

PLANNING
areas, 246
land development and use, of,
244, 246

PLEBISCITE
constitutional—
holding of, provisions as to,
88–90, 473
power to hold, 83, 473
regulations governing, 83
draft Constitution, to approve, 85

POLICE
arrest without warrant by, 215
force, civil, establishment of, 20
Service—
organisation, 180, 489
pensions, safeguarding of, 184,
489

POLITICAL SOVEREIGNTY
distinguished from legal
sovereignty, 113
recognition of, Republican Constitution, in, 112
relation with legal sovereignty,
113–5

POLITICS
religious organisations engaging
in, restrictions on, 236–7

POLL TAX ORDINANCE, 11

PRECEDENT
courts bound by, 173, 487
presumptions as to, 173

PRESIDENT
absence of, provisions for, 135, 143, 479
address to National Assembly, 153, 482
administration of oath to, 108
advice of Cabinet to, 133
affirmation by, 140, 478
assent of, 375–8, 482
assumption of office, 140, 478
Cabinet meetings, attendance at, 333
Commander-in-Chief of Armed Forces, as, 184, 489
death of, provisions in case of, 135, 143, 479
declaration of fundamental principles by, 140 *et seq.*, 478
defamation of, 231
delegation of functions by, 134
election of, 89–90, 137, 477
establishment of office of, 130, 477
first—
    appointment of, 477
    assumption of office by, 108
    election of, 139, 477
    legislative powers, 135–6
    special powers of, 490
functions of, 130 *et seq.*, 477
incapacity of, provisions in case of, 135, 143, 479
legislation relating to, 98
legislative functions, 135, 482
    powers, 94–7, 132, 271, 482
mercy, powers of, 176, 489
Ministers, appointment of, 144
oath of office, 140 *et seq.*, 478
Parliamentary functions and rights, 300
powers of, 93–5, 96, 130 *et seq.*, 477, 482
Presidential Commission appointed by, 143
qualifications for election, 137, 478
resignation of, 137
salary and allowances, 480
term of office, 477

PRESIDENTIAL COMMISSION
appointment and powers, 135, 143, 479
composition, 143

PREVENTIVE DETENTION
appeal against, 225
expiration of Act, 221
habeas corpus, writ of, 225
justification of, 222 *et seq.*
number of persons detained, 224
orders, 222, 224
period of, 221
provisions as to, 219–26

PRICE CONTROL, 248

PRIME MINISTER
Gold Coast, of—
    creation of office, 46
    powers under 1954 Constitution, 49
independent Ghana, of, appointment, 62

PRIVY COUNCIL
appeal to, 33
decisions of, binding effect of, 405

PROCESSION
prohibition of, 255
control of, 237

PROHIBITION
order of, 249, 252

PROPERTY
buildings, control of use of, 244, 246
compulsory acquisition of, 244, 245
conflict of laws in relation to, 449 *et seq.*
damage to, compensation, 249
defence of, 248
detinue, civil remedies, 249
development of land, 244, 246
economic controls, 244, 247
freedom of, 244–9
" intellectual," infringement of rights in, 249
legislation as to, 98
moveable, devolution of, application of customary law, 450, 456
neighbour, duty towards, 244
planning laws, 244, 246
rights of—
    civil remedies, 249
    defence from unlawful interference, 248
    offences, 249
stool, protection of, 249
taxes on, 244
trespass, civil remedies, 249

PROTECTED TERRITORIES
recognition of, 13

PROVINCIAL COUNCILS
Gold Coast Colony, in—
creation of, 30, 31
functions, 31, 32

PUBLIC ACCOUNTS
audit of, 486
Committee, 319

PUBLIC AUTHORITIES
civil actions against, 249
limitation of actions, 251

PUBLIC FUNDS
custody of, 483
meaning, 158–9
payment out of, 159, 165, 483
withdrawal from, 159, 165, 483

PUBLIC LOAN
granting of, 167, 485
raising of, 486
restrictions on, 92, 486

PUBLIC MEETING
control of, 237

PUBLIC SERVICES, 180 *et seq.*,
489

PUBLICATION
comment on matters *sub judice*,
of, 234
laws, of—
colonial system, 284–91
republican system, 291–7
obscene, 234–5
parliamentary proceedings, of,
304, 325

R

RADIO TRANSMITTER
control in emergency, 256
prohibition on use of, 231

RAILWAYS
limitation of actions against, 252

REFERENDUM
Constitution, on, power to hold,
83
reserved powers of Parliament,
on, 147–8

REGIONAL ASSEMBLY
abolition of, 65–6
establishment and functions, provisions as to, 64–5
proposals as to, 54–5

REGIONAL COMMISSIONERS,
129

REGIONS
administration of, 128
definition of boundaries, 54
division into, 64, 128, 477
Houses of Chiefs for, 177–8, 489

RELIGION
blasphemy, 234
churches, disturbances in, 236
fetish worship, restrictions on,
234, 235
freedom of, 234–6
minister of, molestation of, 236
political activities by religious
organisations, 235–6

RENT CONTROL, 248

REPEAL
enactments, of, 275

RIOT
damage by, compensation, 249
provisions of Criminal Code, as
to, 238

RITE
native, restrictions on, 235

ROYAL ASSENT
abolition of need for, 82

ROYAL CHARTER,
1850, of, 9, 10, 11, 15
1874, of, 17
Gold Coast Colony, of, 18

ROYAL NIGER COMPANY, 21

S

SEAL
Presidential, 479
official, 479
public, 479

SEARCH WARRANTS, 248

SECOND CHAMBER
discussions as to, 1954, 51 *et seq.*

SEDITION
law of, Gold Coast, in, 34
seditious statements, 228

SELECT COMMITTEE
ad hoc, 320
Committee of Privileges, 319
consideration of Bill by, 373
definition, 496
House Committee, 311
procedure, 320
Public Accounts Committee, 319
sessional, 319
Standing Orders Committee, 311

SENTENCE
deferment of, 177, 489
remission of, 177, 489

SESSION
parliamentary, duration of, 304,
305, 306

SIERRA LEONE
annexation of possessions to, 5
control of possessions by, 4 *et seq.*
union with, 1866, 15

SLAVERY
provisions as to, 18, 220

SLAVE-TRADING
prohibitions of, 18

SOIL EROSION
prevention of, 246

SOVEREIGNTY
surrender of, powers of Parliament as to, 123, 149, 476

SPEAKER
National Assembly, of—
certification of power to pass
Act by, 148
contempt of Parliament by, 331
defamation of, 232, 330
deputy—
duration of office, 301, 302
election, 301
functions, 302
right to vote, 317
salary and allowances, 302,
303
duration of office, 301
duties, 300, 312 *et seq.*
election, 109, 152, 301, 481
functions, 300, 312 *et seq.*

SPEAKER—*contd.*
National Assembly, of—
interference with, 328
parliamentary privileges, 324-6
procession of, 312
salary and allowances, 301, 303
symbol of authority, 301

SPEECH
freedom of, 226-34
Parliament, in, 322-4

STANDING ORDERS
Committee, 311
making of, 311

STARE DECISIS
principle of, 173

STATUTORY INSTRUMENT. *See
also* LEGISLATION
amendment, 268-9, 276-8
Act, of, by, 269
annulment by National Assembly,
388
commencement, 387
confirmation by National Assembly, 388
construction of, 385-6
definition, 265, 266, 496
drafting of, 342-3, 384, 385
emergency, 268
enabling powers, 382, 386
executive, 265, 295
meaning, 268
publication, 268
initiation, 384
introduction of term, 264
Ghana, in, 265, 266
introductory words, 382
interpretation. *See* INTERPRE-
TATION OF ENACTMENTS
laying before National Assembly,
309, 388
legislative, 265, 266-8
definition, 266-8, 493
numbering, 268
publication, 268, 295
making of, 386
numbered series, 264-5
penal provisions, 386
power to amend, 268-9
make, 267, 269
revoke, 268-9
preparation of, 384-6
publication, 265, 295, 346, 387
revocation of, 275
short title, 381
signature, 384
structure of, 381-4

STOCKS
application of Colonial Stocks Acts, 101

STOOL
disputes—
conduct of, 179
Gold Coast Colony, in, settlement of, 36
provisions as to, 1959...72
property—
protection of, 249
statutory provisions as to, 179

STREET
obstruction of, 239

STRIKE
illegal, 243
railway and dock workers, of, 255

SUPERVISION ORDER
alien, 204

SUPREME COURT
Gold Coast Colony, of—
appeal from, 33
composition, 19
establishment, 18
ex officio judges, 33
jurisdiction, 19
Gold Coast, of—
abolition of, 1866, 15
establishment, 1853, 12
jurisdiction under 1853 Ordinance, 12–3
Republic of Ghana, of—
appeal to, 171, 487
bound by own previous decisions, 173, 487
composition, 172, 487
constitutional questions referred to, 171, 487
definition, 171, 487
establishment, 93, 170, 487
judges—
appointment, 173–4, 488
Chief Justice, 175, 487
judicial oath, 174, 488
pensions, 175–6, 184, 488
qualifications, 174
removal from office, 174, 183, 488
retirement, 174, 488
salaries, 175–6, 183, 488
original jurisdiction, 171, 487
ultra vires enactments, powers as to, 172–3

SUFFRAGE
universal, 119, 476

T

TAXATION
introduction of income tax, 37
restriction of, 483

TERRITORIAL WATERS, 127, 476

TERRITORIES
Republic of Ghana, of, 127, 476

TIMBER
concessions, restrictions on, 247
industry, safeguarding of, 246

TOGOLAND
inclusion in Ghana, 56
Mandate, 28
occupation of, 25
plebiscite as to status, 56–7
trusteeship, 39

TORT
application of common law in cases of, 457

TOWN COUNCILS
Gold Coast Colony, in, 20, 35

TOWN AND COUNTRY PLANNING, 244, 246

TRADE UNION
closed shop principle, 242
Congress, 242
protection in law, 243
registration, 242

TRADITIONAL AREAS
divisions, 178

TRADITIONAL COUNCIL
consideration of customary law by, 429, 502–4

TRAFFIC RESTRICTIONS, 239

TRAINING
military, unlawful, 241

TRANSMITTER
wireless—
control in emergency, 256
prohibitions on use of, 231

TREASON
definition, 226–7
misprision of, 227
provisions relating to, 201
treason felony, 227
treasonable statements, 226–7

TREES
destruction of, restrictions on, 246

TRESPASS
civil remedies, 249
meetings or processions, by, 239

TRIBUNAL
native, Gold Coast Colony, in, administration of justice in, 19

TRUSTEES
investment in Ghanaian securities by, 101

U

ULTRA VIRES ENACTMENTS
powers of Supreme Court, 172–3

UNION OF AFRICAN STATES, 123, 476

UNITED NATIONS ORGANIZATION
diplomatic immunity, 212
military role of, 209

UNITY
African, 120 *et seq.*, 476
constitutional provisions as to, 124, 476
Ghana–Guinea Union, 122–3
realisation of, 476
Union of African States, 123, 476

UPPER REGION
creation of, 96

V

VOTE
right to, 119, 476

W

WAGES
minimum rates, 248

WARRANT
arrest, for, 215
search, 248

WEST AFRICAN COURT OF APPEAL
abolition of right of recourse to, 67
composition, 33
establishment, 33

WIRELESS TRANSMITTER
control in emergency, 256
prohibition on use of, 231

WITNESS
expert, customary law, on, 417
National Assembly, before, privilege, 326
select committee, before—
false evidence, 329
suborning of, 329
summons, immunity of Members of Parliament, 325

WOMEN
Members of Parliament, as, 152, 302